LIVE LONGER
COOKBOOK

READER'S DIGEST

LIVE LONGER
COOKBOOK

The Reader's Digest Association, Inc.
Pleasantville, New York • Montreal

LIVE LONGER COOKBOOK

STAFF

Project Editor	Gayla Visalli
Senior Art Editor	Henrietta Stern
Senior Associate Editor	Barbara C. Loos
Associate Editor	Donna Campbell
Art Associate	Nancy H. Mace
Editorial Assistant	Jeffrey L. Akellian

CONSULTANTS

Chief Consultant	Sally Schneider
Nutrition Consultants	Johanna Dwyer, D.Sc., R.D., Director, Frances Stern Nutrition Center, Tufts New England Medical Center, Boston
	Michele C. Fisher, Ph.D., R.D.

CONTRIBUTORS

Editor	Lee Fowler
Art Editor	Joan Mazzeo
Art Assistant	Stefany Blyn
Researchers	Mary Hart, Joan Walsh
Copy Editor	Virginia Croft
Indexer	Sydney Wolfe Cohen
Writer	Jean Callahan
Recipe Developers	Jo Ann Brett, Sandra Rose Gluck, Georgia Downard, Paul Piccuito, Michele Urvater
Recipe Tester	Hope M. Farrel
Photographer	Michael Molkenthin
Food Stylist	Polly Talbot
Assistant Food Stylist	Margaret A. Neill
Prop Stylist	Deborah E. Donahue
Chart Graphics	Ron Gross
Illustrators	Dick Cole, Ray Skibinski

READER'S DIGEST GENERAL BOOKS

Editor in Chief	John A. Pope, Jr.
Managing Editor	Jane Polley
Executive Editor	Susan J. Wernert
Art Director	David Trooper
Group Editors	Will Bradbury
	Sally French
	Norman B. Mack
	Kaari Ward
Group Art Editors	Evelyn Bauer
	Robert M. Grant
	Joel Musler
Chief of Research	Laurel A. Gilbride
Copy Chief	Edward W. Atkinson
Picture Editor	Richard Pasqual
Rights and Permissions	Pat Colomban
Head Librarian	Jo Manning

The credits that appear on page 340 are
hereby made a part of this copyright page.

Library of Congress Cataloging in Publication Data
Reader's digest Live longer cookbook.
   p. cm.
  Includes index.
  ISBN 0-89577-395-3
  1. Nutrition. 2. Low-fat diet. 3. High-fiber diet. I. Reader's
digest. II. Title: Live longer cookbook.
RA784.R43 1992
641.5'63 — dc20   92-17030

CONTENTS

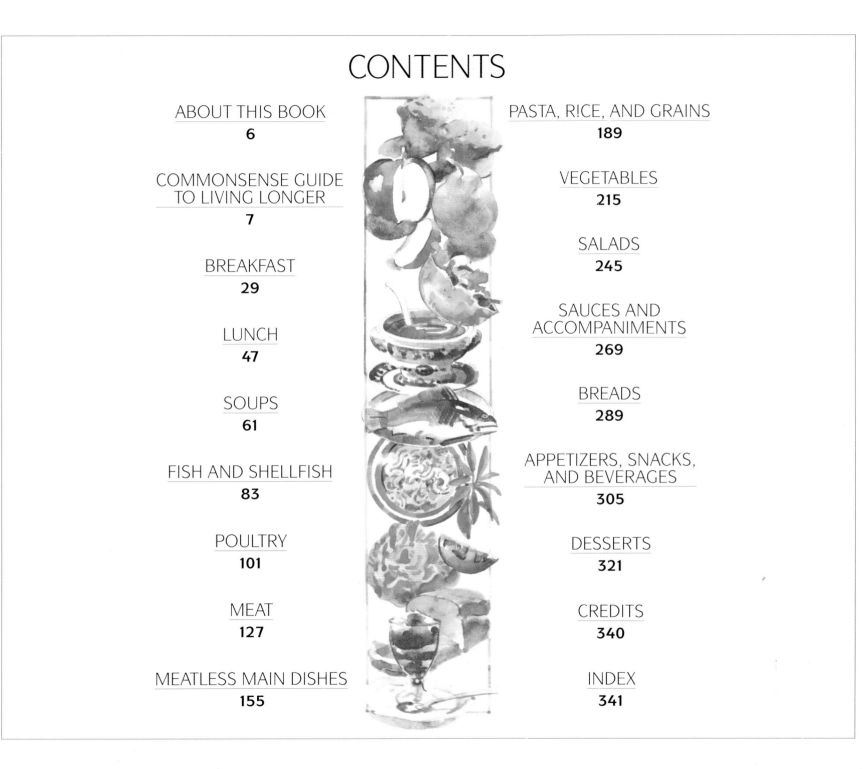

ABOUT THIS BOOK

The *LIVE LONGER COOKBOOK* is dedicated to the premise that you can eat healthfully and pleasurably at the same time. Each of the 500 recipes was created especially for Reader's Digest, using wholesome, mostly fresh, and readily available ingredients and keeping fat, salt, and cholesterol to a minimum. For those who want to explore new eating pleasures, a few recipes include unusual ingredients but suggest more easily found substitutes whenever possible. For busy people, these recipes are a boon because most can be prepared quickly and are easily doubled to have on hand for future meals.

All the recipes have been analyzed for calories, total and saturated fat, protein, carbohydrate, sodium, cholesterol, and dietary fiber content. If you have special diet needs, you can see at a glance if the recipe you have chosen is suitable for you. Preparation and cooking times have also been included, to help you plan your day. (Because people work at different speeds, preparation times should be taken as a guideline, not an exact indicator.)

Serving suggestions, cooking techniques and tips, nutrition information, and menus are given throughout the book — all to make it easy for you and your family to enjoy wonderful, healthful, and satisfying meals every day of the year.

COMMONSENSE GUIDE
TO LIVING LONGER

An important factor that influences longevity is within your power to change as you see fit. What is it? A sensible diet — essentially, one of variety, moderation, and balance. This chapter is designed to help you understand the key factors of a healthful plan. Because nutrition information has exploded over the past decade, it is sometimes hard to sort fact from fiction and useful data from hype. Not long ago, meat and dairy foods were considered the cornerstones of healthy eating habits. Now we know that the saturated fat and cholesterol in animal products are implicated in a number of degenerative diseases. Current recommendations therefore place more emphasis on whole grains, legumes, vegetables, and fruits. Integrate a greater variety of them into your diet and you gain not only more eating pleasure but a broader range of the vitamins, minerals, and other nutrients that contribute to better health. (Some of these plant foods may actually guard against certain cancers and heart disease.) The choices you make about diet and nutrition are vital to your and your family's well-being. In this Commonsense Guide to Living Longer, you can refresh your knowledge of basic nutrition and review the latest findings, then learn how to create a balanced program of diet and exercise to help keep you fit and healthy for a long time to come.

Protein,

the body's main source for growth and tissue repair, is made up of compounds called amino acids. There are 20 amino acids in all; 11 of them can be manufactured in the body, but the remaining 9 — histidine, isoleucine, leucine, lysine, methionine, phenylalanine, threonine, tryptophan, and valine — must be obtained from food; the body then uses them to create proteins, which are the essential building blocks of tissues and also help to regulate many chemical processes of the body. The lack of even one can, over a period of time, cause muscle and tissue loss and impede the ability of your immune system to fight disease. This is why nutritionists recommend a regular intake of foods containing all the essential amino acids. From 10 to 20 percent of daily calories should come from protein. (See page 22 for the equivalent in food.)

Why is protein sometimes called "brain food"?

The same amino acids that build muscle and tissue are also crucial to the production of neurotransmitters — chemical messengers in the brain that convey signals important to such essential functions as memory, pleasure, alertness, and growth. Apparently several amino acids can have a direct effect on the brain's neurotransmitters. For example, the amino acid tryptophan is necessary for production of the neurotransmitter serotonin, which may affect mood and the ability to fall asleep. Milk and turkey are both high in tryptophan, which in turn can increase the amount of sleep-inducing serotonin in the brain. This may explain why most of us feel drowsy after a Thanksgiving meal of turkey and why a glass of milk is a favorite bedtime snack.

Which foods are highest in protein?

Animal foods, such as dairy products, meat, and eggs, provide all the essential amino acids that the body requires. These are called high-quality proteins. Grains, vegetables, and legumes also contain protein but typically lack or are low in one or more of the essential amino acids.

If animal foods have the best protein, why are we hearing that we should eat less meat?

Animal foods, especially meat, are high in saturated fat and cholesterol. Long-term studies have shown a link between high levels of saturated fat in the diet and the development of heart disease and certain types of cancer. On average, North Americans con-

HOW TO CREATE COMPLEMENTARY PROTEINS

Complementary proteins are made by combining plant foods that lack certain amino acids with others that contain them. For instance, beans are typically high in the amino acid lysine but low in methionine. (Soybeans, the closest to animal proteins, are the exception.) Most grains are just the opposite—high in methionine, low in lysine. Combine beans and rice, and you get a complementary protein that is the equivalent of a complete protein. The rule to follow when creating a complementary protein is to combine a legume (a vegetable that bears seed pods) with a grain food, seeds, or nuts.

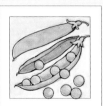 +

Green Peas	Pasta
Kidney Beans	Rice
Lentils	Almonds
Chick Peas	Bulgur
Black-eyed Peas	Couscous
White Beans	Corn
Peanuts	Bread
Lima Beans	Sesame Seeds

sume 75 grams of protein a day, much of it from high-fat animal products, such as lunch meats, hot dogs, hamburgers, and cheese. Epidemiologists studying changes in the contemporary eating habits of rural Chinese people have found that the incidence of heart disease, cancer, diabetes, and other such "diseases of affluence" has increased along with their consumption of more animal fat.

Because meat and dairy products high in fat have been implicated in a number of chronic degenerative diseases, many doctors and nutritionists suggest that we put more emphasis in our diets on whole grains, legumes, fruits, and vegetables and consume high-fat animal foods in moderation.

If we eat less meat, how can we get enough protein?

One way is to eat low-fat or nonfat dairy products such as skim milk and yogurt. Another is to substitute fish, shellfish, and the skinned white meat of poultry. Contrary to popular belief, red meat does not necessarily contain the most protein. In fact, fatty cuts of red meat often have a lower percentage of protein than chicken without skin.

There are two ways to obtain the most benefit from plant proteins: (1) enhancement, combining them with a small amount of high-quality protein, (2) complementing, combining two or more plant proteins in such a way that they form a complete protein equivalent to that of an animal product. To enhance the quality of protein in a dish of pasta, for example, you can add a small portion of meat or cheese to the sauce. To improve the quality of protein in rice, combine it with a little fish, chicken, or egg. For ways to combine plant foods, see Box, left.

Why are plant proteins good for us?

Plant proteins are lower in fat and lack saturated fat altogether. Compare the amount of fat in one egg to that in a dish of beans and rice. Of the 67 calories in an egg, 80 percent is from fat (in the yolk), but in a serving of a dish such as Lentil Fried Rice (page 161), which has 292 calories, only 18 percent comes from fat. Moreover, the legumes, grains, and seeds that combine to make complementary proteins are often also high in fiber, vitamins, and minerals. Studies show that a diet high in soluble fiber can help lower serum cholesterol, and plant foods high in insoluble fiber can reduce risks for certain cancers. Then, too, plant proteins cost less than animal proteins. One nutritionist has likened eating too much animal protein to burning precious mahogany for kindling.

Does our need for protein change as we age?

A common myth holds that people require less protein as they age. In fact, older adults need just as much protein as young adults.

At certain times in life, people should have extra protein. Women who are pregnant or lactating need more protein, as do children and teenagers (to accommodate growth spurts). During recovery from surgery or illness, protein is often broken down faster than it is replaced. Increasing one's intake of protein-rich foods helps speed the repair of tissues.

What happens if we eat too much protein?

Some of the excess may be used for energy, especially if insufficient carbohydrate is present; the rest is converted into fat. Several health risks can result. We know that if protein is consumed without sufficient accompanying phosphorus, calcium is excreted in the urine; excess protein may contribute to osteoporosis. Also, processing the excess nitrogen waste from large quantities of protein puts stress on the kidneys. There is some evidence that eating too much protein over a lifetime may be related to reduced kidney function in old age.

Is it true that athletes need more protein?

Nothing could be further from the truth. Remember, excess protein is converted to fat or carbohydrate, not muscle. Studies show that athletes should eat a diet rich in carbohydrate. Without a sufficient amount, the body will convert muscle protein to glucose in order to fuel the body during exercise.

More than half of an adult's daily calories should come from foods high in carbohydrate, including at least five servings of fruits and vegetables.

Carbohydrate converts into glucose, the body's main source of energy. There are two types of carbohydrate — complex and simple. Simple carbohydrates, or simple sugars, are found principally in fruit and sweet processed foods such as candy. These sugars are quickly absorbed and converted into glucose. The result is a burst of energy that typically burns off just as quickly as it came. Except for fruit and milk (which is composed partly of the sugar lactose), foods of simple carbohydrates also lack vitamins, minerals, and fiber. On the other hand, foods made of complex carbohydrates, or starch — including pasta, whole-wheat bread, vegetables, and legumes — convert more slowly into glucose. The result is that they provide the body with a steadier flow of energy over a longer period of time. Best of all, they contain needed nutrients, so the calories are not empty or wasted. From 50 to 60 percent of daily calories should come from complex carbohydrates.

WHY IS FRUIT GOOD FOR YOU?

Fruit is a good source of simple carbohydrates, fiber, potassium, and vitamins A and C. Greater benefits are derived from fresh or frozen fruits than from canned varieties.

	Apple 1 medium	Orange 1 medium	Banana 1 medium	Pear 1 medium	Grapes 20 seedless	Strawberries 1 cup
Calories	80	60	105	100	70	45
Carbohydrate (gm)	21	15	27	25	18	11
Fiber (gm)	2.8	1.6	2.1	5.0	0.5	0.8
Vitamin A (IU)	74	270	92	33	80	41
Vitamin C (mg)	8	70	10	7	10	85
Potassium (mg)	159	237	451	208	186	247

What happens if you don't have enough carbohydrate in your diet?

Insufficient carbohydrate forces the body to make glucose out of protein and fat, a process that can be dangerous to your health. When the body runs on fat and protein, waste products called ketones build up. High levels of ketones can cause nausea, fatigue, or headache. To clear toxic ketones from the blood, the kidneys must work overtime.

Aren't pasta, potatoes, and beans fattening?

Some dieters swear off such excellent sources of complex carbohydrates as potatoes, pasta, and bread because they think these starchy foods are fattening. The truth is that they are relatively low in calories if eaten without butter or rich sauces. There are only 4 calories in a gram of carbohyrate, compared to 9 calories in a gram of fat. Moreover, foods of complex carbohydrates are often high in fiber, which makes them more filling so that they help dieters ward off hunger pangs.

What difference does it make whether you eat whole grains or enriched grain products?

Whenever whole grains are refined, some portion of their nutritional value is lost. For instance, in the refining of wheat, the bran and germ are removed. This increases the shelf life of products made with refined flour, but it also decreases their vitamin, min-eral, and fiber content. Manufacturers often replace some of the lost nutrients, but they never quite succeed in duplicating what nature created. Stone-ground whole-wheat flour retains as much as 90 percent of its original nutrients plus the fiber. Only four nutrients — niacin, thiamine, riboflavin, and iron — are restored to enriched white flour.

Which is nutritionally best — white sugar, brown sugar, honey, or molasses?

None of these have nutritional merit except black-strap molasses: 1 tablespoon contains 5 milligrams of iron, 137 milligrams of calcium, and 586 milligrams of potassium. Brown sugar is refined white sugar sprayed with molasses, and so it has a minute amount of iron. Sugar is a delightful addition to a balanced diet but is best enjoyed in small amounts because it causes tooth decay. The bacteria present in the mouth's plaque produce acids from sugar that eat away at the teeth's enamel.

To cut down on sugar, try to avoid processed foods that have a sweetener listed on the label as one of the top three ingredients; typical examples are corn syrup, glucose, and sucrose. Also, cut back on sugar in your own cooking whenever possible. This has been done already in the recipes for this book, but most standard recipes work fine with less sweetening. The exception is cakes, which need sugar for tenderness. Even in cakes, however, 1 to 4 tablespoons less usually makes little difference.

Why do some athletes load up on carbohydrate before an athletic event?

Athletes may consume large quantities of complex carbohydrates before an athletic event that requires endurance, such as a 3-mile swimming race or a marathon. Such contests often use up the glucose stored in the muscles. When this happens, fatigue sets in and muscles weaken, a process that runners call "hitting the wall." Eating meals high in complex carbohyrates and cutting back on exercise two to three days before a competition help to build up the body's glucose supply and improve stamina.

Fat

Fat stores extra energy in the body, aids in absorbing the fat-soluble vitamins, A, D, E, and K, helps maintain cell membranes, and is used in the production of certain hormones. It is made up primarily of three types of fatty acids: monounsaturated, polyunsaturated (referred to collectively as unsaturated), and saturated. Although all fats are a mixture of these three, one type usually predominates. Most vegetable fats are mainly unsaturated (see Box, page 13, for comparison of oils), and most animal fats are primarily saturated.

The fat needed in our diets is minuscule — about 1 tablespoon of polyunsaturated fat per day. If we limited ourselves to such a small amount, however, much of our food would be dry and tasteless and our meals less satisfying. On the other hand, many people obtain up to 40 percent of daily calories from fat, which is too much. The recommendation today is that no more than 30 percent, preferably less, of daily calories come from fat; saturated fat should be limited to 10 percent.

What is the difference between saturated and unsaturated fats?

Chemically, the difference is that saturated fatty acids have hydrogen atoms attached to all the carbon chains that comprise them, whereas unsaturated fats have one or more pairs of carbon chains that lack the hydrogen bond. As a rule, fats that are primarily saturated remain solid at room temperature, and unsaturated fats are liquid (coconut and palm oils excepted). In the body, saturated fats promote the buildup of cholesterol, or plaque, in artery walls, thus clogging them. Unsaturated fats do not activate this buildup; some actually help to unclog veins.

What is the purpose of hydrogenation?

Hydrogenation, a process in which hydrogen is added to oil under pressure, makes vegetable oil more saturated, or solid at room temperature. Margarine and vegetable shortening are created in this way. In the case of margarine, the result is a spread that, while more saturated than oil, is less saturated than

HOW TO CALCULATE THE PERCENTAGE OF FAT IN FOOD

To keep a realistic eye on how much fat you're getting from certain foods, it helps to calculate the percentage of fat that the food or dish contains. To find this figure, you need to know the number of fat grams and the total calories. This information can often be found on a package label. There are also books that list these figures for many common foods. In *Live Longer Cookbook*, the analysis has been provided for all recipes.

To find the percentage of fat, first multiply the number of fat grams by 9 to determine the fat calories, then divide this number by the total calories. For example, one glazed doughnut contains 235 calories and 13 grams of fat. Multiply 13 by 9 and divide the result, 117, by 235. You can see that almost 50 percent of the calories in the doughnut comes from fat. Compare this with the amount of fat in one Carrot-Pecan Muffin (page 30). The nutrition analysis shows that one muffin has 137 calories and 2 grams of fat. Multiply the 2 fat grams by 9 (18) and divide by the number of calories (137). Only 13 percent of the muffin's calories is derived from fat.

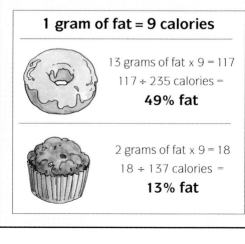

1 gram of fat = 9 calories

13 grams of fat x 9 = 117
117 ÷ 235 calories =
49% fat

2 grams of fat x 9 = 18
18 ÷ 137 calories =
13% fat

butter. Shortening is used by bakers to create tender pastries (butter, margarine, and lard serve a similar purpose). Solid fat coats flour and breaks up dough, making it lighter and moister. Oil, on the other hand, has a tendency to seep through flour, flattening the texture of baked goods.

We now know that hydrogenation also partially alters the chemical structure of unsaturated fat and turns it into a hybrid called trans-fat. Like saturated fat, trans-fat can raise the LDL, or so-called bad cholesterol, level in your blood. (See Cholesterol, page 12.) Studies show that the trans-fats in margarine have this effect, though perhaps the results are no more damaging than from the saturated fat in butter. Used sparingly, neither butter nor margarine should cause health problems.

Why is fat fattening?

One gram of fat yields 9 calories — more than twice the number in 1 gram of carbohydrate or protein, which yields only 4 calories. As any dieter knows, body fat increases when more calories are consumed than can be burned in the body as fuel.

If a label advertises that a food product is 95 percent fat free, does that mean it is low in fat?

Not necessarily. Food manufacturers often base their low-fat claim on the amount of fat as a percentage of a food's *weight* rather than *calories*. Consider this example: The package of a TV dinner reads "95% fat free." This is technically true because the manufacturer is comparing the weight of the fat, 12 grams, to that of the dinner, in this case, 245 grams. A simple calculation shows that fat *is* 5 percent of the meal by weight. However, the 12 grams of fat equal 108 calories, which is actually 41 percent of the meal's 265 calories.

Milk labels can be analyzed in the same way. For example, 99 percent fat-free milk contains 1 percent fat by volume weight. But in fact, 1 cup of 99 percent fat-free milk has 3 grams of milkfat. A quick calculation reveals that, of the 100 calories in a 1-cup serving, 27 percent is from fat.

WAYS TO CUT BACK ON FAT

For an average North American, about 40 percent of daily calories comes from fat. A better amount would be 30 percent or less, with less than 10 percent from saturated fat. In a 2,000-calorie diet, this works out to 66 grams of total fat. (A simple way to calculate the maximum grams of fat you should eat each day is to divide your ideal body weight by 2. For example, if you would like to weigh 120 pounds, keep your fat intake to no more than 60 grams a day.)

If high-fat foods are among your favorites, eat them less often or look for pleasing substitutes (see examples below).

Substitute

for

Substitute	for
Fruit crisp	Fruit pie
Ice milk	Ice cream
Plain popcorn	Potato chips
Bran muffin	Doughnut
Yogurt	Sour cream
Low-fat mayonnaise	Mayonnaise

To reduce fat intake, broil, roast, steam, or poach food instead of frying it. Serve chicken without the skin. Substitute low-fat dairy products such as yogurt and skim milk for sour cream and whole milk. Buy well-trimmed and leaner cuts of meat, such as sirloin tip, round, and top sirloin, and serve smaller portions. A 3-ounce serving supplies an adequate amount of protein. (See page 24 for more ways to cut fat in recipes.)

Cholesterol is a fatty substance

present in every cell of the human body and in the fat of the animal foods we eat — meat, cream, and egg yolks, for example. It performs many important functions, such as constructing cell membranes, aiding in digestion, and helping to produce hormones.

The liver is the primary producer of cholesterol as well as lipoproteins, which carry cholesterol in the bloodstream. High-density lipoproteins (HDL's) provide the best transportation, moving cholesterol safely between the liver and tissue cells. These are often referred to as "good" cholesterol. Low-density lipoproteins (LDL's, or "bad" cholesterol) are not as efficient and lose cholesterol in the arteries, where it accumulates and forms fatty deposits called plaque. A third type of carrier, very-low-density lipoproteins (VLDL's), convert to LDL's after depositing energy-giving triglycerides in the muscles.

Cholesterol deposits eventually impede the flow of blood to the heart and lead to heart disease. The American Heart Association recommends that adults generally limit their dietary cholesterol to 300 milligrams a day.

Why do some people have to restrict their cholesterol intake?

The body manufactures all the cholesterol it needs — about 1,000 milligrams a day. Eating foods that are high in cholesterol may raise the level further, especially in someone whose body is unable to shut off the internal production of cholesterol after a meal high in dietary cholesterol. Because high cholesterol levels are linked to heart disease, anyone over 20 should have a cholesterol check periodically. If the reading is normal, a test once every 3 to 5 years after that is enough. If the results are high, the level should be checked more often. (A test to determine the ratio of HDL's to LDL's is even more telling than an overall figure. The higher the HDL's, the better; not only do they keep cholesterol moving, but they also clean up deposits left by the LDL's.) In general, a desirable level is under 200 milligrams per deciliter; borderline high is 200 to 240; above 240 is considered high.

How does saturated fat affect cholesterol levels in the bloodstream?

Foods high in saturated fat seem to stimulate the body's own production of cholesterol. Egg yolk, cream, and liver are examples of such foods. Although foods of plant origin contain no cholesterol, studies have shown that the ones high in saturated fat — coconut oil, palm and palm kernel oils, and cocoa butter — can also elevate blood cholesterol levels. Commercial baked products and whipped toppings often contain tropical oils.

One Columbia University study found that even young men who did not have excessively high cholesterol levels were able to lower them by cutting their saturated fat intake to 10 percent of total calories. One particularly interesting result of this study was that, when subjects continued to get as much as 38 percent of daily calories from fat, they still lowered their cholesterol counts by limiting their *saturated* fat consumption to 10 percent or less.

How can blood cholesterol levels be lowered?

Since the 1950's, when cholesterol was first linked to heart disease, a number of major studies have revealed the best ways to lower cholesterol. First, cut down on foods high in saturated fat, such as cream-filled dairy products, fatty meats, and tropical oils. Second, limit consumption of foods high in cholesterol, such as egg yolk and organ meats. A diet low in saturated fat and cholesterol and high in fiber is ideal because this combination seems to lower LDL's. Third, exercise. It's been shown that regular exercise is effective in raising HDL's.

What are the benefits of fish oil?

Polyunsaturated fatty acids known as omega-3, present in all fish but especially such cold-water varieties as salmon and tuna, can help reduce incidences of stroke, heart disease, and even certain types of cancer. Research to determine why this happens is still inconclusive. It may be due to the lowering of cholesterol or tryglyceride levels, which

SOME VEGETABLE FATS ARE MORE BENEFICIAL THAN OTHERS.

Most vegetable oils consist primarily of unsaturated fats, which help lower overall levels of cholesterol. But the oils higher in monounsaturated fats (canola and olive, for example) are more discriminating, lowering mainly the LDL (bad cholesterol) levels. Tropical oils, such as coconut, are high in artery-clogging saturated fat. To avoid these oils, check the labels of bakery products.

FAT	% SATURATED	% MONOUNSATURATED	% POLYUNSATURATED
Canola oil	7	62	31
Olive oil	14	77	9
Corn oil	13	25	62
Safflower oil	9	13	78
Palm kernel oil	86	12	2
Coconut oil	92	6	2
Peanut oil	18	49	33
Vegetable shortening	26	47	27
Margarine (hard)	21	46	33
Margarine (soft)	18	37	45

prevents the build-up of fat deposits in artery walls, or perhaps to the fact that omega-3 seems to thin the blood and slow its clotting time.

Whatever takes place, the results present good reasons for eating fish. But what about fish-oil supplements? The advice of leading nutritionists is that supplements should be taken only under the supervision of a doctor. The blood-thinning factor could cause problems for many people, and side effects of large doses are still unknown. Eating fish at least twice a week seems to be the best way to obtain the benefits of fish oil.

Are shellfish high in cholesterol?

Improved tests show that shellfish are lower in cholesterol than previously thought; they contain a substance similar to cholesterol, but it does not affect blood cholesterol levels. A 3½-ounce serving of oysters, for example, has about 55 milligrams of cholesterol, not 300 milligrams as once thought. Lobster, crab, shrimp, and scallops are also fairly low in cholesterol and in saturated fat as well.

Should we limit consumption of eggs?

Ounce for ounce, egg yolk has the highest level of cholesterol of all animal products. A single yolk contains 210 milligrams, about the same amount as in three hamburgers. The white of an egg contains no cholesterol and offers 3.5 grams of high-quality protein. Nutritionists recommend eating no more than three egg yolks a week, fewer if your cholesterol level is high. There is no limit on whites. In recipes, some or all of the yolks can be eliminated by using two egg whites for each whole egg called for.

Fiber is any part of an edible plant that cannot be digested in the gastrointestinal tract. Although it provides no nutrients, fiber is essential to good health. There are two principal types: soluble and insoluble. All vegetables, fruits, plants, grains, and legumes have a mixture of both.

Soluble fiber dissolves in water to form a gel in the intestines, which allows for more even absorption of glucose from the digestive tract and aids elimination by softening stools. Studies show that it may also reduce cholesterol. Insoluble, or crude, fiber does not dissolve in water but retains it instead, thus increasing stool volume and speeding elimination. The two fiber types combined are known as dietary fiber. Both help to keep you regular. (Figures for dietary fiber are given for the recipes in this book.)

One additional benefit of high-fiber foods is that they are filling and generally lessen the appetite for foods high in fat. Though a typical North American diet contains about 10 grams of fiber a day, 20 to 30 grams are recommended.

How can fiber in the diet be increased?

By substituting whole, unprocessed foods — such as brown rice, potatoes with their skins, beans, raw vegetables, and whole-grain bread — for processed foods, you can obtain more fiber. Also, check the labels of processed foods. Many manufacturers now mix whole ingredients with the processed ones for added nutritional value. They may list the amount of fiber per serving too. Nutritionists advise introducing more fiber to your diet slowly; too much too soon may cause discomfort. Also, when increasing fiber, be sure to increase your intake of fluids.

Can a high-fiber diet ward off colon cancer?

Several studies have shown that societies with high-fiber diets have lower rates of colon cancer. Researchers theorize that insoluble fiber especially speeds the elimination of cancer-causing substances in the colon. The less time the colon is exposed to carcinogenic substances, the less chance there is for cancer to develop.

How do oat bran and other foods high in soluble fiber lower cholesterol?

The exact process by which soluble fiber lowers cholesterol levels is not known, but some researchers believe that it binds with cholesterol and removes it in the process of elimination. Cholesterol-lowering benefits are more pronounced when a high intake of soluble fiber — from pectins (found in most fruits), vegetables, legumes, oat bran, and guar gum — is part of a diet that contains moderate amounts of fat and cholesterol.

Vitamins are organic compounds that

perform essential functions in the body. They help to synthesize fats, form hormones, maintain strong bones, metabolize protein, and convert carbohydrate and fat into energy. Obtained from the foods we eat, the 13 known vitamins fall into two groups: fat soluble and water soluble. The fat-soluble vitamins — A, D, E, and K — are stored in the body's fatty tissues. The water-soluble vitamins — C and eight B vitamins — pass out of the body regularly in urine and sweat and must be replenished often.

How are vitamin needs determined?

Recommended Daily Allowances (RDA's) of vitamins are set by the National Academy of Sciences after investigating the nutritional needs of different groups, such as children, men, women, pregnant women, and the elderly. The lowest requirement, or floor, is determined, as well as the highest, or ceiling. Nutritionists then choose a number higher than the floor but lower than the ceiling. Specific recommendations are made for each group by considering the needs of a typical member. For example, the typical adult woman, or reference woman, is 5 feet 4 inches tall and weighs 120 pounds. People who adhere to the recommendations should be getting optimum nutrients. But keep in mind that RDA's are targets to shoot for over time, not every day. You might, for instance, be short on thiamine one day and have more than a sufficient amount the next.

VITAMINS		
VITAMIN	BENEFIT TO THE BODY	SOURCES
A	Needed to maintain good vision and healthy hair, skin, and mucous membranes. Fights infection and may ward off certain cancers.	Dairy products, yellow, orange, and green vegetables, yellow and orange fruits, enriched cereals, organ meats.
D	Aids in forming and maintaining healthy bones and teeth. Necessary in the absorption of calcium.	Fortified milk, egg yolks, fish, liver.
E	Helps create red blood cells and build muscles and other tissues. Maintains essential fatty acids.	Poultry, seafood, vegetable oils, margarine, wheat germ, dried beans.
K	Synthesizes substances necessary for blood clotting and bone metabolism.	Green leafy vegetables, oats, potatoes, cabbage, organ meats.
B_1 Thiamine	Helps convert carbohydrate into energy; maintains healthy appetite, digestion, and nerve function.	Pork, whole grains, enriched cereals, wheat germ, seafood.
B_2 Riboflavin	Helps metabolize carbohydrate, protein, and fat; keeps mucous membranes healthy.	Beef, lamb, poultry (dark meat only), dairy foods, enriched breads and cereals, dark green leafy vegetables.
B_3 Niacin	Necessary to enzymes that convert food into energy; helps maintain healthy appetite, digestion, and nerve function.	Poultry, seafood, seeds and nuts, potatoes, whole-grain bread and cereal.
B_6	Plays a vital role in the metabolism and absorption of protein. Builds red blood cells.	Meat, fish, poultry, whole grains and cereals, spinach, sweet potatoes, avocados.
Folacin Folic Acid	Necessary to the formation of genetic material (DNA and RNA); helps produce red blood cells.	Dark green leafy vegetables, legumes, enriched cereals and breads, fruits, organ meats.
B_{12}	Aids in making red blood cells and genetic material; helps keep the nervous system functioning.	Found only in animal foods, especially liver, eggs, dairy products.
C	Important to the formation of collagen; keeps gums, teeth, and bones healthy; helps prevent infection and aids in healing cuts and wounds.	Citrus fruits, sweet peppers, strawberries, cantaloupe, broccoli.

Are vitamin pills necessary?

People who follow a sensible and varied diet do not need vitamin pills. Generally, there is no harm in taking a supplement that contains 100 percent or less of the RDA's; greater amounts can be toxic (see megadoses, below). Vitamin supplements *are* advised for certain people or special circumstances. Among them are bottle-fed infants, pregnant and nursing women, elderly persons, dieters, and others who may not be getting enough quantity of food to meet all needs. Illnesses and the use of oral contraceptives and some prescription drugs may also create a need for supplements of certain vitamins.

What are megadoses? Are they harmful?

Any supplement that is 10 times the established RDA is considered a megadose. Research has revealed that megadoses of certain vitamins can help in treating some diseases. However, megadoses are not recommended for the general population and, in fact, can be dangerous. Especially harmful are high dosages of the fat-soluble vitamins (A, D, E, and K), because they are not flushed out of the system but are stored in the liver. Over time, excesses of fat-soluble vitamins can become toxic.

Megadoses of water-soluble vitamins are not recommended either. It has been demonstrated that high doses of one vitamin can offset the effectiveness of another. For example, large amounts of vitamin C can interfere with the effectiveness of vitamin B_{12} and the metabolism of copper.

What is beta carotene?

Beta carotene is the natural coloring agent that gives carrots their deep orange color, and collard greens and spinach their dark green color. It converts in the body to vitamin A. Researchers have found that fruits and vegetables rich in beta carotene may help reduce the risk of certain forms of cancer, possibly by undermining the body's production of unstable molecules, or free radicals. These are created when cells are exposed to life-giving oxygen. Once oxygen has passed through a cell, the resulting by-products, free radicals, proceed to attack healthy cell membranes. Vitamins E and C and beta carotene appear to lessen the damage that free radicals inflict on healthy cells.

Does cooking destroy the vitamins in foods?

Heat destroys a portion of some vitamins; vitamin C is the most vulnerable. To minimize vitamin loss, cook vegetables and fruits quickly — the less time they are exposed to heat, the better. Vegetables cooked to the crisp-tender stage retain more vitamins than those cooked until soft (see Vegetable Cooking Chart, pages 232–233). Vegetables that are stir-fried or cooked in a microwave usually retain more of their vitamins because these methods are quick. When vegetables are boiled, some vitamins leach into the cooking water. (Nutritionists advise saving the cooking water and using it in soups and sauces.) Steaming results in less vitamin loss.

Does freezing destroy vitamins?

No. Frozen vegetables, for example, usually have the same vitamin content as fresh produce because they are frozen within a few hours of being picked. Most frozen foods stored at 0° F will retain their nutrients and stay fresh-tasting for up to 12 months.

Minerals are inorganic substances in foods that perform such critical functions as regulating the contractions of the heart, maintaining strong bones and teeth, and keeping body cells energized. Minerals are divided into two groups: macro, needed in larger quantities, and micro, required by the body in minute, or trace, amounts. Minimum daily requirements have been established for three of the minerals and recommended allowances have been determined for seven (see page 22); for others, the needs have only been estimated at this time. In general, a diet that includes a variety of grains, fruits, vegetables, and animal foods provides an adequate, if not generous, amount of all the minerals. Exceptions are iron and calcium, of which some persons do not always obtain a sufficient supply. In the case of sodium (obtained chiefly from table salt), many people in North America consume far too much.

What role does iron play in the body?

Iron is part of hemoglobin, a protein that releases oxygen to body cells. Without sufficient iron, hemoglobin levels eventually drop and red blood cells become small and pale. Less oxygen is given off to the body cells, resulting in fatigue.

The need for iron changes with age. Infants and toddlers demand high levels because of their fast growth rates. And teenagers should have plenty to help them get through growth spurts. Pregnant and nursing women also have a greater need for iron.

The iron in red meat and other other animal foods is readily absorbed by the body. To boost iron absorption from plant sources, eat foods rich in vitamin C and limit iron absorption inhibitors, such as tannins (present in coffee and tea) and phytates (found in unleavened whole-grain bread).

Why is calcium so important?

About 99 percent of the body's calcium is in the bones and teeth. The remaining 1 percent circulates in the blood, where it helps regulate muscle action, blood clotting, cell nourishment, release of energy, and transmission of nerve impulses. Recent, though inconclusive, studies indicate that calcium may also play a role in helping to reduce high blood pressure.

In the early stages of life, insufficient calcium intake can cause poor formation of bones and teeth; in older people, it may lead to tooth loss and bone fractures. For adults in general, the recommended daily allowance is 800 milligrams, but for young people up to age 25 and for pregnant and nursing women, the minimum is 1,200 milligrams.

Too much phosphorus in the diet, from a high consumption of soft drinks or meat, for example, increases the need for calcium. To be absorbed by the body, calcium must be accompanied by vitamin D; vitamin C also aids in absorption.

Is it a good idea to take calcium supplements?

The best way to obtain calcium is from dairy foods and certain fish and plants that are rich in the mineral. People who have an intolerance for or exclude dairy foods from their diet may receive some benefit from supplements. However, not all supplements are equally endowed with calcium, nor are they completely absorbed by the body. (Calcium carbonate, which is about 40 percent calcium, contains the greatest amount.) People at risk for kidney stones should not take supplements. Also, taking too much of a supplement can cause constipation.

Does extra calcium prevent osteoporosis?

There is no conclusive evidence as yet that increased calcium intake, especially in supplement form, can prevent osteoporosis, though it appears to be helpful in slowing the process. This disease of aging, marked by the thinning of bone tissue, can cause back pain and vulnerability to broken bones.

All people lay down bone mass until age 25 or 30, after which there is a gradual loss. Women in particular are vulnerable after menopause, when estrogen levels drop dramatically. (Estrogen seems to protect against bone loss.) For women, estrogen replacement therapy so far has proved the most effective way to ward off osteoporosis, though there are risks and side effects that should be discussed with a doctor. For both women and men, the best way to prepare bones for the aging years is to eat calcium-rich foods throughout childhood and young adulthood so that bones reach their maximum density. Maintaining adequate calcium intake in the adult years is also advised. And there are indications that exercise, especially aerobic exercise, helps modify the loss of bone mass.

How does the body use sodium?

Sodium, in combination with chloride and potassium, regulates the amount and movement of body fluids, transports nutrients across intestinal membranes, controls blood volume, and transmits sig-

Rich sources of calcium are dairy products, an average 8-ounce serving of which contains 300 milligrams. Dark leafy greens, sardines with bones, legumes, eggs, almonds, and tofu also contain a fair amount.

nals affecting nerves and muscles. Sodium regulates fluids outside cells; potassium, inside cells.

A common source of both sodium and chloride in the diet is table salt, 1 gram of which contains 390 milligrams of sodium and 610 milligrams of chloride. Fruits and legumes are good sources of potassium.

What if we get too much sodium?

Excess sodium shifts the balance of fluids in body cells; one consequence can be a build-up of water around body tissues, causing painful swelling, or edema. Another result can be the drawing of more water into the blood, thereby increasing the volume and causing blood pressure to rise and the heart to work harder. The kidneys, responsible for excreting excess sodium, are also overworked.

Does salt (i.e., sodium) cause hypertension?

The exact causes of hypertension, or high blood pressure, are unknown, but salt may be a contributing factor for some people — especially the 10 to 15 percent of the population who are salt sensitive. In these persons the kidneys fail to excrete excess sodium and it builds up. Even in cases in which salt may not be the cause of hypertension, reducing salt intake often helps to correct the condition.

Should everyone cut back on salt?

The people who need to be most concerned about salt intake are those who already suffer from hypertension. (And because sodium is present naturally in most foods, they should also limit consumption of the ones that are high, such as beets, celery, turnips, and milk.) For the rest of the population, some reduction in salt may be a good idea, depending on how excessive their intake is. The actual need for salt is between 200 and 300 milligrams per day, or about ¹⁄₁₀ to ¹⁄₈ of a teaspoon. Nutritionists recommend limiting sodium intake to between 2,200 and 3,300 milligrams (1 to 2 teaspoons of salt) per day. If you are getting more than 3,500 milligrams, you should probably cut back.

What are some ways to limit salt?

The easiest way is to remove the saltshaker from the dining table and cut out such salty snacks as potato chips, pretzels, and pickled foods. Limit your consumption of cheeses and cured meats, such as ham and corned beef. Read the labels of processed foods carefully; many have a great deal of salt. Except for yeast breads, in which salt contributes to the texture, you can eliminate or cut down salt in recipes. (This has been done already for the *Live Longer Cookbook*.) You can also ask your doctor about using a salt substitute such as potassium chloride.

Water, which comprises about two-thirds of the adult human body, is so important to all bodily functions that a person cannot survive more than 2 or 3 days without replenishing lost water. Though we don't drink water for its nutrients, it often contains minerals that we need, such as fluoride, or that we need to be cautious about, such as sodium.

The body loses about 3 quarts of water a day; some will be replaced by the water in foods (fruits and vegetables are 60 to 95 percent water), but the rest should be taken as liquids — at least six to eight 8-ounce glasses. Alcoholic and caffeinated beverages do not count as part of this daily intake because they act as diuretics, removing fluids from the system. In fact, drinking such beverages triggers the need for additional water. So do consumption of highly salted foods, exercise that produces sweat, and weight-loss dieting (the process of burning off fat demands a great deal of fluid).

MINERALS ESSENTIAL TO THE BODY

MINERAL	FUNCTIONS	GOOD SOURCES
Calcium	Is the major building material of bones and teeth; helps regulate muscles, clot blood, nourish cells, and transmit nerve impulses.	Dairy products, dark green vegetables, sardines with bones.
Phosphorus	Works with calcium to build bones and teeth; helps release energy from carbohydrate.	Dairy products, meat, fish, poultry, legumes, grains, nuts.
Magnesium	Is part of bone structure; activates enzymes that release energy from glucose; helps to synthesize protein.	Dark green vegetables, dairy products, nuts, meat, whole-grain cereals, legumes.
Sodium	Aids in regulating passage of nutrients in and out of body cells and also volume of body fluid.	Almost all foods except fruit.
Potassium	Works with sodium and chloride to keep body fluids in balance; aids in carbohydrate and protein metabolism.	Meat, diary products, cereals, many fruits, legumes.
Chloride	With sodium and potassium, helps to keep body fluids in balance; in the stomach, combines with water to form hydrochloric acid for digestion.	Table salt, seafood, meat, dairy products, eggs.
Zinc	Plays an important role in metabolism and protein synthesis.	Dairy products, liver, wheat bran, shellfish.
Iodine	Is part of thyroid hormone that regulates the body's energy metabolism.	Fish and shellfish, iodized salt, dairy products, vegetables.
Copper	Plays a role in the synthesis of hemoglobin; is a component of digestive enzymes.	Liver, shellfish, whole grains, poultry, oysters, nuts.
Manganese	Is involved in synthesis of fatty acids.	Beet greens, fruits, legumes, whole grains.
Fluoride	Can help prevent tooth decay; may minimize bone loss.	Some drinking water, seafood, dark green vegetables, onions.
Selenium	May act as an antioxidant; is associated with fat metabolism.	Fish, organ meats, grains.

GUIDE TO BEANS

Beans, or legumes, are excellent sources of vegetable protein, B vitamins, iron, magnesium, and zinc. They are also high in soluble fiber, which helps lower cholesterol, stabilize blood sugar levels, and reduce the incidence of certain cancers.

Most dried legumes, except lentils and split peas, must be soaked in cold water for at least 4 hours before cooking. The water rehydrates them, ensures uniform texture, and reduces cooking time. It also absorbs some of the indigestible complex sugars in beans that cause gas. Since the soaking water contains these sugars, be sure to discard it and drain and rinse the beans.

There are two soaking methods; for either one, you should sort and rinse the beans first. **(1) Long-soak method:** Place the beans in a large bowl and fill with enough water to cover by 2 inches. Soak for 4 to 8 hours. **(2) Quick-soak method:** Place the beans in a large saucepan and fill with enough water to cover by 1 inch. Bring to a boil, cook for 2 minutes, then remove from the heat and let stand, covered, for 1 hour. The cooking times given here are averages. Freshly dried beans may cook more quickly; older ones may take a little longer. Do not add salt until after beans are cooked.

Black Beans (Black Turtle Beans) are perhaps best known as the main ingredient in black turtle bean soup. Their hearty flavor complements rice, fish, and vegetables. One cup cooked has 15 grams of protein, 7 grams of fiber, and 91 milligrams of magnesium.
Cook: 1 cup beans in 3 cups cold water.
Time: Simmer, covered, for 1 hour.
Yield: 2 ½ cups

Black-eyed Peas. A favorite of the South, the black-eyed pea has a smooth texture and rich flavor. Of all the beans listed here, it is the highest in fiber (16 grams per cup of cooked peas) and the lowest in calories (1 cup has only 179 calories). Legend holds that eating a dish of black-eyed peas on New Year's Day will bring good luck throughout the year.
Cook: 1 cup peas in 3 cups cold water.
Time: Simmer, covered, for 1 to 1 ½ hours.
Yield: 3 cups

Chick Peas (Garbanzo Beans), are ancient legumes that date back to 7,000 B.C. They have a warm nutty flavor and figure in many cuisines. One cup cooked has 15 grams of protein, 6 grams of fiber, and 269 calories. A popular spread is the Middle Eastern purée of chick peas called hummus.
Cook: 1 cup peas in 3 cups cold water.
Time: Simmer, covered, for 1 ½ to 2 hours.
Yield: 2 ½ cups

Cow Peas (Field Peas, Crowder Peas) are grown in many gardens of the South, where they are often served as a side dish.
Cook: 1 cup peas in 3 cups cold water.
Time: Simmer, covered, for 1 hour.
Yield: 3 cups

Great Northern White Beans cook up quickly. Their mild flavor makes them versatile enough to be used in a number of recipes. They are known primarily as an ingredient in the French cassoulet (a casserole of beans and various meats) and in the American ham and bean soup.
Cook: 1 cup beans in 3 cups cold water
Time: Simmer, covered, for 45 minutes.
Yield: 2⅔ cups

Lentils, high in protein and folacin (a B vitamin), are one of the oldest known legumes and even figure in the Bible. In Genesis, Esau sold his birthright for a pot of lentils. There are several varieties. The cooking time below is for the brown (most commonly available) type. Red lentils, which can be cooked in 10 to 15 minutes, are often used for purées; green lentils must cook 20 to 25 minutes.
Cook: 1 cup lentils in 3 cups cold water.
Time: Simmer, covered, for 20 to 25 minutes.
Yield: 3 cups

Lima Beans (Butter Beans) were grown by American Indians between rows of corn so that the corn could act as stakes for the bean vines. This may be the origin of succotash, a well-known dish that combines lima beans and corn.
Cook: 1 cup beans in 3 cups cold water.
Time: Simmer, covered, for 45 minutes to 1 hour.
Yield: 2½ cups

Navy Beans (Boston Beans, Pea Beans) were grown by the Pilgrims, who learned of them from the Indians. Because religious observances kept the Pilgrims from cooking on the Sabbath, a pot of navy beans was baked the night before. The famous Boston baked beans emerged from this tradition.
Cook: 1 cup beans in 3 cups cold water.
Time: Simmer, covered, for 1 to 1½ hours.
Yield: 3 cups

Pigeon Peas have a pleasant roasted flavor that goes wonderfully well with rice, making it a favorite in Latin and Indian cuisine. One cup cooked has 11 grams of protein and 8 grams of fiber.
Cook: 1 cup peas in 3 cups cold water.
Time: Simmer, covered, for 45 minutes to 1¼ hours.
Yield: 3 cups

Pink Beans, as well as pinto beans, are the bean of choice for refried beans. They are milder in taste than the red kidney bean. All beans are an excellent source of complex carbohydrates, with the pink beans leading the pack. One cup cooked has 47 grams of carbohydrate. They are also high in folacin and magnesium.
Cook: 1 cup beans in 3 cups cold water.
Time: Simmer, covered, for 1 hour.
Yield: 3 cups

Pinto Beans (the word *pinto* means "painted" in Spanish) are favorites in the American Southwest, where they are used in chilies and stews. Pintos are good sources of protein, magnesium, and iron.
Cook: 1 cup beans in 3 cups cold water.
Time: Simmer, covered, for 45 minutes to 1 hour.
Yield: 2½ cups

Red Kidney Beans are preferred in chili con carne recipes because of their mild flavor and firm texture. They also go well in salads. One cup cooked has 15 grams of protein and 6 grams of fiber.
Cook: 1 cup beans in 3 cups water.
Time: Simmer, covered, for 45 minutes to 1¼ hours.
Yield: 2½ cups

Split Green Peas are favorites for soups and purées. One cup cooked has 16 grams of protein and 11 grams of fiber. Because they tend to foam when they cook, use a large pot. Split yellow peas cook in the same amount of time as the green and yield the same amount.
Cook: 1 cup peas in 4 cups cold water.
Time: Simmer, covered, for 30 minutes.
Yield: 2 cups

White Kidney Beans (Cannellini) are popular in soups, stews, salads, and pasta. Their smooth, buttery flavor is enhanced by garlic and herbs. One cup cooked has 17 grams of protein and 7 grams of fiber, and provides more than half the recommended daily allowance of iron for adults.
Cook: 1 cup beans in 3 cups cold water.
Time: Simmer, covered, for 45 minutes to 1¼ hours.
Yield: 2½ cups

GUIDE TO GRAINS

Grains are high in complex carbohydrates, fiber, iron, and B vitamins and relatively low in price. They are easy to prepare and make a flavorful, nutritious base for any meal. Before cooking grains, make sure they are free from grit; if necessary, rinse them in cold water and drain. Use a saucepan large enough to allow for their doubling or tripling in volume. Do not stir grains more than necessary because stirring makes them gummy. If using salt, add it at the end. The cooking times below yield a slightly crunchy texture. For a creamier result, cook a little longer.

Barley is high in B vitamins, potassium, and soluble fiber. The type of barley found in supermarkets and health food stores is called pearl or pearled, which means that the outer hull and bran have been removed, leaving the pearl, or endosperm. (Unpearled barley is used for animal feed.)
Cook: 1 cup in 3 cups boiling water.
Time: Simmer, covered, for 45 minutes (quick-cooking pearled barley takes 10 minutes).
Yield: 3 cups
Uses: soup, side dishes

Bulgur is a form of cracked wheat that has been parboiled. Like cracked wheat, bulgur is high in protein and fiber, but it cooks faster. It is available in the pasta and rice sections of most supermarkets and also in health food stores.
Cook: 1 cup bulgur in 2 cups boiling water.
Time: Simmer, covered, for 10 minutes. Remove from heat and let stand, covered, 10 minutes more.
Yield: 3 cups
Uses: cereal, salads, side dishes

Cornmeal comes in 2 colors: white and yellow. While yellow cornmeal contains more beta carotene than the white, both take the same amount of time to cook. Corn that is ground under millstones is called stone-ground cornmeal.
Cook: Stir 1 cup cornmeal into 2 cups cold water until smooth. Add the mixture to 1¾ cups boiling water.
Time: Simmer, covered, for 15 minutes.
Yield: 3¼ cups
Uses: cereal, side dishes, baking

Cracked Wheat is prepared by cutting whole-wheat berries into small pieces. It does not require soaking before cooking. High in fiber and nutrients, cracked wheat is available in health food stores.
Cook: 1 cup cracked wheat in 2 cups boiling water.
Time: Simmer, covered, for 20 minutes.
Yield: 2½ cups
Uses: cereal, salads, side dishes

Hominy Grits are the dried and ground kernels of corn that have been soaked in a mixture of lime and wood ash, causing the outer hulls to burst and the inner kernels to swell. The process yields a sweet, smoke-flavored cereal. (Whole cooked hominy is also available in cans.)
Cook: 1 cup grits in 5 cups boiling water.
Time: Simmer, covered, for 15 minutes.
Yield: 4 cups
Uses: cereal, baking, side dishes

Kasha is roasted buckwheat groats, or whole-grain kernels. Kasha's strong, nutty taste has been featured in Russian cuisine for centuries. For a fluffier texture, place the dry kasha in a skillet, stir in 1 egg, and cook over medium heat for 4 minutes, then add the water, lower the heat, and simmer for 7 minutes.
Cook: 1 cup kasha in 2 cups boiling water.
Time: Simmer, covered, for 7 minutes.
Yield: 3¼ cups
Uses: side dishes, salads

Millet is an ancient grain that dates back to Old Testament times. It is rich in protein, phosphorus, iron, and calcium. Available in specialty and health food stores, millet has a sweet nutty taste similar to that of cashews.
Cook: 1 cup millet in 2¼ cups boiling water.
Time: Simmer, covered, for 30 minutes.
Yield: 3½ cups
Uses: soup, baking, side dishes

Rolled Oats are available in two types. Both are processed by rolling and drying, but one (old-fashioned) is a little thicker and takes a bit longer to cook than the other (quick-cooking) variety. Rolled oats are ⅓ oat bran, which is high in soluble fiber and helps to lower cholesterol.
Cook: 1 cup oats in 2 cups boiing water.
Time: Simmer, uncovered, for 10 minutes, stirring occasionally.
Yield: 1 ¾ cups
Uses: cereal, baking, granola

Steel-cut Oats are found mostly in the specialty section of a supermarket or in health food stores. These are dried and then roughly cut by steel blades. The result is a crunchy, nutty-tasting product.
Cook: 1 cup oats in 2 cups boiling water.
Time: Simmer, covered, for 20 minutes. Remove from heat and let stand, covered, 5 minutes more.
Yield: 2 ½ cups
Uses: cereal, baking

Quinoa (pronounced keen-wa) was grown orignally by the Incas in the Andes Mountains of Peru. This super grain, high in protein, magnesium, and iron, is available in health food and specialty food stores and some supermarkets.
Cook: 1 cup quinoa, rinsed well, in 1 ¾ cups boiling water.
Time: Simmer, covered, for 12 minutes.
Yield: 3 ½ cups
Uses: side dishes, salads, soup, desserts

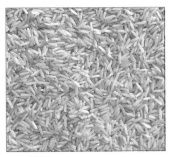

Basmati Rice is an aromatic rice originally from northern India. (A variety of it grown in the United States is called Texmati.) Its saffronlike fragrance is released in the cooking.
Cook: 1 cup white rice, rinsed well, in 3 ¾ cups boiling water.
Time: Simmer, covered, for 10 minutes (brown basmati rice takes 15 minutes longer); do not stir. Remove from heat and let stand, covered, 5 minutes more.
Yield: 3 ¾ cups
Uses: side dishes, desserts

Brown Long-grain Rice, which is unpolished, retains the bran that gives it a tan color and nutlike flavor. Compared to white rice, it is higher in fiber and some B vitamins. Oil in the bran layer of brown rice gives it a shorter shelf life than white.
Cook: 1 cup rice in 2 cups boiling water.
Time: Simmer, covered, for 30 to 35 minutes; do not stir.
Yield: 3 cups
Uses: salads, side dishes, soup, desserts

White Long-grain Rice is grown in North and South Carolina. The process of refining and polishing lightens its color and lowers its fiber content. Long-grain white rice is 4 times longer than it is wide and is fluffy when cooked as directed.
Cook: 1 cup rice in 2 cups boiling water.
Time: Simmer, covered, for 17 minutes; do not stir.
Yield: 3 cups
Uses: cereal, soup, side dishes, desserts

Wild Rice is the seed of a marsh grass that grows principally in the Great Lakes region of the United States. It has an intense, smoky flavor that mixes well with other, blander rices.
Cook: 1 cup well-rinsed wild rice in 3 cups boiling water.
Time: Simmer, covered, for 40 minutes. Remove from heat and let stand, covered, 5 minutes more.
Yield: 4 cups
Uses: side dishes, soups, salads

Wheat Berries are whole-wheat kernels with the inedible hulls removed. They need to be soaked before cooking; cover them with water and soak for 7 hours or overnight in the refrigerator, then drain.
Cook: 1 cup wheat berries in 2 cups boiling water.
Time: Simmer, covered, for 40 minutes.
Yield: 2 ½ cups
Uses: cereal, baking, salads, side dishes

HOW MUCH DO YOU NEED EACH DAY?

PROTEIN	CARBOHYDRATE	FAT	FIBER	VITAMINS	MINERALS
For a healthy adult, a daily intake of protein should equal 10 to 20 percent of total calories. In a diet of 1,800 calories, 13 percent protein equals 59 grams, represented by the foods listed below.	It is recommended that at least 55 percent of a day's calories come from carbohydrate. This is about 250 grams in an 1,800-calorie diet. The sample menu below provides about 250 grams of carbohydrate.	Many health groups recommend limiting fat to 30 percent or less of daily calories (see Box on page 11). In an 1,800-calorie diet, 30 percent comes to 66 grams. The following foods yield about 66 grams of fat.	There are no established dietary guidelines for fiber, but the National Cancer Institute advises consuming 20 to 30 grams per day. The following would provide about 25 grams of fiber.	RDA's have been established for the following vitamins:	The National Research Council has estimated the following minimum requirements for sodium, chloride, and potassium for adults over the age of 18 :
½ cantaloupe (2 grams)	1 cup corn flakes (21 grams)	1 bran muffin (4 grams)	2 slices whole-wheat bread (2.8 grams)	**For adult men**	Sodium: 500 milligrams
½ cup skim milk (4 grams)	½ cup skim milk (6 grams)	1 teaspoon margarine (4 grams)	¾ cup raisin bran cereal (3.6 grams)	Vitamin A: 1 milligram, or 5,000 IU	Chloride: 750 milligrams
¾ cup cooked oatmeal (4 grams)	½ grapefruit (13 grams)	1 cup low-fat yogurt (4 grams)	1 orange (0.8 grams)	Thiamin (B_1): 1.5 milligrams	Potassium: 2,000 milligrams
2 tablespoons peanut butter (8 grams)	2 slices whole-wheat bread (27 grams)	2 ounces Cheddar cheese (18 grams)	2 graham crackers (2.8 grams)	Riboflavin (B_2): 1.7 milligrams	
2 slices whole-wheat bread (5 grams)	1 medium-size carrot (7 grams)	2 slices rye bread (2 grams)	½ cup cooked kidney beans (5.8 grams)	Niacin (B_3): 19 milligrams	RDA's have been established for the following minerals:
1 large peach (1 gram)	1 cup orange juice (24 grams)	2 teaspoons mayonnaise (7 grams)	1 sweet potato (3.8 grams)	Vitamin B_6: 2 milligrams	
1 cup tomato soup (4 grams)	4 ounces cooked pasta (86 grams)	4 ounces poached chicken breast, without skin (5 grams)	¾ cup green beans (3.1 grams)	Folacin: 200 micrograms	**For adult men**
3 ounces broiled cod (23 grams)	½ cup cooked black beans (20 grams)	1 cup cooked peas (1 gram)	1 banana (2.1 grams)	Vitamin B_{12}: 2 micrograms	Calcium: 800 to 1,200 milligrams
½ cup cooked brown rice (2 grams)	½ cup chopped onion (7 grams)	1 teaspoon olive oil (5 grams)		Vitamin C: 60 milligrams.	Phosphorus: 800 to 1,200 milligrams
1 stalk broccoli (4 grams)	½ small sweet green pepper (2 grams)	1 whole-wheat roll (1 gram)		Vitamin D: 5 micrograms, or 400 IU	Magnesium: 350 milligrams
1 enriched roll (2 grams)	1 small tomato (4 grams)	1 tablespoon French dressing (9 grams)		Vitamin E: 10 milligrams, or 30 IU	Iron: 10 milligrams
	1 medium-size apple (21 grams)	1 cup vanilla ice milk (6 grams)		Vitamin K: 80 micrograms	Zinc: 15 milligrams
	1 raisin oatmeal cookie (9 grams)			**For adult women**	Iodine: 150 micrograms
				Vitamin A: 800 micrograms, or 4,000 IU	Selenium: 70 micrograms
				Thiamin (B_1): 1.1 milligrams	
				Riboflavin (B_2): 1.3 milligrams	**For adult women**
				Niacin (B_3): 15 milligrams	Calcium: 800 to 1,200 milligrams
				Vitamin B_6: 1.6 milligrams	Phosphorus: 800 to 1,200 milligrams
				Folacin: 180 micrograms	Magnesium: 280 milligrams
				Vitamin B_{12}: 2 micrograms	Iron: 10 to 15 milligrams
				Vitamin C: 60 milligrams	Zinc: 12 milligrams
				Vitamin D: 10 micrograms, or 400 IU	Iodine: 150 micrograms
				Vitamin E: 8 milligrams, or 24 IU	Selenium: 55 micrograms
				Vitamin K: 65 micrograms	

Living Longer

Why do we age? The question is as old as humanity. One of the first scientists to attempt an answer was Hippocrates, the father of medicine. He believed that body heat was the measure of a person's life force and that aging was simply the result of losing this innate source of energy. Since the discovery of DNA (the genetic code imprinted in our cells), molecular scientists have been investigating aging on a cellular level. They have found that certain cells, such as those of the skin and bone marrow, have the ability to divide continuously, while others, such as liver cells, have a limited lifespan; they can divide only 50 times, after which they stop regenerating and die. Scientists are also looking into a theory of aging that posits an aging hormone. Over time, this hormone slows the metabolism and weakens cells, thus leading to an impairment of the immune system.

While theories of aging abound, new research reveals the impact that external factors can have on longevity. The right lifestyle choices, such as eating sensibly, maintaining proper body weight, and exercising, can increase vitality and help to ward off or lessen the severity of chronic diseases. In fact, a proper diet may be the strongest factor in reducing disease. Large-scale studies indicate that as much as 40 percent of cancer occurrences in men and 60 percent in women are related to diet.

Longevity and Good Food

The evidence is clear: Good nutrition plays a key role in our health and longevity. Unfortunately, when nutrition information makes the news, it is rarely to extol the virture of a well-balanced diet. Studies frequently highlight the health benefits of a particular food. For instance, when it was shown that oat bran could lower serum cholesterol levels, the public immediately clamored for it. Subsequent studies have revealed that it is not oat bran *per se* that lowers cholesterol but the soluble fiber it contains. There are many good sources of soluble fiber, including barley, beans, fruits, and vegetables.

Carrots, too, have made the news as anticancer agents. This is because carrots contain beta caro-

NUTRITIONAL GUIDELINES

Variety, moderation, and balance are the keys to a healthful eating plan. The following are recommendations offered by leading nutritionists and health agencies.

1 Eat a wide variety of foods. Eating many different foods assures you of getting a full range of nutrients.

2 Maintain a healthy weight. A quick way to determine if you are overweight is to compare your waist measurement with that of your hip. For both men and women, the waist should be smaller than the hip.

3 Reduce fat, especially saturated fat. Fat intake should not exceed 30 percent of the day's calories, with less than 10 percent of calories coming from saturated fat.

4 Eat an abundance of vegetables, fruits, and grains. Adults should eat at least three servings of vegetables, two servings of fruit, and six servings of grain products, especially whole grains, every day.

5 Use sugar only in moderation. Sweets offer little nutritional value and have been shown to cause tooth decay.

6 Use salt only in moderation. Ideally, salt consumption from all sources, including the saltshaker, should be no more than 1 to 2 teaspoons a day.

7 If you drink alcohol, do so in moderation. Not only does alcohol offer empty calories, but excessive use of it leads to ailments such as kidney and liver disease. A recommendation is to have no more than two drinks a day. Because alcohol can cause birth defects, pregnant women are urged to abstain from all such beverages.

tene, a coloring agent that converts to vitamin A in the body. Scientists believe that beta carotene (or the vitamin A to which it converts) prevents damage to genes and other substances in cells by neutralizing unstable molecules called free radicals. Free radicals cause a chemical chain reaction in the body that can turn healthy cells into cancerous ones. Beta carotene helps to decrease the production of free radicals, and several studies suggest that it is effective in preventing certain types of cancer, especially of the larynx, esophagus, lung, and bladder. Carrots are far from the only source of beta carotene. It is readily available in a number of vegetables and fruits — in fact, any that are yellow, such as apricots, cantaloupe, and winter squash, or dark green, such as spinach and kale.

Other Cancer Connections

A number of other dietary factors have been identified by cancer researchers as being linked with this disease in either a preventive or a risk category. For example, vitamin C or foods that are high in this vitamin may be a factor in the prevention of esophageal and stomach cancers. So, too, might members of the cabbage family — broccoli, cabbage, Brussels sprouts, and cauliflower. These cruciferous vegetables may help to prevent cancer of the colon as well. Fiber is being investigated as a possible preventive for cancer, but so far the evidence is not consistent. We do know that cancers of the colon and lungs are lower among people who eat more fiber, but the links are not necessarily direct; other factors could be involved. Research continues into the health-enhancing properties of foods. There may be still more substances that reduce the risks of certain types of cancers.

On the negative side are nitrites, used in cured meats such as bacon, and the smoke in smoked fish, ham, and sausage. Eaten frequently or in excessive amounts, these may contribute to the development of stomach and esophageal cancers. Being overweight and drinking to excess appear also to increase greatly a person's chances of contracting many types of cancer.

The Right Measure

In many diets, 40 percent of daily calories comes from fat, 20 percent from protein, and 40 percent from carbohydrate. If this is typical of your own eating patterns, you should aim to increase your proportion of carbohydrate by consuming more grains, vegetables, fruits, and legumes. (See Box, right, for the recommended division of calories.)

One common reason for eating too much fat is that it serves as a flavor enhancer, dissolving the aromatic compounds of foods so that taste buds are activated quickly. Fat also feels good in your mouth, bringing a smooth, satisfying texture to foods.

Healthful Makeovers

Fortunately, fat is not the only way to make your mouth happy. You can season foods more liberally with herbs, marinate meats in fruit juices or wine (which will also tenderize leaner cuts) and try special vinegars for your salads. With the intense flavors of balsamic and raspberry vinegars, for example, less dressing is needed. Flavored mustards also add a special flare to foods. And salsas (spicy vegetable sauces, often tomato based) are good alternatives to cream and butter sauces.

Many reduced-fat and nonfat products are now available to help people lower their fat intake without sacrificing taste. Included are mayonnaise, salad dressings, cured meats such as ham, cakes, ice cream, and other dairy products. On the whole, these are as satisfying as their high-fat counterparts and can be used as substitutes in recipes. The exceptions are some of the low-fat cheeses, which are fine when combined in a sandwich with other ingredients but are less appealing when eaten alone or in recipes that call for melted cheese.

Leading chefs have been experimenting with low-fat alternatives. They have discovered, as many home cooks have, that chicken or beef stock can be substituted satisfactorily for much of the oil in pasta sauces and that vegetable and bean purées combined with stock or low-fat milk make sauces as inviting as those of butter, flour, and cream.

DAILY PROPORTIONS

A diet for a healthy person should have no more than 30 percent of its calories from fat. People with an obesity problem or heart disease may be advised to cut fat to 20 or 25 percent (experiments with having heart patients cut fat to as little as 10 percent have shown some success in unclogging damaged arteries). Another 10 to 20 percent of calories should come from protein, and the remainder, 55 to 65 percent, from carbohydrate. (See Box, page 11, for the way to calculate percentages.)

CARBOHYDRATE 55% TO 65%

FAT 25% TO 30%

PROTEIN 10% TO 20%

Researchers, too, have been seeking ways to reduce fat. A group at the University of Minnesota developed a method for eliminating much of the fat in ground meat. They suggest cooking it in a nonstick pan, draining the fat, rinsing the meat with hot water. The meat can then be used in a pasta sauce or casserole and will have up to 20 percent less fat.

There are other healthful cooking techniques. Bake, broil, or grill meat, fish, and poultry, or poach the last two; frying adds unnecessary fat. Sauté with little oil (no more than 1 teaspoon per serving) or no oil at all by using a nonstick pan and heating it first. Or replace sautéing with "sweating," that is, cooking onions, garlic, and other such ingredients over low heat in a little stock.

If consciously cutting down on fat proves difficult, try another tack: Eat more complex carbohydrates. A big bowl of oatmeal will prove just as filling as a high-fat, high-cholesterol breakfast of bacon, eggs, and buttered toast. At lunch, replace the traditional ham and cheese sandwich with a cup of lentil soup, a fresh salad, and a slice or two of whole-grain bread. Dinner does not have to center around poultry or meat. This cookbook offers dozens of meatless main-dish recipes that can be just as satisfying.

Small Changes, Big Results

The rewards of a lighter, healthier way of eating are many. Just ask the people who live in Wellsburg, West Virginia. From 1988 to 1990, they participated in a wellness program, adopting a low-fat diet, exercising rigorously every day, and, if they were smokers, trying to give up the habit. Those who stayed with the program for the entire 2 years lowered their cholesterol by an average of 12 points. This achievement is impressive. For each point drop in serum cholesterol level, the threat of having a heart attack is cut by 2 percent. Trimming off 12 points means the risk is reduced by almost 25 percent. One Wellsburg citizen who had been fond of fast food lost 80 pounds and shaved 50 points from his cholesterol count. "The program has changed my life completely," he reports.

The Importance of Exercise

A physically active life with regular exercise has proven to be an effective way to slow down, if not turn back, the hands of time. In fact, the more active you are, the more likely it is that you will outlive those who are not. One study of Harvard University alumni found that men who exercised regularly added, on average, 2 years to their lives. The positive impact of exercise on health is so strong that scientists are questioning whether some of the symptoms commonly associated with aging, such as fatigue and hypertension, are related in part to inactivity.

While almost any form of exercise is good for you, studies have shown that aerobic exercise combined with strength training is especially effective. Aerobic exercise entails the sustained movement of the large muscle groups in order to give your heart, circulatory system, and lungs a workout. Strength training involves muscle-building exercises such as weight lifting and isometrics.

A word of caution: If you are 35 or older, have been inactive for some time, or have a risk of heart disease, it is important to consult your doctor before beginning any exercise program.

Aerobic Workouts

Aerobic exercise not only enhances the cardiovascular system, it helps build muscle mass and lower the percentage of body fat. Such workouts three to five times a week can also lower blood pressure and reduce the risk of coronary artery disease. But aerobic exercise does more than increase heart and lung capacity. It improves one's sense of overall well-being, in part by reducing anxiety and depression. Aerobics also burn as much as 400 to 600 calories per hour (the number of calories in an average breakfast), a plus for those wishing to lose weight.

Many activities can be turned into an aerobic workout. Brisk walking or steady bicycling for at least 20 minutes are two examples. Before you start to work out, it is important to spend 5 minutes warming up, slowly stretching out each muscle group. At the end of the exercise period, give yourself 5 minutes of continued activity to let your heart rate gradually return to normal.

Combining an aerobic exercise program with a muscle-strengthing program offers the best of both worlds. One study revealed that those who combined strength training with aerobics lost an average of 10 pounds of fat and gained 2 pounds of muscle in an 8-week period, while those who did only aerobics lost an average of 3 pounds of fat. This is because lean tissue burns more calories than body fat.

Strength and Fitness

If you have never worked with weights before, find an exercise specialist who can teach you how to use the equipment properly. He or she can also design a strength-training program to meet your needs.

When you start weight lifting, begin slowly. Experts suggest selecting one exercise for each major muscle group, then beginning your routine with the large muscles of the lower body before working the smaller muscles of the upper body. Weight lifters advise taking at least 2 seconds to lift a weight and 4 seconds to lower it. To give your muscles time to recuperate, space your workouts at least 2 days apart. Consistency is the key. A few months off will put you right back where you started.

Two sessions a week can increase your strength 20 to 40 percent in just a few months. In one weight-lifting program, men in their 60's and above managed to double their strength in just 12 weeks. The rewards are many. "As I moved into my 50's," reports a 58-year old, "my body felt more and more like a dead weight. I simply accepted it as part of growing older. How wonderful to discover this isn't the way I have to feel at my age — to know that, by working at it, I can actually feel better and more ready for life than I did when I was 22."

More Benefits of Exercise

Studies have shown that exercise can be helpful in coping with two diseases that strike people in their later years: arthritis and osteoporosis. Arthritis sufferers can benefit especially from a regular program of stretching exercises and isometrics (pushing or pulling against resistance), which help stabilize painful joints. For endurance, swimming is particularly recommended. In the case of osteoporosis, weight-bearing exercise, such as walking, jogging, tennis, and aerobics, strengthens bones and stimulates the production of hormones that help protect them.

CALORIES BURNED DURING EXERCISE	
EXERCISE	**CALORIES PER HOUR**
Aerobics	360 to 480
Bicycling (12 mph)	410
Tennis (singles)	400 to 450
Swimming (crawl)	275 to 500
Walking	300 to 440
Jogging	650 to 700
Weight Lifting	480

Getting Started

It's never too late to start an exercise program. But if you haven't exercised in a long time, it would be wise to consult a physician before beginning. You may also want to read up on the subject, join a health club, or consult a personal trainer to help you design a program that best suits your needs. For beginners and older people, walking at a comfortable pace is a great way to start getting fit. Walking outside in pleasant surroundings with a good friend will increase your motivation and your enjoyment of the activity. Once you have begun, you can gradually increase the pace at which you walk. Try joining a walking club or perhaps start your own.

One indicator of your improved fitness will be when your resting heart rate (the rate your heart beats when you are inactive) is lower than before you started your program. The advantage to a lower resting heart rate is simple: The fewer beats per minute, the less wear and tear on the heart. This happens because your heart has become stronger and therefore can pump more blood per beat.

Aside from sparing your heart, feeling fit does wonders for morale. Psychological tests have shown that those who exercise regularly experience a greater sense of self-confidence. Eighty-eight-year-old Ken Beer of Hillsborough, California, is just one example of what regular exercise can do. Beer, a top player on the United States Tennis Association's octogenarian circuit, holds 53 national senior titles. He gets out on the court three times a week. "The only way a person stays alive at my age is to take a keen interest in something and be challenged," Beer says. "For me, that's tennis. It gets me outdoors, helps me meet good people. Frankly, a person without a challenge is on the downhill."

Sensible Dieting

In the 1940's insurance companies first started to correlate weight with longevity. Studies have now proven that obesity, defined as being 20 percent or more over ideal weight, is a health risk. Researchers have found that obesity doubles the risk of develop-

RAISING THE HEARTBEAT

To maximize the benefits of aerobic exercise, you should be raising your heartbeat to at least 60 percent of total capacity for a minimum of 15 minutes. The total heart capacity of different age groups must be taken into consideration.

Age 30: Total capacity: 190 beats / minute. Target zone: 114 to 152 heartbeats / minute.

Age 40: Total capacity: 180 beats / minute. Target zone: 108 to 144 heartbeats / minute.

Age 50: Total capacity: 170 beats / minute. Target zone: 102 to 136 heartbeats / minute.

Age 60: Total capacity: 160 beats / minute. Target zone: 96 to 128 heartbeats / minute.

Age 70: Total capacity: 150 beats / minute. Target zone: 90 to 120 heartbeats / minute.

To find out if you have reached your target heart rate, take your pulse; count the number of beats during a 10-second interval and multiply that number by 6. Do not take your pulse during the peak of an aerobic workout, but wait until you have slowed down a bit. The target zone for your age group indicates if you are exerting too little effort or too much. A pulse reading below your target zone means you are not working hard enough; a reading above it means you are overdoing it and need to slow down.

MEASURING THE PULSE

To obtain a heart rate by feeling the pulse in the neck (the carotid pulse), gently place an index or middle finger on either side of the neck slightly below the jawbone. Be careful not to press too hard, as pressure sensors in these arteries may cause a sudden decrease in heart rate.

ing hypertension and quadruples the risk of an onset of diabetes. At least one-quarter of cardiovascular disease is connected to obesity. And people who weigh 40 percent or more above their ideal weight have a high risk of cancer (as much as 50 percent greater than people of average weight). These are only the most serious implications. Carrying too much weight also exacerbates the symptoms of some forms of arthritis.

The Pitfalls of Crash Diets

The need to keep one's weight within a healthy range is important. Unfortunately, many people who want to lose weight opt for the quick fix and go on a crash diet. Crash diets, however, carry certain risks. They are often so low in calories that the body literally starves for certain nutrients and the brain may not get enough glucose. The result is fatigue and malnutrition, sometimes also depression.

Worse still, 95 percent of the people who lose weight on a crash diet gain it back within a year. There are two principal reasons for this unpleasant statistic: weight plateaus and the yo-yo syndrome.

The frustrating phenomenon known as "hitting a plateau" usually strikes after a dieter has lost a significant amount of weight but, despite continued dieting, cannot lose any more pounds. The body weight simply remains the same, or "plateaus." Scientists believe that the plateau phenomenon harks back to the days when people had to contend with times of feast and famine. During periods of scarcity (when dietary intake might be 1,200 calories per day or less), the body tries to preserve body fat by altering its metabolism so that fewer calories are needed to perform basic functions. When metabolism slows down to conserve body fat, the result is fatigue and a slowing of weight loss. This mechanism can be life-preserving during a famine, but it is a dieter's greatest problem.

Over time, fatigue and lack of further weight loss often send the frustrated dieter back to old ways of eating. Unfortunately, since the body's metabolism has been lowered, fewer calories are now being burned off. With the sudden increase in calories, the weight that was lost is rapidly regained, sometimes along with additional pounds. A dieter may now be prompted to start on yet another crash diet. This unhappy cycle is called the yo-yo syndrome because the dieter's weight constantly fluctuates.

The Secret to Long-term Weight Loss

The effective way to lose weight and keep it off is to diet slowly and sensibly. Nutritionists recommend losing no more than 1/2 to 1 pound a week. The best way to accomplish this is to eat a well-balanced diet and increase physical activity.

When dieting, it is important to eat a wide variety of foods. But the ones you can afford to cut back on drastically are those high in fat. For example, 1 cup of whole milk contains 8 grams of fat and 159 calories, while 1 cup of skim milk has less than 1/2 gram of fat and only 88 calories. Aside from eliminating excess calories, cutting down on fat, particularly the saturated kind, helps guard against heart disease. The best diet is no diet at all; it's a fresh approach to eating that changes habits for life.

Eating Out

If you dine out infrequently, a restaurant meal may represent the chance to pull out all the stops and eat what you please, regardless of calories or fat, or to enjoy a generous helping of food that you normally eat sparingly. However, if you have special diet restrictions or eat out on a regular basis, getting the right foods or maintaining a healthful balance in your diet can be a major challenge. Fortunately, wholesome entrées that feature a minimum of fat and/or salt are becoming more common. Even major fast-food franchises have responded to the demand for healthier fare by adding salad bars and cutting down on the salt and fat used in their recipes. Whether or not a restaurant offers choices that meet your specific diet needs, you can dine happily and healthily by following a few simple guidelines:

If you are watching your sodium:

- Avoid such condiments as pickles, olives, and marinated vegetables.

- Avoid soups; they contain a great deal of salt.
- Order salad without the dressing and request oil and vinegar to dress it.
- Avoid dairy products or eat them sparingly, especially cheese.
- Order foods that are prepared without sauces.
- Request a dish, such as grilled fish, that is not pre-cooked and ask that yours be prepared without salt.

If you are watching your fat intake or trying to lose weight:

- From bread baskets, choose rolls or melba toast and spare the butter; avoid high-fat croissants.
- To avoid overeating with a complete meal that has four courses, order à la carte. Or select half portions when available. Instead of a richly sauced main course, consider having two appetizers, such as a salad and a shrimp cocktail.
- Order foods that are steamed, broiled, grilled, stir-fried, or roasted rather than braised or fried.
- Remove the skin from poultry.
- Order only lean cuts of meat, such as flank or round of beef or tenderloin of pork. Better yet, order fish; it always has less fat than meat.
- Request that sauces and salad dressings be served on the side and use them sparingly.
- Be a wise consumer at the salad bar. Choose greens, crunchy vegetables, croutons, and chick peas and use a reduced-calorie dressing if available. Avoid pasta salads laden with dressing.
- In general, beware of so-called diet plates that offer such fare as hamburger without the roll, tuna salad served on lettuce instead of bread, or canned fruit and a scoop of cottage cheese mounded on iceberg lettuce. They are limited nutritionally and may be higher in fat than you suspect. Hamburger can have as much as 27 percent (by weight) of its calories in fat, and without the bun it isn't balanced by complex carbohydrates. Whether served on bread or lettuce, tuna salad is frequently heavy with mayonnaise. Canned fruit is often high in sugar and iceberg lettuce has minimal nutrients.
- For dessert, ask for fresh seasonal fruit. Avoid whipped cream or sugary toppings.

HOW MANY CALORIES DO YOU NEED?

To maintain an ideal body weight or determine what your caloric intake should be in order to lose weight, you need to know the number of calories that you burn in a typical day. It is a combination of your basal metabolic rate, or BMR, and the calories expended in all your activities. The BMR is the number of calories that your body uses to sustain all normal functions, such as breathing, blinking, and digesting food. Think of it as equivalent to a car's idling speed. A doctor can arrange for you to have your BMR determined accurately. You can also figure your own approximate BMR by multiplying your present weight by 10.

WEIGHT x 10 = BMR
(Example: 150 pounds x 10 = 1,500 calorie BMR)

To determine about how many additional calories you need for everyday activities, such as shopping, working at your desk, and cooking, multiply your BMR by 0.30.

BMR x 0.30 = additional activity calories
(Example: 1,500 calories x 0.30 = 450 calories)

A person with a BMR of 1,500 calories a day must consume an additional 450 calories to maintain a normal level of activity. Now add the calories required for such athletic pursuits as brisk walking, tennis or jogging (see Calories Burned During Exercise, page 25), and you know the approximate number of calories you need each day. If you consistently eat fewer calories than you burn, you will lose weight.

HEALTHFUL MENUS

Each menu below (for one person) was created largely with recipes from the *Live Longer Cookbook* to show you how easy it is to have a day's worth of lively, flavorful dishes and at the same time keep proportions of fat, protein, and carbohydrate within healthful nutritional guidelines. As you can see, the percentages of fat are well below the recommended daily maximum of 30 percent, and because of this, the calories are also quite low. A person who requires more calories could increase serving sizes and/or add more fruits, vegetables, or bread. All three menus include the minimum of five fruit and vegetable servings per day: adding more of these foods would be a nutritional plus.

WEEKDAY EXPRESS

Breakfast
Honey Toasted Granola *(page 40)*

6 Ounces Plain Nonfat Yogurt

1 Large Banana

Coffee or Tea

Lunch
Macaroni Salad with Basil, Tomatoes, and Chick Peas *(page 57)*

1 Slice Olive-Cheddar Bread (page 302)

8 Ounces Vegetable-Juice Cocktail

Dinner
Lemon Rice Soup *(page 62)*

Crispy Baked Fish *(page 84)*

Kale with Chili Sauce *(page 23)*

1 Slice Whole Wheat Italian Bread

1 Teaspoon Butter or Margarine

1 Medium-Size Orange

TOTAL CALORIES: 1,724

FAT: 24 percent

PROTEIN: 14 percent

CARBOHYDRATE: 62 percent

FAMILY FARE

Breakfast
½ Cantaloupe

2 Carrot-Pecan Muffins *(page 30)* with 1 Tablespoon Neufchâtel Cream Cheese

8 Ounces Skim Milk

Lunch
1 Turkey Burger with Sage and Onion *(page 123)*

1 Oat-Bran English Muffin *(page 302)*

½ Medium-Size Tomato, Sliced

1 Tablespoon Ketchup

1 Saltless Dill Pickle *(page 286)*

Cranberry Fizz *(page 319)*

2 Double Ginger Cookies *(page 339)*

Snack
Chili Popcorn *(page 313)*

Dinner
Vegetable Cheese Enchiladas *(page 179)*

Cauliflower, Carrot, and Pepper Vinaigrette *(page 254)*

1 Medium-Size Nectarine

Mocha Ice *(page 333)*

TOTAL CALORIES: 1,645

FAT: 22 percent

PROTEIN: 17 percent

CARBOHYDRATE: 61 percent

SUNDAY SPECIAL

Breakfast
6 Ounces Orange Juice

1 Slice Baked French Toast *(page 37)*

1 Tablespoon Whipped Cheese Topping *(page 39)*

2 Tablespoons Blueberry Sauce *(page 39)*

Citrus Spiced Tea *(page 320)*

Lunch
Chunky Chicken Soup *(page 63)*

2 Basil-Parmesan Biscuits *(page 290)*

2 Teaspoons Butter or Margarine

1 Cup Fresh Pineapple Chunks

Dinner
Double Mushroom Risotto *(page 199)*

2 Cups Escarole

2 Tablespoons Roasted Tomato Vinaigrette *(page 266)*

2 Bread Sticks

Cranberry-Pear Upside Down Cake *(page 326)*

TOTAL CALORIES: 1,676

FAT: 23 percent

PROTFIN: 17 percent

CARBOHYDRATE: 60 percent

BREAKFAST

Start every day with a good breakfast, and this one habit could
increase your chances of living a longer, healthier life. Research has revealed
significantly higher longevity rates for people who eat breakfast regularly. So
why not make it a powerhouse meal while you're at it? Begin with fruit or fruit juice
for vitamin C and enhanced mineral absorption. Add protein for rebuilding body
tissue and for stamina. Good sources are low-fat dairy foods, which also provide calcium.
Then, as the backbone of your healthful breakfast, eat whole-grain cereal — hot
or cold, in bread, biscuits, muffins, waffles, or pancakes — for sustained energy the
whole morning long. Tempting breakfast recipes appear throughout this
chapter. However, if the typical fare doesn't appeal to you, check the box
on page 44 for an abundance of nontraditional breakfast ideas.

To enjoy muffins anytime, store extra muffin batter in the refrigerator and bake just what you need when you want it. The batter will keep for about 5 days. Or freeze muffin batter in cupcake liners and bake them frozen, according to recipe directions, allowing about 10 minutes of extra baking time. Or freeze baked muffins, wrapped individually in aluminum foil. Warm them in their foil wrappers in the oven or toaster oven (but not the microwave), for 20 minutes at 400° F.

Refresh day-old muffins by wrapping them in aluminum foil and warming them in a toaster oven at 400° F for 10 minutes. Or microwave them, unwrapped, on *High* (100% power) for 10 to 15 seconds per muffin.

CARROT-PECAN MUFFINS

These moist whole-grain muffins are sweetened with cider, currants, carrots, and just a touch of brown sugar.

Nonstick cooking spray
⅓ cup golden raisins or currants
¼ cup apple cider or orange juice
¾ cup rye flour
¾ cup whole-wheat flour
¾ cup cornmeal
2 teaspoons baking powder
1 teaspoon baking soda
½ teaspoon salt

1 cup plain low-fat yogurt
2 tablespoons dark brown sugar
1 large egg
1 large egg white
2 medium-size carrots, peeled and shredded (1½ cups)
2 tablespoons coarsely chopped pecans or walnuts

1 Preheat the oven to 400° F. Lightly coat twelve 2½-inch muffin cups with nonstick cooking spray or insert cupcake liners. In a small bowl, soak the raisins in the cider for 15 minutes. Meanwhile, in a large bowl, stir together the rye flour, whole-wheat flour, cornmeal, baking powder, baking soda, and salt. Make a well in the center.

2 In a small bowl, stir together the yogurt, sugar, egg, and egg white until blended. Stir in the carrots, raisins, and cider just until combined. Pour the mixture into the dry ingredients and stir just until combined. Do not overmix.

3 Spoon ¼ cup batter into each muffin cup and sprinkle with the nuts. Bake for 18 to 20 minutes or until golden and a toothpick inserted in the center comes out clean. Makes 12 muffins.

PREPARATION TIME: 20 MIN. COOKING TIME: 18 MIN.

Per muffin: Calories 137; Saturated Fat 0.5 g; Total Fat 2 g; Protein 5 g; Carbohydrate 26 g; Fiber 2 g; Sodium 242 mg; Cholesterol 19 mg

What could be better than beginning the day with oven-fresh Carrot-Pecan Muffins?

BRAN AND CORNMEAL MUFFINS

Bake a double batch of these robust, chewy muffins and freeze the extras.

Nonstick cooking spray
1½ cups skim milk
2 tablespoons corn oil
1½ cups bran cereal
½ cup sifted all-purpose flour
¾ cup yellow cornmeal
2 teaspoons baking powder
¼ teaspoon salt
2 tablespoons sugar
2 large egg whites

1 Preheat the oven to 400° F. Lightly coat twelve 2½-inch muffin cups with the nonstick cooking spray or insert cupcake liners. In a medium-size bowl, pour the milk and oil over the cereal; set aside.

2 In a large bowl, combine the flour, cornmeal, baking powder, salt, and sugar; add the cereal mixture and stir just until combined. Do not overmix.

3 In a perfectly clean medium-size bowl, beat the egg whites with an electric mixer set on high speed until they are stiff but not dry. With a rubber spatula, fold the whites into the batter.

4 Spoon the batter into the muffin cups, filling them to the top. Bake for 22 minutes or until a toothpick inserted in the center comes out clean. Remove from the pan and let cool on a wire rack; serve at room temperature. Makes 12 muffins.

PREPARATION TIME: 12 MIN. COOKING TIME: 22 MIN.

Per muffin: Calories 118; Saturated Fat 0 g; Total Fat 4 g; Protein 6 g; Carbohydrate 22 g; Fiber 4 g; Sodium 245 mg; Cholesterol 1 mg

DATE COFFEE CAKE

If you don't have dates on hand, you can substitute an equal amount of prunes, raisins, or dried apricots.

2 cups unsifted all-purpose flour
¼ cup plus 2 tablespoons firmly packed light brown sugar
1½ teaspoons baking powder
½ teaspoon baking soda
½ teaspoon salt
½ teaspoon ground ginger
1 cup coarsely chopped pitted dates
¾ cup plain nonfat yogurt
3 tablespoons vegetable or corn oil
1 large egg
1 tablespoon grated orange rind
¼ cup toasted wheat germ

1 Preheat the oven to 375° F. Lightly grease and flour a 9" x 9" x 2" baking pan. In a large bowl, combine the flour, ¼ cup of the sugar, the baking powder, baking soda, salt, and ginger; stir in the dates.

2 In a small bowl, stir together the yogurt, oil, egg, and orange rind. Make a well in the center of the flour mixture, pour in the yogurt mixture, and stir just until combined. Do not overmix. Spoon the batter into the prepared pan, smoothing it to the edges.

3 Combine the wheat germ and remaining 2 tablespoons of sugar and sprinkle over the top. Bake for 25 minutes or until a toothpick inserted in the center comes out clean. Serve warm or at room temperature. Serves 6.

PREPARATION TIME: 15 MIN. COOKING TIME: 25 MIN.

Per serving: Calories 393; Saturated Fat 2 g; Total Fat 9 g; Protein 9 g; Carbohydrate 72 g; Fiber 4 g; Sodium 366 mg; Cholesterol 36 mg

BREAKFAST ON THE GO

Grapefruit Juice

Date Coffee Cake

Decaffeinated Tea or Coffee

CAR POOL BREAKFAST

Banana

Oatmeal Breakfast Cookies *(page 34)*

Skim Milk

COMMUTER BREAKFAST

Orange Milk Fizz *(page 45)*

Seven-Grain Toast with Honey

What is the difference between quick-cooking and old-fashioned oats? Very little. Both are of the type called rolled oats, which means they have been formed by rolling the groats after the hulls are removed, but the quick-cooking variety is a little thinner and therefore requires less cooking time. The two are virtually interchangeable, except in baked goods for which the baking time is very brief; in this case the quick-cooking oats are preferable. It's best to use whichever type is called for in a recipe.

APPLE-CHEESE COFFEE CAKE

If you wish, use pears and Gruyère cheese instead of the apples and Cheddar; and if you are watching your sodium, substitute a no-salt-added cheese.

1 cup unsifted all-purpose flour	1 cup shredded Cheddar cheese (4 ounces)
1 cup unsifted whole-wheat flour	2 Golden Delicious apples, peeled, cored, and grated (2 cups)
2 tablespoons sugar	¾ cup buttermilk
1½ teaspoons baking powder	1 large egg
½ teaspoon baking soda	2 tablespoons corn or vegetable oil
½ teaspoon salt	

1 Preheat the oven to 375° F. Lightly grease and flour a 9" x 9" x 2" baking pan. In a large bowl, combine the all-purpose flour, whole-wheat flour, sugar, baking powder, baking soda, and salt; mix in the cheese and apples.

2 In a 1-pint glass measuring cup, stir together the buttermilk, egg, and oil. Make a well in the center of the flour mixture, pour in the buttermilk mixture, and stir just until combined. Spoon the batter into the prepared pan, smoothing it to the edges.

3 Bake for 30 minutes or until a toothpick inserted in the center comes out clean. Let cool for 10 minutes in the pan, then turn onto a serving plate and serve warm or at room temperature. Serves 6.

PREPARATION TIME: 12 MIN. COOKING TIME: 30 MIN.

Per serving: Calories 324; Saturated Fat 5 g; Total Fat 12 g; Protein 12 g; Carbohydrate 43 g; Fiber 4 g; Sodium 489 mg; Cholesterol 56 mg

BANANA CUSTARD OAT BARS

These crunchy bars conceal a luscious fruit and custard filling. Enjoy them for breakfast, lunch, or a snack.

For the oat bars:

- 2 to 3 tablespoons dark brown sugar
- 2 tablespoons unsalted butter or margarine, at room temperature
- 3 tablespoons canola or vegetable oil
- 1 cup whole-wheat flour
- ½ teaspoon ground cinnamon
- ¼ teaspoon salt
- 1 cup old-fashioned or quick-cooking rolled oats

For the filling:

- ½ cup coarsely chopped dried apple or pear
- ½ cup hot water
- 2 large bananas, peeled and cut into 1-inch pieces
- 1 large egg
- 2 large egg whites
- 3 tablespoons honey
- ¼ teaspoon ground ginger

1 Preheat the oven to 375° F. Lightly grease a 9" x 9" x 2" baking pan. In a food processor, whirl the sugar, butter, and oil until smooth. Add the flour, cinnamon, and salt, then process, using on/off pulses, until the texture resembles coarse meal. Add the oats and process until just combined. Set aside ½ cup of the mixture for the topping and press the remainder into the prepared pan.

2 Bake the crust for 20 minutes. Meanwhile, prepare the filling. In a small bowl, soak the apple in the water for 15 minutes, then drain. Place the bananas, egg, egg whites, honey, and ginger in the processor and blend until smooth. Add the apples and pulse just until combined.

3 Pour the banana mixture onto the hot crust; sprinkle the remaining ½ cup oat mixture evenly over the top. Return to the oven and bake 15 minutes more or until set in the center. Let stand in the pan on a rack until warm, then cut into 16 squares. Will keep, tightly wrapped and refrigerated, for up to 4 days.

PREPARATION TIME: 20 MIN. COOKING TIME: 35 MIN.

Per bar: Calories 129; Saturated Fat 2 g; Total Fat 5 g; Protein 3 g; Carbohydrate 20 g; Fiber 2 g; Sodium 48 mg; Cholesterol 17 mg

ALMOND-DATE BARS

You can bake these nutritious bars in advance and freeze them individually. Leave one out overnight for an easy, quick, and portable breakfast the next day.

1 **cup old-fashioned or quick-cooking rolled oats**	2 **cups finely chopped pitted dates**
½ **cup sifted all-purpose flour**	½ **cup finely chopped almonds (2 ounces)**
½ **cup unsifted whole-wheat flour**	1 **cup skim milk**
1 **teaspoon baking powder**	3 **large egg whites**
⅛ **teaspoon salt**	2 **tablespoons firmly packed dark brown sugar**
½ **teaspoon ground cinnamon**	1 **teaspoon vanilla extract**

1 Preheat the oven to 350° F. Grease a 9" x 9" x 2" baking pan. In a large bowl, combine the oats, all-purpose flour, whole-wheat flour, baking powder, salt, and cinnamon. Stir in the dates, almonds, and milk.

2 In a perfectly clean large bowl, beat the egg whites with an electric mixer set on high speed until they form soft peaks. Beat in the sugar, 1 tablespoon at a time, until the whites form stiff peaks, then beat in the vanilla. Using a rubber spatula, gently fold the egg whites into the oat mixture, then spread the batter evenly in the pan.

3 Bake for 30 to 35 minutes or until the top is brown and a toothpick inserted in the center comes out clean. Let cool for 10 minutes in the pan, then transfer to a wire rack and let cool to room temperature. Cut into 12 bars.

PREPARATION TIME: 20 MIN. COOKING TIME: 30 MIN.

Per bar: Calories 196; Saturated Fat 0.5 g; Total Fat 4 g; Protein 6 g; Carbohydrate 38 g; Fiber 4 g; Sodium 77 mg; Cholesterol 0 mg

OATMEAL BREAKFAST COOKIES

Cookies for breakfast? Well, why not, when they are as wholesome as these. They also make an excellent snack or pick-me-up with a glass of milk.

- ¾ cup unsifted all-purpose flour
- ½ teaspoon baking soda
- ½ teaspoon salt
- ⅓ cup no-sugar-added apricot jam
- 3 tablespoons vegetable or olive oil
- 2 tablespoons honey
- 2 large egg whites
- 1½ cups old-fashioned rolled oats
- ¾ cup wheat germ
- ¼ cup chopped walnuts or pecans (optional)

1 Preheat the oven to 350° F. Line 2 baking sheets with aluminum foil. On a sheet of wax paper, sift together the flour, baking soda, and salt.

2 In a large bowl, stir together the jam, oil, honey, and egg whites until well combined. Stir in the flour mixture, oats, wheat germ, and walnuts if desired. Drop the dough by heaping tablespoons on the baking sheet, spacing the mounds 1 inch apart. Bake for 17 minutes or until the cookies are set and browned. Let cool for 1 to 2 minutes on the baking sheets, then, using a spatula, transfer to wire racks to cool completely. The cookies can be frozen or stored in the refrigerator for up to 3 days. Makes about twenty-four 2½-inch cookies.

PREPARATION TIME: 10 MIN. COOKING TIME: 17 MIN.

Per cookie: Calories 85; Saturated Fat 0.5 g; Total Fat 2 g; Protein 3 g; Carbohydrate 14 g; Fiber 1 g; Sodium 67 mg; Cholesterol 0 mg

SESAME-CHEDDAR SCONES

Vegetable shortening gives these scones an especially good texture. If you don't have any on hand, use an equal amount of unsalted butter or margarine.

- 1¼ cups sifted unbleached flour
- 1 cup cornmeal
- 1 tablespoon baking powder
- ½ teaspoon salt
- 2 tablespoons each vegetable shortening and cold unsalted butter or margarine, cut into bits
- ½ cup shredded sharp Cheddar cheese (2 ounces)
- ⅔ cup skim milk
- 1 large egg white
- 2 tablespoons sesame seeds

1 Preheat the oven to 425° F. Grease a large baking sheet. In a large bowl, stir together the flour, cornmeal, baking powder, and salt. Add the shortening and butter and blend with your fingers until the mixture resembles coarse meal; mix in the cheese.

2 In a medium-size bowl, blend ½ cup of the milk with the egg white; add to the flour mixture and stir until combined enough to gather into a ball, adding more of the milk if needed. Lightly knead the dough on a floured surface, then pat or roll it into a 9-inch round ½ inch thick.

3 Place the dough on the baking sheet. Brush the top with water and sprinkle with the sesame seeds. Cut it into 8 wedges and bake for 15 to 18 minutes or until golden brown. Makes 8 scones.

PREPARATION TIME: 10 MIN. COOKING TIME: 15 MIN.

Per scone: Calories 235; Saturated Fat 4 g; Total Fat 10 g; Protein 7 g; Carbohydrate 29 g; Fiber 2 g; Sodium 320 mg; Cholesterol 16 mg

RED PEPPER SPOON BREAD

Serve this popular southern bread for a special Sunday morning breakfast or a brunch. Accompany it, if you like, with a green salad.

1 ½ **cups Chicken Stock (page 62) or low-sodium chicken broth**	1 **medium-size sweet red pepper, cored, seeded, and finely chopped (¾ cup)**
1 ½ **cups skim milk**	1 **small yellow onion, finely chopped (½ cup)**
1 **tablespoon sugar**	1 **cup fresh or frozen corn kernels, thawed**
½ **teaspoon salt**	2 **large eggs, separated**
1 **cup cornmeal**	4 **large egg whites**
4 **teaspoons unsalted butter**	2 **teaspoons baking powder**
⅛ **teaspoon each ground red pepper (cayenne) and nutmeg**	

1 Preheat the oven to 350° F. Butter a 1-quart flame-proof baking dish. In a medium-size saucepan, stir together the stock, milk, sugar, salt, and cornmeal, then bring to a boil over moderate heat. Add 2 teaspoons of the butter and cook the mixture over low heat, whisking occasionally, for 5 minutes. Transfer to a large bowl and stir in the ground red pepper and nutmeg.

2 In a 9-inch nonstick skillet, cook the sweet red pepper and onion in the remaining 2 teaspoons of butter over moderate heat for 3 minutes or until softened, stirring occasionally; add the corn and cook the mixture, stirring, 1 minute more. Stir into the cornmeal mixture. In a small bowl, whisk the egg yolks with the baking powder, then stir them into the cornmeal mixture.

3 In a perfectly clean large bowl, beat the egg whites with an electric mixer set on high speed until stiff but not dry. Stir ¼ of the whites into the cornmeal mixture, then gently fold in the rest. Pour the mixture into the prepared

baking dish and bake for 40 minutes or until puffed, then broil 4 inches from the heat for 1 to 2 minutes or until golden brown. Serve at once directly from the dish. Serves 6.

PREPARATION TIME: 15 MIN. COOKING TIME: 40 MIN.

Per serving: Calories 204; Saturated Fat 2 g; Total Fat 5 g; Protein 9 g; Carbohydrate 31 g; Fiber 2 g; Sodium 376 mg; Cholesterol 79 mg

Melt-in-the-mouth Sesame-Cheddar Scones could be the highlight of your weekend brunch.

To make perfect waffles every time, have your waffle iron well seasoned according to the manufacturer's instructions (with proper seasoning, a waffle iron does not need oiling each time) and fully preheated. For easy pouring, mix your batter in a 2-quart measuring cup. Pour the batter slowly into the center of the iron, filling it ⅔ full; the batter will spread to the edges when you close the lid. The waffle is completely baked when steam stops escaping through the sides.

Bake extra waffles, wrap them individually in aluminum foil, and freeze them. When you want one, all you have to do is unwrap it and pop it in the toaster.

BROWN RICE WAFFLES

Here is a tasty way to get your fiber and B vitamins. If you like, make the batter ahead. It will keep for 3 days, refrigerated.

1 cup sifted whole-wheat flour	3 tablespoons honey
¾ cup sifted all-purpose flour	4 teaspoons vegetable oil
2 teaspoons baking powder	1 ½ cups low-fat milk
½ teaspoon ground cinnamon (optional)	1 cup cooked brown rice
¼ teaspoon salt	3 large egg whites
	¼ teaspoon lemon juice
	Nonstick cooking spray or vegetable oil

1 Preheat a waffle iron. In a large bowl or 2-quart measuring cup, stir together the whole-wheat flour, all-purpose flour, baking powder, cinnamon if desired, and salt and make a well in the center.

2 In a small bowl, beat the honey and oil until blended. Add the milk and beat until well combined, then pour the mixture into the dry ingredients and beat just until incorporated. Fold in the brown rice. Do not overmix.

3 In a perfectly clean medium-size bowl, beat the egg whites and lemon juice with an electric mixer set on high speed until soft peaks form. Gently fold the whites into the batter. Lightly coat the waffle iron with cooking spray; spoon or pour the batter into the center of the iron, filling it ⅔ full. Cook the waffles until golden. Repeat until all the batter has been used. Makes six 5-inch waffles.

PREPARATION TIME: 20 MIN. COOKING TIME: 20 MIN.

Per waffle: Calories 254; Saturated Fat 1 g; Total Fat 5 g; Protein 9 g; Carbohydrate 45 g; Fiber 3 g; Sodium 260 mg; Cholesterol 3 mg

•

Brown Rice Pancake Variation: Prepare the batter as directed. Preheat a nonstick griddle or skillet over moderately low heat and coat with nonstick cooking spray. For each pancake, pour ¼ *cup batter* onto the griddle and cook for 1 minute or until bubbles form on the surface. Turn the pancake and cook about 1 minute more or until golden. Makes 24 pancakes. *Per pancake: Calories 64; Saturated Fat 0 g; Total Fat 1 g; Protein 2 g; Carbohydrate 11 g; Fiber 1 g; Sodium 65 mg; Cholesterol 1 mg.*

To get the day off to a good beginning, top Brown Rice Waffles with maple syrup or Blueberry Sauce (page 39) and Creamy Yogurt Spread (page 287).

BAKED FRENCH TOAST

This variation on traditional French toast tastes like Danish pastry. To save time in the morning, soak the bread overnight.

2/3 cup low-fat (1% milk-fat) cottage cheese
1/4 cup skim milk
2 tablespoons sugar
1 large egg
1 large egg white
1/2 teaspoon vanilla extract
4 slices (1 ounce each) whole-wheat, oatmeal, or other whole-grain bread

1 Preheat the oven to 425° F. In a food processor or blender, whirl the cottage cheese, milk, sugar, egg, egg white, and vanilla for about 1 minute or until smooth. Transfer the mixture to a shallow dish, place the bread in it, and let stand for 10 minutes. Turn the bread over and let stand another 10 minutes. Meanwhile, grease a baking sheet and place it in the preheated oven for 7 minutes.

2 Remove the baking sheet from the oven, place the bread on it, and bake for 6 minutes. Turn the bread over and bake 5 to 6 minutes longer or until golden brown. Serve with no-sugar-added jam. Makes 4 servings.

PREPARATION TIME: 4 MIN. COOKING TIME: 12 MIN.
STANDING TIME: 20 MIN.

Per serving: Calories 149; Saturated Fat 1 g; Total Fat 3 g; Protein 10 g; Carbohydrate 21 g; Fiber 3 g; Sodium 369 mg; Cholesterol 55 mg

ALMOND BUCKWHEAT PANCAKES

Serve these hearty, nutty pancakes with honey, maple syrup, or one of the toppings on page 39.

3/4 cup sifted all-purpose flour
1/2 cup unsifted buckwheat flour
1/4 cup ground almonds (1 ounce)
2 tablespoons sugar
1 1/2 teaspoons baking powder
1/4 teaspoon salt
2 large eggs, separated
2 tablespoons vegetable or peanut oil
1 cup skim milk
Nonstick cooking spray

1 In a large bowl, combine the all-purpose flour, buckwheat flour, almonds, sugar, baking powder, and salt; set aside.

2 In a large glass measuring cup, stir the egg yolks and oil into the milk and blend with a fork. Add to the flour mixture and stir just until moistened.

3 In a perfectly clean medium-size bowl, beat the egg whites with an electric mixer set on high speed until they are stiff but not dry; gently fold them into the batter.

4 Lightly coat a 12-inch nonstick skillet with the cooking spray and set over moderate heat. When the skillet is hot, cook the pancakes 4 at a time, using 1/4 cup batter for each. Cook for 2 1/2 to 3 minutes on one side or until bubbles form on top of the pancakes; turn, then cook about 1 minute longer or until the bottom of each pancake is deep brown. Makes 12 pancakes.

PREPARATION TIME: 20 MIN. COOKING TIME: 12 MIN.

Per pancake: Calories 107; Saturated Fat 1 g; Total Fat 5 g; Protein 4 g; Carbohydrate 13 g; Fiber 1 g; Sodium 107 mg; Cholesterol 36 mg

•

Pecan Whole-Wheat Pancake Variation: Substitute *1/2 cup unsifted whole-wheat pastry flour* for the buckwheat flour and *1/4 cup ground pecans (1 ounce)* for the almonds. *Per pancake: Calories 106; Saturated Fat 1 g; Total Fat 5 g; Protein 3 g; Carbohydrate 13 g; Fiber 1 g; Sodium 107 mg; Cholesterol 36 mg.*

Pancake pointers: To test the temperature of a griddle, drop a little cold water on it. If the water flattens, the griddle is not hot enough; if it vanishes, the griddle is too hot; if the drops bounce, start pouring the batter.

To make small, uniform pancakes, drop the batter from a tablespoon; use a 1/4-cup measure to produce large ones.

If possible, serve pancakes as soon as they are cooked. Otherwise, place them in a single layer on a baking sheet in a 200° F oven until serving time.

You can store unused pancake batter in the refrigerator for up to 5 days. Or make some extra pancakes and refrigerate or freeze them; reheat them in a toaster oven or in a microwave oven on *High* (100% power) for 20 to 50 seconds.

Buttermilk is often used in baking because it makes the texture of biscuits, cakes, waffles, and pancakes tenderer while adding a pleasing flavor. For anyone concerned with health, the big plus is that when buttermilk is substituted for whole milk, it provides rich taste with less fat. The name *buttermilk* is misleading, for this tangy beverage is actually very low in milkfat, containing only 1 percent milkfat when made from skim milk and 1.5 to 2 percent milkfat when made from low-fat milk.

On Sunday, treat yourself and your family to a very special breakfast — Whole-Grain Buttermilk Pancakes, Whipped Cheese Topping, Crushed Red Berry Sauce, and Turkey Sausage (page 124).

WHOLE-GRAIN BUTTERMILK PANCAKES

A blend of grains provides a nutty flavor that is sure to please at your breakfast table. If you like, you can use a combination of buckwheat and whole-wheat flours, just as long as there is ⅔ cup in all.

- ⅔ cup unsifted whole-wheat flour
- ¼ cup oat bran
- 1 tablespoon cornmeal
- 1 tablespoon brown sugar
- 1½ teaspoons baking powder
- ¼ teaspoon baking soda
- ¼ teaspoon salt
- 1 cup buttermilk
- 2 large eggs, separated
- 2 tablespoons corn oil
- Nonstick cooking spray or vegetable oil

1 In a medium-size bowl, combine the whole-wheat flour, oat bran, cornmeal, sugar, baking powder, baking soda, and salt. In a 1-pint glass measuring cup, combine the buttermilk, egg yolks, and oil.

2 In a perfectly clean large bowl, beat the egg whites with an electric mixer set on high speed until they form stiff peaks. Stir the buttermilk mixture into the flour mixture. Fold in the egg whites.

3 Lightly coat a 12-inch nonstick skillet with the cooking spray and set over moderate heat. When the skillet is hot, cook the pancakes 4 at a time, using ¼ cup batter for each. Cook for about 2 minutes on one side or until bubbles appear on the surface; turn, then cook 2 minutes longer or until golden brown on each side and cooked through. Makes 12 pancakes.

PREPARATION TIME: 15 MIN. COOKING TIME: 12 MIN.

Per pancake: Calories 76; Saturated Fat 1 g; Total Fat 4 g; Protein 3 g; Carbohydrate 9 g; Fiber 1 g; Sodium 135 mg; Cholesterol 36 mg

BLUEBERRY SAUCE

Serve this quick and delicious topping on waffles, pancakes, yogurt, or ice cream.

- ¾ cup unsweetened apple juice
- 4 teaspoons honey
- 1 tablespoon cornstarch
- ½ teaspoon grated fresh ginger or ⅛ teaspoon ground ginger (optional)
- 2 cups blueberries or 1 package (12 ounces) frozen dry-pack blueberries, thawed
- 1 teaspoon lime or lemon juice

1 In a small saucepan, stir together the apple juice, honey, cornstarch, and, if desired, ginger until the cornstarch dissolves. Add the blueberries, then bring to a simmer over moderate heat; cook, stirring, for 2 minutes. Remove from the heat and stir in the lime juice. Serve hot or warm. Makes 1 ⅓ cups.

PREPARATION TIME: 5 MIN. COOKING TIME: 8 MIN.

Per tablespoon: Calories 18; Saturated Fat 0 g; Total Fat 0 g; Protein 0 g; Carbohydrate 5 g; Fiber 0 g; Sodium 1 mg; Cholesterol 0 mg

CRUSHED RED BERRY SAUCE

High in natural vitamin C and low in calories, this luscious topping is suitable for pancakes, waffles, and French toast.

- 1½ cups thinly sliced strawberries or frozen dry-pack strawberries, thawed
- 3 tablespoons sugar
- 1 cup raspberries or frozen dry-pack raspberries, thawed

1 In a medium-size bowl, sprinkle the strawberries with the sugar. Cover and let stand for 1 hour at room temperature, allowing the berries to form their own syrup.

2 Mash the strawberries with a potato masher or wooden spoon, then add the raspberries and mix well. Cover and refrigerate for at least 1 hour to let the flavors mellow. Serve chilled or at room temperature. Will keep, refrigerated, for up to 5 days. Makes 1 ⅓ cups.

PREPARATION TIME: 10 MIN., PLUS 2 HR. REFRIGERATION

Per tablespoon: Calories 12; Saturated Fat 0 g; Total Fat 0 g; Protein 0 g; Carbohydrate 3 g; Fiber 1 g; Sodium 0 mg; Cholesterol 0 mg

WHIPPED CHEESE TOPPING

This light fruity topping is so good you'll want to eat it with a spoon. Try it on pancakes, waffles, berries, or toast. It adds protein but virtually no fat.

- 1 pound low-fat (1% milk-fat) cottage cheese
- 2 tablespoons sugar
- ½ teaspoon grated orange rind
- 2 tablespoons orange juice

1 In a food processor or blender, whirl the cottage cheese, sugar, orange rind, and orange juice for about 30 seconds or until smooth. Will keep, covered, in the refrigerator for 1 to 2 weeks, depending on the freshness of the cottage cheese. Makes 2 cups.

PREPARATION TIME: 4 MIN.

Per tablespoon: Calories 14; Saturated Fat 0 g; Total Fat 0 g; Protein 2 g; Carbohydrate 1 g; Fiber 0 g; Sodium 58 mg; Cholesterol 1 mg

SUNDAY BRUNCH

Whole-Grain Buttermilk Pancakes

Drained Crushed Pineapple

Creamy Yogurt Spread
(page 287)

Turkey Sausage
(page 124)

Orange Spice Herbal Tea

WORKDAY BREAKFAST

Sliced Strawberries with Whipped Cheese Topping

Whole-Wheat Toast

Skim Milk

Ready-to-eat cereal can be a good way to start the day, if carefully selected. Before you buy your next box, check the label to see what has been added. *Enriched* cereals are those in which any nutrients destroyed during processing have been replaced. *Fortified* cereals are those to which nutrients, such as vitamin D, have been added, regardless of whether they were present in the grains themselves. *Natural* cereals have no added artificial ingredients and have been processed minimally.

Cereals containing nuts and fruits are a good choice, but avoid those with added sugar. You will be getting extra calories with no nutritional value.

BREAKFAST BROWN RICE PUDDING

A comforting dessert is converted here to a delicious breakfast dish — a great substitute for the usual cereal and milk.

- 1 ½ cups plus 2 tablespoons water
- ½ cup apple juice or water
- 1 cup quick-cooking brown rice
- ¼ teaspoon salt
- ¾ cup skim milk
- 2 medium-size cooking apples, peeled, cored, and diced
- ¼ cup raisins or currants
- ¼ cup firmly packed light brown sugar
- ¾ teaspoon ground cinnamon
- 1 large egg
  Nutmeg or granola (optional garnish)

1 In a medium-size saucepan, combine 1 ½ cups of the water, the apple juice, rice, and salt; bring to a boil over moderate heat. Reduce the heat to low and cook, covered, for 15 minutes or until the rice is tender. Add the milk, apples, raisins, sugar, and cinnamon; return to a simmer and cook, uncovered, 15 minutes more, stirring occasionally.

2 Beat the egg and the remaining 2 tablespoons water in a small bowl. Stir about ½ cup of the rice mixture into the egg, then stir the egg mixture into the saucepan and simmer for 1 minute, stirring. Serve hot or cold, sprinkled with nutmeg or granola if desired. Will keep in the refrigerator for up to 4 days. Makes four 1-cup servings.

PREPARATION TIME: 5 MIN.   COOKING TIME: 45 MIN.

> *Per serving: Calories 295; Saturated Fat 1 g; Total Fat 3 g; Protein 7 g; Carbohydrate 65 g; Fiber 4 g; Sodium 190 mg; Cholesterol 55 mg*

•

Baked Breakfast Pudding Variation: Follow the directions in Step 1, but simmer the water, apple juice, rice, and salt for just 10 minutes. Preheat the oven to 350° F. In a 6-cup baking dish, combine the rice mixture, milk, apples, raisins, sugar, and cinnamon. Beat the egg in a small bowl and combine with the rest of the ingredients; bake, stirring once, for 40 minutes or until the rice and apples are tender. *Per serving: Calories 295; Saturated Fat 1 g; Total Fat 3 g; Protein 7 g; Carbohydrate 65 g; Fiber 4 g; Sodium 190 mg; Cholesterol 55 mg.*

HONEY TOASTED GRANOLA

Eat homemade granola with low-fat milk or yogurt for breakfast, or snack on it any time of day.

- 3 cups old-fashioned rolled oats
- ½ cup each oat bran and wheat germ or 1 cup wheat germ
- ½ cup raw sunflower seeds
- ⅓ cup sliced almonds
- 1 teaspoon ground cinnamon
- ⅓ cup honey
- ⅓ cup orange juice
- 2 tablespoons unsalted butter
- ½ cup diced dried apricots
- ½ cup diced pitted prunes

1 Preheat the oven to 350° F. In a large ungreased baking pan, mix the oats, oat bran, wheat germ, sunflower seeds, almonds, and cinnamon.

2 In a small saucepan, combine the honey, orange juice, and butter. Cook, stirring, over moderate heat until the butter is melted; do not let boil. Pour the liquid over the oat mixture and toss to combine.

3 Toast the mixture in the oven for 15 minutes, stirring every 5 minutes. Let cool, then stir in the apricots and prunes. Will keep in an airtight container in a cool, dark place for up to 2 months. Makes 6 ½ cups.

PREPARATION TIME: 10 MIN.   COOKING TIME: 15 MIN.

> *Per ½ cup: Calories 218; Saturated Fat 2 g; Total Fat 8 g; Protein 7 g; Carbohydrate 34 g; Fiber 3 g; Sodium 3 mg; Cholesterol 5 mg*

MUESLI WITH WHEAT BERRIES

High in protein, fiber, and some B vitamins, wheat berries are available in health food stores. Here they are cooked to a slightly crunchy stage; if you prefer a softer texture, cook them an additional 10 to 15 minutes.

1 cup wheat berries	3 tablespoons shredded coconut
3½ cups cold water	2 tablespoons sesame seeds
⅓ cup raisins	
¼ cup dried apricots, chopped	1½ tablespoons light brown sugar
¼ cup blanched or unblanched almonds, coarsely chopped	2 cups skim milk

1 The night before, rinse the wheat berries and place them in a large bowl with the water. Soak for 12 hours, preferably in the refrigerator.

2 Transfer the wheat berries and water to a large saucepan and bring to a boil over moderate heat. Lower the heat and simmer, covered, for 30 to 35 minutes or until the wheat berries are tender but somewhat crunchy.

3 Remove from the heat and stir in the raisins, apricots, almonds, coconut, sesame seeds, and sugar. Spoon into bowls and top with the milk. Serves 4.

PREPARATION TIME: 4 MIN., PLUS 12 HR. SOAKING

COOKING TIME: 30 MIN.

Per serving: Calories 373; Saturated Fat 2 g; Total Fat 9 g; Protein 15 g; Carbohydrate 63 g; Fiber 5 g; Sodium 82 mg; Cholesterol 3 mg

•

Quick Muesli Variation: Mix *1 cup bulgur* with the raisins, apricots, almonds, coconut, sesame seeds, sugar, and *¼ teaspoon salt*. In a large saucepan, heat *4 cups skim milk* or *2 cups low-fat (1% milkfat) milk plus 2 cups water* over low heat. When bubbles begin to appear around the edges, add the bulgur mixture and cook, uncovered, stirring occasionally, until the milk has been absorbed and the bulgur is tender, about 6 minutes. Serves 4. *Per serving: Calories 380; Saturated Fat 3 g; Total Fat 9 g; Protein 16 g; Carbohydrate 63 g; Fiber 11 g; Sodium 152 mg; Cholesterol 5 mg*

Easy to make, delicious, and nutritious, Muesli with Wheat Berries is an adaptation of a popular Swiss breakfast cereal.

COUSCOUS WITH RAISINS AND NUTS

Not usually considered a breakfast dish, couscous (a form of semolina) is high in protein and low in fat.

2 cups skim milk	⅓ cup raisins
1 tablespoon molasses	⅓ cup unblanched almonds, coarsely chopped
1 teaspoon grated lemon rind	
¼ teaspoon salt	1 tablespoon sesame seeds
1 cup couscous	

1 In a medium-size saucepan, combine the milk, molasses, lemon rind, and salt; bring to a gentle boil over moderate heat. Add the couscous and raisins, remove from the heat, cover, and let stand for 5 minutes; stir in the almonds. Spoon the mixture into bowls and sprinkle the sesame seeds on top. Serves 4.

PREPARATION TIME: 6 MIN. COOKING TIME: 5 MIN.

Per serving: Calories 344; Saturated Fat 1 g; Total Fat 7 g; Protein 13 g; Carbohydrate 57 g; Fiber 9 g; Sodium 206 mg; Cholesterol 3 mg

Zesty Eggs in Tortilla Flowers are pretty enough for company but easy enough to please yourself with now and then.

2 Pour the mixture into the baking dish, cover, and place in a larger baking dish or pan; add enough hot water to come halfway up the sides. Bake for 45 minutes, then uncover and bake 30 minutes longer or until a knife inserted in the center comes out clean. Serve the pudding hot or at room temperature. Serves 4.

PREPARATION TIME: 10 MIN. COOKING TIME: 1 HR.

Per serving: Calories 246; Saturated Fat 4 g; Total Fat 10 g; Protein 18 g; Carbohydrate 20 g; Fiber 2 g; Sodium 683 mg; Cholesterol 126 mg

ONION EGG SCRAMBLE

For an extra measure of protein without accompanying cholesterol, mix tofu with your eggs. Soft tofu can be substituted for the firm type but will give off some liquid in the cooking process.

8 ounces firm tofu (soybean curd)	½ teaspoon honey
3 large eggs	¼ teaspoon salt
2 green onions, chopped, or 2 tablespoons snipped fresh or freeze-dried chives	8 drops hot red pepper sauce
	Nonstick cooking spray

1 Place the tofu on paper toweling, press it to blot out excess moisture, then cut into 4 pieces. Place the tofu, eggs, green onions, honey, salt, and red pepper sauce in a food processor or blender. Whirl until smooth.

2 Coat a 10-inch nonstick skillet with cooking spray, then heat it for 1 minute over moderate heat. Add the egg mixture and cook for 5 minutes, stirring occasionally, or until the eggs are set. Serve immediately. Serves 4.

PREPARATION TIME: 6 MIN. COOKING TIME: 5 MIN.

Per serving: Calories 142; Saturated Fat 2 g; Total Fat 9 g; Protein 14 g; Carbohydrate 4 g; Fiber 1 g; Sodium 189 mg; Cholesterol 160 mg

CHEDDAR AND RYE BREAD PUDDING

4 slices rye bread with caraway seeds, cut into 1-inch cubes (2 cups)	2 large eggs
	2 large egg whites
1½ cups shredded low-fat Cheddar cheese (6 ounces)	1 tablespoon Dijon mustard
1 cup skim milk	⅛ teaspoon ground red pepper (cayenne), or to taste
3 green onions, including tops, chopped (about ⅓ cup)	

1 Preheat the oven to 350° F. Grease a 1½-quart baking dish. In a large bowl, combine the bread cubes, cheese, milk, green onions, eggs, egg whites, mustard, and red pepper.

EGGS IN TORTILLA FLOWERS

Nonstick cooking spray
4 corn tortillas, 6 inches in diameter
2 teaspoons canola or vegetable oil
6 large eggs
4 large egg whites
2 tablespoons water
¼ teaspoon black pepper, or to taste
1 large sweet red pepper, cored, seeded, and finely chopped (1 cup)
4 ounces reduced-sodium ham, finely cubed (½ cup)
2 green onions, including tops, sliced
Mild salsa (optional topping)

1 Preheat the oven to 325° F. Invert 4 small custard cups or ovenproof glasses on a baking sheet and coat the bottoms with nonstick cooking spray. Brush each tortilla with ¼ teaspoon oil, then cut 8 evenly spaced 2-inch-deep slits around the edge. Center each tortilla, oiled side up, on top of a cup, letting the cut edges drape down the sides. Bake for 20 minutes or until crisp.

2 After the tortillas have baked for 10 minutes, start the eggs. In a medium-size bowl, beat together the eggs, egg whites, water, and black pepper. Heat the remaining oil in a 10-inch nonstick skillet over moderately low heat. Add the red pepper, ham, and green onions. Cover and cook for 6 minutes or until softened.

3 Add the egg mixture and cook, uncovered, 3 minutes more, scrambling the eggs lightly, until they are just set. Remove the tortillas from the custard cups and invert them on 4 individual serving plates. They will have formed a shallow flowerlike cup. Fill each tortilla flower with the egg mixture and serve immediately. Top with salsa if desired. Serves 4.

PREPARATION TIME: 15 MIN. COOKING TIME: 20 MIN.

Per serving: Calories 266; Saturated Fat 3 g; Total Fat 13 g; Protein 21 g; Carbohydrate 16 g; Fiber 2 g; Sodium 414 mg; Cholesterol 334 mg

PIPERADE

Calories and cholesterol have been cut from this traditional French open-faced omelet by using less oil and eliminating the yolks from two of the eggs.

4 teaspoons olive oil
1 small yellow onion, thinly sliced (½ cup)
1 small sweet green pepper, cored, seeded, and thinly sliced (½ cup)
¼ teaspoon each salt and black pepper, or to taste
1 clove garlic, minced
3 medium-size plum tomatoes, chopped, or 1 can (14½ ounces) low-sodium tomatoes, drained and chopped
2 large eggs
2 large egg whites
2 teaspoons water
2 tablespoons minced fresh basil, chives, parsley, or oregano

1 In a 9-inch skillet, heat 2 teaspoons of the oil over moderate heat. Add the onion, green pepper, and ⅛ teaspoon each of the salt and black pepper; sauté, stirring occasionally, for 3 minutes or until softened. Add the garlic and tomatoes and sauté, stirring occasionally, 4 to 5 minutes longer or until the mixture is dry. Transfer the vegetables to a medium-size bowl and set aside.

2 In a small bowl, whisk together the eggs, egg whites, water, and remaining ⅛ teaspoon each of salt and black pepper. In the same skillet, heat the remaining 2 teaspoons of oil over moderate heat. Add the eggs, reduce the heat to moderately low, and cook, covered, for 1 minute. Spoon the vegetable mixture on top, cover, and cook 2 minutes more or until the vegetables are heated through and the eggs are set. Serve immediately, sprinkled with the basil. Serves 2.

PREPARATION TIME: 10 MIN. COOKING TIME: 10 MIN.

Per serving: Calories 232; Saturated Fat 2 g; Total Fat 14 g; Protein 12 g; Carbohydrate 14 g; Fiber 4 g; Sodium 404 mg; Cholesterol 214 mg

Egg advice: Although eggs have gained a bad reputation in recent years because they are high in cholesterol, they do have many virtues. Eggs provide high-quality protein (all nine essential amino acids) and are a rich source of phosphorus, iron, and vitamins A, B₁₂, and D, among other nutrients. Because the yolks contain the cholesterol, nutritionists suggest eating no more than 4 egg yolks a week; whites need not be limited.

When buying eggs, check to see that they are clean and unbroken. If you accidentally break one, use it the same day and cook it thoroughly.

Refrigerate eggs, pointed end down, in the carton and use them within 2 weeks of purchase.

Eggs will keep for 6 months in the freezer but should not be frozen in their shells. Blend the whites and yolks, place the mixture in a small container with a tight-fitting lid, label it with the date and number of eggs, then freeze. Do not refreeze thawed eggs.

TROPICAL PINEAPPLE-BANANA SHAKE

This refreshing drink is a simple, healthful way to start the day. If you like your shakes extra cold, refrigerate the pineapple and banana overnight.

1 **cup crushed pineapple in juice (8-ounce can)**	1 **tablespoon honey**
1 **large banana, peeled and quartered**	2 **teaspoons finely chopped candied ginger (optional)**
1 **cup buttermilk**	1 **drop coconut extract (optional)**

1 In a food processor or blender, combine the pineapple, banana, buttermilk, honey, and, if desired, the ginger and coconut extract. Whirl for 1 minute or until smooth. Pour into 2 tall glasses and serve immediately. Serves 2.

PREPARATION TIME: 5 MIN.

Per serving: Calories 223; Saturated Fat 1 g; Total Fat 2 g; Protein 5 g; Carbohydrate 51 g; Fiber 2 g; Sodium 132 mg; Cholesterol 5 mg

Who says you have to eat toast or cereal for breakfast day after day? You can create a nourishing and pleasing morning meal from a number of foods. Just be sure you include protein and complex carbohydrates.

"Sundaes." Using yogurt or cottage cheese as the "ice cream," top with nuts, honey, such seeds as sunflower or sesame, dried or fresh fruits, preserves with no sugar added, or wheat germ. Round out the meal with bread, preferably one containing a whole grain.

Sandwiches. Combine sliced banana and peanut butter on whole-grain bread; chutney and chicken on whole-wheat pita bread. Broil any of these combinations: low-fat mozzarella cheese and tuna on pumpernickel bread; low-fat cottage cheese plus fruit, sprinkled with sugar and cinnamon, on whole-wheat bread; applesauce mixed with a little butter on cinnamon raisin bread; tomato sauce and low-fat Muenster cheese on an English muffin; tomato, reduced-sodium ham, and low-fat Cheddar cheese on rye bread.

Fruits plus. Top fresh orange or pineapple slices, berries, or a fruit salad with yogurt or cottage cheese and oat bran or granola.

Leftovers. Make use of almost any lunch or dinner food for the first meal of the day: soups; meat, poultry, fish, or pasta (preferably made without garlic); bean dishes; casseroles; rice or baked potatoes, perhaps topped with melted low-fat cheese; milk-based puddings; carrot cake.

CRANBERRY-PEAR WHIP

1 **ripe pear, peeled, cored, and cubed**	2 **teaspoons honey**
2 **tablespoons oat bran**	1 **teaspoon lime or lemon juice**
¾ **cup cranberry juice**	4 **ice cubes**

1 In a food processor or blender, whirl the pear, oat bran, cranberry juice, honey, lime juice, and ice cubes for 1 to 2 minutes or until smooth. Serve immediately. Serves 2.

PREPARATION TIME: 5 MIN.

Per serving: Calories 141; Saturated Fat 0 g; Total Fat 1 g; Protein 1 g; Carbohydrate 36 g; Fiber 3 g; Sodium 5 mg; Cholesterol 0 mg

CHERRY-MELON BREAKFAST DRINK

For a slushy drink, put the melon in the freezer the night before and don't thaw the cherries.

1½ **cups cubed cantaloupe or watermelon**	1 **tablespoon light brown sugar**
1 **cup (about 24) pitted fresh or frozen dry-pack cherries, thawed**	1 **tablespoon honey**
1 **cup plain low-fat yogurt**	⅛ **teaspoon ground cloves**

1 In a food processor or blender, combine the melon, cherries, yogurt, sugar, honey, and cloves. Whirl for about 1 minute or until smooth. Pour into glasses and serve immediately. Serves 2.

PREPARATION TIME: 10 MIN.

Per serving: Calories 232; Saturated Fat 1 g; Total Fat 3 g; Protein 8 g; Carbohydrate 47 g; Fiber 2 g; Sodium 93 mg; Cholesterol 7 mg

ORANGE MILK FIZZ

Loaded with vitamin C and calcium, this citrus-flavored drink is quick to prepare. For variety, try tangerine or orange-pineapple juice concentrate instead of orange.

- **3 tablespoons frozen orange juice concentrate**
- **2 tablespoons nonfat dry milk**
- **1 tablespoon brown sugar**
- **⅛ teaspoon vanilla extract**
- **½ cup cold water**
- **4 ice cubes**

1 In a food processor or blender, combine the orange juice concentrate, dry milk, sugar, vanilla, water, and ice cubes. Whirl for 1 minute or until blended and frothy. Pour into a tall glass and serve immediately. Serves 1.

PREPARATION TIME: 5 MIN.

Per serving: Calories 151; Saturated Fat 0 g; Total Fat 0 g; Protein 4 g; Carbohydrate 34 g; Fiber 0 g; Sodium 52 mg; Cholesterol 2 mg

FRUIT AND YOGURT BREAKFAST

If you prefer, substitute low-fat cottage cheese for the yogurt.

- **1 cup Creamy Yogurt Spread (page 287)**
- **1 tablespoon brown sugar**
- **1 large banana**
- **1 cup seedless grapes**

1 Place the yogurt spread in a medium-size bowl. Blend in the sugar with a fork. Peel and thinly slice the banana into the yogurt; add the grapes and mix with a fork. Makes 2 servings.

PREPARATION TIME: 6 MIN.

Per serving: Calories 234; Saturated Fat 0 g; Total Fat 1 g; Protein 14 g; Carbohydrate 45 g; Fiber 2 g; Sodium 178 mg; Cholesterol 4 mg

For a beautiful start to your morning, sip a Cherry-Melon Breakfast Drink.

45

BAKED APPLES WITH CURRANTS

The apples can be prepared, then covered and refrigerated for up to a day before baking.

4 medium-size baking apples, such as Rome Beauty, Cortland, or Granny Smith	2 tablespoons currants
	1 tablespoon chopped pecans (optional)
½ cup bran cereal	4 teaspoons brown sugar
	4 teaspoons maple syrup

1 Preheat the oven to 350° F. With an apple corer, a melon baller, or a thin, sharp knife, scoop out all but the bottom ½ inch of each apple core; with a vegetable peeler, peel a ½-inch-wide strip around the top of the cavity. Stand the apples in a shallow baking dish just large enough to accommodate all of them in a single layer.

2 In a small bowl, combine the cereal, currants, and pecans if desired. Spoon ¼ of the mixture into the cavity of each apple, then sprinkle with the sugar. Drizzle the syrup over the apples and bake for 40 to 45 minutes or until tender when pierced with a knife. Serves 4.

PREPARATION TIME: 15 MIN. COOKING TIME: 40 MIN.

Per serving: Calories 158; Saturated Fat 0 g; Total Fat 1 g; Protein 2 g; Carbohydrate 42 g; Fiber 6 g; Sodium 135 mg; Cholesterol 0 mg

SPICED PRUNES

A good source of vitamin A, prunes are a sweet treat for breakfast.

1 package (1 pound) pitted prunes	¼ teaspoon each ground cloves and nutmeg
½ teaspoon each ground cinnamon and ginger	1 slice lemon, ¼ inch thick
	Water

1 In a medium-size saucepan, combine the prunes, cinnamon, ginger, cloves, and nutmeg. Squeeze the juice from the lemon slice over the prunes, then add the lemon to the pan. Add just enough water to cover the prunes. Bring to a boil over moderate heat, then lower the heat and simmer, uncovered, for 20 minutes. Remove the lemon from the pan and discard. Let cool, then transfer the prunes and liquid to a bowl; cover and refrigerate for up to 1 week. Serves 6.

PREPARATION TIME: 5 MIN. COOKING TIME: 25 MIN.

Per serving: Calories 183; Saturated Fat 0 g; Total Fat 0 g; Protein 2 g; Carbohydrate 48 g; Fiber 5 g; Sodium 3 mg; Cholesterol 0 mg

APRICOTS WITH CINNAMON AND ORANGE

1 package (8 ounces) dried apricots	6 tablespoons sugar
	Water
1 cinnamon stick (about 2½ inches)	½ teaspoon vanilla extract
Grated rind of 1 orange	

1 In a medium-size saucepan, combine the apricots, cinnamon stick, orange rind, and sugar. Add just enough water to cover the apricots. Bring to a boil over moderate heat, then lower the heat and simmer, uncovered, for 12 to 15 minutes or until tender. Let cool for a few minutes, then stir in the vanilla. Let cool completely, then transfer the apricots and liquid to a bowl; refrigerate, covered, for up to a week. Serves 4.

PREPARATION TIME: 4 MIN. COOKING TIME: 15 MIN.

Per serving: Calories 207; Saturated Fat 0 g; Total Fat 0 g; Protein 2 g; Carbohydrate 54 g; Fiber 4 g; Sodium 6 mg; Cholesterol 0 mg

LUNCH

Mention lunch and the thought that probably comes first to most people's minds is a sandwich. This wonderful English invention of the 18th century is embraced wholeheartedly today by every working person and youngster whose workplace or school is too far from home to return for a midday meal. And with today's fast pace, the sandwich may be the most convenient food any time of day. If you favor sandwiches, make them work in your nutritional favor. Use mostly whole-grain breads and eschew high-fat luncheon meats for fillings of fish, chicken, low-fat cheese, and beans plus greens and other vegetables. And don't overlook the satisfaction and portability of a luncheon salad made with grains and vegetables or nuts and fruits. The recipes in this chapter show you how.

Packing your lunch for work is one way to ensure balanced nutrition and to control salt, fat, and cholesterol in your midday meal. To make certain that sandwiches are never soggy, pack any greens and fresh vegetables separately. Add them to the sandwich just before you plan to eat.

When preparing a meat sandwich, spread a very thin layer of butter or margarine on the bread. It will keep meat juices from making the bread soggy.

If your sandwich filling is a very moist one, such as tuna salad, pack the bread and filling separately. Put the sandwich together when you are ready to eat.

Keep condiments such as ketchup, mustard, and relish at work and add them at the last minute.

HONEY CHICKEN MUFFINS

This is a meal in a muffin and a great make-ahead. Just store in the freezer, wrapped in aluminum foil, then pop them into your lunch bag in the morning. They will be thawed by noon.

Nonstick cooking spray
1 cup unsifted all-purpose flour
1 cup cornmeal
1 tablespoon baking powder
1 tablespoon dry mustard
½ teaspoon baking soda
½ teaspoon salt
2 cups coarsely chopped cooked chicken (8 ounces)
1 cup buttermilk
¼ cup vegetable oil
2 large egg whites
2 tablespoons honey

1 Preheat the oven to 375° F. Coat twelve 2½-inch muffin cups with nonstick cooking spray or insert cupcake liners. In a large bowl, stir together the flour, cornmeal, baking powder, mustard, baking soda, and salt. Stir in the chicken and make a well in the center.

2 In a 1-pint measuring cup, stir together the buttermilk, oil, egg whites, and honey. Pour the liquid into the dry ingredients and stir just until combined.

3 Fill each muffin cup about ¾ full. Bake for 20 minutes or until a cake tester inserted in the center comes out clean. Will keep, wrapped in aluminum foil and refrigerated, for 2 days. Makes 12 muffins.

PREPARATION TIME: 13 MIN. COOKING TIME: 20 MIN.

Per muffin: Calories 174; Saturated Fat 1 g; Total Fat 6 g; Protein 9 g; Carbohydrate 21 g; Fiber 1 g; Sodium 250 mg; Cholesterol 17 mg

CHICKEN TORTILLA SANDWICH

You can enjoy these tasty sandwiches hot or at room temperature. Tomato Salsa (page 280) and an avocado salad would make fine accompaniments.

6 flour tortillas, 7 inches in diameter
1 cup diced cooked chicken or turkey (4 ounces)
1 cup shredded low-fat Monterey Jack cheese (4 ounces)
1 small red onion, finely chopped (½ cup)
½ cup drained, chopped roasted sweet red peppers
1 can (4 ounces) chopped green chilies, drained
1 clove garlic, minced
1 teaspoon ground cumin
2 tablespoons minced fresh cilantro (coriander) or 2 tablespoons minced parsley mixed with ¾ teaspoon dried cilantro
1 tablespoon olive or vegetable oil

1 Preheat the oven to 400° F. Wrap the tortillas in aluminum foil and heat in the oven for 5 minutes or until warm. Preheat the broiler, setting the rack 6 inches from the heat.

2 Meanwhile, in a medium-size bowl, combine the chicken, cheese, onion, peppers, chilies, garlic, cumin, and cilantro. Spread an equal amount of the mixture in the center of each tortilla, then fold the tortilla in half to enclose the filling.

3 Brush both sides of each sandwich with the oil and transfer to a baking sheet. Broil for 2½ to 3 minutes on each side or until crisp and blistered. Serve immediately or wrap the sandwiches in aluminum foil and refrigerate for up to 2 days, letting them come to room temperature before serving. Makes 6 sandwiches.

PREPARATION TIME: 20 MIN. COOKING TIME: 5 MIN.

Per sandwich: Calories 218; Saturated Fat 3 g; Total Fat 9 g; Protein 14 g; Carbohydrate 21 g; Fiber 2 g; Sodium 79 mg; Cholesterol 29 mg

CURRIED CHICKEN AND APPLE SANDWICH

If you prepare this sandwich more than 2 hours in advance, withhold the lettuce and tuck it in at the last minute.

¼ cup reduced-calorie mayonnaise

¼ cup plain low-fat yogurt

¾ teaspoon curry powder, or to taste

⅛ teaspoon each salt and ground red pepper

1 clove garlic, minced

2 cups diced cooked chicken or turkey (8 ounces)

5 green onions, including tops, chopped (about ⅔ cup)

1 large sweet green or red pepper, cored, seeded, and chopped (1 cup)

1 small Golden or Red Delicious apple, cored and diced (1 cup)

2 tablespoons minced fresh cilantro (coriander) or 2 tablespoons minced parsley mixed with ¾ teaspoon dried cilantro

Lettuce leaves

4 whole-wheat pita rounds, halved

1 In a medium-size bowl, whisk together the mayonnaise, yogurt, curry powder, salt, ground red pepper, and garlic. Stir in the chicken, green onions, green pepper, apple, and cilantro.

2 Tuck several lettuce leaves into each pita half, then stuff with the filling. Cover with plastic food wrap and chill until ready to serve. Will keep, refrigerated, for up to 2 days. Makes 4 sandwiches.

PREPARATION TIME: 20 MIN.

Per sandwich: Calories 279; Saturated Fat 1 g; Total Fat 7 g; Protein 23 g; Carbohydrate 30 g; Fiber 2 g; Sodium 337 mg; Cholesterol 54 mg

A Curried Chicken and Apple Sandwich is hearty enough for a man-sized appetite.

CONFETTI TURKEY SALAD SANDWICH

Sweet red peppers, corn, and green onions add crunchiness, color, and vitamins to this spicy turkey salad.

Salmon-Cucumber Sandwiches look dainty enough for a tea party, but they are packed with protein and fiber.

- 2 **cups diced cooked turkey or chicken (8 ounces)**
- 1 **small sweet red pepper, cored, seeded, and finely chopped (½ cup)**
- ½ **cup frozen corn kernels, thawed and drained**
- 2 **green onions, including tops, sliced (¼ cup)**
- ½ **cup plain low-fat yogurt**
- ¾ **teaspoon ground cumin**
- ⅛ **teaspoon salt, or to taste**
- 8 **slices whole-grain bread**

1 In a large bowl, combine the turkey, pepper, corn, green onions, yogurt, cumin, and salt. Spread about ¾ cup of the turkey salad on each of 4 bread slices. Top with the remaining bread slices and cut each sandwich in half. Makes 4 sandwiches.

PREPARATION TIME: 10 MIN.

Per sandwich: Calories 244; Saturated Fat 0.5 g; Total Fat 3 g; Protein 24 g; Carbohydrate 30 g; Fiber 4 g; Sodium 323 mg; Cholesterol 49 mg

BEEF OR HAM SALAD SANDWICH WITH TANGY MUSTARD DRESSING

This flavorful combination can be made with any leftover cooked meat or poultry. Omit the gherkins if you are watching your sodium.

- 1 **cup diced cooked beef, ham, pork, or chicken (4 ounces)**
- 1 **small carrot, peeled and shredded (½ cup)**
- 3 **tablespoons reduced-calorie mayonnaise**
- 2 **sweet gherkins, chopped (about 2 tablespoons)**
- 1½ **teaspoons Dijon mustard**
- 1 **teaspoon bottled horseradish**
- 4 **slices pumpernickel or whole-wheat bread**

1 In a small bowl, combine the beef, carrot, mayonnaise, gherkins, mustard, and horseradish. Spread each of 2 slices of the bread with half of the mixture, then top with the remaining bread and cut in half. Makes 2 sandwiches.

PREPARATION TIME: 10 MIN.

Per sandwich: Calories 448; Saturated Fat 3 g; Total Fat 17 g; Protein 33 g; Carbohydrate 41 g; Fiber 5 g; Sodium 605 mg; Cholesterol 89 mg

SALMON-CUCUMBER SANDWICH

Neufchâtel, a delicious light cream cheese, has about 50 percent less fat than standard cream cheese.

- ¼ cup Neufchâtel cream cheese
- 3 tablespoons plain low-fat yogurt
- 1 tablespoon lemon juice
- 1 can (15½ ounces) salmon in water, drained
- ¼ cup finely chopped red onion
- ½ teaspoon dill weed
- 2 small cucumbers (4 ounces each), peeled and thinly sliced (1 cup)
- 8 slices whole-grain bread

1 Using a food processor or an electric mixer at medium speed, beat the cheese, yogurt, and lemon juice for 1 minute or until smooth. In a medium-size bowl, flake the salmon, then add the cheese mixture, onion, and dill weed and mix well. Place half the cucumber slices on 4 bread slices and spread a generous ½ cup of the salmon mixture on each. Top with the remaining cucumber slices and bread. Makes 4 sandwiches.

PREPARATION TIME: 9 MIN.

> Per sandwich: Calories 300; Saturated Fat 2 g;
> Total Fat 9 g; Protein 27 g; Carbohydrate 27 g;
> Fiber 4 g; Sodium 813 mg; Cholesterol 58 mg

•

Sardine Variation: Increase the *Neufchâtel to ⅓ cup* and the *lemon juice to 2 tablespoons*. Add *1 ½ teaspoons each prepared mustard* and *vegetable or olive oil*, then blend with the yogurt as directed. For the salmon, substitute *3 cans sardines in water (4⅜ ounces each),* mashing them well. Increase the *dill weed to 3 teaspoons,* then proceed as directed. *Per sandwich: Calories 388; Saturated Fat 3 g; Total Fat 20 g; Protein 23 g; Carbohydrate 29 g; Fiber 4 g; Sodium 408 mg; Cholesterol 147 mg.*

TUNA NIÇOISE IN PITA POCKETS

For a change of pace, you can make the filling using turkey, chicken, or salmon in place of the tuna.

- 1 cup frozen cut green beans
- 1 can (6½ ounces) tuna in water, drained
- 2 plum tomatoes, diced
- 8 black olives (preferably Niçoise or calamata), pitted and finely chopped
- 2 tablespoons finely chopped red onion
- 2 tablespoons snipped fresh dill or minced fresh basil or parsley
- 2 teaspoons olive oil
- 2 tablespoons lemon juice
- ⅛ teaspoon black pepper, or to taste
- Lettuce leaves (preferably red leaf or Boston)
- 2 whole-wheat pita rounds, halved

1 In a medium-size saucepan of boiling water, cook the green beans for 1 minute. Drain, rinse under cold running water to cool, drain again, and set aside.

2 In a large bowl, mix the tuna, green beans, tomatoes, olives, onion, dill, oil, lemon juice, and pepper. Tuck several lettuce leaves into each pita half, then fill with the tuna Niçoise. Makes 2 sandwiches.

PREPARATION TIME: 10 MIN. COOKING TIME: 1 MIN.

> Per sandwich: Calories 346; Saturated Fat 2 g;
> Total Fat 10 g; Protein 32 g; Carbohydrate 34 g;
> Fiber 4 g; Sodim 743 mg; Cholesterol 38 mg

For those days when you don't have time to make a sandwich, toss a can of water-packed tuna, salmon, or sardines (the ones with bones are a good source of calcium) into your lunch bag along with a lemon, crackers or a whole-grain roll, and some fruit for dessert. When it's time to eat, drain the fish, squeeze lemon juice over it, and enjoy a high-protein, low-fat lunch.

If this becomes a favorite meal, keep a jar of dill weed in your desk. Canned fish is always enhanced by it.

To create perfect egg salad, begin with a perfectly hard-cooked egg. Place eggs in an enamel or stainless steel saucepan (they discolor aluminum), then add enough cold water to cover them by 1 inch. Bring the water to a full boil, cover the pan, and turn off the heat. Let the eggs sit for 15 minutes, then pour off the hot water and cool the eggs immediately under cold running water.

Cooking the eggs at a low temperature prevents toughening and discoloration of the yolk, and cooling them quickly makes the peeling easy.

EGG SALAD SANDWICH

Tofu (see Tip, page 166) works the magic here. Combined with egg whites and just one whole egg, it makes a rich, creamy sandwich spread that is high in protein and lower in cholesterol than the usual egg salad sandwich. For variety, you can add some minced capers, minced black or green olives, or toasted sesame seeds, or omit the paprika and turmeric and season the spread with dried dill weed.

- 5 ounces firm tofu
- 1 tablespoon prepared mustard
- 1/4 cup water
- 1 hard-cooked large egg, coarsely chopped
- 2 hard-cooked large egg whites, coarsely chopped
- 1/3 cup finely chopped yellow onion
- 1/3 cup finely chopped sweet red pepper
- 1/4 teaspoon each ground turmeric and paprika
- 1/8 teaspoon each salt and black pepper, or to taste
- 8 slices whole-grain or rye bread

1 In a food processor or blender, whirl the tofu, mustard, and water for about 30 seconds or until smooth. Transfer the mixture to a medium-size bowl and add the egg, egg whites, onion, red pepper, turmeric, paprika, salt, and black pepper. Toss to mix.

2 Spread each of 4 bread slices with 1/2 cup of the mixture, top with the remaining bread, and cut in half. Makes 4 sandwiches.

PREPARATION TIME: 12 MIN.

Per sandwich: Calories 219; Saturated Fat 1 g; Total Fat 6 g; Protein 14 g; Carbohydrate 27 g; Fiber 4 g; Sodium 370 mg; Cholesterol 53 mg

HERBED CHEESE AND WATERCRESS SANDWICH

If you are making this sandwich to take to work, pack the watercress separately and add it at the last minute.

- 1 1/2 cups low-fat (1% milk-fat) cottage cheese
- 1/3 cup finely chopped pimientos, patted dry
- 1/3 cup finely chopped seeded cucumber
- 1 green onion, including top, thinly sliced (2 tablespoons)
- 2 tablespoons snipped fresh dill or minced fresh basil, chives, or parsley
- 1/2 teaspoon grated lemon rind
- 1/8 teaspoon black pepper, or to taste
- 8 slices whole-grain bread
- 1 large bunch watercress, rinsed, patted dry, and coarse stems removed

1 In a medium-size bowl, combine the cottage cheese, pimientos, cucumber, green onion, dill, lemon rind, and pepper. Spread an equal amount of the mixture on 4 slices of the bread, then top with the watercress. Place the remaining bread slices on top and cut in half. Makes 4 sandwiches.

PREPARATION TIME: 15 MIN.

Per sandwich: Calories 200; Saturated Fat 1 g; Total Fat 3 g; Protein 16 g; Carbohydrate 28 g; Fiber 4 g; Sodium 558 mg; Cholesterol 4 mg

MOZZARELLA, TOMATO, AND PESTO SANDWICH

If you prefer, you can substitute roasted sweet red peppers for the tomatoes.

For the pesto:
- 1 cup packed fresh basil leaves
- 1 clove garlic, crushed
- 1 tablespoon olive oil
- 1/8 teaspoon black pepper

For the sandwich filling:
- 2 loaves (10 inches long) whole-wheat French or Italian bread
- 4 ounces sun-dried tomatoes, blanched and patted dry on paper toweling
- 8 ounces low-fat, low-sodium mozzarella cheese, thinly sliced

1 To make the pesto: In a food processor or blender, whirl the basil, garlic, oil, and pepper for about 40 seconds or until smooth.

2 Cut each bread loaf in half horizontally. Spread each bottom slice with half of the pesto; top with half of the tomatoes and mozzarella cheese. Cover with the top slice of bread and cut in half. Makes 4 sandwiches.

PREPARATION TIME: 10 MIN.

Per sandwich: Calories 447; Saturated Fat 6 g; Total Fat 14 g; Protein 27 g; Carbohydrate 49 g; Fiber 3 g; Sodium 760 mg; Cholesterol 0 mg

Sun-dried tomatoes, carried in the produce department of many supermarkets, have a rich and intense flavor. They are particularly good in sandwiches because they don't get mushy or make the bread soggy.

Before use, they must be blanched in boiling water for 2 minutes, drained, and patted dry on paper toweling. You can also buy sun-dried tomatoes already blanched and packed in oil. Blot off the excess oil on paper toweling before using them.

Help yourself to a taste of summer's bounty — Mozzarella, Tomato, and Pesto Sandwich.

Though sandwiches and salads come first to mind for a midday meal, don't overlook soup. When you're packing a lunch, pour hot soup — or in warm weather a chilled soup — into a wide-mouth thermos; it will be ready when you are.

A soup that contains meat, fish, poultry, or rice and beans as well as vegetables is nutritionally complete with just a whole-grain bread. You can augment the protein in an all-vegetable soup with a meat or fish sandwich or crackers and cheese. For a host of ideas, see the soup chapter, which begins on page 61.

PIMIENTO AND GREEN ONION SPREAD

2 green onions, sliced
¼ cup finely chopped pimientos
1 cup Creamy Yogurt Spread (page 287)
¼ teaspoon salt
⅛ teaspoon black pepper

1 In a small bowl, mix together the green onions, pimientos, and yogurt spread. Stir in the salt and pepper. Cover and refrigerate for 1 hour before serving. Makes about 1¼ cups.

PREPARATION TIME: 7 MIN.

Per ¼ cup: Calories 54; Saturated Fat 0g; Total Fat 0g; Protein 5g; Carbohydrate 8g; Fiber 0g; Sodium 176mg; Cholesterol 2mg

GARLIC-HERB SANDWICH SPREAD

A mixture of herbs gives this spread the best flavor. Use it also as a dip for crisp vegetables.

1 cup Creamy Yogurt Spread (page 287)
1 clove garlic, minced
¼ cup minced fresh basil, dill, mint, parsley, or a combination
¼ teaspoon salt, or to taste
⅛ teaspoon black pepper

1 In a small bowl, stir together the yogurt spread, garlic, herbs, salt, and pepper until well blended. Cover with plastic food wrap and refrigerate for 1 hour before serving. Makes about 1¼ cups.

PREPARATION TIME: 7 MIN.

Per tablespoon: Calories 53; Saturated Fat 0g; Total Fat 0g; Protein 5g; Carbohydrate 7g; Fiber 0g; Sodium 178mg; Cholesterol 2mg

You can enjoy this tasty duo — Lemon-Garlic Chick Pea Spread (top) and Pimiento and Green Onion Spread (bottom) — as a sandwich spread or a dip for raw vegetables.

HERBED CHEESE SPREAD

This creamy spread tastes like one of the imported full-fat herb cheeses, but it is lower in fat and calories and much less expensive. Serve it on crackers, accompanied by fruit, or make a sandwich with it using rye bread.

1 **clove garlic**	¼ **teaspoon dried basil, crumbled**
8 **ounces low-fat (1% milkfat) cottage cheese**	⅛ **teaspoon black pepper**
¼ **cup parsley leaves**	1½ **tablespoons snipped fresh chives or green onion tops**

1 In a small saucepan of boiling water, cook the garlic for 1 minute. Drain off the water and transfer the garlic to a food processor or blender.

2 Add the cottage cheese, parsley, basil, pepper, and chives to the food processor or blender and whirl for 30 seconds or until smooth. Cover and refrigerate for 2 hours to let the flavors mellow. Will keep, covered and refrigerated, for up to 10 days. Makes 1 cup.

PREPARATION TIME: 5 MIN. COOKING TIME: 1 MIN.

Per tablespoon: Calories 44; Saturated Fat 0 g; Total Fat 1 g; Protein 7 g; Carbohydrate 2 g; Fiber 0 g; Sodium 232 mg; Cholesterol 3 mg

LEMON-GARLIC CHICK PEA SPREAD

This versatile spread can be served as a dip for raw vegetables or as a sandwich filling. For variety as well as extra nutrition, stir in a chopped small sweet red pepper or 8 ounces of chopped fresh spinach. For a Tex-Mex flavor, omit the garlic and hot red pepper sauce and stir in ¼ cup chopped mild green chilies and a minced green onion.

1 **can (1 pound) chick peas, drained and rinsed (2 cups)**	1 **tablespoon vegetable or olive oil**
1 **package (10 ounces) frozen green peas, thawed**	1 **teaspoon ground cumin**
	1 **clove garlic, minced**
¼ **cup lemon juice**	½ **teaspoon salt, or to taste**
	4 **drops hot red pepper sauce, or to taste**

1 In a food processor or blender, whirl the chick peas, green peas, lemon juice, oil, cumin, garlic, salt, and red pepper sauce for 1 minute or until puréed. Refrigerate, covered, for 1 hour before serving. Will keep, covered and refrigerated, for 2 days. Makes 3 cups.

PREPARATION TIME: 8 MIN.

Per ¼ cup: Calories 67; Saturated Fat 0 g; Total Fat 2 g; Protein 3 g; Carbohydrate 10 g; Fiber 3 g; Sodium 260 mg; Cholesterol 0 mg

Good nutrition doesn't have to take a lot of time. With a little imagination plus whole-grain bread and one of the convenient old standbys — canned tuna, peanut butter, or cream cheese — you can make a healthful and appealing sandwich in minutes.

Of these three fillings, canned tuna in water has the least fat. Peanut butter is a low-cost, easily obtainable plant protein; the unhydrogenated form, carried by health food stores and increasingly by supermarkets, has higher levels of linoleic acid and vitamin E and lower amounts of saturated fat and sugar. When buying cream cheese, get Neufchâtel, which has about half the fat of the regular type.

Almost any raw vegetable added to a sandwich filling contributes not only nutritional value but texture and bulk as well. A few suggestions are given below.

___

Tuna combos:
* plain low-fat yogurt, finely chopped cucumber and red onion, dill
* reduced-calorie mayonnaise, non-fat yogurt, sunflower seeds, raisins, curry powder
* finely chopped tomato, onion, and sweet pepper; vinaigrette dressing

Peanut butter combos:
* shredded carrot or chopped celery
* sliced fresh banana, pear, or apple
* chopped dried fruit or raisins
* fruit chutney
* chopped reduced-sodium ham

Cream cheese combos:
* fruit butter, such as peach or apple
* chopped roasted sweet red peppers, arugula or watercress
* chutney, sliced reduced-sodium ham
* chopped raw nuts, such as walnuts

PASTA SALAD WITH ARTICHOKE HEARTS, CHEESE, AND PEPPERS

8 ounces medium-size pasta shells, ditalini, or elbow macaroni

1 jar (6 ounces) artichoke hearts in marinade

⅓ cup apple juice

2 tablespoons white wine vinegar or cider vinegar

1 teaspoon dried marjoram, crumbled

¼ teaspoon salt, or to taste

⅛ teaspoon hot red pepper sauce

1 jar (7 ounces) roasted sweet red peppers, drained, rinsed, and sliced into ¼-inch strips

3 green onions, including tops, sliced (about ⅓ cup)

8 ounces low-fat mozzarella or Monterey Jack cheese, cut into ½-inch cubes

1 Cook the pasta in unsalted water according to package directions. Meanwhile, in a small bowl, whisk together 3 tablespoons of the artichoke marinade, the apple juice, vinegar, marjoram, salt, and red pepper sauce until well blended.

2 Drain the artichoke hearts, discarding the remaining marinade, and put them in a large bowl with the peppers and green onions.

3 When the pasta is done, drain and rinse it under cold running water, drain again, and add it to the vegetable mixture. Pour half the dressing over the salad and refrigerate, covered, for up to 2 days. Just before serving, stir in the remaining dressing and the cheese. Serve chilled or at room temperature. Serves 4.

PREPARATION TIME: 15 MIN. COOKING TIME: 10 MIN.

Per serving: Calories 394; Saturated Fat 6 g; Total Fat 10 g; Protein 22 g; Carbohydrate 54 g; Fiber 4 g; Sodium 427 mg; Cholesterol 32 mg

It's picnic perfect: Pasta Salad with Artichoke Hearts, Cheese, and Peppers.

TRICOLOR PASTA SALAD WITH CHEESE DRESSING

If you like, you can make this dish a day ahead and keep it refrigerated. If the pasta absorbs too much of the dressing, stir in 1 or 2 tablespoons of water just before serving to restore the creamy texture.

- 8 ounces tricolor rotini, medium-size pasta shells, or elbow macaroni
- 4 cups cauliflower florets (8 ounces)
- 3 medium-size carrots, peeled and thinly sliced on the diagonal (1 cup)
- 2 medium-size stalks celery, thinly sliced on the diagonal
- 1 small yellow summer squash, halved and thinly sliced on the diagonal (1 cup)

For the dressing:
- 1 cup low-fat (1% milkfat) cottage cheese
- 2 tablespoons grated Parmesan cheese
- 2 tablespoons apple juice
- 2 tablespoons cider vinegar
- 1 teaspoon Dijon mustard
- 1 clove garlic, minced
- 1 ¼ teaspoons dried basil, crumbled
- ¼ teaspoon each salt and black pepper, or to taste
- 2 green onions, including tops, sliced (optional garnish)

1 Bring a stockpot of water to a boil, then add the pasta. When the water returns to a boil, add the cauliflower and carrots and cook for 4 minutes. Add the celery and cook 3 minutes more or until the pasta is firm-tender. Add the squash, remove from the heat, and drain in a colander. Rinse well under cold water and transfer to a large bowl.

2 To make the dressing: In a food processor or blender, whirl the cottage cheese, Parmesan, apple juice, vinegar, mustard, garlic, basil, salt, and pepper until smooth. Pour the dressing over the pasta-vegetable mixture and toss to coat. Cover with plastic food wrap and chill for 4 hours. Garnish with green onions if desired. Serves 4.

PREPARATION TIME: 20 MIN.   COOKING TIME: 8 MIN.

Per serving: Calories 309; Saturated Fat 1 g; Total Fat 2 g; Protein 18 g; Carbohydrate 56 g; Fiber 8 g; Sodium 500 mg; Cholesterol 5 mg

MACARONI SALAD WITH BASIL, TOMATOES, AND CHICK PEAS

If fresh basil isn't available, substitute ¼ cup flat-leaf parsley mixed with 1 teaspoon dried basil.

- 8 ounces elbow macaroni or medium-size pasta shells
- 1 can (19 ounces) chick peas, drained and rinsed (2 ¼ cups)
- 2 plum tomatoes, cut into ½-inch pieces (about 1 cup)
- 2 green onions, including tops, sliced (¼ cup)
- ¼ cup firmly packed basil leaves, coarsely chopped
- 3 tablespoons lemon juice
- ¼ teaspoon black pepper
- ⅓ cup olive oil
- 3 cloves garlic, halved
- ¾ teaspoon each dried rosemary and marjoram, crumbled

1 Cook the pasta in unsalted water according to package directions. Drain, rinse under cold running water to stop the cooking, and drain again, then transfer to a large bowl. Add the chick peas, tomatoes, green onions, basil, lemon juice, and pepper and toss together.

2 In an 8-inch skillet, heat the oil over low heat and add the garlic, rosemary, and marjoram. Cook for about 5 minutes, turning the garlic as it colors, until it is golden and the oil is fragrant. Strain the oil onto the pasta mixture, discarding the garlic and herbs, then toss to combine. Serve either at room temperature or chilled. Will keep, refrigerated, for 2 days. Serves 6.

PREPARATION TIME: 6 MIN.   COOKING TIME: 12 MIN.

Per serving: Calories 346; Saturated Fat 2 g; Total Fat 14 g; Protein 9 g; Carbohydrate 46 g; Fiber 7 g; Sodium 363 mg; Cholesterol 0 mg

EASY SUMMER LUNCH

Crudités with Herbed Cheese Spread
(page 55)

Macaroni Salad with Basil, Tomatoes, and Chick Peas

Rye Bread

Peaches with Yogurt and Brown Sugar

Low-fat cheese and grapes are dandy accompaniments to Asparagus, Mushroom, and Kasha Salad.

ASPARAGUS, MUSHROOM, AND KASHA SALAD

1 large egg
1 cup kasha (toasted buckwheat groats)
1 ⅓ cups Chicken Stock (page 62) or low-sodium chicken broth
1 medium-size yellow onion, chopped (1 ¼ cups)
3 tablespoons olive oil
8 ounces mushrooms, sliced (2 ½ cups)
8 ounces asparagus, cut into 1 ½-inch lengths (about 3 cups)

2 cloves garlic, minced
⅛ teaspoon each salt and black pepper
¼ cup water
1 large sweet red pepper, cored, seeded, and chopped (1 cup)
1 medium-size stalk celery, diced (½ cup)
2 tablespoons minced parsley or snipped fresh dill
2 tablespoons sherry vinegar or balsamic vinegar

1 In a small bowl, beat the egg lightly, then add the kasha and stir to coat. Pour the mixture into a 10-inch non-stick skillet and cook over moderate heat, stirring, for about 2 minutes or until the kasha is completely dry. Add the stock and onion and bring to a boil. Cover and simmer over low heat for 15 minutes or until the kasha is tender.

2 Meanwhile, in a 12-inch skillet, heat 2 tablespoons of the oil over moderately high heat. Add the mushrooms and sauté for 3 minutes or until they begin to release their juices. Add the asparagus, garlic, salt, and black pepper and sauté, stirring, for 1 minute. Add the water to the skillet, cover, and steam the vegetables for 2 minutes or until the asparagus are crisp-tender. Remove the cover from the pan, raise the heat to high, and cook until all the remaining liquid has evaporated.

3 In a large bowl, combine the kasha, vegetable mixture, red pepper, celery, and parsley. Sprinkle with the vinegar and remaining tablespoon of oil and toss to combine. Serve at room temperature. The salad will keep, covered, in the refrigerator for up to 24 hours. Serves 6.

PREPARATION TIME: 25 MIN. COOKING TIME: 25 MIN.

Per serving: Calories 219; Saturated Fat 1 g;
Total Fat 9 g; Protein 8 g; Carbohydrate 30 g;
Fiber 4 g; Sodium 83 mg; Cholesterol 36 mg

58

COUSCOUS SALAD WITH SUMMER VEGETABLES

1 ½ cups Chicken Stock (page 62) or low-sodium chicken broth
1 tablespoon olive oil
1 cup couscous
3 small eggplants, halved lengthwise and sliced ½ inch thick (4 ½ cups)
1 medium-size zucchini, halved lengthwise and sliced ½ inch thick (about 2 cups)
2 cloves garlic, minced
½ teaspoon each ground cumin and cinnamon
⅛ teaspoon each salt and black pepper, or to taste
¼ cup water

1 can (10 ½ ounces) chick peas, drained and rinsed
2 plum tomatoes, diced
1 small red onion, finely chopped (½ cup)
2 tablespoons minced fresh mint or parsley

For the dressing:
¼ cup orange juice
2 tablespoons lemon juice
1 teaspoon grated orange rind
1 teaspoon Dijon mustard
⅛ teaspoon each salt and black pepper, or to taste
2 tablespoons olive oil

1 In a medium-size saucepan, bring the stock to a boil; stir in 1 teaspoon of the olive oil and the couscous. Cover, remove from the heat, and let stand for 10 minutes.

2 Meanwhile, in a 10-inch nonstick skillet, heat the remaining 2 teaspoons of oil over moderate heat until very hot but not smoking. Add the eggplants and sauté, stirring, for 2 minutes. Add the zucchini, garlic, cumin, cinnamon, salt, and pepper; sauté, stirring, for 1 minute. Add the water, cover, and cook 1 to 2 minutes longer or until the vegetables are crisp-tender.

3 To make the dressing: In a large bowl, combine the orange juice, lemon juice, lemon rind, mustard, salt, and pepper, then whisk in the oil. Add the couscous, vegetable mixture, chick peas, tomatoes, onion, and mint and toss to combine. The salad will keep, refrigerated, for 2 days. Serves 6.

PREPARATION TIME: 20 MIN. COOKING TIME: 15 MIN.

Per serving: Calories 277; Saturated Fat 1 g; Total Fat 8 g; Protein 9 g; Carbohydrate 43 g; Fiber 11 g; Sodium 322 mg; Cholesterol 0 mg

PORK, RICE, AND LENTIL SALAD

This high-protein salad is easy to make, and you cook it in just one pot, so there is hardly any cleanup.

3 cups water
1 cup dried lentils, sorted and rinsed
3 cloves garlic, crushed
3 strips lemon zest (colored part of the rind), 2 inches long by ¼ inch wide
½ teaspoon salt, or to taste

½ cup long-grain white rice
1 cup frozen green peas
6 radishes, halved and thinly sliced
4 ounces cooked pork, cut into thin strips
1 ½ tablespoons lemon juice

1 In a large saucepan, bring the water to a boil. Add the lentils, garlic, lemon zest, and salt. Cover and simmer over low heat for 5 minutes. Add the rice, cover, and simmer for 17 minutes, stirring occasionally with a fork. Add the peas, cover, and simmer 3 minutes longer or until the rice, lentils, and peas are tender.

2 Transfer to a large bowl and stir in the radishes, pork, and lemon juice. Serve at room temperature or chilled. Will keep, refrigerated, for 2 days. Serves 4 to 6.

PREPARATION TIME: 12 MIN. COOKING TIME: 25 MIN.

Per serving (for 4): Calories 248; Saturated Fat 2 g; Total Fat 5 g; Protein 17 g; Carbohydrate 36 g; Fiber 5 g; Sodium 340 mg; Cholesterol 27 mg

Tossed green salads are welcome additions to any lunch but don't travel well because the greens easily wilt. So what does a health-minded person do? Leave out the greens and pack instead a mélange of diced vegetables such as cucumbers, peppers, and carrots in a vinaigrette dressing. Or make up a batch of coleslaw. It keeps for 2 to 3 days and is easily transported in a small plastic container.

RICE SALAD PRIMAVERA

You can be as creative as you like with this recipe — substitute snow peas, corn, yellow squash, or green beans for any of the vegetables, or use a combination of wild and brown rice.

- 2 cups Chicken Stock (page 62), low-sodium chicken broth, or water
- 1 cup long-grain brown rice
- 2 cups broccoli florets (5 ounces)
- 2 medium-size carrots, peeled and thinly sliced (1½ cups)
- 2 small zucchini, halved lengthwise and sliced ½ inch thick (2 cups)
- 8 ounces firm-textured tofu, cut into ¾-inch cubes
- 1 medium-size sweet green pepper, cored, seeded, and chopped (¾ cup)
- 3 green onions, including tops, finely chopped (about ⅓ cup)
- ½ cup chopped walnuts (optional garnish)

For the dressing:
- ¼ cup lemon juice
- 1 teaspoon grated lemon rind
- 2 teaspoons Dijon mustard
- ¼ teaspoon each salt and black pepper, or to taste
- 3 tablespoons walnut or olive oil
- 2 tablespoons olive or vegetable oil
- 2 tablespoons snipped fresh dill or 2 teaspoons dill weed, crumbled

1 In a medium-size saucepan, bring the stock to a boil. Add the rice, cover, and simmer over low heat for 40 minutes or until the rice is tender. Let stand for 5 minutes.

2 Meanwhile, bring a large saucepan of water to a boil. Add the broccoli and carrots and cook for 2 minutes. Add the zucchini and cook 1 minute more or until the vegetables are crisp-tender. Drain the vegetables, rinse under cold running water, and pat dry.

3 To make the dressing: In a large bowl, combine the lemon juice, rind, mustard, salt, and black pepper. Add the oils in a thin stream, whisking constantly until the dressing is blended and slightly thickened. Stir in the dill, rice, vegetables, tofu, green pepper, and green onions and toss to coat. Sprinkle with the walnuts if desired. Serves 6.

PREPARATION TIME: 15 MIN. COOKING TIME: 40 MIN.

Per serving: Calories 309; Saturated Fat 2 g;
Total Fat 16 g; Protein 11 g; Carbohydrate 33 g;
Fiber 5 g; Sodium 156 mg; Cholesterol 0 mg

NUTTED FRUIT AND CHEESE SALAD

Apples, pears, nuts, and a bit of cheese make a perfect fall lunch. Serve with a whole-grain roll. If you can't find fresh mint or basil, substitute ⅓ cup flat-leaf parsley mixed with 1 teaspoon mint flakes.

For the dressing:
- ⅓ cup firmly packed fresh mint or basil leaves
- ½ cup buttermilk
- 2 tablespoons honey
- 2 teaspoons lime juice
- 2 teaspoons olive oil

For the fruit salad:
- 1 large Granny Smith apple, cored and cut into 12 wedges
- 1 large Empire, McIntosh or Red Delicious apple, cored and cut into 12 wedges
- 2 large Bartlett pears, cored and each cut into 8 wedges
- 4 ounces low-fat Cheddar cheese, cut into ½-inch cubes
- ¼ cup pecans, coarsely chopped
- Mint leaves (optional garnish)

1 To make the dressing: In a food processor or blender, whirl the mint, buttermilk, honey, lime juice, and oil for about 30 seconds or until smooth. Transfer to a jar with a tight-fitting lid and refrigerate for several hours or overnight. Will keep, refrigerated, for up to 4 days.

2 To make the salad: In a large bowl, place the apples, pears, cheese, and pecans and toss together. Shake the dressing well and drizzle it over the fruit. Garnish the salad with the mint if desired. Serves 4.

PREPARATION TIME: 7 MIN.

Per serving: Calories 304; Saturated Fat 4 g;
Total Fat 13 g; Protein 10 g; Carbohydrate 42 g;
Fiber 5 g; Sodium 175 mg; Cholesterol 21 mg

SOUPS

Soup has myriad virtues. Among them is its versatility — you can
serve it hot or cold, as an opener or main course, for lunch or dinner. Then too, almost
any food can be used in soup making, but vegetables, of which we should
have at least 3 servings a day, are included in most recipes. And soup can be one of
the most nourishing and satisfying yet relatively low-calorie dishes on the menu,
provided that fat is kept to a minimum. Perhaps the only drawback to soup is that it
can absorb an enormous amount of salt without your ever tasting it. Many
canned soups have a high sodium content. Making your own salt-free stock (recipes
on page 62) makes sense if you are salt sensitive. Having a repertoire of
savory soups to serve all year round is not only savvy but also one of the most
healthful things you can do for yourself and your family.

CHICKEN STOCK

The secret to a rich-tasting stock is simmering it for a long time to draw all the flavor out of the ingredients. About 4 hours is ideal, although 2 hours will do. A stewing hen makes the most flavorful stock; however, the meat, which you can save for another recipe, is a bit tough. A broiler-fryer yields more tender meat but not quite as much flavor. Another option is to save and freeze less-desirable parts, such as wings, necks, and backs, from a whole chicken and use them for stock.

1 **stewing or roasting chicken (5 to 6 pounds) or 5 to 6 pounds chicken parts**	6 **sprigs parsley**
	2 **bay leaves**
	12 **black or green peppercorns**
1 **large yellow onion, quartered**	½ **teaspoon salt, or to taste**
2 **medium-size stalks celery, quartered**	1 **teaspoon each dried rosemary and thyme, crumbled**
2 **medium-size carrots, quartered**	2 **cloves garlic (optional)**
1 **parsnip or turnip, quartered (optional)**	3 **quarts water**

1 In a large stockpot, combine the chicken, onion, celery, carrots, parsnip if desired, parsley, bay leaves, peppercorns, salt, rosemary, thyme, garlic if desired, and water. Bring to a boil over high heat, lower the heat, and partially cover, leaving about 1 inch of space for the steam to escape. Cook at a barely bubbling simmer for at least 2 hours or up to 4 hours, occasionally skimming off any scum that collects on the surface.

2 If using a roasting chicken, remove it from the stock after 1½ hours or when the juices run clear if the skin is pricked. Remove the meat from the bones, return the bones to the pot, and continue simmering. Save the meat for another purpose. Discard the skin.

3 If using a stewing chicken or chicken parts, remove them when the stock has finished simmering and set aside to cool. Strain the liquid through a sieve or cheesecloth-lined colander into a large heatproof bowl. Let cool slightly, cover, and refrigerate. Discard the vegetables and other solids. Meanwhile, remove the meat from the bones and save for another use. Discard the skin and bones.

4 Refrigerate the stock until chilled, then skim off the fat. The stock will keep, refrigerated, in a tightly covered container for up to 3 days. The yield varies according to how long the stock has simmered. Makes 2 to 2½ quarts.

PREPARATION TIME: 10 MIN. COOKING TIME: 2 HR.

Per 1-cup serving: Calories 21; Saturated Fat 0g; Total Fat 1g; Protein 3g; Carbohydrate 1g; Fiber 0g; Sodium 133mg; Cholesterol 0mg

•

Vegetable Stock Variation Omit the chicken. Heat *2 tablespoons unsalted butter or margarine or olive oil* in the stockpot over low heat. Add the onion, celery, *4 carrots, quartered,* and *2 parsnips or turnips, quartered;* cook, uncovered, stirring occasionally, for 10 minutes. Add the remaining ingredients and simmer, partially covered, for 2 hours. Follow directions in Steps 3 and 4 for straining and storing. Makes about 2 quarts.
Per 1-cup serving: Calories 15; Saturated Fat 0g; Total Fat 0g; Protein 0g; Carbohydrate 4g; Fiber 0g; Sodium 53mg; Cholesterol 0mg.

LEMON RICE SOUP

2 **quarts Chicken Stock (above) or 4 cups low-sodium chicken broth mixed with 4 cups water**	6 **green onions, including tops, sliced (¾ cup)**
	½ **cup minced parsley**
	1 **teaspoon grated lemon rind**
¾ **cup long-grain white rice**	⅓ **cup lemon juice**

1 In a stockpot or 5-quart Dutch oven, bring the stock to a boil over moderate heat. Add the rice, green onions, parsley, and lemon rind. Return to a boil, adjust the heat so that the mixture simmers gently, cover, and cook for 20 minutes or until the rice is tender. Remove from the heat and stir in the lemon juice. Serve hot or cold. Makes four 1½-cup servings.

PREPARATION TIME: 5 MIN. COOKING TIME: 25 MIN.

Per serving: Calories 181; Saturated Fat 0g; Total Fat 2g; Protein 9g; Carbohydrate 33g; Fiber 1g; Sodium 301mg; Cholesterol 0mg

Chicken stock lends flavor to so many dishes besides soup — poultry, meat, and vegetables, for example — it is useful to keep a ready supply in your freezer. Making your own stock for this purpose allows you to regulate the sodium, which is usually high in canned versions.

To freeze stock, let it cool to room temperature, then pour it into labeled 1-quart freezer bags (2 servings to a bag). For smaller portions, freeze the stock in ice cube trays and seal the cubes in freezer bags. Frozen chicken stock will keep for up to 6 months at 0° F.

CHUNKY CHICKEN SOUP, MEDITERRANEAN STYLE

*This colorful soup can also be made
with skinless boneless turkey.*

1 tablespoon olive oil
1 medium-size yellow onion, coarsely chopped (1 cup)
1 medium-size sweet green pepper, cored, seeded, and coarsely chopped (¾ cup)
2 cloves garlic, minced
1 can (14½ ounces) low-sodium tomatoes, chopped, with their juice
4 cups Chicken Stock (page 62) or low-sodium chicken broth
2 cups water
½ cup long-grain white rice

1 tablespoon minced fresh basil or 1 teaspoon dried basil, crumbled
6 medium-size carrots, peeled and sliced ½ inch thick (4½ cups)
1 pound skinned and boned chicken breasts, cut into ¾-inch cubes
1 package (10 ounces) frozen green beans
½ cup chopped black olives
¼ teaspoon black pepper

1 In a stockpot or 5-quart Dutch oven, heat the oil over moderate heat. Add the onion, green pepper, and garlic and sauté, stirring occasionally, for 5 minutes or until the vegetables are soft.

2 Stir in the tomatoes with their juice, the stock, water, rice, and basil and bring to a boil. Adjust the heat so that the mixture simmers gently, cover, and cook for 10 minutes. Add the carrots and cook 5 minutes longer.

3 Add the chicken, green beans, and olives and cook, uncovered, for 5 minutes or until the chicken is just cooked through. Stir in the black pepper. Makes four 1¼-cup servings.

PREPARATION TIME: 20 MIN.   COOKING TIME: 25 MIN.

*Per serving: Calories 376; Saturated Fat 1 g;
Total Fat 8 g; Protein 34 g; Carbohydrate 44 g;
Fiber 7 g; Sodium 308 mg; Cholesterol 66 mg*

With Chunky Chicken Soup, Mediterranean Style, just add a crusty loaf of bread and dinner is on the table.

TURKEY MEATBALL SOUP

For the meatballs:
- 2 slices day-old bread, cubed
- 2 tablespoons low-fat (1% milkfat) milk
- 12 ounces ground turkey
- 2 tablespoons minced parsley
- 1 large egg white
- ¼ teaspoon salt
- ¼ teaspoon ground sage
- 3 dashes hot red pepper sauce

For the soup:
- 3¾ cups Chicken Stock (page 62) or 1 can (14 ounces) low-sodium chicken broth mixed with 2 cups water
- 1 medium-size stalk celery, diced (½ cup)
- 2 medium-size carrots, peeled, halved lengthwise, and thinly sliced (1½ cups)
- 3½ ounces mushrooms, sliced (1 cup)
- 1 tablespoon dry sherry (optional)
- ¼ teaspoon salt, or to taste
- ⅛ teaspoon each dried thyme, crumbled, and ground sage
- ⅛ teaspoon black pepper
- 3 green onions, including tops, sliced (⅓ cup)

Optional garnishes:
- 1 tablespoon slivered almonds
- 1 tablespoon minced parsley

1 To prepare the meatballs: In a medium-size bowl, soak the bread in the milk for 3 minutes or until soft. Mash the bread with a fork, then stir in the turkey, parsley, egg white, salt, sage, and red pepper sauce; mix well. With moistened hands, form the mixture into balls, using 1 tablespoon for each ball. Place on wax paper; set aside.

2 To prepare the soup: In a large saucepan or 4-quart Dutch oven, combine the stock, celery, carrots, mushrooms, sherry, salt, thyme, sage, and pepper. Bring to a simmer, cover, and cook for 15 minutes.

3 Drop the meatballs into the broth. Add the green onions, cover, and cook for 15 minutes or until the meatballs are cooked through. Garnish with the almonds or parsley if desired. Makes four 1½-cup servings.

PREPARATION TIME: 25 MIN. COOKING TIME: 30 MIN.

Per serving: Calories 204; Saturated Fat 1 g; Total Fat 4 g; Protein 31 g; Carbohydrate 11 g; Fiber 2 g; Sodium 524 mg; Cholesterol 59 mg

VEGETABLE BEEF SOUP

Serve this hearty soup as a main course, accompanied by crusty whole-wheat rolls or bread sticks.

- 2 teaspoons vegetable oil
- 1 pound boneless beef chuck, cut into 1-inch cubes and patted dry
- ½ teaspoon salt, or to taste
- ¼ teaspoon black pepper
- 1 large yellow onion, sliced (1½ cups)
- 1 medium-size stalk celery, thinly sliced (½ cup)
- 2 cloves garlic, minced
- 1 can (14½ ounces) tomatoes, chopped, with their juice
- 4 cups low-sodium beef broth
- ½ teaspoon each dried thyme and marjoram, crumbled
- 1 bay leaf
- 2 large Idaho or russet potatoes, peeled and cut into 1-inch cubes (2½ cups)
- 2 small carrots, peeled and sliced 1 inch thick (1 cup)
- 2 cups shredded cabbage (8 ounces)

1 In a 10-inch nonstick skillet, heat the oil over moderate heat. Add the beef, season it with ¼ teaspoon of the salt and ⅛ teaspoon of the pepper, and cook for 5 minutes or until browned on all sides. Using a slotted spoon, transfer the beef to a 5-quart Dutch oven.

2 Add the onion and celery to the skillet and sauté in the beef drippings, stirring occasionally, for 5 minutes or until softened. Transfer the mixture to the Dutch oven.

3 Add the garlic, tomatoes, broth, thyme, marjoram, bay leaf, and remaining salt and pepper to the Dutch oven. Bring the mixture to a boil, then lower the heat, cover, and simmer gently for 30 minutes. Add the potatoes, carrots, and cabbage and bring the liquid to a boil. Lower the heat and simmer, covered, for 25 to 30 minutes or until the vegetables and meat are tender. Makes four 1½-cup servings.

PREPARATION TIME: 15 MIN. COOKING TIME: 1 HR.

Per serving: Calories 391; Saturated Fat 4 g; Total Fat 11 g; Protein 42 g; Carbohydrate 31 g; Fiber 5 g; Sodium 573 mg; Cholesterol 103 mg

Portuguese Kale Soup makes a wonderful Sunday night supper. Why not make extra for Monday lunch?

PORTUGUESE KALE SOUP

Vitamin-rich kale tastes great teamed with sausage, potatoes, and kidney beans. If it's unavailable, you can substitute spinach or chard for similar results.

- 4 ounces spicy turkey sausage or Italian sausage
- 1 ½ ounces sliced pepperoni, slivered
- 1 large yellow onion, quartered and thinly sliced (1 ½ cups)
- 1 medium-size stalk celery, coarsely chopped (½ cup)
- 4 cups Chicken Stock (page 62) mixed with 4 cups water or 1 can (14 ¼ ounces) low-sodium chicken broth mixed with 6 cups water
- 8 ounces kale, thick stems removed and leaves sliced (about 8 cups), or 2 packages (10 ounces each) frozen kale, thawed and squeezed dry
- ½ teaspoon minced garlic
- 12 ounces red skin potatoes, halved and sliced (2 cups)
- ½ teaspoon hot red pepper sauce, or to taste
- ¼ teaspoon salt, or to taste
- 1 ½ cups cooked red kidney beans or cannellini (white kidney beans)

1 Remove the casings from the sausage and discard; crumble the meat. In a stockpot or 5-quart Dutch oven, cook the sausage, stirring, over moderately low heat for 4 minutes. Add the pepperoni and cook 2 minutes more or until the fat is rendered. Drain the sausage and pepperoni on paper toweling. Pour all but 1 teaspoon of the fat from the stockpot and discard.

2 Add the onion and celery to the stockpot and cook, covered, stirring occasionally, over low heat for 8 minutes or until softened. Return the sausage to the stockpot and add the stock, kale, and garlic. Bring to a simmer, cover, and cook for 10 minutes.

3 Stir in the potatoes, red pepper sauce, and salt and simmer, covered, 20 minutes more or until the potatoes and kale are tender. Add the beans and cook just until heated through. Makes six 1 ½-cup servings.

PREPARATION TIME: 20 MIN. COOKING TIME: 45 MIN.

Per serving: Calories 229; Saturated Fat 2 g; Total Fat 7 g; Protein 13 g; Carbohydrate 30 g; Fiber 6 g; Sodium 498 mg; Cholesterol 13 mg

Hearty Cabbage Soup, a colorful blend of cabbage, carrots, and tomatoes, is brimming with vitamin C.

HAM AND GREENS SOUP WITH TOMATOES

A small ham hock gives this soup a rich flavor. If you like, you can dice the meat into the soup when it has finished cooking. Spinach or kale can be substituted for the collards.

1 tablespoon vegetable oil	1 ½ pounds collard greens, thick stems removed, leaves shredded (8 cups), or 2 packages (10 ounces each) frozen collard greens
1 large yellow onion, finely chopped (1 ½ cups)	
3 green onions, including tops, thinly sliced (⅓ cup)	1 small smoked ham hock (8 ounces)
3 cloves garlic, slivered	9 cups water
8 ounces mushrooms, thickly sliced (2 cups)	¾ teaspoon salt, or to taste
1 large yam or sweet potato, peeled and cut into 1-inch cubes (2 cups)	½ teaspoon dried savory, crumbled
	¼ teaspoon ground red pepper (cayenne)
6 plum tomatoes, cored and chopped (2 cups)	2 tablespoons red wine vinegar

1 In a stockpot or 5-quart Dutch oven, heat the oil over low heat. Add the yellow onion, green onions, and garlic and cook, stirring occasionally, for 5 minutes or until the onions have softened. Add the mushrooms and cook 2 minutes longer. Stir in the yam, tomatoes, and collard greens and cook 2 minutes more.

2 Add the ham hock, water, salt, savory, and red pepper and bring to a boil over moderate heat. Adjust the heat so that the mixture simmers gently, cover, and cook for 35 minutes or until the yam and greens are tender. Remove the ham hock and, if desired, dice the meat and return it to the pot; discard the fat. Skim any fat from the surface of the soup; stir in the vinegar. Makes ten 1 ½-cup servings.

PREPARATION TIME: 20 MIN.   COOKING TIME: 45 MIN.

Per serving: Calories 118; Saturated Fat 1 g; Total Fat 3 g; Protein 7 g; Carbohydrate 18 g; Fiber 3 g; Sodium 410 mg; Cholesterol 8 mg

TOMATO-HOMINY SOUP

Hominy gives this soup an appealing tortilla-like flavor. Serve it for lunch with dark pumpernickel bread or for dinner, accompanied by a main-dish salad or pasta.

- 1 can (1 pound) white or yellow hominy, drained and rinsed
- 1 can (14 ounces) low-sodium tomatoes, drained, with juice reserved
- 1 tablespoon olive oil
- 1 medium-size yellow onion, coarsely chopped (1 cup)
- 1 medium-size sweet red pepper, cored, seeded, and finely chopped (¾ cup)
- 1 teaspoon chili powder
- 4 cups Chicken Stock (page 62) or low-sodium chicken broth
- 1 package (10 ounces) frozen corn kernels
- ½ teaspoon dried oregano, crumbled
- 1 cup finely diced smoked ham, 95% or more fat free (6 ounces)
- 1 tablespoon lemon juice
- ¼ teaspoon black pepper

1 In a food processor or blender, coarsely chop the hominy and tomatoes and set aside. In a stockpot or 5-quart Dutch oven, heat the oil over moderate heat. Add the onion and red pepper and sauté, stirring constantly, for 2 to 3 minutes. Stir in the chili powder, stock, corn, oregano, hominy-tomato mixture, and reserved tomato juice and bring to a boil. Adjust the heat so that the mixture simmers gently, cover, and cook for 10 minutes.

2 Stir in the ham, lemon juice, and black pepper and cook, uncovered, 1 minute more or until the ham is heated through. Makes six 1¼-cup servings.

PREPARATION TIME: 15 MIN. COOKING TIME: 15 MIN.

> *Per serving: Calories 186; Saturated Fat 1 g; Total Fat 5 g; Protein 10 g; Carbohydrate 27 g; Fiber 5 g; Sodium 529 mg; Cholesterol 7 mg*

HEARTY CABBAGE SOUP

Serve this rich-tasting soup with yogurt and dark bread. To make a main-dish meal, add 3 cups cooked noodles and 2 cups diced cooked chicken or ham along with the vinegar in Step 2. Cook just until heated through.

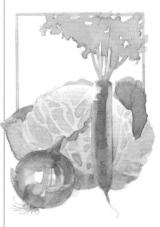

- 1 teaspoon vegetable or olive oil
- 1 small yellow onion, finely chopped (½ cup)
- 4 cloves garlic, minced
- 6 cups Chicken Stock (page 62) or 3 cups low-sodium chicken broth mixed with 3 cups water
- 2 pounds green or red cabbage, cored and shredded (7 cups)
- 3 medium-size carrots, peeled, halved lengthwise, and thinly sliced (1½ cups)
- 2 medium-size tomatoes, chopped, with their juice (2 cups)
- 2 tablespoons tomato paste
- ⅓ cup snipped fresh dill or 1½ tablespoons dill weed
- 3 cups water
- 2 tablespoons red wine vinegar
- 1½ teaspoons sugar
- ¼ teaspoon salt, or to taste

1 In a stockpot or 5-quart Dutch oven, heat the oil over low heat. Add the onion and garlic and cook, stirring constantly, for 2 minutes. Add ⅓ cup of the stock, cover, and cook for 5 minutes, stirring occasionally.

2 Stir in the cabbage, the remaining 5⅔ cups stock, the carrots, tomatoes, tomato paste, dill, and water. Bring to a boil over moderate heat, adjust the heat so that the mixture simmers gently, cover, and cook for 35 minutes. Stir in the vinegar, sugar, and salt, cover, and simmer 5 minutes more. Makes eight 1½-cup servings.

PREPARATION TIME: 15 MIN. COOKING TIME: 47 MIN.

> *Per serving: Calories 78; Saturated Fat 0 g; Total Fat 1 g; Protein 4 g; Carbohydrate 14 g; Fiber 4 g; Sodium 299 mg; Cholesterol 0 mg*

Toasted garlic bread is a wonderful companion to soup. Instead of preparing it with butter, which is high in saturated fat, why not try an Italian favorite: olive oil and garlic. Studies have shown that the monounsaturated fat in olive oil may actually be beneficial to the heart.

Preheat the oven to 400° F. For an 8-ounce loaf of bread (4 servings), mix 4 tablespoons of olive oil with 4 to 6 crushed cloves of garlic. Cut the bread in half and with a pastry brush, spread the mixture evenly on the two halves, then make 1-inch slices cutting not quite all the way through. Bake for 5 to 8 minutes or until heated through and crusty on the edges.

MANHATTAN CLAM CHOWDER

This blend of clams and vegetables is lower in fat and calories than creamy New England–style chowder. Serve it with toasted garlic bread.

- 2 teaspoons unsalted butter or margarine
- 1 medium-size yellow onion, chopped (1 cup)
- 1 small carrot, peeled and diced (½ cup)
- 1 small stalk celery, diced (⅓ cup)
- ⅛ teaspoon salt, or to taste
- ¼ teaspoon black pepper
- 1 medium-size all-purpose potato, peeled and diced (1¼ cups)
- 1 can (14½ ounces) low-sodium tomatoes, puréed with their juice
- 1 cup water
- 1 cup minced fresh or canned clams, with their liquid
- 1 bottle (8 ounces) clam juice
- 2 tablespoons minced parsley

1 In a large saucepan, melt the butter over low heat. Add the onion, carrot, celery, salt, and pepper. Cover and cook, stirring occasionally, for 5 minutes or until the vegetables are softened.

2 Add the potato, tomatoes, and water and bring to a boil. Lower the heat, cover, and simmer for 15 to 20 minutes or until the vegetables are just tender.

3 Stir in the clams, their liquid, and the clam juice. Bring the soup to a boil, then lower the heat and simmer, covered, for 5 minutes or until the flavors have blended. Sprinkle with the parsley. Makes four 1½-cup servings.

PREPARATION TIME: 15 MIN. COOKING TIME: 25 MIN.

Per serving: Calories 131; Saturated Fat 1 g; Total Fat 3 g; Protein 10 g; Carbohydrate 18 g; Fiber 3 g; Sodium 255 mg; Cholesterol 24 mg

ZUPPA DI PESCE

Serve this easy Italian-style fish soup with garlic bread or Parmesan toast. For extra flavor, substitute 1 cup bottled clam juice for 1 cup of the chicken stock.

- 1 tablespoon olive oil
- 2 medium-size leeks, rinsed and coarsely chopped (1¼ cups)
- ⅔ cup chopped fennel or celery (4 ounces)
- 3 cloves garlic, minced
- ⅛ teaspoon each salt and black pepper, or to taste
- 4½ cups Chicken Stock (page 62) or low-sodium chicken broth
- ½ cup dry white wine or chicken stock
- 1 can (14½ ounces) low-sodium tomatoes with their juice
- ½ teaspoon dried thyme, crumbled
- ¼ teaspoon crumbled saffron (optional)
- 1 bay leaf
- 12 clams or mussels, scrubbed and beards removed from mussels
- 8 ounces large shrimp, shelled and deveined
- 8 ounces firm-fleshed white fish, such as cod, monkfish, or halibut, cut into 2-inch pieces
- Minced fresh basil or parsley (optional garnish)

1 In a large saucepan, heat the oil over moderate heat. Add the leeks, fennel, garlic, salt, and pepper and sauté, stirring occasionally, for 3 to 5 minutes or until the leeks are softened. Add the stock, wine, tomatoes, thyme, saffron if using, and bay leaf and bring to a boil. Lower the heat and simmer the mixture, covered, for 20 minutes.

2 Add the clams to the saucepan, cover, and simmer for 5 minutes or until they have opened. (Discard any that do not open.) Using a slotted spoon, transfer the clams to a bowl and cover loosely with foil. Add the shrimp and fish to the saucepan and simmer, stirring occasionally, for about 3 minutes or until cooked through. Remove and discard the bay leaf. Ladle the soup into 4 soup bowls and top each serving with 3 clams and a sprinkling of basil if desired. Makes four 2-cup servings.

PREPARATION TIME: 20 MIN. COOKING TIME: 32 MIN.

Per serving: Calories 293; Saturated Fat 1 g; Total Fat 7 g; Protein 33 g; Carbohydrate 19 g; Fiber 2 g; Sodium 556 mg; Cholesterol 127 mg

CHINESE HOT-AND-SOUR SOUP

This spicy soup makes a fine prelude to a stir-fried dish or lo-mein noodles. Look for dried shiitake mushrooms in an Oriental food store or substitute whatever dried mushrooms are available in your supermarket. You can use 1 ½ cups leftover chicken instead of the chicken breast; however, it should be added in Step 3 along with the tofu.

1 ¼ cups water	2 ½ cups Chicken Stock (page 62) or 1 can (14 ounces) low-sodium chicken broth mixed with ¾ cup water
¾ cup canned bamboo shoots, drained	
¼ ounce dried shiitake mushrooms (4 large)	2 to 3 tablespoons reduced-sodium soy sauce
2 teaspoons dark sesame oil	2 teaspoons honey
8 ounces skinned and boned chicken breast, cut into 2" x ¼" x ¼" strips	1 ½ tablespoons cornstarch
	8 ounces firm tofu, cut into ½" x ½" x 2" strips
7 ounces fresh mushrooms, sliced (2 cups)	2 tablespoons rice vinegar or white wine vinegar
3 green onions, including tops, sliced (⅓ cup)	¼ teaspoon hot red pepper sauce, or to taste

1 In a small saucepan, bring 1 cup of the water to a boil. Place the bamboo shoots in a small heatproof bowl and pour ½ cup of the boiling water over them. Let them soak for 5 minutes, then drain. Meanwhile, add the dried mushrooms to the water remaining in the saucepan and let soak for 15 minutes. Drain the mushrooms through a sieve, lined with cheesecloth or paper toweling, set over a bowl; reserve the soaking liquid. Slice the mushrooms, discarding the stems.

2 In a large saucepan, heat the oil over moderate heat. Add the chicken and sauté, stirring occasionally, for 4 minutes or until no longer pink on the outside. Add the soaked mushrooms, fresh mushrooms, green onions, stock, soy sauce, honey, and reserved mushroom soaking liquid. Bring the saucepan mixture to a simmer.

3 Meanwhile, in a small bowl, mix the cornstarch with the remaining ¼ cup water. Stir the cornstarch mixture into the simmering soup and cook for 5 minutes. Stir in the tofu, vinegar, and red pepper sauce and cook until the tofu is heated through. Makes four 1 ½-cup servings.

PREPARATION TIME: 30 MIN. COOKING TIME: 12 MIN.

Per serving: Calories 259; Saturated Fat 2 g; Total Fat 10 g; Protein 30 g; Carbohydrate 15 g; Fiber 2 g; Sodium 379 mg; Cholesterol 48 mg

Zuppa di Pesce combines the fruits of the sea with a flavorsome broth.

CHICK PEA SOUP WITH SAUSAGE

This soup is hearty enough to serve as a main dish, accompanied by salad and bread. If you prefer, you can substitute black-eyed peas for the chick peas. Allow extra time to soak the beans or peas using either the overnight or quick soaking method (see Box, page 173).

- 2 tablespoons olive oil
- 1 large yellow onion, coarsely chopped (1 ½ cups)
- 1 large sweet red pepper, cored, seeded, and coarsely chopped (1 cup)
- 2 medium-size carrots, peeled, halved, and thinly sliced (1 ½ cups)
- 3 cloves garlic, minced
- 1 tablespoon paprika
- 4 ounces chorizo, pepperoni, or kielbasa, halved lengthwise and thinly sliced (1 cup)
- 8 cups Chicken Stock (page 62) or 2 cups low-sodium chicken broth mixed with 6 cups water
- 1 pound dried chick peas or black-eyed peas, rinsed, sorted, and soaked
- 2 bay leaves
- ½ cup minced parsley
- ½ teaspoon black pepper

1 In a stockpot or 5-quart Dutch oven, heat the oil over low heat. Add the onion and cook, stirring frequently, for 5 minutes or until soft. Stir in the red pepper, carrots, and garlic and cook 5 minutes longer.

2 Stir in the paprika and cook 1 minute longer. Add the chorizo, stock, chick peas, and bay leaves and bring to a boil over moderate heat. Adjust the heat so that the mixture simmers gently, cover, and cook for 1 ½ hours or until chick peas are tender. Skim any fat from the surface of the soup and discard. Remove the bay leaves; stir in the parsley and black pepper. Makes eight 1 ½-cup servings.

PREPARATION TIME: 20 MIN. COOKING TIME: 1 HR. 40 MIN.

Per serving: Calories 343; Saturated Fat 3 g; Total Fat 12 g; Protein 19 g; Carbohydrate 42 g; Fiber 1 g; Sodium 157 mg; Cholesterol 15 mg

ITALIAN BEAN SOUP WITH PASTA AND BASIL

Here is a very flexible recipe that you can make with kidney beans, chick peas, or cannellini, and any medium-size pasta such as elbow macaroni, shells, or wagon wheels.

1 tablespoon olive oil	4 cups Chicken Stock (page 62) or low-sodium chicken broth
1 medium-size yellow onion, finely chopped (1 cup)	½ teaspoon each dried thyme and basil, crumbled
1 medium-size stalk celery, finely chopped (½ cup)	⅔ cup small pasta shells, elbow macaroni, or wagon wheel pasta
1 small carrot, peeled and finely chopped (⅓ cup)	1 can (15½ ounces) red kidney beans, cannellini (white kidney beans), or chick peas, drained and rinsed
2 cloves garlic, minced	
¼ teaspoon salt	
⅛ teaspoon black pepper	¼ cup minced fresh basil or parsley
1 can (28 ounces) crushed tomatoes	

1 In a large heavy saucepan, heat the oil over moderately low heat. Add the onion, celery, carrot, garlic, salt, and pepper and cook, stirring occasionally, for 5 minutes. Stir in the tomatoes, stock, thyme, and basil and bring to a boil. Adjust the heat so that the mixture simmers gently, cover, and cook for 15 minutes.

2 Bring the soup back to a boil over moderately high heat, add the pasta, and cook, stirring occasionally, for 5 minutes. Add the beans and cook 5 minutes more or until the pasta is tender and the beans are heated through. Stir in the basil. Makes six 1½-cup servings.

PREPARATION TIME: 15 MIN. COOKING TIME: 30 MIN.

Per serving: Calories 158; Saturated Fat 0 g; Total Fat 4 g; Protein 8 g; Carbohydrate 25 g; Fiber 6 g; Sodium 639 mg; Cholesterol 0 mg

CARIBBEAN EGGPLANT AND BLACK BEAN SOUP

You can turn this sweet and spicy soup into a one-dish meal by adding 2 cups diced cooked pork, chicken, or shrimp along with the beans. Zucchini or yellow summer squash can be substituted for the eggplant.

1 tablespoon canola or olive oil	¼ teaspoon salt
1 medium-size sweet green pepper, cored, seeded, and coarsely chopped (¾ cup)	1 can (28 ounces) tomatoes in purée
	2 tablespoons dry sherry, orange juice, or water
1 medium-size stalk celery, coarsely chopped (½ cup)	1 tablespoon honey
	½ teaspoon grated lime rind
1 clove garlic, minced	1 small eggplant (9 ounces), peeled and cut into ½-inch cubes (about 2¼ cups)
2 small carrots, peeled and thinly sliced (1 cup)	
1½ teaspoons ground cumin	1 cup cooked black beans
¾ teaspoon each ground allspice and dried oregano, crumbled	6 drops hot red pepper sauce, or to taste

1 In a 5-quart Dutch oven, heat the oil over moderately low heat. Add the green pepper, celery, garlic, and carrots. Cover and cook, stirring occasionally, for 8 minutes or until the vegetables are soft. Stir in the cumin, allspice, oregano, and salt and cook for 2 minutes.

2 Add the tomatoes, breaking them up with a spoon, and the sherry, honey, and lime rind. Bring to a boil, then adjust the heat so that the mixture simmers gently, cover, and cook for 15 minutes. Add the eggplant and cook, covered, for 10 minutes or until tender. Stir in the beans and red pepper sauce and cook just until heated through. Makes four 1½-cup servings.

PREPARATION TIME: 20 MIN. COOKING TIME: 40 MIN.

Per serving: Calories 229; Saturated Fat 1 g; Total Fat 4 g; Protein 8 g; Carbohydrate 43 g; Fiber 8 g; Sodium 197 mg; Cholesterol 0 mg

Canned beans, though a boon to cooking, are high in salt. For example, one 19-ounce can of kidney beans may contain as much as 950 milligrams of sodium. You can get rid of about half the salt by putting the beans in a colander and rinsing them with running water. Better yet, cook your own beans without salt (see pages 18 – 19 for specific instructions) and freeze them in handy 1-cup portions in heavy-duty plastic food bags. They will keep for up to 3 months at 0° F.

FRENCH WHITE BEAN SOUP

You can serve this hearty vegetable soup plain or with a robust garlic and cheese pesto. A tablespoon of the pesto will add about 30 calories per serving.

2 teaspoons olive oil
1 medium-size yellow onion, finely chopped (1 cup)
8 ounces fennel or celery, finely chopped (1 cup)
2 medium-size carrots, peeled and diced (1 cup)
⅛ teaspoon each salt and black pepper, or to taste
1 can (14 ounces) low-sodium tomatoes, puréed with their juice
2½ cups Chicken Stock (page 62) or low-sodium chicken broth
¼ teaspoon dried basil, crumbled
¼ teaspoon fennel seeds, crushed
1 can (19 ounces) cannellini (white kidney beans), drained and rinsed

For the garlic pesto:
1 clove garlic, minced
1 tablespoon minced fresh basil or 1 teaspoon dried basil, crumbled
1 tablespoon minced parsley
1 tablespoon grated Parmesan cheese
1 tablespoon olive oil

1 In a large saucepan, heat the oil over moderate heat. Add the onion, fennel, carrots, salt, and pepper and sauté, stirring occasionally, for 5 minutes.

2 Add the tomatoes, stock, basil, and fennel seeds and bring to a boil. Cover, lower the heat, and simmer for 10 minutes. Add the cannellini and simmer 3 minutes more or until they are heated through.

3 Meanwhile, if using the pesto, combine the garlic, basil, parsley, cheese, and oil in a small bowl. With the back of a spoon, mash the mixture into a paste. Ladle the soup into bowls and garnish each one with a dollop of the pesto. Makes four 1½-cup servings.

PREPARATION TIME: 20 MIN. COOKING TIME: 20 MIN.

Per serving: Calories 200; Saturated Fat 0 g; Total Fat 4 g; Protein 11 g; Carbohydrate 32 g; Fiber 7 g; Sodium 629 mg; Cholesterol 0 mg

EASY BLACK BEAN SOUP

2 cups dried black beans (12 ounces), rinsed and sorted
7 cups water
1 large yellow onion, coarsely chopped (1½ cups)
1 large sweet green pepper, cored, seeded, and coarsely chopped (1 cup)
4 cloves garlic, slivered
2 teaspoons mild chili powder
2 bay leaves
1 cinnamon stick, split lengthwise
¾ teaspoon dried marjoram, crumbled
1 package (10 ounces) frozen corn kernels
1 teaspoon salt
½ cup minced cilantro (coriander) or ½ cup minced parsley mixed with 3 teaspoons dried cilantro
2 tablespoons lime juice
1 teaspoon hot red pepper sauce (optional)

Optional garnishes:
Plain low-fat yogurt
Chopped green onions

1 In a large stockpot or 5-quart Dutch oven, bring the beans and enough cold water to cover them to a boil over moderate heat. Boil for 2 minutes, then remove from the heat and let stand for 1 hour. Drain and rinse.

2 Return the beans to the stockpot, add the water, onion, pepper, garlic, chili powder, bay leaves, cinnamon stick, and marjoram and bring to a boil over high heat. Adjust the heat so that the mixture simmers gently, cover, and cook for 1 hour or until beans are tender.

3 Remove and discard the bay leaves and cinnamon stick. Stir in the corn, salt, cilantro, lime juice, and red pepper sauce if desired. Cook for 4 minutes or until the corn is heated through. Garnish with a dollop of yogurt and a sprinkling of green onions if desired. Makes eight 1¼-cup servings.

PREPARATION TIME: 15 MIN. COOKING TIME: 1 HR. 5 MIN.
SOAKING TIME: 1 HR.

Per serving: Calories 217; Saturated Fat 0 g; Total Fat 1 g; Protein 13 g; Carbohydrate 42 g; Fiber 2 g; Sodium 27 mg; Cholesterol 0 mg

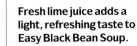
Fresh lime juice adds a light, refreshing taste to Easy Black Bean Soup.

MINTED LENTIL SOUP

This hearty soup can be served chunky or puréed.
It can be frozen for up to 3 months.

2 **tablespoons olive oil**	2 **cups Chicken Stock (page 62) or low-sodium chicken broth**
4 **medium-size yellow onions, coarsely chopped (4 cups)**	3 **cups water**
1 **clove garlic, minced**	¼ **teaspoon salt, or to taste**
4 **medium-size carrots, peeled and coarsely chopped (3 cups)**	¼ **teaspoon black pepper**
¼ **cup mint flakes, crumbled**	½ **cup plain low-fat yogurt (optional garnish)**
1 **cup dried brown lentils, rinsed and sorted**	

1 In a large heavy saucepan, heat the oil over moderate heat. Add the onions, garlic, and carrots and sauté for 2 to 3 minutes. Stir in the mint, lentils, stock, and water and bring to a boil.

2 Adjust the heat so that the mixture simmers gently, cover, and cook for 35 minutes or until the lentils are tender. Stir in the salt and pepper. Serve chunky style with a dollop of yogurt if desired, or purée the soup as directed in Step 3.

3 To purée, drain the mixture in a sieve set over a bowl, reserving the liquid. Place the lentil mixture and ½ cup of the reserved liquid in a blender or food processor and whirl for 1 minute or until puréed. Return the lentils to the saucepan, stir in the remaining liquid, and heat to serving temperature. Garnish each portion with a dollop of yogurt if desired. Makes six 1 ¼-cup servings.

PREPARATION TIME: 10 MIN. COOKING TIME: 40 MIN.

Per serving: Calories 212; Saturated Fat 1 g;
Total Fat 5 g; Protein 10 g; Carbohydrate 32 g;
Fiber 3 g; Sodium 162 mg; Cholesterol 0 mg

MEXICAN RED ONION SOUP

Serve this delicately spiced soup plain or topped with shredded Monterey Jack cheese. To save preparation time, slice the onions in a food processor using the slicing attachment. You can substitute 8 large yellow onions or 4 Spanish onions for the red.

3 tablespoons olive oil
6 large red onions, thinly sliced (12 cups)
1 tablespoon sugar
1 teaspoon dried oregano, crumbled
¾ teaspoon each ground coriander and cumin
¼ teaspoon each ground allspice and cinnamon
½ cup red wine vinegar

⅓ cup orange juice
1½ tablespoons all-purpose flour
7 cups Chicken Stock (page 62) or 3½ cups low-sodium chicken broth mixed with 3½ cups water
½ teaspoon salt, or to taste
¼ teaspoon black pepper

1 In a stockpot or 5-quart Dutch oven, heat the oil over low heat. Add the onions and cook, stirring frequently, for 30 minutes or until softened and lightly colored. Sprinkle the onions with the sugar, oregano, coriander, cumin, allspice, and cinnamon and cook 20 minutes more, stirring occasionally.

2 Stir in the vinegar and orange juice and cook 4 minutes longer. Sprinkle with the flour and cook, stirring constantly, for 1 minute. Stir in the stock and bring to a boil over moderate heat. Adjust the heat so that the mixture simmers gently, cover, and cook 20 minutes longer. Stir in the salt and pepper. Makes eight 1½-cup servings.

PREPARATION TIME: 7 MIN. COOKING TIME: 1¼ HR.

Per serving: Calories 159; Saturated Fat 1 g; Total Fat 6 g; Protein 5 g; Carbohydrate 23 g; Fiber 4 g; Sodium 256 mg; Cholesterol 0 mg

MISO SOUP WITH CABBAGE AND ROOT VEGETABLES

Here is a very nourishing yet light soup. You will find miso — soybean paste — in Oriental, health, or specialty food stores. Though it is relatively high in sodium, a small amount provides a lot of flavor.

2 teaspoons vegetable oil
1 medium-size yellow onion, finely chopped (1 cup)
1 small stalk celery, finely chopped (⅓ cup)
2 cloves garlic, minced
2 teaspoons minced fresh ginger
1 large carrot, peeled and thinly sliced (¾ cup)
1 large parsnip, peeled and thinly sliced (¾ cup)
3 turnips (8 ounces), peeled and cut into ½-inch cubes

1½ cups coarsely chopped savoy cabbage (5 ounces)
6 cups Chicken Stock or Vegetable Stock (page 62) or low-sodium chicken broth
1 tablespoon miso (soybean paste)
¼ teaspoon salt, or to taste
⅛ teaspoon red pepper flakes
2 tablespoons minced fresh cilantro (coriander) or parsley (optional garnish)

1 In a large saucepan, heat the oil over moderate heat. Add the onion, celery, garlic, and ginger and sauté for 5 minutes, stirring occasionally. Add the carrot, parsnip, turnips, cabbage, stock, miso, salt, and pepper flakes. Bring the liquid to a boil, stirring to dissolve the miso. Lower the heat, cover, and simmer for 20 to 25 minutes or until the vegetables are tender. Garnish with the cilantro if desired. Makes six 1¼-cup servings.

PREPARATION TIME: 20 MIN. COOKING TIME: 25 MIN.

Per serving: Calories 87; Saturated Fat 0 g; Total Fat 3 g; Protein 5 g; Carbohydrate 13 g; Fiber 3 g; Sodium 365 mg; Cholesterol 0 mg

SPLIT PEA AND CAULIFLOWER SOUP

1 tablespoon olive oil
1 medium-size yellow onion, finely chopped (1 cup)
1 medium-size stalk celery, finely chopped (½ cup)
1 tablespoon minced garlic
1 tablespoon minced fresh ginger or 1 teaspoon ground ginger
2 teaspoons each ground cumin and coriander
¼ teaspoon each red pepper flakes and ground turmeric
4 cups water

¾ cup dried green or yellow split peas, rinsed and sorted
1 bay leaf
½ teaspoon salt, or to taste
1 head cauliflower (1 ½ pounds), broken into florets, or 2 packages (10 ounces each) frozen cauliflower
2 tablespoons minced fresh cilantro (coriander) or 2 tablespoons minced parsley mixed with 1 teaspoon dried cilantro
Plain low-fat yogurt (optional garnish)

1 In a large heavy saucepan, heat the oil over moderately low heat. Add the onion and celery, cover, and cook, stirring occasionally, for 5 minutes. Add the garlic, ginger, cumin, coriander, red pepper flakes, and turmeric and cook, stirring, 1 minute more.

2 Add the water, split peas, bay leaf, and salt and bring to a boil. Adjust the heat so that the mixture simmers gently, cover, and cook for 30 minutes or until the peas are tender. Remove the bay leaf.

3 In a food processor or blender, working in batches if necessary, whirl the soup until puréed. Return the purée to the saucepan and bring to a boil over moderate heat, then add the cauliflower. Lower the heat, cover, and simmer until the cauliflower is tender — about 20 minutes for fresh cauliflower, 12 to 15 minutes for frozen. Sprinkle each portion with the cilantro and top with a dollop of yogurt if desired. Makes four 1 ½-cup servings.

PREPARATION TIME: 20 MIN.   COOKING TIME: 1 HR.

Per serving: Calories 260; Saturated Fat 1 g; Total Fat 5 g; Protein 16 g; Carbohydrate 44 g; Fiber 9 g; Sodium 344 mg; Cholesterol 0 mg

For a subtle blend of winter vegetables and spices, try Miso Soup with Cabbage and Root Vegetables.

75

SUMMER SQUASH SOUP WITH LEEKS

You can make this delectable blend of garden vegetables with either squash of summer — green (zucchini) or yellow.

- 2 **large leeks or 1 large yellow onion, coarsely chopped (1 ½ cups)**
- 2 **tablespoons vegetable oil**
- 2 **medium-size all-purpose potatoes (1 pound), peeled and cubed (3 cups)**
- 4 **cups Chicken Stock (page 62) or low-sodium chicken broth**
- ½ **teaspoon dried thyme, crumbled**
- 1 **bay leaf**
- ¼ **teaspoon salt, or to taste**
- ⅛ **teaspoon black pepper**
- 1 **large sweet red pepper, cored, seeded, and cut into 1-inch squares (1 ¼ cups)**
- 8 **ounces mushrooms, sliced (3 cups)**
- 2 **cloves garlic, minced**
- 2 **medium-size zucchini or yellow summer squash, cut into 1-inch cubes (4 cups)**
- 3 **tablespoons snipped fresh chives**

1 In a large heavy saucepan, heat 1 tablespoon of the oil over moderately low heat. Add the leeks, cover, and cook, stirring occasionally, for 3 minutes or until softened.

Add the potatoes, stock, herbs, salt, and pepper and bring to a boil. Adjust the heat so that the mixtures simmers gently, cover, and cook for 15 minutes or until the potatoes are tender.

2 Meanwhile, heat the remaining tablespoon of oil in a 10-inch nonstick skillet over moderately low heat. Add the red pepper and mushrooms, cover, and cook, stirring occasionally, for 3 minutes. Stir in the garlic and cook 1 minute more. Remove from the heat and set aside.

3 In a food processor or blender, working in batches if necessary, whirl the potato mixture until puréed. Return purée to the saucepan and stir in the skillet mixture and squash. Cover and simmer over moderately low heat, stirring occasionally, for 5 minutes or until the squash is tender. Discard the bay leaf. Ladle soup into bowls and sprinkle with the chives. Makes four 1 ½-cup servings.

PREPARATION TIME: 15 MIN. COOKING TIME: 30 MIN.

*Per serving: Calories 259; Saturated Fat 1 g;
Total Fat 8 g; Protein 9 g; Carbohydrate 41 g;
Fiber 6 g; Sodium 290 mg; Cholesterol 0 mg*

A feast for the eyes as well as the appetite is Puréed Carrot Soup with Tomatoes.

ROASTED VEGETABLE SOUP WITH GARLIC

The pleasing combination of vegetables in this soup is enhanced by roasting, which imparts a smoky flavor.

1 **large eggplant (1 pound), halved lengthwise**	3 **cloves garlic**
2 **large yellow onions (7 ounces each), quartered**	1/2 **teaspoon each dried thyme and basil, crumbled**
1 **tablespoon olive oil**	1/4 **teaspoon salt, or to taste**
1 **large sweet red pepper (8 ounces), cored, seeded, and quartered**	1/8 **teaspoon black pepper**
3 **plum tomatoes, halved and seeded**	6 **cups Chicken Stock (page 62) or low-sodium chicken broth**

1 Preheat the oven to 400° F. Arrange the eggplant and onions in a large shallow baking pan, brush the cut sides with 1 1/2 teaspoons of the oil, and bake for 20 minutes. Add the red pepper, tomatoes, and garlic to the pan; brush the cut sides with the remaining 1 1/2 teaspoons oil. Sprinkle the thyme, basil, salt, and black pepper over the vegetables and bake 20 minutes more or until very tender.

2 Set aside the red pepper and 1 eggplant half. Chop the remaining half eggplant, the onions, tomatoes, and garlic and transfer them to a large saucepan. Add the stock, bring it to a boil, then lower the heat and simmer the mixture, stirring occasionally, for 20 minutes. Meanwhile, peel the red pepper, discard the skin, and dice the pulp. Dice the reserved eggplant.

3 In a food processor or blender, working in batches if necessary, whirl the cooked mixture until puréed. Return the purée to the saucepan and stir in the diced eggplant and red pepper. Simmer the soup for 5 minutes or until heated through. Makes six 1 1/2-cup servings.

PREPARATION TIME: 10 MIN. COOKING TIME: 1 HR.

Per serving: Calories 107; Saturated Fat 0 g; Total Fat 3 g; Protein 5 g; Carbohydrate 16 g; Fiber 3 g; Sodium 232 mg; Cholesterol 0 mg

PURÉED CARROT SOUP WITH TOMATOES

This thick creamy soup is delicately spiced with ginger and studded with chunks of plum tomatoes.

1 **tablespoon vegetable oil**	1/4 **teaspoon salt, or to taste**
1 **large yellow onion, coarsely chopped (1 1/2 cups)**	1/4 **teaspoon sugar**
9 **medium-size carrots, peeled and thinly sliced (4 1/2 cups)**	1/8 **teaspoon black pepper**
	1 **bay leaf**
3 **tablespoons minced fresh ginger, or to taste**	1 **pound plum tomatoes, peeled, cored, seeded, and diced (1 1/4 cups)**
4 **cups Chicken Stock (page 62) or low-sodium chicken broth**	2 **tablepoons minced fresh basil, dill, or parsley**

1 In a large heavy saucepan, heat the oil over moderately low heat. Add the the onion, carrots, and ginger. Cover and cook, stirring occasionally, for 5 minutes or until the onion is tender. Stir in the stock, salt, sugar, pepper, and bay leaf; simmer the mixture, covered, for 25 minutes or until the carrots are tender. Remove the bay leaf.

2 In a food processor or blender, working in batches if necessary, whirl the mixture until puréed. Return the purée to the saucepan, stir in the tomatoes, and simmer, stirring occasionally, for 5 minutes or until the tomatoes are heated through. Garnish the soup with the basil. Makes six 1 1/2-cup servings.

PREPARATION TIME: 15 MIN. COOKING TIME: 35 MIN.

Per serving: Calories 112; Saturated Fat 0 g; Total Fat 3 g; Protein 4 g; Carbohydrate 19 g; Fiber 5 g; Sodium 223 mg; Cholesterol 0 mg

Puréed soups are easy to make with a blender or food processor. Here is a tip to help speed your cleanup: Fill half of the food processor or blender bowl with water, add a drop of dishwashing soap, cover, and turn on a low speed for a few seconds. Rinse and dry.

CURRIED CAULIFLOWER SOUP

1 tablespoon unsalted butter or margarine
1 medium-size yellow onion, coarsely chopped (1 cup)
2 teaspoons curry powder
½ teaspoon ground ginger
2 cups Chicken Stock (page 62) or low-sodium chicken broth
2 cups water
⅓ cup long-grain white rice
3 cups cauliflower florets (1 medium-size head) or 2 packages (10 ounces each) frozen cauliflower florets
⅛ teaspoon salt, or to taste
¼ teaspoon black pepper
½ cup tomato juice
Optional garnishes:
Parsley sprigs
1 green onion, sliced

1 In a large heavy saucepan, melt the butter over moderate heat. Add the onion and sauté for 3 minutes, stirring occasionally. Stir in the curry powder, ginger, stock, water, rice, and cauliflower and bring to a boil. Adjust the heat so that the mixture simmers gently, cover, and cook for 20 minutes. Stir in the salt and pepper.

2 Drain the mixture in a large sieve set over a bowl, reserving the liquid. Place the vegetables in a blender or food processor, add the tomato juice, and whirl until puréed. Return the vegetable purée to the saucepan, stir in the reserved liquid, and bring to serving temperature over moderate heat. Garnish with the parsley or green onion if desired. Makes four 1¼-cup servings.

PREPARATION TIME: 12 MIN. COOKING TIME: 25 MIN.

Per serving: Calories 140; Saturated Fat 2 g; Total Fat 4 g; Protein 6 g; Carbohydrate 22 g; Fiber 3 g; Sodium 162 mg; Cholesterol 9 mg

•

Broccoli Variation: In Step 1, substitute *3 cups broccoli florets* for the cauliflower. In Step 2, substitute *½ cup low-fat (1% milkfat) milk* for the tomato juice. Makes four 1½-cup servings. *Per serving: Calories 133; Saturated Fat 2 g; Total Fat 4 g; Protein 5 g; Carbohydrate 21 g; Fiber 3 g; Sodium 264 mg; Cholesterol 8 mg.*

CREAM OF BROCCOLI SOUP

Enjoy all the richness of a cream soup with none of the fat and excess calories.

1 tablespoon olive or vegetable oil
2 medium-size yellow onions, coarsely chopped (2 cups)
5 cloves garlic, slivered
1 bunch broccoli (1¼ pounds), heads cut into florets, stalks trimmed, peeled, and thinly sliced, or 2 packages (10 ounces each) frozen broccoli
3 medium-size all-purpose potatoes (1 pound), peeled and thinly sliced
½ teaspoon dried basil, crumbled
⅛ teaspoon ground nutmeg
5 cups Chicken Stock (page 62) or 2 cups low-sodium chicken broth mixed with 3 cups water
2 cups low-fat (1% milkfat) milk
¼ teaspoon each salt and black pepper
Optional garnishes:
3 tablespoons minced fresh parsley
2 green onions, sliced
3 tablespoons plain nonfat yogurt

1 In a stockpot or 5-quart Dutch oven, heat the oil over low heat. Add the onions and garlic and cook, stirring frequently, for 5 minutes or until softened.

2 Add the broccoli, potatoes, basil, nutmeg, and stock and bring to a boil over moderate heat. Adjust the heat so that the mixture simmers gently, cover, and cook for 20 minutes or until the broccoli and potatoes are very tender.

3 In a food processor or blender, working in batches if necessary, whirl the mixture until puréed. Return the purée to the Dutch oven, stir in the milk, salt, and pepper, and set over moderate heat for 4 minutes or just until heated through. Garnish with the parsley, green onions, or yogurt if desired. Makes six 1½-cup servings.

PREPARATION TIME: 15 MIN. COOKING TIME: 30 MIN.

Per serving: Calories 184; Saturated Fat 1 g; Total Fat 4 g; Protein 10 g; Carbohydrate 30 g; Fiber 4 g; Sodium 273 mg; Cholesterol 3 mg

Beneath the golden topping of Baked Squash Soup with Cheddar Cheese is a savory purée that is well worth the digging.

BAKED SQUASH SOUP WITH CHEDDAR CHEESE

2 medium-size butternut or acorn squash (1 ½ pounds)	¼ cup Chicken Stock (page 62) or low-sodium chicken broth
¼ teaspoon each salt and black pepper, or to taste	1 cup skim milk
1 teaspoon vegetable oil	4 slices (½ inch thick) French or Italian bread
4 shallots, finely chopped (½ cup)	1 cup shredded low-fat Cheddar or Gruyère cheese (4 ounces)
¼ cup dry white wine or water	2 tablespoons snipped fresh chives or minced parsley (optional)

1 Preheat the oven to 400° F. Halve the squash lengthwise and sprinkle with ⅛ teaspoon each of the salt and pepper. Place on a baking sheet, cover loosely with aluminum foil, and bake for 50 to 60 minutes or until tender. Scoop the squash from the shells and transfer the pulp to a food processor or blender. Set aside. Discard the shells.

2 In a small saucepan, heat the oil over moderate heat. Add the shallots and sauté, stirring, for 3 minutes or until softened. Add the wine and cook, uncovered, for 2 minutes or until reduced to 2 tablespoons. Stir in the stock, milk, and remaining ⅛ teaspoon each of salt and pepper. Add the mixture to the food processor with the squash; whirl until puréed, working in batches if necessary.

3 Divide half of the soup among four 1 ½-cup ovenproof bowls or baking dishes or a 2-quart casserole. Place a slice of bread on top of each portion, then sprinkle each with 2 tablespoons of the cheese. Top with the remaining soup and sprinkle with the remaining cheese. Set the bowls on a baking sheet and bake the soup for 25 minutes or until bubbling. If you like, run the soup briefly under a preheated broiler to brown the cheese, then sprinkle with the chives if desired. Makes four 1 ½-cup servings.

PREPARATION TIME: 10 MIN. COOKING TIME: 1 HR. 20 MIN.

Per serving: Calories 338; Saturated Fat 6 g; Total Fat 12 g; Protein 15 g; Carbohydrate 43 g; Fiber 4 g; Sodium 559 mg; Cholesterol 31 mg

Curly-leaf parsley is often relegated to the garnish category, but cooks are rediscovering its spirited flavor, which can brighten the taste of many foods. This most common of parsleys is also high in vitamin C and potassium.

Two other parsleys are winning approval with cooks. *Italian,* or *flat-leaf, parsley* has an intense flavor that goes beautifully with salads and soups. *Chinese parsley,* similar in appearance to flat-leaf parsley, is actually the herb known as *coriander* or *cilantro.* Its pretty green leaves make a lovely garnish, while its pungent taste enlivens vegetables, soups, salads, and main dishes, especially from the southwestern states. The dried seed of this plant is also used for flavoring.

CREAMY PARSNIP SOUP

- 1 tablespoon vegetable oil
- 1 medium-size yellow onion, thinly sliced (1 cup)
- 3 cloves garlic, slivered
- 1 tablespoon minced fresh ginger or 1 teaspoon ground ginger
- 1 medium-size McIntosh apple, peeled, cored, and thinly sliced (1 cup)
- 1 pound parsnips, peeled and thinly sliced (4 cups)
- 1 white turnip (5 ounces), peeled, halved, and thinly sliced (1 cup)
- 1 medium-size all-purpose potato, peeled, halved, and thinly sliced (1 cup)
- 2 small carrots, peeled and thinly sliced (1 cup)
- ¾ teaspoon salt, or to taste
- ½ teaspoon ground cinnamon
- ⅛ teaspoon ground allspice
- 4 cups water
- 3 cups low-fat (1% milkfat) milk
- ¼ teaspoon black pepper

Optional garnishes:
Parsley sprigs
Thin apple slices

1 In a large heavy saucepan or 5-quart Dutch oven, heat the oil over low heat. Add the onion and cook, stirring frequently, for 5 minutes or until soft. Add the garlic and ginger and cook for 2 minutes. Add the apple and cook, stirring frequently, for 5 minutes or until the apple is soft.

2 Stir in the parsnips, turnip, potato, carrots, salt, cinnamon, allspice, and 1 cup of the water and bring to a boil. Adjust the heat so that the mixture simmers gently, cover, and cook for 20 minutes. Add the remaining 3 cups water, cover, and simmer 20 minutes longer or until the vegetables are tender.

3 In a food processor or blender, working in batches if necessary, whirl the mixture until puréed. Return the mixture to the saucepan, stir in the milk and pepper, and cook over moderate heat, stirring, for 5 minutes or until heated through. Garnish each serving with parsley sprigs or apple slices if desired. Makes six 1½-cup servings.

PREPARATION TIME: 25 MIN. COOKING TIME: 1 HR.

Per serving: Calories 213; Saturated Fat 1 g; Total Fat 4 g; Protein 7 g; Carbohydrate 40 g; Fiber 8 g; Sodium 362 mg; Cholesterol 5 mg

SWEET POTATO-PEANUT BUTTER SOUP

This velvety smooth soup is delicious hot or cold. You can garnish it with either sliced green onions or chopped peanuts. The peanuts will add about 50 calories per serving.

- 1¾ cups Chicken Stock (page 62) or 1 can (14¼ ounces) low-sodium chicken broth
- 1 cup water
- 1 large yellow onion, coarsely chopped (1½ cups)
- 2 medium-size stalks celery, coarsely chopped (1 cup)
- ½ teaspoon minced garlic
- 2 medium-size sweet potatoes, peeled and cut into ½-inch cubes (about 3 cups)
- 1 bay leaf
- ¼ teaspoon dried thyme, crumbled
- ¼ teaspoon hot red pepper sauce, or to taste
- 3 tablespoons creamy peanut butter
- 2 teaspoons rice vinegar or white wine vinegar

Optional garnishes:
¼ cup chopped dry-roasted peanuts
¼ cup chopped green onions

1 In a 4-quart Dutch oven or large saucepan, combine the stock, water, onion, celery, garlic, sweet potatoes, bay leaf, thyme, and red pepper sauce and bring to a boil over moderate heat. Adjust the heat so that the mixture simmers gently, cover, and cook for 20 to 25 minutes or until the potatoes are tender. Remove from the heat, discard the bay leaf, and stir in the peanut butter and vinegar.

2 In a food processor or blender, working in batches if necessary, whirl the vegetable mixture until puréed. Serve hot or chilled, garnished with the peanuts or green onions if desired. Makes four 1½-cup servings.

PREPARATION TIME: 15 MIN. COOKING TIME: 22 MIN.

Per serving: Calories 222; Saturated Fat 1 g; Total Fat 7 g; Protein 7 g; Carbohydrate 35 g; Fiber 5 g; Sodium 147 mg; Cholesterol 0 mg

Watercress and
Parsley Soup makes
an elegant start
to any meal.

WATERCRESS AND PARSLEY SOUP

*Here is a light, elegant soup that is rich
in vitamin A. Serve it for lunch with a sandwich
or as a first course for a company dinner.*

2 tablespoons unsalted
butter or margarine

1 small yellow onion,
coarsely chopped (½
cup)

¼ cup all-purpose flour

2¼ cups Chicken Stock
(page 62) or low-
sodium chicken broth

1 can (12 ounces)
evaporated skim milk

2½ cups flat-leaf parsley

2 cups watercress leaves

⅛ teaspoon ground
nutmeg

⅛ teaspoon salt, or to
taste

¼ teaspoon black pepper

1 In a large heavy saucepan, melt the butter over moderately low heat. Add the onion, cover, and cook for 5
minutes or until softened. Add the flour and cook, stirring,
for about 3 minutes or until smooth and straw colored.
Gradually stir in the stock and milk and bring to a boil over
moderate heat, whisking constantly.

2 Adjust the heat so that the mixture simmers gently,
then add 2 cups of the parsley and the watercress,
nutmeg, salt, and pepper. Cover and cook for 5 minutes.

3 Drain the mixture in a large sieve set over a bowl,
reserving the liquid. Place the solids, 1 cup of the
reserved liquid, and the remaining ½ cup parsley in a
blender or food processor and whirl for 30 to 40 seconds
or until puréed. Return the purée to the saucepan, add the
remaining liquid, and reheat over moderate heat. Makes
four 1¼-cup servings.

PREPARATION TIME: 10 MIN.   COOKING TIME: 15 MIN.

*Per serving: Calories 176; Saturated Fat 4 g;
Total Fat 7 g; Protein 10 g; Carbohydrate 20 g;
Fiber 3 g; Sodium 264 mg; Cholesterol 19 mg*

•

Cream of Spinach Variation: In Step 2, substitute *4 cups
coarsely chopped fresh spinach* or *1 package (10 ounces) thawed
frozen chopped spinach* for the parsley and watercress and *⅛
teaspoon ground mace* for the nutmeg. In Step 3, purée the soup
as directed with *½ cup flat-leaf parsley* to brighten the color.
Makes four 1¼-cup servings. *Per serving: Calories 176; Saturated
Fat 4 g; Total Fat 7 g; Protein 11 g; Carbohydrate 20 g; Fiber 2 g; Sodium
288 mg; Cholesterol 19 mg.*

ASPARAGUS-HAZELNUT SOUP

This elegant soup is actually very easy to make. Toasting the hazelnuts gives the soup a richer flavor and makes it possible to remove the skins. If you prefer, you can substitute blanched almonds for the hazelnuts.

½ cup shelled hazelnuts (2 ounces)

1 tablespoon vegetable oil

1 large leek (8 ounces), trimmed, rinsed, and cut into ½-inch cubes (¾ cup)

3 cloves garlic, thinly sliced

1 medium-size all-purpose potato, peeled and thinly sliced (1¼ cups)

¼ cup firmly packed parsley leaves

1½ pounds asparagus, trimmed, or 2 packages (10 ounces each), frozen asparagus, cut into 1-inch lengths

4½ cups water

½ teaspoon salt, or to taste

½ teaspoon dried marjoram or savory, crumbled

1 green onion, including top, thinly sliced

1 Preheat the oven to 400° F. Spread the hazelnuts on a baking sheet and toast for 10 minutes or until the skins have loosened and the nuts are fragrant. Place them on a clean dish towel and rub vigorously to remove the skins (some will remain). Discard the skins and coarsely chop ⅓ of the nuts; leave the remainder whole. Set the nuts aside.

2 In a stockpot or 5-quart Dutch oven, heat the oil over low heat. Add the leek and cook, stirring frequently, for 7 minutes or until softened. Add the garlic and cook for 1 minute, stirring frequently. Add the potato and parsley, cover, and cook for 5 minutes, stirring occasionally.

3 Set aside 1 cup of the asparagus tips. Add the remaining tips and stalks to the saucepan along with the whole nuts, water, salt, and marjoram. Bring to a boil over moderate heat, adjust the heat so that the mixture simmers gently, cover, and cook for 20 minutes or until the asparagus and potato are tender. In a food processor or blender, working in batches if necessary, whirl the mixture until puréed. Return the mixture to the saucepan, add the

reserved asparagus tips, and reheat over moderate heat. Garnish with the chopped hazelnuts and green onion. Makes six 1½-cup servings.

PREPARATION TIME: 12 MIN.   COOKING TIME: 45 MIN.

Per serving: Calories 160; Saturated Fat 1 g; Total Fat 9 g; Protein 5 g; Carbohydrate 18 g; Fiber 4 g; Sodium 195 mg; Cholesterol 0 mg

APRICOT BUTTERMILK SOUP

So good and so easy to make, this refreshing light soup can be served as a first course or for lunch, accompanied by rolls and a salad.

3 cups apricot nectar

1 cup buttermilk

2 teaspoons grated orange rind

Juice of 1 orange (about ⅓ cup)

1 tablespoon honey

1 teaspoon lemon juice

⅛ to ¼ teaspoon ground allspice

⅛ teaspoon ground nutmeg

Mint sprigs (optional garnish)

1 In a large bowl, stir together the apricot nectar, buttermilk, orange rind, orange juice, honey, lemon juice, allspice, and nutmeg until thoroughly blended. Cover and refrigerate until cold. Serve chilled, garnished with mint if desired. Makes four 1-cup servings.

PREPARATION TIME: 5 MIN.   CHILLING TIME: 2 HR.

Per serving: Calories 157; Saturated Fat 0 g; Total Fat 1 g; Protein 3 g; Carbohydrate 37 g; Fiber 1 g; Sodium 71 mg; Cholesterol 2 mg

FISH AND SHELLFISH

There are many reasons to recommend that fish be eaten at least twice a week. First, fish are relatively low in calories and saturated fat; shellfish are even lower. And though some people used to shun shellfish because of their high cholesterol levels, more sophisticated testing procedures have revealed that these are much lower than once thought. Another plus for fish is that omega-3 fatty acids, prevalent in cold-water varieties such as tuna, cod, and salmon, may help prevent stroke and heart disease by keeping fatty plaque from building up in artery walls. Fish is high in protein and phosphorus and potassium. What more could you ask except that it taste good without your resorting to frying or rich sauces? Try the recipes throughout this chapter and see if it doesn't.

When buying whole fish, allow about 12 ounces per serving. For a *dressed* fish — one that has had its head, tail, fins, entrails, and scales removed — allow about 8 ounces per serving. Neither a *fillet*, a long boneless piece cut from the sides of the fish, nor a *steak*, which is a cross section (with backbone), has much waste; allow 4 to 6 ounces per person.

CRISPY BAKED FISH

Use almost any kind of fish fillet — flounder, sole, scrod, or perch, for example — in this delectable recipe.

Nonstick cooking spray
4 fish fillets (about 5 ounces each)
1/3 cup lemon juice
1 tablespoon plus 1 teaspoon olive oil
1 teaspoon dried oregano, crumbled

1/4 teaspoon each salt and white pepper, or to taste
2 cups instant mashed potato buds
Lemon wedges (optional)

1 Preheat the oven to 500° F. Coat a wire rack with the cooking spray, place the rack on a baking sheet, and set aside. Pat dry the fish fillets on paper toweling.

2 In a medium-size shallow dish, whisk together the lemon juice, oil, oregano, salt, and pepper. Place the potato buds in another medium-size shallow dish. Dip each fish fillet first in the liquid mixture, then in the potato buds, making sure both sides are well coated.

3 Place the coated fillets on the prepared wire rack and bake for 10 minutes. Transfer the fish to individual serving plates and serve with lemon wedges on the side if desired. Accompany with Escarole Sautéed with Garlic (page 229). Serves 4.

PREPARATION TIME: 10 MIN. BAKING TIME: 10 MIN.

Per serving: Calories 381; Saturated Fat 1 g; Total Fat 6 g; Protein 29 g; Carbohydrate 54 g; Fiber 0 g; Sodium 268 mg; Cholesterol 99 mg

•

Cornmeal Variation: Substitute a mixture of *1/4 cup yellow cornmeal, 1/4 cup plain dry bread crumbs,* and *1/4 teaspoon salt* for the potato buds. After dipping the fillets in the coating, be sure to shake off the excess. *Per serving: Calories 199; Saturated Fat 1 g; Total Fat 6 g; Protein 23 g; Carbohydrate 13 g; Fiber 1 g; Sodium 392 mg; Cholesterol 99 mg.*

•

Parmesan Variation: Substitute a mixture of *1/4 cup grated Parmesan cheese* and *1/2 cup plain dry bread crumbs* for the potato buds. After dipping the fillets in the coating, be sure to shake off excess. *Per serving: Calories 220; Saturated Fat 2 g; Total Fat 8 g; Protein 25 g; Carbohydrate 11 g; Fiber 1 g; Sodium 421 mg; Cholesterol 104 mg.*

TANDOORI FISH KEBABS

You can use cod, halibut, or monkfish for these quick and easy kebabs and cook them on an outdoor grill if you like.

2 tablespoons lemon juice
2 tablespoons plain low-fat yogurt
1 tablespoon minced fresh garlic
1 tablespoon minced fresh ginger or 1 teaspoon ground ginger
1 teaspoon finely chopped fresh green chili pepper
1 teaspoon each ground cumin and coriander
1/2 teaspoon ground turmeric (optional)
1/4 teaspoon salt

1 1/2 pounds firm-fleshed white fish, cut into 1-inch pieces; large shrimp, shelled and deveined; or sea scallops
1 medium-size yellow onion (8 ounces), cut into 1-inch wedges
1 medium-size sweet red pepper (6 ounces), cored, seeded, and cut into 1 1/2-inch squares

Optional garnishes:
Minced fresh cilantro
Lemon wedges

1 In a large bowl, combine the lemon juice, yogurt, garlic, ginger, chili pepper, cumin, coriander, turmeric if desired, and salt. Add the fish or shellfish, toss to coat with the marinade, cover, and chill for 30 minutes.

2 Preheat the broiler, setting the rack 5 inches from the heat. Lightly grease four 12- or 14-inch metal skewers. Thread the fish alternately with the onion and red pepper on the skewers and arrange on the rack of a broiler pan. Broil the kebabs for 3 minutes on each side or until the fish is firm but still springs back when touched. When the kebabs are done, transfer them to a warm platter and garnish with cilantro and lemon wedges if desired. Serve with sliced cucumbers topped with a dressing of low-fat yogurt and dill. Serves 4.

PREPARATION TIME: 20 MIN. COOKING TIME: 6 MIN.
MARINATING TIME: 30 MIN.

Per serving: Calories 169; Saturated Fat 0 g; Total Fat 1 g; Protein 31 g; Carbohydrate 6 g; Fiber 1 g; Sodium 232 mg; Cholesterol 74 mg

Serve Tandoori Fish Kebabs — succulent chunks of fish coated with a spicy marinade and quickly grilled — with rice and peas plus a tossed green salad.

ZESTY SEAFOOD SALAD

This main-dish salad is especially refreshing on a hot summer day. It can also be served as an appetizer.

⅔ cup bottled clam juice	1¼ pounds bay scallops; shrimp, shelled and deveined; or cod fillets, cut into 2-inch chunks
⅓ cup water	
1 tablespoon plus 1 teaspoon tomato paste	
1 tablespoon orange juice	1 medium-size carrot, peeled and cut into matchstick strips
1 tablespoon lime juice	2 tablespoons olive oil
1 3- by ½-inch strip orange zest (colored part of the rind), slivered crosswise	3 tablespoons minced parsley
	6 cups salad greens Croutons (optional garnish)
½ teaspoon fennel seeds	

1 In a 12-inch skillet, combine the clam juice, water, tomato paste, orange juice, lime juice, orange zest, and fennel seeds. Bring to a boil over moderate heat, then lower the heat and add the scallops and carrot. Cover and simmer for 5 minutes or until the scallops are cooked through and the carrot is tender. With a slotted spoon, transfer the solids to a medium-size bowl and set aside.

2 Return the skillet to high heat. Bring the liquid to a boil, add the oil, and cook, uncovered, for 4 minutes or until the sauce is slightly thickened; stir in the parsley. Let the sauce cool to room temperature, then pour it over the scallops; cover and refrigerate until well chilled (for up to 2 days). Serve over salad greens and sprinkle with croutons if desired. Serves 4 as a main course, 6 as an appetizer.

PREPARATION TIME: 10 MIN. COOKING TIME: 10 MIN.

CHILLING TIME: 2HR.

Per serving (for 4): Calories 216; Saturated Fat 1 g; Total Fat 8 g; Protein 26 g; Carbohydrate 10 g; Fiber 2 g; Sodium 374 mg; Cholesterol 47 mg

Fresh fish should have a pleasant odor with no trace of ammonia. The eyes should be clear and bulging, the gills pink or red, the scales shimmering, the flesh firm and springy. If you're buying fillets or steaks, avoid any with dry, brown edges.

Whole fish should be presented on a bed of ice; fish fillets and steaks should be set on a tray or paper above — not directly on — the ice.

Fish damages easily, so make the fish market your last stop on the way home. If this is impossible, place the wrapped fish on top of frozen food or in a plastic bag surrounded by ice.

FISH TERRINE

You can prepare this dish with any variety of mild, white-fleshed fish: flounder, sole, cod, scrod, or bass.

1 medium-size all-purpose potato, peeled and cubed (1 cup)	1 large egg
	1 large egg white
	¾ teaspoon salt
3 cloves garlic, peeled	⅛ teaspoon ground red pepper (cayenne)
5 large green onions, trimmed	¾ cup buttermilk
1 small carrot, peeled and cut into matchstick strips	1 small roasted sweet red pepper or 3 ounces pimientos, cut into strips ½ inch wide
1¼ pounds scrod fillets, cut into chunks	Lemon quarters (optional garnish)

1 In a large saucepan of lightly salted boiling water, cook the potato and garlic for 8 minutes. Place a colander over the pan, lay the green onions and carrot strips in the colander, cover, and steam for 5 minutes or until the vegetables are tender and the potato is cooked through. Drain well.

2 Preheat the oven to 375° F. Line an 8" x 4" x 3" loaf pan with plastic food wrap, extending it up and over the long sides so that it overhangs 3 inches on each side; set aside. In a food processor, purée the fish, scraping down the sides occasionally, until it is smooth. Add the potato and garlic mixture and purée until no lumps remain. Add the egg, egg white, salt, red pepper, and buttermilk and whirl until well combined.

3 Spread 1 cup of the fish mixture in the prepared pan. Lay the carrot strips in 4 rows down the length of the pan. Spread another cup of the mixture over the carrots and lay the green onions down the length of the pan. Spread another cup of the mixture over the green onions and lay the pepper strips down the length of the pan in 4 rows. Spread the last cup of the mixture over the pepper strips and smooth the top. Fold the plastic wrap over the fish, then cover with aluminum foil.

4 Set the pan in a larger pan and pour enough hot water in the larger pan to come halfway up the sides of the loaf pan. Bake for 1 hour 10 minutes or until set. Remove the loaf pan from the water and let cool to room tempera-

For special occasions, this elegant Fish Terrine is well worth the effort. Offer Cucumber-Yogurt Sauce (page 278) alongside.

ture. Remove the foil and peel the plastic wrap off the top of the terrine. Invert onto a serving platter and discard any liquid. Remove the plastic wrap. Chill. Slice and serve cold with lemon quarters, if desired, and Cucumber-Yogurt Sauce (page 278). Makes 12 slices or 6 servings.

PREPARATION TIME: 20 MIN. COOKING TIME: 1 HR. 25 MIN.

Per serving: Calories 164; Saturated Fat 2 g; Total Fat 4 g; Protein 21 g; Carbohydrate 11 g; Fiber 1 g; Sodium 444 mg; Cholesterol 82 mg

GINGERED SEA BASS EN PAPILLOTE

This recipe enhances the light and delicate flavor of sea bass. It works well also with flounder, snapper, sole, or scrod.

2 teaspoons finely grated fresh ginger
2 teaspoons lemon juice
1 teaspoon reduced-sodium soy sauce
1 teaspoon peanut oil
1 teaspoon honey
4 sea bass fillets (5 ounces each)
2 ounces mushrooms, thinly sliced (1 cup)
2 green onions, thinly sliced (¼ cup)

1 Preheat the oven to 450° F. In a small bowl, whisk together the ginger, lemon juice, soy sauce, oil, and honey. Place each fillet in the center of a 12-inch square of parchment paper or aluminum foil. Scatter ¼ of the mushrooms and green onions over each and spoon ¼ of the ginger mixture on top. Fold the paper around the fish to make closed packets.

2 Place the packets on a baking sheet and bake for 8 to 10 minutes. To test for doneness, open one packet carefully (watch for steam) and see if the fish flakes easily with a fork. When done, transfer the packets to dinner plates, cut an X in the center of each one with a sharp knife, and carefully peel back the paper. Serve with orzo and steamed broccoli. Serves 4.

PREPARATION TIME: 15 MIN. COOKING TIME: 8 MIN.

Per serving: Calories 158; Saturated Fat 1 g; Total Fat 4 g; Protein 27 g; Carbohydrate 3 g; Fiber 0 g; Sodium 138 mg; Cholesterol 58 mg

BAKED BLUEFISH WITH GREEN CHILI SAUCE

If there are any leftovers, serve them chilled — reheating will toughen the fish.

2 tablespoons olive oil
2 cloves garlic, minced
2 medium-size sweet green peppers, cored, seeded, and chopped (1½ cups)
2 cans (14½ ounces each) low-sodium tomatoes, drained and chopped
2 cans (4 ounces each) chopped green chilies, drained
1 teaspoon dried oregano, crumbled
1 teaspoon ground cumin
½ teaspoon salt, or to taste
¼ teaspoon black pepper
6 bluefish fillets (4 ounces each)

1 In a heavy 12-inch skillet, heat the oil over moderate heat; add the garlic and green peppers and sauté, uncovered, for 2 minutes. Stir in the tomatoes, chilies, oregano, cumin, salt, and black pepper. Cover and cook for 10 minutes.

2 Place the fillets, skin side down, on top of the sauce in the skillet. Cover and cook for 10 minutes or until the fish flakes easily when tested with a fork. Transfer the fish to dinner plates and spoon some sauce over each fillet. Serve with black beans, rice, and a green salad. Serves 6.

PREPARATION TIME: 10 MIN. COOKING TIME: 23 MIN.

Per serving: Calories 224; Saturated Fat 2 g; Total Fat 10 g; Protein 25 g; Carbohydrate 10 g; Fiber 2 g; Sodium 265 mg; Cholesterol 67 mg

Easy-to-make Bluefish with Chili Crumbs has such a zesty flavor, you'll want to try the topping with other fish as well.

BLUEFISH WITH CHILI CRUMBS

Red snapper, scrod, or sea bass would also taste wonderful with this crunchy topping.

1 tablespoon each butter and olive oil
½ teaspoon minced garlic
1½ teaspoons chili powder
¼ teaspoon each ground cumin and dried oregano, crumbled
¼ teaspoon salt, or to taste

1 cup fresh bread crumbs (2 slices)
2 tablespoons minced parsley
4 bluefish fillets (5 ounces each)
2 tablespoons cornmeal
Nonstick cooking spray
Lemon wedges

1 In a 10-inch nonstick skillet, heat the butter with the oil over moderately low heat. Add the garlic, chili powder, cumin, oregano, and salt and cook for 2 minutes, stirring frequently. Add the bread crumbs and parsley; stir and cook for 5 minutes or until crisp. Transfer the crumb mixture to a small bowl and set aside.

2 Dredge the fillets in the cornmeal. Wipe out the skillet with paper toweling and coat with the nonstick cooking spray. Heat the pan over moderately low heat. Add the fish fillets and cook, partially covered, for 4 minutes. Turn the fillets over and continue cooking 4 minutes longer. Transfer the fish to warm dinner plates and sprinkle the crumb mixture on top of each fillet. Serve with the lemon wedges, steamed rice, and Roasted Pepper Mélange (page 235). Serves 4.

PREPARATION TIME: 10 MIN. COOKING TIME: 15 MIN.

Per serving: Calories 285; Saturated Fat 4 g;
Total Fat 13 g; Protein 30 g; Carbohydrate 13 g;
Fiber 1 g; Sodium 317 mg; Cholesterol 91 mg

BLUEFISH MARINATED IN YOGURT AND HERBS

Although bluefish has a reputation for being oily, it is actually quite low in fat and cholesterol.

1 **small yellow onion, coarsely chopped**	¼ **teaspoon ground turmeric**
2 **tablespoons snipped fresh dill or 2 teaspoons dill weed**	⅛ **teaspoon black pepper**
	1 **cup plain low-fat yogurt**
2 **teaspoons lemon juice**	4 **bluefish fillets (5 ounces each)**
1½ **teaspoons minced fresh ginger or ½ teaspoon ground ginger**	½ **cucumber, peeled, seeded, and diced (1 cup)**
½ **teaspoon prepared mustard**	¾ **cup radishes, trimmed and quartered**

1 In a food processor, combine the onion, dill, lemon juice, ginger, mustard, turmeric, and pepper; whirl for 30 seconds to 1 minute or until minced. Add the yogurt and whirl 10 seconds longer or until well combined.

2 Spoon ⅔ cup of the yogurt mixture into a small bowl, cover, and refrigerate. Place the bluefish fillets in a greased ovenproof dish just large enough to hold them in a single layer. Spoon the remaining yogurt mixture over them. Cover with plastic food wrap and refrigerate for at least 4 hours or overnight.

3 Preheat the oven to 400° F. Bake the fish for 10 minutes or until it flakes easily when tested with a fork. Transfer the fillets to heated dinner plates. Stir the cucumber and radishes into the reserved yogurt mixture and spoon over the fish. Accompany with rice and steamed asparagus. Serves 4.

PREPARATION TIME: 15 MIN. COOKING TIME: 10 MIN.
MARINATING TIME: 4 HR.

Per serving: Calories 228; Saturated Fat 2 g; Total Fat 7 g; Protein 32 g; Carbohydrate 8 g; Fiber 1 g; Sodium 137 mg; Cholesterol 87 mg

COD WITH CAPER SAUCE

This creamy sauce only tastes rich. You can also serve it with perch, trout, flounder, or salmon.

Nonstick cooking spray	2 **tablespoons capers, drained and chopped**
4 **cod or scrod fillets (about 5 ounces each)**	1 **can (12 ounces) evaporated skim milk**
1 **tablespoon unsalted butter or margarine**	¼ **cup minced parsley**
1½ **tablespoons flour**	¼ **teaspoon black or white pepper**
1 **green onion, including some of the top, thinly sliced**	

1 Preheat the oven to 375° F. Lightly coat a 9" x 9" x 2" baking pan with the cooking spray. Place the fish fillets in the pan and cover with aluminum foil. Bake the fish for 10 minutes or until it flakes easily when tested with a fork.

2 While the fish is baking, prepare the sauce. In a small heavy saucepan, melt the butter over moderately low heat. Blend in the flour and cook, stirring, for 2 minutes or until smooth and straw colored. Add the green onion and capers, then slowly stir in the milk and cook, stirring constantly, for 5 minutes or until thickened and smooth. Stir in the parsley and pepper.

3 Transfer the fish to warm dinner plates and spoon some sauce over each fillet. Serve with steamed new potatoes and broccoli. Serves 4.

PREPARATION TIME: 7 MIN. COOKING TIME: 10 MIN.

Per serving: Calories 229; Saturated Fat 2 g; Total Fat 4 g; Protein 33 g; Carbohydrate 13 g; Fiber 0 g; Sodium 305 mg; Cholesterol 73 mg

Before buying frozen fish, be sure that it's frozen solid. Don't forget to check the expiration date on the package. Buy frozen fish at the end of your shopping expedition so that it has less chance of thawing.

When freezing fresh fish, wrap it tightly in freezer paper or heavy-duty aluminum foil. Freeze fillets or steaks individually or place wax paper between them; freeze no more than 1 pound per package.

Place packages of fish in the coldest part of the freezer, against the walls and away from the door. Lean fish can be frozen for up to 6 months; fatty fish, no longer than 3 months.

When thawing fish, place it, wrapped, on a plate in the refrigerator — not on a countertop. If you're in a hurry, put the packaged fish in very cold water to thaw, allowing 30 minutes per pound.

You can also thaw fish in the microwave; for precise instructions, consult the manufacturer's manual. Never cook frozen fish in the microwave without defrosting it first.

Use thawed fish within a day — do not refreeze it.

Omega-3 fatty acids, found in fish oils, especially from the fatty cold-water types of fish, are believed to lower blood cholesterol levels, leading to less buildup of artery-clogging plaque.

Among the fish that are especially good sources of omega-3 fatty acids are anchovies, bluefish, clams, cod, crab, halibut, trout, salmon, snapper, tuna, and lake whitefish.

Even if there were no special benefits from fish oils, it would still be a good idea to make fish a regular part of your diet. They contain complete protein and are lower in fat than many other protein foods. They are also an excellent source of iodine, fluoride, and selenium; this last helps prevent cell damage from oxidation.

COD, LEEKS, AND POTATOES IN ORANGE-TOMATO SAUCE

1 tablespoon olive oil	1 cup water
3 large leeks, rinsed, trimmed, and diced (1 ¾ cups)	⅓ cup pitted green olives, quartered
1 large sweet red pepper, cored, seeded, and diced (1 cup)	1 medium-size tomato, chopped, with its juice (1 cup)
3 cloves garlic, slivered	½ cup orange juice
3 medium-size all-purpose potatoes, peeled and cubed (2 cups)	4 cod fillets (5 ounces each)
	3 tablespoons minced parsley or fresh cilantro (coriander)

1 In a 12-inch skillet, heat the oil over low heat. Add the leeks and cook, uncovered, stirring occasionally, for 5 minutes or until soft. Add the pepper and garlic and cook for 2 minutes. Add the potatoes, water, and olives, cover, and simmer for 20 minutes. Stir in the tomato and orange juice.

2 Lay the fillets on top of the vegetable mixture, cover, and cook for 10 to 12 minutes or until the fish flakes easily when tested with a fork. Transfer the fish to warm dinner plates; stir the parsley into the sauce, then spoon the sauce over each fillet. Serve with a green salad and Four-Grain Rolls (page 304). Serves 4.

PREPARATION TIME: 20 MIN.   COOKING TIME: 37 MIN.

Per serving: Calories 322; Saturated Fat 1 g; Total Fat 6 g; Protein 29 g; Carbohydrate 40 g; Fiber 4 g; Sodium 206 mg; Cholesterol 62 mg

CREOLE HALIBUT STEW

When halibut isn't available, substitute cod, scrod, mackerel, or bluefish.

1 tablespoon olive oil	½ teaspoon finely chopped jalapeño pepper, or to taste (wash your hands after handling the pepper)
3 green onions, thinly sliced (⅓ cup)	
4 cloves garlic, minced	
1 small sweet green pepper, cored, seeded, and finely chopped (1 cup)	1 large tomato, chopped, with its juice (1 ½ cups)
2 small carrots, peeled and thinly sliced (1 cup)	⅓ cup clam broth or bottled clam juice
1 ounce spicy dry sausage (pepperoni, soppresata, or chorizo), cut into matchstick strips (¼ cup)	¼ teaspoon ground cumin
	⅛ teaspoon ground red pepper (cayenne)
	4 halibut steaks (6 ounces each)

1 In a 12-inch skillet, heat the oil over moderate heat. Add the green onions and sauté, stirring frequently, for 2 minutes. Add the garlic and cook for 1 minute. Stir in the green pepper, carrots, sausage, and jalapeño pepper; reduce the heat to low, cover, and cook for 5 minutes. Stir in the tomato and clam broth and cook 4 minutes more.

2 Rub the cumin and red pepper over the halibut steaks and place them on top of the vegetable mixture. Cover and cook over low heat for 10 minutes or until the fish flakes easily when tested with a fork. Transfer the halibut to warm dinner plates and spoon some vegetables over each portion. Serve with crusty French bread. Serves 4.

PREPARATION TIME: 20 MIN.   COOKING TIME: 22 MIN.

Per serving: Calories 283; Saturated Fat 2 g; Total Fat 11 g; Protein 38 g; Carbohydrate 8 g; Fiber 2 g; Sodium 302 mg; Cholesterol 54 mg

POACHED SALMON ON A BED OF SPINACH

Salmon, rich in health-promoting omega-3 fatty acids, is served atop spinach for a colorful and nutritious main course.

- 1 pound spinach, trimmed and rinsed
- 3 tablespoons lemon juice
- 1 teaspoon Dijon mustard
- ½ teaspoon grated lemon rind
- ¼ teaspoon each salt and black pepper
- 2 tablespoons plus 2 teaspoons olive oil
- 2 tablespoons red wine vinegar
- 4 salmon fillets or steaks (6 ounces each)
- 2 tablespoons minced shallot
- 2 tablespoons minced fresh tarragon or chives or 2 teaspoons dried tarragon or chives

1 In a 10-inch skillet, place the spinach with just the water that clings to its leaves. Cover and steam over moderate heat, tossing occasionally, for 3 to 4 minutes or until wilted. Drain; refresh under cold water to stop the cooking and drain again; gently squeeze dry and set aside.

2 In a small bowl, whisk together the lemon juice, mustard, lemon rind, and ⅛ teaspoon each of the salt and pepper. Slowly drizzle in 2 tablespoons of the oil, whisking vigorously until well blended, and set aside.

3 Fill a fish poacher, shallow 10-inch skillet, or flameproof casserole with 2 inches of water. Add the vinegar and bring to a simmer. Gently place the fish in the simmering water and cook, covered, over moderately low heat for 4 to 5 minutes for fillets, 6 to 7 minutes for steaks, or until the fish just flakes when tested with a fork.

4 Meanwhile, in a 10-inch skillet, cook the shallot in the remaining 2 teaspoons of oil over moderate heat, stirring, for about 2 minutes or until softened. Add the spinach and remaining ⅛ teaspoon each of salt and pepper and cook, stirring, for 3 to 4 minutes or until heated through.

A hearty one-dish meal, Cod, Leeks, and Potatoes in Orange-Tomato Sauce goes well with a green salad and crusty bread.

5 With a spatula, carefully transfer the fish to a platter lined with paper toweling to drain. Divide the spinach among 4 warm dinner plates and top each with a portion of salmon. Whisk ¼ cup of the poaching liquid into the dressing and spoon the dressing over the fish and spinach. Sprinkle with the tarragon. Serves 4.

PREPARATION TIME: 15 MIN. COOKING TIME: 10 MIN.

Per serving: Calories 360; Saturated Fat 4 g; Total Fat 19 g; Protein 40 g; Carbohydrate 7 g; Fiber 3 g; Sodium 318 mg; Cholesterol 66 mg

Snapper with Cumin-Citrus Sauce, delicious with herbed rice and steamed asparagus, is special enough for company but easy enough for family.

SALMON HASH

For a satisfying weekend brunch, serve this hearty hash with a tossed green salad.

2½ cups diced cooked potatoes
1 can (15½ ounces) water-packed salmon, drained and flaked
1 small sweet green pepper, cored, seeded, and diced (¾ cup)
4 green onions, finely chopped (½ cup)
3 tablespoons snipped fresh dill or minced parsley or 1 tablespoon dill weed or parsley flakes
1 teaspoon grated lemon rind
½ teaspoon salt, or to taste
¼ teaspoon black pepper
2 tablespoons vegetable oil
1 large egg
1 large egg white
¼ cup skim milk
Minced fresh parsley (optional garnish)

1 In a large bowl, combine the potatoes, salmon, green pepper, green onions, dill, lemon rind, ¼ teaspoon of the salt, and ⅛ teaspoon of the black pepper.

2 In a 10-inch nonstick skillet, heat the oil over moderate heat. Add the salmon mixture, flattening it into a cake. Cook, covered, over moderately low heat for 7 to 10 minutes or until the underside is golden. Shake the pan frequently to prevent the bottom of the hash from burning.

3 In a large bowl, whisk together the egg, egg white, milk, and remaining salt and pepper. Make an indentation in the hash, pour in the egg-milk mixture, and cook over moderately low heat for 2 to 3 minutes or until the eggs are set. Loosen the hash around the edges with a spatula, place a plate over the skillet, and invert onto the plate. Sprinkle with parsley if desired. Serves 4.

PREPARATION TIME: 15 MIN. COOKING TIME: 10 MIN.

Per serving: Calories 284; Saturated Fat 2 g; Total Fat 12 g; Protein 24 g; Carbohydrate 19 g; Fiber 1 g; Sodium 852 mg; Cholesterol 100 mg

SARDINE CAKES

Sardines are loaded with beneficial omega-3 fatty acids and are an excellent source of calcium as well. If you don't have sardines in your cupboard, use 3 cans (3¼ ounces each) of canned tuna.

3 cans (3½ ounces each) water-packed sardines, drained, boned, and flaked (1½ cups)
1¼ cups mashed potato (1 large potato, cooked and mashed)
2 green onions, finely chopped (¼ cup)
2 tablespoons minced parsley
2 cloves garlic, minced
1 tablespoon Dijon mustard
1 large egg, lightly beaten
¼ teaspoon salt, or to taste
⅛ teaspoon ground red pepper (cayenne), or to taste
⅓ cup toasted fresh bread crumbs

1 Preheat the oven to 400° F. Lightly grease a baking sheet. In a large bowl, combine the sardines, potato, green onions, parsley, garlic, mustard, egg, salt, and red pepper.

2 Form the mixture into 8 patties, dredge them in the bread crumbs, and arrange on the baking sheet. Bake for 25 minutes; turn the patties and bake 10 minutes longer or until golden. Serve hot with Cucumber-Yogurt Sauce (page 278) and steamed zucchini sticks. Serves 4.

PREPARATION TIME: 20 MIN.   COOKING TIME: 35 MIN.

Per serving: Calories 219; Saturated Fat 2 g; Total Fat 9 g; Protein 20 g; Carbohydrate 23 g; Fiber 2 g; Sodium 640 mg; Cholesterol 160 mg

SNAPPER WITH CUMIN-CITRUS SAUCE

If red snapper is unavailable, flounder or scrod goes well with the cumin-citrus sauce.

1 bay leaf
2 lemon slices
4 red snapper fillets (5 ounces each)
For the sauce:
⅓ cup water
1½ tablespoons cornstarch
⅓ cup orange juice
2 teaspoons reduced-sodium soy sauce
¾ teaspoon ground cumin
1 green onion, thinly sliced (2 tablespoons)

1 In a 12-inch skillet, bring 2 inches of water to a simmer with the bay leaf and lemon slices. Add the fillets, cover, and barely simmer for 4 to 6 minutes or until the fish flakes easily when tested with a fork.

2 Meanwhile, prepare the sauce. In a small saucepan, stir together the water and cornstarch until dissolved. Add the orange juice, soy sauce, and cumin and bring to a simmer, stirring, over moderate heat. Add the green onion and cook for 1 minute. With a slotted spatula, transfer the fillets to individual plates and spoon the sauce over them. Serve with orzo and steamed Brussels sprouts. Serves 4.

PREPARATION TIME: 5 MIN.   COOKING TIME: 5 MIN.

Per serving: Calories 165; Saturated Fat 0 g; Total Fat 2 g; Protein 29 g; Carbohydrate 6 g; Fiber 0 g; Sodium 171 mg; Cholesterol 52 mg

•

Pan-Fried Variation: Soak the fillets in *2 tablespoons skim milk* for 5 minutes, then dip them in *3 tablespoons flour*, shaking off the excess. In a 12-inch nonstick skillet, heat *2 teaspoons canola or vegetable oil* over moderate heat. Add the fish and cook, partially covered, for 8 minutes, turning the fillets 3 times while cooking.
Per serving: Calories 206; Saturated Fat 1 g; Total Fat 4 g; Protein 30 g; Carbohydrate 10 g; Fiber 0 g; Sodium 175 mg; Cholesterol 52 mg.

If storing fresh fish for more than a few hours, first wrap it tightly in aluminum foil, then place it in a plastic food bag in the refrigerator. Use it within 2 days.

Keep fish in the coldest part of your refrigerator, preferably at 32° F, perhaps at the back of the meat compartment. If you don't want to keep your refrigerator that cold, put the fish in a plastic bag and pack it in ice.

RED SNAPPER WITH BLACK BEANS

The fish, beans, and garnishes for this remarkably easy dish can be prepared a couple of hours in advance and refrigerated until cooking time.

- 2 tablespoons reduced-sodium soy sauce
- 1 tablespoon dark sesame oil
- ½ teaspoon ground ginger
- ¼ teaspoon garlic powder
- 3 tablespoons dry sherry or orange juice
- ¼ teaspoon black pepper
- 4 red snapper fillets (about 5 ounces each)
- 3 cups cooked black beans
- 1 tablespoon finely chopped sweet red pepper
- 1 green onion, including top, thinly sliced

1 In a small bowl, combine the soy sauce, oil, ginger, garlic powder, sherry, and black pepper. Lay the fillets, skin side down, on a large plate and rub 1 teaspoon of the mixture into the flesh side of each fillet.

2 In a heavy 10-inch skillet, combine the remaining soy sauce mixture with the beans. Bring to a simmer over moderate heat, cover, and cook for 3 minutes or until the beans are heated through. Place the fillets, skin side down, on top of the beans, cover, and cook for another 6 minutes or until the fish flakes easily when tested with a fork. Transfer the fish to a heated serving platter, spoon the beans and cooking liquid over each fillet, and sprinkle with the red pepper and green onion. Serve with Escarole Sautéed with Garlic (page 229) or steamed wax beans. Serves 4.

PREPARATION TIME: 7 MIN. COOKING TIME: 10 MIN.

Per serving: Calories 491; Saturated Fat 1 g; Total Fat 7 g; Protein 49 g; Carbohydrate 56 g; Fiber 10 g; Sodium 273 mg; Cholesterol 52 mg

LEMON SOLE BLANKETED IN MUSHROOMS

This elegant, richly flavored sauce also goes well with flounder or other white fish fillets, although they may take a minute or so longer to cook.

- 4 lemon sole fillets (about 5 ounces each)
- 1 tablespoon unsalted butter or margarine
- 12 ounces mushrooms, thinly sliced (about 3¾ cups)
- 2 tablespoons dry white wine or water
- 2 tablespoons flour
- 1 can (12 ounces) evaporated skim milk
- 2 tablespoons low-sodium tomato paste
- 4 green onions, including tops, thinly sliced (½ cup)
- ¼ teaspoon white or black pepper

1 Preheat the oven to 350° F. Lightly grease a 9" x 9" x 2" baking pan. Arrange the fish fillets in the baking pan, skinned side down, and set aside.

2 In a 10-inch nonstick skillet, heat the butter over moderate heat until bubbling. Add the mushrooms and sauté for 1 minute. Stir in the wine and cook, covered, for 3 minutes or until the mushrooms are almost tender. Blend in the flour and cook, stirring, for 1 minute. Slowly add the milk and cook, stirring constantly, for about 5 minutes or until thickened and smooth.

3 Remove the skillet from the heat and stir in the tomato paste, green onions, and pepper. Spoon the mushrooms and sauce over the fish fillets and bake, uncovered, for 6 minutes or until the fish flakes easily when tested with a fork. Transfer the fish to warm dinner plates and spoon some sauce over each fillet. Serve with parsleyed new potatoes and steamed asparagus. Serves 4.

PREPARATION TIME: 10 MIN. COOKING TIME: 17 MIN.

Per serving: Calories 234; Saturated Fat 2 g; Total Fat 4 g; Protein 31 g; Carbohydrate 18 g; Fiber 2 g; Sodium 202 mg; Cholesterol 110 mg

SWORDFISH WITH PINEAPPLE SALSA

Fresh pineapple makes a splendid accompaniment to broiled fish (or chicken, for that matter). This dish may be served hot, at room temperature, or chilled.

For the salsa:
- 1 small red onion, thinly sliced (½ cup)
- ½ pineapple, peeled, cored, and cut into ½-inch cubes (2 cups), or 2 cups canned pineapple chunks in juice, drained
- 1 small sweet red pepper, cored, seeded, and finely chopped (½ cup)
- 2 tablespoons minced fresh cilantro (coriander) or 2 tablespoons minced parsley mixed with 1 teaspoon dried cilantro
- 1 tablespoon lime juice
- ½ teaspoon honey
- ¼ teaspoon salt, or to taste

For the swordfish:
- 1 tablespoon plus 1 teaspoon lime juice
- 2 teaspoons olive oil
- ¼ teaspoon ground cumin
- 2 swordfish steaks (10 ounces each), halved to make 4 steaks

1 To prepare the salsa: Place the onion in a small bowl, cover with ice water, and let stand for 30 minutes; drain and pat dry with paper toweling. In a medium-size bowl, toss together the pineapple, pepper, cilantro, lime juice, honey, salt, and onion. Cover and refrigerate for 1 hour to allow the flavors to blend.

2 To prepare the swordfish: Preheat the broiler, setting the rack 6 inches from the heat. In a small bowl, stir together the lime juice, oil, and cumin; brush the mixture on the swordfish. Arrange the swordfish on a broiler pan and broil for 4 minutes; turn and broil 3 minutes longer or until the fish flakes easily when tested with a fork. Transfer the swordfish steaks to a warm platter and spoon the salsa over them. Serve with rice and sugar snap peas. Serves 4.

PREPARATION TIME: 20 MIN. COOKING TIME: 7 MIN.

STANDING TIME: 1½ HR.

> *Per serving: Calories 246; Saturated Fat 2 g; Total Fat 8 g; Protein 29 g; Carbohydrate 13 g; Fiber 2 g; Sodium 262 mg; Cholesterol 55 mg*

Swordfish with Pineapple Salsa and Vegetable Kebabs (page 241) are inviting any time of year, but especially in summer, when you can grill them outdoors.

Vegetable-Stuffed Trout with rice and wild rice, broiled tomatoes, and steamed carrots — it's a meal fit for a monarch.

VEGETABLE-STUFFED TROUT

You can prepare the stuffing for this elegant but easy dish up to 2 days ahead and refrigerate it.

- 1 **tablespoon plus 1 teaspoon olive oil**
- 6 **green onions, including tops, thinly sliced (¾ cup)**
- 6 **ounces mushrooms, coarsely chopped (2 cups)**
- 1 **package (10 ounces) frozen chopped spinach, thawed and squeezed dry**
- ¼ **cup Neufchâtel cream cheese**
- 1 **tablespoon sesame seeds**
- 4 **brook or rainbow trout (10 to 12 ounces each), cleaned and boned**
- 2 **teaspoons lemon juice**
- ½ **teaspoon salt**
  Lemon slices (optional garnish)

1 Preheat the oven to 400° F. Lightly grease a large baking sheet; set aside. In a 12-inch nonstick skillet, heat the oil over moderate heat. Add the green onions and cook for 1 minute; add the mushrooms and cook 3 to 4 minutes longer or until soft. Remove from the heat and stir in the spinach, cheese, and sesame seeds.

2 Make 3 shallow slashes on one side of each trout and sprinkle with the lemon juice and salt. Fill each fish cavity with the stuffing and place on the baking sheet, slashed side up. Bake for 15 minutes or until the fish flakes easily when tested with a fork. Transfer to warm dinner plates and garnish with lemon slices if desired. Serve with rice and steamed wax beans. Serves 4.

PREPARATION TIME: 12 MIN. COOKING TIME: 20 MIN.

Per serving: Calories 323; Saturated Fat 4 g;
Total Fat 15 g; Protein 40 g; Carbohydrate 7 g;
Fiber 3 g; Sodium 432 mg; Cholesterol 107 mg

GRILLED TUNA TERIYAKI

*Though broiling is called for in this recipe,
you can also cook the tuna steaks on an outdoor
grill or a well-seasoned stovetop grill.*

2 **tablespoons reduced-sodium soy sauce**
1 **tablespoon rice wine, dry sherry, or rice vinegar**
1 **large clove garlic, minced**

1 **tablespoon minced fresh ginger or 1 teaspoon ground ginger**
4 **tuna steaks, ¾ inch thick (6 ounces each)**
1 **tablespoon vegetable oil**

1 In a shallow dish large enough to hold the tuna, combine the soy sauce, rice wine, garlic, and ginger. Place the tuna in the marinade and turn to coat it; cover and refrigerate for at least 30 minutes.

2 Preheat the broiler, setting the rack 6 inches from the heat. Discard the marinade and pat the tuna steaks dry with paper toweling, then brush both sides with the oil. Arrange the tuna on a broiler pan and broil for 3 minutes on each side or until the fish flakes easily when tested with a fork. Serve with Sautéed Peppers (variation, page 235) and steamed brown rice. Serves 4.

PREPARATION TIME: 7 MIN. COOKING TIME: 6 MIN.
MARINATING TIME: 30 MIN.

*Per serving: Calories 225; Saturated Fat 1 g;
Total Fat 5 g; Protein 40 g; Carbohydrate 1 g;
Fiber 0 g; Sodium 304 mg; Cholesterol 76 mg*

CURRIED CRAB AND ASPARAGUS QUICHE

*Serve this light crustless quiche for a festive brunch
or as a first course for a special dinner.*

1 **can (7½ ounces) crabmeat or 8 ounces fresh lump crabmeat, drained, picked over, and patted dry**
6 **medium-size asparagus, cooked, patted dry, and sliced into ¼-inch pieces (1 cup)**
⅔ **cup part-skim ricotta cheese**
⅔ **cup low-fat (1% milkfat) milk**
2 **green onions, including tops, thinly sliced (¼ cup)**

1 **large egg**
2 **large egg whites**
2 **tablespoons grated Parmesan cheese**
2 **tablespoons flour**
2 **teaspoons Dijon mustard**
2 **teaspoons curry powder**
¼ **teaspoon each salt and ground red pepper (cayenne), or to taste**

1 Preheat the oven to 375° F. Lightly grease a 9-inch pie pan and set aside. In a large bowl, mix together the crabmeat, asparagus, ricotta cheese, milk, green onions, egg, egg whites, 1 tablespoon of the Parmesan cheese, the flour, mustard, curry powder, salt, and red pepper. Pour the mixture into the pie pan and bake for 40 to 45 minutes or until set.

2 Remove the quiche from the oven and raise the temperature to broil. Sprinkle the remaining tablespoon of Parmesan over the quiche, then place under the broiler about 3 inches from the heat for 1 minute or until golden brown. Serve with a tossed salad and hard rolls. Serves 4 as an entrée, 6 to 8 as a first course or appetizer.

PREPARATION TIME: 15 MIN. COOKING TIME: 45 MIN.

*Per serving (for 4): Calories 191; Saturated Fat 4 g;
Total Fat 8 g; Protein 22 g; Carbohydrate 11 g;
Fiber 1 g; Sodium 609 mg; Cholesterol 123 mg*

EASY WEEKDAY DINNER

Grilled Tuna Teriyaki

Parsleyed Rice

Steamed Spinach

Honeydew Melon

SIMPLE SUNDAY SUPPER

Tomato-Hominy Soup
(page 67)

Curried Crab and Asparagus Quiche

Whole-Wheat Bread Sticks

Chocolate Angel Food Cake
(page 323)

MUSSELS IN TOMATO-GINGER SAUCE

You can serve these mussels in their shells, or scoop them out and toss them and their sauce with 1 pound of hot pasta, or chill and arrange them on lettuce as a salad. If mussels are unavailable, try fresh clams.

1 tablespoon olive oil
1 medium-size yellow onion, finely chopped (1 cup)
2 cloves garlic, slivered
1 large carrot, peeled, halved lengthwise, and thinly sliced (1 cup)
2 teaspoons minced fresh ginger or ¾ teaspoon ground ginger
1 can (14½ ounces) low-sodium tomatoes, chopped, with their juice
1 cup water
5 pounds mussels in their shells, scrubbed and beards removed
Croutons (optional garnish)

1 In a 5-quart Dutch oven, heat the oil over moderate heat. Add the onion and garlic and sauté, stirring, for 5 minutes or until softened. Add the carrot and ginger and cook 4 minutes longer. Stir in the tomatoes and water, then bring to a boil over moderate heat.

2 Place ⅓ of the mussels in the liquid, cover, and reduce the heat to moderately low; cook for 5 minutes or until the shells have opened. With a slotted spoon, transfer to a serving bowl and keep warm. Continue adding the remaining mussels to the liquid until all are cooked. (Discard any mussels that do not open.) Pour the sauce over the mussels and top with croutons if desired. Accompany with bread, to soak up any sauce, and Pasta Salad with Italian Green Beans and Mushrooms (page 251). Serves 4.

PREPARATION TIME: 20 MIN.   COOKING TIME: 25 MIN.

Per serving: Calories 291; Saturated Fat 1 g; Total Fat 9 g; Protein 34 g; Carbohydrate 18 g; Fiber 2 g; Sodium 671 mg; Cholesterol 127 mg

ASPARAGUS AND SCALLOP SAUTÉ

If you can't find fresh asparagus, green beans make an acceptable substitute in this quick, easy, and colorful dish.

1¼ pounds asparagus, trimmed and cut into 1-inch pieces
1½ tablespoons Dijon mustard
1 tablespoon honey
1 teaspoon minced fresh basil or ¼ teaspoon dried basil, crumbled
1 teaspoon unsalted butter
1¼ pounds sea scallops

1 In a 12-inch nonstick skillet, bring 1 inch of water to a boil. Add the asparagus and simmer for 4 to 6 minutes or until crisp-tender; drain in a colander; rinse under cold running water, then drain again. In a small bowl, stir together the mustard, honey, and basil.

2 Melt the butter in the skillet over moderate heat. Add the scallops and sauté for 6 minutes, turning them after 3 minutes. Add the asparagus and the mustard mixture and cook and stir for 2 to 3 minutes or until the scallops are firm and opaque but still spring back when touched. Serve with rice or angel hair pasta. Serves 4.

PREPARATION TIME: 10 MIN.   COOKING TIME: 15 MIN.

Per serving: Calories 190; Saturated Fat 1 g; Total Fat 3 g; Protein 28 g; Carbohydrate 14 g; Fiber 2 g; Sodium 312 mg; Cholesterol 49 mg

SCALLOP SALAD WITH ORANGE-GINGER DRESSING

Serve this unusual combination of broiled scallops and baby greens with whole-grain biscuits.

- ¼ cup orange juice
- 1 tablespoon plus 1 teaspoon rice vinegar or white wine vinegar
- 2 teaspoons minced fresh ginger or ¾ teaspoon ground ginger
- 2 teaspoons minced garlic
- 1 teaspoon honey
- 1 teaspoon reduced-sodium soy sauce
- 1 teaspoon grated orange rind
- 1¼ pounds sea scallops
- 2 tablespoons minced shallot

- ½ cup low-sodium chicken broth
- 1 tablespoon vegetable oil
- 1 teaspoon Dijon mustard
- 4 cups baby greens, such as bibb, lamb's, or red oak lettuce, mustard or dandelion greens, or a combination, rinsed and dried
- 2 tablespoons minced fresh cilantro (coriander) or 2 tablespoons minced parsley mixed with 1 teaspoon dried cilantro

1 In a shallow dish large enough to hold the scallops, combine the orange juice, vinegar, ginger, garlic, honey, soy sauce, and orange rind; add the scallops, toss to coat with the marinade, cover, and refrigerate for at least 30 minutes. Drain the scallops, setting the marinade aside. Thread the scallops on 4 lightly greased 12- to 14-inch metal skewers.

2 In a small saucepan, boil the marinade and shallot, uncovered, over high heat for 1 to 2 minutes or until the mixture is reduced to 2 tablespoons. Add the broth and boil 2 minutes more to reduce the mixture to ⅓ cup. Whisk in the oil and mustard.

3 Preheat the broiler, setting the rack 6 inches from the heat. Arrange the skewers on a broiler pan and broil for 3 minutes on each side or until the scallops are firm and opaque but still spring back when touched.

4 In a large bowl, toss the greens with half the dressing and divide them among 4 dinner plates. Top each plate with a skewer of scallops and spoon the remaining dressing over the scallops. Sprinkle with the cilantro. Serves 4.

PREPARATION TIME: 20 MIN. COOKING TIME: 10 MIN.
MARINATING TIME: 30 MIN.

Per serving: Calories 225; Saturated Fat 1 g; Total Fat 5 g; Protein 21 g; Carbohydrate 10 g; Fiber 1 g; Sodium 300 mg; Cholesterol 47 mg

Asparagus and Scallop Sauté, served over angel hair pasta, combines delicate flavors from both the sea and the garden.

Cleaning shrimp is a simple procedure. For the way to peel and devein them, see below.

1. With the feet of the shrimp facing you, grasp an edge of the shell at the head end and peel it away from the body, working toward the tail. If you wish, pinch off the tail shell.

2. To remove the gritty intestinal vein, hold the shrimp as shown, with the back facing away from you, and make a slit with a small sharp knife.

3. With the vein now exposed, use your fingers to pull it out, then rinse the shrimp in cold water.

SAUTÉED SHRIMP WITH TOMATO-HERB SAUCE

1 ¼ pounds large shrimp (about 24), shelled, deveined, and patted dry
1 tablespoon flour
1 tablespoon olive oil
¼ teaspoon each salt and black pepper
4 shallots, finely chopped (½ cup)
⅓ cup dry white wine or water
⅓ cup Chicken Stock (page 62) or low-sodium chicken broth
1 teaspoon grated orange rind
1 medium-size tomato, seeded and chopped (1 cup), or 1 cup canned tomatoes, drained and chopped
2 cloves garlic, minced
¼ teaspoon each dried thyme and marjoram, crumbled
3 tablespoons minced fresh basil or parsley

1 Dredge the shrimp in the flour, shaking off any excess. In a 10-inch nonstick skillet, heat 2 teaspoons of the oil over moderate heat. Add the shrimp and ⅛ teaspoon each of the salt and pepper; sauté for 30 seconds on each side or until golden. Transfer the shrimp to a plate.

2 Heat the remaining oil in the skillet over moderate heat, then add the shallots and cook, stirring, for 1 minute. Add the wine, stock, and orange rind and cook for 2 minutes or until the liquid is reduced to ½ cup. Add the tomato, garlic, thyme, marjoram, and remaining ⅛ teaspoon each of the salt and pepper. Bring the liquid to a boil, then lower the heat and simmer, stirring occasionally, for 3 minutes.

3 Return the shrimp to the skillet and cook for 2 to 3 minutes or until they are heated through and the sauce is slightly thickened. Transfer to a heated serving dish and sprinkle with the basil. Serve with pasta, steamed rice, or rice pilaf and peas. Serves 4.

PREPARATION TIME: 20 MIN. COOKING TIME: 10 MIN.

Per serving: Calories 225; Saturated Fat 1 g; Total Fat 6 g; Protein 30 g; Carbohydrate 8 g; Fiber 1 g; Sodium 373 mg; Cholesterol 217 mg

SHRIMP DUMPLINGS

Nonstick cooking spray
4 large dried mushrooms, such as tree ear or shiitake
3 green onions, quartered crosswise
½ clove garlic
8 ounces shrimp, shelled and deveined
6 ounces ground turkey
2 teaspoons reduced-sodium soy sauce
1 teaspoon dark sesame oil
3 dashes hot red pepper sauce
6 egg roll wrappers (each 6 inches square), each cut into 4 squares, or 24 wonton skins (each 2½ inches square)

For the dipping sauce:
2 tablespoons reduced-sodium soy sauce
2 teaspoons rice wine vinegar
½ teaspoon honey
½ teaspoon dark sesame oil
½ teaspoon minced fresh ginger or ⅛ teaspoon ground ginger

1 Coat a steamer basket with the nonstick cooking spray and set aside. In a small saucepan, soak the mushrooms in boiling water to cover for 15 minutes, then drain. Remove and discard the stems; cut the caps into quarters.

2 In a food processor, combine the mushroom caps, green onions, and garlic and whirl until coarsely chopped. Add the shrimp and whirl until finely chopped. Transfer to a medium-size bowl and stir in the ground turkey, soy sauce, oil, and red pepper sauce.

3 Place 1 tablespoon of the shrimp mixture in the center of each wrapper square. Dampen the edges with water, then fold up the sides around the filling, pleating the edges. Place in the steamer basket, leaving ½ inch of space between the dumplings for the steam to circulate. Set over boiling water, cover, and steam for 15 minutes.

4 Meanwhile, prepare the dipping sauce. In a small bowl, whisk together the soy sauce, vinegar, honey, oil, and ginger. Serve the dumplings hot with the dipping sauce. Makes 24 dumplings.

PREPARATION TIME: 20 MIN. COOKING TIME: 15 MIN.
SOAKING TIME: 15 MIN.

Per dumpling: Calories 50; Saturated Fat 0 g; Total Fat 1 g; Protein 5 g; Carbohydrate 5 g; Fiber 0 g; Sodium 52 mg; Cholesterol 19 mg

POULTRY

Health-conscious people today are aware that poultry can be a
very good source of relatively low-fat animal protein. The way to benefit most from
this quality is to cook the meat by broiling, poaching, stir-frying, roasting, or
braising (not frying); remove the skin before eating — about 50 percent of the fat is
in the skin; and stay with a portion of 4 ounces or less. Of the various
kinds of poultry, chicken and turkey have the least fat; duck and goose have the
most. (On page 126 you will find recipes for cooking duck as fat free as
possible, if you wish to enjoy it now and then.) When choosing between light and
dark poultry meat, remember that the dark has less protein and about
twice the fat of the light. Take advantage of poultry's versatility. In this chapter,
we give you at least 40 different ways to prepare it.

ROAST CHICKEN WITH COUSCOUS AND RED PEPPER STUFFING

The buttery flavor of couscous goes particularly well with chicken and makes an appealing change from bread stuffings. To keep the meat moist and juicy, the chicken is roasted with the skin on; to reduce the fat content, the skin is removed as the bird is being carved.

For the stuffing:

1 ½ cups Chicken Stock (page 62) or low-sodium chicken broth	2 cloves garlic, minced
3 teaspoons olive oil	¼ teaspoon salt, or to taste
1 cup couscous	½ teaspoon black pepper
1 medium-size sweet red pepper, cored, seeded, and diced (¾ cup)	¼ cup snipped fresh chives, minced basil, or parsley
1 medium-size yellow onion, finely chopped (1 cup)	3 tablespoons grated Parmesan cheese
	1 small roasting chicken or whole broiler-fryer (3 pounds)

1 To prepare the stuffing: In a small saucepan, combine the stock and 1 teaspoon of the oil. Bring to a boil over moderately high heat and stir in the couscous. Remove the pan from the heat and let stand, covered, for 10 minutes.

2 Meanwhile, heat the remaining 2 teaspoons of oil in a 10-inch nonstick skillet over moderate heat. Add the red pepper, onion, garlic, salt, and black pepper; cook, stirring occasionally, for 5 minutes or until the onion is softened. Transfer the mixture to a large bowl, add the couscous, chives, and cheese, and mix well.

3 Preheat the oven to 350° F. Spoon 1 cup of the stuffing into the cavity of the chicken and truss the chicken (see illustration, opposite page). Place the chicken on a rack in a roasting pan. Transfer the remaining stuffing to a lightly greased gratin dish and cover it with aluminum foil.

4 Roast the chicken, basting it every 15 minutes with the pan juices, for 1 to 1 ¼ hours or until the juices run clear when a thigh is pricked with a fork or a leg moves easily in its socket. Bake the extra stuffing for the last 30 minutes of cooking time. Let the chicken stand for 10 minutes, then carve it, discarding the skin. Serves 4.

PREPARATION TIME: 30 MIN. COOKING TIME: 1 HR.
STANDING TIME: 10 MIN.

Per serving: Calories 493; Saturated Fat 3 g; Total Fat 12 g; Protein 53 g; Carbohydrate 40 g; Fiber 8 g; Sodium 434 mg; Cholesterol 147 mg

Here is a winning combination for Sunday supper, Roast Chicken with Couscous and Red Pepper Stuffing. To complete the menu, add a salad of escarole, yellow squash, and tomatoes.

ROAST CHICKEN WITH ORANGE RICE STUFFING AND CITRUS SAUCE

This delectable combination of brown rice, pecans, and orange juice is more nutritious than packaged stuffings, and it tastes great. The stuffing is also good with turkey, but remember to double or triple the recipe, depending on the size of the bird.

2 cups cooked brown rice	¼ teaspoon salt
¼ cup coarsely chopped pecans, walnuts, or pine nuts (1 ounce)	1 tablespoon lemon juice
3 tablespoons minced parsley	**For the citrus sauce:**
	1 cup orange juice
2 tablespoons orange juice	2 tablespoons honey
	1 tablespoon lemon juice
½ teaspoon grated lemon rind	1 tablespoon cornstarch mixed with 3 tablespoons water
1 small roasting chicken or whole broiler-fryer (3 pounds)	

1 Preheat the oven to 400° F. In a medium-size bowl, combine the rice, pecans, parsley, orange juice, and lemon rind. Sprinkle the inside of the chicken with the salt and lemon juice. Stuff the breast cavity with the rice mixture and truss the chicken (see Tip, at right). Place the chicken on a rack in a roasting pan and roast for 55 minutes or until the juices run clear when a thigh is pricked with a fork and a leg moves easily in its socket.

2 When the chicken is done, transfer to a platter, cover to keep warm, and let stand for 10 minutes. Meanwhile, prepare the sauce. In a small saucepan, combine the orange juice, honey, and lemon juice and bring to a boil over moderate heat, stirring constantly. Whisk the cornstarch-water mixture briefly, then add it to the saucepan and bring the mixture to a boil. Boil the sauce for 1 minute, stirring constantly. Carve the chicken, discarding the skin, and serve with the sauce, rice stuffing, and steamed broccoli. Serves 4.

PREPARATION TIME: 15 MIN. COOKING TIME: 55 MIN.
STANDING TIME: 10 MIN.

Per serving: Calories 472; Saturated Fat 2 g; Total Fat 12 g; Protein 47 g; Carbohydrate 42 g; Fiber 3 g; Sodium 297 mg; Cholesterol 143 mg

CHICKEN STEAMED IN SPICED BROTH

You can drink the aromatic broth of this succulent chicken like a soup or serve it as a light sauce.

1 whole broiler-fryer (2½ to 3 pounds)	1 cinnamon stick, split lengthwise
¼ teaspoon salt	½ teaspoon each ground cumin and coriander
1 lemon, rind pricked all over with a fork	⅛ teaspoon each ground cardamom, ginger, and red pepper (cayenne)
2 cloves garlic, crushed	
3 cups Chicken Stock (page 62) or low-sodium chicken broth	

1 Rub the chicken cavity with the salt. Place the lemon and garlic inside the cavity and truss the chicken (see Tip, at right).

2 In a Dutch oven large enough to hold a rack or colander, bring the stock, cinnamon stick, cumin, coriander, cardamom, ginger, and red pepper to a boil. Place a rack in the Dutch oven, set the chicken on top, cover, and simmer over low heat for 1 hour. Transfer the chicken to a cutting board, remove and discard the skin, and cut into serving pieces. Serve with couscous or barley and Broiled Mixed Vegetables (page 242). Serves 4.

PREPARATION TIME: 7 MIN. COOKING TIME: 1 HR.

Per serving: Calories 248; Saturated Fat 2 g; Total Fat 6 g; Protein 44 g; Carbohydrate 1 g; Fiber 0 g; Sodium 307 mg; Cholesterol 143 mg

Trussing **a chicken** before roasting keeps the shape more compact and ensures even cooking.

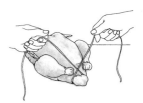

1. Place the bird on its back, leg tips facing you. Center a 3- to 4-foot length of white string under the tail. Cross the string over the top of the tail and bring it around the legs. Cross it over again and pull the legs tightly together.

2. Bring the string under the tip of the breastbone and back toward the wings.

3. Turn the bird over onto its breast. Bring the string up and over the wings, pulling them snugly against the body. Tie a knot, leaving no slack.

Before poultry is cooked, it's a good idea to rinse and pat it dry with paper toweling. Drying is necessary because spices adhere better to a dry surface and you want the spices on the bird, not in the pan. It is especially important to remove surface moisture if you are going to sauté poultry. Otherwise the meat will steam rather than brown.

Salmonella, a type of bacteria that causes food poisoning, is sometimes found in poultry. Heat kills the bacteria; just make sure that the meat is cooked until no longer pink. If you use a thermometer when roasting poultry, place it in the thickest part between the breast and a thigh and not touching the bone. Cook the bird to 180° F.

There is some danger of salmonella being transferred from raw poultry to your hands or a work surface and then onto other foods. If the newly contaminated food is one that is served uncooked, the bacteria will not be killed. After handling poultry, thoroughly wash your hands, the work surface, sink, and utensils with hot water and detergent.

CHICKEN IN SALSA MARINADE

Accompany this south-of-the border dish with Potato-Corn Patties (page 234). The patties require 1 to 12 hours of chilling before frying; the chicken 1 to 12 hours of marinating — a well-teamed make-ahead meal.

- 1 clove garlic, sliced
- ¼ cup fresh cilantro (coriander) leaves or ¼ cup parsley plus 2 teaspoons dried cilantro
- 1 green onion, including top, cut into 2-inch lengths
- ½ cup medium-hot salsa
- 1 tablespoon lime juice
- 1 tablespoon low-sodium ketchup
- ¼ cup water
- 1 broiler-fryer or small roasting chicken (2 ½ to 3 pounds), quartered and skinned
- 2 tablespoons minced fresh cilantro or parsley

1 In a food processor or blender, whirl the garlic, cilantro, green onion, salsa, lime juice, ketchup, and water for 30 seconds or until blended. Pour the mixture into a 1-gallon plastic food storage bag, add the chicken, and secure with a twist tie, pushing out all the air. Or arrange the chicken in a large shallow dish, coat with the marinade, and cover with plastic food wrap. Let marinate in the refrigerator for at least 1 hour or up to 12 hours.

2 Preheat the oven to 400° F. Remove the chicken from the marinade and place in a foil-lined broiler pan. Bake for 15 minutes, then spoon the marinade over the chicken. Bake 15 minutes more or until the juices run clear when the chicken is pricked with a fork. Garnish with minced cilantro. Serve hot or warm. Serves 4.

PREPARATION TIME: 15 MIN. COOKING TIME: 30 MIN.
MARINATING TIME: 1 HR.

Per serving: Calories 218; Saturated Fat 1 g; Total Fat 6 g; Protein 37 g; Carbohydrate 3 g; Fiber 0 g; Sodium 266 mg; Cholesterol 119 mg

CHICKEN POACHED WITH FENNEL, TURNIPS, AND CARROTS

- 1 broiler-fryer (2 ½ to 3 pounds), skinned and cut into 8 serving pieces
- 1 small yellow onion, peeled and stuck with 3 whole cloves
- 1 medium-size stalk celery with leaves, thinly sliced (¾ cup)
- 1 fennel bulb or celery heart (8 ounces), trimmed and quartered
- ½ teaspoon dried thyme, crumbled
- ¼ teaspoon each salt and black pepper
- 1 bay leaf
- 3 cups Chicken Stock (page 62) or low-sodium chicken broth
- 2 medium-size turnips, peeled and quartered
- 2 small carrots, peeled and cut into 2-inch lengths
- 1 large leek (6 ounces), including green top, halved lengthwise and rinsed thoroughly

1 Place the chicken legs and thighs, the onion, celery, and fennel in a 5-quart Dutch oven. Sprinkle with the thyme, salt, and pepper. Add the bay leaf and stock and, if necessary, enough water to just cover the chicken. Bring the liquid to a boil over high heat, then lower the heat, cover, and simmer for 20 minutes.

2 Add the remaining chicken pieces, the turnips, carrots, and leek to the Dutch oven and simmer, covered, over moderate heat for 15 minutes or until the juices run clear when the chicken is pricked with a fork and the vegetables are tender.

3 Arrange the chicken in a shallow serving dish surrounded by the fennel, turnips, carrots, and leek. Cover with aluminum foil and keep warm. Meanwhile, skim any fat from the stock. Remove the onion and bay leaf and discard. Over high heat, boil the stock for 5 minutes or until reduced to 1 cup; pour it over the chicken and vegetables. Serve with a green salad and whole-grain rolls. Serves 4.

PREPARATION TIME: 20 MIN. COOKING TIME: 40 MIN.

Per serving: Calories 317; Saturated Fat 1 g; Total Fat 6 g; Protein 41 g; Carbohydrate 24 g; Fiber 6 g; Sodium 487 mg; Cholesterol 119 mg

RASPBERRY CHICKEN

Raspberry vinegar gives this dish a special taste and aroma. If it is unavailable, you can make your own (see recipe, page 288) or substitute balsamic vinegar, which lends a very good but somewhat different flavor.

- 1 **broiler-fryer (2½ pounds), skinned and cut into serving pieces**
- ¼ **teaspoon each salt and black pepper**
- 1 **tablespoon olive oil**
- 1 **medium-size yellow onion, finely chopped (1 cup)**
- 1 **medium-size stalk celery, diced (½ cup)**
- 1 **medium-size carrot, peeled and diced (¾ cup)**
- 6 **cloves garlic, peeled**
- ¼ **cup raspberry or balsamic vinegar**
- 1 **cup Chicken Stock (page 62) or low-sodium chicken broth**
- 1 **can (14½ ounces) low-sodium tomatoes, drained and chopped**
- 1 **tablespoon tomato paste**
- ½ **teaspoon each dried rosemary and basil, crumbled**

1 Sprinkle the chicken with ⅛ teaspoon each of the salt and pepper. In a 12-inch nonstick skillet, heat the oil over moderate heat. Add the chicken and sauté for 2 minutes on each side or until lightly browned. Transfer the chicken to a 5-quart Dutch oven.

2 Add the onion, celery, carrot, garlic, and remaining ⅛ teaspoon each of the salt and pepper to the skillet and sauté over moderate heat, stirring occasionally, for 5 minutes or until the onion is softened. Add the vinegar and cook, stirring, 1 minute longer.

3 Transfer the onion mixture to the Dutch oven and stir in the stock, tomatoes, tomato paste, rosemary, and basil. Bring the liquid to a boil over high heat. Lower the heat and simmer, covered, for 10 minutes or until the breast meat is tender and no longer pink inside. Remove the breast pieces to a serving platter and cover to keep warm. Cook the remaining chicken 20 minutes more or until the juices run clear when the meat is pricked with a fork. Transfer chicken to the serving platter.

4 Skim any fat from the surface of the sauce. Cook the sauce over moderately high heat for 2 to 3 minutes or until slightly thickened, then pour it over the chicken. Serve with orzo and steamed summer squash. Serves 4.

PREPARATION TIME: 20 MIN. COOKING TIME: 40 MIN.

Per serving: Calories 291; Saturated Fat 2 g; Total Fat 9 g; Protein 39 g; Carbohydrate 13 g; Fiber 2 g; Sodium 365 mg; Cholesterol 119 mg

Chicken Poached with Fennel, Turnips, and Carrots is just the comforting dish to serve on a blustery day.

Chickens are sold by weight. Generally speaking, young birds are more tender and the best choice for roasting, frying, poaching, and barbecuing. Older, tougher birds are more flavorful and better suited to stewing or preparing soups. When selecting a whole bird, look for a plump breast and blemish-free skin. The skin color will vary from white to yellow, depending on what the chicken has been fed. It does not indicate quality. The meatiest chickens with the best appearance often bear a USDA Grade A stamp.

Roasting Chicken: A young, plump chicken, 4 to 8 pounds.

Capon: A neutered male chicken, 6 to 8 pounds, that has a higher proportion of breast meat than other birds. It makes an excellent roasting chicken.

Broiler-Fryer: An all-purpose chicken weighing 2 to 4 pounds. You can broil, fry, or poach this chicken with excellent results.

Hen: A mature bird, 2½ to 8 pounds, that is very flavorful. Hens must be cooked slowly for at least 2 to 3 hours to make them tender.

COQ AU VIN WITH BALSAMIC VINEGAR

Balsamic vinegar gives a zesty new twist to a classic French dish. Serve it with rice, pasta, or potatoes.

- 1 slice thick-cut bacon (2 ounces)
- 1 broiler-fryer (2½ to 3 pounds), skinned and cut into serving-size pieces
- ¼ teaspoon each salt and black pepper, or to taste
- 1 package (10 ounces) frozen pearl onions
- 8 ounces small mushrooms, quartered
- ¼ cup balsamic vinegar
- ½ cup dry red wine
- 1½ cups Chicken Stock (page 62) or low-sodium chicken broth
- 1 can (14½ ounces) low-sodium tomatoes, drained and chopped
- 1 teaspoon each dried rosemary and thyme, crumbled
- 1 tablespoon arrowroot or cornstarch mixed with 2 tablespoons water
- 2 tablespoons minced fresh tarragon or parsley

1 In a 12-inch nonstick skillet, cook the bacon over moderate heat for 2 minutes or until crisp. Transfer the bacon to paper toweling to drain, then crumble it and set aside. Pour off all but 1 tablespoon of the fat from the skillet and discard. Sprinkle the chicken with ⅛ teaspoon each of the salt and pepper. Set the skillet over moderate heat and, when the bacon fat is hot, add the chicken and sauté for 2 minutes on each side or until lightly browned. Transfer the chicken to a 5-quart Dutch oven.

2 Add the onions, mushrooms, and remaining ⅛ teaspoon each of the salt and pepper to the skillet and sauté over moderate heat, stirring occasionally, for 5 minutes. Transfer the vegetables to a bowl. Add the vinegar and wine to the skillet and bring to a boil over moderately high heat. Boil the mixture, stirring, for 1 minute, then add it to the Dutch oven with the chicken.

3 Add the stock, tomatoes, rosemary, and thyme to the Dutch oven; bring to a boil. Cover and simmer over low heat for 15 minutes or until the breast meat is no longer pink inside. Transfer the breast pieces to a plate; add the onions and mushrooms to the Dutch oven. Cover and simmer 8 to 10 minutes more or until the onions are tender and the juices run clear when a thigh is pricked with a fork.

Coq au Vin with Balsamic Vinegar is steeped in a flavorful sauce that renders the chicken moist and tender.

4 Return the breast pieces to the Dutch oven and bring the liquid to a boil. Stir in the arrowroot mixture and simmer over low heat for 2 to 3 minutes or until the sauce has thickened. Sprinkle with the tarragon. Serves 4.

PREPARATION TIME: 15 MIN.   COOKING TIME: 40 MIN.

Per serving: Calories 380; Saturated Fat 4 g; Total Fat 13 g; Protein 45 g; Carbohydrate 16 g; Fiber 3 g; Sodium 578 mg; Cholesterol 131 mg

DEVILED OVEN-FRIED CHICKEN

Use a food processor to grind the matzohs or crackers into crumbs, or crush them in a towel with a rolling pin.

⅔ cup buttermilk
2 teaspoons Dijon mustard
1 clove garlic, minced
⅛ teaspoon ground red pepper (cayenne)
2 pounds chicken leg quarters, skinned and separated into drumsticks and thighs

⅔ cup whole-wheat matzoh crumbs or cracker crumbs
2 tablespoons grated Parmesan cheese
¼ teaspoon each dried sage and rosemary, crumbled
1 tablespoon unsalted butter
1 tablespoon olive oil

1 In a large bowl, combine the buttermilk, mustard, garlic, and red pepper. Add the chicken pieces, cover, and let them marinate in the refrigerator for at least 30 minutes or as long as overnight.

2 Preheat the oven to 375° F. In a shallow bowl, combine the crumbs, cheese, sage, and rosemary. In a small saucepan, melt the butter and stir in the oil. Dredge the chicken pieces in the crumb mixture. Place them on a rack in a baking pan and drizzle with the butter and oil. Bake for 40 to 45 minutes or until the juices run clear when the chicken is pricked with a fork. If desired, run under the broiler for 1 or 2 minutes or until golden. Serve with Sautéed Summer Squash (page 239). Serves 4.

PREPARATION TIME: 18 MIN. COOKING TIME: 42 MIN.
MARINATING TIME: 30 MIN.

*Per serving: Calories 321; Saturated Fat 4 g;
Total Fat 14 g; Protein 32 g; Carbohydrate 15 g;
Fiber 0 g; Sodium 253 mg; Cholesterol 121 mg*

CHICKEN, GREENS, AND SWEET POTATO STEW

¼ cup all-purpose flour
2 tablespoons cornmeal
1 broiler-fryer (2½ to 3 pounds), skinned and cut into 8 serving pieces
2 tablespoons olive or corn oil
2 cups Chicken Stock (page 62) or low-sodium chicken broth

3 medium-size sweet potatoes (1 pound), peeled and cut into 1-inch cubes
6 cloves garlic, slivered
2 tablespoons slivered fresh ginger
1 pound kale, spinach, or mustard or collard greens, rinsed, stems removed, and torn into bite-size pieces

1 On a sheet of wax paper, combine the flour and cornmeal. Dredge the chicken in the mixture, shaking off any excess. In a 5-quart Dutch oven, heat the oil over moderately high heat. Add the chicken and sauté for about 3 minutes on each side or until golden brown.

2 Add the stock, potatoes, garlic, and ginger and bring to a boil. Lower the heat and simmer, covered, for 20 minutes. Place the kale on top of the chicken and potatoes, cover, and cook 5 minutes longer or until the kale is tender and the chicken is cooked through. Serve with Herbed Buttermilk Biscuits (page 291). Serves 4.

PREPARATION TIME: 20 MIN. COOKING TIME: 31 MIN.

*Per serving: Calories 464; Saturated Fat 2 g;
Total Fat 13 g; Protein 44 g; Carbohydrate 43 g;
Fiber 7 g; Sodium 301 mg; Cholesterol 119 mg*

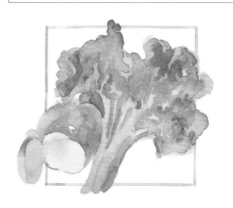

**It is crispy, crunchy, tasty, and low in fat too —
Chicken with Sage Corn-Bread Crust.**

CHICKEN MOLE WITH ALMONDS AND RAISINS

This recipe is a mild version of the traditional Mexican sauce (pronounced mō-lā or mō-lē). For a spicier dish, increase the chili powder to 1 ½ teaspoons.

1 teaspoon olive or canola oil

2 green onions, including tops, finely chopped (¼ cup)

1 clove garlic, minced

1 teaspoon each unsweetened cocoa powder and chili powder

½ teaspoon ground cumin

¼ teaspoon salt

1 can (8 ounces) low-sodium tomato sauce

1 tablespoon raisins

1 tablespoon slivered almonds or hulled pumpkin seeds

¼ cup water

2 tablespoons minced fresh cilantro (coriander) or 2 tablespoons minced parsley plus 1 teaspoon dried cilantro

4 skinned and boned chicken thighs (4 ounces each)

1 Preheat the oven to 400° F. Line a 13″ x 9″ x 2″ baking pan with aluminum foil. In a 10-inch nonstick skillet, heat the oil over moderate heat. Add the green onions and garlic and sauté for 2 minutes. Stir in the cocoa powder, chili powder, cumin, and salt and cook for 1 minute.

2 Stir in the tomato sauce, raisins, and almonds. Lower the heat and simmer, uncovered, for 8 minutes or until the flavors have blended and the sauce has thickened slightly. Transfer the mixture to a food processor or blender, add the water and cilantro, and whirl for 30 seconds or until smooth.

3 Place the chicken in the baking pan and bake for 10 minutes. Spoon about 2 tablespoons sauce over each piece of chicken and bake 10 minutes more or until the juices run clear when a thigh is pricked with a fork. Pass the remaining sauce on the side. Serve with rice and a salad of mixed greens. Serves 4

PREPARATION TIME: 15 MIN. COOKING TIME: 31 MIN.

Per serving: Calories 191; Saturated Fat 1 g; Total Fat 7 g; Protein 25 g; Carbohydrate 8 g; Fiber 2 g; Sodium 255 mg; Cholesterol 91 mg

CHICKEN WITH SAGE CORN-BREAD CRUST

Though a chicken thigh looks small, the meat is rich and satisfying, and a 4-ounce boneless portion is sufficient. This recipe is best when prepared with unsweetened corn bread. You can make the crumbs in the food processor.

- 4 skinned and boned chicken thighs (4 ounces each)
- ⅛ teaspoon each salt and black pepper
- 1 tablespoon plus 1 teaspoon Dijon mustard
- 1 teaspoon olive oil
- ⅔ cup fine corn bread crumbs or fresh bread crumbs
- 1 tablespoon minced fresh sage, thyme, or rosemary or 1 teaspoon dried sage, thyme, or rosemary, crumbled

1 Preheat the oven to 400° F. Sprinkle the chicken with the salt and pepper and arrange it on a rack in a baking pan. Bake for 20 to 25 minutes or until the juices run clear when the chicken is pricked with a fork. Meanwhile, in a small bowl, combine the mustard and oil. In another small bowl, combine the crumbs and sage.

2 Preheat the broiler, setting the rack 6 inches from the heat. Brush the chicken with half of the mustard mixture and sprinkle with half of the crumbs, then transfer the baking pan to the broiler. Broil the chicken for 1 minute or until golden brown. Turn the chicken, coat it with the remaining mustard and crumbs, and broil 1 minute more or until golden brown. Serve with corn on the cob and steamed green beans or broiled tomatoes. Serves 4.

PREPARATION TIME: 10 MIN. COOKING TIME: 25 MIN.

Per serving: Calories 178; Saturated Fat 1 g; Total Fat 7 g; Protein 24 g; Carbohydrate 4 g; Fiber 0 g; Sodium 264 mg; Cholesterol 91 mg

CHICKEN AND CHILI

Chicken thighs were used in this recipe because dark meat is juicier than white and is less likely to dry out. If you prefer breasts, cook them for only 10 minutes after browning. Corn bread or baked corn chips would be a nice accompaniment. Round out the meal with a watercress salad.

- 4 skinned and boned chicken thighs (4 ounces each)
- 3 tablespoons all-purpose flour
- 1 tablespoon olive oil
- 1 large yellow onion, finely chopped (1 ½ cups)
- 3 cloves garlic, minced
- ¼ cup water
- 2½ tablespoons chili powder
- ¾ teaspoon ground cumin
- ½ teaspoon dried oregano, crumbled
- 1 can (14½ ounces) low-sodium tomatoes, chopped, with their juice
- 1 cup cooked red kidney beans
- 1 tablespoon lime juice

1 Dredge the chicken in the flour, shaking off any excess. In a large heavy saucepan or 4-quart Dutch oven, heat the oil over moderately high heat. Add the chicken and sauté for about 3 minutes on each side or until golden brown. Transfer the chicken to a bowl.

2 Reduce the heat to low, add the onion and garlic, and cook, stirring frequently, for 5 minutes. Add the water, then cook, uncovered, stirring occasionally, for 5 minutes or until the onion is tender. Stir in the chili powder, cumin, and oregano; cook for 1 minute.

3 Stir in the tomatoes, beans, and chicken and bring to a boil over moderate heat. Lower the heat, cover, and simmer for 20 minutes or until the juices run clear when the chicken is pricked with a fork. Stir in the lime juice. Serves 4.

PREPARATION TIME: 12 MIN. COOKING TIME: 40 MIN.

Per serving: Calories 241; Saturated Fat 1 g; Total Fat 7 g; Protein 20 g; Carbohydrate 26 g; Fiber 6 g; Sodium 331 mg; Cholesterol 54 mg

EASY PARTY MENU
Minted Spinach Dip
(page 309)
Crudités
Chicken and Chili
Watercress with Creamy Tomato Vinaigrette
(page 266)
Apricot-Buttermilk Sherbet
(page 333)
Double Ginger Cookies
(page 339)

Pepper, once the prized fare of royalty and literally worth its weight in gold, is today probably the world's most popular spice. It comes from the fruit of the *piper nigrum*, a vine native to India. The plant yields berrylike fruits that we know as black, white, or green peppercorns. To obtain black peppercorns, the fruit is picked when green, then fermented and dried in the sun until either dark brown or black. For white peppercorns, the fruit is picked ripe, the husk is removed, and the berry dried until white. It is preferred for light-colored sauces and foods. If pepper is picked before it is mature and freeze-dried or packed in brine or vinegar, green peppercorns are the result. Their taste is milder than that of either black or white pepper.

Black and white peppercorns will retain their flavor for a fairly long time if stored in a cool, dark place. Once opened, green peppercorns should be refrigerated.

Since ground pepper loses its aroma and freshness quickly, a pepper mill is a useful addition to any kitchen. The best are those with metal mechanisms.

PEPPER CHICKEN WITH MUSTARD SAUCE

2 teaspoons crushed black peppercorns or a combination of black and green peppercorns
2 whole skinned and boned chicken breasts (1 pound), halved
2 teaspoons olive oil
¼ teaspoon salt
¼ cup dry white wine or water
2 shallots, finely chopped (¼ cup)

1 cup Chicken Stock (page 62) or low-sodium chicken broth
⅓ cup reduced-fat sour cream mixed with 2 teaspoons cornstarch
2 teaspoons honey mustard or Dijon mustard, or to taste
Snipped fresh chives (optional garnish)

1 Preheat the oven to 425° F. Lightly grease a shallow baking dish large enough to hold the chicken. Press the crushed peppercorns into the chicken and sprinkle with the oil and salt. Arrange the chicken in the baking dish and bake for 15 to 20 minutes or until the juices run clear when the chicken is pricked with a fork.

2 Meanwhile, in a small saucepan, boil the wine and shallots, uncovered, over moderately high heat for 2 minutes or until the wine is reduced to 2 tablespoons. Add the stock and boil 2 minutes more or until the liquid is reduced to 1 cup. Reduce the heat to low and add the sour cream, whisking for 1 minute. Stir in the mustard.

3 On a cutting board, cut each breast diagonally into ¼-inch slices and arrange on 4 dinner plates. Spoon the sauce over the breasts and garnish with chives if desired. Serve with boiled new potatoes and broccoli purée. Serves 4.

PREPARATION TIME: 10 MIN. COOKING TIME: 20 MIN.

Per serving: Calories 206; Saturated Fat 3 g; Total Fat 7 g; Protein 28 g; Carbohydrate 4 g; Fiber 0 g; Sodium 304 mg; Cholesterol 66 mg

ORANGE-GINGER CHICKEN BREASTS

Orange and ginger combine beautifully with chicken. You can marinate the breasts for as little as 4 hours, but they absorb more flavor if you let them marinate overnight.

⅓ cup orange juice
2 cloves garlic, minced
1 tablespoon reduced-sodium soy sauce
1 tablespoon brown sugar
1 tablespoon rice vinegar or cider vinegar
1 tablespoon minced fresh ginger or 1 teaspoon ground ginger

2 teaspoons Dijon mustard
1 teaspoon grated orange rind
⅛ teaspoon red pepper flakes
2 whole skinned and boned chicken breasts (1 pound), halved

1 In a shallow baking dish, combine the orange juice, garlic, soy sauce, sugar, vinegar, ginger, mustard, orange rind, and red pepper flakes. Add the chicken, turning to coat, cover with plastic food wrap, and marinate in the refrigerator for at least 4 hours or overnight.

2 Preheat the broiler, setting the rack 7 inches from the heat. Arrange the chicken on a broiler pan and broil for 4 to 5 minutes. Turn and broil 4 to 5 minutes more or until the juices run clear when the flesh is pricked with a fork.

3 Transfer the chicken to a serving dish and brush with the pan juices. Serve with rice or couscous and steamed carrots. Serves 4.

PREPARATION TIME: 10 MIN. COOKING TIME: 10 MIN.
MARINATING TIME: 4 HR.

Per serving: Calories 154; Saturated Fat 0 g; Total Fat 2 g; Protein 27 g; Carbohydrate 7 g; Fiber 0 g; Sodium 230 mg; Cholesterol 66 mg

CHICKEN BREASTS STUFFED WITH HAM AND MUSHROOMS

For the stuffing:

- 1 tablespoon unsalted butter or margarine
- 2 shallots, finely chopped (¼ cup)
- 4 mushrooms, finely chopped
- 2 slices smoked ham, such as Black Forest or Westphalian, or prosciutto (1 ounce), finely chopped
- 2 tablespoons dry bread crumbs
- 1 tablespoon grated Parmesan cheese
- 2 tablespoons snipped fresh chives or minced parsley
- 2 whole chicken breasts (2 pounds), halved
- ¼ teaspoon each salt and black pepper

1 To prepare the stuffing: In an 8-inch nonstick skillet, melt the butter over moderate heat. Add the shallots and sauté, stirring constantly, for 1 minute. Add the mushrooms and sauté, stirring, for 2 minutes or until softened. Transfer the mixture to a bowl and add the ham, bread crumbs, cheese, and chives. Mix well, then let cool to room temperature.

2 Preheat the broiler, setting the rack 7 inches from the heat. Using a sharp knife, cut a pocket in the thickest part of each chicken breast (the breastbone side). It should be cut into the meat, parallel to the rib bones, not between the meat and bones, and should be large enough to hold 2 tablespoons of stuffing. Fill each pocket with the stuffing and close the opening with a toothpick. Arrange the breasts, skin side up, on a lightly greased broiler pan and sprinkle them with the salt and pepper.

3 Broil for 4 to 5 minutes or until lightly browned. Turn the breasts over and broil 4 to 5 minutes more or until the juices run clear when the flesh is pricked with a fork. Transfer the breasts to a cutting board, remove the skin and bones, and cut diagonally into slices. Serve with Sautéed Leeks, Potatoes, and Cabbage (page 234). Serves 4.

PREPARATION TIME: 20 MIN. COOKING TIME: 12 MIN.

Per serving: Calories 251; Saturated Fat 3 g; Total Fat 6 g; Protein 42 g; Carbohydrate 5 g; Fiber 0 g; Sodium 378 mg; Cholesterol 110 mg

Pepper Chicken with Mustard Sauce — only the taste is rich. The creamy sauce, capturing the best of both worlds, is low in fat and calories but high in flavor.

Warm Chicken Salad with Walnuts and Blue Cheese Dressing is a winning combination that can be served as a light supper or when guests come for lunch.

POACHED CHICKEN WITH AVOCADO SAUCE

This elegant dish, which is served cold, is ideal for summer entertaining. If you like, you can poach the chicken as much as 3 days ahead, then whip up the sauce at the last minute.

1 small yellow onion, halved	¼ cup plain low-fat yogurt
2 bay leaves	2 tablespoons snipped fresh chives
8 black peppercorns	1 tablespoon lemon juice
¼ teaspoon salt	⅛ teaspoon salt, or to taste
2 whole skinned and boned chicken breasts (1 pound), halved	¼ teaspoon hot red pepper sauce, or to taste

For the sauce:

1 avocado (14 ounces), peeled, pitted, and diced (1 cup)

Snipped fresh chives (optional garnish)

1 Place the onion, bay leaves, peppercorns, and salt in a 12-inch skillet, add 2 inches of water, and bring just to a simmer. Add the chicken, cover, and cook over low heat for 8 to 10 minutes or until the juices run clear when a breast is pricked with a fork. Set aside 2 tablespoons of the poaching water for the sauce. Transfer the chicken to a bowl, add enough of the poaching water to cover, and let cool to room temperature. Cover with plastic food wrap and refrigerate until ready to serve.

2 Just before serving, prepare the avocado sauce. In a food processor or blender, whirl the avocado, yogurt, chives, reserved poaching water, lemon juice, salt, and red pepper sauce for 30 seconds or until smooth. Serve the chicken breasts whole or sliced with 2 tablespoons of the avocado sauce spooned over each serving. Garnish with the chives if desired. Pass the remaining sauce on the side. Serve with Confetti Rice Salad (page 253) and French baguettes. Serves 4.

PREPARATION TIME: 15 MIN. COOKING TIME: 15 MIN.

Per serving: Calories 212; Saturated Fat 2 g; Total Fat 9 g; Protein 28 g; Carbohydrate 4 g; Fiber 2 g; Sodium 228 mg; Cholesterol 67 mg

WARM CHICKEN SALAD WITH WALNUTS AND BLUE CHEESE DRESSING

Here is an inviting supper for a warm summer evening.

- 2 whole skinned and boned chicken breasts (1 pound), halved
- ¼ teaspoon each salt and black pepper
- 5 cups mixed lettuce, such as watercress, arugula, Boston, or bibb
- 1 medium-size cucumber, peeled, halved lengthwise, and thinly sliced (1 cup)
- 1 medium-size tomato, diced (1 cup)
- 2 green onions, including tops, finely chopped (¼ cup)
- 1 tablespoon plus 1 teaspoon chopped walnuts

For the dressing:
- ⅓ cup crumbled blue cheese, such as Roquefort (1 ½ ounces)
- 1 tablespoon reduced-calorie mayonnaise
- 3 tablespoons skim milk
- 2 teaspoons white wine vinegar
- 1 teaspoon walnut oil or vegetable oil

1 Preheat the broiler, setting the rack 7 inches from the heat. Arrange the chicken on a broiler pan, sprinkle with the salt and pepper, and broil for 4 to 5 minutes. Turn and broil 4 to 5 minutes more or until the juices run clear when the chicken is pricked with a fork.

2 Meanwhile, in a large salad bowl, combine the greens, cucumber, tomato, and green onions. In a blender or food processor, whirl all the dressing ingredients for 30 seconds or until smooth.

3 Cut the chicken into bite-size pieces and add it to the salad bowl. Pour the dressing over all and toss lightly. Divide the salad among 4 salad plates and sprinkle with the nuts. Serve with crusty French bread. Serves 4.

PREPARATION TIME: 20 MIN. COOKING TIME: 10 MIN.

Per serving: Calories 228; Saturated Fat 3 g; Total Fat 8 g; Protein 31 g; Carbohydrate 7 g; Fiber 2 g; Sodium 371 mg; Cholesterol 75 mg

CHICKEN AND RICE SKILLET

Here is a quick and nourishing one-dish meal. If using chicken thighs, double the cooking time in Step 1.

- 1 pound skinned and boned chicken breasts or thighs, cut into strips ½ inch wide
- ½ teaspoon each salt and black pepper
- 1 tablespoon olive oil
- 8 ounces sweet or spicy Italian sausage or chorizo, sliced ¼ inch thick (optional)
- 1 medium-size yellow onion, finely chopped (1 cup)
- 1 medium-size sweet red pepper, cored, seeded, and cut into strips ¼ inch wide
- 2 cloves garlic, minced
- 1 cup long-grain white rice
- 2 cups Chicken Stock (page 62) or low-sodium chicken broth
- 3 plum tomatoes, chopped (1 cup)
- 1 teaspoon each ground cumin and dried thyme, crumbled
- 1 cup frozen peas, thawed
- 8 black or green pitted olives, sliced (optional)

1 Sprinkle the chicken with ¼ teaspoon each of the salt and black pepper. In a 12-inch nonstick skillet, heat the oil over moderate heat. Add the chicken breasts and, if desired, the sausage and sauté, stirring frequently, for 5 minutes or until lightly browned. Transfer to a plate.

2 Add the onion and red pepper to the skillet, sprinkle with the remaining ¼ teaspoon each of salt and black pepper, and sauté, stirring, for 5 minutes or until softened. Add the garlic and rice and sauté, stirring, for 1 minute. Add the stock, tomatoes, cumin, and thyme and bring to a boil over high heat. Lower the heat and simmer, covered, for 15 minutes or until the rice is tender.

3 Add the peas, chicken, sausage, and olives, if using, to the skillet and mix well. Simmer for 5 minutes or until the peas are tender and the chicken and sausage are heated through. Serve with a green salad. Serves 4.

PREPARATION TIME: 20 MIN. COOKING TIME: 32 MIN.

Per serving: Calories 401; Saturated Fat 1 g; Total Fat 6 g; Protein 34 g; Carbohydrate 51 g; Fiber 4 g; Sodium 453 mg; Cholesterol 66 mg

SUMMER DINNER
Summer Squash Soup with Leeks
(page 76)

Poached Chicken with Avocado Sauce

Roasted Red Peppers

Herbed Buttermilk Biscuits
(page 291)

Frozen Yogurt Parfait
(page 333)

If **chicken cutlets are** not carried in your market, you can make them quickly and easily from skinned and boned chicken breasts. Using a sharp knife, cut a breast horizontally in half. Place each half between two pieces of wax paper and, with a meat mallet, small heavy skillet, or a rolling pin, pound or roll them to a thickness of ¼ inch.

SPICY CHICKEN CUTLETS

1 tablespoon each paprika and onion powder	4 chicken cutlets (4 ounces each)
¼ teaspoon garlic salt	1 tablespoon plus 1 teaspoon olive or canola oil
¼ teaspoon each dried oregano and basil, crumbled	1 can (8 ounces) low-sodium tomato sauce
⅛ teaspoon ground red pepper (cayenne), or to taste	1 teaspoon cider vinegar
	⅛ teaspoon salt, or to taste

1 On a sheet of wax paper, combine the paprika, onion powder, garlic salt, oregano, basil, and red pepper. Coat both sides of the cutlets with the mixture.

2 In a 12-inch nonstick skillet, heat the oil over moderately high heat. Add the cutlets and cook for 2 to 3 minutes or until lightly browned. Turn the cutlets over and cook 2 to 3 minutes more or until the juices run clear when the flesh is pricked with a fork. Transfer the cutlets to a serving platter and keep warm.

3 Add the tomato sauce, vinegar, and salt to the skillet and cook, stirring, for 2 minutes or until heated through. Pour the sauce over the cutlets. Serve with coleslaw or Baked Eggplant Slices (page 228) and corn-bread sticks. Serves 4.

PREPARATION TIME: 8 MIN. COOKING TIME: 7 MIN.

> *Per serving: Calories 197; Saturated Fat 1 g; Total Fat 6 g; Protein 28 g; Carbohydrate 7 g; Fiber 1 g; Sodium 286 mg; Cholesterol 66 mg*

•

Glazed Variation: Preheat the broiler, setting the rack 6 inches from the heat; cover a broiler pan with aluminum foil. In a small bowl, combine the spices, vinegar, and salt with the tomato sauce, omitting the paprika. Also omit the oil. Arrange the cutlets on the broiler pan and broil for 1 minute on each side. Brush the sauce on one side of each cutlet and broil 1 to 2 minutes more; coat the other side with the sauce and broil 1 to 2 minutes longer or until the juices run clear when the flesh is pricked with a fork. Serve with Spinach Fettuccine with Vegetables (page 191). *Per serving: Calories 161; Saturated Fat 1 g; Total Fat 2 g; Protein 28 g; Carbohydrate 7 g; Fiber 1 g; Sodium 286 mg; Cholesterol 66 mg*

CRISPY CHICKEN CUTLETS WITH LEMON-MUSHROOM SAUCE

Instant mashed potato flakes are the secret ingredient here. They are used to make the crispy crust and to thicken the sauce.

¼ cup instant mashed potato flakes (not granules)	**For the sauce:**
	⅔ cup Chicken Stock (page 62) or low-sodium chicken broth
¼ cup whole-wheat cracker crumbs	8 ounces mushrooms, sliced (2½ cups)
¼ teaspoon ground sage	2 tablespoons potato flakes
1 large egg white	2 tablespoons lemon juice
1 teaspoon lemon juice	
4 chicken cutlets (4 ounces each)	½ teaspoon minced garlic
2 tablespoons olive oil	⅛ teaspoon ground sage

1 On a sheet of wax paper, combine the potato flakes, cracker crumbs, and sage. In a 9-inch pie pan, beat the egg white and lemon juice with a fork until blended. One at a time, dip the cutlets first in the egg white, then in the crumb mixture; transfer to a sheet of wax paper.

2 In a 10-inch nonstick skillet, heat 1 tablespoon of the oil over moderately high heat. Add 2 of the cutlets and cook for 2 to 3 minutes or until lightly browned. Turn and cook 2 to 3 minutes more or until the juices run clear when the flesh is pricked with a fork. Transfer the cutlets to a serving platter, cover with aluminum foil, and keep warm. Repeat with the remaining 1 tablespoon of oil and cutlets.

3 To prepare the sauce: Add the stock, mushrooms, potato flakes, lemon juice, garlic, and sage to the skillet. Bring the liquid to a boil and cook over moderate heat, stirring frequently, for 5 minutes or until thickened. Pour the sauce over the cutlets. Serve with rice and steamed Brussels sprouts or green beans. Serves 4.

PREPARATION TIME: 13 MIN. COOKING TIME: 13 MIN.

> *Per serving: Calories 301; Saturated Fat 1 g; Total Fat 10 g; Protein 31 g; Carbohydrate 22 g; Fiber 1 g; Sodium 127 mg; Cholesterol 66 mg*

HERBED CHICKEN AND VEGETABLES IN PACKETS

For this easy recipe, you simply sprinkle the chicken and vegetables with herbs, wrap them in parchment paper or aluminum foil, and bake. There are no pots and pans to wash, and the wrapping keeps the chicken moist and succulent.

1 large carrot, peeled and cut into 2" x ¼" x ¼" strips (1 cup)

1 medium-size white turnip, peeled and cut into 2" x ¼" x ¼" strips (⅔ cup)

1 large parsnip (3 ounces), peeled and cut into 2" x ¼" x ¼" strips (⅔ cup)

1 tablespoon plus 1 teaspoon lemon juice

1 teaspoon olive oil

1 teaspoon sugar

½ teaspoon dried rosemary, crumbled

4 chicken cutlets (4 ounces each)

¼ cup snipped fresh dill

1 Preheat the oven to 400° F. In a medium-size bowl, toss together the carrot, turnip, parsnip, lemon juice, oil, sugar, and rosemary.

2 Cut 4 pieces of parchment paper or aluminum foil 12 by 14 inches. Place a chicken cutlet in the center of each piece of paper. Spread ¼ of the vegetable mixture on top of each cutlet and sprinkle with 1 tablespoon of the dill.

3 Roll the long sides of the paper or foil over the chicken and vegetables as if you were wrapping a package, then fold and seal the ends. Place the packets on a baking sheet and bake for 20 minutes. Place the packets on individual dinner plates and cut an X in the center of each to release the steam, being careful not to burn your fingers. When the steam has been released, peel back the paper to reveal the chicken and vegetables. Serve with rice, whole-wheat rolls, and Spinach Salad with Pears and Walnuts (page 259). Serves 4.

PREPARATION TIME: 16 MIN.   COOKING TIME: 20 MIN.

Per serving: Calories 176; Saturated Fat 1 g; Total Fat 3 g; Protein 27 g; Carbohydrate 10 g; Fiber 3 g; Sodium 99 mg; Cholesterol 66 mg

For fine down-home fare, try Spicy Chicken Cutlets, accompanied by Tricolored Coleslaw (page 256) and corn-bread sticks.

Broccoli rabe is steadily gaining favor in the United States under a handful of different names and spellings (*raab, broccoli rabe, broccoli rab, broccoli di rapa, broccoli di rape, rapini, Italian turnip,* and *turnip broccoli*). This vegetable can be used in recipes that call for broccoli and is particularly good in pasta and stir-fried dishes. Its flavor, a cross between that of broccoli and spinach, has a slightly robust bitter edge.

To prepare broccoli rabe, trim the ends of the stems, then use the entire vegetable, leaves and all.

STIR-FRIED CHICKEN WITH BROCCOLI RABE

- **4 large dried shiitake mushrooms (1 ounce)**
- **1 cup hot water**
- **3 teaspoons vegetable oil**
- **2 teaspoons minced fresh ginger**
- **2 teaspoons minced garlic**
- **1 pound skinned and boned chicken breasts, cut into 1-inch cubes**
- **2 green onions, including tops, finely chopped (¼ cup)**
- **8 ounces broccoli rabe, cut into 2-inch lengths**
- **1 tablespoon reduced-sodium soy sauce**
- **2 tablespoons rice wine, dry sherry, or water**
- **2 teaspoons cornstarch mixed with 1 tablespoon water**
- **1 tablespoon dark sesame oil**

1 Place the mushrooms in a shallow bowl, add the hot water, then weight down the mushrooms with a plate so that they remain submerged. Let soak for 20 minutes. Over a glass measuring cup drain the mushrooms through a sieve lined with paper toweling and reserve ½ cup of the soaking liquid. Slice the mushrooms, discarding the stems.

2 In a 12-inch nonstick skillet, heat 2 teaspoons of the vegetable oil over moderately high heat until hot but not smoking. Add the ginger and garlic and stir-fry for 30 seconds. Add the chicken and mushrooms and stir-fry for 2 minutes or until the chicken is no longer pink. Transfer the mixture to a plate.

3 Heat the remaining teaspoon of vegetable oil in the skillet. Add the green onions and stir-fry for 30 seconds, then add the broccoli rabe and stir-fry 1 minute more. Return the chicken and mushrooms to the skillet, then add the reserved soaking liquid, the soy sauce, and wine. Bring to a boil and cook, covered, for 1 minute.

4 Stir the cornstarch mixture, add it to the skillet, and cook, stirring, for 2 to 3 minutes or until the sauce is slightly thickened. Stir in the sesame oil. Serve with steamed rice. Serves 4.

PREPARATION TIME: 12 MIN.   COOKING TIME: 8 MIN.
SOAKING TIME: 20 MIN.

Per serving: Calories 240; Saturated Fat 1 g; Total Fat 9 g; Protein 29 g; Carbohydrate 11 g; Fiber 2 g; Sodium 212 mg; Cholesterol 66 mg

Stir-fried Chicken with Broccoli Rabe partners the slightly bitter Italian vegetable with tender, sweet chunks of chicken.

STIR-FRIED CHICKEN WITH SNOW PEAS AND BABY CORN

4 teaspoons reduced-sodium soy sauce
4 teaspoons dark sesame oil
1 tablespoon rice wine, dry sherry, or rice vinegar
1 pound skinned and boned chicken breasts, cut into 1-inch cubes
½ cup Chicken Stock (page 62) or low-sodium chicken broth mixed with 2 teaspoons cornstarch

1 tablespoon vegetable oil
1 tablespoon minced fresh ginger
1 tablespoon minced garlic
4 green onions, white part only, sliced (⅓ cup)
4 ounces snow peas, trimmed (1 cup)
1 can (14 ounces) baby corn, drained and rinsed

1 In a medium-size bowl, mix 2 teaspoons each of the soy sauce and sesame oil with the wine. Add the chicken and let marinate for 30 minutes. In a small bowl, combine the stock-cornstarch mixture with the remaining 2 teaspoons each of soy sauce and sesame oil.

2 In a 12-inch nonstick skillet, heat the vegetable oil over moderately high heat. Add the ginger, garlic, and green onions and stir-fry for 30 seconds. Add the chicken and stir-fry for about 2 minutes or until no longer pink on the outside. Add the snow peas and corn and stir-fry 2 minutes more.

3 Add the cornstarch-stock mixture to the skillet, lower the heat, and simmer, stirring, for 2 to 3 minutes or until the sauce is slightly thickened and the juices run clear when the chicken is pricked with a fork. Serves 4.

PREPARATION TIME: 20 MIN. COOKING TIME: 8 MIN.
MARINATING TIME: 30 MIN.

Per serving: Calories 302; Saturated Fat 2 g; Total Fat 11 g; Protein 31 g; Carbohydrate 23 g; Fiber 2 g; Sodium 536 mg; Cholesterol 66 mg

CHICKEN PRIMAVERA

You can make this stir-fried dish in minutes. To save even more time, prepare the vegetables while the chicken marinates.

¼ cup plain low-fat yogurt
½ teaspoon chopped garlic
¾ teaspoon dill weed
1 pound chicken cutlets, cut into strips ¼ inch wide
½ teaspoon cornstarch
¼ teaspoon salt

2 teaspoons olive or vegetable oil
1 small yellow onion, cut into ¾-inch cubes
2 small yellow summer squash or zucchini, cut into 2" x ¼" x ¼" strips
1½ cups sugar snap peas or snow peas, trimmed
1 cup cherry tomatoes

1 In a medium-size bowl, combine the yogurt, garlic, and ¼ teaspoon of the dill weed. Add the chicken and let marinate for 20 minutes.

2 Heat a 12-inch nonstick skillet over moderate heat. Add the chicken and marinade and cook, stirring, for 5 minutes or until the chicken is no longer pink.

3 Using a slotted spoon, transfer the chicken to a plate and keep warm. Spoon ¼ cup of the marinade into a small bowl; stir in the cornstarch and salt until dissolved. Wipe out the skillet, discarding any remaining marinade.

4 Add the oil to the skillet and heat over moderate heat. Add the onion, squash, and remaining ½ teaspoon of dill weed. Cover and cook, stirring occasionally, for 8 minutes or until the vegetables are crisp-tender. Add the sugar snap peas and tomatoes and cook 3 minutes more or until the peas are crisp-tender. Stir in the chicken and cornstarch mixture, bring the liquid to a boil, and cook for 1 minute or until the sauce has thickened and the chicken is heated through. Serve warm with steamed rice, or serve chilled as a main-dish salad, accompanied by Rosemary Dinner Rolls (page 304). Serves 4.

PREPARATION TIME: 15 MIN. COOKING TIME: 18 MIN.
MARINATING TIME: 20 MIN.

Per serving: Calories 206; Saturated Fat 1 g; Total Fat 4 g; Protein 30 g; Carbohydrate 11 g; Fiber 3 g; Sodium 225 mg; Cholesterol 67 mg

S tir-frying is a quick method of cooking that preserves nutrients and fresh color. For best results, all ingredients should be cut into uniform, preferably bite-size, pieces. For the cooking, a wok or a heavy skillet is suitable, but in either case, the oil should be heated until very hot but not smoking before adding the other ingredients.

The technique is to stir the food quickly and constantly, until it is cooked on all sides and is the desired degree of doneness. As a rule, foods are added to the wok in a certain order. Such flavoring ingredients as garlic and ginger go in first, then the items that take the longest to cook; quickly cooked foods are added last.

Two favorite Thanksgiving foods are rolled into one in Turkey, Spinach, and Mashed Potato Roll.

CHICKEN BURGERS WITH MUSHROOMS, BARLEY, AND PEPPER

Barley adds moisture to these flavorful burgers and extends the chicken, yielding man-sized portions with just 12 ounces of poultry.

1 clove garlic, minced	½ teaspoon ground marjoram or poultry seasoning
3 green onions, including tops, finely chopped (⅓ cup)	¼ teaspoon black pepper
1 small sweet red or yellow pepper, cored, seeded, and finely chopped (½ cup)	2 teaspoons reduced-sodium soy sauce
	12 ounces ground chicken or turkey
4 ounces mushrooms, finely chopped (1 ½ cups)	1 cup cooked pearl barley
¼ teaspoon salt	¼ cup fine dry bread crumbs
	2 teaspoons olive or canola oil

1 In a 12-inch nonstick skillet, cook the garlic, green onions, red pepper, mushrooms, salt, and marjoram over moderate heat for 6 minutes or until the vegetables are tender and most of the liquid has evaporated.

2 Transfer the mixture to a large bowl. Add the black pepper, soy sauce, chicken, barley, and bread crumbs and mix well. Using moistened hands, shape the mixture into 4 patties, 4 inches in diameter. The mixture will be moist. Place the patties on 4 small squares of wax paper.

3 Heat the oil in the skillet over moderate heat. Add the patties to the skillet, using the wax paper to lift and invert them, and cook for 3 to 4 minutes or until lightly browned. Turn and cook 3 to 4 minutes more or until golden brown and the juices run clear when a patty is pricked with a fork. Serve on toasted whole-wheat English muffins and top with lettuce and tomatoes. Serves 4.

PREPARATION TIME: 20 MIN. COOKING TIME: 12 MIN.

Per serving: Calories 200; Saturated Fat 1 g; Total Fat 4 g; Protein 22 g; Carbohydrate 18 g; Fiber 3 g; Sodium 318 mg; Cholesterol 49 mg

TURKEY, SPINACH, AND MASHED POTATO ROLL

This succulent stuffed turkey breast slices easily into beautiful green and white swirls. Serve it hot or at room temperature.

- 2 medium-size all-purpose potatoes (12 ounces), peeled and cut into 1-inch cubes
- 3 cloves garlic, peeled
- ¼ cup grated Parmesan cheese
- 1 large egg white
- ¼ teaspoon black pepper
- ⅛ teaspoon ground nutmeg
- ½ skinned and boned turkey breast (2½ pounds)
- 1 package (10 ounces) frozen chopped spinach, thawed and squeezed dry
- 2 teaspoons olive oil
- ¼ teaspoon salt, or to taste

1 In a large saucepan of boiling water, cook the potatoes and garlic for about 15 minutes or until the potatoes are tender. Drain, reserving 2 tablespoons of the cooking water. Return the potatoes, garlic, and reserved cooking water to the saucepan and mash them until smooth. Stir in the cheese, egg white, pepper, and nutmeg and combine well; set aside.

2 Preheat the oven to 400° F. Place the turkey breast, which is oblong in shape, on a cutting board with one of the short ends facing you. Using a sharp knife and beginning at one of the long sides, split the turkey breast almost in half, leaving just ½ inch uncut at the other long side. Now open the breast up like a book so that you have one thin rectangular piece of meat. Cover the turkey with the spinach and spread the potato mixture on top.

3 Starting at one of the long sides, roll up the turkey breast jelly-roll fashion. Tie with string about every 2 inches to prevent the stuffing from coming out. Place the turkey roll, seam side down, on a lightly greased roasting pan, brush it with the oil, and sprinkle with the salt. Roast for 1 hour or until the meat is cooked through. Let stand for 10 minutes before slicing. Serve with baby carrots, accompanied, if you like, with Greek Lemon Sauce (page 276), and a salad of radicchio and escarole. Serves 6 to 8.

PREPARATION TIME: 10 MIN. COOKING TIME: 1¼ HR.

Per serving (for 6): Calories 317; Saturated Fat 2 g; Total Fat 3 g; Protein 49 g; Carbohydrate 18 g; Fiber 2 g; Sodium 339 mg; Cholesterol 117 mg

TURKEY CUTLETS IN SPICY GREEN SAUCE

- 4 turkey cutlets (4 ounces each)
- ¼ cup all-purpose flour
- 2 tablespoons olive oil
- 3 cloves garlic, minced
- 2 tablespoons lime juice
- 1 teaspoon finely chopped jalapeño pepper, or to taste
- ½ cup Chicken Stock (page 62) or low-sodium chicken broth
- ⅓ cup minced fresh cilantro (coriander) or ⅓ cup minced parsley mixed with 1 tablespoon dried cilantro
- ¼ cup minced flat-leaf parsley

1 Dredge the turkey in the flour, shaking off any excess. In a 12-inch skillet, heat the oil over moderately high heat. Add the cutlets and sauté for 1½ minutes or until golden brown. Turn and cook 1½ minutes on the other side or until golden and the juices run clear when the flesh is pricked with a fork. Transfer the cutlets to a plate.

2 Lower the heat, add the garlic to the skillet, and cook for 30 seconds. Add the lime juice and jalapeño pepper and cook 30 seconds more. Stir in the stock, cilantro, and parsley, then add the turkey and cook for about 2 minutes or until the turkey is heated through and the sauce is slightly thickened. Serve with corn and a salad of romaine lettuce and tomatoes. Serves 4.

PREPARATION TIME: 15 MIN. COOKING TIME: 6 MIN.

Per serving: Calories 227; Saturated Fat 2 g; Total Fat 7 g; Protein 28 g; Carbohydrate 10 g; Fiber 1 g; Sodium 103 mg; Cholesterol 68 mg

TURKEY CUTLETS IN LIME CREAM

This refreshing dish is elegant enough for company and easy enough to make any night of the week. Serve it over noodles.

- 4 turkey cutlets (4 ounces each)
- 1 tablespoon plus 1 teaspoon lime juice
- ¼ teaspoon each salt and black pepper
- 1 tablespoon unsalted butter or margarine
- ⅓ cup finely chopped shallots
- ⅓ cup dry white wine or water
- 1 cup Chicken Stock (page 62) or low-sodium chicken broth
- 1 teaspoon grated lime rind
- ¼ cup reduced-fat sour cream mixed with 1 teaspoon arrowroot or cornstarch
- 2 tablespoons snipped fresh chives or thinly sliced green onion tops

1 Sprinkle the turkey with 1 tablespoon of the lime juice and the salt and pepper; let stand for 10 minutes. In a 12-inch nonstick skillet, melt the butter over moderate heat until bubbling. Add the turkey and cook for 1 ½ minutes on each side or until golden and the juices run clear when the flesh is pricked with a fork; transfer to a plate.

2 Add the shallots to the skillet and cook, stirring, for 1 minute. Add the wine and cook for 1 minute or until the liquid is reduced to 2 tablespoons. Add the stock and lime rind and simmer the mixture, uncovered, for about 5 minutes or until the liquid is reduced to ¾ cup. If necessary, boil the mixture over moderate heat until it is reduced.

3 Lower the heat, stir in the sour cream mixture, and simmer, stirring constantly, for 1 to 2 minutes or until the sauce has thickened. Add the turkey cutlets along with any juices on the plate and simmer for 2 minutes or until the turkey is heated through. Add the remaining teaspoon of lime juice and sprinkle with the chives. Serve with Broiled Mixed Vegetables (page 244). Serves 4.

PREPARATION TIME: 12 MIN. COOKING TIME: 14 MIN.
MARINATING TIME: 10 MIN.

*Per serving: Calories 214; Saturated Fat 4 g;
Total Fat 5 g; Protein 28 g; Carbohydrate 6 g;
Fiber 0 g; Sodium 266 mg; Cholesterol 76 mg*

TURKEY CUTLETS IN SWEET-AND-SOUR MINT SAUCE

Sugar gives this sauce not only sweetness but a deep, rich color.

- 4 turkey cutlets (4 ounces each)
- ¼ cup all-purpose flour
- 2 tablespoons vegetable oil
- 2 tablespoons sugar
- ⅓ cup red wine vinegar
- ⅔ cup Chicken Stock (page 62) or low-sodium chicken broth
- 3 tablespoons minced fresh mint or 1 tablespoon mint flakes

1 Dredge the turkey in the flour, shaking off any excess. In a 12-inch skillet, heat the oil over moderately high heat. Add the cutlets and sauté for 1 ½ minutes or until golden brown. Turn and cook 1 ½ minutes more or until golden and the juices run clear when the flesh is pricked with a fork; transfer the cutlets to a plate.

2 Lower the heat, add the sugar to the skillet, and swirl the skillet for about 1 minute or until the sugar is amber colored. Stir in the vinegar and cook 1 minute longer or until the sugar has melted. Stir in the stock, increase the heat to high, and cook for 2 minutes. Lower the heat, add the mint and turkey, and cook for 1 minute or until the turkey is heated through. Serve with brown rice and stir-fried carrot sticks. Serves 4.

PREPARATION TIME: 5 MIN. COOKING TIME: 8 MIN.

*Per serving: Calories 244; Saturated Fat 2 g;
Total Fat 7 g; Protein 28 g; Carbohydrate 15 g;
Fiber 0 g; Sodium 95 mg; Cholesterol 68 mg*

Turkey Quesadillas are a sensational blend of ground turkey, spices, and vegetables heaped on flour tortillas and topped, if you like, with salsa.

TURKEY QUESADILLAS

This spicy southwestern dish can also be made with ground chicken, beef, or pork.

6 flour tortillas, 7 inches in diameter	1 jalapeño pepper, seeded and finely chopped (1 tablespoon) (optional)
2 teaspoons olive oil	½ cup low-sodium tomato sauce
1 medium-size yellow onion, finely chopped (1 cup)	2 tablespoons minced fresh cilantro (coriander) or 2 tablespoons minced parsley mixed with ¾ teaspoon dried cilantro
1 medium-size sweet red pepper, cored, seeded, and diced (¾ cup)	
1¼ pounds ground turkey	
¼ teaspoon salt	½ cup grated Monterey Jack cheese (2 ounces)
2 cloves garlic, minced	1 cup Tomato Salsa (page 280) (optional)
1 teaspoon each ground cumin, chili powder, and dried oregano, crumbled	

1 Preheat the oven to 350° F. Wrap the tortillas in aluminum foil and heat them in the oven for 8 minutes. Meanwhile, in a 12-inch nonstick skillet, heat the oil over moderate heat. Add the onion and red pepper and sauté, stirring occasionally, for 5 minutes or until the onion is soft.

2 Add the turkey and salt to the skillet and sauté, stirring, for 3 minutes or until the turkey is no longer pink. Add the garlic, cumin, chili powder, oregano, and, if desired, the jalapeño pepper; sauté, stirring, for 1 minute or until the mixture is dry. Stir in the tomato sauce and cilantro.

3 Increase the oven temperature to 450° F. Unwrap the tortillas and place them on greased baking sheets. Spread an equal amount of the turkey mixture on each one and sprinkle with the cheese. Bake for 8 to 10 minutes or until the cheese is melted and the tortillas are golden. Serve with salsa if desired. Accompany with a salad of avocado and tomatoes. Serves 6.

PREPARATION TIME: 20 MIN.   COOKING TIME: 25 MIN.

Per serving: Calories 277; Saturated Fat 1 g; Total Fat 9 g; Protein 26 g; Carbohydrate 22 g; Fiber 2 g; Sodium 213 mg; Cholesterol 61 mg

Tortillas are thin, unleavened breads used in Mexican cooking. There are two varieties: corn and flour. Corn tortillas have a slightly more robust flavor than the flour kind and go well with spicy sauces. Because corn tortillas are fairly sturdy, they can be fried and folded into half-moon shapes for tacos or they can be shredded and added to soups.

Flour tortillas are softer and have a more delicate flavor. They are most often served open, like a pizza, with meat or vegetables piled on top. Most supermarkets carry both corn and flour tortillas in the frozen food section.

TURKEY TORTILLA CASSEROLE

This low-fat version of the popular Mexican casserole can be assembled and refrigerated a day ahead; just allow an extra 20 minutes of baking time. Serve it with salsa and a salad of oranges, red onion, and avocado.

- 1 tablespoon vegetable oil
- 1 medium-size yellow onion, coarsely chopped (1 cup)
- 1 large sweet green pepper, cored, seeded, and coarsely chopped (1 cup)
- ¼ teaspoon salt
- 4 ounces mushrooms, thinly sliced (1¼ cups)
- 1¼ pounds ground turkey
- 1 tablespoon each ground cumin, coriander, and chili powder
- 1 can (28 ounces) crushed tomatoes in purée
- 3 cloves garlic, minced
- 1 can (4 ounces) chopped green chilies, drained
- 8 corn tortillas, softened according to package directions
- 1 cup shredded Monterey Jack cheese (4 ounces)
- 3 tablespoons minced fresh cilantro (coriander) (optional garnish)

1 Preheat the oven to 400° F. In a 12-inch nonstick skillet, heat 1½ teaspoons of the oil over moderate heat. Add the onion, green pepper, and ⅛ teaspoon of the salt and sauté, stirring occasionally, for 3 minutes or until slightly softened. Add the mushrooms and sauté, stirring occasionally, 3 minutes more or until all the vegetables are tender.

2 Add the turkey to the skillet and sauté, stirring occasionally, for 3 minutes or until no longer pink. Stir in the cumin, coriander, chili powder, and remaining ⅛ teaspoon of salt and cook the mixture, stirring constantly, for 1 minute. Stir in the tomatoes, garlic, and chilies and bring the mixture to a simmer.

3 In a 13″ x 9″ x 2″ baking dish, spread just enough of the turkey mixture to cover the bottom. Cover the turkey with 4 tortillas, then top with half of the remaining turkey mixture; sprinkle with half of the cheese. Top with the remaining tortillas, turkey mixture, and cheese. Bake for 25 minutes or until bubbling and lightly browned. Sprinkle with the cilantro if desired. Serves 6.

PREPARATION TIME: 20 MIN. COOKING TIME: 35 MIN.

Per serving: Calories 342; Saturated Fat 1 g; Total Fat 13 g; Protein 30 g; Carbohydrate 28 g; Fiber 4 g; Sodium 545 mg; Cholesterol 61 mg

Poultry is a perishable product and for safety's sake should be kept as cold as possible until you are ready to cook it. Put poultry last on your shopping list and do not leave it in the car while you do other errands. Also avoid letting it sit on a countertop to marinate or while you prepare other foods; bacteria multiply rapidly at room temperature.

When you refrigerate poultry, store it in the meat compartment if there is one; this is the coldest area. It should be left in the store wrapper and, if necessary, set inside a plastic bag or on a plate to collect any juices. It will keep this way for up to 3 days. Frozen poultry, in addition to the store wrap, should be covered with heavy-duty aluminum foil, freezer wrap, or a freezer bag to prevent freezer burn. It will keep for up to 9 months at 0° F.

There are 3 safe ways to thaw poultry: in the refrigerator, submerged in cold water, and in a microwave oven. **In the refrigerator,** a chicken will usually thaw overnight, a duck in 1 to 2 days, and a turkey in 2 to 4 days, depending on the weight (allow 3 to 4 hours per pound). **In cold water,** a chicken or duck requires only 1 to 4 hours to thaw, a turkey 3 to 8 hours (roughly 20 minutes per pound). The water should be changed about every 30 minutes. **In a microwave oven,** thawing times vary depending on the model. It's best to follow the manufacturer's instructions, but allow roughly 6 to 7 minutes per pound plus 5 to 10 minutes of standing time. Plan on cooking poultry immediately after thawing it in a microwave.

It is possible to cook a frozen bird, allowing half again as much time as it would take to cook when thawed. The results, however, may not be entirely satisfactory because the outside tends to overcook before the inside is done.

TURKEY BURGERS WITH SAGE AND ONION

- 1 **pound ground turkey**
- 1 **small yellow onion, grated, drained, and squeezed dry**
- 1 **tablespoon minced fresh sage or 1 teaspoon ground sage**
- ½ **cup soft whole-wheat bread crumbs (1 slice)**
- ¼ **teaspoon each salt and black pepper**

1 Preheat the broiler, setting the rack 6 inches from the heat. In a medium-size bowl, combine the turkey, onion, sage, bread crumbs, salt, and pepper. With moistened hands, form the mixture into 4 patties.

2 Place the patties on a lightly greased broiler pan and broil for 5 minutes. Turn the patties over and broil 5 minutes more or until the juices run clear when a patty is pricked with a fork. Serves 4.

PREPARATION TIME: 10 MIN. COOKING TIME: 10 MIN.

> *Per patty: Calories 159; Saturated Fat 1 g;*
> *Total Fat 4 g; Protein 26 g; Carbohydrate 5 g;*
> *Fiber 1 g; Sodium 258 mg; Cholesterol 74 mg*

QUICK TURKEY CHILI

- 2 **teaspoons olive oil**
- 1 **medium-size yellow onion, finely chopped (1 cup)**
- 1 **large sweet green pepper, cored, seeded, and diced (1 cup)**
- 1 **pound ground turkey**
- 2 **teaspoons each ground cumin and chili powder**
- ¼ **teaspoon salt**
- 2 **cloves garlic, minced**
- 1 **can (14½ ounces) low-sodium tomatoes, chopped, with their juice**
- ½ **teaspoon each dried basil and oregano, crumbled**
- 1½ **cups cooked red kidney beans**
- 1 **tablespoon minced fresh cilantro (coriander) (optional garnish)**

1 In a 12-inch nonstick skillet, heat the oil over moderate heat. Add the onion and green pepper and sauté, stirring occasionally, for 5 minutes or until the onion is softened. Add the turkey and sauté for 3 minutes or until no longer pink. Add the cumin, chili powder, salt, and garlic and sauté, stirring, 1 minute more.

2 Stir in the tomatoes, basil, and oregano and lower the heat. Simmer, stirring occasionally, for 20 minutes. Stir in the beans and simmer 5 to 7 minutes more or until the beans are heated through. Garnish with the cilantro if desired. Serve with rice and a salad of lettuce and tomatoes. Serves 4.

PREPARATION TIME: 12 MIN. COOKING TIME: 35 MIN.

> *Per serving: Calories 283; Saturated Fat 1 g;*
> *Total Fat 6 g; Protein 32 g; Carbohydrate 25 g;*
> *Fiber 7 g; Sodium 541 mg; Cholesterol 74 mg*

Add a spoonful of low-sodium ketchup or your favorite relish before you bite into a Turkey Burger with Sage and Onion. Round off the meal with crudités and fruit.

TURKEY SAUSAGE

These spicy homemade patties are easy to make, low in fat, and additive free.

1 tablespoon plus 2 teaspoons vegetable oil	⅓ cup fresh bread crumbs
1 small yellow onion, finely chopped (½ cup)	3 tablespoons skim milk
1 clove garlic, minced	½ teaspoon ground sage
3 tablespoons water	¼ teaspoon salt
12 ounces ground turkey	⅛ teaspoon black pepper
	1 tablespoon all-purpose flour

1 In a 12-inch nonstick skillet, heat 2 teaspoons of the oil over moderate heat. Add the onion and garlic and sauté, stirring often, for 5 minutes or until softened. Add the water and cook for 4 minutes or until it has evaporated and the onion is soft.

2 In a medium-size bowl, combine the turkey, bread crumbs, milk, sage, salt, and pepper. Add the onion mixture and mix well. Shape the mixture into 8 oblong patties, each about ½ inch thick.

3 Dredge the patties in the flour, shaking off any excess. Heat the remaining tablespoon of oil in the skillet over moderate heat. Add the patties and cook for 4 minutes or until golden brown. Turn the patties over and cook 4 minutes more or until golden brown and cooked through. Serve with eggs or pancakes. Makes 8 patties.

PREPARATION TIME: 10 MIN. COOKING TIME: 17 MIN.

Per patty: Calories 101; Saturated Fat 1 g; Total Fat 4 g; Protein 10 g; Carbohydrate 5 g; Fiber 0 g; Sodium 130 mg; Cholesterol 28 mg

HERBED CORNISH HENS

*If you have time, let the hens marinate
in the herbs for up to 3 hours so that they absorb
as much flavor as possible. This marinade is
also good with pork or chicken.*

½ teaspoon coarse (kosher) salt
¾ teaspoon ground sage
½ teaspoon each ground allspice, black pepper, and dried rosemary, crumbled

2 Cornish hens (1½ pounds each), split and skinned
1 tablespoon plus 1 teaspoon olive oil

1 In a small bowl, combine the salt, sage, allspice, pepper, and rosemary. Coat the hens first with the oil, then with the herb mixture, rubbing them well. Cover the hens with plastic food wrap and refrigerate for at least 1 hour or up to 3 hours.

2 Preheat the broiler, setting the rack 8 inches from the heat. Arrange the hens on a broiler pan and broil for 8 minutes, then them turn over and broil 7 to 8 minutes longer or until the juices run clear when a thigh is pricked with a fork and a leg moves easily in its socket. If the hens are overbrowning, tent them with aluminum foil during the last few minutes of broiling. Serve with Puréed Squash with Orange and Cinnamon (page 240). Serves 4.

PREPARATION TIME: 10 MIN. COOKING TIME: 16 MIN.
MARINATING TIME: 1 HR.

*Per serving: Calories 272; Saturated Fat 2 g;
Total Fat 11 g; Protein 41 g; Carbohydrate 0 g;
Fiber 0 g; Sodium 246 mg; Cholesterol 119 mg*

LEMON-GARLIC CORNISH HENS

*This recipe calls for 6 cloves of garlic. However, they
mellow as they cook, leaving a rich, almost sweet flavor.
You can cook the hens on the barbecue if you prefer.*

6 cloves garlic, minced
¼ cup plus 2 tablespoons lemon juice

2 Cornish hens (1¼ pounds each), split and skinned
½ teaspoon black pepper
1 teaspoon sugar

1 In a small bowl, mix the garlic with ¼ cup of the lemon juice, then rub the mixture over the hens. Cover the hens with plastic food wrap and let them marinate in the refrigerator for 2 hours.

2 Preheat the broiler, setting the rack 8 inches from the heat. Sprinkle the hens with the pepper, then arrange them on a broiler pan. Broil for 8 minutes, turn the hens over, and broil 7 to 8 minutes longer or until the juices run clear when a thigh is pricked with a fork. If the hens start to overbrown, tent them with aluminum foil.

3 Meanwhile, in a small bowl, combine the remaining 2 tablespoons of lemon juice and the sugar. When the hens have finished cooking, remove them from the oven and brush them with the lemon-sugar mixture. Serve with steamed asparagus and wild rice. Serves 4.

PREPARATION TIME: 10 MIN. COOKING TIME: 16 MIN.
MARINATING TIME: 2 HR.

*Per serving: Calories 247; Saturated Fat 2 g;
Total Fat 7 g; Protein 41 g; Carbohydrate 5 g;
Fiber 0 g; Sodium 114 mg; Cholesterol 119 mg*

Cornish hens are small young chickens that weigh 1 to 1½ pounds each. Some producers call the tiny birds Cornish "game" hens, and they do have a slightly gamy taste. However, the birds carried in supermarkets are usually not game birds but a cross between domestic chickens and Cornish hens. When Cornish birds are crossed with White Plymouth Rock chickens, the progeny are called Rock Cornish hens.

With a plump breast and delicate flavor, the Cornish hen makes wonderful eating. One hen will feed two people. For company or holiday dinners, however, you might want to serve each guest a whole stuffed bird. Any of the stuffings given in this chapter for chicken or duck will go nicely with Cornish hens. Bake any excess stuffing separately.

DUCK WITH WINE, FIGS, AND COUSCOUS

Here is the Chinese technique of steaming duck to remove some of the fat and then roasting it until the skin is crisp and brown. The crispy skin is especially delicious, but if you remove it, you reduce the fat to 14 grams and almost halve the calories to 559 per serving.

1 duck (3½ pounds), tail, wing tips, and visible fat removed
½ teaspoon salt
½ teaspoon ground cinnamon
¼ teaspoon black pepper
⅛ teaspoon ground allspice
6 ounces dried figs, quartered
1 cup dry red wine or low-sodium chicken broth
2 tablespoons sugar
¾ teaspoon dried thyme, crumbled
¾ cup boiling water
½ cup couscous

1 Using a fork, prick the skin of the duck all over. In a small bowl, mix together the salt, cinnamon, pepper, and allspice, then rub the mixture into the skin and cavity of the duck.

2 In a Dutch oven large enough to hold the duck on a rack, bring 2 inches of water to a boil. Lightly grease the rack and adjust it so that the duck will sit above the water. Place the duck in the Dutch oven, adjust the heat so that the water simmers, cover, and cook for 1 hour. Remove the duck, pat dry, then air-dry for 30 minutes.

3 Preheat the oven to 400° F. Meanwhile, in a medium-size saucepan, combine the figs, wine, sugar, and thyme and bring to a boil over moderate heat. Adjust the heat so that the mixture simmers, cover, and cook for 10 minutes or until the figs are soft.

4 In a medium-size bowl, pour the boiling water over the couscous and let stand for 5 minutes. Using a slotted spoon, remove the figs from the saucepan and stir them into the couscous, reserving the wine mixture. Spoon the couscous mixture into the duck cavity and brush the duck with a little of the reserved wine mixture.

5 Place the duck on a rack in a roasting pan. Roast, basting it every 10 minutes with the wine mixture, for 30 minutes or until the skin is crisp and a leg moves easily in its socket. Serve with steamed carrots. Serves 4.

PREPARATION TIME: 15 MIN. COOKING TIME: 1 HR. 40 MIN.
DRYING TIME: 30 MIN.

Per serving: Calories 1018; Saturated Fat 22 g; Total Fat 64 g; Protein 45 g; Carbohydrates 53 g; Fiber 8 g; Sodium 444 mg; Cholesterol 189 mg

BRAISED DUCK WITH CHUTNEY SAUCE

1 duck (3½ pounds), skinned and quartered
3 tablespoons all-purpose flour
1 tablespoon canola, olive, or corn oil
3 tablespoons minced fresh ginger
5 cloves garlic, thinly slivered
¼ cup red wine vinegar
¾ cup water
¼ cup mango chutney, chopped
¼ teaspoon ground ginger

1 Dredge the duck in the flour, shaking off any excess. In a 12-inch skillet, heat the oil over moderately high heat. Add the duck and cook for 3 to 4 minutes or until golden brown. Turn and repeat on the other side. Transfer the duck to a platter and set aside.

2 Reduce the heat to low. Add the fresh ginger and garlic to the skillet and cook, stirring frequently, for 2 minutes. Add the vinegar and cook for 1 minute. Stir in the water, chutney, and ground ginger, scraping up bits from the bottom of the skillet. Return the duck to the skillet and bring the liquid to a boil over moderate heat. Adjust the heat so that the liquid simmers, cover, and cook for 30 minutes or until the duck is cooked through. Serves 4.

PREPARATION TIME: 10 MIN. COOKING TIME: 40 MIN.

Per serving: Calories 378; Saturated Fat 6 g; Total Fat 17 g; Protein 42 g; Carbohydrate 12 g; Fiber 0 g; Sodium 273 mg; Cholesterol 175 mg

MEAT

Meat, an outstanding source of protein, iron, and B vitamins, is
also high in fat and cholesterol. If you want to limit the fat and cholesterol in
your diet, can you still include meat? The answer is yes, but with
controls. Eat smaller portions; a 3- to 4-ounce serving is adequate. Select leaner
cuts, such as round and sirloin tip, and trim away all visible surface fat. Also,
eat meat less often — once or twice a week instead of every day — and broil, stir-fry,
roast, or braise it rather than frying. Begin thinking of meat more as an
accompaniment to or flavor enhancer of vegetables and starchy foods than as the
main course. And when you do include meat on the menu, enjoy it to the
fullest with palate-pleasing recipes such as the ones that follow.

Standing time, usually 10 to 15 minutes for both meat and poultry, is the amount of time a roast needs to rest before it is carved. This interval allows the juices to be reabsorbed into the meat, making carving easier and the meat moister. When ready to cut a roast, transfer it from the baking pan to the cutting board with tongs or a carving fork; untie and discard any trussing strings.

ROSEMARY-LEMON ROAST BEEF

The secret to making this flavorful roast is to cut slits in the surface and fill them with the garlic-herb mixture so that the taste penetrates the meat. Because the recipe serves 12, it makes a wonderful party dish.

¼ cup fresh rosemary, minced, or 1 ½ tablespoons dried rosemary, crumbled
2 cloves garlic, minced
2 teaspoons grated lemon rind
½ teaspoon black pepper
4¼ pounds beef sirloin tip or top round roast, tied
¼ teaspoon salt

1 Preheat the oven to 350° F. Line a roasting pan with aluminum foil. In a small bowl, mix the rosemary, garlic, lemon rind, and ¼ teaspoon of the pepper. Using a narrow sharp knife, make 12 slits, each ¾ inch long and 1 inch deep, across the top of the roast. Use a chopstick to widen the slits and then to push a rounded ¼ teaspoon of the garlic-herb mixture into each one. Sprinkle the roast with any remaining mixture, the salt, and the remaining ¼ teaspoon of pepper.

2 Place the roast on a rack in the roasting pan and roast for 1 hour 20 minutes for medium-rare or until a meat thermometer registers 140° F; for medium, roast 1 ½ hours or to 160° F. Let stand for 15 minutes before carving. Serve with baked sweet potatoes and steamed green beans. Serves 12.

PREPARATION TIME: 15 MIN.   COOKING TIME: 1 HR. 20 MIN.
STANDING TIME: 15 MIN.

Per serving: Calories 268; Saturated Fat 2 g; Total Fat 16 g; Protein 47 g; Carbohydrate 0 g; Fiber 0 g; Sodium 156 mg; Cholesterol 230 mg

POT ROAST, NEW ORLEANS STYLE

A spicy Creole sauce flavors the meat and keeps it moist and juicy.

2½ pounds lean chuck roast, patted dry
½ teaspoon each ground red pepper (cayenne) and black pepper, or to taste
¼ teaspoon salt
2 teaspoons vegetable oil
1 large yellow onion, coarsely chopped (1 ½ cups)
1 large stalk celery, coarsely chopped (½ cup)
1 small sweet green pepper, cored, seeded, and coarsely chopped (½ cup)
2 cloves garlic, minced
2 tablespoons flour
1 can (28 ounces) crushed tomatoes in purée
1 cup low-sodium beef broth
½ teaspoon each dried thyme and basil, crumbled
1 bay leaf

1 Rub the meat all over with the red pepper, black pepper, and salt. In a 5-quart Dutch oven or flameproof casserole, heat the oil over moderately high heat. Add the meat and cook, turning, for 5 to 7 minutes or until browned on all sides. Transfer the beef to a plate. Add the onion, celery, green pepper, and garlic to the Dutch oven and sauté for 5 to 7 minutes or until the onion is golden.

2 Add the flour to the vegetables and cook the mixture over low heat, stirring constantly, for 2 minutes. Add the tomatoes, broth, thyme, basil, and bay leaf, stirring until well blended, then return the meat to the Dutch oven. Bring the liquid to a boil over high heat. Lower the heat, cover, and simmer for 2 ½ to 3 hours or until the roast is tender. Skim any fat from the surface of the cooking liquid and remove the bay leaf before serving. Serve with grits and steamed okra. Serves 8.

PREPARATION TIME: 15 MIN.   COOKING TIME: 2 HR. 40 MIN.

Per serving: Calories 347; Saturated Fat 4 g; Total Fat 11 g; Protein 46 g; Carbohydrate 14 g; Fiber 3 g; Sodium 341 mg; Cholesterol 129 mg

STUFFED FLANK STEAK WITH ONION-MUSHROOM SAUCE

For convenience, you can prepare the stuffing several hours ahead and stuff the meat when ready to cook.

For the stuffing:
- 2 teaspoons unsalted butter or margarine
- 1 medium-size yellow onion, finely chopped (1 cup)
- 1 medium-size stalk celery, finely chopped (½ cup)
- 2 cloves garlic, minced
- 1 cup fresh bread crumbs (2 slices)
- ¼ cup minced parsley
- 1 large egg white
- ¼ teaspoon each dried thyme and sage, crumbled
- ¼ teaspoon each salt and black pepper

For the steak:
- 1 pound flank steak
- 2 teaspoons vegetable oil
- 2 large yellow onions, thinly sliced (3 cups)
- 3½ ounces mushrooms, thinly sliced (1 cup)
- ¼ teaspoon each salt and black pepper
- ¼ teaspoon each dried thyme and sage, crumbled
- ½ cup dry red wine or low-sodium beef broth
- 2 cups low-sodium beef broth
- 1 tablespoon tomato paste

1 To prepare the stuffing: In a 10-inch nonstick skillet, melt the butter over moderate heat. Add the onion, celery, and garlic and sauté, stirring occasionally, for 5 minutes or until the onion is softened. Remove from the heat and let cool. When cool, add the bread crumbs, parsley, egg white, thyme, sage, salt, and pepper to the skillet and mix well.

2 Preheat the oven to 325° F. Using a sharp knife, cut a pocket in the steak. First, make a shallow horizontal slit along one long side, leaving 1 inch uncut at both ends. Then cut the slit more deeply to make a horizontal pocket through the center of the steak, leaving about 1 inch uncut on 3 sides.

3 Fill the pocket with stuffing and tie the steak with string at 2-inch intervals to close the opening. In a medium-size flameproof casserole, heat the oil over moderate heat. Add the steak and cook for 5 minutes or until browned on both sides; transfer to a plate. Add the onions, mushrooms, salt, pepper, thyme, and sage to the casserole and cook, stirring occasionally, for 5 minutes or until the onions are softened. Stir in the wine, broth, and tomato paste, return the steak to the casserole, and bring the liquid to a boil. Transfer the casserole to the oven and bake, covered, for 1 to 1½ hours or until the steak is tender.

4 Transfer the steak to a cutting board and remove the string. Skim any fat from the surface of the sauce and simmer it, uncovered, over moderately high heat for 3 minutes or until slightly thickened. Slice the steak ½ inch thick, arrange the slices on a warm platter, and drizzle with the sauce. Serve with Creamy Mashed Potatoes (page 236) or noodles and a tossed green salad. Serves 4.

PREPARATION TIME: 25 MIN. COOKING TIME: 1½ HR.

Per serving: Calories 360; Saturated Fat 6 g; Total Fat 16 g; Protein 29 g; Carbohydrate 21 g; Fiber 4 g; Sodium 615 mg; Cholesterol 62 mg

Don't count on having leftovers with this succulent Rosemary-Lemon Roast Beef.

London Broil in Ginger and Onion Marinade updates an American classic. Keep the menu contemporary and light with Vegetable Kebabs (page 243) and a tossed salad with Roasted Tomato Vinaigrette (page 266).

FLANK STEAK WITH RED ONIONS

If flank is unavailable, substitute top round London broil.

2 **medium-size red onions, sliced ½ inch thick**	2 **tablespoons black currant or seedless raspberry jam**
2 **cloves garlic, crushed**	½ **teaspoon salt**
⅔ **cup balsamic or malt vinegar**	⅛ **teaspoon ground red pepper (cayenne)**
1 **tablespoon olive oil**	1 **pound flank steak**

1 Place the onions, garlic, vinegar, oil, jam, salt, and red pepper in a self-sealing plastic food storage bag. Push out all the air and seal the bag, then knead the marinade through the bag until it is combined. Using a sharp knife and cutting a scant ⅛ inch deep, score the steak on both sides in a diamond pattern. Add the steak to the marinade, coat the steak well, and reseal the bag. Place the bag on a plate and marinate the steak in the refrigerator for at least 30 minutes or up to 3 hours.

2 Preheat the broiler, setting the rack 5 inches from the heat. Place an 8-inch square of aluminum foil on one end of the broiler pan. Using a slotted spoon, remove the onions from the marinade and arrange them on the foil. Place the steak directly on the pan next to the onions. Broil the onions for 5 minutes on each side, and the steak for 5 to 6 minutes on each side for medium-rare, 7 to 8 minutes for medium.

3 Transfer the steak to a cutting board and let stand for 10 minutes; then thinly slice it against the grain, holding the knife at a slight angle. Place the slices on individual plates and spoon any juices over them. Serve with the broiled onions, Sautéed Peppers (variation, page 235) or Braised Endive (page 228), and Italian bread. Serves 4.

PREPARATION TIME: 10 MIN. COOKING TIME: 10 MIN.

MARINATING AND STANDING TIME: 40 MIN.

Per serving: Calories 264; Saturated Fat 6 g; Total Fat 14 g; Protein 24 g; Carbohydrate 16 g; Fiber 1 g; Sodium 352 mg; Cholesterol 57 mg

LONDON BROIL IN GINGER AND ONION MARINADE

For a more piquant flavor, increase the balsamic vinegar to 2 tablespoons.

2 **large yellow onions, thinly sliced (3 cups)**
1 **piece (about 1 inch) fresh ginger, peeled and cut into matchstick strips, or ½ teaspoon ground ginger**

1¾ **pounds London broil (top round), about 1 inch thick**
½ **teaspoon each salt and black pepper**
2 **teaspoons olive oil**
1 **tablespoon balsamic or red wine vinegar**

1 In a shallow ceramic or glass dish, spread half of the onions and ginger. Sprinkle the meat with ¼ teaspoon each of the salt and pepper and place it on top. Spread the remaining onions and ginger on top of the meat. (If using ground ginger, sprinkle it on both sides of the beef along with the salt and pepper.) Cover the dish with plastic food wrap and refrigerate for 1 to 3 hours.

2 Preheat the broiler, setting the rack 6 inches from the heat. Place the steak on a broiler pan. In a 10-inch nonstick skillet, heat the oil over moderate heat. Add the onions and ginger and the remaining ¼ teaspoon each of salt and pepper and sauté, stirring occasionally, for 8 to 10 minutes or until the onions are golden brown. Stir in the vinegar.

3 Meanwhile, broil the meat to the desired degree of doneness: 5 minutes on each side for medium-rare, 7 minutes for medium, and 9 minutes for well-done. Transfer the meat to a cutting board and let stand for 5 minutes before cutting it diagonally into thin slices. Serve with the onions and broiled or grilled vegetables. Serves 8.

PREPARATION TIME: 10 MIN. COOKING TIME: 15 MIN.
MARINATING AND STANDING TIME: 1 HR. 5 MIN.

Per serving: Calories 164; Saturated Fat 2 g; Total Fat 5 g; Protein 24 g; Carbohydrate 5 g; Fiber 1 g; Sodium 187 mg; Cholesterol 57 mg

SKIRT STEAK IN A CRISPY POTATO CRUST

1 **medium-size all-purpose potato, peeled and sliced ⅛ inch thick (1¼ cups)**
4 **skirt or blade steaks (4 ounces each), about ½ inch thick**
½ **teaspoon salt**
¼ **teaspoon black pepper**

1 **large egg white mixed with 1 teaspoon water**
2 **teaspoons vegetable oil**
Optional garnishes:
   Reduced-fat sour cream
   Snipped fresh chives

1 In a large saucepan of boiling water, cook the potato slices for 4 to 5 minutes or until almost tender but not breaking; drain and rinse. Meanwhile, sprinkle the steaks with ¼ teaspoon of the salt and the pepper. Brush both sides of the steaks with the egg white mixture.

2 Using half of the potato slices, cover one side of the steaks, overlapping the slices slightly and pressing them into the meat. Carefully turn the steaks over and press the remaining potato slices into the second side. Sprinkle with the remaining ¼ teaspoon salt.

3 Heat a 12-inch nonstick skillet over moderately high heat. Add the oil and heat until hot but not smoking. Carefully place the steaks in the skillet and cook for 3 minutes or until the potato crust is crisp. Turn the steaks over and cook 3 minutes longer or until the second side is crisp. The steaks will be medium-rare. If you prefer them well-done, transfer them to a baking sheet and bake in a preheated 450° F oven for another 8 minutes. If you like, garnish with sour cream and chives. Serve with Creamed Artichokes, Peppers, and Corn (page 216). Serves 4.

PREPARATION TIME: 5 MIN. COOKING TIME: 10 MIN.

Per serving: Calories 253; Saturated Fat 5 g; Total Fat 13 g; Protein 24 g; Carbohydrate 9 g; Fiber 1 g; Sodium 365 mg; Cholesterol 57 mg

Broiling is a healthful way to cook meat because intense direct heat helps cook out much of the fat. To prepare for broiling, trim the meat of excess fat to prevent flare-ups. Preheat the broiler, setting the rack 5 to 9 inches from the heat source. (The broiler pan will bring the meat closer to the heat by another 1 to 2 inches.) Cuts that are up to 1½ inches thick should be 3 to 4 inches from the heat source, thicker cuts 5 to 8 inches away.

BEEF GOULASH

Here's a new slimmed-down version of an old favorite. Why not make two batches and store one in the freezer? It will keep for up to 3 months.

- 2 teaspoons vegetable oil
- 12 ounces lean beef round or chuck, cut into ¾-inch cubes
- 1 large yellow onion, finely chopped (1½ cups)
- 1 medium-size sweet red pepper, cored, seeded, and coarsely chopped (1 cup)
- 1 medium-size carrot, peeled and thinly sliced (½ cup)
- 2 cloves garlic, crushed
- ¼ cup white wine or water
- 1 tablespoon tomato paste
- ¾ cup Chicken Stock (page 62) or low-sodium chicken broth
- ¼ teaspoon salt
- 3 tablespoons reduced-fat sour cream

1 Heat the oil in a 5-quart Dutch oven or large heavy saucepan over moderately high heat. Add the beef and sauté for 4 minutes or until browned on all sides. Using a slotted spoon, transfer the beef to a plate and set aside.

2 Lower the heat and add the onion, pepper, carrot, and garlic to the Dutch oven. Cover and cook, stirring occasionally, for 12 minutes or until the onion has softened. Add the wine and cook for 1 minute. Stir in the tomato paste, stock, and salt, then return the meat to the Dutch oven and bring the liquid to a boil. Lower the heat, cover, and simmer for 1 hour or until the meat is tender.

3 Using a slotted spoon, transfer the meat to the plate. Skim off any fat, then transfer the vegetables and stock to a food processor or blender and whirl for 1 minute or until smooth. Return the puréed vegetable mixture to the Dutch oven and stir in the sour cream. Add the meat and gently reheat for 1 minute or until the sauce is heated through. Do not allow the sauce to boil. Serves 4.

PREPARATION TIME: 18 MIN. COOKING TIME: 1 HR. 20 MIN.

Per serving: Calories 256; Saturated Fat 4 g; Total Fat 11 g; Protein 28 g; Carbohydrate 9 g; Fiber 2 g; Sodium 265 mg; Cholesterol 77 mg

GINGERED BEEF STEW WITH WHITE BEANS AND APRICOTS

- ½ cup dried apricots, coarsely chopped (2 ounces)
- 1½ cups hot water
- 1 tablespoon olive oil
- 12 ounces boneless beef round, cut into ¾-inch cubes
- 1 medium-size yellow onion, finely chopped (1 cup)
- 3 cloves garlic, minced
- 1 tablespoon minced fresh ginger or 1 teaspoon ground ginger
- 2 tablespoons tomato paste
- 1 tablespoon apricot jam
- 1 teaspoon ground sage
- 1 medium-size all-purpose potato, peeled and cut into ¾-inch cubes (1 cup)
- 1½ cups cooked cannellini (white kidney beans)

1 In a small bowl, soak the apricots in the hot water for 30 minutes. Drain, reserving both the soaking liquid and the apricots.

2 In a 5-quart Dutch oven or large heavy saucepan, heat the oil over moderately high heat. Add the beef and sauté for 4 minutes or until browned on all sides. Using a slotted spoon, transfer the beef to a plate.

3 Lower the heat, add the onion, garlic, and ginger, and cook, stirring occasionally, for 5 minutes or until the onion is softened. Stir in the apricot soaking liquid and cook 5 minutes more.

4 Stir in the tomato paste, jam, sage, apricots, and beef. Bring the liquid to a boil, lower the heat, cover, and simmer for 45 minutes. Add the potato, cover, and cook 15 minutes more. Add the beans, cover, and cook 8 minutes longer or until the potatoes and meat are tender. Serve with crusty bread and a green salad. Serves 4.

PREPARATION TIME: 20 MIN. COOKING TIME: 1 HR. 25 MIN
SOAKING TIME: 30 MIN.

Per serving: Calories 325; Saturated Fat 2 g; Total Fat 7 g; Protein 26 g; Carbohydrate 39 g; Fiber 5 g; Sodium 384 mg; Cholesterol 48 mg

STIR-FRIED FLANK STEAK WITH HONEY-TOMATO GLAZE

This quick dish can be served either hot or at room temperature. If flank steak is unavailable, substitute top round steak. The special technique in Step 2 is called velveting (see explanation, Pork Stir-fry with Noodles, page 149).

- 1 **large egg white**
- 1 **tablespoon cornstarch**
- 2 **teaspoons reduced-sodium soy sauce**
- 1 **teaspoon water**
- 12 **ounces flank steak, sliced ¼ inch thick and cut into strips ½ inch wide**
- 2 **teaspoons canola or peanut oil**
- 1 **small yellow onion, cut into ½-inch cubes (¾ cup)**

- 1 **medium-size sweet red pepper, cored, seeded, and cut into ½-inch squares (¾ cup)**
- 1 **small tomato, finely chopped, with its juice (½ cup)**
- 2 **teaspoons honey**
- 2 **cloves garlic, minced**
- ½ **teaspoon ground ginger**
- 2 **green onions, including tops, thinly sliced on the diagonal (¼ cup)**

1 In a medium-size bowl, stir together the egg white, cornstarch, 1 teaspoon of the soy sauce, and the water. Add the steak and toss to coat. Cover with plastic food wrap and refrigerate for at least 30 minutes or as long as overnight.

2 Drop the steak into a large saucepan of boiling water and cook for 20 seconds; drain, then rinse quickly with cold water and pat dry with paper toweling.

3 In a 12-inch nonstick skillet, heat the oil over moderately high heat. Add the onion and pepper and stir-fry for 2 minutes. Add the steak and stir-fry for 1 minute. Add the tomato, honey, garlic, ginger, and remaining 1 teaspoon of soy sauce and stir-fry 2 minutes more. Stir in the green onions. Serve over rice or with noodles tossed with a little peanut or sesame oil. Serves 4.

PREPARATION TIME: 20 MIN. COOKING TIME: 5 MIN.
MARINATING TIME: 30 MIN.

Per serving: Calories 210; Saturated Fat 4 g; Total Fat 10 g; Protein 19 g; Carbohydrate 10 g; Fiber 1 g; Sodium 161 mg; Cholesterol 43 mg

Gingered Beef Stew with White Beans and Apricots doubles as hearty family fare or an easy company entrée.

ORANGE BEEF STIR-FRY

4 strips orange zest (colored part of the rind), each 3 inches long and ½ inch wide
1 large egg white
1 tablespoon plus 1 teaspoon cornstarch
1 teaspoon water
12 ounces flank steak, ¼ inch thick, cut into strips ½ inch wide
2 teaspoons peanut oil
1 medium-size carrot, peeled and thinly sliced (½ cup)
1 large cucumber, peeled, halved lengthwise, seeded, and sliced ¼ inch thick (8 ounces)
1 clove garlic, minced
1 cup orange juice
½ teaspoon each ground coriander and cumin
½ teaspoon salt
¼ teaspoon each ground cinnamon and ginger
2 green onions, including tops, thinly sliced (¼ cup)

1 Preheat the oven to 300° F. Place the orange zest on a small cake rack set on a baking sheet and bake for 10 minutes or until dry. Let cool, then mince and set aside.

2 Meanwhile, in a medium-size bowl, stir together the egg white, 1 tablespoon of the cornstarch, and the water. Add the beef to the cornstarch mixture, toss to coat, and marinate in the refrigerator, covered with plastic food wrap, for at least 30 minutes or as long as overnight.

3 Drop the beef into a large saucepan of boiling water and cook for 20 seconds; drain and rinse. In a 12-inch nonstick skillet, heat the oil over moderately high heat until hot but not smoking. Add the carrot, cucumber, garlic, and orange zest and stir-fry for 2 minutes or until the vegetables are slightly softened. Add the beef and stir-fry 2 minutes longer or until lightly browned.

4 In a small bowl, combine the orange juice, remaining 1 teaspoon of cornstarch, the coriander, cumin, salt, cinnamon, and ginger. Add the mixture to the skillet and cook, stirring, for 1 minute or until slightly thickened; stir in the green onions. Serve over rice. Serves 4.

PREPARATION TIME: 22 MIN.   COOKING TIME: 16 MIN.

MARINATING TIME: 30 MIN.

Per serving: Calories 226; Saturated Fat 4 g; Total Fat 11 g; Protein 19 g; Carbohydrate 14 g; Fiber 2 g; Sodium 351 mg; Cholesterol 43 mg

Your guests will think you're a super chef when you present Beef Rolls with Currant Stuffing. Only you will know how deceptively simple they are to prepare.

BEEF ROLLS WITH CURRANT STUFFING

For this impressive dish, paper-thin slices of beef are wrapped around a light stuffing of currants, green onions, and spices.

1 **pound beef top round, cut horizontally into thin slices**
4 **green onions, including tops, finely chopped (½ cup)**
3 **tablespoons dried currants or raisins**
1 **tablespoon minced garlic**
1 **teaspoon minced fresh ginger or ¼ teaspoon ground ginger**
½ **teaspoon ground ginger**
¼ **teaspoon salt**
⅛ **teaspoon black pepper**
2 **large egg whites**
1 **tablespoon water**
⅓ **cup plain dry bread crumbs**
1 **tablespoon plus 1 teaspoon vegetable oil**
1 **lemon, cut into 4 wedges**

1 Place each slice of meat between 2 sheets of wax paper and, using a mallet or the bottom of a small heavy pan, pound it paper-thin. Cut into rectangles measuring about 4 by 6 inches.

2 In a small bowl, mix together the green onions, currants, garlic, fresh ginger, ground ginger, salt, and pepper. In a shallow bowl, mix the egg whites with the water. Spread the bread crumbs on a plate.

3 Brush the top side of each piece of meat with the egg white mixture and spread a tablespoon of the green onion mixture over it. Starting at a short end, roll up each piece of meat and secure with a toothpick. Dip each roll in the egg white, then coat with the crumbs.

4 Heat a 12-inch nonstick skillet over moderately high heat. When it is hot, add the oil and heat until it is hot but not smoking. Add the beef rolls and, working in batches if necessary, sauté for 4 to 5 minutes or until golden brown all over. Garnish with the lemon wedges and serve with orzo and sautéed spinach. Serves 4.

PREPARATION TIME: 20 MIN. COOKING TIME: 5 MIN.

Per serving: Calories 262; Saturated Fat 3 g; Total Fat 10 g; Protein 30 g; Carbohydrate 15 g; Fiber 1 g; Sodium 283 mg; Cholesterol 65 mg

BEEF ROLLS WITH MUSHROOM STUFFING

1 **ounce dried mushrooms, such as porcini or shiitake, or 4 ounces fresh mushrooms, coarsely chopped**
¾ **cup hot water**
12 **ounces beef top round, cut into 8 thin slices about 5″ x 3″ x ⅛″**
4 **cloves garlic, minced**
½ **cup minced fresh basil or parsley**
1½ **teaspoons grated lemon rind**
¼ **teaspoon salt**
2 **tablespoons all-purpose flour**
2 **teaspoons olive oil**
⅓ **cup dry red wine or low-sodium beef broth**
1 **medium-size tomato, coarsely chopped (1 cup), or 1 cup canned crushed tomatoes**

1 In a small bowl, soak the dried mushrooms in the hot water for 30 minutes. Using a slotted spoon, transfer the mushrooms to a cutting board. Strain the soaking liquid through a sieve lined with cheesecloth or paper toweling into a measuring cup. Set aside ½ cup of the liquid and discard the rest. Finely chop the mushrooms.

2 Using a mallet or a small heavy skillet, pound the meat slightly. In a small bowl, combine the mushrooms, garlic, basil, lemon rind, and salt. Spread 2 rounded tablespoons of the mixture on top of each beef slice, then roll the beef and secure with a toothpick. Dredge the beef rolls in the flour, shaking off any excess.

3 In a 12-inch nonstick skillet, heat the oil over moderately high heat until hot but not smoking. Add the beef rolls and sauté for 4 minutes or until lightly browned on all sides. Add the wine and reserved mushroom soaking liquid and cook for 3 minutes. (If using fresh mushrooms, add ½ cup water.) Lower the heat, add the tomato, cover, and simmer, turning the rolls occasionally, for 20 minutes or until the sauce has thickened and the rolls are cooked through. Serve with rice and steamed zucchini. Serves 4.

PREPARATION TIME: 20 MIN. COOKING TIME: 25 MIN.
SOAKING TIME: 30 MIN.

Per serving: Calories 195; Saturated Fat 2 g; Total Fat 6 g; Protein 21 g; Carbohydrate 11 g; Fiber 1 g; Sodium 198 mg; Cholesterol 48 mg

BEEF, BULGUR, AND SPINACH LOAF

The bulgur and spinach add extra fiber and nutrition to this meat loaf and extend the beef so that you get 8 servings from just 1 ½ pounds.

⅓ cup bulgur	1 ½ pounds lean ground beef
½ cup cold water	1 large egg white
2 teaspoons unsalted butter	½ teaspoon each dried savory and marjoram, crumbled
1 large yellow onion, finely chopped (1 ½ cups)	¼ teaspoon each salt and black pepper
2 cloves garlic, minced	
1 package (10 ounces) frozen chopped spinach, thawed and squeezed dry	

1 Preheat the oven to 375° F. In a medium-size bowl, combine the bulgur with the water and let the mixture stand for 15 minutes or until the bulgur is tender. In a colander or strainer, drain the bulgur, then, with your hands, gently press it dry.

2 In a 10-inch nonstick skillet, melt the butter over moderate heat. Add the onion and sauté, stirring occasionally, for 3 minutes or until softened. Add the garlic and sauté, stirring, 1 minute more.

3 In a large bowl, combine the bulgur, onion mixture, spinach, beef, egg white, savory, marjoram, salt, and pepper. Using your hands, shape the mixture into a 9" x 4" x 1 ½" loaf. Place the meat loaf in a greased baking pan and bake for 40 to 45 minutes or until the juices run clear when the meat is pricked with a fork. Serve with Creamy Mashed Potatoes (page 236) and Carrots with Orange-Ginger Glaze (page 223). Serves 8.

PREPARATION TIME: 12 MIN. COOKING TIME: 45 MIN.

STANDING TIME: 15 MIN.

Per serving: Calories 165; Saturated Fat 2 g; Total Fat 5 g; Protein 22 g; Carbohydrate 9 g; Fiber 3 g; Sodium 150 mg; Cholesterol 51 mg

TEX-MEX MEAT LOAF

You can make this meat loaf as spicy as you like by using mild, medium, or hot salsa. Use any leftovers for sandwiches or make mini meat loaves (see below) and tuck a couple of them in your lunch bag.

1 **pound lean ground beef**	2 **green onions, including tops, finely chopped (¼ cup)**
1½ **cups Tomato Salsa (page 280) or prepared salsa**	¼ **cup plain dry bread crumbs**
1 **cup frozen corn kernels, thawed and drained**	2 **large egg whites**
	¼ **teaspoon salt**
6 **ounces mushrooms, finely chopped (2 cups)**	

1 Preheat the oven to 375° F. Lightly grease a 9" x 5" x 4" loaf pan. In a large bowl, combine the beef, 1 cup of the salsa, the corn, mushrooms, green onions, bread crumbs, egg whites, and salt. Press the mixture into the loaf pan.

2 Bake the meat loaf, uncovered, for 50 minutes or until the juices run clear and the loaf is set. Remove from the oven and carefully invert onto a large serving platter. Spoon the remaining ½ cup of salsa over the top and serve with Sautéed Summer Squash (page 239) and corn bread. Serves 4 to 6.

PREPARATION TIME: 9 MIN.   COOKING TIME: 50 MIN.

> *Per serving (for 4): Calories 253; Saturated Fat 1 g; Total Fat 7 g; Protein 31 g; Carbohydrate 19 g; Fiber 1 g; Sodium 591 mg; Cholesterol 64 mg*

•

Mini Meat Loaf Variation: To make mini meat loaves, spoon the mixture into twelve 2½-inch muffin cups that have been coated with nonstick cooking spray or lined with aluminum foil cupcake liners. Bake in the preheated oven for 25 minutes or until the juices run clear and the loaves are set. *Per mini loaf: Calories 85; Saturated Fat 1 g; Total Fat 2 g; Protein 11 g; Carbohydrate 7 g; Fiber 1 g; Sodium 197 mg; Cholesterol 22 mg.*

GREEN CHILI BURGERS

Here are burgers in a new lean and spicy guise. Ground chicken or pork can be substituted for the turkey with equally good results.

3 **green onions, including tops, sliced (⅓ cup)**	1 **can (4 ounces) chopped green chilies, drained**
1 **teaspoon minced garlic**	12 **ounces lean ground beef**
¾ **teaspoon dried marjoram, crumbled**	8 **ounces ground turkey**
¼ **teaspoon dried thyme, crumbled**	½ **cup Homemade Ketchup (page 281) or prepared low-sodium ketchup (optional topping)**
⅛ **teaspoon ground red pepper (cayenne)**	

1 In a 10-inch nonstick skillet, cook the green onions, garlic, marjoram, thyme, red pepper, and chilies over moderate heat for 5 minutes or until the onions are softened. Transfer the mixture to a medium-size bowl and let cool to room temperature.

2 Add the ground beef and turkey to the chili mixture and mix well. Using your hands, shape the mixture into 6 patties about ½ inch thick. (It is easier to shape the patties if you wet your hands first.) Wipe out the skillet and set it over moderate heat. Add the patties and cook, turning once, for 6 to 8 minutes or until the juices run clear when the burgers are pierced with a fork. Serve on whole-wheat buns, topped with sliced tomatoes and cucumbers and the ketchup if desired. Serves 6.

PREPARATION TIME: 10 MIN.   COOKING TIME: 12 MIN.

> *Per patty: Calories 127; Saturated Fat 1 g; Total Fat 3 g; Protein 22 g; Carbohydrate 1 g; Fiber 0 g; Sodium 56 mg; Cholesterol 57 mg*

MEXICAN BBQ FOR SIX

Baked Tortilla Chips

Tomato Salsa
(page 280)

Green Chili Burgers on Whole-Wheat Rolls

Black Beans with Corn and Winter Squash
(page 158)

Sliced Tomatoes and Avocados

Frozen Peach Yogurt

For a speedy Sunday supper, cook up a sizzling skilletful of Golden Beef Hash.

HAMBURGERS STUFFED WITH MOZZARELLA AND RED PEPPERS

Cheeseburger lovers rejoice! Creamy mozzarella oozes from the center of this very special burger, giving you a calcium boost with your protein.

¼ **cup diced roasted red pepper, patted dry**	1 **teaspoon balsamic or red wine vinegar**
¼ **cup diced part-skim mozzarella cheese (1 ounce)**	1 **pound lean ground beef**
4 **black olives, pitted and coarsely chopped**	2 **cloves garlic, minced**
1 **tablespoon minced fresh basil or 1 teaspoon dried basil, crumbled**	¼ **teaspoon each salt and black pepper**

1 In a medium-size bowl, combine the red pepper, cheese, olives, basil, and vinegar. In another medium-size bowl, combine the beef, garlic, salt, and black pepper.

2 Using your hands, shape the beef mixture into 8 thin patties about 3½ inches in diameter. (It is easier to shape the patties if you wet your hands first.) Spread the cheese mixture on top of 4 patties, dividing the amount equally. Place the 4 remaining patties on top and pinch the edges to seal.

3 Preheat the broiler, setting the rack 6 inches from the heat. Arrange the stuffed burgers on a broiler pan and broil for 3 to 4 minutes on each side for medium-rare, 4 to 5 minutes for medium, or 5 to 6 minutes for well-done. Serve on whole-wheat English muffins, accompanied by carrot and cucumber sticks. Serves 4.

PREPARATION TIME: 15 MIN.   COOKING TIME: 6 MIN.

Per serving: Calories 179; Saturated Fat 2 g; Total Fat 6 g; Protein 28 g; Carbohydrate 1 g; Fiber 0 g; Sodium 246 mg; Cholesterol 69 mg

MEATBALLS WITH CREAMY DILL SAUCE

With this easy recipe, you can turn ground beef into an elegant, rich-tasting dish in minutes. If you prefer, substitute ground lamb, veal, or pork for the beef.

- 12 **ounces lean ground beef**
- 3 **tablespoons low-fat (1% milkfat) milk**
- 1 **large egg white**
- 2 **tablespoons plain dry bread crumbs**
- 3 **tablespoons snipped fresh dill or 1 teaspoon dill weed, crumbled**
- ½ **teaspoon prepared mustard**
- ¼ **teaspoon salt**
- 3 **tablespoons all-purpose flour**
- 2 **teaspoons vegetable oil**
- ½ **cup Chicken Stock or Vegetable Stock (page 62) or low-sodium chicken broth**
- ¼ **cup plain low-fat yogurt**

1 In a medium-size bowl, combine the beef, milk, egg white, bread crumbs, 2 tablespoons of the dill, the mustard, and salt. Using your hands, shape the mixture into 24 meatballs about 1 ½ inches in diameter. (It is easier to shape the meatballs if you wet your hands first.)

2 Dredge the meatballs in the flour, shaking off any excess. In a 12-inch nonstick skillet, heat the oil over moderately high heat until very hot but not smoking. Add the meatballs and sauté for 4 minutes or until browned on all sides.

3 Lower the heat, add the stock to the skillet, cover, and simmer for 5 minutes. Remove from the heat and stir in the yogurt and remaining 1 tablespoon of dill. Serve with egg noodles and steamed green beans. Serves 4.

PREPARATION TIME: 10 MIN. COOKING TIME: 10 MIN.

Per serving: Calories 189; Saturated Fat 2 g; Total Fat 6 g; Protein 23 g; Carbohydrate 8 g; Fiber 0 g; Sodium 248 mg; Cholesterol 50 mg

GOLDEN BEEF HASH

This is an ideal dish to make with leftover steak or roast beef. Corned beef, chicken, or turkey are also suitable. Instead of cooking the potatoes and parsnips separately, you can mix the uncooked vegetables with the meat and cook the skillet mixture for an extra 10 minutes.

- 1 **medium-size all-purpose potato, peeled and diced (1 cup)**
- 1 **medium-size size parsnip, peeled and diced (1 cup)**
- 8 **ounces cooked beef round or chuck, diced (2 cups)**
- 1 **medium-size yellow onion, finely chopped (1 cup)**
- ¼ **cup minced parsley**
- 2 **teaspoons Worcestershire sauce**
- ½ **teaspoon black pepper**
- ¼ **teaspoon salt**
- 2 **teaspoons vegetable oil**
- 1 **tablespoon grated Parmesan cheese**

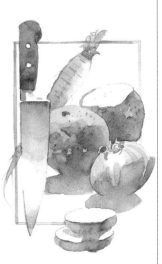

1 In a medium-size saucepan of boiling water, cook the potato and parsnip for 10 minutes or until tender; drain and transfer to a large bowl. Add the beef, onion, parsley, Worcestershire sauce, pepper, and salt and mix well.

2 In a 10-inch nonstick skillet, heat the oil over moderate heat. Add the beef mixture and flatten it evenly with a spatula. Lower the heat and cook, uncovered, for 15 minutes or until the edges are golden brown.

3 Preheat the broiler, setting the rack 6 inches from the heat. Sprinkle the top of the hash with the cheese. Wrap the handle of the skillet with heavy-duty aluminum foil and run the hash under the broiler for 2 minutes or until the top is golden and crisp. Serve with Broiled Tomatoes (page 242) and a green salad. Serves 4.

PREPARATION TIME: 15 MIN. COOKING TIME: 27 MIN.

Per serving: Calories 231; Saturated Fat 3 g; Total Fat 8 g; Protein 20 g; Carbohydrate 18 g; Fiber 3 g; Sodium 224 mg; Cholesterol 56 mg

FRUIT-STUFFED PORK LOIN

This fragrant stuffing calls for a mixture of dried fruits. If you are lacking one ingredient, just add more of the others or devise your own combination to equal ½ cup chopped fruit. You can make the stuffing up to 6 hours in advance and refrigerate until you're ready to roast the meat.

- 1 tablespoon olive oil
- 1 Spanish onion, chopped (2 cups)
- 8 ounces fresh spinach, trimmed, rinsed, and chopped (4 cups), or 5 ounces (½ package) frozen chopped spinach, thawed and squeezed dry
- 1 teaspoon dried basil, crumbled
- 1 ounce each dried apples, apricots, and pitted prunes, chopped, and golden raisins (½ cup total)
- 6 slices whole-wheat toast, cut into ½-inch cubes
- ¼ cup chopped walnuts or pecans (2 ounces)
- ½ teaspoon salt
- ¼ teaspoon black pepper
- 3 tablespooons apple jack or cider
- 1 egg white
- 2 pounds boneless pork loin
- Nonstick cooking spray

1 In a 10-inch nonstick skillet, heat the oil over moderate heat. Add the onion and sauté, stirring frequently, for 5 minutes or until softened. Stir in the spinach, basil, and dried fruit; cook, uncovered, for 5 minutes or until most of the liquid has evaporated.

2 Add the toast cubes, walnuts, salt, and pepper, stir until combined, and remove from the heat. In a glass measuring cup, beat together the apple jack and egg white. Stir into the skillet and set aside.

3 Preheat the oven to 400° F. Trim the pork loin of excess fat. Using a sharp knife and beginning at one of the long sides, split the roast almost in half, leaving ½ inch uncut at the other long side. Lay the pork loin open between 2 sheets of plastic food wrap. Using a meat mallet or a small heavy skillet, pound the pork to an even ⅝-inch thickness. Remove the plastic food wrap. Spoon about 2½ cups of the filling down the center of the meat, spreading it evenly and shaping into a log. Gently wrap both sides of the meat around the filling and temporarily secure the edges with toothpicks. Tie the meat with string at 1-inch intervals and remove the toothpicks.

4 Tear off a sheet of heavy-duty aluminum foil about 16 inches long and coat it with nonstick cooking spray. Place the roast, seam side down, on the foil and wrap, crimping the edges to seal. Place the remaining stuffing in a covered ovenproof dish and set aside.

5 Place the meat on a baking sheet and roast for 30 minutes. Reduce the oven temperature to 350° F and place the covered dish of stuffing in the oven. Open the foil around the roast so that the top and sides can brown and roast an additional 25 minutes or until a meat thermometer inserted into the thickest part of the pork registers 160° F. Remove the roast and covered dish. Let the roast stand for 15 minutes before carving. Serve warm or cold with steamed butternut squash. Serves 8.

PREPARATION TIME: 25 MIN. COOKING TIME: 1 HR. 5 MIN.
STANDING TIME: 15 MIN.

Per serving: Calories 349; Saturated Fat 3 g; Total Fat 15 g; Protein 30 g; Carbohydrate 25 g; Fiber 5 g; Sodium 374 mg; Cholesterol 71 mg

A meat thermometer allows you to check on the doneness of meat without cutting into it. The traditional type is inserted, usually into a roast, before cooking and registers the temperature as the meat cooks. For accurate results, insert the thermometer in the thickest part of the meat, making sure the tip does not touch bone.

The newer, instant-read thermometer can be put into meat anytime during the cooking process and will give an immediate reading of the internal temperature. Instant-read thermometers are ideal for checking the temperature of meat cooked in a microwave because a traditional thermometer is made of metal and cannot be used there.

Meat that is either undercooked or overcooked can cause health problems. The USDA therefore recommends cooking meat to the following internal temperatures, which equate to medium well-done:
Beef 160° F
Lamb 170° F
Poultry 180° F
Veal 170° F
Pork 170° F

PORK TENDERLOIN WITH CRANBERRY-APPLE RELISH

Pork goes beautifully with any kind of fruit sauce. This recipe calls for a piquant combination of cranberries and apples.

- 1 **pound pork tenderloin**
- ¼ **teaspoon each salt and black pepper**
- ¼ **teaspoon ground sage**
- 1 **small yellow onion, finely chopped (½ cup)**
- ¼ **cup dry red wine, Chicken Stock (page 62), or low-sodium chicken broth**
- 1 **teaspoon unsalted butter**
- 1 **cup Cranberry-Apple Relish (page 286) or canned cranberry applesauce**
- 1 **teaspoon lemon juice**

1 Preheat the oven to 425° F. Sprinkle both sides of the pork with ⅛ teaspoon each of the salt and pepper and the sage. Place the pork in an 11″ x 7″ x 2″ baking pan, tucking the narrow end under so that the meat is an even thickness. Add the onion and wine to the pan.

2 Roast for 25 minutes or until a meat thermometer registers 165° F and the juices run clear when the meat is pricked with a fork. (The liquid in the pan should be almost evaporated.) Place the meat on a cutting board and let stand for 10 minutes.

3 Meanwhile, add the butter to the baking pan and let it melt. Stir in the remaining ⅛ teaspoon each of salt and pepper, the relish, and lemon juice, scraping up any browned bits from the pan. Slice the pork thinly against the grain, holding the knife at a slight angle; stir any pork juices from the cutting board into the fruit mixture. Arrange the meat on a platter and serve the sauce on the side. Accompany with Creamy Mashed Potatoes (page 236) and Escarole Sautéed with Garlic (page 229). Serves 4.

PREPARATION TIME: 7 MIN. COOKING TIME: 25 MIN.

STANDING TIME: 10 MIN.

*Per serving: Calories 290; Saturated Fat 2 g;
Total Fat 7 g; Protein 25 g; Carbohydrate 32 g;
Fiber 1 g; Sodium 195 mg; Cholesterol 76 mg*

Dazzle your most discerning diners with this glamorous Fruit-Stuffed Pork Loin, beautifully garnished with rosettes of Puréed Squash with Orange and Cinnamon (page 240).

Today's hog is a leaner animal than his 1940's counterpart, thanks to improvements in the feeding and breeding of pigs. Instead of their former high-fat diet, pigs are now being fed soybeans, which are low in saturated fat. (Improved feeding has also nearly eliminated the threat of trichinosis from pork.)

The leanest cuts of pork, which come from the top and center of the loin, are almost as lean as chicken. A 3-ounce serving of pork tenderloin has 4 grams of fat and 67 milligrams of cholesterol; the same size serving of boneless, skinless chicken breast has 3 grams of fat and 72 milligrams of cholesterol. Closer trimming by meat processors is also helping to eliminate excess fat.

1940's Hog

Today's Hog

ORANGE BRAISED HAM STEAK

The marinade in this recipe calls for dark rum; if you prefer, you can substitute orange juice.

3 tablespoons orange juice	1 lean reduced-sodium ham steak (1 ¼ pounds)
2 tablespoons dark rum or orange juice	1 teaspoon cornstarch
1 tablespoon honey	⅓ cup low-sodium beef broth
2 cloves garlic, minced	2 teaspoons olive or canola oil
½ teaspoon dried thyme, crumbled	1 medium-size orange, peeled and sliced crosswise (optional garnish)
½ teaspoon grated orange rind	
¼ teaspoon ground allspice	

1 In a shallow baking dish, combine the orange juice, rum, honey, garlic, thyme, orange rind, and allspice. Score the edge of the ham with a knife at 1-inch intervals to prevent curling. Add the ham to the marinade, cover with plastic food wrap, and marinate, refrigerated, for 30 minutes to 1 hour. Drain the ham, reserving the marinade, and pat it dry.

2 In a glass measuring cup, mix the cornstarch with the broth until dissolved. In a 10-inch nonstick skillet, heat the oil over moderate heat. Add the ham and cook it for 1 minute on each side. Add the marinade and broth mixture to the skillet and bring to a boil. Reduce the heat to low and cook the ham, basting it occasionally, for 10 minutes or until tender.

3 Transfer the ham to a warm platter and pour the sauce over it. If you wish, garnish with the orange slices. Serve with sugar snap peas or steamed asparagus and Carrot-Turnip Salad with Cumin-Lime Dressing (page 254). Serves 4.

PREPARATION TIME: 15 MIN. COOKING TIME: 12 MIN.
MARINATING TIME: 30 MIN.

Per serving: Calories 271; Saturated Fat 3 g; Total Fat 10 g; Protein 30 g; Carbohydrate 9 g; Fiber 0 g; Sodium 1,070 mg; Cholesterol 75 mg

HAM STEAK WITH SUGAR-MUSTARD GLAZE

Here is a simple supper dish that is sure to please. Lean ham is available in most supermarkets.

4 teaspoons dark brown sugar	⅛ teaspoon ground cloves
1 teaspoon Dijon mustard	1 lean reduced-sodium ham steak (1 ¼ pounds)
1 teaspoon cider vinegar	

1 In a small bowl, combine the sugar, mustard, vinegar, and cloves. Score the edge of the ham at 1-inch intervals with a knife to prevent curling. Coat one side of the ham with half of the mixture.

2 Preheat the broiler, setting the rack 5 inches from the heat. Place the ham on a broiler pan, coated side up, and broil for 3 minutes. Turn the ham, coat it with the remaining glaze mixture, and broil 3 minutes more. Serve with Potato and Chick Pea Salad (page 261) or baked beans and coleslaw. Serves 4.

PREPARATION TIME: 5 MIN. COOKING TIME: 6 MIN.

Per serving: Calories 183; Saturated Fat 2 g; Total Fat 6 g; Protein 24 g; Carbohydrate 6 g; Fiber 0 g; Sodium 857 mg; Cholesterol 60 mg

SAGE-MARINATED PORK CHOPS

This super-quick recipe is simply delicious.

- 3 tablespoons olive oil
- 2 tablespoons dry sherry or apple cider
- 2 tablespoons minced fresh sage or 1 ½ teaspoons ground sage
- ⅛ teaspoon black pepper
- 4 center-cut pork chops, about ½ inch thick (4 ounces each)

1 In a self-sealing plastic food storage bag, combine the oil, sherry, sage, and pepper. Add the pork chops, push out all the air, and seal tightly. Refrigerate for 30 minutes or up to 2 hours.

2 Heat a 12-inch nonstick skillet over moderate heat. Add the chops and cook for 3 minutes on each side or until no longer pink on the inside. Serve with white beans and tomatoes or Braised Fennel (page 230). Serves 4.

PREPARATION TIME: 5 MIN. COOKING TIME: 6 MIN.
MARINATING TIME: 30 MIN.

Per serving: Calories 235; Saturated Fat 4 g; Total Fat 16 g; Protein 19 g; Carbohydrate 1 g; Fiber 0 g; Sodium 56 mg; Cholesterol 54 mg

Orange Braised Ham Steak — its sauce is a sumptuous way to dress up ham.

BRAISED PORK CHOPS WITH MUSHROOMS AND ONIONS

This mushroom and onion sauce turns ordinary pork chops into a French country dinner. It is also delicious on lamb or veal chops.

2 teaspoons olive oil
2 large yellow onions, halved and thinly sliced (3 cups)
1 medium-size carrot, peeled and thinly sliced (½ cup)
2 cloves garlic, minced
6 ounces mushrooms, thinly sliced (1¾ cups)

⅓ cup Chicken Stock (page 62) or low-sodium chicken broth
½ teaspoon salt
1 teaspoon dried rosemary, crumbled
¼ teaspoon ground sage
4 loin pork chops (5 ounces each)

1 In a 12-inch nonstick skillet, heat the oil over low heat. Add the onions and cook, uncovered, stirring frequently, for 20 minutes or until very soft. Add the carrot and garlic and cook 5 minutes longer. Add the mushrooms, stir to combine, and cook another 5 minutes.

2 Raise the heat to moderate and stir in the stock, salt, rosemary, and sage. Place the pork chops on top, cover, and cook for 4 minutes. Turn the chops over, cover, and cook 4 minutes longer or until they are no longer pink on the inside. Serve with ¼ of the onion mixture on top of each chop. Accompany with Carrot Pudding (page 224) and steamed broccoli. Serves 4.

PREPARATION TIME: 10 MIN. COOKING TIME: 38 MIN.

Per serving: Calories 250; Saturated Fat 3 g; Total Fat 11 g; Protein 27 g; Carbohydrate 10 g; Fiber 2 g; Sodium 362 mg; Cholesterol 71 mg

In this lighter version of a classic recipe, Pork Cutlets in Madeira Sauce are a beautiful blend of simplicity and elegance. Accompany them with Wild and Brown Rice with Toasted Pecans (page 201) and steamed wax beans.

PORK CHOPS MARINATED IN HERBS

This easy-to-prepare dry marinade is a perfect sweet and spicy blend that is delicious with lamb as well as pork. For safety's sake, be sure that the bay leaves are very finely crushed or ground, and for best results, marinate the chops for at least 6 hours.

- ¾ teaspoon ground allspice
- 2 bay leaves, finely crushed or ground in a spice grinder
- ½ teaspoon each sugar and salt
- ¼ teaspoon each ground cinnamon, ginger, and black pepper
- 4 loin pork chops, about ½ inch thick (5 ounces each)

1 In a small bowl, combine the allspice, bay leaves, sugar, salt, cinnamon, ginger, and pepper. Rub the mixture into both sides of each pork chop; wrap the chops in plastic food wrap and marinate in the refrigerator for at least 6 hours or overnight.

2 Preheat the broiler, setting the rack 6 inches from the heat. Arrange the chops on a broiler pan and broil for 5 minutes. Turn the chops over and broil 3 minutes longer. Serve with Hominy and Red Pepper Sauté (page 211) and steamed dandelion greens. Serves 4.

PREPARATION TIME: 4 MIN. COOKING TIME: 8 MIN.
MARINATING TIME: 6 HR.

Per serving: Calories 184; Saturated Fat 3 g; Total Fat 8 g; Protein 25 g; Carbohydrate 1 g; Fiber 0 g; Sodium 342 mg; Cholesterol 71 mg

PORK CUTLETS IN MADEIRA SAUCE

The pleasing character of Madeira wine (a cross between port and sherry) greatly enhances meats and soups.

- 4 slices boneless pork loin (4 ounces each)
- ¼ teaspoon each salt and white pepper
- 1 teaspoon each unsalted butter and vegetable oil
- 2 large shallots, finely chopped (⅓ cup)
- ⅓ cup dry Madeira, Chicken Stock (page 62), or low-sodium chicken broth
- 1 cup Chicken Stock or low-sodium chicken broth
- 1 teaspoon cornstarch
- ⅓ cup half-and-half
- 1 teaspoon Dijon mustard, or to taste

1 With a meat mallet or heavy skillet, pound each slice of pork until ¼ inch thick. Sprinkle on both sides with the salt and pepper. In a 10-inch nonstick skillet, heat the butter and oil over moderate heat. Add the pork and brown for 2 minutes on each side. Transfer the pork to a plate and set aside.

2 Add the shallots to the skillet and cook, stirring, for 1 minute. Add the Madeira and cook for 2 minutes or until the liquid is reduced to ¼ cup. Add the stock and cook for 5 minutes or until the liquid is reduced to ¾ cup.

3 In a glass measuring cup, stir the cornstarch with the half-and-half until dissolved. Add the mixture to the sauce and simmer for 2 minutes or until thickened. Stir in the mustard. Return the pork cutlets to the skillet and simmer for 2 to 3 minutes or until they are heated through. Serve with Creamy Mashed Potatoes (page 236) and a green salad. Serves 4.

PREPARATION TIME: 8 MIN. COOKING TIME: 18 MIN.

Per serving: Calories 263; Saturated Fat 5 g; Total Fat 13 g; Protein 27 g; Carbohydrate 4 g; Fiber 0 g; Sodium 269 mg; Cholesterol 81 mg

Cooking with wine or spirits tenderizes meat, fish, and poultry and adds wonderful flavor. However, even after extensive cooking, some of the alcohol may remain. For this reason, recipes in the *Live Longer Cookbook* offer substitutions for wines and spirits when appropriate. For example, chicken, beef, or vegetable stock or even water can be substituted in equal measure when preparing a sauce. In marinades, every cup of wine should be replaced with 2 tablespoons of vinegar, such as cider, rice, or wine vinegar, plus enough chicken stock or water to fill a cup. Vinegar, like wine, tenderizes meat.

GLAZED PORK KEBABS

The wonderful sweet and spicy glaze for these kebabs goes equally well on chicken or turkey, either broiled or grilled.

1 small can (5 1/2 ounces) prune juice	1/8 teaspoon salt
2 tablespoons low-sodium ketchup	1/8 teaspoon ground allspice
1 tablespoon each granulated sugar and brown sugar	Pinch ground red pepper (cayenne)
1 tablespoon honey	1 tablespoon cider vinegar
1 green onion, sliced	1 pound boneless pork tenderloin, cut into 1-inch cubes
1/2 teaspoon ground ginger	

1 Preheat the broiler, setting the rack 5 inches from the heat. In a small saucepan, combine the prune juice, ketchup, granulated sugar, brown sugar, honey, green onion, ginger, salt, allspice, and red pepper. Bring to a boil, lower the heat, and simmer, uncovered, for 12 to 15 minutes or until reduced to 1/3 cup. Remove from the heat, stir in the vinegar, and set aside.

2 Arrange the pork on four 8-inch-long skewers. Broil, turning once, for 8 to 10 minutes or until the juices run clear when the meat is pierced. Using a pastry brush, coat each cube with the glaze and broil 1 more minute. Serve hot or at room temperature, accompanied by the remaining glaze. Serve with steamed rice and Sautéed Collard Greens with Carrots (page 225). Serves 4.

PREPARATION TIME: 10 MIN.   COOKING TIME: 22 MIN.

Per serving: Calories 200; Saturated Fat 1 g; Total Fat 3 g; Protein 24 g; Carbohydrate 19 g; Fiber 0 g; Sodium 170 mg; Cholesterol 74 mg

---

PORK STEW WITH COCONUT AND LIME

Unsweetened coconut is available in health food stores; sweetened coconut from a supermarket can be used instead.

1 cup boiling water	2 strips lime zest (colored part of the rind), each 2 inches long and 1/4 inch wide
1/2 cup plus 2 tablespoons shredded unsweetened coconut	3 tablespoons lime juice
1 small yellow onion, sliced (1/2 cup)	1 pound boneless pork shoulder, trimmed and cut into 3/4-inch cubes
1/2 cup packed fresh cilantro (coriander) or 1/2 cup packed parsley plus 1 teaspoon dried cilantro	3 tablespoons all-purpose flour
2 cloves garlic, quartered	1 tablespoon olive oil
2 tablespoons canned chopped green chilies	1/2 cup Chicken Stock (page 62) or low-sodium chicken broth
	1 tablespoon grated lime rind (optional garnish)

1 In a small bowl, pour the boiling water over 1/2 cup of the coconut; let stand for 30 minutes. Strain the liquid through a sieve into a measuring cup, pressing the coconut to extract the juice. Discard the pulp and reserve the juice.

2 In a food processor or blender, combine the onion, cilantro, garlic, chilies, lime zest, and lime juice and whirl for 30 seconds or until puréed. Set aside.

3 Dredge the pork in the flour, shaking off any excess. In a 5-quart Dutch oven, heat the oil over moderately high heat. Add the pork and sauté for 5 minutes or until lightly browned all over. Add the stock, reserved coconut juice, and puréed onion mixture and bring to a boil. Lower the heat, cover, and simmer for 1 hour or until the meat is tender. Serve over steamed rice, garnished with the remaining 2 tablespoons of shredded coconut and the lime rind if desired. Serves 4.

PREPARATION TIME: 15 MIN.   COOKING TIME: 1 HR. 5 MIN.

STANDING TIME: 30 MIN.

Per serving: Calories 303; Saturated Fat 7 g; Total Fat 17 g; Protein 24 g; Carbohydrate 14 g; Fiber 1 g; Sodium 136 mg; Cholesterol 76 mg

---

PORK STEW WITH GREMOLATA

Gremolata is a classic Italian garnish, traditionally served over braised veal shanks. When sprinkled over this succulent pork stew, it adds a pleasing pungent flavor.

- ⅓ cup all-purpose flour
- ¼ teaspoon white pepper
- 1 pound boneless lean pork shoulder, cut into ¾-inch cubes
- 2 tablespoons olive or canola oil
- 1 can (13¾ ounces) low-sodium beef broth
- ½ cup dry white wine or apple cider
- 3 medium-size carrots, peeled and sliced ¼ inch thick (1½ cups)
- 3 small white turnips, peeled and cut into ¾-inch wedges (1½ cups)
- ¼ teaspoon each dried oregano and thyme, crumbled
- ½ cup low-fat (1% milkfat) milk
- 3 ounces small mushrooms, quartered (1 cup)
- 1 cup frozen pearl onions

For the gremolata:
- 2 tablespoons minced parsley
- 1 clove garlic, minced
- 1 teaspoon grated lemon rind

1 Combine the flour and pepper in a plastic food storage bag. Add the pork and shake to coat. Remove the pork from the bag, shaking off the excess flour, and reserve the flour. In a 5-quart Dutch oven, heat 1 tablespoon of the oil over moderately high heat. Add the pork and cook for 5 minutes, turning until browned on all sides.

2 Add the broth, wine, carrots, turnips, oregano, and thyme to the Dutch oven and simmer, uncovered, for 20 minutes. Meanwhile, in a small bowl, whisk 3½ tablespoons of the reserved flour with just enough of the milk to make a smooth paste. Blend in the remaining milk.

3 Stir the milk-flour mixture, mushrooms, and pearl onions into the stew and simmer, partially covered, stirring occasionally, for 20 minutes or until both the meat and vegetables are tender.

4 Meanwhile, prepare the gremolata. In a small bowl, combine the parsley, garlic, and lemon rind; cover and set aside. Ladle the stew over brown rice on individual serving plates and sprinkle some of the gremolata on each serving. Accompany with steamed spinach and Four-Grain Rolls (page 304). Serves 4.

PREPARATION TIME: 25 MIN. COOKING TIME: 45 MIN.

Per serving: Calories 364; Saturated Fat 4 g; Total Fat 16 g; Protein 27 g; Carbohydrate 22 g; Fiber 4 g; Sodium 272 mg; Cholesterol 77 mg

For a terrific Caribbean combo, serve Pork Stew with Coconut and Lime alongside a crunchy Dilled Cucumber and Carrot Salad (page 257).

PORK AND CHICK PEA STEW

Adding chick peas to this stew allows you to cut down on the amount of meat used and also gives this dish a Mediterranean nuance. Beef chuck can be substituted for the pork if you prefer.

12 ounces boneless pork shoulder, cut into 1-inch cubes
2 tablespoons all-purpose flour
1 tablespoon olive or vegetable oil
1 medium-size yellow onion, finely chopped (1 cup)
2 cloves garlic, minced
2 small carrots, peeled and sliced diagonally ½ inch thick (1 cup)
1 teaspoon ground ginger
⅛ teaspoon each salt and ground red pepper (cayenne), or to taste
½ cup low-sodium beef broth or water
⅔ cup cooked chick peas
1 teaspoon lemon juice

1 Dredge the pork in the flour. In a 12-inch nonstick skillet, heat the oil over moderately high heat. Add the pork in 1 layer and cook for about 5 minutes or until browned on all sides. With a slotted spoon, transfer to a plate lined with paper toweling and set aside.

2 Lower the heat to moderate. Add the onion and garlic to the skillet and cook, stirring frequently, for 5 minutes or until the onion is soft. Add the carrots, ginger, salt, red pepper, and broth and bring to a boil. Lower the heat, cover, and simmer for 1 hour 15 minutes or until the pork is tender. Stir in the chick peas and cook 5 minutes longer or until heated through. Stir in the lemon juice. Serve with couscous and cucumbers drizzled with Roasted Tomato Vinaigrette (page 266). Serves 4.

PREPARATION TIME: 18 MIN. COOKING TIME: 1½ HR.

Per serving: Calories 242; Saturated Fat 3 g; Total Fat 11 g; Protein 20 g; Carbohydrate 16 g; Fiber 3 g; Sodium 325 mg; Cholesterol 57 mg

PORK AND RED BEANS

Here is a healthful version of a favorite dish: pork and beans. To keep the sodium content to a minimum, cook your own red beans. If using canned beans, drain and rinse them thoroughly.

12 ounces boneless pork shoulder, trimmed and cut into ¾-inch cubes
3 tablespoons all-purpose flour
4 teaspoons canola or olive oil
1 medium-size yellow onion, finely chopped (1 cup)
4 cloves garlic, slivered
2 teaspoons minced fresh ginger or ¾ teaspoon ground ginger
3 tablespoons red wine vinegar
2 tablespoons light corn syrup
1 can (14½ ounces) low-sodium tomatoes, chopped, with their juice
2 tablespoons low-sodium ketchup
½ teaspoon each ground ginger and allspice
¼ teaspoon black pepper
2 cups cooked red beans

1 Dredge the pork in the flour, shaking off any excess. In a 5-quart Dutch oven or large heavy saucepan, heat 2 teaspoons of the oil over moderately high heat. Add the pork; sauté for 5 minutes or until lightly browned all over.

2 With a slotted spoon, transfer the meat to a plate. Lower the heat and add the remaining 2 teaspoons of oil, the onion, garlic, and fresh ginger. Cook, stirring frequently, for 5 minutes or until the onion is softened. Return the meat to the Dutch oven and stir in the vinegar, corn syrup, tomatoes, ketchup, ground ginger, allspice, and pepper. Bring to a boil over moderate heat, then lower the heat, cover, and cook for 50 minutes. Add the beans, cover, and simmer 20 minutes longer or until the meat is tender. Serve with brown rice and a green salad. Serves 4.

PREPARATION TIME: 15 MIN. COOKING TIME: 1 HR. 20 MIN.

Per serving: Calories 385; Saturated Fat 3 g; Total Fat 12 g; Protein 26 g; Carbohydrate 44 g; Fiber 8 g; Sodium 138 mg; Cholesterol 57 mg

PORK STIR-FRY WITH NOODLES

This delectable stir-fry calls for a Chinese cooking technique known as velveting in which meat, fish, or chicken pieces are coated with cornstarch, cooked briefly, then rinsed under cold water. Velveting seals in the juices, tenderizes the meat, and gives it a pleasing texture.

1 large egg white	3 ounces green beans, trimmed and halved lengthwise (1 cup)
2 tablespoons cornstarch	
1 tablespoon cold water	½ teaspoon ground ginger
12 ounces boneless pork loin, cut into 2" x ¼" x ¼" strips	1¾ cups Chicken Stock (page 62) or low-sodium chicken broth
1 tablespoon vegetable oil	1 tablespoon reduced-sodium soy sauce
1 medium-size yellow onion, cut into ½-inch cubes (1 cup)	6 ounces spaghetti, fettuccine, or egg noodles, cooked and drained
1 medium-size carrot, peeled and thinly sliced (½ cup)	2 green onions, including tops, thinly sliced (¼ cup)
4 ounces mushrooms, thinly sliced (1¼ cups)	

1 In a medium-size bowl, stir together the egg white, 1 tablespoon of the cornstarch, and the water. Add the pork and toss to coat. Cover with plastic food wrap and refrigerate for at least 30 minutes or as long as overnight.

2 In a large saucepan of boiling water, cook the coated pork strips for 45 seconds. Drain, then rinse quickly with cold water and pat dry with paper toweling.

3 In a 12-inch nonstick skillet, heat 2 teaspoons of the oil over high heat. Add the onion and carrot and stir-fry for 2 minutes. Add the mushrooms, green beans, and ginger, reduce the heat to low, and cook, covered, for 3 minutes. Meanwhile, in a small bowl, mix together the stock, soy sauce, and remaining 1 tablespoon of corn-starch and set aside. With a slotted spoon, transfer the vegetables to a plate.

4 Raise the heat to high and add the remaining 1 tea-spoon of oil to the skillet. Add the pork and spaghetti and stir-fry for 1 minute. Stir in the stock mixture, then add

the vegetables and cook, stirring occasionally, for 2 minutes or until the sauce has thickened. Stir in the green onions and serve. Serves 4.

PREPARATION TIME: 20 MIN. COOKING TIME: 10 MIN.
MARINATING TIME: 30 MIN.

Per serving: Calories 394; Saturated Fat 3g; Total Fat 11g; Protein 28g; Carbohydrate 45g; Fiber 2g; Sodium 260mg; Cholesterol 54mg

Pork Stir-Fry with Noodles brings the ancient cuisine of China to your 20th-century table.

To keep frozen food at its peak, the freezer temperature should always be kept at 0° F. Using an inexpensive freezer thermometer (available at most hardware stores) is a good way to check on your freezer's temperature.

In case of a power outage or a freezer door left ajar, a freezer thermometer can tell you how high the temperature has risen. If the temperature does not go above 40° F (the average temperature of a refrigerator) and ice crystals are visible on packages, the food can be refrozen. Should the temperature go above 40° F, all frozen raw foods should be cooked. Any uncooked items that are kept above 40° F for more than 6 hours must be discarded for safety's sake.

PORK STIR-FRY WITH BLACK BEAN SAUCE

This delightful stir-fry calls for an unusual ingredient: fermented black beans, available at Oriental markets. If you prefer, substitute black bean sauce and skip the soaking.

2 tablespoons fermented black beans or 1 tablespoon black bean sauce

4 green onions (white part only), finely chopped (¼ cup)

1 tablespoon minced fresh ginger

2 cloves garlic, minced

½ cup Chicken Stock (page 62) or low-sodium chicken broth

1 tablespoon each soy sauce and dry sherry or water

1 teaspoon sugar

1 teaspoon cornstarch

1 pound mustard greens or spinach, trimmed, rinsed, and drained

2 teaspoons peanut oil

1 pound boneless pork loin, cut into ½-inch cubes

2 teaspoons dark sesame oil

1 In a small bowl, soak the beans in 2 tablespoons cold water for 10 minutes; drain and mince. Return to the bowl, stir in the green onions, ginger, and garlic, and set aside. In another small bowl, mix the stock, soy sauce, sherry, sugar, and cornstarch and set aside.

2 In a large saucepan of boiling water, cook the mustard greens for 2 minutes. Drain in a colander, rinse under cold running water to stop the cooking, and drain again. Squeeze the greens dry, then coarsely chop.

3 In a 12-inch wok or nonstick skillet, heat the peanut oil over moderately high heat until very hot but not smoking. Add the black bean mixture and stir-fry for 1 minute. Add the pork and stir-fry for 2 minutes or until no longer pink. Add the greens and stock mixture and bring to a boil. Lower the heat and simmer, covered, for 5 minutes or until the meat is tender. Stir in the sesame oil. Serve with steamed rice. Serves 4.

PREPARATION TIME: 20 MIN. COOKING TIME: 10 MIN.

SOAKING TIME: 10 MIN.

Per serving: Calories 273; Saturated Fat 4 g; Total Fat 13 g; Protein 29 g; Carbohydrate 9 g; Fiber 3 g; Sodium 459 mg; Cholesterol 71 mg

SAUSAGE PATTIES

Making your own sausage patties is easy. It is also an excellent way to avoid the fat and additives found in many prepared meat products. If you like, prepare this recipe ahead of time and refrigerate overnight. Or seal the patties individually in plastic sandwich or freezer bags, label, and freeze for up to 1 month at 0° F.

12 ounces lean ground pork or turkey

¼ cup fresh bread crumbs

3 tablespoons skim milk

2 cloves garlic, minced

¼ teaspoon rubbed sage, crumbled

¼ teaspoon fennel seeds, crushed

¼ teaspoon each salt and black pepper

2 tablespoons minced parsley

2 teaspoons olive oil

1 In a medium-size bowl, combine the pork, bread crumbs, milk, garlic, sage, fennel seeds, salt, pepper, and parsley. Using your hands, form the mixture into six 3½-inch patties. (It is easier to shape the patties if you wet your hands in cold water first.)

2 In a 10-inch nonstick skillet, heat the oil over moderate heat. Add the patties and cook for 4 to 5 minutes on each side or until the juices run clear. Serve with Braised Red Cabbage with Apples (page 222) and Herbed Buttermilk Biscuits (page 291), or serve with poached eggs and toasted whole-grain English muffins. Makes 6 patties.

PREPARATION TIME: 10 MIN. COOKING TIME: 10 MIN.

Per patty: Calories 110; Saturated Fat 2 g; Total Fat 6 g; Protein 11 g; Carbohydrate 2 g; Fiber 0 g; Sodium 146 mg; Cholesterol 38 mg

Served here with
Celery Victor (page 255),
Leg of Lamb
with Lime-Honey
Marinade ushers
in the spring.

LEG OF LAMB WITH LIME-HONEY MARINADE

Serve this tender, succulent roast hot or at room temperature. It can be barbecued instead of roasted; omit the folding and tying and lay the roast open on the grill.

3 **tablespoons lime juice**	½ **teaspoon salt**
2 **tablespoons honey**	¼ **teaspoon black pepper**
¾ **teaspoon dried oregano, crumbled**	½ **leg of lamb, boned and butterflied (2½ pounds boned weight)**
½ **teaspoon each ground allspice and ginger**	

1 In a shallow glass or ceramic dish, whisk together the lime juice, honey, oregano, allspice, ginger, salt, and pepper. Add the lamb, turning it several times to coat; cover with plastic food wrap and refrigerate for at least 3 hours or overnight.

2 Preheat the oven to 375° F. Fold the 2 halves of the lamb together and tie with string at 1½-inch intervals. Place the lamb in a small roasting pan and roast, brushing occasionally with the marinade, for 35 minutes for rare or until the meat thermometer registers 140° F. For lamb that is medium, roast for 42 minutes or until the meat thermometer registers 150° F. For lamb that is well-done, roast for 50 minutes or until the meat thermometer registers 170° F. Let the roast stand for 15 minutes before carving. Serve with potato salad and Celery Victor (page 255) or rice and steamed green beans. Serves 8.

PREPARATION TIME: 10 MIN.   COOKING TIME: 35 MIN.

MARINATING TIME: 3 HR.

*Per serving: Calories 199; Saturated Fat 2 g;
Total Fat 6 g; Protein 29 g; Carbohydrate 5 g;
Fiber 0 g; Sodium 230 mg; Cholesterol 91 mg*

When the winds blow cold, heat things up with Lamb Couscous, a rich, spicy Mediterranean stew of vegetables, chick peas, and meat, served over fluffy semolina.

LAMB COUSCOUS

Vegetables, lamb, and couscous (the pasta-like grains of semolina available in most supermarkets) combine to create a complete and hearty meal.

1 ½ pounds boneless lamb shoulder, cut into 1-inch cubes
½ teaspoon each salt and black pepper
2 teaspoons olive or canola oil
2 large yellow onions, sliced (3 cups)
2 cloves garlic, minced
1 can (1 pound) low-sodium tomatoes, chopped, with their juice
½ teaspoon each ground ginger and cumin
½ teaspoon dried thyme, crumbled

1 cinnamon stick
4 cups low-sodium beef broth
2 medium-size carrots, peeled and sliced ½ inch thick (1 ¼ cups)
2 medium-size zucchini, sliced ½ inch thick (2 ½ cups)
1 medium-size yellow squash, cut into 1-inch cubes (1 ½ cups)
1 cup cooked chick peas
2 cups couscous, prepared according to package instructions

1 Season the lamb with ¼ teaspoon each of the salt and pepper. In a 5-quart Dutch oven, heat the oil over moderate heat. Add the lamb and cook, turning frequently, for 5 minutes or until evenly browned on all sides. With a slotted spoon, transfer the lamb to a plate lined with paper toweling.

2 Add the onions and remaining salt and pepper to the Dutch oven and sauté, stirring occasionally, for 7 minutes or until the onions are golden.

3 Add the garlic, tomatoes, ginger, cumin, thyme, cinnamon stick, broth, and lamb to the Dutch oven and bring to a boil. Lower the heat and simmer, covered, for 1 hour. Add the carrots and simmer, covered, for 10 minutes. Add the zucchini, yellow squash, and chick peas and simmer, covered, 10 minutes more or until the vegetables are just tender. Remove the cinnamon stick. Serve the lamb and vegetables over the couscous. Serves 8.

PREPARATION TIME: 20 MIN. COOKING TIME: 1 ½ HR.

Per serving: Calories 280; Saturated Fat 2 g; Total Fat 8 g; Protein 24 g; Carbohydrate 28 g; Fiber 7 g; Sodium 487 mg; Cholesterol 56 mg

LAMB AND BARLEY STEW

*Pearl barley adds a wonderful nutty flavor to stews.
It's also an excellent source of soluble fiber.*

- 12 ounces boneless lamb shoulder, trimmed and cut into ½-inch cubes
- 2 tablespoons all-purpose flour
- 1 tablespoon olive oil
- 1 medium-size yellow onion, chopped (1 cup)
- 3 cloves garlic, minced
- 2¼ cups water
- 2 medium-size carrots, peeled, halved lengthwise, and thinly sliced (⅔ cup)
- 1½ cups low-sodium tomato-vegetable juice
- ½ cup medium pearl barley
- ¼ teaspoon each ground cinnamon and ginger
- ¼ teaspoon salt
- ⅛ teaspoon black pepper

1 Preheat the oven to 350° F. Dredge the lamb in the flour, shaking off any excess. In a 5-quart Dutch oven, heat the oil over moderate heat. Add the lamb and sauté for about 4 minutes or until lightly browned. Remove the lamb with a slotted spoon and set aside.

2 Add the onion and garlic to the Dutch oven, stirring to coat, then add ½ cup of the water. Cook, stirring occasionally, for 5 minutes or until the onions are translucent. Add the carrots and cook 4 minutes longer. Return the lamb to the saucepan. Stir in the tomato juice, the remaining 1¾ cups water, the barley, cinnamon, ginger, salt, and pepper. Bring to a boil over moderate heat. Cover and transfer to the oven. Bake for 55 minutes or until the lamb is tender and the barley is cooked through. Serve with crusty French bread and a green salad. Serves 4.

PREPARATION TIME: 18 MIN. COOKING TIME: 1 HR. 10 MIN.

Per serving: Calories 302; Saturated Fat 3 g; Total Fat 10 g; Protein 22 g; Carbohydrate 34 g; Fiber 7 g; Sodium 219 mg; Cholesterol 56 mg

LAMB MEATBALLS IN YOGURT-MINT SAUCE

These marvelous meatballs can be prepared in advance through Step 2. Make the sauce just before serving, and accompany the dish with noodles and a cucumber salad.

- 1 pound lean ground lamb
- ¼ cup fresh bread crumbs (½ slice)
- 1 large egg, separated
- 2 cloves garlic, minced
- 2 tablespoons minced fresh mint or 2 teaspoons mint flakes, crumbled
- 2 tablespoons minced parsley
- ¼ teaspoon ground cinnamon
- ¼ teaspoon each salt and black pepper
- 2 cups Chicken Stock (page 62) or low-sodium chicken broth
- ½ cup plain low-fat yogurt
- 1 tablespoon cornstarch
- 2 tablespoons lemon juice, or to taste
- Minced fresh mint (optional garnish)

1 In a medium-size bowl, combine the lamb, bread crumbs, egg white, garlic, mint, parsley, cinnamon, salt, and pepper. Using your hands, form the mixture into 1-inch meatballs. (It is easier to shape the meatballs if you wet your hands in cold water first.)

2 In a medium-size saucepan, bring the stock to a boil. Add the meatballs, lower the heat, and simmer, covered, for 20 minutes or until tender. With a slotted spoon, transfer the meatballs to a plate and cover with aluminum foil to keep them warm. Set the stock aside.

3 In a medium-size bowl, whisk the yogurt, cornstarch, and egg yolk until well combined. Add the hot stock in a stream, continuing to whisk. Transfer the yogurt mixture to the saucepan and simmer over low heat, stirring, for 2 minutes or until the sauce is slightly thickened. Add the lemon juice. Strain the sauce over the meatballs. Garnish with the mint. Makes 24 meatballs or enough to serve 4.

PREPARATION TIME: 15 MIN. COOKING TIME: 25 MIN.

Per meatball: Calories 39; Saturated Fat 1 g; Total Fat 2 g; Protein 5 g; Carbohydrate 1 g; Fiber 0 g; Sodium 55 mg; Cholesterol 22 mg

Couscous — granules of semolina, which is milled from the heart of durum wheat — is a traditional part of many North African dishes. There it is cooked in a *couscousiere*, a colander fitted over a large pot. When the lower pot is filled with a simmering lamb or vegetable stew, the steam rises and cooks the couscous in the colander nestled above. The type of couscous used in steaming can be found in health food stores.

For easier and faster cooking, precooked couscous is available in most supermarkets. For this type, steaming is not advisable. Instead, put boiling water or stock in a bowl, stir in the couscous, cover, and let stand for 5 to 10 minutes. To serve couscous Moroccan style, mound it on a platter, hollow out the center, and fill the hollow with stewed vegetables or meats.

SAUTÉED VEAL ON A BED OF GREENS

Succulent veal on a bed of crisp, cool greens and tomatoes makes a lovely summer dish. Balsamic vinegar is slightly sweet and nutty tasting. If you cannot find it, use red wine vinegar. You can also substitute turkey or chicken cutlets for the veal.

2	egg whites
1	tablespoon water
12	ounces veal cutlets, cut into 8 pieces
½	cup plain dry bread crumbs
1	tablespoon olive oil
3	tablespoons low-sodium tomato juice or tomato-vegetable juice
1 ½	tablespoons balsamic vinegar

1	large or 2 small bunches arugula or watercress (about 10 ounces), trimmed and rinsed well
2	medium-size tomatoes, thickly sliced
¼	teaspoon salt, or to taste

1 In a shallow bowl, stir together the egg whites and water until combined. Dip the cutlets first in the egg white mixture, then in the bread crumbs. (This may be done up to 3 hours before serving time.)

2 Heat the oil in a 12-inch nonstick skillet over moderately high heat. Add the veal cutlets and sauté for 2 to 3 minutes on each side or until golden brown and the juices run clear when the meat is pricked with a fork.

3 In a medium-size bowl, whisk together the tomato juice and vinegar. Add the arugula and toss to coat. Divide the arugula among 4 serving plates. Top with the tomato slices and sprinkle them with the salt. Arrange the veal on top and serve immediately. Serves 4.

PREPARATION TIME: 10 MIN. COOKING TIME: 5 MIN.

Per serving: Calories 210; Saturated Fat 3 g; Total Fat 7 g; Protein 23 g; Carbohydrate 14 g; Fiber 2 g; Sodium 367 mg; Cholesterol 68 mg

ROSEMARY-LEMON VEAL WITH RICE AND MUSHROOMS

For this versatile dish, you can use sweet red pepper instead of green if you like, or add a cup of chopped tomato and substitute a grating of orange rind for the lemon.

2	teaspoons olive oil
12	ounces boneless veal shoulder, cut into ¾-inch cubes
1	medium-size yellow onion, finely chopped (1 cup)
1	medium-size sweet green pepper, cored, seeded, and diced (¾ cup)
2	cloves garlic, crushed
6	ounces mushrooms, sliced ¼ inch thick (about 1 ¾ cups)

2	teaspoons dried rosemary, crumbled
2	teaspoons grated lemon rind
2⅔	cups Chicken Stock (page 62) or low-sodium chicken broth
¼	teaspoon salt, or to taste
1	cup long-grain white rice
1	tablespoon lemon juice

1 In a 10-inch nonstick skillet, heat the oil over moderately high heat. Add the veal and sauté for 5 minutes or until lightly browned. With a slotted spoon, transfer the veal to a bowl. Lower the heat and add the onion, pepper, and garlic to the skillet. Cook, stirring frequently, for 5 minutes or until the onion is soft. Add the mushrooms, cover, and cook for 5 minutes or until the mushrooms are soft.

2 Return the meat to the skillet and add the rosemary, lemon rind, ⅔ cup of the stock, and the salt. Bring to a boil, lower the heat, cover, and simmer for 20 minutes. Stir in the rice and remaining 2 cups stock, bring to a boil, lower the heat, and simmer, covered, 25 minutes longer or until the rice is tender. Stir in the lemon juice. Serve with steamed carrot sticks or peas. Serves 4.

PREPARATION TIME: 20 MIN. COOKING TIME: 1 HR.

Per serving: Calories 330; Saturated Fat 1 g; Total Fat 7 g; Protein 24 g; Carbohydrate 45 g; Fiber 2 g; Sodium 306 mg; Cholesterol 73 mg

MEATLESS MAIN DISHES

Preparing main courses without meat brings both challenges
and rewards. The challenge is to create dishes that please the palate while providing
sufficient protein to meet a substantial portion of daily needs. This chapter
presents you with an enticing choice of such recipes. Once you have the knack of
cooking this way, you will realize that variations are nearly endless.
Variety is just one of the many rewards. Most of the typical ingredients for
meatless dishes — beans, grains, and vegetables — are also inexpensive
compared with meat. Best of all, they are generally high in fiber, vitamins, and
minerals and low in fat. The fiber makes them filling and satisfying;
less fat makes them good for your heart.

Complete protein, one that contains all 9 of the essential amino acids, should equal 50 to 63 grams a day in the diet of an average adult. Whereas meat, poultry, fish, and dairy products all furnish complete protein, plant foods either lack or contain an insufficient amount of some essential amino acids. For example, corn is low in tryptophan and lysine but high in methionine; beans, on the other hand, contain more lysine and tryptophan and less methionine. Eaten together, they provide all the essential amino acids. In the two columns below, any of the legumes paired with any of the grains adds up to a complete protein.

Legumes

Kidney Beans
Black-eyed Peas
Chick Peas
Navy Beans
Lentils
Split Peas
Lima Beans
Peanuts

Grains

Corn
Rice
Wheat
Oats
Barley
Rye

CHICK PEAS AND CORN WITH MUSTARD-CHILI SAUCE

This dish will keep in the refrigerator for up to 3 days or in the freezer for up to 1 month at 0° F. The best way to reheat it is in a casserole, in a 375° F oven, for 30 to 40 minutes.

1 ½ cups fresh or frozen corn kernels
4 cups cooked chick peas or cannellini (white kidney beans)
2 tablespoons finely chopped pimiento
⅓ cup Tomato Chili Sauce (page 271) or bottled chili sauce
2 teaspoons Dijon mustard
1 can (14 ½ ounces) low-sodium tomatoes, chopped, with their juice (1 ½ cups)
6 parsley sprigs (optional garnish)

1 In a large saucepan, combine the corn, chick peas, and pimiento. Add the chili sauce and mustard and stir until thoroughly mixed. Stir in the tomatoes and their juice. Cover and bring to a boil over moderate heat. Lower the heat and simmer for 15 minutes to mellow the flavors. Garnish individual portions with the parsley if desired. Serve with spinach tossed with Buttermilk Dressing (page 268). Serves 4 to 6.

PREPARATION TIME: 8 MIN. COOKING TIME: 20 MIN.

Per serving (for 4): Calories 359; Saturated Fat 0 g; Total Fat 5 g; Protein 18 g; Carbohydrate 66 g; Fiber 3 g; Sodium 89 mg; Cholesterol 0 mg

WHITE BEANS WITH TOMATO, BASIL, AND PARMESAN

Here is a versatile recipe that can be served hot or cold, as a main course or side dish. It is especially nice served over cooked pasta.

1 tablespoon olive oil
3 cloves garlic, minced
3 cups cooked navy beans, Great Northern beans, or cannellini (white kidney beans)
1 large tomato, chopped (1 ½ cups)
¼ cup minced fresh basil or parsley
½ cup grated Parmesan cheese (2 ounces)
1 tablespoon lemon juice
Basil leaves (optional garnish)

1 In a 12-inch nonstick skillet, heat the oil over low heat. Add the garlic and cook, stirring occasionally, for 4 minutes or until lightly colored and fragrant. Stir in the beans, tomato, and minced basil and cook for 7 minutes or until heated through and the tomato has released its juices. Stir in the cheese and lemon juice. Serve hot or at room temperature. (Will keep, refrigerated, for 2 days.) Garnish with the basil leaves if desired. Serves 4 as a main course, 8 as a side dish.

PREPARATION TIME: 15 MIN. COOKING TIME: 11 MIN.

Per serving (for 4): Calories 276; Saturated Fat 3 g; Total Fat 8 g; Protein 18 g; Carbohydrate 34 g; Fiber 8 g; Sodium 279 mg; Cholesterol 11 mg

BLACK AND WHITE BEANS, ORIENTAL STYLE

*Lemon gives this quick bean dish a fresh spring taste.
Try it reheated the next day – it's just as good.*

- **4 medium-size carrots,** peeled and sliced ¼ inch thick (3 cups)
- **8 medium-size mushroom caps, sliced** ¼ inch thick (2 cups)
- **2 tablespoons reduced-sodium soy sauce**
- **1 tablespoon dark sesame oil**
- **¼ cup lemon juice**
- **2 tablespoons water**
- **1 teaspoon grated lemon rind**
- **2 cups cooked black beans or red kidney beans**
- **2 cups cooked white California beans, navy beans, or chick peas**
- **4 green onions, including tops, thinly sliced (½ cup)**

1 In a large heavy saucepan, combine the carrots, mushrooms, soy sauce, sesame oil, lemon juice, water, and lemon rind. Bring to a boil over moderate heat and cook, covered, for 4 minutes or until the carrots are just tender.

2 Add the black beans and white beans, cover, and cook, stirring occasionally, over moderate heat for 8 minutes or until the beans are very hot and the liquid has thickened. Stir in the green onions and cook, covered, for 2 minutes or until they are slightly softened. Serve with brown rice and Dilled Cucumber-Carrot Salad (page 257). Serves 4.

PREPARATION TIME: 18 MIN. COOKING TIME: 15 MIN.

*Per serving: Calories 303; Saturated Fat 1 g;
Total Fat 5 g; Protein 17 g; Carbohydrate 51 g;
Fiber 11 g; Sodium 275 mg; Cholesterol 0 mg*

White Beans with Tomatoes, Basil, and Parmesan — ready in about 25 minutes — will become a mainstay in your kitchen.

157

To reduce the time and effort of preparing dried beans for each recipe, why not cook a couple of big batches and store them in the freezer? (See pages 18–19 for cooking times.) With the exception of lentils, which become mushy, most beans freeze well. Place 1 to 3 cups of beans in a container or plastic freezer bag and label it with the contents, quantity, and date. They will keep for up to 6 months at 0° F.

BLACK BEANS WITH CORN AND WINTER SQUASH

This hearty dish is packed with good nutrition: winter squash and sweet potatoes are the leading vegetable sources of vitamin A; green peppers, tomatoes, and potatoes are high in vitamin C; black beans add a healthy amount of fiber.

- 1 tablespoon olive oil
- 1 large yellow onion, coarsely chopped (1½ cups)
- 2 cloves garlic, thinly sliced
- 1 medium-size sweet green pepper, cored, seeded, and cut into 1-inch squares (¾ cup)
- 1 small acorn or butternut squash (1 pound), peeled and cut into 1-inch cubes
- 1 small sweet potato, peeled and cut into 1-inch cubes (½ cup)
- 2 medium-size tomatoes, chopped (2 cups)
- ½ cup water
- ½ teaspoon dried oregano, crumbled
- ½ teaspoon ground cumin
- ¼ teaspoon salt, or to taste
- 1 cup cooked black beans
- ⅔ cup fresh or frozen corn kernels, thawed
- 2 tablespoons lime juice

1 In a 12-inch nonstick skillet, heat the oil over moderate heat. Add the onion and garlic and sauté, stirring occasionally, for 5 minutes or until the onion is soft. Add the pepper and cook 5 minutes longer.

2 Stir in the squash, sweet potato, tomatoes, water, oregano, cumin, and salt. Bring to a boil over moderate heat. Lower the heat and simmer, covered, for 40 minutes or until the squash is tender. Stir in the beans and corn and cook for about 4 minutes or until heated through. Stir in the lime juice. Serve with rice and a spinach salad. Serves 4 as an entrée, 8 as a side dish.

PREPARATION TIME: 25 MIN. COOKING TIME: 55 MIN.

Per serving (for 4): Calories 236; Saturated Fat 1 g; Total Fat 4 g; Protein 8 g; Carbohydrate 47 g; Fiber 7 g; Sodium 150 mg; Cholesterol 0 mg

CAJUN BEANS WITH "DIRTY" RICE

"Dirty" rice is traditionally made with chopped chicken livers and gizzards. But this meatless version still has down-home taste. For a crowd pleaser, make a double batch of this classic from the Deep South. After the liquid boils, cover the casserole and cook in a preheated 325° F oven for 30 minutes.

- 2 tablespoons vegetable oil
- 1 large yellow onion, finely chopped (1½ cups)
- 2 cloves garlic, minced
- 2 medium-size sweet green peppers, cored, seeded, and finely chopped (1½ cups)
- 1 medium-size stalk celery, finely chopped (½ cup)
- 1½ teaspoons dried thyme, crumbled
- 1 teaspoon ground cumin
- ¼ teaspoon each salt and ground red pepper (cayenne), or to taste
- 3 cups Chicken Stock or Vegetable Stock (page 62), low-sodium chicken broth, or water
- 1½ cups long-grain white rice
- 4 cups cooked red kidney beans or black beans

1 In a 4-quart flameproof casserole, heat the oil over moderately high heat until very hot but not smoking. Add the onion, garlic, half of the green peppers, and the celery. Sauté, stirring frequently, for 7 minutes or until the onions just begin to turn golden.

2 Add the thyme, cumin, salt, red pepper, stock, rice, and beans. Bring to a boil over high heat, then lower the heat, cover, and simmer for 20 minutes or until the rice has absorbed all of the liquid and is very tender. Serve each portion topped with the remaining chopped green pepper. Serves 6.

PREPARATION TIME: 15 MIN. COOKING TIME: 30 MIN.

Per serving: Calories 405; Saturated Fat 1 g; Total Fat 6 g; Protein 16 g; Carbohydrate 72 g; Fiber 10 g; Sodium 172 mg; Cholesterol 0 mg

For authentic "home-on-the-range" taste, rustle up a bowl of Vegetarian Chili to feed a hungry hombre.

VEGETARIAN CHILI

Your family won't believe this flavorful chili contains no meat. Jalapeños add an extra kick, but can be omitted for a milder taste.

- 1 tablespoon olive oil
- 1 large yellow onion, finely chopped (1 ½ cups)
- 2 medium-size sweet red peppers, cored, seeded, and finely chopped (1 ½ cups)
- 2 cloves garlic, minced
- 1 medium-size stalk celery, finely chopped (½ cup)
- 1 ½ tablespoons chili powder
- 2 teaspoons ground cumin
- 1 teaspoon finely chopped pickled jalapeño pepper
- ¼ teaspoon salt, or to taste
- 4 medium-size carrots (12 ounces), peeled and sliced ¼ inch thick
- 8 ounces mushrooms, thinly sliced (2 ½ cups)
- 1 cup water
- 1 can (14 ½ ounces) low-sodium tomatoes with their juice
- 3 cups cooked black beans or pinto beans
- ½ cup plain nonfat yogurt
- 2 tablespoons minced fresh cilantro (coriander) or parsley

1 In a large heavy saucepan, heat the oil over moderately high heat until very hot but not smoking. Add the onion, red peppers, garlic, and celery. Sauté, stirring frequently, for 7 minutes or until the onion just begins to turn golden.

2 Stir in the chili powder, cumin, jalapeño pepper, salt, carrots, mushrooms, water, and tomatoes. Bring the liquid to a boil over high heat, then lower the heat, cover, and simmer for 10 minutes or until the carrots are barely tender. Add the beans, cover, and cook for 5 minutes or until they are heated through. Uncover the saucepan and continue to cook for 10 minutes or until the liquid has thickened slightly. Top each portion with 2 tablespoons of yogurt and a sprinkling of the cilantro. Serve with a grain such as rice or bulgur. Serves 4.

PREPARATION TIME: 25 MIN. COOKING TIME: 35 MIN.

Per serving: Calories 318; Saturated Fat 1 g; Total Fat 6 g; Protein 17 g; Carbohydrate 55 g; Fiber 12 g; Sodium 243 mg; Cholesterol 1 mg

Serve Bean Burritos, topped with yogurt and Tomato Salsa (page 280), the next time you're in the mood for Mexican food.

INDIAN LENTILS WITH RICE

If you wish, substitute green split peas for the lentils and parsnips for the carrots.

2 tablespoons vegetable oil

2 medium-size yellow onions, thinly sliced (2½ cups)

3 cups Chicken Stock or Vegetable Stock (page 62), low-sodium chicken broth, or water

2 cloves garlic, minced

1 teaspoon each ground cumin and curry powder

½ teaspoon each ground cardamom, cinnamon, and ginger

⅛ teaspoon ground red pepper (cayenne)

⅛ teaspoon sugar

1 cup tomato juice

¾ cup long-grain brown rice

¾ cup dried brown lentils, sorted and rinsed

4 small carrots, peeled and sliced ¼ inch thick (2 cups)

1 cup plain nonfat yogurt

1 tablespoon minced fresh mint, cilantro (coriander), or parsley (optional garnish)

1 In a large heavy saucepan, heat the oil over moderately high heat until very hot but not smoking. Add the onions and stir to coat with the oil. Add ¼ cup of the stock, reduce the heat to low, cover, and cook for 5 minutes or until the onions are soft. Uncover, raise the heat to moderate, and continue to cook, stirring constantly, 3 minutes more or until the onions are golden.

2 Add the garlic, cumin, curry powder, cardamom, cinnamon, ginger, red pepper, sugar, remaining 2¾ cups of stock, tomato juice, rice, lentils, and carrots. Bring the liquid to a boil, then lower the heat, cover, and simmer for 30 minutes.

3 Uncover and stir the mixture. If it seems dry, add ¼ to ½ cup of water until the liquid just covers it. Continue to cook for 10 to 15 minutes or until the lentils are tender. Top each portion with ¼ cup of yogurt and a sprinkling of fresh herbs if desired. Serves 4.

PREPARATION TIME: 20 MIN.   COOKING TIME: 50 MIN.

*Per serving: Calories 429; Saturated Fat 2 g;
Total Fat 9 g; Protein 19 g; Carbohydrate 70 g;
Fiber 6 g; Sodium 399 mg; Cholesterol 1 mg*

LENTIL FRIED RICE

This recipe lends itself to substitutions. For the rice, feel free to use any cooked grain, such as barley or bulgur. For the lentils, try cooked green split peas, and for the sweet pepper, substitute 1 small zucchini or yellow summer squash.

2 teaspoons peanut oil	1 ½ tablespoons reduced-sodium soy sauce
2 teaspoons dark sesame oil	2 tablespoons rice vinegar
1 clove garlic, minced	4 ounces snow peas, trimmed
2 teaspoons minced fresh ginger or ½ teaspoon ground ginger	2 cups cooked brown rice
	2 cups cooked lentils
2 small carrots, peeled and sliced ¼ inch thick (1 cup)	1 cup rinsed and drained bean sprouts
1 medium-size sweet yellow pepper, cored, seeded, and cut into matchstick strips (1 cup)	

1 In a heavy 12-inch skillet or wok, heat the peanut and sesame oils over moderately high heat until very hot but not smoking. Add the garlic and ginger and stir-fry for 30 seconds. Stir in the carrots and pepper and stir-fry for 1 minute to coat with the oil. Add the soy sauce and vinegar, reduce the heat to low, cover, and cook for 2 minutes or until the vegetables are crisp-tender.

2 Add the snow peas, rice, lentils, and bean sprouts. Raise the heat to moderately high and stir-fry, stirring continuously, for 2 minutes or until the mixture is hot and the snow peas are bright green and still crunchy. Serve immediately. Serves 4.

PREPARATION TIME: 20 MIN. COOKING TIME: 7 MIN.

Per serving: Calories 292; Saturated Fat 1 g; Total Fat 6 g; Protein 13 g; Carbohydrate 50 g; Fiber 9 g; Sodium 227 mg; Cholesterol 0 mg

BEAN BURRITOS

2 teaspoons vegetable oil	2 tablespoons canned chopped green chilies
1 small sweet green pepper, cored, seeded, and diced (½ cup)	½ teaspoon each ground cumin and chili powder
2 green onions, including tops, thinly sliced (¼ cup)	8 flour tortillas, 7 inches in diameter
2 cloves garlic, minced	½ cup shredded low-fat Monterey Jack cheese (2 ounces)
1 ¼ cups water	
2 cups cooked pinto beans	**Optional garnishes:**
3 tablespoons tomato paste	½ cup Tomato Salsa (page 280) or prepared salsa
	½ cup plain nonfat yogurt

1 Preheat the oven to 350° F. Lightly grease an 11" x 7" x 2" baking dish and set aside. In a 12-inch nonstick skillet, heat the oil over moderate heat. Add the pepper, green onions, and garlic and cook, covered, stirring occasionally, for 5 minutes or until the onions are lightly browned. Add ¾ cup of the water and cook, uncovered, another 5 minutes or until the vegetables are very soft and almost all the liquid has evaporated.

2 Add the beans, tomato paste, green chilies, cumin, chili powder, and remaining ½ cup of water and cook, covered, stirring occasionally, for 5 minutes. With a potato masher or spoon, mash the mixture until smooth.

3 Place about 2 tablespoons of the bean mixture on each tortilla and sprinkle with 1 tablespoon of the cheese. Roll up the tortillas and place them, seam side down, in a single layer in the prepared baking dish. Using a pastry brush, brush each tortilla with a little water. Cover the dish with aluminum foil and bake for 15 minutes or until the tortillas are piping hot. Top with salsa and yogurt if desired. Serves 4.

PREPARATION TIME: 20 MIN. COOKING TIME: 30 MIN.

Per serving: Calories 406; Saturated Fat 0 g; Total Fat 9 g; Protein 18 g; Carbohydrate 65 g; Fiber 7 g; Sodium 145 mg; Cholesterol 10 mg

Sprouts are a favorite with health-conscious cooks because they are nutritious and require no advance preparation. Just toss a handful into a salad or stir-fry and reap the benefit of extra vitamins A, B, C, and E. Most seeds, particularly those of beans and grains, produce an edible sprout. The exceptions are fava and lima beans.

Supermarkets usually carry 2 varieties of sprouts: alfalfa, light green filaments that are popular in tossed salads, and mung bean, which have a crunchy texture that is particularly good in stir-fries. If refrigerated in a covered container, sprouts will keep for up to 4 days, after which they begin to turn brown and smell stale.

THREE-BEAN TERRINE

*This unusual, colorful, and low-calorie terrine
is quite easy to make. If you are using canned beans,
be sure to drain and rinse them thoroughly.
If using home-cooked beans, blend ¼ teaspoon
of salt with each of the three bean purées.*

Nonstick cooking spray
1 ½ **cups cooked black beans**
¼ **cup plus 3 tablespoons plain low-fat yogurt**
7 **large egg whites**
6 **cloves garlic, peeled**
¾ **teaspoon ground coriander**
¼ **cup plus 3 tablespoons water**

1 ½ **cups cooked cannellini (white kidney beans) or navy beans**
1 **tablespoon lemon juice**
½ **teaspoon ground sage**
1 ½ **cups cooked red kidney beans or pinto beans**
¼ **cup tomato paste**
½ **teaspoon hot red pepper sauce, or to taste**

1 Preheat the oven to 350° F. Coat a 9" x 5" x 3" loaf pan with the cooking spray. Line the bottom of the loaf pan with wax paper and coat the paper with cooking spray.

2 In a food processor or blender, whirl the black beans, 3 tablespoons of the yogurt, 2 of the egg whites, 2 of the garlic cloves, the coriander, and ¼ cup of the water for 1 minute or until smooth. Spoon the purée into the bottom of the prepared pan and smooth the top.

3 Wash and dry the food processor or blender, then whirl in it the cannellini, the remaining ¼ cup of yogurt, 3 of the egg whites, 2 of the garlic cloves, the lemon juice, and sage for 1 minute or until smooth. Gently spread this purée on top of the black bean purée.

4 In the food processor or blender, whirl the red kidney beans, remaining 2 egg whites, remaining 2 garlic cloves, tomato paste, remaining 3 tablespoons of water, and red pepper sauce for 1 minute or until smooth. Gently spoon this purée on top of the cannellini purée, spreading and smoothing it to the edges of the pan. Cover with aluminum foil and place in a larger baking pan. Pour enough hot water into the larger pan to come 1 inch up the sides of the loaf pan.

Layers of white, black, and red bean purées are featured in this unique Three-Bean Terrine, enhanced by a cool Cucumber-Yogurt Sauce (page 278).

5 Bake for 1 ¼ hours or until a toothpick inserted in the center comes out clean. Let cool on a wire rack for 30 minutes, then run a spatula around the edges and invert the loaf onto a serving platter. Remove the wax paper and slice. Serve at room temperature with Confetti Rice Salad (page 253) and crusty bread. Serves 8.

PREPARATION TIME: 20 MIN. COOKING TIME: 1 ¼ HR.
STANDING TIME: 30 MIN.

Per serving: Calories 161; Saturated Fat 0 g; Total Fat 1 g; Protein 13 g; Carbohydrate 27 g; Fiber 6 g; Sodium 282 mg; Cholesterol 1 mg

BLACK BEAN PANCAKES WITH SALSA

Hold the syrup and pass the salsa! These unusual and unusually good pancakes are a wonderful entrée or a festive first course for a company dinner.

2 teaspoons ground cumin	3 cups cooked black beans
1 teaspoon each ground coriander and ginger	1 large egg, lightly beaten
¼ teaspoon ground cinnamon	2 tablespoons flour
⅛ teaspoon ground red pepper (cayenne)	1 cup Tomato Salsa (page 280) or prepared salsa
½ teaspoon salt	½ cup plain nonfat yogurt
1 tablespoon vegetable oil	1 green onion, including top, thinly sliced
1 clove garlic, minced	

1 Preheat the oven to 300° F. In a small bowl, mix the cumin, coriander, ginger, cinnamon, red pepper, and salt. In an 8-inch nonstick skillet, heat the oil over moderate heat. Add the garlic and spice mixture and stir-fry for 15 seconds or just until the garlic is soft and fragrant; remove the skillet from the heat before the garlic browns.

2 In a food processor or blender, purée the beans with the egg, flour, and garlic-spice mixture for 1 minute or until smooth. Transfer the mixture to a medium-size bowl and refrigerate for 15 minutes.

3 Heat a 12-inch nonstick skillet over moderately high heat until very hot. Drop 2 tablespoons of the bean purée into the skillet and flatten slightly to form a 2-inch pancake. Continue until the skillet is filled, leaving about 1 inch between each pancake, then cook the pancakes, without moving them, for 5 minutes. Using a spatula, turn them over and cook another 3 minutes. Transfer the pancakes to a baking pan and keep them warm in the oven. Repeat with the remaining purée. For each main-course serving, spoon ¼ cup salsa onto the middle of a plate. Surround the salsa with pancakes, top each pancake with a teaspoon of yogurt, and sprinkle some of the green onion over the yogurt. Makes about 20 pancakes, enough to serve 4 as a main course or 6 as a first course.

PREPARATION TIME: 20 MIN. COOKING TIME: 18 MIN.
CHILLING TIME: 15 MIN.

Per pancake: Calories 119; Saturated Fat 0 g; Total Fat 1 g; Protein 7 g; Carbohydrate 20 g; Fiber 0 g; Sodium 68 mg; Cholesterol 11 mg

BULGUR WITH WHITE BEANS AND SPINACH

1 cup bulgur	2 large sweet red peppers, cored, seeded, and finely chopped (2 cups)
1½ cups boiling water	
1 pound spinach, rinsed, trimmed, and torn into bite-size pieces	1 tablespoon Dijon mustard
2 cups cooked cannellini (white kidney beans), navy beans, or chick peas	2 tablespoons cider vinegar
	3 tablespoons grated Parmesan cheese
4 medium-size radishes, thinly sliced	¼ teaspoon black pepper, or to taste
4 green onions, including tops, sliced (½ cup)	3 tablespoons olive oil
2 medium-size cucumbers, peeled, halved lengthwise, and thinly sliced (2 cups)	

1 In a large heatproof bowl, soak the bulgur in the boiling water for 15 minutes or until it has absorbed the water and is soft. Stir in the spinach, beans, radishes, green onions, cucumbers, and red peppers.

2 In a small bowl, combine the mustard, vinegar, cheese, and black pepper. Whisk in the oil until well blended. Pour the dressing over the salad and toss to mix. Serve at room temperature or chilled. Serves 4.

PREPARATION TIME: 20 MIN. SOAKING TIME: 15 MIN.

Per serving: Calories 403; Saturated Fat 3 g; Total Fat 14 g; Protein 19 g; Carbohydrate 59 g; Fiber 18 g; Sodium 245 mg; Cholesterol 4 mg

Bean purée can be used as a thickening agent and nutrition booster. Consider adding it to soups, sauces, and breads; about 1 tablespoon of purée for each cup of liquid is a good proportion. Your soups and sauces will have richer flavor without added fat, and breads will be slightly denser and moister.

Prepare bean purée in a blender or food processor; store it in the refrigerator for up to 6 days or in the freezer for up to 6 weeks.

Bulgur is cracked wheat that has been parched (steamed and dried) and had part of the bran removed. To cook it, simply add boiling water and let it soak for the time indicated on the package, usually 10 to 15 minutes. Cracked wheat, which still has all of the bran and has not been parched, should be cooked for at least 20 minutes to be palatable. Longer cooking will yield a softer, less chewy cereal.

Some cooks like bulgur because it is so easy to prepare; others prefer cracked wheat because it yields a larger, fluffier grain. However, both products boast a delicious wheaty taste that is a fine foil for spicy foods.

CRACKED WHEAT WITH CHICK PEAS AND SPINACH

Because this dish cooks for 40 minutes, you can't substitute bulgur for the cracked wheat — it would get too mushy. However, you can use brown rice instead.

- 2 **tablespoons vegetable oil**
- 1 **medium-size yellow onion, finely chopped (1 cup)**
- 1 **clove garlic, minced**
- 1 **medium-size sweet red pepper, cored, seeded, and finely chopped (¾ cup)**
- 2 **tablespoons lemon juice**
- 1 **cup chopped cooked spinach, squeezed dry (1 pound fresh or 10 ounces frozen)**
- 1 **tablespoon minced fresh mint or 1 teaspoon mint flakes, crumbled**
- 1 **teaspoon ground cumin**
- ¼ **teaspoon salt, or to taste**
- ⅛ **teaspoon ground red pepper (cayenne)**
- 1 **cup cracked wheat**
- 2 **cups cooked chick peas**
- ¾ **cup raisins or currants**
- 2¾ **cups Chicken Stock or Vegetable Stock (page 62), low-sodium chicken broth, or water**
- 1 **cup plain low-fat yogurt**
- 4 **sprigs parsley (optional garnish)**

1 Preheat the oven to 350° F. In a 4-quart flameproof casserole, heat the oil over moderately high heat. Add the onion, garlic, and sweet red pepper; stir to coat with the oil. Stir in the lemon juice, reduce the heat to low, cover, and cook for 5 minutes or until the onion is softened.

2 Add the spinach, mint, cumin, salt, ground red pepper, cracked wheat, chick peas, raisins, and stock. Raise the heat to high and bring the liquid to a boil. Cover, transfer the casserole to the oven, and bake for 35 minutes or until the mixture has absorbed all the liquid. Top each portion with ¼ cup of yogurt and garnish with the parsley if desired. Serves 4.

PREPARATION TIME: 22 MIN.   COOKING TIME: 40 MIN.

Per serving: Calories 494; Saturated Fat 2 g; Total Fat 12 g; Protein 21 g; Carbohydrate 85 g; Fiber 13 g; Sodium 371 mg; Cholesterol 4 mg

SPICY RICE WITH BULGUR AND PASTA

This is a delicious way to get your grains; bulgur is available at most health food stores, as is basmati rice — a wonderfully fragrant rice that originated in India.

- 2 **teaspoons olive oil**
- 1 **large yellow onion, chopped (1½ cups)**
- 1 **medium-size sweet green pepper, cored, seeded, and chopped (¾ cup)**
- 1 **clove garlic, minced**
- ¾ **cup white basmati or long-grain white rice**
- ½ **cup orzo or elbow macaroni**
- 1 **cup Chicken Stock or Vegetable Stock (page 62) or low-sodium chicken broth**
- 2¼ **cups boiling water**
- ¼ **cup bulgur**
- 2 **teaspoons each chili powder and ground cumin**
- ¼ **teaspoon each salt and black pepper, or to taste**
- 4 **ounces Monterey Jack cheese with jalapeño peppers, cut into ½-inch cubes**

1 In a large saucepan, heat the oil over moderate heat. Add the onion, green pepper, and garlic and sauté for 5 minutes or until the vegetables are softened. Stir in the rice and pasta and cook, stirring, 5 minutes more or until the rice and pasta are lightly golden.

2 Stir in the stock, water, bulgur, chili powder, cumin, salt, and black pepper. Lower the heat and simmer, covered, for 20 minutes, stirring once or twice to prevent sticking. Before serving, stir in the cheese. Accompany with pinto beans and cucumber salad. Serves 4.

PREPARATION TIME: 20 MIN.   COOKING TIME: 30 MIN.

Per serving: Calories 396; Saturated Fat 0 g; Total Fat 12 g; Protein 15 g; Carbohydrate 57 g; Fiber 4 g; Sodium 338 mg; Cholesterol 0 mg

BULGUR-STUFFED CABBAGE

If you prefer, substitute couscous for the bulgur, preparing it according to package directions.

½ **cup bulgur**	½ **teaspoon salt**
¾ **cup boiling water**	¼ **teaspoon each dried thyme and mint flakes, crumbled**
1 **head cabbage (2½ pounds), tough outer leaves removed**	
2 **teaspoons olive or canola oil**	¼ **teaspoon black pepper, or to taste**
1 **medium-size red onion, chopped (1 cup)**	1 **large egg white**
	2 **teaspoons lemon juice**
1 **small sweet red pepper, cored, seeded, and chopped (½ cup)**	1¼ **cups shredded low-fat Monterey Jack or mozzarella cheese (5 ounces)**
4 **ounces mushrooms, sliced (1¼ cups)**	
1 **small zucchini, quartered and sliced (1 cup)**	⅛ **teaspoon hot red pepper sauce, or to taste**
	1 **can (8 ounces) low-sodium tomato sauce**
1½ **teaspoons dried basil, crumbled**	

1 In a medium-size heatproof bowl, soak the bulgur in the boiling water for 15 minutes or until all the liquid is absorbed. Meanwhile, bring a stockpot of unsalted water to a boil. Place the whole cabbage in the boiling water for about 2 minutes. Remove the cabbage and cut off 4 leaves at the core. Repeat twice more, removing 12 leaves altogether. (Reserve the remaining cabbage for another dish.) Return the leaves to the boiling water and cook for 4 minutes or until crisp-tender. Drain, rinse under cold water to stop the cooking, and pat dry with paper toweling.

2 Heat the oil in a 10-inch nonstick skillet over moderate heat. Add the onion, red pepper, and mushrooms and sauté for 5 minutes. Stir in the zucchini, basil, salt, thyme, mint, and black pepper. Partially cover and cook, stirring occasionally, for 10 minutes or until the vegetables are soft and the liquid has evaporated. Stir in the bulgur. In a small bowl, beat the egg white and lemon juice and add to the bulgur-vegetable mixture. Stir in 1 cup of the cheese.

3 Preheat the oven to 400° F. Lightly grease a 13″ x 9″ x 2″ baking dish. Spoon ¼ cup of the bulgur mixture into the center of a cabbage leaf. Fold the sides of the leaf toward the center, then roll up the leaf and place, seam side down, in the prepared baking dish. Repeat with the remaining leaves and filling.

4 Stir the red pepper sauce into the tomato sauce and spoon the sauce over the cabbage rolls. Sprinkle the remaining ¼ cup of cheese on top. Cover with aluminum foil and bake for 25 minutes. Remove the foil and bake 10 minutes more or until the cheese is golden and bubbling. Accompany with rye bread. Serves 4.

PREPARATION TIME: 25 MIN. COOKING TIME: 1 HR.

SOAKING TIME: 15 MIN.

Per serving: Calories 299; Saturated Fat 4 g; Total Fat 11 g; Protein 19 g; Carbohydrate 39 g; Fiber 13 g; Sodium 470 mg; Cholesterol 25 mg

Bulgur-Stuffed Cabbage rolls are filled abundantly with a colorful medley of vegetables and grain.

Tofu, or soybean curd, a white custard-like substance made from coagulated soy milk, is high in protein, calcium, potassium, and iron and contains no cholesterol. Although tofu is also relatively high in fat (some 50 percent of its calories), the fat is mainly unsaturated.

Tofu comes in three types: soft, firm, and extra-firm. Soft tofu is best for recipes in which it is to be mashed or blended with other ingredients, as in Tofu Egg Salad Sandwich (page 52). The firm type should be used in dishes that call for sliced or cubed tofu; the extra-firm (if available) is particularly suited to stir-fries.

Many people like tofu because it is bland and readily absorbs the flavors of other ingredients. It can be added to almost any dish to boost the protein without changing the taste significantly.

Tofu is usually sold vacuum packed with water. Once it has been opened, it will keep for about a week if covered with water, which should be changed daily. Tofu can also be drained, wrapped, and frozen for up to 3 months, but the texture will be altered.

TOFU WITH PEPPERS, PEANUTS, AND MUSHROOMS

Here is an interesting combination of textures, flavors, and colors that pleases both the palate and the eye.

- 1/4 cup reduced-sodium soy sauce
- 1/4 cup lemon juice
- 2 tablespoons dark sesame oil
- 1 1/2 pounds firm tofu, cut into 1-inch cubes
- 2 cloves garlic, minced
- 2 large sweet red peppers, cored, seeded, and finely chopped (2 cups)
- 8 ounces mushrooms, sliced 1/8 inch thick (3 cups)
- 1/2 cup unsalted dry-roasted peanuts, chopped
- 1 teaspoon grated lemon rind
- 2 bunches watercress (10 ounces), rinsed and stems removed, or 1 pound fresh spinach, rinsed and chopped

1 In a large bowl, combine the soy sauce, lemon juice, and 1 tablespoon of the sesame oil. Add the tofu, toss to coat, and marinate for 10 minutes.

2 In a heavy 10-inch skillet, heat the remaining 1 tablespoon of sesame oil over moderately high heat until very hot but not smoking. Add the garlic and peppers and stir-fry for 1 minute or until the garlic is fragrant. Lower the heat; add the mushrooms and the marinade from the tofu and simmer, covered, for 5 minutes or until the mushrooms are tender. Add the peanuts, lemon rind, and tofu and simmer, covered, another 5 minutes or until the tofu is heated through. Stir in the watercress and simmer, covered, for about 1 minute or until the watercress is wilted. Serve over steamed brown rice. Serves 6.

PREPARATION TIME: 25 MIN. COOKING TIME: 13 MIN.
MARINATING TIME: 10 MIN.

Per serving: Calories 307; Saturated Fat 3 g; Total Fat 21 g; Protein 23 g; Carbohydrate 14 g; Fiber 3 g; Sodium 361 mg; Cholesterol 0 mg

VEGETABLE SUKIYAKI

This recipe calls for ramen, or dried Oriental noodles. You can find these clear quick-cooking noodles in the Oriental section of your supermarket or a food specialty store.

- 1 cup Chicken Stock or Vegetable Stock (page 62) or low-sodium chicken broth
- 2 1/2 cups water
- 2 tablespoons reduced-sodium soy sauce
- 2 cups thinly sliced cabbage (6 ounces)
- 2 medium-size stalks celery, thinly sliced (1 1/2 cups)
- 1 medium-size sweet red pepper, cored, seeded, and thinly sliced lengthwise (3/4 cup)
- 4 green onions, including tops, sliced diagonally 1/2 inch thick
- 6 ounces mushrooms, sliced (2 cups)
- 1 package (3 ounces) ramen noodles or vermicelli
- 8 ounces firm tofu, cut into 2" x 2/3" x 3/8" sticks
- 1 tablespoon minced fresh cilantro (coriander) or parsley
- 1 tablespoon honey
- 1 tablespoon rice vinegar or white wine vinegar
- 1/4 teaspoon hot red pepper sauce, or to taste

1 In a large saucepan, combine the stock, water, and soy sauce and bring to a simmer. Add the cabbage, celery, pepper, and the white parts of the green onions. Simmer, covered, for 8 minutes.

2 Stir in the mushrooms. Submerge the block of noodles and gently place the tofu on top. Cook, covered, for 3 minutes or until the noodles are tender. Stir in the cilantro, honey, vinegar, red pepper sauce, and green onion tops. Ladle into bowls and serve hot, accompanied by rice cakes and a salad of bean sprouts. Serves 4.

PREPARATION TIME: 20 MIN. COOKING TIME: 12 MIN.

Per serving: Calories 155; Saturated Fat 1 g; Total Fat 6 g; Protein 12 g; Carbohydrate 17 g; Fiber 3 g; Sodium 389 mg; Cholesterol 0 mg

Fragrant Vegetable Sukiyaki with noodles, tofu, and crisp-tender vegetables is a simply elegant meal in a bowl.

TOFU TOSTADOS

East meets Southwest in these mildly spiced, open-faced versions of tacos. Tofu makes a fine meat substitute here, because it readily absorbs all the flavors.

- 1 tablespoon olive or vegetable oil
- 1 medium-size sweet red pepper, cored, seeded, and diced (¾ cup)
- 1 small sweet green pepper, cored, seeded, and diced (½ cup)
- 1 pound firm tofu, cut into 1-inch cubes
- 2 cups mild salsa
- 1 can (4 ounces) chopped green chilies
- ¾ teaspoon dried oregano, crumbled
- ¾ teaspoon each ground coriander and cumin
- 1 cup frozen corn kernels
- 3 tablespoons minced fresh cilantro (coriander) or 3 tablespoons minced parsley mixed with 1 teaspoon dried cilantro
- 4 corn tortillas, 7 inches in diameter

1 In a 12-inch nonstick skillet, heat the oil over moderately high heat. Add the red and green peppers and sauté, stirring frequently, for 2 to 3 minutes or until the peppers are slightly softened. Add the tofu, tossing to coat. Stir in the salsa, green chilies, oregano, coriander, cumin, and corn and cook, stirring occasionally, for 3 minutes or until the mixture is heated through. Stir in the cilantro.

2 Heat a 10-inch nonstick skillet over moderate heat and toast the tortillas, one at a time, for 2 to 3 minutes on each side or until hot. Place the tortillas on 4 individual plates and spoon the tofu mixture on top. Serve with steamed zucchini and black beans. Serves 4.

PREPARATION TIME: 17 MIN. COOKING TIME: 25 MIN.

Per serving: Calories 351; Saturated Fat 2 g; Total Fat 17 g; Protein 23 g; Carbohydrate 38 g; Fiber 5 g; Sodium 517 mg; Cholesterol 0 mg

TOFU ON A BED OF SEASONED NOODLES

This tofu, glazed with a flavorful marinade, can also be served on a bed of brown rice or steamed spinach.

6 pieces firm tofu, each 2 ½ to 3 inches square and about 1 inch thick (2 pounds)
¼ cup teriyaki sauce
½ cup plus 2 tablespoons rice vinegar
¼ cup reduced-sodium soy sauce
2 tablespoons dark sesame oil
1 clove garlic, crushed
1 teaspoon grated orange rind
1 teaspoon minced fresh ginger or ½ teaspoon ground ginger
¼ teaspoon ground red pepper (cayenne)
1 pound linguine or vermicelli, cooked and rinsed with cold water

Garnishes:
2 green onions, including tops, thinly sliced (¼ cup)
¼ cup minced fresh cilantro (coriander) or parsley
⅓ cup unsalted dry-roasted peanuts, finely chopped

Ginger, soy sauce, and teriyaki sauce delicately flavor Tofu on a Bed of Seasoned Noodles.

1 Set the pieces of tofu on a double layer of paper toweling. Cover them with another sheet of paper toweling and put a weight, such as a heavy skillet, on top; let stand for 30 minutes while you do Step 2.

2 In a large bowl, combine the teriyaki sauce with ¼ cup of the vinegar and set aside. In another large bowl, combine the remaining ¼ cup plus 2 tablespoons vinegar with the soy sauce, oil, garlic, orange rind, ginger, and red pepper. Add the linguine and toss to coat; cover and marinate at room temperature for 4 hours or in the refrigerator overnight.

3 Remove the weight from the tofu and slice each piece in half horizontally so that you have twelve ½-inch-thick squares. Dip both sides of the pieces in the teriyaki and vinegar marinade. Set the pieces on a plate, cover with plastic food wrap, and marinate at room temperature for 4 hours or in the refrigerator overnight.

4 Preheat the broiler, setting the rack about 6 inches from the heat. Arrange the tofu on a broiler pan and broil for 4 minutes or until the tops are brown. Turn the tofu over, spoon any remaining teriyaki marinade over the second side, and broil 4 minutes more or until brown. Toss the noodles again. To serve, spoon a portion of noodles in the center of each dinner plate. Slice each piece of broiled tofu in 3 narrow fingers. Spread 6 overlapping slices on top of each portion of noodles and sprinkle some green onion, cilantro, and peanuts on top. Accompany with steamed snow peas or sugar snap peas. Serves 6.

PREPARATION TIME: 35 MIN.   COOKING TIME: 10 MIN.
MARINATING AND STANDING TIME: 4 ½ HR.

Per serving: Calories 643; Saturated Fat 4 g; Total Fat 23 g; Protein 37 g; Carbohydrate 69 g; Fiber 2 g; Sodium 808 mg; Cholesterol 0 mg

TORTILLA PIZZAS WITH PEPPERS AND CHEESE

4 flour tortillas, 7 inches in diameter
3 teaspoons olive oil
1 medium-size red onion, sliced
½ teaspoon each ground cumin and dried oregano, crumbled
¼ teaspoon salt
1 large sweet green pepper, cut into thin rings

1 pickled jalapeño pepper, seeded and finely chopped
1 cup shredded Monterey Jack cheese (4 ounces)
8 pitted black olives, sliced
2 tablespoons minced fresh cilantro (coriander) or parsley

1 Preheat the oven to 450° F. Brush one side of the tortillas with 1 teaspoon of the oil and arrange them, oiled sides up, on a baking sheet. Warm them in the oven for 5 minutes or until softened. Set aside.

2 Meanwhile, in a 10-inch nonstick skillet, heat the remaining 2 teaspoons of oil over moderate heat. Add the onion, cumin, oregano, and salt and sauté, stirring occasionally, for 3 minutes. Lay the red pepper rings on top of the onion, cover, and cook over low heat 2 to 3 minutes more or until the pepper is softened.

3 Arrange ¼ of the onion and pepper mixture on top of each tortilla and sprinkle with the jalapeño pepper, cheese, and olives. Bake for 10 minutes or until the cheese is melted and gently bubbling. Sprinkle with the cilantro. Serve with a salad of lettuce, tomatoes, and shredded carrots. Serves 4.

PREPARATION TIME: 20 MIN.   COOKING TIME: 20 MIN.

Per serving: Calories 262; Saturated Fat 1 g; Total Fat 15 g; Protein 10 g; Carbohydrate 22 g; Fiber 2 g; Sodium 450 mg; Cholesterol 0 mg

PITA-BREAD PIZZAS

This is a quick and delicious pizza recipe that is perfect for unexpected lunch guests.

2 whole-wheat pita rounds, split horizontally into halves
4 teaspoons olive oil
3 shallots, finely chopped (¼ cup)
8 ounces broccoli florets, cut into 1-inch pieces (3 cups), or 1 package (10 ounces) frozen broccoli florets, thawed
¼ teaspoon each salt and red pepper flakes

2 cloves garlic, minced
¼ cup water
4 ounces crumbled goat cheese or shredded mozzarella cheese
8 large sun-dried tomatoes, blanched (page 53) and finely chopped
12 whole basil leaves
4 teaspoons grated Parmesan cheese

1 Preheat the broiler, setting the rack 6 inches from the heat. Arrange the pita rounds, cut sides up, on a baking sheet and toast for 1 to 2 minutes or until lightly golden.

2 Preheat the oven to 450° F. In a 10-inch nonstick skillet, heat 2 teaspoons of the oil over moderate heat. Add the shallots and sauté, stirring, for 1 minute. Add the broccoli, salt, pepper flakes, and garlic and cook, stirring, 1 minute more. Add the water to the skillet, cover, and steam the broccoli for 3 minutes or until just tender. Uncover the skillet and, if necessary, boil any remaining liquid until evaporated.

3 Spread ¼ of the broccoli mixture in an even layer on top of each pita round, then top with the goat cheese and sun-dried tomatoes and garnish with the basil. Sprinkle the pizzas with the Parmesan cheese and drizzle with the remaining 2 teaspoons of oil. Arrange on a baking sheet and bake for 10 to 12 minutes or until the cheese is melted and the topping is hot. Serves 4.

PREPARATION TIME: 20 MIN.   COOKING TIME: 20 MIN.

Per serving: Calories 259; Saturated Fat 5 g; Total Fat 12 g; Protein 13 g; Carbohydrate 28 g; Fiber 6 g; Sodium 429 mg; Cholesterol 24 mg

Pastry brushes, used to coat foods with egg white, oil, water, or a marinade, can be expensive as well as difficult to clean. For an ideal substitute, try inexpensive 1-inch paint brushes. They are less costly than pastry brushes and can be cleaned easily in the dishwasher.

WHOLE-WHEAT PIZZA DOUGH

Nothing quite compares with homemade pizza. This recipe tells you how to make dough both the old-fashioned way and with a food processor. The dough can be refrigerated for 2 days or frozen for up to 2 months.

1 package (¼ ounce) active dry yeast	1 tablespoon olive oil
¼ cup warm water (105°–115° F)	½ teaspoon salt
1 teaspoon honey	1 cup whole-wheat flour
¾ cup cold water	1¾ to 2 cups unbleached all-purpose flour

1 In a large bowl, stir together the yeast, warm water, and honey and set aside for 10 minutes or until foamy. Meanwhile, in a glass measuring cup, combine the cold water, oil, and salt. Add the cold water mixture to the yeast mixture and stir in the whole-wheat flour and 1¾ cups of the all-purpose flour. Beat the mixture, adding more all-purpose flour as needed to make a soft but manageable dough. Knead the dough on a lightly floured surface for 5 to 10 minutes or until smooth and elastic.

2 Alternatively, to prepare the dough in a food processor, combine the whole-wheat flour and 1¾ cups of the all-purpose flour in the bowl. With the motor running, add the cold water mixture and the yeast mixture in a steady stream and process for about 15 seconds or until well combined. Gradually add enough of the remaining all-purpose flour until the mixture forms a ball, then knead the dough by processing for 20 seconds.

3 Put the dough in a lightly greased bowl and turn to coat with grease. Let the dough rise, covered loosely with plastic food wrap, in a warm, draft-free place for 45 minutes to 1 hour or until doubled in bulk. Punch down the dough and proceed as directed in the following recipes. Makes enough dough for one 14-inch pizza or 4 servings.

PREPARATION TIME: 20 MIN. RISING TIME: 45 MIN.

Per serving: Calories 341; Saturated Fat 1 g; Total Fat 4 g; Protein 11 g; Carbohydrate 66 g; Fiber 6 g; Sodium 269 mg; Cholesterol 0 mg

WHOLE-WHEAT PIZZA WITH SPINACH, CHEESE, AND MUSHROOMS

4 teaspoons olive oil	1 tablespoon minced garlic
1 medium-size yellow onion, finely chopped (1 cup)	2 tablespoons cornmeal
4 large mushrooms (4 ounces), sliced	1 recipe Whole-Wheat Pizza Dough (left)
¼ teaspoon each salt and black pepper	1 cup shredded smoked mozzarella or other smoked cheese (4 ounces)
2 pounds spinach, chopped, cooked, and squeezed dry, or 2 packages (10 ounces each) frozen chopped spinach, thawed and squeezed dry	¼ cup minced fresh basil or parsley
	2 tablespoons grated Parmesan cheese

1 Preheat the oven to 450° F. In a 10-inch nonstick skillet, heat 2 teaspoons of the oil over moderate heat. Add the onion and sauté, stirring occasionally, for 5 minutes or until golden. Add the mushrooms, salt, and pepper and cook, stirring occasionally, 3 minutes more or until the mushrooms are tender. Add the spinach and garlic and cook, stirring, for 1 to 2 minutes or until the mixture is dry.

2 Sprinkle a 14-inch pizza pan with the cornmeal. Lightly dust a work surface with whole-wheat flour, roll out the dough into a 14-inch circle, and fit it into the pan. Spread the spinach-mushroom mixture over the dough, sprinkle it with the mozzarella cheese, basil, and Parmesan cheese, and drizzle it with the remaining 2 teaspoons oil. Bake the pizza on the bottom shelf of the oven for 20 minutes or until the crust is golden brown. Cut in wedges and serve immediately. Serves 4.

PREPARATION TIME: 25 MIN. COOKING TIME: 30 MIN.

Per serving: Calories 521; Saturated Fat 6 g; Total Fat 17 g; Protein 21 g; Carbohydrate 75 g; Fiber 9 g; Sodium 633 mg; Cholesterol 24 mg

CALZONES WITH RICOTTA AND BROCCOLI

- 2 tablespoons cornmeal
- 1 tablespoon olive oil
- 4 large shallots, sliced (1 cup)
- 8 ounces broccoli florets, cut into ½-inch pieces (3 cups), or 1 package (10 ounces) frozen broccoli florets, thawed
- 2 teaspoons minced garlic
- 1½ teaspoons minced fresh thyme or ½ teaspoon dried thyme, crumbled
- ¼ teaspoon each salt and black pepper, or to taste
- ¼ cup water
- 1 large egg
- ⅔ cup part-skim ricotta cheese
- ⅔ cup part-skim mozzarella cheese, diced (2 ounces)
- 2 tablespoons grated Parmesan cheese
- 1 recipe Whole-Wheat Pizza Dough (opposite page)

1 Preheat the oven to 450° F. Sprinkle a baking sheet with the cornmeal and set aside. In a 10-inch nonstick skillet, heat 1 teaspoon of the oil over moderately low heat. Add the shallots and cook, stirring occasionally, for 5 minutes or until the shallots are golden brown.

2 Stir in the broccoli, garlic, thyme, salt, and pepper and cook for 1 minute. Raise the heat to moderately high, add the water, and cover. Steam the vegetables for 3 to 4 minutes or until the broccoli is just tender and the liquid has evaporated. If necessary, raise the heat and boil off any remaining liquid. Remove pan from the heat. Meanwhile, in a small bowl, combine the egg and the 3 cheeses.

3 Divide the pizza dough into 4 pieces. On a lightly floured surface, roll each piece with a rolling pin into an 8-inch circle. Spoon about ¼ of the cheese mixture onto half of each round, leaving a 1-inch border. Top the cheese with ¼ of the broccoli mixture. Brush the edge of the dough with water. Fold the other half of each circle over the filling and pinch the edges together to seal.

4 Arrange the calzones on the prepared baking sheet and place the sheet in the lower third of the oven. Bake for 15 minutes or until the dough is golden brown. Brush the calzones with the remaining 2 teaspoons of oil. Serve with sliced tomatoes. Serves 4.

PREPARATION TIME: 25 MIN.   COOKING TIME: 25 MIN.

Per calzone: Calories 544; Saturated Fat 6 g; Total Fat 16 g; Protein 24 g; Carbohydrate 79 g; Fiber 7 g; Sodium 613 mg; Cholesterol 76 mg

In Calzones with Ricotta and Broccoli, you have a complete meal tucked into a whole-wheat pocket.

A perfectly ripe eggplant has firm, glossy, purple-black skin that springs back when you touch it. If the eggplant is too ripe, the skin won't spring back and the vegetable will be slightly bitter when cooked. When an eggplant is underripe, there is no give at all to the skin and the vegetable doesn't have its full flavor. You can store eggplant in a plastic bag for up to 6 days in the refrigerator.

Every bite of Provençale Pizza evokes the south of France: crusty bread, earthy black olives, pungent garlic, and vine-ripened tomatoes.

PROVENÇALE PIZZAS

- 1 **French baguette or Italian loaf, about 22 inches long, 2½ inches in diameter (6 ounces)**
- 4 **teaspoons olive oil**
- 1 **medium-size yellow onion, thinly sliced (1 cup)**
- ½ **teaspoon each dried rosemary and thyme, crumbled**
- ¼ **teaspoon each salt and black pepper, or to taste**
- 1 **can (14½ ounces) low-sodium tomatoes, drained and chopped**
- 2 **cloves garlic, minced**
- 2 **medium-size tomatoes, thinly sliced and seeded**
- 8 **pitted Calamata or other black olives, chopped**
- 4 **anchovies, drained and chopped (optional)**
- 2 **tablespoons grated Parmesan cheese**

1 Preheat the broiler, setting the rack 6 inches from the heat. Cut the bread crosswise into 4 pieces and halve each piece horizontally. Arrange the bread, cut sides up, on a baking sheet and toast it under the broiler for 1 to 2 minutes or until lightly golden.

2 Preheat the oven to 450° F. In a 10-inch nonstick skillet, heat 2 teaspoons of the oil over moderate heat. Add the onion, rosemary, thyme, salt, and pepper and sauté, stirring occasionally, for 6 minutes or until the onion is golden. Add the canned tomatoes and garlic and cook the mixture, stirring, for about 2 minutes or until thick.

3 Spread the onion-tomato mixture, dividing it evenly, on the pieces of bread. Top with the sliced tomatoes and garnish with the olives, anchovies if desired, and cheese. Drizzle the tops of the pizzas with the remaining 2 teaspoons of oil and bake them for 8 to 10 minutes or until the cheese is melted and the topping is hot. Serves 4.

PREPARATION TIME: 25 MIN. COOKING TIME: 18 MIN.

Per serving: Calories 231; Saturated Fat 2 g; Total Fat 9 g; Protein 8 g; Carbohydrate 32 g; Fiber 3 g; Sodium 484 mg; Cholesterol 2 mg

FOCACCIA WITH EGGPLANT, ONION, AND TOMATOES

Focaccia is a dense bread that is topped with herbs and olive oil and sometimes other ingredients as well. This version, with its topping of vegetables and cheese, can be the glorious centerpiece of a Sunday brunch.

- 1 recipe Whole-Wheat Pizza Dough (page 170)
- ½ tablespoon each minced fresh sage and rosemary or 1 teaspoon each ground sage and dried rosemary, crumbled
- 2 tablespoons cornmeal
- 2 teaspoons extra-virgin olive oil

For the topping:
- 2 small eggplants (6 ounces each), sliced lengthwise ¼ inch thick
- 1 small red onion, sliced ¼ inch thick
- ¼ teaspoon each salt and black pepper
- 2 teaspoons extra-virgin olive oil
- 2 plum tomatoes, halved lengthwise, seeded, and cut into ¼-inch slices
- 2 teaspoons minced fresh garlic
- 1 teaspoon each minced fresh sage and rosemary or ½ teaspoon each ground sage and dried rosemary, crumbled
- ⅔ cup diced part-skim mozzarella cheese (2 ounces)
- 1 tablespoon grated Parmesan cheese

1 Prepare the pizza dough according to instructions, adding the sage and rosemary along with the flour. Sprinkle a pizza pan with the cornmeal. On a lightly floured surface, roll out the dough into a 10-inch circle. Arrange the dough on the pizza pan, brush with the oil, and with your fingertips make impressions, about 1 inch apart, across the entire surface of the dough. Let the dough rise in a warm place for 20 minutes.

2 Meanwhile, prepare the topping. Preheat the broiler, setting the rack 6 inches from the heat. Lightly grease a baking sheet. Arrange the eggplant and onion slices on the baking sheet and sprinkle them with the salt and pepper. Brush the vegetables with 1 teaspoon of the oil and broil for 3 to 4 minutes or until golden brown. Turn, coat the other sides with the remaining teaspoon of oil, and broil 3 minutes more.

3 Preheat the oven to 450° F. Arrange the eggplant, onion, and tomato slices on the dough. Sprinkle the vegetables with the garlic, sage, rosemary, and the mozzarella and Parmesan cheeses. Bake the focaccia in the lower third of the oven for 20 minutes or until the dough is golden brown. Serves 4.

PREPARATION TIME: 40 MIN. COOKING TIME: 26 MIN.
RISING TIME: 1 HR. 5 MIN.

Per serving: Calories 416; Saturated Fat 3 g; Total Fat 11 g; Protein 15 g; Carbohydrate 67 g; Fiber 7 g; Sodium 770 mg; Cholesterol 9 mg

Beans and peas are often a main ingredient in meatless dishes because they are such good sources of low-fat protein, especially when combined with a grain or a pasta. (See page 156 for information on combining proteins.) Beans are also excellent sources of carbohydrate, fiber, vitamins, and minerals.

While canned beans are convenient to use, they are often high in salt — an average of 370 milligrams of sodium per ½ cup. You can eliminate about half of the salt by draining and rinsing the beans, but it is healthier and less expensive to use dried beans and peas and cook them yourself. A good way to speed the preparation time, which includes a soaking period of at least 8 hours, is to do a quick soak. In a large saucepan or Dutch oven, cover the beans with 2 to 3 inches of cold water. (Some beans require rinsing and picking over before cooking. Check the package instructions.) Bring the water to a boil and cook for 2 minutes, then turn off the heat and let the beans stand for 1 hour. Drain and cover them with fresh water before cooking. (See pages 18–19 for specific cooking times of different beans.)

Pressure cookers offer an even faster way to cook beans; they eliminate the need for soaking and cook the beans in half to three-quarters of the time.

Because foods cook so rapidly in pressure cookers, they retain more of their vitamins and minerals. This is especially true for vegetables. For example, broccoli retains 88 percent of its vitamin C and 85 percent of its B vitamins.

Concerns about safety have steered some cautious cooks away from pressure cookers in the past. Recent improvements, however, include back-up systems that track the pressure and keep it from building up too much.

Eggplant absorbs oil like a sponge, so any recipe that calls for fried eggplant is generally high in fat and calories. You can easily lower the fat in your favorite recipes with this simple trick. Cut the eggplant in half, place it face down on a greased baking sheet, and bake in a 350° F oven for about 30 minutes or until tender. Then slice or chop the eggplant and proceed as the recipe directs.

EGGPLANT ROLLATINI

1 tablespoon plus 1 teaspoon olive oil
1 large eggplant about 8 inches long (1 ½ pounds), cut lengthwise into 12 slices
1 medium-size yellow onion, chopped (1 cup)
1 small sweet red pepper, cored, seeded, and chopped (½ cup)
1 small sweet green pepper, cored, seeded, and chopped (½ cup)
4 ounces small mushrooms, halved and sliced (1 ¼ cups)

1 tablespoon minced fresh basil or 1 ½ teaspoons dried basil, crumbled
½ teaspoon salt
¼ teaspoon black pepper
1 cup part-skim ricotta cheese
2 tablespoons grated Parmesan cheese
¾ cup shredded part-skim mozzarella cheese (3 ounces)
1 cup Herbed Tomato Sauce (page 270) or 1 can (8 ounces) low-sodium tomato sauce

1 In a small bowl, place 1 tablespoon of the oil. Using a pastry brush, brush 1 side of each eggplant slice with the oil. Heat a 12-inch nonstick skillet over moderately high heat. Place a layer of the eggplant slices in the skillet, oiled sides down, and cook, covered, for 6 minutes, turning once. Transfer the eggplant to a plate and let cool. Repeat with the remaining slices.

2 In the same skillet, heat the remaining 1 teaspoon of oil over moderate heat. Add the onion and red and green peppers and sauté for 5 minutes or until softened. Add the mushrooms, basil, salt, and black pepper and cook 5 minutes more or until the liquid has evaporated and the vegetables are tender. Remove from the heat, spoon into a medium-size bowl, and let cool. Stir in the ricotta cheese, Parmesan cheese, and ¼ cup of the mozzarella.

3 Preheat the oven to 375° F. Lightly grease a 13" x 9" x 2" baking dish. Spoon about ¼ cup of the vegetable-cheese mixture in the center of each eggplant slice. Roll up the slices and arrange them, seam sides down, in the prepared baking dish. Top with the tomato sauce and sprinkle with the remaining ½ cup of mozzarella. Cover the dish with aluminum foil and bake for 45 minutes, then remove the foil. Bake, uncovered, 15 minutes more or until the cheese is bubbling and beginning to brown. Serve with Four-Grain Rolls (page 304) and a green salad. Makes 12 rollatini. Serves 4.

PREPARATION TIME: 30 MIN. COOKING TIME: 1 ½ HR.

Per roll: Calories 96; Saturated Fat 2 g; Total Fat 5 g; Protein 6 g; Carbohydrate 8 g; Fiber 1 g; Sodium 175 mg; Cholesterol 11 mg

EGGPLANT PARMESAN

This version of an Italian favorite is lower in fat than the traditional recipe and is very easy to prepare: just slice, dip, and bake.

½ cup plain dry bread crumbs
½ cup grated Parmesan cheese (2 ounces)
1 large egg
1 tablespoon water
1 medium-size eggplant (1 pound), peeled and sliced crosswise ½ inch thick

1 tablespoon olive oil
1 cup Herbed Tomato Sauce (page 270) or 1 can (8 ounces) low-sodium tomato sauce
1 ½ cups shredded part-skim mozzarella cheese (6 ounces)

1 Preheat the oven to 400° F. Lightly grease a 9" x 11" x 2" baking dish. In a shallow bowl or pie pan, combine the bread crumbs and Parmesan cheese. In another shallow bowl, beat together the egg and water. Dip the eggplant slices in the egg mixture, then into the crumb mixture. Place the slices in a single layer in the prepared baking dish. Drizzle the oil over the top.

2 Bake for 30 minutes or until golden and tender. Pour the tomato sauce over the eggplant, then sprinkle with the mozzarella cheese. Bake another 7 to 10 minutes or until the cheese has melted. Serve with a lettuce and tomato salad and crusty bread. Serves 4.

PREPARATION TIME: 15 MIN. COOKING TIME: 37 MIN.

Per serving: Calories 324; Saturated Fat 8 g; Total Fat 15 g; Protein 24 g; Carbohydrate 23 g; Fiber 1 g; Sodium 569 mg; Cholesterol 89 mg

EGGPLANT-RICOTTA LOAF

This substitute for meat loaf will keep, refrigerated, for up to 3 days. Serve it as a main course or part of a buffet. If you like, top it with a favorite tomato sauce.

- 1 large eggplant about 10 inches long (1 ½ pounds), sliced lengthwise ¼ inch thick
- 4 ounces medium-size pasta shells
- 1 container (15 ounces) part-skim ricotta cheese
- 3 large egg whites
- 1 large egg
- ¼ teaspoon salt
- ¼ cup minced fresh basil
- 2 teaspoons grated lemon rind
- 2 teaspoons minced garlic
- 1 jar (7 ounces) roasted red peppers, rinsed, drained, and sliced ½ inch thick
- 1 medium-size tomato (6 ounces), cut into 6 slices

1 Preheat the oven to 400° F. Lightly grease a baking sheet. Arrange the eggplant slices on the baking sheet and sprinkle them with a few tablespoons of water. Bake for 15 minutes or until tender; remove from the oven and let cool. Meanwhile, bring a large saucepan of unsalted water to a boil and cook the pasta for 8 minutes or until tender but still firm to the bite. Drain, rinse under cool water, and set aside.

2 Lightly grease a 9" x 5" x 3" loaf pan, line the bottom with wax paper, and grease the paper. Place the eggplant slices crosswise in rows so that they overhang the sides of the pan. Overlap the slices where necessary. If there are any remaining slices, cover the short ends of the pan as well.

3 In a medium-size bowl, stir together the ricotta cheese, egg whites, whole egg, salt, 2 tablespoons of the basil, 1 teaspoon of the lemon rind, and 1 teaspoon of the garlic. Spoon ⅓ of the mixture into the loaf pan. Spread the pasta on top. Cover with half of the remaining cheese mixture. Lay the roasted pepper slices on top. Cover with the remaining cheese mixture, lay the tomato slices on top of the cheese, and sprinkle with the remaining 2 tablespoons of basil, 1 teaspoon of lemon rind, and 1 teaspoon of garlic. Fold the eggplant over the top of the mixture to cover.

4 Cover the pan with aluminum foil and place in a larger baking pan. Fill the larger pan with enough hot water to come halfway up the sides of the loaf pan. Bake for 30 minutes. Uncover and bake 15 minutes longer. Let cool for 20 minutes, then run a knife around the sides of the loaf and invert onto a serving platter. Pour off any liquid that accumulates and remove the wax paper. Serve at room temperature or chilled. Serves 8.

PREPARATION TIME: 25 MIN. COOKING TIME: 1 HR.
STANDING TIME: 20 MIN.

Per serving: Calories 176; Saturated Fat 3 g; Total Fat 5 g; Protein 11 g; Carbohydrate 21 g; Fiber 0 g; Sodium 167 mg; Cholesterol 43 mg

Thin slices of eggplant envelop layers of cheese, pasta, and roasted red peppers. Served at room temperature or chilled, Eggplant-Ricotta Loaf, with a salad of mixed greens, makes a summery fresh supper.

boil. Lower the heat and simmer, stirring occasionally, for 20 minutes or until the sauce has thickened and reduced to about 3 cups. Remove from the heat and set aside.

2 Preheat the oven to 425° F. Line a baking sheet with aluminum foil. Place the zucchini slices in a single layer on the baking sheet. Brush the top sides with about 1 tablespoon of the egg white, then sprinkle the bread crumbs and pepper evenly over the slices.

3 Bake for 20 minutes or until the zucchini is golden and crisp-tender when pierced with a knife. Remove from the oven and set aside until cool enough to handle. Reduce the oven temperature to 350° F. In a medium-size bowl, combine the ricotta cheese, remaining egg white, parsley, and 3 tablespoons of the Parmesan cheese.

4 Grease an 11" x 7" x 2" baking dish. Spread 1 cup of the tomato-basil sauce evenly in the dish. Arrange half of the zucchini on top of the sauce in a single layer, trimming the slices to fit if necessary. Spread the ricotta-Parmesan mixture evenly over the zucchini. Sprinkle ¼ cup of the mozzarella cheese over the top; spoon ¾ cup sauce over the mozzarella.

5 Place the remaining zucchini in a single layer on top, again trimming to fit. Spread the remaining 1¼ cups sauce evenly over the zucchini layer, then scatter the remaining ½ cup mozzarella cheese and 1 tablespoon of Parmesan cheese over the sauce. Place the dish on a baking sheet in case the lasagne bubbles over.

6 Bake for 35 to 45 minutes or until the cheese is bubbling and the lasagne is hot in the center. Cover the pan loosely with foil if the top browns too quickly. Remove from the oven and let stand for 15 minutes before cutting into rectangles. Serves 6.

PREPARATION TIME: 35 MIN. COOKING TIME: 45 MIN.

STANDING TIME: 15 MIN.

Per serving: Calories 263; Saturated Fat 6 g; Total Fat 10 g; Protein 18 g; Carbohydrate 25 g; Fiber 5 g; Sodium 310 mg; Cholesterol 30 mg

Serve Zucchini, Potato, and Cheese Pancakes as a light entrée or as a stylish partner to pork or lamb chops.

ZUCCHINI LASAGNE

Zucchini replaces pasta in this version of an old favorite.

- 2 teaspoons olive oil
- 1 medium-size yellow onion, chopped (1 cup)
- 2 teaspoons minced garlic
- 1 recipe Herbed Tomato Sauce (page 270) or 4 cans (8 ounces each) low-sodium tomato sauce
- ¼ cup minced fresh basil or 1 tablespoon dried basil, crumbled
- 5 medium-size zucchini (1¾ pounds), sliced lengthwise ¼ inch thick
- 1 large egg white, lightly beaten
- ¼ cup plain dry bread crumbs
- ⅛ teaspoon black pepper, or to taste
- 1½ cups (12 ounces) part-skim ricotta cheese
- ¼ cup minced flat-leaf parsley
- ¼ cup grated Parmesan cheese (1 ounce)
- ¾ cup shredded part-skim mozzarella cheese (3 ounces)

1 In a large heavy saucepan, heat the oil over moderate heat. Add the onion and garlic and sauté for 5 minutes or until soft. Add the tomato sauce and basil and bring to a

ZUCCHINI, POTATO, AND CHEESE PANCAKES

Pancakes aren't just for breakfast. Serve these savory treats anytime.

- 3 medium-size zucchini, shredded (4 cups)
- 3 medium-size all-purpose potatoes, peeled and shredded (2¾ cups)
- 4 green onions, including tops, thinly sliced (½ cup)
- ½ cup grated Parmesan cheese (2 ounces)
- ⅓ cup all-purpose flour
- 2 large egg whites
- ¼ teaspoon dried oregano, crumbled
- ¼ teaspoon each salt and black pepper, or to taste
- 4 teaspoons olive or vegetable oil
- 1 cup plain nonfat yogurt
- ½ cup Tomato Salsa (page 280) (optional garnish)

1 Preheat the oven to 250° F. In a large bowl, stir together the zucchini, potatoes, green onions, cheese, flour, egg whites, oregano, salt, and pepper until well combined.

2 In a 12-inch nonstick skillet, heat 1 teaspoon of the oil over moderate heat. Spoon a scant ⅓ cup of the zucchini mixture, including some of the zucchini liquid, into the skillet. With a spatula, flatten the mixture into a 4-inch pancake. Spoon in 3 more pancakes and cook for 3 minutes on each side or until cooked through and golden brown. Transfer the pancakes to a baking sheet and keep warm in the oven. Repeat with the remaining batter, adding a teaspoon of oil after each batch of 4. Makes 16 pancakes. Place 4 pancakes on each of 4 plates and spoon ¼ cup of yogurt and some salsa, if desired, alongside. Accompany with a tomato salad. Serves 4.

PREPARATION TIME: 15 MIN. COOKING TIME: 25 MIN.

Per serving: Calories 290; Saturated Fat 3 g; Total Fat 9 g; Protein 15 g; Carbohydrate 39 g; Fiber 4 g; Sodium 446 mg; Cholesterol 11 mg

CHEESE-AND-PASTA STUFFED PEPPERS

If you are using fresh broccoli, save the stalks for vegetable stock.

- 4 large sweet red peppers (8 ounces each), cored, seeded, and halved
- 2 teaspoons olive oil
- 1 large yellow onion, chopped (1½ cups)
- 3 cloves garlic, minced
- 2 cups fresh or frozen small broccoli florets (4 ounces)
- 2 tablespoons water
- ⅔ cup part-skim ricotta cheese
- 2 tablespoons raisins
- 2 tablespoons minced parsley
- ¼ teaspoon each black pepper
- ⅛ teaspoon ground red pepper (cayenne)
- 2 ounces orzo, cooked according to package directions
- 1 can (14½ ounces) low-sodium tomatoes, chopped, with their juice

1 Preheat the oven to 400° F. In a stockpot of boiling water, cook the sweet red peppers for 5 minutes or until crisp-tender. Drain on paper toweling.

2 In a 10-inch skillet, heat the oil over moderately low heat. Add the onion and garlic and cook, stirring occasionally, for 5 minutes or until the onion is softened. Stir in the broccoli and water, cover, and cook for 5 minutes or until the broccoli is tender. Stir in the ricotta cheese, raisins, parsley, salt, black pepper, ground red pepper, and orzo. Spoon the mixture into the pepper halves.

3 Arrange the peppers in an 11" x 7" x 2" baking dish, spoon the tomatoes around them, and cover with aluminum foil. Bake for 15 to 20 minutes or until peppers are tender and the filling is piping hot. Serve the peppers hot or at room temperature with the tomatoes spooned over them and accompanied by crusty bread. Serves 4.

PREPARATION TIME: 20 MIN. COOKING TIME: 30 MIN.

Per serving: Calories 250; Saturated Fat 3 g; Total Fat 7 g; Protein 11 g; Carbohydrate 40 g; Fiber 6 g; Sodium 216 mg; Cholesterol 13 mg

SPICY STUFFED PEPPERS

4 large sweet green peppers (8 ounces each)
1 ⅓ cups water
⅔ cup long-grain white rice
3 green onions, including tops, thinly sliced (¾ cup)
3 tablespoons minced fresh cilantro (coriander) or 1 teaspoon dried cilantro, crumbled
1 ¼ teaspoons each ground cumin and dried oregano, crumbled
1 teaspoon chopped jalapeño pepper
1 cup frozen corn kernels, thawed
1 cup cooked black beans
2 tablespoons lime juice
¼ cup shredded Monterey Jack cheese (1 ounce)

1 Slice the tops off the peppers and set aside. Remove and discard the seeds. If the peppers won't stand upright, slice a little off the bottoms. In a stockpot of boiling water, cook the peppers and their tops for 5 minutes or until crisp-tender; drain upside down on paper toweling.

2 In a medium-size saucepan, bring the water to a boil over moderate heat. Add the rice, green onions, cilantro, ¾ teaspoon each of the cumin and oregano, and the jalapeño pepper. Lower the heat and simmer, covered, for 15 minutes or until the rice is fluffy and has absorbed all the water.

3 Preheat the oven to 400° F. Stir the corn, beans, lime juice, and cheese into the rice mixture; spoon the mixture into the peppers. Cover with the pepper tops and place in an 8" x 8" x 2" baking dish. Pour 1 inch of water around the peppers; stir the remaining ½ teaspoon each of cumin and oregano into the water. Cover with aluminum foil and bake for 25 minutes or until the peppers are tender. Serve hot or at room temperature with a tossed green salad and French bread. Serves 4.

PREPARATION TIME: 20 MIN. COOKING TIME: 45 MIN.

Per serving: Calories 331; Saturated Fat 0 g;
Total Fat 4 g; Protein 14 g; Carbohydrate 64 g;
Fiber 8 g; Sodium 60 mg; Cholesterol 0 mg

ORZO-CORN SALAD IN TOMATO SHELLS

The stuffing for this summer delight can be made up to 2 days ahead and refrigerated. Orzo, the rice-shaped pasta in the filling, also makes a fine side dish in place of rice.

4 ounces orzo
3 strips lemon zest (colored part of the rind)
2 cups cooked corn kernels or frozen corn, thawed
1 cup diced low-fat Swiss or Monterey Jack cheese (4 ounces)
2 green onions, including tops, sliced (⅓ cup)
⅔ cup diced celery or fennel
¼ cup apple juice
2 tablespoons lemon juice
2 tablespoons olive or canola oil
½ teaspoon salt
¼ teaspoon hot red pepper sauce, or to taste
4 large tomatoes (2¼ pounds)
1 cup shredded lettuce (optional garnish)

1 Bring a large saucepan of unsalted water to a boil. Add the orzo and lemon zest and cook for about 8 minutes or until the orzo is tender but still firm to the bite. Drain in a colander, rinse with cold water to stop the cooking, and drain again. Discard the lemon zest.

2 In a large bowl, combine the orzo, corn, cheese, green onions, celery, apple juice, lemon juice, oil, salt, and red pepper sauce. Trim the bottoms of the tomatoes so that they stand upright. Cut off the tops and remove the cores. Dice the tomato trimmings and add them to the corn salad. Scoop out the tomato pulp and discard or save for a sauce. Invert the tomatoes onto a plate lined with paper toweling and let drain.

3 Fill the hollow of each tomato with about ½ cup of corn salad mixture. To serve, place a tomato in the center of a serving plate and ring with about 1 cup of the remaining salad plus lettuce if you like. Serve cold or at room temperature, accompanied by bread sticks. Serves 4.

PREPARATION TIME: 20 MIN. COOKING TIME: 10 MIN.

Per serving: Calories 392; Saturated Fat 1 g;
Total Fat 15 g; Protein 18 g; Carbohydrate 54 g;
Fiber 6 g; Sodium 345 mg; Cholesterol 19 mg

VEGETABLE-CHEESE ENCHILADAS

This low-fat version of a Mexican favorite is a fine dish for enticing youngsters to eat their vegetables.

For the filling:
- 8 corn tortillas, 6 inches in diameter
- 1 medium-size zucchini (8 ounces), cut into ½-inch cubes
- 1 cup cooked brown rice
- 2 green onions, including tops, finely chopped (¼ cup)
- ⅓ cup reduced-fat sour cream
- 1 cup shredded low-fat Monterey Jack cheese, (4 ounces)
- ¼ teaspoon each salt and black pepper, or to taste

For the sauce:
- 2 teaspoons olive oil
- 1 medium-size yellow onion, finely chopped (1 cup)
- 2 cloves garlic, minced
- 1 tablespoon chili powder, or to taste
- 1 can (14½ ounces) low-sodium tomatoes, crushed, with their juice (1½ cups)
- ½ cup Chicken Stock or Vegetable Stock (page 62) or low-sodium chicken broth
- 1 jalapeño pepper, seeded and finely chopped (optional)
- 3 tablespoons minced fresh cilantro (coriander) or 3 tablespoons minced parsley mixed with 1 teaspoon dried cilantro

Stuff the pick of the vine with vegetables and pasta for Orzo-Corn Salad in Tomato Shells.

1 Preheat the oven to 350° F. Wrap the tortillas in aluminum foil and heat in the oven for 7 to 10 minutes or until softened. Meanwhile, in a medium-size saucepan of boiling water, blanch the zucchini for 2 minutes or until just tender. Drain, rinse under cold water to stop the cooking, and pat dry with paper toweling. In a large mixing bowl, combine the zucchini, rice, green onions, sour cream, ½ cup of the cheese, salt, and pepper.

2 Lightly grease an 11" x 9" x 2" baking dish. Spoon ⅛ of the filling onto each tortilla and spread it down the center. Roll the tortilla to enclose the filling and arrange, seam side down, in the prepared baking dish. Cover the baking dish with aluminum foil and bake the enchiladas for 10 minutes or until heated through.

3 Meanwhile, prepare the sauce. In a medium-size saucepan, heat the oil over moderate heat. Add the onion and sauté, stirring occasionally, for 5 minutes or until softened. Add the garlic and chili powder and sauté, stirring, for 1 minute. Add the tomatoes, stock, and jalapeño pepper if using and simmer, stirring occasionally, for 10 minutes or until the sauce has thickened slightly. Stir in the cilantro. Spoon the sauce over the enchiladas, sprinkle with the remaining ½ cup cheese, and bake 8 to 10 minutes longer or until the cheese has melted and the sauce is bubbling. Serve with black beans and sliced avocado. Serves 4.

PREPARATION TIME: 30 MIN. COOKING TIME: 45 MIN.

Per enchilada: Calories 377; Saturated Fat 6 g; Total Fat 15 g; Protein 17 g; Carbohydrate 49 g; Fiber 7 g; Sodium 411 mg; Cholesterol 20 mg

VEGETABLE COUSCOUS

You can adapt this mellow dish to the seasons, replacing carrots and parsnips with spring's young green beans or sugar snap peas and slender asparagus.

2 tablespoons olive oil

2 medium-size yellow onions, thinly sliced (4 cups)

2 large carrots, peeled and sliced ½ inch thick

2 medium-size red-skinned potatoes (6 ounces each), cut into ½-inch cubes

3 cloves garlic, minced

4 cups Chicken Stock or Vegetable Stock (page 62) or low-sodium chicken broth

1 can (14½ ounces) low-sodium tomatoes, chopped, with their juice

½ teaspoon each dried thyme and basil, crumbled

½ teaspoon each salt and black pepper, or to taste

1 bay leaf

2 parsnips (7 ounces), peeled and sliced ½ inch thick

1 medium-size zucchini (6 ounces), cut into 1-inch cubes

1 medium-size yellow squash (6 ounces), cut into 1-inch cubes

2 cups cooked chick peas

¼ cup golden raisins

1 cup couscous

1 In a 5-quart Dutch oven, heat 1 tablespoon of the oil over moderate heat. Add the onions and sauté, stirring occasionally, for 5 to 7 minutes or until golden. Add the carrots, potatoes, and garlic and cook, stirring, for 2 minutes. Stir in the stock, tomatoes, thyme, basil, salt, pepper, and bay leaf. Bring the liquid to a boil, then lower the heat and simmer the vegetables, covered, for 5 minutes. Add the parsnips and simmer, covered, for 3 minutes. Add the zucchini, yellow squash, and chick peas and simmer, covered, for 8 minutes or until the vegetables are just tender. Remove and discard the bay leaf.

2 Using a 1-pint glass measuring cup, transfer 1½ cups of the cooking liquid from the Dutch oven to a small saucepan. Stir in the raisins and the remaining 1 tablespoon of oil, then bring the liquid to a boil and stir in the couscous. Remove the saucepan from the heat and let

Tempt the most reluctant vegetable eater with this wonderful version of a North African favorite — Vegetable Couscous.

stand, covered, for 10 minutes or until the liquid is absorbed and the couscous is tender. Serve the vegetables over the couscous. Serves 4 to 6.

PREPARATION TIME: 25 MIN. COOKING TIME: 25 MIN.

STANDING TIME: 10 MIN.

Per serving (for 4): Calories 570; Saturated Fat 1 g; Total Fat 11 g; Protein 20 g; Carbohydrate 103 g; Fiber 14 g; Sodium 453 mg; Cholesterol 0 mg

VEGETARIAN PICADILLO

Eggplant takes the place of chopped meat in this healthful version of a favorite Spanish dish.

4 teaspoons olive oil	½ teaspoon each chili powder and ground cumin
1 large yellow onion, diced (1 ½ cups)	
3 cloves garlic, minced	¼ teaspoon salt, or to taste
1 small eggplant (6 ounces), cut into ½-inch cubes but not peeled (2 cups)	1 can (14½ ounces) low-sodium tomatoes, crushed, with their juice
1 small sweet red pepper (4 ounces), cored, seeded, and cut into ½-inch squares	2 tablespoons cider vinegar (optional)
	2 cups cooked pinto beans or kidney beans
1 small yellow squash, sliced ¼ inch thick (1 cup)	¼ cup raisins
	2 tablespoons chopped almonds (optional)
¾ teaspoon ground coriander	

1 In a 5-quart Dutch oven or large heavy saucepan, heat 2 teaspoons of the oil over moderate heat. Add the onion and garlic and sauté, stirring frequently, for 6 minutes or until the onion is golden. Add the remaining 2 teaspoons of oil, the eggplant, red pepper, and squash; cook, stirring, for 2 minutes. Lower the heat, cover, and cook for 10 minutes or until all the vegetables are tender.

2 Stir in the coriander, chili powder, cumin, salt, tomatoes, and vinegar if using, and cook over moderate heat, stirring occasionally, for 7 minutes or until thickened. Stir in the beans, raisins, and almonds if desired, and cook 5 minutes longer. Serve with brown rice. Serves 4.

PREPARATION TIME: 20 MIN. COOKING TIME: 30 MIN.

Per serving: Calories 283; Saturated Fat 1 g; Total Fat 6 g; Protein 12 g; Carbohydrate 50 g; Fiber 7 g; Sodium 152 mg; Cholesterol 0 mg

CABBAGE-CARAWAY NOODLE PUDDING

Here is a one-dish meal that is richly satisfying.

4 ounces egg noodles	1 cup Chicken Stock (page 62) or low-sodium chicken broth
1 tablespoon unsalted butter	
1 medium-size yellow onion, finely chopped (1 cup)	1 tablespoon cornstarch
	1 cup skim milk
	½ cup reduced-fat sour cream
1 ½ pounds cabbage, cored and shredded (6 cups)	2 tablespoons white wine vinegar or rice vinegar
1 tablespoon caraway seeds	2 teaspoons Dijon mustard
½ teaspoon each salt and black pepper	½ cup fresh bread crumbs
	2 tablespoons grated Parmesan cheese

1 Preheat the oven to 375° F. Lightly grease an 11" x 9" x 2" baking dish. Cook the noodles according to package directions, drain, rinse with cold water, and drain again. Meanwhile, in a medium-size saucepan, heat 2 teaspoons of the butter over moderate heat. Add the onion and sauté, stirring occasionally, for 5 minutes or until softened. Stir in the cabbage, caraway seeds, salt, and pepper and cook for 1 minute. Stir in the stock, bring the liquid to a boil, then lower the heat, cover, and simmer for 5 minutes.

2 In a glass measuring cup, dissolve the cornstarch in the milk and pour into the saucepan. Bring the liquid to a boil, lower the heat, and simmer, stirring, for 3 minutes or until the liquid is thick and smooth. Remove from the heat and stir in the sour cream, vinegar, mustard, and noodles.

3 Transfer the cabbage mixture to the prepared baking dish. Sprinkle the top with the bread crumbs and cheese and dot with the remaining teaspoon of butter. Bake for 15 to 20 minutes or until bubbling and golden. Serve with Four-Grain Rolls (page 304). Serves 4 to 6.

PREPARATION TIME: 15 MIN. COOKING TIME: 30 MIN.

Per serving (for 4): Calories 311; Saturated Fat 6 g; Total Fat 11 g; Protein 13 g; Carbohydrate 43 g; Fiber 5 g; Sodium 519 mg; Cholesterol 34 mg

Dutch ovens are large heavy pots with tight-fitting lids that are used in recipes calling for long, slow cooking. In colonial times, Dutch ovens were made exclusively from cast iron and were often hung on a hook in an open fireplace. Nowadays they are made from a number of materials, including stainless steel, aluminum, copper, and enamel on a stainless steel or cast iron base.

Unlike baking dishes and casseroles made of glass or ceramic, Dutch ovens can be used on the stovetop as well as in the oven. This makes them ideal for recipes that combine both stovetop cooking and baking. Dutch ovens range in size from 4 to 7 quarts; the 5-quart size is most common.

If you can flip a flapjack, you can easily create award-worthy Ricotta-Filled Crêpes. Unveil these whole-wheat winners at your next brunch or luncheon and collect the compliments.

RICOTTA, BASIL, AND PINE NUT LOAF

In combination, these simple flavors are quite earthy. The loaf can be prepared and refrigerated up to 2 days ahead. It makes an excellent appetizer as well as an entrée.

- 3 tablespoons plain dry bread crumbs
- 2 tablespoons pine nuts
- 1 container (15 ounces) part-skim ricotta cheese
- ⅓ cup plain low-fat yogurt
- 4 large egg whites
- ¾ cup basil leaves
- 2 tablespoons grated Parmesan cheese
- ⅓ cup sun-dried tomatoes, blanched (page 53) and finely chopped
- 2 tablespoons golden raisins

1 Preheat the oven to 350° F. Lightly grease a 9" x 5" x 3" loaf pan and dust with the bread crumbs; set aside. Toast the pine nuts on a baking sheet in the oven for 5 minutes or until fragrant and very slightly browned.

2 In a food processor or blender, whirl the ricotta cheese and yogurt for 30 seconds or until smooth. Add the egg whites, basil, and Parmesan cheese and whirl 30 seconds longer. Stir in the sun-dried tomatoes, raisins, and pine nuts.

3 Spoon the mixture into the prepared loaf pan and cover with aluminum foil. Place the pan in a slightly larger baking pan and pour enough hot water into the larger pan to come halfway up the sides of the loaf pan. Bake for 45 minutes, uncover, and bake 30 minutes longer or until set. Let cool for 20 minutes, then run a metal spatula around the edges; invert the loaf onto a serving platter and slice. Serve at room temperature or chilled, accompanied by a salad of mixed greens and crusty whole-wheat Italian bread. Serves 4 as a main dish or makes 16 appetizer servings.

PREPARATION TIME: 12 MIN. COOKING TIME: 1 HR. 20 MIN.
STANDING TIME: 20 MIN.

Per serving (for 4): Calories 271; Saturated Fat 7 g; Total Fat 14 g; Protein 21 g; Carbohydrate 18 g; Fiber 2 g; Sodium 303 mg; Cholesterol 36 mg

RICOTTA-FILLED CRÊPES

The crêpes can be made up to 2 days ahead, covered with plastic food wrap, and refrigerated until ready to use. If you wish, assemble several hours in advance and bake just before serving.

For the crêpes:
- 1¼ cups buttermilk
- 1 cup whole-wheat flour
- 4 large egg whites
- Pinch salt
- Nonstick cooking spray

For the filling:
- 1 teaspoon olive or vegetable oil
- 1 medium-size yellow onion, finely chopped (1 cup)
- 1 clove garlic, minced
- 1 medium-size zucchini (6 ounces), quartered lengthwise and thinly sliced
- 3 tablespoons water
- 1 cup part-skim ricotta cheese, drained in a sieve for 1 hour
- ¼ cup grated Parmesan cheese (1 ounce)
- 2 large tomatoes, chopped (3 cups)
- 3 tablespoons tomato paste

1 To prepare the crêpes: In a food processor or blender, combine the buttermilk, flour, egg whites, and salt and whirl for 30 seconds or until well blended. Let stand at room temperature for 1 hour.

2 Coat an 8-inch nonstick skillet with the cooking spray. Heat the skillet over moderately high heat. Pour a scant ¼ cup of the batter into the skillet and quickly tilt it to coat the bottom of the pan with the batter. Cook for 30 to 45 seconds or until the underside of the crêpe is cooked and lightly colored. With a spatula, turn the crêpe over and cook 30 seconds longer. Transfer to a plate. Repeat with the remaining batter, placing sheets of wax paper between the crêpes as you stack them. You should have 12 crêpes.

3 To prepare the filling: In an 8-inch nonstick skillet, heat the oil over moderate heat. Add the onion and garlic and sauté, stirring frequently, for 6 minutes or until golden. Add the zucchini and water and cook, covered, 5 minutes more or until the zucchini is tender.

4 Preheat the oven to 450° F. Lightly grease an 11" x 7" x 2" baking dish. In a medium-size bowl, combine the ricotta cheese, 2 tablespoons of the Parmesan cheese, and the zucchini mixture. Spoon 3 tablespoons of the filling onto 1 quarter section of each crêpe. Fold the crêpe in half, then in quarters, forming a fan shape (see photograph, opposite page).

5 In a medium-size bowl, combine the tomatoes and tomato paste. Spread ¼ cup of the mixture in the bottom of the prepared baking dish. Place the filled crêpes in a single layer on top and spoon the rest of the tomato mixture over them. Sprinkle with the remaining 2 tablespoons of Parmesan cheese. Bake for 20 minutes or until bubbling. Serve with a green salad. Serves 4.

PREPARATION TIME: 25 MIN. COOKING TIME: 40 MIN.
STANDING TIME: 1 HR.

> *Per serving: Calories 326; Saturated Fat 5 g; Total Fat 10 g; Protein 22 g; Carbohydrate 40 g; Fiber 7 g; Sodium 505 mg; Cholesterol 27 mg*

•

Cheese Blintz Variation Prepare the crêpes as directed. Preheat the oven to 450° F. Lightly grease a 9" x 9" x 2" baking dish and set aside. To prepare the filling: Peel, cook, and mash *1 large all-purpose potato (1 cup)*. In a 6-inch nonstick skillet, heat *1 teaspoon olive oil* over moderate heat. Add *1 small yellow onion, finely chopped (½ cup)*, and sauté, stirring frequently, for 6 minutes or until the onion is golden. In a medium-size bowl, combine the potato, onion, *1 cup low-fat (1% milkfat) cottage cheese,* and *⅛ teaspoon black pepper*. Spoon 3 tablespoons of the filling onto the center of the lower half of each crêpe, fold the sides over the filling, then roll up the crêpes; place them, seam sides down, in the prepared dish. Bake for 10 minutes or until lightly crisped and hot. Serve with plain low-fat yogurt and unsweetened applesauce if desired. Serves 4. *Per serving: Calories 245; Saturated Fat 1 g; Total Fat 3 g; Protein 18 g; Carbohydrate 38 g; Fiber 5 g; Sodium 422 mg; Cholesterol 5 mg.*

SPINACH DUMPLINGS WITH PEPPER SAUCE

2 cups mashed potatoes (from 2 large all-purpose potatoes)
2 large eggs, separated
1 cup part-skim ricotta cheese
1 pound spinach, chopped, cooked, and squeezed dry, or 1 package (10 ounces) frozen chopped spinach, thawed and squeezed dry
½ cup all-purpose flour
¼ cup grated Parmesan cheese (1 ounce)
¼ teaspoon each salt and black pepper
2 teaspoons olive oil

For the pepper sauce:
2 jars (7 ounces each) roasted red peppers, rinsed and drained
1 cup basil leaves, rinsed and patted dry
1 clove garlic, sliced
1 tablespoon olive oil
1 tablespoon balsamic or red wine vinegar
¼ teaspoon each salt and black pepper

1 In a large bowl, combine the potatoes, egg yolks, ricotta cheese, spinach, flour, 2 tablespoons of the Parmesan, salt, and pepper. In a very clean medium-size bowl, using an electric mixer set on high speed, beat the egg whites until they hold stiff peaks. Stir ⅓ of the whites into the potato mixture, then gently fold in the remainder.

2 Preheat the oven to 400° F. Lightly grease an 11" x 9" x 2" baking dish. With dampened hands, shape the mixture into oval balls, using ¼ cup per ball, and place in the prepared baking dish (you should have 16 dumplings). Sprinkle with the remaining Parmesan cheese and drizzle with the oil. Bake for 20 to 25 minutes or until golden.

3 Meanwhile, prepare the pepper sauce. In a food processor or blender, whirl the peppers, basil, and garlic for about 30 seconds or until puréed. Add the oil, vinegar, salt, and pepper and whirl several seconds more or until well blended. (If the sauce is too thick, add 1 or 2 tablespoons of water.) Arrange 4 dumplings on each serving plate and spoon some sauce over each serving. Serves 4.

PREPARATION TIME: 30 MIN. COOKING TIME: 20 MIN.

Per serving: Calories 384; Saturated Fat 6 g;
Total Fat 16 g; Protein 20 g; Carbohydrate 43 g;
Fiber 5 g; Sodium 592 mg; Cholesterol 130 mg

CHEESE POLENTA WITH HERBED TOMATO SAUCE

Polenta, a rustic Italian dish made with cornmeal, can be served for brunch or a light lunch. All you need is a salad and crusty bread to complete the meal.

2 cups cold water
2 cups Chicken Stock or Vegetable Stock (page 62) or low-sodium chicken broth
1½ cups yellow cornmeal
¼ teaspoon each salt and black pepper
1½ cups shredded part-skim mozzarella cheese (6 ounces)
¼ cup grated Parmesan cheese (1 ounce)
2 teaspoons olive oil
1 recipe Herbed Tomato Sauce (page 270)

1 Preheat the oven to 400° F. Lightly grease a 1½-quart soufflé dish or deep baking dish. In a medium-size saucepan, combine the water, stock, cornmeal, salt, and pepper. Bring to a boil over moderate heat, whisking constantly. Lower the heat and simmer, whisking occasionally, for 5 minutes or until thick.

2 Spoon half of the cornmeal mixture into the prepared soufflé dish, smoothing the surface with the back of the spoon. Sprinkle the top with 1 cup of the mozzarella cheese and 2 tablespoons of the Parmesan cheese. Smooth the remaining cornmeal mixture on top and sprinkle with the remaining cheeses. Drizzle the oil over all and bake for 35 minutes or until bubbling and golden. Cut the polenta into 8 wedges. Place 2 wedges on each of 4 serving plates and spoon some of the tomato sauce over each serving. Serves 4.

PREPARATION TIME: 15 MIN. COOKING TIME: 43 MIN.

Per serving: Calories 434; Saturated Fat 6 g;
Total Fat 15 g; Protein 21 g; Carbohydrate 54 g;
Fiber 5 g; Sodium 426 mg; Cholesterol 30 mg

SPINACH AND POTATO SOUFFLÉ

Gruyère adds a wonderful flavor to this easy-to-make soufflé. Look for this excellent cheese in the imported cheese section of your supermarket or in a specialty food shop.

- 2 medium-size red-skinned potatoes, peeled and cut into ½-inch cubes
- 2 teaspoons unsalted butter
- 1 medium-size yellow onion, finely chopped (1 cup)
- 1 package (10 ounces) frozen chopped spinach, thawed and squeezed dry
- ¼ teaspoon each salt and black pepper, or to taste
- ¾ cup skim milk
- ¼ cup reduced-fat sour cream
- 1 teaspoon Dijon mustard
- ½ cup shredded Gruyère or Swiss cheese (2 ounces)
- 4 large egg whites

1 Preheat the oven to 400° F. Lightly grease a 1 ½-quart soufflé dish. In a small saucepan of boiling water, cook the potatoes, covered, for 8 minutes or until tender. Drain the potatoes and mash them. You should have 1 cup.

2 In a 10-inch nonstick skillet, melt the butter over moderate heat. Add the onion and sauté, stirring occasionally, for 5 minutes or until softened. Add the spinach and ⅛ teaspoon each of the salt and pepper and cook, stirring, for 2 minutes. Remove from the heat.

3 In a medium-size bowl, combine the potatoes, milk, sour cream, mustard, the remaining ⅛ teaspoon each of the salt and pepper, and all but 2 tablespoons of the cheese. Stir in the spinach mixture.

4 In a very clean medium-size bowl, beat the egg whites with an electric mixer set on high speed until they hold firm peaks. Gently fold the whites into the potato-spinach mixture. Pour the mixture into the prepared dish and sprinkle the top with the remaining cheese. Place the soufflé dish in the oven, reduce the oven temperature to 375° F, and bake for 30 to 35 minutes or until puffed and golden. Serve with crusty bread and Cauliflower, Carrot, and Pepper Vinaigrette (page 254). Serves 4.

PREPARATION TIME: 20 MIN.   COOKING TIME: 45 MIN.

Per serving: Calories 242; Saturated Fat 6 g; Total Fat 9 g; Protein 14 g; Carbohydrate 27 g; Fiber 3 g; Sodium 358 mg; Cholesterol 21 mg

In Italy, they're called *gnocchi*, but don't wait for your next vacation to try feathery-light Spinach Dumplings with Pepper Sauce.

SAVORY NOODLE AND CHEESE PUDDING

*Rich and satisfying, this homey dish
is good for lunch or dinner.*

2 teaspoons olive oil	2 large egg whites
1 medium-size yellow onion, chopped (1 cup)	½ cup milk
1 head cabbage, cut into 1-inch pieces (5 cups)	¼ teaspoon each salt and black pepper, or to taste
½ cup water	4 ounces broad egg noodles, cooked according to package directions
2 tablespoons snipped fresh dill	
2 cups low-fat (1% milkfat) cottage cheese	

1 Preheat the oven to 350° F. Lightly grease a 9" x 9" x 2" baking dish. In a 12-inch skillet, heat the oil over moderate heat. Add the onion and sauté, stirring frequently, for 6 minutes or until golden. Add the cabbage and cook, stirring, for 1 minute. Add the water, reduce the heat to low, cover, and cook, stirring occasionally, for 5 minutes or until the cabbage is wilted. Stir in the dill.

2 In a large bowl, whisk together the cottage cheese, egg whites, milk, salt, and pepper. Fold in the cabbage mixture and noodles and transfer to the prepared baking dish. Cover with aluminum foil and bake for 10 minutes. Uncover and bake 10 minutes longer or until slightly crusty on top. Serve hot, accompanied by rye bread and Carrot-Parsnip Salad with Cumin-Lime Dressing (page 254). Serves 4.

PREPARATION TIME: 15 MIN. COOKING TIME: 32 MIN.

*Per serving: Calories 269; Saturated Fat 2 g;
Total Fat 6 g; Protein 22 g; Carbohydrate 31 g;
Fiber 2 g; Sodium 655 mg; Cholesterol 32 mg*

CRUSTLESS LEEK AND POTATO QUICHE

*Here is a low-calorie version of a classic dish that
is perfect for brunch, lunch, or a light supper.*

2 teaspoons unsalted butter	¼ teaspoon each salt and black pepper, or to taste
3 medium-size leeks (1 pound), quartered lengthwise, sliced crosswise ½ inch thick, and rinsed well	⅓ cup water
	2 large eggs
	1 large egg white
1 large all-purpose potato (8 ounces), peeled and cut into ½-inch cubes	1 cup skim milk
	½ cup part-skim ricotta cheese
	3 tablespoons grated Parmesan cheese

1 Preheat the oven to 375° F. Lightly grease a 10-inch quiche dish or pie pan and set aside. In a 10-inch non-stick skillet, melt the butter over moderate heat. Add the leeks, potato, salt, and pepper and cook, stirring, for 1 minute. Add the water and simmer, covered, for 12 minutes, stirring occasionally.

2 Meanwhile, in a large bowl, combine the eggs, egg white, milk, ricotta cheese, and 2 tablespoons of the Parmesan cheese. Add the leek mixture and stir to combine. Pour the egg-leek mixture into the prepared dish and sprinkle the top with the remaining 1 tablespoon of Parmesan cheese. Bake for 30 minutes or until set. Cut into 4 wedges and serve with Four-Grain Rolls (page 304) and a salad of endive and tomatoes. Serves 4.

PREPARATION TIME: 15 MIN. COOKING TIME: 43 MIN.

*Per serving: Calories 262; Saturated Fat 4 g;
Total Fat 9 g; Protein 14 g; Carbohydrate 33 g;
Fiber 3 g; Sodium 362 mg; Cholesterol 126 mg*

CHEESE SQUARES

These flavorful squares are filled with ricotta cheese, spinach, and black olives. To remove the pits from the olives, pound or "stone" them lightly with a can or meat pounder. This will split the olives, easing pit removal.

1 teaspoon olive or canola oil

1 large yellow onion, chopped (1 ½ cups)

6 ounces mushrooms, coarsely chopped (2 cups)

1 package (10 ounces) frozen chopped spinach, thawed and squeezed dry

1 tablespoon chopped dry-cured black olives

¼ teaspoon each ground nutmeg and red pepper (cayenne)

4 large egg whites

Nonstick cooking spray

1 container (15 ounces) part-skim ricotta cheese

¼ cup low-fat (1% milkfat) milk

2 teaspoons lemon juice

⅓ cup uncooked farina (wheat) cereal

1 teaspoon baking powder

¼ cup minced fresh basil or 2 teaspoons dried basil, crumbled

3 tablespoons grated Parmesan cheese

1 In a 12-inch nonstick skillet, heat the oil over moderate heat. Add the onion and sauté for 5 minutes or until softened. Raise the heat to moderately high and add the mushrooms. Cook for 6 minutes, stirring occasionally, or until the mushrooms are golden. Stir in the spinach and cook 2 minutes more or until the liquid has evaporated. Remove the skillet from the heat and stir in the olives. Add ⅛ teaspoon each of the nutmeg and red pepper. Set aside to cool, then stir in 1 egg white.

2 Meanwhile, preheat the oven to 350° F. Line a 7" x 5" x 2" baking pan with aluminum foil and coat the foil with cooking spray. In a medium-size bowl, combine the ricotta cheese, milk, remaining 3 egg whites, lemon juice, farina, baking powder, basil, Parmesan cheese, and remaining ⅛ teaspoon each of nutmeg and red pepper.

3 Pour half of the cheese mixture into the prepared pan and spread evenly. Gently spread the vegetable mixture evenly on top. Spread the remaining cheese mixture evenly over all. Bake for 25 minutes or until firm in the center. Let cool for 5 minutes, then cut into 4, 6, or 12 pieces. Serve as a main dish, topped with Quick Tomato-

Pepper Sauce (page 272), or serve plain as a side dish or appetizer. Serves 4 as a main dish, 6 as a side dish, or makes 12 appetizers.

PREPARATION TIME: 25 MIN. COOKING TIME: 38 MIN.

Per serving (for 4): Calories 311; Saturated Fat 6 g; Total Fat 12 g; Protein 24 g; Carbohydrate 29 g; Fiber 4 g; Sodium 435 mg; Cholesterol 37 mg

Crustless Leek and Potato Quiche is a stunning version of a long-time favorite but with only half the calories and fat.

The frittata, an Italian specialty, is a wonderfully versatile egg dish similar to an omelet. Any combination of cooked filling ingredients — potatoes, onions, spaghetti, mushrooms, vegetables, and herbs, for example — is layered in the skillet and the eggs are poured over them. Once the eggs are set, the top of a frittata is cooked in one of two ways: The skillet is placed under the broiler for a few minutes, or a plate is held over the skillet and the frittata is flipped onto the plate and then slid back into the pan. When done, a frittata is cut into wedges like pizza. It is equally good served hot or at room temperature.

POTATO FRITTATA

1 large all-purpose potato (8 ounces), peeled and sliced ⅛ inch thick	2 large egg whites
	¼ cup part-skim ricotta cheese or low-fat (1% milkfat) cottage cheese
1 tablespoon olive oil	
2 large shallots, finely chopped (⅔ cup)	3 tablespoons grated Parmesan cheese
4 ounces mushrooms, sliced (1 ½ cups)	⅔ cup diced part-skim mozzarella cheese
¼ teaspoon each salt and black pepper	2 tablespoons snipped fresh chives or minced parsley
2 large eggs	

1 Using paper toweling, pat dry the potato slices. Heat a 12-inch nonstick skillet over moderate heat. Add the potatoes in a single layer and cook for 3 to 4 minutes on each side or until golden. Transfer to a plate and set aside. In the same skillet, heat 1 teaspoon of the oil over moderate heat. Stir in the shallots, mushrooms, and ⅛ teaspoon each of the salt and pepper and sauté for 4 minutes, stirring occasionally; remove from the heat.

2 In a large bowl, whisk together the eggs and egg whites. Whisk in the ricotta cheese, 2 tablespoons of the Parmesan cheese, the remaining ⅛ teaspoon each of salt and pepper, and the mushroom mixture.

3 Preheat the broiler, setting the rack about 6 inches from the heat. In a 10-inch nonstick skillet, heat the remaining 2 teaspoons of oil over moderate heat. Arrange the potato slices in a single layer in the skillet and pour the egg-mushroom mixture on top. Lower the heat and cook, uncovered, for 10 minutes or until the eggs are set. Sprinkle the top of the frittata with the mozzarella cheese and remaining 1 tablespoon of Parmesan cheese. Wrap the handle of the skillet with heavy-duty aluminum foil and broil the frittata for 2 minutes or until the top is golden brown and set. Garnish with the chives. Serve with whole-grain bread and a tossed green salad. Serves 4.

PREPARATION TIME: 25 MIN. COOKING TIME: 22 MIN.

Per serving: Calories 228; Saturated Fat 4 g; Total Fat 11 g; Protein 14 g; Carbohydrate 19 g; Fiber 1 g; Sodium 372 mg; Cholesterol 123 mg

SPAGHETTI FRITTATA

In this Italian omelet, leftover pasta is put to good use.

1 tablespoon olive oil	2 cloves garlic, minced
1 small yellow onion, thinly sliced (⅔ cup)	2 large eggs
	2 large egg whites
1 large sweet red pepper, seeded and sliced lengthwise into ¼-inch strips	¼ cup skim milk
	2 tablespoons grated Parmesan cheese
1 teaspoon dried oregano, crumbled	2 cups cooked spaghetti, linguine, or fettuccine (6 ounces uncooked)
¼ teaspoon each salt and black pepper	⅔ cup diced part-skim mozzarella cheese
2 large tomatoes, seeded and chopped (3 cups)	2 tablespoons minced fresh basil or parsley

1 In a 10-inch nonstick skillet, heat 1 teaspoon of the oil over moderate heat. Add the onion, red pepper, oregano, and ⅛ teaspoon each of the salt and black pepper. Sauté, stirring occasionally, for 4 minutes or until the vegetables are tender. Add the tomatoes and garlic and cook, stirring occasionally, for 3 minutes or until thickened. Transfer the mixture to a plate and set aside. In a medium-size bowl, whisk together the eggs, egg whites, milk, and 1 tablespoon of the Parmesan cheese.

2 Preheat the broiler, setting the rack 6 inches from the heat. In the same skillet, heat the remaining 2 teaspoons of oil over moderate heat. Add the spaghetti, tossing to coat. Using a spatula, flatten the spaghetti to form a pancake. Pour in the egg mixture and top it with the vegetable mixture, spreading it in an even layer. Reduce the heat to low and cook, uncovered, for 10 minutes or until the eggs are set. Sprinkle the top of the frittata with the mozzarella cheese and remaining 1 tablespoon of Parmesan cheese. Wrap the handle of the skillet with heavy-duty aluminum foil and broil the frittata for 2 minutes or until the top is golden brown and set. Garnish with the basil. Serves 4.

PREPARATION TIME: 25 MIN. COOKING TIME: 20 MIN.

Per serving: Calories 277; Saturated Fat 3 g; Total Fat 10 g; Protein 16 g; Carbohydrate 33 g; Fiber 4 g; Sodium 341 mg; Cholesterol 117 mg

PASTA, RICE, AND GRAINS

North Americans are fortunate in having access to a variety of grains
from around the world — bulgur, barley, oats, millet, corn, kasha, rice, wild rice, even
the ancient Peruvian grain quinoa (pronounced keen-wa) — and every
shape of pasta that's been invented. Amid this wealth, whole grains have the greatest
nutritional value, offering not only more vitamins and minerals but also fiber. Polished
and refined grains, with their longer shelf life and shorter cooking time, also serve
us well and remain staples in today's busy lives. This chapter presents
grain recipes of every guise to please all members of your family. Many are suited to
the starring role in a meal; others are best in supporting roles. All are satisfying
and high in complex carbohydrates. Enjoy them for good health.

Parmesan cheese adds a mellow, rich flavor to pasta. To enjoy this cheese at its best, use it freshly grated. When buying Parmesan, look for a wedge that is slightly moist and crumbly, aged at least 2 years, and pale golden beige in color.

Although Parmesan is made partly with skim milk, it is high in fat and sodium. One tablespoon has, on average, 2 grams of fat and 93 milligrams of sodium. Because of its intense flavor, however, a little goes a long way.

SPAGHETTI WITH FOUR ONIONS

Slow cooking of onions releases their natural sweetness, creating a surprisingly rich sauce—without cream or butter.

- 1 tablespoon olive oil
- 2 large red onions, chopped (3 cups)
- 1 large yellow onion, chopped (1½ cups)
- 6 green onions, including tops, thinly sliced (¾ cup)
- 4 shallots, chopped (½ cup)
- 3 cloves garlic, minced
- 3 tablespoons brandy or apple juice
- 2½ cups Chicken Stock or Vegetable Stock (page 62) or low-sodium chicken broth
- ½ teaspoon salt, or to taste
- 1 teaspoon dried rosemary, crumbled
- 2 tablespoons all-purpose flour
- ⅛ teaspoon black pepper, or to taste
- 1 pound spaghetti
- ¼ cup chopped green onion tops (optional garnish)

1 In a 12-inch nonstick skillet, heat the oil over low heat. Add the red, yellow, and green onions and the shallots. Cook, stirring frequently, for 15 minutes or until lightly golden. Add the garlic and cook 2 minutes more. Stir in the brandy and cook for 1 minute.

2 Stir in 1½ cups of the stock, cover, and cook for 25 minutes. Stir in the salt and rosemary. Cook, uncovered, for 10 minutes or until the liquid has evaporated. Add the flour and cook, stirring, for 2 minutes. Add the remaining 1 cup of stock and the pepper; bring to a boil over moderate heat. Cook, stirring, for 2 minutes or until thick.

3 Meanwhile, bring a stockpot of unsalted water to a boil, add the spaghetti, and cook for 8 minutes or until tender but still firm to the bite. Drain and transfer to a warm serving bowl. Pour the sauce over the spaghetti and garnish with the green onion tops if desired. Serves 4 or 5 as a main course, 6 as a first course.

PREPARATION TIME: 20 MIN. COOKING TIME: 1 HR.

Per serving (for 4): Calories 592; Saturated Fat 1g; Total Fat 6g; Protein 19g; Carbohydrate 110g; Fiber 3g; Sodium 361mg; Cholesterol 0mg

PAPPARDELLE IN CREAMY TOMATO SAUCE WITH SEAFOOD

You can substitute bite-size chunks of your favorite fish or seafood for the scallops. Cod, shrimp, and lobster all go well with the delicate seasonings. If you make this dish in advance, add the scallops when you reheat the sauce for serving.

- 2 teaspoons olive oil
- 3 cloves garlic, minced
- 3 medium-size tomatoes, chopped, with their juice (3 cups)
- ½ teaspoon sugar
- ¼ teaspoon ground cinnamon
- ¾ cup bottled clam juice
- ⅓ cup part-skim ricotta cheese or low-fat (1% milkfat) cottage cheese
- 12 ounces bay scallops or halved sea scallops
- 12 ounces pappardelle (broad noodles)
- Fresh basil leaves or parsley sprigs (optional garnish)

1 In a 12-inch nonstick skillet, heat the oil over low heat. Add the garlic and cook for 1 minute or until fragrant. Add the tomatoes, sugar, and cinnamon and cook, uncovered, for 12 minutes or until thickened. Stir in the clam juice and cook 3 minutes longer.

2 Transfer the tomato mixture to a food processor or blender and whirl for 1 minute or until smooth. Add the ricotta and process 30 seconds more. Return to the skillet and bring to a boil over moderate heat. Add the scallops, lower the heat, and simmer, covered, for 2 to 3 minutes or until the scallops are opaque but still springy to the touch.

3 Meanwhile, bring a stockpot of unsalted water to a boil. Add the pappardelle and cook for 8 minutes or until tender but still firm to the bite. Drain and transfer to a warm serving bowl. Add the sauce and toss to coat. Garnish each serving with a fresh basil leaf or parsley sprig if desired. Serves 4 or 5 as a main course, 6 as a first course.

PREPARATION TIME: 13 MIN. COOKING TIME: 20 MIN.

Per serving (for 4): Calories 473; Saturated Fat 2g; Total Fat 8g; Protein 30g; Carbohydrate 69g; Fiber 1g; Sodium 286mg; Cholesterol 115mg

SPINACH FETTUCCINE WITH VEGETABLES

1 tablespoon olive oil
3 shallots, finely chopped (⅓ cup)
1 each small sweet red and yellow peppers, cored, seeded, and cut into ½-inch squares (1½ cups)
1 medium-size carrot, peeled and thinly sliced (¾ cup)
2 cloves garlic, minced
¼ teaspoon each salt and black pepper, or to taste

¼ cup Chicken Stock (page 62) or low-sodium chicken broth
1 medium-size zucchini, sliced (¾ cup)
1 cup red or yellow cherry tomatoes, halved, or 2 medium-size tomatoes, cut into ¾-inch cubes
12 ounces spinach fettuccine
1 tablespoon each minced fresh basil and parsley

1 In a 10-inch nonstick skillet, heat the oil over moderately low heat. Add the shallots and cook for 1 minute. Add the sweet peppers, carrot, garlic, salt, and black pepper and cook, stirring, for 1 minute. Add the stock, bring to a boil, lower the heat, and simmer, covered, for 3 minutes. Stir in the zucchini and tomatoes and cook, covered, for 1 to 2 minutes or until the tomatoes are heated through and the vegetables are just tender.

2 Meanwhile, bring a stockpot of unsalted water to a boil. Add the fettuccine and cook for 8 minutes or until tender but still firm to the bite. Drain, transfer to a warm serving bowl, and add the vegetable mixture, basil, and parsley. Toss until well combined. Serve with the Glazed Variation of Spicy Chicken Cutlets (page 114). Serves 4 as a first course or side dish.

PREPARATION TIME: 20 MIN. COOKING TIME: 15 MIN.

Per serving: Calories 388; Saturated Fat 1 g; Total Fat 5 g; Protein 13 g; Carbohydrate 73 g; Fiber 2 g; Sodium 160 mg; Cholesterol 0 mg

Spaghetti with Four Onions is a sweet, simple, and fragrant dish that takes the versatile onion to new heights.

FETTUCCINE WITH TUNA, MUSHROOMS, AND TOMATOES

Canned tuna is a busy cook's lifesaver, but this is no ordinary dish. Dried porcini or cèpe mushrooms add a rich, smoky flavor—less exotic and expensive types work too.

½ ounce dried porcini or cèpe mushrooms
½ cup boiling water
1 tablespoon olive oil
3 cloves garlic, minced
6 ounces fresh mushrooms, sliced (about 1¾ cups)
1 can (1 pound) low-sodium tomatoes with their juice

1 teaspoon dried tarragon, crumbled
¼ teaspoon salt, or to taste
1 can (12½ ounces) tuna in water, drained
¼ teaspoon black pepper
1 pound fettuccine

1 In a small heatproof bowl, soak the dried mushrooms in the water for 15 minutes or until softened. Over a small bowl, drain the mushrooms in a sieve lined with cheesecloth or paper toweling; reserve mushrooms and liquid.

2 Meanwhile, in a 12-inch nonstick skillet, heat the oil over moderate heat. Add the garlic and fresh mushrooms and sauté, stirring occasionally, for 5 minutes or until softened. Add the tomatoes, soaked mushrooms and their liquid, tarragon, and salt and bring to a boil. Lower the heat and simmer, uncovered, for 10 minutes or until thickened. Stir in the tuna and pepper and simmer for 5 minutes or until hot.

3 Meanwhile, bring a stockpot of unsalted water to a boil. Add the fettuccine and cook for 6 to 8 minutes or until tender but still firm to the bite. Drain and transfer to a heated serving bowl. Add the sauce and toss well to coat. Serves 4 or 5 as a main course, 6 as a first course.

PREPARATION TIME: 10 MIN.   COOKING TIME: 20 MIN.

STANDING TIME: 15 MIN.

Per serving (for 4): Calories 616; Saturated Fat 1 g; Total Fat 7 g; Protein 40 g; Carbohydrate 96 g; Fiber 1 g; Sodium 500 mg; Cholesterol 37 mg

Fettuccine with Tuna, Mushrooms, and Tomatoes transforms an old standby — canned tuna — into a fresh-tasting entrée for busy weeknights.

LINGUINE WITH GREEN BEAN PESTO

When you're craving pesto and pasta, don't limit yourself to just basil. This garden-fresh variation is every bit as good as the original recipe.

1 ½ cups water	2 tablespoons lemon juice
½ teaspoon salt	2 tablespoons olive oil
1 pound green beans, trimmed	¼ teaspoon black pepper
½ cup each packed fresh basil and parsley leaves	1 pound linguine or spaghetti
2 cloves garlic, sliced	¼ cup grated Parmesan cheese (optional)
½ cup white wine or water	

1 In a large saucepan, bring the water and salt to a boil over moderate heat. Add the green beans, cover, and cook for 8 minutes or until tender. Let cool slightly but do not drain. Transfer the green beans and their cooking water to a food processor. Add the basil, parsley, garlic, wine, lemon juice, oil, and pepper. Whirl for 1 minute or until puréed. Return to the saucepan and rewarm over low heat, adding a little water if the sauce seems too thick.

2 Meanwhile, bring a stockpot of unsalted water to a boil. Add the linguine and cook for 8 minutes or until tender but still firm to the bite. Drain and transfer to a heated serving bowl. Add the sauce and toss until coated. Serve topped with the cheese if desired. Serves 4 or 5 as a main course, 6 as a first course.

PREPARATION TIME: 15 MIN. COOKING TIME: 20 MIN.

Per serving (for 4): Calories 548; Saturated Fat 1 g; Total Fat 9 g; Protein 17 g; Carbohydrate 96 g; Fiber 3 g; Sodium 299 mg; Cholesterol 0 mg

SOBA NOODLES WITH SESAME SAUCE

Soba noodles are a Japanese pasta made primarily of buckwheat, a grain that is high in protein. Associated with longevity, soba noodles are usually included in a New Year's feast. They can be eaten hot, cold, or at room temperature.

8 ounces soba noodles	2 teaspoons dark sesame oil
⅓ cup Chicken Stock (page 62) or low-sodium chicken broth	2 green onions, including tops, thinly sliced
2 tablespoons reduced-sodium soy sauce	¼ teaspoon each salt and black pepper, or to taste
1 tablespoon minced fresh ginger	

1 Bring a stockpot of unsalted water to a boil. Add the soba and cook for 5 to 8 minutes or until tender. Drain and rinse to prevent sticking. Meanwhile, in a large bowl, combine the stock, soy sauce, ginger, sesame oil, green onions, salt, and pepper. Add the soba and toss to coat. Serves 4 as a first course or side dish.

PREPARATION TIME: 5 MIN. COOKING TIME: 6 MIN.

Per serving: Calories 219; Saturated Fat 0 g; Total Fat 3 g; Protein 9 g; Carbohydrate 44 g; Fiber 1 g; Sodium 704 mg; Cholesterol 0 mg

ORIENTAL SUPPER

Grilled Tuna Teriyaki
(page 97)

Soba Noodles with Sesame Sauce

Vegetable Medley Stir-Fry
(page 244)

Sliced Oranges

Green Tea

SIMPLE SUMMER LUNCH

Sliced Tomatoes and Low-Fat Mozzarella Cheese

Whole-Wheat Italian Bread

Linguine with Green Bean Pesto

Fresh Fruit

Fresh herbs greatly enhance pasta dishes. Most supermarkets carry fresh parsley year round and other herbs in season. To store herbs, rinse and spin or pat them dry, wrap loosely in paper toweling, seal in a plastic food bag, and store in the refrigerator. They will keep for up to 2 weeks. The exception is fresh basil, which will turn black in the refrigerator. Stand it in a glass of water on the countertop, or put the leaves in a jar, cover with olive oil, and store in the refrigerator. They will keep for up to 6 months. You can use the oil as well as the leaves to flavor soups, stews, and sauces.

You can also freeze herbs. After rinsing and drying them, chop, snip or mince, seal in a plastic food bag, label, and store at 0° F. They will keep for up to 6 months.

PASTA SHELLS WITH EGGPLANT, TOMATOES, AND CHICK PEAS

Turn the first tomatoes of the season into something special: a garden-fresh dish that you can serve at room temperature or hot. For variety, try summer squash instead of eggplant.

- 5 teaspoons olive oil
- 1 large eggplant (1 pound), peeled and cut into 1-inch cubes
- ¼ cup water
- 4 cloves garlic, minced
- 3 large tomatoes, chopped, with their juice (4½ cups)
- 1 cup cooked chick peas
- 2 teaspoons grated orange rind
- ½ teaspoon ground ginger
- ¼ teaspoon salt, or to taste
- ¼ cup minced fresh basil
- 1 pound medium-size pasta shells

1 In a 12-inch nonstick skillet, heat 2 teaspoons of the oil over moderately high heat. Add half of the eggplant and cook, stirring frequently, for 5 minutes or until lightly colored. Add 2 tablespoons of the water and cook 1 minute longer or until the water has evaporated. Transfer the cooked eggplant to a bowl and set aside. Repeat with 2 more teaspoons of the oil, the remaining eggplant, and the remaining 2 tablespoons of water.

2 Lower the heat, add the remaining teaspoon of oil and the garlic, and cook for 1 minute. Stir in the eggplant, tomatoes, chick peas, orange rind, ginger, and salt. Raise the heat slightly and cook for 5 minutes; add the basil and cook 2 minutes longer or until the eggplant is tender.

3 Meanwhile, bring a stockpot of unsalted water to a boil and cook the pasta for 8 minutes or until tender but still firm to the bite. Drain and transfer to a warm serving bowl. Add the vegetable mixture and toss well. Serves 4 or 5 as a main course, 6 as a first course.

PREPARATION TIME: 15 MIN. COOKING TIME: 20 MIN.

Per serving (for 4): Calories 595; Saturated Fat 1 g; Total Fat 9 g; Protein 21 g; Carbohydrate 109 g; Fiber 2 g; Sodium 153 mg; Cholesterol 0 mg

PASTA TWISTS WITH BROCCOLI RABE

Here is an example of how bacon can be used to enhance the flavor of a dish without adding a great deal of fat. If broccoli rabe is not available, substitute 1¼ pounds of broccoli.

- 1¼ cups water
- ¼ teaspoon salt, or to taste
- 1 bunch broccoli rabe (1¼ pounds), rinsed, trimmed, and cut into 1½-inch pieces
- 2 cloves garlic, minced
- 2 medium-size tomatoes, chopped, with their juice (2 cups)
- ¼ teaspoon ground red pepper (cayenne), or to taste
- 3 slices lean bacon (3 ounces), diced
- 1 pound pasta twists, broad egg noodles, or medium-size pasta shells

1 In a large saucepan, bring the water and ⅛ teaspoon of the salt to a boil over moderate heat. Add the broccoli rabe and garlic, cover, and cook for 6 minutes or until rabe stems are crisp-tender. Stir in tomatoes and red pepper.

2 In a 6-inch skillet, cook the bacon over moderately low heat, stirring occasionally, for 6 to 8 minutes or until crisp. Drain on paper toweling.

3 Meanwhile, bring a stockpot of unsalted water to a boil. Add the pasta twists and cook for 8 minutes or until tender but still firm to the bite. Drain and transfer to a warm serving bowl. Add the broccoli rabe with its cooking liquid, the bacon, the remaining ⅛ teaspoon of salt, and more red pepper if desired. Toss well. Serves 4 or 5 as a main course, 6 as a first course.

PREPARATION TIME: 12 MIN. COOKING TIME: 15 MIN.

Per serving (for 4): Calories 486; Saturated Fat 1 g; Total Fat 4 g; Protein 20 g; Carbohydrate 93 g; Fiber 4 g; Sodium 250 mg; Cholesterol 4 mg

Eye-catching pasta spirals are tossed with a julienne of vegetables for Fusilli with Peppers and Onions.

FUSILLI WITH PEPPERS AND ONIONS

- 2 tablespoons olive oil
- 3 medium-size yellow onions, thinly sliced (about 4 cups)
- 3 cloves garlic, minced
- 2 large sweet green peppers, cored, seeded, and thinly sliced lengthwise (about 3 cups)
- 2 tablespoons minced fresh basil or 2 teaspoons dried basil, crumbled
- 1 teaspoon dried thyme, crumbled
- 2 tablespoons flour
- 2 cups Chicken Stock or Vegetable Stock (page 62) or low-sodium chicken broth
- ½ teaspoon salt, or to taste
- ¼ teaspoon black pepper
- 1 pound fusilli, corkscrew pasta, or twists

1 In a 12-inch nonstick skillet, heat 1 tablespoon of the oil over moderate heat. Add the onions and sauté for 5 minutes or until softened. Reduce the heat to moderately low, add the garlic, green peppers, basil, and thyme, and cook, stirring occasionally, for 15 minutes or until soft.

2 In a small saucepan, heat the remaining tablespoon of oil over moderate heat. Stir in the flour and cook for 30 seconds. Gradually add the stock and bring to a boil. Cook, stirring constantly, for 5 minutes or until smooth and thickened. Stir in the salt and black pepper.

3 Meanwhile, bring a stockpot of unsalted water to a boil. Add the fusilli and cook for 8 minutes or until tender but still firm to the bite. Drain and transfer to a warm serving bowl. Stir the sauce into the cooked vegetables and toss the mixture with the hot cooked pasta. Serves 4 or 5 as a main course, 6 as a first course.

PREPARATION TIME: 14 MIN. COOKING TIME: 32 MIN.

Per serving (for 4): Calories 585; Saturated Fat 1 g; Total Fat 10 g; Protein 19 g; Carbohydrate 107 g; Fiber 4 g; Sodium 344 mg; Cholesterol 0 mg

•

Peas and Onions Variation: Substitute *2 large yellow onions, chopped (3 cups),* for the sliced onions, *2 teaspoons dried rosemary* for the basil, and *2 cups frozen green peas* for the green peppers. In Step 1, cook the onions, garlic, rosemary, and thyme for 8 to 10 minutes or until the onions are lightly golden. Proceed as directed in Step 2, stirring the peas into the sauce after it comes to a boil. Serves 4 or 5 as a main course, 6 as a first course. *Per serving (for 4): Calories 614; Saturated Fat 1 g; Total Fat 10 g; Protein 22 g; Carbohydrate 110 g; Fiber 5 g; Sodium 411 mg; Cholesterol 0 mg.*

•

Zucchini and Onions Variation: Substitute *2 large yellow onions, chopped (3 cups),* for the sliced onions, *1 teaspoon dried oregano* for the basil, and *2 medium-size zucchini or yellow squash, grated (1 pound),* for the peppers. In Step 1, cook the onions, garlic, oregano, and thyme for 8 minutes or until the onions are lightly golden. Stir in the zucchini and cook 2 minutes more. Proceed as directed in Steps 2 and 3. Serves 4 or 5 as a main course, 6 as a first course. *Per serving (for 4): Calories 553; Saturated Fat 1 g; Total Fat 10 g; Protein 22 g; Carbohydrate 99 g; Fiber 3 g; Sodium 344 mg; Cholesterol 0 mg.*

PENNE WITH PEPPERS, ALMONDS, AND GARLIC

Loosely based on a Spanish sauce called romesco, *this versatile sweet pepper purée is also terrific over cooked shrimp or grilled poultry. For a method of roasting peppers, see Roasted Pepper Mélange (page 233).*

8 cloves garlic, unpeeled
3 small roasted sweet red or green peppers, cored, seeded, and peeled, or 2 jars (7 ounces each) roasted red peppers, drained
½ cup water
¼ cup unblanched almonds
¼ cup fine dry bread crumbs

2 tablespoons red wine vinegar
1 tablespoon olive oil
½ teaspoon salt, or to taste
¼ teaspoon ground red pepper (cayenne)
1 pound penne, ziti, or fusilli
2 tablespoons minced parsley for garnish

1 Preheat the oven to 400° F. Wrap the garlic in aluminum foil, place on a baking sheet, and bake for 20 minutes or until the package feels soft when pressed. Or put the garlic in a glass measuring cup, cover with plastic food wrap, and microwave on high (100 percent power) for 1 minute. When cool enough to handle, squeeze the garlic cloves out of their skins.

2 In a food processor or blender, whirl the garlic, roasted peppers, water, almonds, bread crumbs, vinegar, oil, salt, and ground red pepper for 1 minute or until the mixture is puréed but still has texture.

3 Bring a stockpot of unsalted water to a boil and cook the penne for 8 minutes or until tender but still firm to the bite. Meanwhile, transfer the sauce to a medium-size saucepan and warm over low heat, stirring occasionally. Drain the pasta and transfer it to a warm serving bowl. Add the sauce and parsley and toss to coat. Serves 4 or 5 as a main course, 6 as a first course.

PREPARATION TIME: 10 MIN. COOKING TIME: 30 MIN.

Per serving (for 4): Calories 557; Saturated Fat 1 g; Total Fat 11 g; Protein 18 g; Carbohydrate 99 g; Fiber 1 g; Sodium 320 mg; Cholesterol 0 mg

BAKED ZITI WITH EGGPLANT

Cooked pasta that will be added to a baked dish should be slightly underdone because it continues cooking in the oven. You can use zucchini instead of eggplant in this recipe and reduce the cooking time in Step 1 to 6 minutes.

Nonstick cooking spray
1 medium-size eggplant, halved lengthwise, then sliced crosswise ⅛ inch thick (3 cups)
1 tablespoon olive oil
2 large tomatoes (12 ounces each), quartered
8 ounces part-skim ricotta cheese or low-fat (1% milkfat) cottage cheese

1 cup skim milk
1 large egg
1 large egg white
½ cup grated Parmesan cheese (2 ounces)
¼ teaspoon each salt and black pepper, or to taste
¼ teaspoon ground allspice
12 ounces ziti

1 Preheat the oven to 400° F. Lightly grease a shallow 1½-quart baking dish. Line a baking sheet with aluminum foil and coat it with the cooking spray. Arrange the eggplant slices in a single layer and drizzle the oil over them. Bake for 10 minutes or until soft. Set aside until the slices are cool enough to handle.

2 Place the tomatoes, ricotta cheese, milk, egg, and egg white in a food processor and whirl for 1 minute or until smooth. Add the Parmesan cheese, salt, pepper, and allspice and whirl until combined. Meanwhile, in a stockpot of boiling unsalted water, cook the ziti for 8 minutes or until barely tender and still very firm to the bite.

3 Arrange a layer of the eggplant slices in the baking dish, place the ziti on top, and cover with the remaining eggplant. Spread the tomato mixture over the top and bake for 25 minutes or until set and lightly browned. Serves 4 or 5 as a main course, 6 as a first course.

PREPARATION TIME: 16 MIN. COOKING TIME: 35 MIN.

Per serving (for 4): Calories 545; Saturated Fat 6 g; Total Fat 15 g; Protein 29 g; Carbohydrate 76 g; Fiber 1 g; Sodium 493 mg; Cholesterol 81 mg

RISOTTO PRIMAVERA

Risotto is a traditional Italian dish in which stock is slowly stirred into rice to create a creamy mixture with tender but firm grains. In this recipe, crisp green vegetables are added at the last minute. Once you've mastered the basic technique for making risotto, you can experiment with different stocks or try adding meat, shellfish, or different cheeses.

4 ounces broccoli florets (1½ cups)

4 ounces green beans or asparagus, cut into 1-inch lengths (1 cup)

3 cups Chicken Stock or Vegetable Stock (page 62) or low-sodium chicken broth

4 teaspoons unsalted butter or margarine

1 medium-size yellow onion, finely chopped (1 cup)

1 cup arborio, basmati, or long-grain white rice

½ cup dry white wine, Chicken Stock (page 62), or low-sodium chicken broth

½ teaspoon salt

¼ teaspoon black pepper

½ cup minced fresh basil or parsley

3 tablespoons grated Parmesan cheese

1 In a large saucepan of boiling water, cook the broccoli and green beans for 3 to 4 minutes or until crisp-tender; drain, rinse under cold water to stop the cooking, and drain again. Meanwhile, in a medium-size saucepan, bring the stock to a simmer, then reduce the heat to the lowest setting and keep warm.

2 In a 12-inch nonstick skillet, melt 2 teaspoons of the butter over moderate heat. Add the onion and sauté, stirring occasionally, for 3 minutes or until slightly softened. Add the rice and cook, stirring, for 2 minutes or until well coated with the oil. Add the wine and cook, stirring, for 2 to 3 minutes or until it has been absorbed by the rice.

3 Using a ladle, add ½ cup of the stock to the skillet and cook, stirring frequently, until most of it has been absorbed. Continue adding the stock, ½ cup at a time, keeping the liquid in the skillet at a simmer and stirring frequently, for about 20 minutes or until the rice is tender and most of the liquid has been absorbed.

4 Add the broccoli, beans, salt, pepper, and basil and cook, stirring frequently, until they are heated through. Stir in the cheese and the remaining butter. Serves 4 as a first course, 2 as a main course.

PREPARATION TIME: 15 MIN. COOKING TIME: 30 MIN.

Per serving (for 4): Calories 298; Saturated Fat 4 g; Total Fat 7 g; Protein 9 g; Carbohydrate 46 g; Fiber 3 g; Sodium 488 mg; Cholesterol 15 mg

There can be much more to pasta than tomato sauce; try this terrific Penne with Peppers, Almonds, and Garlic.

Risotto is usually made with arborio, an Italian rice that absorbs liquid easily, giving the dish its distinctive creamy consistency. You can also use white basmati or long-grain rice; with these types, the consistency will be slightly drier.

The traditional Italian recipe calls for risotto to be stirred constantly over moderate heat for about 20 minutes. If you are discouraged at the prospect of so much stirring, set the pan over low heat and stir every few minutes while you prepare the rest of the meal. The risotto will take a few minutes longer to cook but the results will be just as good.

SMOKED TURKEY RISOTTO

2 1/2 cups Chicken Stock or Vegetable Stock (page 62) or low-sodium chicken broth	1/2 cup white wine or water
	1/4 teaspoon salt
1 tablespoon olive oil	1/8 teaspoon crushed red pepper flakes
4 green onions, white and green thinly sliced separately	2 teaspoons minced fresh sage or 3/4 teaspoon ground sage
1 cup arborio, basmati, or long-grain white rice	3 ounces smoked turkey, slivered
1 clove garlic, minced	3 tablespoons grated Parmesan cheese

1 In a medium-size saucepan, heat the stock over low heat. Meanwhile, in a 12-inch nonstick skillet, heat the oil over moderate heat. Add the white part of the green onions, the rice, and garlic. Cook, stirring frequently, for 3 minutes or until the onions are slightly softened.

2 Add the wine and 1/2 cup of the hot stock to the skillet. Stir in the salt and red pepper flakes and cook, stirring occasionally, until almost all of the stock has been absorbed. Continue adding the stock, 1/2 cup at a time, keeping the liquid at a simmer and stirring frequently for about 20 minutes or until the rice is tender and most of the liquid has been absorbed. Stir in the sage and the green part of the green onions with the last of the stock.

3 Stir in the turkey and cook for 1 minute or until heated through. Top each serving with some of the cheese. Serves 4 as a first course, 2 as a main course.

PREPARATION TIME: 15 MIN. COOKING TIME: 30 MIN.

Per serving (for 4): Calories 293; Saturated Fat 1 g; Total Fat 8 g; Protein 11 g; Carbohydrate 39 g; Fiber 1 g; Sodium 324 mg; Cholesterol 4 mg

RISOTTO WITH SPINACH AND ARTICHOKE HEARTS

3 cups Chicken Stock or Vegetable Stock (page 62) or low-sodium chicken broth	1 cup arborio, basmati, or long-grain white rice
	1/2 teaspoon dried oregano, crumbled
1 package (10 ounces) frozen artichoke hearts	1/2 teaspoon salt
2 teaspoons olive or canola oil	1/4 teaspoon black pepper
	4 ounces spinach, rinsed, trimmed, and thinly sliced (2 cups)
3 green onions, including tops, sliced (1/3 cup)	3 tablespoons grated Parmesan cheese
1 clove garlic, minced	

1 In a medium-size saucepan, bring the stock to a boil over moderate heat. Lower the heat, add the artichoke hearts, cover, and simmer for about 10 minutes or until tender. With a slotted spoon, transfer the artichoke hearts to a bowl and cover to keep warm.

2 Meanwhile, in a 12-inch nonstick skillet, heat the oil over moderate heat. Add the green onions, garlic, and rice and cook, stirring, for 3 minutes or until the garlic is golden. Stir in the oregano, salt, and pepper. Using a ladle, add about 1/2 cup of the simmering stock and cook, stirring frequently, until most of the liquid has been absorbed. Continue adding the hot stock to the skillet, 1/2 cup at a time, keeping the liquid at a simmer and stirring frequently, for about 20 minutes or until the rice is tender and most of the stock has been absorbed.

3 Stir in the artichoke hearts and spinach and cook, stirring constantly, for 3 minutes or until the spinach is wilted. Spoon onto individual serving plates and top each serving with some of the cheese. Serves 4 as a first course, 2 as a main course.

PREPARATION TIME: 10 MIN. COOKING TIME: 35 MIN.

Per serving (for 4): Calories 266; Saturated Fat 1 g; Total Fat 5 g; Protein 10 g; Carbohydrate 47 g; Fiber 4 g; Sodium 525 mg; Cholesterol 4 mg

DOUBLE MUSHROOM RISOTTO

This dish is made with both fresh and dried mushrooms. If you prefer to make it with fresh mushrooms only, increase the amount to 12 ounces, eliminate the boiling water, and increase the stock to 2¾ cups. For an especially rich flavor, you can make the risotto with all dried mushrooms, increasing the quantity to 1 ounce and the boiling water to 2 cups; reduce the chicken stock to 1¼ cups.

½ ounce dried mushrooms, such as porcini, shiitake, or cèpes

1 cup boiling water

2 cups Chicken Stock or Vegetable Stock (page 62) or low-sodium chicken broth

1 tablespoon olive oil

4 large shallots, finely chopped (½ cup)

8 ounces fresh mushrooms, sliced (3 cups)

¼ teaspoon each salt and black pepper, or to taste

1 cup arborio, basmati, or long-grain white rice

½ cup dry white wine or water

3 tablespoons grated Parmesan cheese

1 teaspoon unsalted butter or margarine

1 In a small heatproof bowl, soak the dried mushrooms in the water for 20 minutes or until softened. Drain in a sieve lined with cheesecloth or paper toweling, reserving the liquid. Slice the mushrooms, removing tough stems.

2 In a medium-size saucepan, bring the stock and mushroom liquid to a simmer. Reduce the heat to the lowest setting and keep the stock mixture warm. Meanwhile, in a 12-inch nonstick skillet, heat 2 teaspoons of the oil over moderate heat. Add the shallots and cook, stirring occasionally, for 2 minutes. Stir in the fresh mushrooms, soaked dried mushrooms, salt, and pepper and cook, stirring occasionally, for 3 minutes or until the fresh mushrooms are lightly browned.

3 Push the mushroom mixture to the sides of the skillet and place the remaining 1 teaspoon of oil in the center. Add the rice to the oil and cook, stirring, for 2 minutes or until well coated. Add the wine, stir in the mushrooms from the sides of the skillet, and cook, stirring frequently, for 3 minutes or until the wine has been absorbed.

4 Using a ladle, add ½ cup of the stock mixture to the skillet and cook, stirring frequently, for 2 to 3 minutes or until almost all the liquid has been absorbed. Continue adding the stock to the skillet, ½ cup at a time, keeping the liquid at a simmer and stirring frequently, for about 20 minutes or until the rice is tender and creamy and most of the liquid has been absorbed. Stir in the cheese and butter and serve. Serves 4 as a first course, 2 as a main course.

PREPARATION TIME: 19 MIN. COOKING TIME: 32 MIN.

SOAKING TIME: 20 MIN.

Per serving (for 4): Calories 299; Saturated Fat 2 g; Total Fat 7 g; Protein 9 g; Carbohydrate 47 g; Fiber 1 g; Sodium 311 mg; Cholesterol 6 mg

Creamy grains of rice tickle your palate in Risotto with Spinach and Artichoke Hearts.

For an American harvest menu, match the nutty flavors of Wild and Brown Rice with Toasted Pecans and Herbed Cornish Hens (page 125).

RICE AND CHEESE PUDDING WITH PEAS

*This dish has the creamy texture of
a risotto but is higher in protein because
it is made with milk. If you like, you
can add leftover cooked vegetables in
Step 2 along with the peas.*

1 cup long-grain white rice	¼ teaspoon ground nutmeg
2¼ cups low-fat (1% milkfat) milk	⅛ teaspoon ground allspice
¾ cup water	⅔ cup frozen green peas
1 medium-size yellow onion, finely chopped (1 cup)	½ cup shredded low-fat fontina or Monterey Jack cheese (2 ounces)
1 bay leaf	⅛ teaspoon black pepper, or to taste
¼ teaspoon salt	

1 Bring a medium-size saucepan of water to a boil. Add the rice and boil for 2 minutes. Drain and rinse under cold water to stop the cooking. In the same saucepan, bring the milk, water, onion, bay leaf, salt, nutmeg, and allspice to a simmer over moderate heat. Add the rice, lower the heat, and cook, uncovered, stirring frequently, for 25 minutes or until the rice is very tender and creamy. If all the liquid evaporates before the rice is tender, add a little more water.

2 Remove and discard the bay leaf. Stir in the peas and cook for 2 minutes. Stir in the cheese and pepper and cook for 1 minute or until the cheese has melted. Serve as a side dish with poached chicken or fish or as a main course, followed by Tricolor Coleslaw (page 256). Serves 4 as a side dish, 2 as a main course.

PREPARATION TIME: 8 MIN.   COOKING TIME: 30 MIN.

*Per serving (for 4): Calories 302; Saturated Fat 3 g;
Total Fat 5 g; Protein 14 g; Carbohydrate 50 g;
Fiber 2 g; Sodium 277 mg; Cholesterol 16 mg*

SPICED RICE WITH CURRANTS AND CARROTS

This colorful side dish goes especially well with Indian dishes or grilled meat, fish, or poultry. You can also convert it to a salad by stirring in 1 to 2 tablespoons of vinegar and serving it at room temperature.

- **2 teaspoons canola or vegetable oil**
- **1 cup basmati or long-grain white or brown rice**
- **½ teaspoon each ground cumin, curry powder, and turmeric**
- **2¼ cups water**
- **1 medium-size yellow onion, coarsely chopped (1 cup)**
- **1 clove garlic, minced**
- **½ teaspoon salt**
- **½ cup frozen green peas**
- **1 medium-size carrot, peeled and shredded (¾ cup)**
- **2 tablespoons dried currants**
- **¼ teaspoon black pepper**

1 In a medium-size saucepan, heat the oil over moderate heat. Add the rice, cumin, curry powder, and turmeric and cook, stirring constantly, for 2 to 3 minutes or until the spices are fragrant and the rice is coated.

2 Stir in the water, onion, garlic, and salt and bring to a simmer. Cover and cook until the rice is almost tender — 15 minutes for white rice, 30 to 35 for brown. Stir in the peas, carrot, currants, and pepper. Cover and cook 5 minutes more or until the rice is tender. Serves 4.

PREPARATION TIME: 10 MIN. COOKING TIME: 25 MIN.

Per serving: Calories 241; Saturated Fat 1 g; Total Fat 3 g; Protein 5 g; Carbohydrate 49 g; Fiber 3 g; Sodium 294 mg; Cholesterol 0 mg

WILD AND BROWN RICE WITH TOASTED PECANS

Get twice the rice plus earthy flavor in this versatile side dish. Serve it with roasted meat, poultry, or seafood. If you have any leftovers, toss them with a dressing for a super rice salad.

- **⅔ cup wild rice**
- **1⅓ cups brown rice**
- **½ cup coarsely chopped pecans**
- **1 tablespoon unsalted butter or margarine**
- **½ teaspoon each salt and black pepper**
- **¼ cup snipped fresh chives or minced parsley**

1 Preheat the oven to 300° F. Bring a large saucepan of unsalted water to a boil over moderate heat. Add the wild rice and boil, uncovered, for 15 minutes. Add the brown rice and boil 20 minutes more. Drain.

2 Meanwhile, scatter the pecans on a baking sheet and toast in the oven, stirring occasionally to prevent burning, for 10 to 15 minutes or until lightly toasted; set aside.

3 Transfer the boiled rice to a steamer or colander. Set over boiling water in a large saucepan, cover, and steam for 15 to 20 minutes or until tender. Transfer the rice to a warm serving bowl and stir in the butter, pecans, salt, pepper, and chives. Serves 6 to 8.

PREPARATION TIME: 10 MIN. COOKING TIME: 50 MIN.

Per serving (for 6): Calories 294; Saturated Fat 2 g; Total Fat 9 g; Protein 7 g; Carbohydrate 47 g; Fiber 3 g; Sodium 182 mg; Cholesterol 6 mg

Wild rice, with its nutty flavor and crunchy texture, has been a favorite with gourmets for many years; it goes particularly well with game or poultry and makes a superb stuffing. The seeds, which range from dark brown to purplish black, are difficult to harvest and so command a high price. For the sake of economy as well as varied texture, wild rice is often mixed with brown or white rice.

A water grass native to North America, wild rice grows most abundantly in the Great Lakes region. In the past it played an important part in the diets of many Native Americans and battles were fought over control of the areas where it thrived.

Lemon Rice Pilaf beautifully complements a simply prepared fish such as broiled salmon.

MINTED RICE WITH PEAS

Fluffy white rice, dressed up with emerald green peas and refreshing mint, makes an elegant escort for most lamb entrées.

1 **tablespoon unsalted butter or margarine**	¼ **teaspoon each salt and black pepper**
3 **large shallots, finely chopped (½ cup)**	1 **package (10 ounces) frozen green peas**
1 **cup long-grain white rice**	2 **tablespoons minced fresh mint or 2 teaspoons mint flakes, crumbled**
2 **cups Chicken Stock or Vegetable Stock (page 62) or low-sodium chicken broth**	2 **tablespoons minced parsley**

1 In a medium-size saucepan, melt 2 teaspoons of the butter over moderate heat. Add the shallots and sauté, stirring, for 1 minute. Add the rice and cook, stirring, for 1 minute or until well coated. Add the stock, salt, and pepper and bring the liquid to a boil. Cover, lower the heat, and simmer for 15 minutes or until the rice is almost tender but still a little firm to the bite.

2 Sprinkle the peas over the rice and continue to simmer, covered, 5 minutes more or until the rice and peas are tender. Let stand for 5 minutes, then stir in the remaining 1 teaspoon of butter and the mint and parsley. Serves 4.

PREPARATION TIME: 10 MIN. COOKING TIME: 22 MIN.

STANDING TIME: 5 MIN.

Per serving: Calories 277; Saturated Fat 2 g; Total Fat 4 g; Protein 9 g; Carbohydrate 51 g; Fiber 3 g; Sodium 267 mg; Cholesterol 8 mg

SPICY RICE PILAF

Here is an easy way to dress up rice. You can easily double or triple this recipe for company fare.

2 teaspoons olive oil
1 cup long-grain white or brown rice
2 cups Chicken Stock or Vegetable Stock (page 62) or low-sodium chicken broth
1 teaspoon fennel seeds, crushed
1 bay leaf
¾ teaspoon each ground cardamom and cinnamon
¼ cup slivered almonds
¼ teaspoon black pepper

1 Preheat the oven to 300° F. In a medium-size nonstick saucepan, heat the oil over moderately high heat. Add the rice and cook, stirring constantly, for 2 to 3 minutes or until lightly golden.

2 Stir in the stock, fennel seeds, bay leaf, cardamom, and cinnamon and bring to a boil. Lower the heat, cover, and simmer until the rice is tender and all of the liquid has been absorbed — 15 to 20 minutes for white rice, 35 to 40 minutes for brown.

3 Meanwhile, scatter the almonds on a baking sheet and toast, stirring occasionally to avoid burning, for 10 to 12 minutes or until lightly toasted; set aside. When the rice is done, remove and discard the bay leaf and stir in the pepper. Garnish each serving with the toasted almonds. Serve with roast chicken or pork. Serves 4.

PREPARATION TIME: 3 MIN. COOKING TIME: 20 MIN.

Per serving: Calories 244; Saturated Fat 1 g; Total Fat 7 g; Protein 6 g; Carbohydrate 39 g; Fiber 1 g; Sodium 70 mg; Cholesterol 0 mg

LEMON RICE PILAF

This light dish is a wonderful accompaniment for fish or poultry. Lemon zest and parsley make attractive garnishes.

2 teaspoons unsalted butter or margarine
1 medium-size yellow onion, finely chopped (1 cup)
2 cups long-grain white or brown rice
4 cups Chicken Stock or Vegetable Stock (page 62) or low-sodium chicken broth
2 tablespoons lemon juice
1 teaspoon grated lemon rind
1 bay leaf
½ teaspoon salt
¼ teaspoon white pepper
Optional garnishes:
    Slivered lemon zest (colored part of the rind)
    2 tablespoons minced parsley

1 Preheat the oven to 350° F. In a medium-size saucepan, melt the butter over moderate heat. Add the onion and sauté, stirring occasionally, for 5 minutes or until softened. Add the rice and cook, stirring, for 1 minute or until well coated. Add the stock, lemon juice, lemon rind, bay leaf, salt, and pepper and bring to a boil. Lower the heat, cover, and simmer until the rice is tender and all liquid has been absorbed — 15 to 20 minutes for white rice, 35 to 40 minutes for brown. Remove and discard the bay leaf. Serves 6 to 8. Top each serving with a few slivers of lemon zest and a sprinkling of parsley if desired.

PREPARATION TIME: 10 MIN. COOKING TIME: 25 MIN.

Per serving (for 6): Calories 262; Saturated Fat 1 g; Total Fat 2 g; Protein 6 g; Carbohydrate 53 g; Fiber 1 g; Sodium 270 mg; Cholesterol 4 mg

Preparing perfect rice is easy if you follow two basic rules. First, be sure to cook the rice in water that is just simmering. Do not let it boil or too much steam will escape and the rice may burn dry before it is done.

Second, keep the pot covered and don't stir the rice while it is cooking. When rice is left to cook undisturbed, small holes form on the surface that allow steam to flow evenly through the grains, cooking each one to plump perfection. If rice is stirred, the steam is not properly distributed and the grains become gummy rather than light and fluffy.

SOUTH-OF-THE-
BORDER SUPPER

Tex-Mex
Meat Loaf
(page 137)

Spanish
Rice

Tossed Green
Salad

Sliced Honeydew
Melon

RICE GRATIN WITH SUMMER SQUASH AND RED PEPPER

This colorful combination makes an ideal party dish because you can assemble it hours ahead and bake it just before serving. It goes well with fish, meat, or poultry and also makes a fine meatless entrée. To vary it, substitute goat cheese for the Cheddar, and plain dry bread crumbs for the Parmesan.

- 2 teaspoons olive oil
- 1 small yellow onion, finely chopped (½ cup)
- 1 medium-size sweet red pepper, cored, seeded, and diced (¾ cup)
- 1 medium-size zucchini, diced (2 cups)
- 1 medium-size yellow squash, diced (2 cups)
- 2 cloves garlic, minced
- ½ teaspoon each salt and black pepper
- 2 cups cooked brown rice
- 2 large eggs, lightly beaten
- ½ cup shredded Cheddar cheese (2 ounces)
- ½ cup minced fresh basil, chives, or parsley or a combination
- 2 tablespoons grated Parmesan cheese

1 Preheat the oven to 375° F. In a 12-inch nonstick skillet, heat the oil over moderate heat. Add the onion and sauté, stirring, for 1 minute. Add the red pepper and sauté, stirring, for 2 minutes. Add the zucchini, yellow squash, garlic, salt, and black pepper and sauté, stirring occasionally, for 3 to 5 minutes or until the squash is barely tender.

2 In a large bowl, combine the squash mixture with the rice, eggs, Cheddar cheese, and basil. Transfer to a greased 1½-quart gratin dish or shallow casserole and sprinkle with the Parmesan cheese. Bake for 30 minutes or until the gratin is set. If desired, brown under a preheated broiler, about 4 inches from the heat, for 1 to 2 minutes. Serves 6 as a side dish, 4 as a main course.

PREPARATION TIME: 20 MIN. COOKING TIME: 36 MIN.

Per serving (for 6): Calories 188; Saturated Fat 3 g; Total Fat 8 g; Protein 9 g; Carbohydrate 22 g; Fiber 3 g; Sodium 304 mg; Cholesterol 83 mg

SPANISH RICE

This old family favorite makes a zesty accompaniment to grilled meat, poultry, or fish. Or you can turn it into a meatless main dish by adding 1½ cups cooked chick peas. For added flavor, stir in some chopped green chilies or sliced Spanish olives. For extra nutrition, add a small chopped zucchini along with the green pepper.

- 2 teaspoons olive oil
- 1 medium-size yellow onion, finely chopped (1 cup)
- 1 medium-size sweet green pepper, cored, seeded, and diced (¾ cup)
- 1 can (1 pound) low-sodium tomatoes, drained and chopped
- 2 cloves garlic, minced
- 1½ cups long-grain white or brown rice
- 3 cups Chicken Stock or Vegetable Stock (page 62) or low-sodium chicken broth
- ¾ teaspoon dried thyme, crumbled
- ½ teaspoon salt, or to taste
- ¼ teaspoon each ground turmeric and black pepper
- 1 bay leaf
- 2 tablespoons minced parsley (optional garnish)

1 In a medium-size saucepan, heat the oil over moderate heat. Add the onion and green pepper and sauté, stirring occasionally, for 5 minutes or until softened. Add the tomatoes and garlic and sauté, stirring, for 2 minutes.

2 Add the rice, stock, thyme, salt, turmeric, black pepper, and bay leaf and bring to a boil. Lower the heat, cover, and simmer until the rice is tender and all the liquid has been absorbed — 15 to 20 minutes for white rice, 35 to 40 minutes for brown. Remove and discard the bay leaf. Garnish each serving with parsley if desired. Serves 6.

PREPARATION TIME: 10 MIN. COOKING TIME: 25 MIN.

Per serving: Calories 222; Saturated Fat 0 g; Total Fat 2 g; Protein 6 g; Carbohydrate 44 g; Fiber 2 g; Sodium 257 mg; Cholesterol 0 mg

Serve Rice Gratin with Summer Squash and Red Pepper at the next family get-together.

RICE AND SPINACH TIMBALES

These attractive molded rounds look lovely on a platter with roast meat or poultry. If you don't have timbale molds, use 4-ounce custard cups or soufflé dishes.

2 teaspoons unsalted butter or margarine	1 ¾ cups Chicken Stock or Vegetable Stock (page 62) or low-sodium chicken broth
3 small shallots, finely chopped (⅓ cup)	¼ teaspoon each salt and black pepper
1 cup long-grain white or brown rice	3 tablespoons grated Parmesan cheese
5 ounces (½ package) frozen chopped spinach, thawed	½ teaspoon grated lemon rind

1 In medium-size saucepan, melt the butter over moderate heat. Add the shallots and sauté, stirring occasionally, for 3 minutes or until softened. Add the rice and cook, stirring, for 1 minute. Add the spinach, stock, salt, and pepper and bring to a simmer. Cover and simmer until the rice is tender and all the liquid has been absorbed — 15 to 20 minutes for white rice, 35 to 40 minutes for brown.

2 Stir in the cheese and lemon rind, mixing well, then spoon the mixture into 6 lightly greased 4-ounce timbale molds or custard cups, packing it lightly. Invert the molds onto individual serving plates or a platter. Serves 6.

PREPARATION TIME: 10 MIN. COOKING TIME: 20 MIN.

Per serving: Calories 158; Saturated Fat 1 g; Total Fat 3 g; Protein 5 g; Carbohydrate 28 g; Fiber 1 g; Sodium 120 mg; Cholesterol 6 mg

SHRIMP FRIED RICE

*Here is a great way to use up
leftover rice. Cooked chicken or pork
could be substituted for the shrimp.*

2 teaspoons vegetable oil

4 green onions, including tops, sliced diagonally 1 inch thick (1 cup)

1 small red chili pepper, cored, seeded, and cut into strips ¼ inch wide

2 cloves garlic, minced

1 tablespoon minced fresh ginger or 1 teaspoon ground ginger

4 ounces medium-size shrimp, shelled and deveined

3 cups cooked brown rice

2 large egg whites, lightly beaten

1 tablespoon oyster sauce (optional)

1 tablespoon reduced-sodium soy sauce

1 tablespoon dark sesame oil

¼ teaspoon salt, or to taste

1 In a 12-inch nonstick skillet, heat 1 teaspoon of the vegetable oil over moderate heat. Add the green onions and stir-fry for 2 to 3 minutes or until tender. Using a slotted spoon, transfer the onions to a bowl and set aside.

2 Add the chili pepper, garlic, and ginger to the skillet and stir-fry for 1 to 2 minutes. Transfer them to the bowl with the green onions. Add the remaining teaspoon of oil to the skillet and, when hot but not smoking, add the shrimp and stir-fry for 2 to 3 minutes or until pink. Transfer the shrimp to the bowl with the vegetables.

3 Add the rice to the skillet and stir-fry for 3 minutes or until warm but not brown. Lower the heat and make a slight well in the center of the rice. Add the egg whites and stir until softly scrambled. Stir in the reserved vegetables and shrimp, the oyster sauce if desired, soy sauce, sesame oil, and salt and cook until heated through. Serves 4.

PREPARATION TIME: 20 MIN.   COOKING TIME: 12 MIN.

*Per serving: Calories 259; Saturated Fat 1 g;
Total Fat 8 g; Protein 12 g; Carbohydrate 36 g;
Fiber 3 g; Sodium 358 mg; Cholesterol 43 mg*

Create an authentic Chinese dish in no time: Shrimp Fried Rice, flavored with fresh ginger, chili peppers, and soy sauce. Accompany the rice with green beans — the extra-long Chinese kind if available.

RICE PANCAKES

*These savory pancakes go well with any
dish that has a sauce, such as Pork Cutlets
in Madeira Sauce (page 145). Or you
could serve them as an entrée with Herbed
Tomato Sauce (page 270). For breakfast,
top them with orange marmalade.*

3 teaspoons olive oil	½ cup low-fat (1% milkfat) milk
1 small yellow onion, finely chopped (½ cup)	¼ cup cooked brown rice
⅔ cup all-purpose flour	¼ cup cooked wild rice
1 teaspoon baking powder	¼ cup finely chopped pecans (1 ounce)
¼ teaspoon each salt and black pepper	1 tablespoon minced parsley
2 large egg whites, lightly beaten	2 teaspoons grated orange rind

1 Preheat the oven to 300° F. In a 12-inch nonstick skillet, heat 1 teaspoon of the oil over moderate heat. Add the onion and sauté, stirring occasionally, for 5 minutes or until soft.

2 In a medium-size bowl, combine the flour, baking powder, salt, and pepper. Add the egg whites, milk, and 1 teaspoon of the oil, stirring with a fork just until the flour is moistened (the batter will be lumpy). Fold in the onion, white rice, wild rice, pecans, parsley, and orange rind.

3 Wipe out the skillet, add the remaining 1 teaspoon of the oil, and heat over moderate heat. Drop the batter in the skillet by slightly rounded tablespoonfuls and flatten slightly with a spatula. Cook for 1 to 2 minutes or until golden. Turn and cook 1 to 2 minutes more or until golden. Transfer the pancakes to a baking sheet and keep warm in the oven. Repeat until all of the batter has been used up. Makes twelve 2½- to 3-inch pancakes. Serves 4 as a side dish, 2 as a main course.

PREPARATION TIME: 20 MIN. COOKING TIME: 15 MIN.

*Per serving (for 4): Calories 204; Saturated Fat 1 g;
Total Fat 9 g; Protein 6 g; Carbohydrate 25 g;
Fiber 2 g; Sodium 260 mg; Cholesterol 1 mg*

LENTIL AND WHEAT BERRY PILAF

*High in protein and carbohydrate and low
in fat, this side dish could also be the centerpiece
of your menu. Serve it with Vegetable Medley
Stir-fry (page 244) or Sautéed Collard Greens with
Carrots (page 225) for a light, satisfying meal.
You can substitute brown lentils for red; simmer an
additional 10 to 15 minutes in Step 2.*

½ cup wheat berries	¼ teaspoon each ground sage and crushed red pepper flakes
2 green onions, white and green chopped separately	¼ teaspoon salt, or to taste
1¼ cups Chicken Stock or Vegetable Stock (page 62) or low-sodium chicken broth	2 medium-size carrots, peeled and finely chopped (1½ cups)
1 cup water	⅔ cup dried red lentils

1 Rinse the wheat berries and place them in a medium-size bowl with enough cool water to cover. Soak for 12 hours in the refrigerator. Drain.

2 In a medium-size saucepan, combine the wheat berries with the white part of the green onions, stock, water, sage, red pepper flakes, and salt. Bring to a boil over moderate heat. Lower the heat and simmer, covered, for 40 minutes. Stir in the carrots and lentils and simmer, covered, 10 minutes more or just until the lentils are tender. Remove from the heat, stir in the green onion tops, and let stand for 10 minutes. Serves 4.

PREPARATION TIME: 10 MIN. COOKING TIME: 50 MIN.
SOAKING TIME: 12 HR. STANDING TIME: 10 MIN.

*Per serving: Calories 213; Saturated Fat 0 g;
Total Fat 1 g; Protein 12 g; Carbohydrate 42 g;
Fiber 2 g; Sodium 197 mg; Cholesterol 0 mg*

Lentils are rich in potassium and phosphorus and are a good source of protein, especially when paired with a grain such as rice. Red lentils, a staple of Middle Eastern cuisines, cook to a soft purée and are excellent in soups. The green lentils found in Europe hold their shape when cooked and can be served as a side dish. The more common brown lentils are a staple of the Indian diet and are used for preparing *dhal,* a thick lentil porridge that is served over rice. Most supermarkets carry brown lentils. Look for the red and green ones in specialty food stores.

Nutritious millet, which is high in iron, phosphorus, and calcium, is a staple grain in North Africa and India, where it is used to thicken soups and stews and to make bread. The tiny round yellow grains, which have a flavor somewhere between that of egg noodles and corn, make a superb hot breakfast cereal. To make 4 servings, stir 1 cup of millet into 2 ¼ cups of boiling water, then cover and simmer for 30 minutes or until all of the liquid has been absorbed. If you like, you can cook some sliced peaches or apples or chopped dried fruit along with the millet. Serve hot with milk and a sweetener such as maple syrup.

TABBOULEH

This colorful and healthful Middle Eastern dish can be refrigerated for up to 4 days (if you use radishes, add them just before serving). For a summer luncheon or light supper, core, seed, and halve sweet peppers and fill them with tabbouleh.

Boiling water	**2 tablespoons minced fresh mint or 2 teaspoons mint flakes, crumbled**
¾ **cup bulgur**	
1 **medium-size red onion, chopped (1 cup)**	
1 **medium-size tomato, coarsely chopped, with its juice (1 cup)**	**1 tablespoon olive or canola oil**
½ **cucumber, seeded and coarsely chopped (½ cup)**	**1 teaspoon grated lemon rind**
	3 tablespoons lemon juice
4 **large radishes, slivered (optional)**	¾ **teaspoon salt**
1 **cup flat-leaf parsley, coarsely chopped**	**8 to 10 drops hot red pepper sauce**

1 In a large heatproof serving bowl, pour 1 cup of boiling water over the bulgur and let stand for 20 minutes or until the water is absorbed. Meanwhile, in a small bowl, pour just enough boiling water over the onion to cover and let stand for 10 minutes. Drain.

2 Add the onion, tomato, cucumber, radishes if desired, parsley, mint, oil, lemon rind, lemon juice, salt, and red pepper sauce to the bulgur. Toss until combined thoroughly. Refrigerate, covered, for 6 hours or until chilled. Serve cold or at room temperature. Serves 4.

PREPARATION TIME: 20 MIN. STANDING AND CHILLING TIME: 6 HR. 20 MIN.

Per serving: Calories 153; Saturated Fat 1 g; Total Fat 4 g; Protein 5 g; Carbohydrate 28 g; Fiber 8 g; Sodium 418 mg; Cholesterol 0 mg

GINGERED BULGUR RISOTTO

Bulgur gives versatile risotto a new crunch.

2 **cups Chicken Stock or Vegetable Stock (page 62) or low-sodium chicken broth**	1 **small sweet green pepper, cored, seeded, and chopped (½ cup)**
	1 **cup bulgur**
1 **teaspoon olive oil**	1 **teaspoon minced fresh ginger or ½ teaspoon ground ginger**
1 **medium-size yellow onion, chopped (1 cup)**	
1 **large carrot, peeled and grated (1 cup)**	⅛ **teaspoon each salt and black pepper, or to taste**

1 In a small saucepan, heat the stock over low heat. Meanwhile, in a medium-size nonstick saucepan, heat the oil over moderate heat. Add the onion, carrot, and green pepper and sauté for 3 minutes or until almost tender. Add the bulgur, ginger, salt, and pepper and cook, stirring occasionally, 2 minutes more. Lower the heat, add 1 cup of the hot stock, and cook, stirring constantly, until most of the liquid has been absorbed. Continue stirring in the hot stock, ½ cup at a time, for about 15 minutes or until the bulgur is cooked but still slightly crunchy and most of stock has been absorbed. Serves 4.

PREPARATION TIME: 16 MIN. COOKING TIME: 20 MIN.

Per serving: Calories 167; Saturated Fat 0 g; Total Fat 2 g; Protein 6 g; Carbohydrate 33 g; Fiber 10 g; Sodium 148 mg; Cholesterol 0 mg

MILLET CORN PUDDING

Instead of the usual mashed potatoes, start a new tradition and serve this colonial classic with the Thanksgiving turkey.

- 1 tablespoon unsalted butter
- 1 tablespoon canola oil
- ¼ cup all-purpose flour
- 1 ½ cups low-fat (1% milkfat) milk
- ¾ teaspoon dried basil, crumbled
- ⅛ teaspoon ground nutmeg
- ½ teaspoon salt, or to taste
- 1 ½ cups fresh or frozen corn kernels
- 1 cup cooked millet
- 1 large egg
- 1 large egg white
- 8 drops hot red pepper sauce
- 3 tablespoons shredded Cheddar cheese

1 Preheat the oven to 350° F. Lightly grease a 1 ½-quart casserole; set aside. In a medium-size saucepan, melt the butter with the oil over moderate heat. Add the flour and cook, stirring, for 2 minutes or until bubbling and golden. Whisk in the milk, basil, nutmeg, and salt. Bring the mixture to a boil and cook, continuing to whisk, for 2 minutes or until smooth and thickened. Stir in the corn and simmer for 5 minutes. Remove from the heat and let stand for 5 minutes.

2 Stir the millet into the corn pudding. In a small bowl, beat the egg, egg white, and red pepper sauce, then add this mixture to the pudding and mix well. Pour the pudding into the casserole and sprinkle the cheese on top. Bake for 30 to 35 minutes or until the center of the pudding is almost firm. Let stand for at least 10 minutes before serving. Serve hot or at room temperature. Serves 4.

PREPARATION TIME: 10 MIN.   COOKING TIME: 40 MIN.
STANDING TIME: 15 MIN.

Per serving: Calories 277; Saturated Fat 5 g; Total Fat 11 g; Protein 11 g; Carbohydrate 37 g; Fiber 1 g; Sodium 381 mg; Cholesterol 71 mg

Tabbouleh, a traditional Lebanese salad of finely chopped vegetables and bulgur, fills halved yellow peppers, artfully arranged on a bed of summer greens.

Serve Hominy and Red Pepper Sauté with Deviled Oven-Fried Chicken (page 107) and Herbed Buttermilk Biscuits (page 291), hot from the oven.

MILLET PILAF WITH GREEN PEPPER AND EGGPLANT

Pale green Italian peppers are more slender and slightly milder than their bell-shaped sweet-pepper cousins. If you have trouble finding them, substitute a small sweet red or green pepper. You can also serve this dish as a salad. Simply stir in ¼ cup of vinaigrette and chill.

2 teaspoons olive or canola oil	1 small eggplant, peeled and cut into ½-inch cubes (1½ cups)
3 green onions, white and green chopped separately	¾ cup water
1 medium-size Italian pepper, cored, seeded, and chopped (½ cup)	1 tablespoon tomato paste
	1 tablespoon red wine vinegar
½ cup millet	1 teaspoon honey
½ teaspoon each dried oregano and thyme, crumbled	½ teaspoon salt, or to taste
	⅛ teaspoon black pepper

1 In a medium-size saucepan, heat the oil over moderate heat. Sauté the white of the green onions and the Italian pepper for 5 minutes or until softened. Add the millet, oregano, and thyme and mix thoroughly. Stir in the eggplant, water, tomato paste, vinegar, honey, salt, and black pepper. Bring to a simmer and cook, covered, for 25 minutes or just until the millet is tender. Stir in the green onion tops and cook 2 minutes more. Serve with Three-Bean Terrine (page 162) or broiled chicken, pork, or fish and toasted pita bread. Serves 4.

PREPARATION TIME: 15 MIN. COOKING TIME: 33 MIN.

Per serving: Calories 82; Saturated Fat 0 g; Total Fat 3 g; Protein 2 g; Carbohydrate 15 g; Fiber 1 g; Sodium 211 mg; Cholesterol 43 mg

HOMINY AND RED PEPPER SAUTÉ

Add cooked chunks of ham or sausage to this southern-style side dish to turn it into a main course winner. If hominy is hard to come by, you can substitute 1 1/2 cups of cooked corn.

- 2 teaspoons olive or canola oil
- 1 large yellow onion, chopped (1 1/2 cups)
- 1 large sweet red pepper, cored, seeded, and chopped (1 cup)
- 1 clove garlic, minced
- 1 teaspoon dried tarragon, crumbled
- 1 can (1 pound) hominy, drained and rinsed
- 2 teaspoons grated lemon rind
- 1/4 teaspoon salt, or to taste
- 1 tablespoon lemon juice
- 6 drops hot red pepper sauce or 1 jalapeño pepper, seeded and minced

1 In a 10-inch nonstick skillet, heat the oil over moderate heat. Add the onion, red pepper, garlic, and tarragon. Sauté, stirring occasionally, for 10 minutes or until the vegetables are tender. Stir in the hominy, lemon rind, and salt. Cook for 2 minutes or until heated through. Stir in the lemon juice and red pepper sauce. Serve hot or at room temperature. Serves 4.

PREPARATION TIME: 15 MIN. COOKING TIME: 13 MIN.

Per serving: Calories 130; Saturated Fat 1 g; Total Fat 4 g; Protein 3 g; Carbohydrate 23 g; Fiber 5 g; Sodium 375 mg; Cholesterol 0 mg

GARLIC GRITS

Hominy grits, or just plain grits, are ground from hulled kernels of corn. When you expect a hungry crowd, make this stick-to-your-ribs dish the day before and refrigerate. Then add an extra 15 minutes to the baking time.

- 3 cups Chicken Stock or Vegetable Stock (page 62) or low-sodium chicken broth
- 1 cup quick-cooking hominy grits
- 2 tablespoons unsalted butter or margarine
- 3 cloves garlic, minced
- 1/4 teaspoon each salt and black pepper
- 1/8 teaspoon ground red pepper (cayenne), or to taste
- 2 egg whites
- 1 egg
- 3/4 cup low-fat (1% milkfat) milk
- 1/4 cup grated Parmesan cheese (1 ounce)

1 Preheat the oven to 325° F. Lightly grease a shallow 1 1/2- or 2-quart baking dish. In a large saucepan, bring the stock to a boil over high heat. Gradually add the grits, whisking until completely incorporated. Lower the heat to moderate and cook, whisking occasionally, for 3 to 5 minutes or until tender and slightly thickened. Remove from the heat and stir in the butter, garlic, salt, black pepper, and red pepper.

2 In a medium-size bowl, beat together the egg whites, egg, and milk. Slowly add about a quarter of the hot grits to the eggs, whisking constantly. Stir this mixture into the saucepan with the rest of the grits.

3 Pour the grits into the baking dish and bake, uncovered, for 20 minutes. Remove from the oven and sprinkle with the cheese. Bake 10 minutes more. Serve hot with Turkey Sausage (page 124) or Ham Steak with Sugar-Mustard Glaze (page 142). Serves 8 to 10.

PREPARATION TIME: 10 MIN. COOKING TIME: 35 MIN.

Per serving (for 8): Calories 92; Saturated Fat 3 g; Total Fat 5 g; Protein 5 g; Carbohydrate 6 g; Fiber 0 g; Sodium 209 mg; Cholesterol 38 mg

The pearl barley called for in recipes is barley from which the outer husk has been removed. It can be found in any supermarket. High in fiber, pearl barley makes a nutritious addition to soups or stews. The chewy texture is especially good in pilaf-type dishes. Scotch barley, which can be found in health food stores, must be soaked overnight and is used in recipes less often.

CORN TIMBALES

Timbales are custards containing vegetables, cheese, meat, or fish that are baked in individual molds. The secret to obtaining a satiny texture for these elegant dishes is the bain-marie, or "hot bath," which allows the custard to bake slowly and evenly. A fitting garnish for these corn timbales is fresh cilantro.

1½ cups water
½ cup cornmeal
1 teaspoon ground cumin
¾ teaspoon chili powder
½ teaspoon salt, or to taste
2 large egg whites

1 package (10 ounces) frozen corn kernels, thawed and drained
¼ teaspoon black pepper
1 teaspoon unsalted butter or margarine

1 Preheat the oven to 350° F. Lightly grease 4 timbale molds or 4-ounce custard cups. In a medium-size heavy saucepan, combine the water, cornmeal, cumin, chili powder, and salt. Bring to a boil, stirring occasionally, over moderate heat. Lower the heat, cover, and cook, stirring occasionally, for 8 to 10 minutes or until very thick. Remove from the heat.

2 In a medium-size bowl, beat the egg whites until foamy. Whisk about a quarter of the hot cornmeal into the beaten whites, then slowly pour the whites into the remaining cornmeal mixture, stirring quickly. Stir in the corn, pepper, and butter and cook, stirring constantly, about 1 minute more or just until thickened.

3 Divide the mixture among the prepared molds, pressing the surfaces with the back of a spoon. Cover loosely with aluminum foil. Place the molds in an 8" x 8" x 2" baking dish filled halfway with hot water. Bake for 20 to 25 minutes or until heated through. Let stand for a few minutes to set. Run a small spatula or knife around the sides of each mold and invert carefully onto serving plates. Serve with Vegetarian Chili (page 159) or Pork Stew with Coconut and Lime (page 146). Serves 4.

PREPARATION TIME: 10 MIN. COOKING TIME: 35 MIN.

Per serving: Calories 139; Saturated Fat 1 g; Total Fat 1 g; Protein 5 g; Carbohydrate 28 g; Fiber 2 g; Sodium 298 mg; Cholesterol 3 mg

BARLEY PILAF WITH BEETS AND DILL

You can make this pretty pink dish in advance, leaving out the watercress, dill, and yogurt until just before serving; reheat it in the oven at 325° F for 30 minutes. Brown rice can replace the barley; in Step 2, cook it for 40 minutes or until just tender.

1 tablespoon vegetable oil
1 medium-size yellow onion, finely chopped (1 cup)
2 cups medium pearl barley
1 jar (1 pound) pickled beets, juice reserved, beets finely chopped
4 cups Chicken Stock or Vegetable Stock (page 62) or low-sodium chicken broth

1 teaspoon sugar
¼ teaspoon each salt and black pepper, or to taste
1 teaspoon Dijon mustard
1 bunch watercress, stems removed (1 cup leaves)
¼ cup snipped fresh dill or minced parsley
1 cup plain nonfat yogurt

1 In a medium-size heavy saucepan, heat the oil over moderate heat. Add the onion and sauté, stirring, for 2 minutes or until it begins to turn translucent. Stir in the barley, beet juice, stock, sugar, salt, and pepper and bring to a boil. Lower the heat, cover, and simmer for 25 minutes or until the barley is just tender.

2 Stir in the beets and mustard, cover, and cook for 5 minutes or until the beets are hot. Remove from the heat and stir in the watercress, dill, and yogurt. Cover and let stand for 5 minutes or until the yogurt is warm and the watercress leaves are wilted. Serves 6.

PREPARATION TIME: 15 MIN. COOKING TIME: 40 MIN.
STANDING TIME: 5 MIN.

Per serving: Calories 353; Saturated Fat 1 g; Total Fat 4 g; Protein 12 g; Carbohydrate 71 g; Fiber 11 g; Sodium 427 mg; Cholesterol 1 mg

BARLEY-MUSHROOM CASSEROLE

Dried mushrooms intensify the robust flavor of this hearty dish. Serve with roast chicken and Brussels Sprouts with Oriental Sauce (page 220) on a crisp early autumn evening.

½ ounce dried mushrooms
1 cup boiling water
4 teaspoons unsalted butter or margarine
1 cup medium pearl barley
1 medium-size yellow onion, chopped (1 cup)
5 medium-size fresh mushrooms, sliced (1¼ cups)

2 cups Chicken Stock or Vegetable Stock (page 62) or low-sodium chicken broth
½ teaspoon each salt and black pepper, or to taste
1 bay leaf
¼ cup snipped fresh chives or minced parsley

1 Preheat the oven to 350° F. In a small heatproof bowl, soak the dried mushrooms in the water for 10 minutes or until softened. Drain in a sieve lined with cheesecloth or paper toweling over a bowl and reserve the liquid. Chop the mushrooms.

2 In a medium-size flameproof casserole, melt 2 teaspoons of the butter over moderate heat. Add the barley and sauté, stirring, for 1 minute or until lightly browned. Transfer the barley to a small bowl.

3 Melt the remaining 2 teaspoons of butter in the casserole. Add the onion and sauté, stirring, for 1 minute or until it just begins to turn translucent. Add the fresh mushrooms and sauté, stirring occasionally, for 3 minutes. Return the barley to the casserole, add the soaked mushrooms and their liquid, the stock, salt, pepper, and bay leaf, and bring to a boil. Transfer to the oven and bake, covered, for 1 to 1¼ hours or until the barley is tender. Before serving, remove and discard the bay leaf and stir in the chives. Serves 6.

PREPARATION TIME: 15 MIN. COOKING TIME: 1 HR. 10 MIN.
SOAKING TIME: 10 MIN.

Per serving: Calories 169; Saturated Fat 2 g; Total Fat 3 g; Protein 5 g; Carbohydrate 31 g; Fiber 6 g; Sodium 227 mg; Cholesterol 7 mg

Corn kernels and cumin transform plain cornmeal into Corn Timbales, a terrific accompaniment for a spicy but simple dish such as monkfish served with Tomato Salsa (page 280).

SAVORY BAKED WHOLE-WHEAT FARINA

*Here a nutritional breakfast food is adapted
to make a super side dish for supper.*

1½ cups low-fat (1% milkfat) milk
1½ cups water
1 cup whole-wheat farina
¼ teaspoon each dried marjoram and sage, crumbled
¼ teaspoon each salt and black pepper
⅛ teaspoon ground nutmeg

1 cup shredded fontina or Monterey Jack cheese (4 ounces)
2 teaspoons olive oil
3 cloves garlic, minced
2 large or 3 medium-size tomatoes, chopped, with their juice (3 cups)
Pinch sugar

1 Lightly grease an 11" x 7" x 2" baking pan or dish; set aside. In a medium-size saucepan, combine the milk and water and bring to a simmer over moderate heat. Lower the heat and gradually stir in the farina. Add the marjoram, sage, salt, pepper, and nutmeg and cook, stirring frequently, for 10 minutes or until thick and creamy. Stir in the cheese. Spread the mixture in the prepared pan and let stand for 45 minutes or until firm.

2 Preheat the oven to 425° F. In a 10-inch nonstick skillet, heat the oil over low heat. Add the garlic and cook for 3 to 4 minutes or until fragrant. Add the tomatoes and sugar, partly cover, and cook, stirring occasionally, for 10 minutes or until thick but not all of the liquid has evaporated. Spoon the sauce over the farina and bake for 20 minutes or until bubbling and piping hot. Serves 4.

PREPARATION TIME: 15 MIN.   COOKING TIME: 45 MIN.

STANDING TIME: 45 MIN.

*Per serving: Calories 349; Saturated Fat 6 g;
Total Fat 12 g; Protein 16 g; Carbohydrate 43 g;
Fiber 4 g; Sodium 188 mg; Cholesterol 37 mg*

QUINOA SALAD

*A sacred food of the ancient Incas in Peru,
quinoa (pronounced keen-wa) is making a culinary
comeback. This mild-tasting grain is high in
protein and very versatile. You can use it as you
would bulgur or rice—in pilafs, soups, casseroles, or
salads. Look for these small pale yellow seeds
in gourmet and health food stores.*

1 cup quinoa
2 cups Chicken Stock or Vegetable Stock (page 62) or low-sodium chicken broth
1 small red onion, finely chopped (½ cup)
1 medium-size sweet red pepper, cored, seeded, and chopped (¾ cup)
1 medium-size cucumber, peeled, seeded, and chopped (¾ cup)
¼ cup minced fresh basil, parsley, or chives, or a mixture of all 3

¼ cup orange juice
1 tablespoon balsamic or white wine vinegar
1 teaspoon grated orange rind
¼ teaspoon each salt and black pepper, or to taste
1 tablespoon olive oil

Optional garnishes:
Red leaf lettuce
3 tablespoons toasted pine nuts or pecan pieces

1 In a colander, rinse the quinoa thoroughly and drain. In a medium-size saucepan, bring the stock to a boil, stir in the quinoa, and return to a boil. Lower the heat and simmer, covered, for 20 to 25 minutes or until all of the liquid has been absorbed. Let stand for 5 minutes, then transfer to a large bowl and stir in the onion, red pepper, cucumber, and herbs.

2 In a small bowl, combine the orange juice, vinegar, orange rind, salt, and black pepper and whisk in the oil. Pour this dressing over the quinoa and vegetables and toss well. If desired, arrange each serving on the lettuce and garnish with pine nuts. Serve at room temperature. Serves 4 as a main dish, 6 as a side dish.

PREPARATION TIME: 15 MIN.   COOKING TIME: 25 MIN.

STANDING TIME: 5 MIN.

*Per serving (for 4): Calories 190; Saturated Fat 1 g;
Total Fat 4 g; Protein 7 g; Carbohydrate 34 g;
Fiber 10 g; Sodium 210 mg; Cholesterol 0 mg*

VEGETABLES

Gone are the days when vegetables were overcooked, often tasteless
entities that we were urged to eat because they were "good for us." Today we know
they are actually better for us (and better tasting too) when cooked minimally
and with the cooking water reserved (see pages 232–233 for Vegetable Cooking Times).
We also know that vegetables creatively prepared at the peak of freshness can
be the most exciting dishes on the menu. Most of the recipes in this chapter were
developed as accompaniments for a main course. But there's no reason
why two or three combined couldn't be an entire meal, and not just for dinner. Broiled
Vegetable Mélange (page 244), for example, makes a delectable sandwich
filling; Sweet Potato Pancakes (page 241) are fine for breakfast. With such choices,
it's easy to fulfill the need for two to three vegetable servings a day.

CREAMED ARTICHOKES, PEPPERS, AND CORN

This unusual dish, high in vitamins and fiber, can be prepared a day ahead, refrigerated, and baked just before serving (see Baked Variation below).

1 tablespoon unsalted butter or margarine	½ cup skim milk
1 small yellow onion, finely chopped (½ cup)	⅛ teaspoon ground nutmeg
1 medium-size sweet red pepper, cored, seeded, and finely chopped (¾ cup)	1 package (9 ounces) frozen artichoke hearts, thawed and chopped
1½ tablespoons all-purpose flour	1 cup fresh or frozen corn kernels
½ cup Chicken Stock (page 62) or low-sodium chicken broth	¼ teaspoon each salt and black pepper, or to taste

1 In a medium-size heavy saucepan, melt the butter over moderate heat. Stir in the onion and red pepper and sauté, stirring occasionally, for 5 minutes or until soft.

2 Lower the heat, stir in the flour, and cook, stirring, for 1 minute. Add the stock, milk, and nutmeg and cook, stirring constantly, for 5 minutes or until thickened and smooth. Add the artichoke hearts, corn, salt, and black pepper and cook, stirring constantly, 2 minutes more or until hot. Serve with Turkey Sausage (page 124). Serves 4.

PREPARATION TIME: 10 MIN. COOKING TIME: 15 MIN.

Per serving: Calories 124; Saturated Fat 2 g; Total Fat 4 g; Protein 5 g; Carbohydrate 21 g; Fiber 4 g; Sodium 211 mg; Cholesterol 9 mg

---

•

Baked Variation: Preheat the oven to 375° F. Lightly grease a 1-quart baking dish. Prepare vegetables and sauce as directed; spoon the mixture into the prepared baking dish. Combine *1 tablespoon fine dry bread crumbs* and *1 tablespoon grated Parmesan cheese*. Sprinkle over the vegetable mixture and bake, uncovered, for 15 minutes (40 minutes from the refrigerator) or until heated through. Serves 4. *Per serving: Calories 127; Saturated Fat 2 g; Total Fat 4 g; Protein 6 g; Carbohydrate 22 g; Fiber 4 g; Sodium 252 mg; Cholesterol 10 mg.*

•

Cauliflower Variation: Substitute *3 cups cauliflower florets* for the artichoke hearts. Cook them in unsalted boiling water for 6 to 8 minutes or until crisp-tender. Add them to the sauce in Step 2 along with the corn and seasonings. Serves 4. *Per serving: Calories 114; Saturated Fat 2 g; Total Fat 4 g; Protein 5 g; Carbohydrate 18 g; Fiber 3 mg; Sodium 180 mg; Cholesterol 9 mg.*

ARTICHOKE HEARTS WITH TOMATO AND ORANGE

This quick and delicious dish is good hot or cold. Artichokes are high in vitamin A, calcium, and potassium.

⅔ cup orange juice	¼ teaspoon salt
3 plum tomatoes, finely chopped, with their juice (1 cup)	1 bay leaf
	Pinch sugar
1 tablespoon olive oil	1 package (9 ounces) frozen artichoke hearts
¼ teaspoon dried oregano, crumbled	

1 In a medium-size enameled or stainless steel saucepan, combine the orange juice, tomatoes, oil, oregano, salt, bay leaf, and sugar. Add the artichoke hearts and bring to a boil over moderate heat. Lower the heat, cover, and simmer for 8 minutes or until the artichoke hearts are tender. Discard the bay leaf. Serve hot with leg of lamb or cold with poached salmon. Serves 4.

PREPARATION TIME: 5 MIN. COOKING TIME: 10 MIN.

Per serving: Calories 95; Saturated Fat 1 g; Total Fat 4 g; Protein 3 g; Carbohydrate 15 g; Fiber 4 g; Sodium 186 mg; Cholesterol 0 mg

---

ASPARAGUS WITH LEMON-PARSLEY SAUCE

For best results, let the asparagus marinate in this delectable lemon-parsley sauce for 1 to 2 hours before serving.

⅓ cup minced parsley
2 canned anchovies, patted dry
2 tablespoons lemon juice
2 tablespoons Chicken Stock (page 62) or low-sodium chicken broth
1 tablespoon capers
1 tablespoon olive oil
1 pound asparagus, trimmed

1 In a food processor or blender, whirl the parsley, anchovies, lemon juice, stock, and capers for about 1 minute or until puréed. Add the oil and whirl 30 seconds longer; set aside.

2 Arrange the asparagus in a steamer and set over boiling water in a large saucepan. Steam the asparagus for 6 to 7 minutes or until crisp-tender. Rinse under cold water to stop the cooking and pat dry on paper toweling. Transfer the asparagus to a serving dish, toss with the parsley dressing, and let marinate for 1 to 2 hours at room temperature or overnight in the refrigerator. Serve as an appetizer or as an accompaniment to cold poached chicken. Serves 4.

PREPARATION TIME: 10 MIN. COOKING TIME: 5 MIN.
MARINATING TIME: 1 HR.

Per serving: Calories 67; Saturated Fat 2 g; Total Fat 5 g; Protein 4 g; Carbohydrate 6 g; Fiber 2 g; Sodium 114 mg; Cholesterol 2 mg

A simple preparation, such as Asparagus with Lemon-Parsley Sauce, enhances the delicate flavor of this springtime vegetable.

Spiced Beets explode with crimson color, making any meal festive. They're also high in potassium and vitamins A and C. Serve them hot or cold the next time your table needs brightening.

SPICED BEETS

Serve this popular beet dish warm, cold, or at room temperature. If you serve it chilled, do not use the optional butter.

6 **medium-size beets (1½ pounds), peeled and quartered**
1 **cup Chicken Stock (page 62) or low-sodium chicken broth**
¼ **cup cider vinegar**
3 **whole cloves**

8 **whole coriander seeds**
8 **whole black peppercorns**
¼ **teaspoon ground allspice**
1 **whole garlic clove**
1 **teaspoon sugar**
1 **tablespoon butter or margarine (optional)**

1 In a medium-size enameled or stainless steel sauce-pan, bring the beets, stock, vinegar, cloves, coriander seeds, peppercorns, allspice, garlic, and sugar to a boil over moderate heat. Lower the heat and simmer, covered, for 35 minutes or until the beets are just tender. With a slotted spoon, transfer the beets to a serving dish.

2 Boil the remaining liquid for 5 minutes or until reduced to ¼ cup. Stir in the butter if desired and pour the liquid over the beets. Serve with broiled salmon or scrod and steamed new potatoes. Serves 4.

PREPARATION TIME: 7 MIN. COOKING TIME: 40 MIN.

Per serving: Calories 62; Saturated Fat 0 g; Total Fat 0 g; Protein 2 g; Carbohydrate 14 g; Fiber 4 g; Sodium 117 mg; Cholesterol 0 mg

BROCCOLI ORIENTAL

The aromatic sauce in this recipe can be used with a number of vegetables. Try it with Brussels sprouts, carrots, or artichokes instead of the broccoli.

1 bunch broccoli (1¼ pounds)
1 large yellow onion, halved and thinly sliced (1½ cups)
½ cup Chicken Stock (page 62), low-sodium chicken broth, or water
1 teaspoon dark sesame oil

1 teaspoon grated fresh ginger or ¼ teaspoon ground ginger
¾ teaspoon cornstarch
2 teaspoons water
1 tablespoon rice vinegar
1 tablespoon plus 1 teaspoon reduced-sodium soy sauce

1 Cut the florets off the broccoli and set aside. Peel the broccoli stems and slice ½ inch thick. In a 12-inch skillet, bring the onion, stock, sesame oil, and ginger to a boil over moderate heat. Add the broccoli stems, lower the heat, cover, and simmer for 3 minutes or until the broccoli stems are slightly tender but still firm. Add the florets, cover, and simmer 3 to 4 minutes longer or until both stems and florets are crisp-tender.

2 Meanwhile, in a small bowl, stir together the cornstarch, water, vinegar, and soy sauce. Pour the mixture over the broccoli, bring to a boil, and cook, stirring, for 1 minute or until the sauce has thickened. Serve hot with steamed rice and Grilled Tuna Teriyaki (page 97). Serves 4.

PREPARATION TIME: 13 MIN. COOKING TIME: 10 MIN.

Per serving: Calories 73; Saturated Fat 0 g; Total Fat 2 g; Protein 5 g; Carbohydrate 12 g; Fiber 5 g; Sodium 218 mg; Cholesterol 0 mg

BROCCOLI WITH SPICY CHICK PEA SAUCE

You can prepare the sauce in advance and bring it to room temperature before dressing the broccoli. The sauce will keep for 3 days in the refrigerator.

½ cup cooked chick peas
¼ cup plain nonfat yogurt
2 cloves garlic, peeled and blanched in boiling water for 2 minutes
2 tablespoons water
1 teaspoon olive oil
1 teaspoon lemon juice

¼ teaspoon ground cumin
⅛ teaspoon ground red pepper (cayenne)
⅛ teaspoon salt, or to taste
1 bunch broccoli (1¼ pounds)

1 In a food processor or blender, whirl the chick peas, yogurt, garlic, water, oil, lemon juice, cumin, red pepper, and salt for 1 minute or until smooth; set aside.

2 Cut the florets off the broccoli and peel and slice the stems ½ inch thick. Arrange the broccoli in a steamer or colander and set over boiling water in a large saucepan. Cover and steam for 6 to 7 minutes or until crisp-tender. Transfer to a warm serving dish. Spoon the sauce over the broccoli and toss to coat. Serve with roast lamb or chicken and orzo. Serves 4.

PREPARATION TIME: 10 MIN. COOKING TIME: 6 MIN.

Per serving: Calories 93; Saturated Fat 0 g; Total Fat 2 g; Protein 7 g; Carbohydrate 15 g; Fiber 4 g; Sodium 118 mg; Cholesterol 0 mg

Fresh ginger adds a unique spicy flavor to any dish. When buying fresh ginger, choose a firm root that is light brown in color, with no cuts on the skin or withered knobs. Place fresh ginger in a plastic food bag and store in the refrigerator; it will keep for up to 1 month. You can also wrap it in aluminum foil and freeze it for up to 4 months. (Thawed ginger will be soft but still flavorful.)

To cook with fresh ginger, cut off a small portion and peel the skin down to the flesh, then slice, mince, or grate it.

BRUSSELS SPROUTS WITH ORIENTAL SAUCE

Dress up Brussels sprouts with a piquant sauce that is sure to tempt even your most reluctant vegetable eater.

1 **pint Brussels sprouts (about 10 ounces), trimmed and quartered, or 1 package (10 ounces) frozen Brussels sprouts, thawed and quartered**	2 **tablespoons rice vinegar**
	¼ **teaspoon dry mustard**
	⅛ **teaspoon red pepper flakes**
	1 **tablespoon dark sesame oil**
½ **cup Chicken Stock or Vegetable Stock (page 62) or low-sodium chicken broth**	2 **green onions, including tops, finely sliced**
2 **tablespoons reduced-sodium soy sauce**	1 **teaspoon cornstarch mixed with 1 tablespoon cold water**

1 In a large saucepan, bring 2 quarts of unsalted water to a boil over moderately high heat. Cut a small X into the base of each sprout to ensure that they cook evenly. Add the Brussels sprouts and cook, uncovered, for 8 to 10 minutes or until just tender. Meanwhile, in a measuring cup, combine the stock, soy sauce, vinegar, mustard, and red pepper flakes and set aside.

2 In a small saucepan, heat the sesame oil over moderately high heat. Add the green onions and sauté for 30 seconds, then add the stock mixture and cook for 1 minute. Stir in the cornstarch-water mixture and bring to a boil. Cook, stirring constantly, for 1 minute or until thickened. Transfer the Brussels sprouts to a warm serving bowl, add the sauce, and toss lightly. Serve with grilled tuna and brown rice. Serves 4.

PREPARATION TIME: 12 MIN. COOKING TIME: 14 MIN.

Per serving: Calories 67; Saturated Fat 1 g; Total Fat 4 g; Protein 3 g; Carbohydrate 8 g; Fiber 3 g; Sodium 274 mg; Cholesterol 0 mg

BRUSSELS SPROUTS AND PEARL ONIONS IN HONEY-LEMON SAUCE

Brussels sprouts, the smallest member of the cabbage family, are available from September to May.

1 **pint Brussels sprouts (about 10 ounces), trimmed, or 1 package (10 ounces) frozen Brussels sprouts**	1 **package (8 ounces) frozen pearl onions**
	2 **tablespoons lemon juice**
½ **cup Chicken Stock (page 62), low-sodium chicken broth, or water**	¼ **teaspoon salt**
	⅛ **teaspoon black pepper**
1 **tablespoon honey**	1 **teaspoon cornstarch mixed with 2 teaspoons water**
¼ **teaspoon caraway seeds**	

1 Cut a small X into the base of each sprout to ensure that they cook evenly. In a 10-inch skillet, bring the stock, honey, and caraway seeds to a boil over moderate heat. Add the sprouts, lower the heat, and simmer, covered, for 3 minutes. Add the onions and cook, covered, 7 minutes more or until the vegetables are tender.

2 Stir in the lemon juice, salt, pepper, and cornstarch-water mixture. Bring to a boil and cook for 1 minute, stirring to coat the vegetables. Serve with roast turkey and sweet potatoes. Serves 6.

PREPARATION TIME: 10 MIN. COOKING TIME: 12 MIN.

Per serving: Calories 47; Saturated Fat 0 g; Total Fat 0 g; Protein 2 g; Carbohydrate 11 g; Fiber 3 g; Sodium 111 mg; Cholesterol 0 mg

CABBAGE STUFFED WITH VEGETABLES

Dried mushrooms add intense flavor to this hearty vegetable dish. If they are unavailable, you can substitute 3 ounces of sliced fresh mushrooms and omit the soaking in Step 1.

1 **ounce dried mushrooms**
1 **cup boiling water**
1 **head cabbage (2 to 2½ pounds), tough outer leaves removed**
1 **tablespoon olive oil**
2 **large yellow onions, chopped (3 cups)**
2 **cloves garlic, minced**

3 **medium-size carrots, peeled, halved, and thinly sliced (2 cups)**
3 **tablespoons snipped fresh dill or 1 tablespoon dill weed**
1 **can (14½ ounces) low-sodium tomatoes, chopped, with their juice**

1 In a glass measuring cup or small heatproof bowl, soak the mushrooms in the water for 30 minutes. Drain in a sieve lined with cheesecloth or paper toweling, reserving ½ cup of the liquid.

2 Meanwhile, bring a stockpot of unsalted water to a boil. Place the cabbage in the boiling water for about 2 minutes. Remove the cabbage and cut off 4 leaves at the core, taking care not to tear them. Repeat twice, removing 12 leaves altogether (use the remaining cabbage for another dish). Return the leaves to the boiling water and cook for 4 minutes or until tender. Drain and rinse under cold water to stop the cooking; pat dry with paper toweling.

3 In a 10-inch nonstick skillet, heat the oil over low heat. Add the onions and garlic and cook, uncovered, stirring frequently, for 5 minutes. Add the mushrooms, reserved mushroom liquid, and 1 cup of the carrots and cook, uncovered, stirring frequently, another 5 minutes or until the carrots are tender. Remove from the heat and stir in 2 tablespoons of the dill.

4 Spoon ¼ cup of the vegetable mixture into the center of a cabbage leaf. Fold the sides of the leaf toward the center, then roll up the leaf and place, seam side down, in a 12-inch skillet. Repeat with the remaining cabbage leaves and filling. Add the tomatoes to the skillet along with the remaining carrots and dill. Bring to a boil over

moderate heat. Lower the heat and simmer, covered, for 8 to 10 minutes or until the cabbage is tender. Serve with grilled veal chops and whole-wheat rolls or, for a meatless meal, serve on a bed of brown rice. Serves 4 to 6.

PREPARATION TIME: 20 MIN. COOKING TIME: 30 MIN.

SOAKING TIME: 30 MIN.

Per serving (for 4): Calories 191; Saturated Fat 1 g; Total Fat 5 g; Protein 7 g; Carbohydrate 37 g; Fiber 9 g; Sodium 77 mg; Cholesterol 0 mg

Next Thanksgiving include in the feast Brussels Sprouts and Pearl Onions in Honey-Lemon Sauce as well as Sweet Potatoes Roasted with Garlic (page 240).

BRAISED RED CABBAGE WITH APPLES

Apples and red cabbage, both high in fiber, are especially appealing with pork or ham.

1 medium-size head red cabbage (about 1¾ pounds), cored and thinly sliced

2 medium-size Granny Smith apples, peeled, cored, and grated (1½ cups)

1 tablespoon brown sugar

2 tablespoons all-purpose flour

¼ teaspoon black pepper

1 cup dry red wine or unsweetened apple juice

1 In a large enameled or stainless steel saucepan, mix the cabbage, apples, sugar, flour, and pepper. (Iron or aluminum will react with the cabbage and turn it brown.) Stir in the wine and bring to a boil over high heat. Lower the heat, cover, and simmer, stirring occasionally, for 25 to 30 minutes or until the cabbage is tender. Serve with Pork Chops Marinated in Herbs (page 145). Serves 6.

PREPARATION TIME: 10 MIN. COOKING TIME: 25 MIN.

Per serving: Calories 108; Saturated Fat 0 g; Total Fat 1 g; Protein 2 g; Carbohydrate 20 g; Fiber 4 g; Sodium 40 mg; Cholesterol 0 mg

CARROTS AND PARSNIPS WITH MUSTARD CREAM

This simple vegetable dish can be served hot or cold. Its piquant flavor especially complements grilled fish, meat, or poultry.

¼ cup Chicken Stock or Vegetable Stock (page 62), low-sodium chicken broth, or water

½ teaspoon dried tarragon, crumbled

½ teaspoon salt

⅛ teaspoon black pepper

4 medium-size carrots, peeled and shredded (3 cups)

2 medium-size parsnips, peeled and shredded (2 cups)

3 tablespoons reduced-fat sour cream

2 teaspoons Dijon mustard

1 teaspoon lemon juice

1 In a 10-inch skillet, bring the stock, tarragon, salt, and pepper to a boil over moderate heat. Add the carrots and parsnips, cover, and cook, stirring occasionally, for 6 minutes or until crisp-tender. Remove from the heat. Meanwhile, in a small bowl, stir together the sour cream, mustard, and lemon juice. Combine the mixture with the carrots and parsnips. Serve with grilled chicken and small boiled new potatoes. Serves 4.

PREPARATION TIME: 10 MIN. COOKING TIME: 6 MIN.

Per serving: Calories 100; Saturated Fat 2 g; Total Fat 2 g; Protein 2 g; Carbohydrate 19 g; Fiber 5 g; Sodium 351 mg; Cholesterol 0 mg

Braised Red Cabbage with Apples beautifully complements hearty winter casseroles and roasts.

CARROTS WITH ORANGE-GINGER GLAZE

This simple glaze turns the everyday carrot into an elegant side dish that goes beautifully with meats, poultry, grains, or legumes.

- 1 **teaspoon grated orange rind**
- ¾ **cup orange juice**
- 1 ½ **teaspoons unsalted butter or margarine**
- 1 **teaspoon honey**
- ½ **teaspoon ground ginger**
- ¼ **teaspoon salt**
- ⅛ **teaspoon black pepper**
- 4 **large carrots, peeled and cut diagonally into ½-inch slices (about 5 cups)**

1 In a 10-inch nonstick skillet, combine the orange rind, orange juice, butter, honey, ginger, salt, and pepper and bring to a boil. Add the carrots, lower the heat, and simmer, covered, for 5 minutes or until the carrots are slightly tender but still firm.

2 Raise the heat to high and boil the mixture, uncovered, shaking the pan frequently, for 5 minutes or until the liquid has reduced to 3 tablespoons and the carrots are crisp-tender and nicely glazed. Serves 4.

PREPARATION TIME: 7 MIN. COOKING TIME: 11 MIN.

Per serving: Calories 74; Saturated Fat 1 g; Total Fat 2 g; Protein 1 g; Carbohydrate 14 g; Fiber 3 g; Sodium 165 mg; Cholesterol 4 mg

1. In a large saucepan, melt the butter over moderate heat. Add the onion and sauté, stirring frequently, for 5 minutes or until soft. Add the rice and stock, cover, and cook over moderately low heat for 10 minutes. Add the carrots, tarragon, salt, and pepper and cook, covered, 10 minutes more or until the rice and carrots are very tender.

2. Preheat the oven to 375° F. Grease a 1-quart baking dish and set aside. In a food processor or blender, whirl the rice and carrot mixture for 20 seconds or until smooth. If the mixture is too thick, add the skim milk and purée another 10 seconds. Transfer to a large bowl.

3. In a perfectly clean medium-size bowl, beat the egg whites with an electric mixer set on high speed until they are stiff but not dry. Gently stir ¼ of the whipped egg whites into the carrot purée to loosen it, then fold in the remainder. Transfer the mixture to the baking dish and bake for 30 minutes or until puffed and golden. Serve with roast turkey or Sage-Marinated Pork Chops (page 143) and steamed broccoli. Serves 4.

PREPARATION TIME: 15 MIN. COOKING TIME: 55 MIN.

Per serving: Calories 147; Saturated Fat 2 g;
Total Fat 4 g; Protein 6 g; Carbohydrate 23 g;
Fiber 4 g; Sodium 264 mg; Cholesterol 8 mg

•

Summer Squash Variation: Grate *4 medium-size yellow squash or zucchini (about 1 ½ pounds).* In a colander set in the sink, toss the squash with *¼ teaspoon salt* and let drain for 15 minutes. In a large heavy saucepan, melt the butter over moderate heat. Add the onion and sauté for 2 minutes. Add the rice, *1 cup Chicken Stock, 1 ½ teaspoons dill weed,* and the pepper. Cover and cook over moderately low for 5 minutes. Meanwhile, working in small batches, squeeze the salted squash with your hands to rid it of water. Add the squash to the rice mixture, cover, and cook for 15 minutes or until the rice and squash are tender. Purée as directed, adding *1 large egg* to the purée. Proceed as in Step 3. Serves 4. *Per serving: Calories 152; Saturated Fat 2 g; Total Fat 5 g; Protein 8 g; Carbohydrate 20 g; Fiber 3 g; Sodium 228 mg; Cholesterol 62 mg.*

You're missing only the fat in these homey helpings of vegetables — Sautéed Collard Greens with Carrots and a baked potato topped with Creamy Yogurt Spread (page 287).

CARROT PUDDING

This recipe lends itself to seasonal variations. Try it also with winter squash, turnips, parsnips, or rutabagas or a combination of these. With the turnips and parsnips, you might substitute 1 teaspoon of curry powder for the tarragon.

1 tablespoon unsalted butter or margarine	6 medium-size carrots, peeled and finely chopped (4½ cups)
1 small yellow onion, finely chopped (½ cup)	1½ teaspoons dried tarragon, crumbled
¼ cup long-grain white rice	¼ teaspoon each salt and black pepper, or to taste
1½ cups Chicken Stock (page 62) or low-sodium chicken broth	2 tablespoons skim milk (optional)
	3 large egg whites

SAUTÉED COLLARD GREENS WITH CARROTS

Collard greens and carrots — two superstars of nutrition — combine beautifully in this simple recipe.

1¼ pounds collard greens, stems removed, rinsed well, and torn in half (10 cups), or 1 package (10 ounces) frozen collard greens
1 tablespoon olive oil
2 large carrots, peeled, quartered lengthwise, and thinly sliced (about 2½ cups)
1 small stalk celery, finely chopped (⅓ cup)
1 teaspoon sugar
1 teaspoon ground ginger
⅛ teaspoon ground nutmeg

1 Bring a large saucepan of unsalted water to a boil. Add the collard greens and cook for 15 minutes or until tender. Before draining, reserve 3 tablespoons of the cooking liquid.

2 In a 12-inch nonstick skillet, heat the oil over low heat; add the carrots and celery and cook, stirring occasionally, for 5 minutes or until the carrots are crisp-tender. In a small bowl, combine the sugar, ginger, and nutmeg. Add the cooked collard greens to the skillet along with the sugar mixture and reserved cooking liquid. Cook, stirring constantly, for about 2 minutes or until heated through. Serve with roast chicken or grilled pork chops and baked potatoes. Serves 4.

PREPARATION TIME: 10 MIN. COOKING TIME: 23 MIN.

Per serving: Calories 120; Saturated Fat 1 g; Total Fat 4 g; Protein 6 g; Carbohydrate 18 g; Fiber 7 g; Sodium 109 mg; Cholesterol 0 mg

CAULIFLOWER AND TOMATO AU GRATIN

1 medium-size cauliflower, cored and cut into florets (4 cups)
1 tablespoon unsalted butter or margarine
2 tablespoons all-purpose flour
1 can (14½ ounces) low-sodium tomatoes, puréed with their juice
¼ cup skim milk
1 teaspoon dried thyme or oregano, crumbled
¼ teaspoon each salt and black pepper
1 tablespoon grated Parmesan cheese
2 tablespoons fine dry bread crumbs

1 Preheat the oven to 375° F. Lightly grease a shallow 1-quart baking dish. In a steamer or colander placed over a large saucepan of boiling water, steam the cauliflower for 10 to 12 minutes or until crisp-tender.

2 Meanwhile, in a large heavy saucepan, melt the butter over moderately low heat. Add the flour and cook, stirring constantly, for 30 seconds or until smooth. Stir in the tomatoes, milk, thyme, salt, and pepper. Simmer the mixture, stirring constantly, for 5 minutes or until thick. Remove from the heat and stir in the cheese and cauliflower.

3 Spoon the mixture into the prepared baking dish, sprinkle the top with the bread crumbs, and bake, covered, for 15 minutes or until bubbling. Serve with baked fish, roast chicken, or Spicy Rice with Bulgur and Pasta (page 164). Serves 4.

PREPARATION TIME: 12 MIN. COOKING TIME: 32 MIN.

Per serving: Calories 119; Saturated Fat 2 g; Total Fat 4 g; Protein 6 g; Carbohydrate 17 g; Fiber 4 g; Sodium 228 mg; Cholesterol 10 mg

DOWN-HOME DINNERS

Orange Braised Ham Steak
(page 142)

Sautéed Collard Greens with Carrots

Corn Bread Sticks

Sweet Potato Pancakes
(page 241)

Deviled Oven-Fried Chicken
(page 107)

Carrot Pudding

Braised Okra

Herbed Buttermilk Biscuits
(page 291)

Baked Apples

CAULIFLOWER WITH RAISINS AND SUN-DRIED TOMATOES

Cauliflower and raisins are both high in fiber. Sun-dried tomatoes add vitamin C as well as wonderful flavor to this recipe. If using sun-dried tomatoes that are packed in oil, be sure to refrigerate the jar after opening it.

½ cup raisins
⅓ cup sun-dried tomatoes, finely chopped
1 cup boiling water
1 medium-size head cauliflower (1¼ pounds), cored and cut into florets

1 tablespoon olive oil
¼ teaspoon salt
3 tablespoons plain dry bread crumbs

1 In a small bowl, soak the raisins and sun-dried tomatoes in the water for 10 minutes or until plumped. In a steamer or metal colander set over a large saucepan of boiling water, steam the cauliflower for 5 minutes or until slightly tender.

2 In a 12-inch nonstick skillet, heat the oil over moderate heat. Add the cauliflower and cook, stirring frequently, for 3 minutes or until lightly colored. Add the raisins and sun-dried tomatoes, their soaking liquid, and the salt. Raise the heat to high and cook for 5 minutes or until the liquid has almost evaporated. Stir in the bread crumbs and cook, stirring constantly, 2 minutes more or until the sauce has thickened slightly. Serve warm or at room temperature with roast meat or poultry. Serves 4.

PREPARATION TIME: 8 MIN. COOKING TIME: 15 MIN.
SOAKING TIME: 10 MIN.

Per serving: Calories 175; Saturated Fat 1 g; Total Fat 4 g; Protein 6 g; Carbohydrate 34 g; Fiber 5 g; Sodium 208 mg; Cholesterol 0 mg

Pasta Variation: In a stockpot of boiling unsalted water, cook *1 pound pasta* (bow-tie or elbow macaroni) according to package directions. Drain in a colander. To the same stockpot, add *2 cups Chicken Stock (page 62) or low-sodium chicken broth* and bring to a simmer. Stir in the pasta, the cooked cauliflower mixture, and *3 tablespoons minced fresh parsley.* Serve immediately. *Per serving: Calories 606; Saturated Fat 1 g; Total Fat 7 g; Protein 22 g; Carbohydrate 119 g; Fiber 6 g; Sodium 280 mg; Cholesterol 0 mg.*

Snow-white florets and emerald-green peas, lightly seasoned with cumin and curry, make Indian-Style Cauliflower a dish fit for a raja.

INDIAN-STYLE CAULIFLOWER

- 1 large yellow onion, quartered and sliced
- ½ cup Chicken Stock or Vegetable Stock (page 62) or low-sodium chicken broth
- 2 tablespoons chutney or apricot preserves
- 2 teaspoons Dijon mustard
- ¾ teaspoon dried basil, crumbled
- ¾ teaspoon each ground ginger and cumin
- ½ teaspoon salt
- ¼ teaspoon each ground cinnamon and curry powder
- 1 medium-size head cauliflower (1 ¼ pounds), cored and cut into florets
- 1 cup frozen green peas
- 1 tablespoon cornstarch dissolved in 2 tablespoons water
- 2 tablespoons white wine vinegar or cider vinegar
- 6 drops hot red pepper sauce

1 In a 10-inch nonstick skillet, combine the onion, stock, chutney, mustard, basil, ginger, cumin, salt, cinnamon, and curry powder. Bring to a simmer and cook, covered, for 6 minutes. Add the cauliflower and cook, covered, for 5 minutes over moderately low heat. Add the peas, cover, and cook 4 to 5 minutes more or until the cauliflower is crisp-tender. Stir in the cornstarch mixture, vinegar, and red pepper sauce and cook for 1 minute or until the sauce has thickened. Serve hot or at room temperature with roast chicken and couscous or rice. Serves 4 to 6.

PREPARATION TIME: 15 MIN. COOKING TIME: 17 MIN.

Per serving (for 4): Calories 117; Saturated Fat 0 g; Total Fat 1 g; Protein 6 g; Carbohydrate 25 g; Fiber 6 g; Sodium 407 mg; Cholesterol 0 mg

BROILED EGGPLANT ORIENTAL

Broiling is a simple, low-fat way to cook eggplant, which tends to absorb a great deal of oil when fried.

- 1 large eggplant (1 pound), sliced ½ inch thick
- 2 tablespoons reduced-sodium soy sauce
- 1 tablespoon rice vinegar or white wine vinegar
- 2 teaspoons each vegetable oil and dark sesame oil
- 1 teaspoon minced fresh ginger or ½ teaspoon ground ginger
- 1 clove garlic, minced
- ¼ teaspoon crumbled red pepper flakes or black pepper

1 Preheat the broiler, setting the rack 4 inches from the heat. Lightly grease a baking sheet and arrange the eggplant slices on it. In a small bowl, whisk together the soy sauce, vinegar, vegetable oil, sesame oil, ginger, garlic, and red pepper flakes. Brush the mixture over both sides of each eggplant slice.

2 Broil the eggplant slices for 3 to 4 minutes on each side or until golden brown and tender. Serve with broiled fish or shrimp and steamed sugar snap peas. Serves 4.

PREPARATION TIME: 5 MIN. COOKING TIME: 8 MIN.

Per serving: Calories 76; Saturated Fat 1 g; Total Fat 5 g; Protein 2 g; Carbohydrate 8 g; Fiber 1 g; Sodium 245 mg; Cholesterol 0 mg

Cornstarch comes from the heart of dried corn. Used as a thickener for sauces, especially sweet-sour and sweet ones, it has twice the thickening power of all-purpose flour. A sauce thickened with cornstarch is translucent and will become thin and watery if overcooked.

OVEN-FRIED EGGPLANT

Serve this as a side dish, or create your own eggplant pizzas by topping each slice with tomato sauce and low-fat mozzarella cheese. For best results, use an eggplant that is 3 to 4 inches in diameter.

- 6 tablespoons all-purpose flour
- ¼ cup toasted wheat germ
- 3 tablespoons sesame seeds
- ¼ teaspoon salt
- 2 large egg whites
- 1 tablespoon water
- 1 large eggplant (1 pound), peeled and sliced ¼ inch thick
- 2 tablespoons olive oil
- 4 lemon wedges, (optional garnish)

1 Preheat the oven to 450° F. Lightly grease a baking sheet. On a large plate, combine the flour, wheat germ, sesame seeds, and salt. In a shallow bowl, stir together the egg whites and water. Dip the eggplant slices first in the egg white mixture, then in the flour mixture to coat. Arrange on the baking sheet; drizzle each slice with the oil and bake for 10 minutes.

2 Lower the oven temperature to 400° F and bake 10 minutes longer. Turn the eggplant slices over and bake another 10 minutes or until crisp, golden, and tender. Serve with lemon wedges if desired. Serves 4.

PREPARATION TIME: 10 MIN. COOKING TIME: 30 MIN.

Per serving: Calories 204; Saturated Fat 2 g; Total Fat 11 g; Protein 8 g; Carbohydrate 21 g; Fiber 3 g; Sodium 165 mg; Cholesterol 0 mg

BRAISED ENDIVE

Braising vegetables in chicken or vegetable stock is a wonderful way to enhance their flavor.

- 4 Belgian endive, halved lengthwise
- 2 cups Chicken Stock or Vegetable Stock (page 62) or low-sodium chicken broth
- 2 teaspoons lemon juice
- ¼ teaspoon salt
- ⅛ teaspoon black pepper
- ¼ cup plain dry bread crumbs
- 2 tablespoons grated Parmesan cheese

1 Preheat the broiler, setting the rack 6 inches from the heat. In a large shallow flameproof casserole, arrange the endive, cut sides down. Add the stock, lemon juice, salt, and pepper and cover with wax paper and a lid. Simmer for 15 to 20 minutes or until the endive is tender. Sprinkle the endive with the bread crumbs and cheese. Broil for 1 to 2 minutes or until the topping is golden brown. Serve with baked or poached fish and steamed carrots. Serves 4.

PREPARATION TIME: 10 MIN. COOKING TIME: 18 MIN.

Per serving: Calories 58; Saturated Fat 1 g; Total Fat 2 g; Protein 4 g; Carbohydrate 7 g; Fiber 0 g; Sodium 316 mg; Cholesterol 2 mg

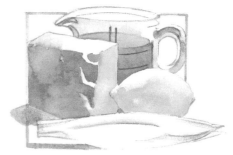

ESCAROLE SAUTÉED WITH GARLIC

Garlic highlights the assertive flavor of escarole, which is high in iron and calcium. This dish beautifully complements broiled meat, fish, or poultry, as well as meatless entrées. You can also make it with romaine lettuce and substitute lemon rind and lemon juice for the orange rind and juice.

1 large head escarole (1 ½ pounds), cored and rinsed	1 teaspoon grated orange rind
1 tablespoon olive oil	1 tablespoon orange juice
2 cloves garlic, minced	¼ teaspoon black pepper

1 Shake the excess water from the escarole and tear the leaves in half. In a 12-inch nonstick skillet, heat the oil over high heat until very hot but not smoking. Stir in the garlic, orange rind, orange juice, pepper, and escarole. Immediately lower the heat to moderate and cook, uncovered, stirring constantly, for 1 to 2 minutes or until the escarole has just wilted.

2 Transfer the escarole with tongs or a fork to a platter. If necessary, boil the liquid remaining in the skillet for 1 to 2 minutes or until reduced to 1 tablespoon, then pour over the escarole. Serve with Beef Rolls with Currant Stuffing (page 135) or Herbed Cornish Hens (page 125). Serves 4.

PREPARATION TIME: 6 MIN.   COOKING TIME: 4 MIN.

Per serving: Calories 72; Saturated Fat 1 g; Total Fat 4 g; Protein 5 g; Carbohydrate 7 g; Fiber 4 g; Sodium 135 mg; Cholesterol 0 mg

Oven-Fried Eggplant never looked so good — its succulence enhanced by a crunchy coating of sesame seeds and wheat germ.

BRAISED FENNEL

Fennel, a green and white bulb-shaped vegetable that resembles celery in its crunchy texture, has a subtle anise, or licorice, flavor. It is usually available from September until May and, like celery, can be eaten raw or cooked.

2 teaspoons olive oil	½ teaspoon dried thyme, crumbled
1 medium-size yellow onion, finely chopped (1 cup)	¼ teaspoon each salt and black pepper, or to taste
1 large clove garlic, minced	2 bulbs fennel (about 2¼ pounds), trimmed and cut lengthwise into strips ¼ inch wide
1 can (1 pound) low-sodium tomatoes, puréed with their liquid	Snipped fennel sprigs (garnish)
1 cup Chicken Stock or Vegetable Stock (page 62) or low-sodium chicken broth	

1 In a 5-quart Dutch oven or 12-inch nonstick skillet, heat the oil over moderately low heat. Add the onion and garlic and cook, stirring occasionally, for 5 minutes. Add the tomatoes, stock, thyme, salt, and pepper. Place the fennel in the Dutch oven and spoon the tomato mixture on top. (The liquid should just cover the fennel; if necessary, add a few teaspoons of water.) Bring the mixture to a boil, cover, and cook for 15 to 20 minutes or until the fennel is tender. Raise the heat and cook another 5 minutes or until the sauce has thickened. Garnish with the fennel sprigs. Serve with Sage-Marinated Pork Chops (page 143) or Crispy Baked Fish (page 84). Serves 6.

PREPARATION TIME: 15 MIN.   COOKING TIME: 25 MIN.

Per serving: Calories 88; Saturated Fat 0 g; Total Fat 2 g; Protein 4 g; Carbohydrate 17 g; Fiber 6 g; Sodium 386 mg; Cholesterol 0 mg

Roasted Jerusalem Artichokes, high in iron and B vitamins, and calcium-rich Kale with Chili Sauce are just the duo to accompany a simply grilled chicken.

ROASTED JERUSALEM ARTICHOKES

The Jerusalem artichoke, also known as the sunchoke, has a nutty flavor and potato-like texture. It is available year round and is an outstanding source of iron.

1 ½ tablespoons olive oil
8 cloves garlic, peeled
1 pound Jerusalem artichokes, rinsed and cut into 1-inch cubes
⅓ cup water

3 tablespoons lemon juice
½ teaspoon each dried rosemary and sage, crumbled
¼ teaspoon salt

1 Preheat the oven to 400° F. In a small roasting pan, mix the oil and garlic and heat in the oven for 5 minutes. Add the artichokes and toss to coat with the oil. Roast, tossing occasionally, for 25 minutes.

2 In a glass measuring cup, mix the water, lemon juice, rosemary, sage, and salt and pour over the artichokes. Roast for an additonal 20 minutes or until the liquid has almost evaporated and the artichokes are tender on the inside and crisp on the outside. Serve with grilled pork chops or chicken and a green salad. Serves 4.

PREPARATION TIME: 6 MIN. COOKING TIME: 50 MIN.

Per serving: Calories 139; Saturated Fat 1 g;
Total Fat 5 g; Protein 3 g; Carbohydrate 22 g;
Fiber 2 g; Sodium 135 mg; Cholesterol 0 mg

KALE WITH CHILI SAUCE

Both kale and collard greens are high in health-promoting beta carotene, a form of vitamin A. This spicy recipe makes eating your greens a pleasure.

1 large bunch kale or collard greens (1 ¼ pounds), trimmed, rinsed, and patted dry
1 tablespoon olive oil
¼ teaspoon red pepper flakes, or to taste

⅓ cup finely chopped sweet red pepper
2 tablespoons red wine vinegar
2 tablespoons water
1 tablespoon bottled chili sauce

1 Tear the kale leaves in half (you should have about 12 cups). In a large saucepan of boiling water, cook the kale for 5 minutes or until tender. Drain, rinse under cold water to stop the cooking, and drain again. Transfer to a serving bowl.

2 In an 8-inch skillet, heat the oil over low heat; add the red pepper flakes and cook for 5 minutes. Raise the heat to moderately high, add the sweet red pepper, and cook for 3 minutes. Add the vinegar, water, and chili sauce and boil for 30 seconds. Pour the sauce over the kale and toss. Serve with poached fish and rice or Crustless Leek and Potato Quiche (page 186). Serves 4.

PREPARATION TIME: 10 MIN. COOKING TIME: 14 MIN.

Per serving: Calories 81; Saturated Fat 1 g;
Total Fat 3 g; Protein 3 g; Carbohydrate 10 g;
Fiber 5 g; Sodium 83 mg; Cholesterol 0 mg

Garlic has been in use for more than 5,000 years. Researchers have found recently that garlic has at least 3 different chemical compounds beneficial to our health: one works to lower blood pressure; the second has the ability to reduce low-density cholesterol, the so-called bad cholesterol; the third compound helps shield the stomach from cancer. Scientists do not know how much garlic is needed to obtain these health benefits, but one thing is certain: garlic is a boon to cooks. Such root vegetables as potatoes, turnips, and carrots are especially enhanced by it.

When sautéing garlic, cook it briefly until soft and translucent and be careful not to scorch it. In soups, stews, and sauces, it can be cooked for a long period and will gradually become mellower.

VEGETABLE COOKING TIMES

Ideally, vegetables should be cooked to the crisp-tender stage, that is, softened but still slightly crunchy. In this state, they retain not only their best appearance and flavor but also maximum vitamins and minerals. The cooking times below are for supermarket vegetables, which often travel some distance. If you buy locally grown produce, it is usually fresher and will cook faster. **To steam** vegetables, arrange them in a steamer basket or colander and set in a large saucepan containing just enough boiling water to reach the bottom of the basket. Cover the saucepan and simmer for the times listed below. **To boil**, add the vegetables to a saucepan of boiling water and cook, uncovered, following the times indicated. **To microwave**, use a 1- or 2-quart microwave-safe casserole with a cover. Where noted, stir the vegetables or rotate the dish a half turn to ensure even cooking. Let the vegetables stand for a few minutes before serving. **To bake** vegetables, use a covered baking dish and preheat the oven for 10 minutes.

VEGETABLE (4 servings)	STEAM	BOIL	MICROWAVE	BAKE
Artichoke 4 medium size (7 ounces each) trimmed	25 minutes (replenish water if necessary)	25 minutes (lay on side) 1½ quarts boiling water	15 minutes ¼ cup water (rotate each artichoke halfway through)	45 minutes at 350° F 1 cup water
Asparagus 1¼ pounds, medium size	7 minutes (lay spears horizontally in steamer basket)	4½ minutes 3 quarts boiling water	5½ minutes ¼ cup water (rotate halfway through)	20 minutes at 350° F ¼ cup water
Beets 4 medium size (1 pound) whole, trimmed	45 minutes (replenish water if necessary)	35 minutes start with cold water to cover (about 7 cups)	10 minutes ¼ cup water (rotate halfway through)	1 hour at 350° F ¾ cup water
Broccoli 1½ pounds cut into florets	7 minutes	5 minutes 4 quarts boiling water	6 minutes ¼ cup water (rotate halfway through)	
Brussels sprouts 10-ounce carton trimmed, crosses cut in stems	12 minutes	10 minutes 2 quarts boiling water	6 minutes ¼ cup water (stir halfway through)	
Cabbage 2 pounds trimmed, cored, sliced	10 minutes	7 minutes 4 quarts boiling water	15 minutes ¼ cup water (stir every 3 minutes)	
Carrots 6 to 7 medium size (1 pound) sliced ¼ inch thick	12 minutes	6 minutes 2 quarts boiling water	7 minutes ¼ cup water (stir halfway through)	40 minutes at 350° F ¼ cup water
Cauliflower 1 head (2 pounds) trimmed, cut into 2-inch florets	12 minutes	8 minutes 4 quarts boiling water	8 minutes ¼ cup water (rotate halfway through)	

VEGETABLE (4 servings)	STEAM	BOIL	MICROWAVE	BAKE
Corn 4 ears, husked	7 minutes	6 minutes 4 quarts boiling water	9 minutes (leave in husk and shuck after cooking)	20 minutes at 425° F wrapped in aluminum foil
Green beans 1 pound trimmed	12 minutes	9 minutes 2 quarts boiling water	9 minutes 1 ¼ cups water (stir every 3 minutes)	
Parsnips 1 pound cut into ½ -inch cubes	7 minutes	6 minutes 2 quarts boiling water	5 minutes ¼ cup water (stir halfway through)	30 minutes at 350° F ¼ cup water
Peas 2 pounds (2 cups shelled)	7 minutes	4 minutes 2 quarts boiling water	7 minutes ¼ cup water (stir halfway through)	
Potatoes 4 medium size (1½ pounds)	18 minutes peeled, quartered	17 minutes 2 quarts boiling water peeled, quartered	10 minutes whole, unpeeled, pricked with fork	60 minutes at 350° F (uncovered) whole, unpeeled
Spinach 1 ¼ pounds trimmed	4 minutes	3 minutes 4 quarts boiling water	8 minutes ¼ cup water (stir halfway through)	
Squash, acorn 2 large (1 pound each) halved	12 minutes peeled and cut into 2-inch chunks		10 minutes covered, no water (rotate halfway through)	30 minutes at 400° F ¼ cup water (uncovered)
Squash, butternut 1 large (2 pounds)	20 minutes peeled, cut into 2-inch chunks		15 minutes covered, no water	45 minutes at 400° F ¼ cup water (uncovered)
Squash, summer 4 small (4 ounces each) sliced ½ inch thick (except to bake)	6 minutes		5 minutes no water (stir halfway through)	30 minutes at 350° F 1 tablespoon water halved lengthwise
Sweet Potatoes 4 medium size (1½ pounds)	15 minutes peeled, quartered	16 minutes 2 quarts boiling water peeled, quartered	8 minutes whole, unpeeled, pricked with fork	60 minutes at 350° F (uncovered) whole, unpeeled
Turnips (white) 1 pound cut into ½-inch cubes	15 minutes	8 minutes 2 quarts boiling water	8 minutes ¼ cup water (stir halfway through)	40 minutes at 350° F ¼ cup water

Fresh vegetables are easy to prepare in a microwave oven, and the speed of cooking helps preserve their vitamins, minerals, texture, and color. For best results, keep in mind these tips:
• If the power of your microwave is less than 700 watts, you may need to cook vegetables a bit longer than the suggested time, but still use the specified amount of water.
• For even cooking, cut vegetables to uniform size.
• With uncut pieces, arrange tender parts, such as tips or florets, toward the center of the dish, tougher stalks toward the outside where they will cook more quickly.
• If using salt, add it at the table; during microwaving, salt can cause dark spots.
• Save any leftover cooking liquid for a soup or sauce; it contains vitamins and minerals leached out during the cooking process.

Dicing is a simple technique used to cut vegetables, poultry, or meat into neat, uniform pieces, usually about ¼ inch in size. The same technique can also be used to cut these ingredients into cubes larger than ¼ inch. Dicing is illustrated below using a potato.

1. Cut the potato in half lengthwise. Place the flat side down on a cutting board and slice it lengthwise into sections about ¼ inch wide.

2. Steadying the potato with your hand on top, halve it horizontally.

3. Finish by cutting the potato crosswise in ¼-inch-wide sections.

BRAISED LEEKS, POTATOES, AND CABBAGE

2 **medium-size leeks, halved lengthwise, sliced crosswise into ½-inch pieces, and rinsed well**	1 **tablespoon unsalted butter**
4 **all-purpose potatoes (1 pound), peeled and cut into ½-inch cubes**	¾ **teaspoon dill weed**
	¾ **teaspoon salt**
	¼ **teaspoon black pepper**
½ **cup Chicken Stock or Vegetable Stock (page 62), low-sodium chicken broth, or water**	½ **small head green cabbage, halved, cored, and cut into strips ½ inch wide**

1 In a 12-inch nonstick skillet, combine the leeks, potatoes, stock, butter, dill weed, salt, and pepper. Bring to a simmer, cover, and cook for 8 minutes. Add the cabbage, cover, and cook 10 minutes more or until the cabbage and potatoes are tender. Serve with roast chicken or meat loaf. Serves 4.

PREPARATION TIME: 12 MIN. COOKING TIME: 18 MIN.

> *Per serving: Calories 182; Saturated Fat 2 g; Total Fat 3 g; Protein 5 g; Carbohydrate 36 g; Fiber 5 g; Sodium 447 mg; Cholesterol 9 mg*

•

Salad Variation: Transfer the cooked vegetables to a large bowl. In a small bowl, whisk together *3 tablespoons red wine vinegar, 2 tablespoons olive oil,* and *¼ teaspoon dill weed.* Pour the dressing over the vegetables, cover, and refrigerate for at least 2 hours. Will keep for up to 3 days. Refrigerate until ready to serve.
Per serving: Calories 242; Saturated Fat 3 g; Total Fat 11 g; Protein 5 g; Carbohydrate 36 g; Fiber 5 g; Sodium 499 mg; Cholesterol 9 mg.

CURRIED PARSNIP AND CHICK PEA PURÉE

Curry turns this nutritious purée into an unusual side dish — the perfect accent for roast chicken or turkey.

1 **tablespoon vegetable or canola oil**	1 **can (14½ ounces) low-sodium tomatoes with their juice**
2 **cloves garlic, sliced**	½ **cup cooked chick peas**
1½ **teaspoons curry powder**	2 **tablespoons plain nonfat yogurt**
1 **small carrot (2 ounces), peeled and thinly sliced**	¼ **teaspoon each salt and black pepper, or to taste**
5 **medium-size parsnips (about 1 pound), peeled and thinly sliced**	

1 In a large heavy saucepan, heat the oil over moderate heat. Stir in the garlic and curry powder, then add the carrot, parsnips, and tomatoes. Cook, covered, for 20 minutes or until the parsnips are just tender. Add the chick peas and cook, covered, another 5 minutes.

2 In a food processor or blender, combine the mixture with the yogurt, salt, and pepper and purée until smooth. If necessary, return to the saucepan and reheat over low heat. Serves 4.

PREPARATION TIME: 10 MIN. COOKING TIME: 25 MIN.

> *Per serving: Calories 190; Saturated Fat 1 g; Total Fat 5 g; Protein 5 g; Carbohydrate 35 g; Fiber 7 g; Sodium 170 mg; Cholesterol 0 mg*

ROASTED PEPPER MÉLANGE

2 **large sweet red peppers (10 ounces each)**	½ **teaspoon salt**
2 **large sweet green peppers (10 ounces each)**	¼ **teaspoon black pepper, or to taste**
2 **large sweet yellow peppers (10 ounces each)**	1 **tablespoon olive oil**
	2 **tablespoons each minced fresh basil and parsley or snipped chives or a combination**
2 **tablespoons white wine vinegar or cider vinegar**	
2 **cloves garlic, crushed**	1 **tablespoon drained capers, chopped (optional garnish)**

1 Preheat the broiler, setting the rack 6 inches from the heat. Line a broiler pan with aluminum foil and arrange the sweet peppers on their sides on the pan. Broil the peppers, turning frequently, for 10 to 12 minutes or until they are charred on all sides. Gently lift the aluminum foil off the broiler pan and wrap it around the peppers. Place on a cutting board and let stand for 5 minutes.

2 Using a thin knife, scrape the skin off the peppers and discard. Remove the core, seeds, and ribs; cut the peppers lengthwise into 1-inch-wide strips and rinse them under cold water to remove black bits. Arrange the strips on a platter. In a small bowl, whisk together the vinegar, garlic, salt, black pepper, and oil. Pour the dressing over the peppers and top with the basil, parsley, and, if desired, the capers. Serve with Pork Cutlets in Madeira Sauce (page 145). Serves 6.

PREPARATION TIME: 18 MIN. COOKING TIME: 11 MIN.
STANDING TIME: 5 MIN.

Per serving: Calories 98; Saturated Fat 0 g; Total Fat 3 g; Protein 3 g; Carbohydrate 19 g; Fiber 5 g; Sodium 184 mg; Cholesterol 0 mg

•

Sautéed Variation: Core and seed the peppers and cut lengthwise into ½-inch strips. Omit the vinegar and garlic. Chop *1 medium-size yellow onion.* In a 12-inch skillet, heat the oil over moderate heat. Add the onion and sauté for 3 minutes or until slightly softened. Add the peppers and sauté, stirring, for 5 minutes or until lightly browned and tender but still slightly crisp. Stir in the salt, pepper, and herbs and cook 1 minute more. Serve hot. Serves 6. *Per serving: Calories 107; Saturated Fat 0 g; Total Fat 3 g; Protein 3 g; Carbohydrate 21 g; Fiber 5 g; Sodium 185 mg; Cholesterol 0 mg.*

Peppers — one of Columbus's great discoveries in the New World — are presented here in all their glory as a vibrant Roasted Pepper Mélange.

Potatoes are an excellent source of vitamin C and potassium. When selecting potatoes, choose firm ones; avoid any with skins that are cut or wrinkled. If skins have a greenish tint, the potatoes have been overexposed to light and will have a somewhat bitter taste.

Store potatoes in a dark, ventilated space that is cool (between 45° and 50° F). Do not refrigerate them because temperatures below 40° F turn their starch to sugar. Also, do not store potatoes next to onions; a chemical reaction takes place between the two vegetables that shortens the shelf life of both.

CREAMY MASHED POTATOES

Onions add a wonderful flavor to this low-fat version of a long-time favorite. If you prefer, substitute ¼ cup plain nonfat yogurt for the warm skim milk.

- **4 medium-size all-purpose potatoes (1 ½ pounds), peeled and cubed**
- **1 small yellow onion, finely chopped (½ cup)**
- **⅓ cup warm skim milk**
- **2 teaspoons unsalted butter or margarine**
- **½ teaspoon salt**
- **¼ teaspoon white pepper**

1 In a medium-size saucepan, combine the potatoes and onion with just enough salted water to cover. Bring the water to a boil and simmer, covered, for 15 to 20 minutes or until the potatoes are tender. Drain.

2 In a large bowl, mash the potatoes and onion with a potato masher or force them through a ricer into the bowl. Beat in the milk, butter, salt, and pepper. Serve with Rosemary-Lemon Roast Beef (page 128) and steamed broccoli. Serves 4.

PREPARATION TIME: 8 MIN. COOKING TIME: 21 MIN.

Per serving: Calories 179; Saturated Fat 1 g; Total Fat 2 g; Protein 4 g; Carbohydrate 37 g; Fiber 2 g; Sodium 287 mg; Cholesterol 6 mg

•

Mashed Potatoes au Gratin: Preheat the broiler, setting the rack 6 inches from the heat. Lightly grease a shallow 1-quart flameproof baking dish. In a large bowl, combine the mashed potatoes with *½ cup part-skim ricotta cheese* and *2 tablespoons grated Parmesan cheese*. Transfer the mixture to the prepared baking dish, sprinkle the top with *¼ teaspoon paprika* and *1 tablespoon grated Parmesan cheese*. Dot with *1 teaspoon unsalted butter*. Broil for 1 to 2 minutes or until the top is golden brown. Serves 4. *Per serving: Calories 252; Saturated Fat 4 g; Total Fat 7 g; Protein 9 g; Carbohydrate 39 g; Fiber 2 g; Sodium 412 mg; Cholesterol 22 mg.*

POTATO-CORN PATTIES

This easy recipe turns the potato into a festive dish for company. The mixture can be prepared a day ahead and shaped and baked just before serving. If you serve the patties with a spicy entrée, omit the jalapeño pepper.

- **8 small all-purpose potatoes (1 ½ pounds), peeled and quartered**
- **¼ cup skim milk**
- **1 large egg white**
- **¼ teaspoon each salt and black pepper, or to taste**
- **½ cup fresh or frozen corn kernels**
- **2 green onions, including tops, finely chopped (¼ cup)**
- **1 pickled jalapeño pepper, cored, seeded, and finely chopped (optional)**
- **2 tablespoons all-purpose flour**
- **1 tablespoon unsalted butter or margarine**

1 In a large saucepan of boiling unsalted water, cook the potatoes, covered, over moderately high heat for 12 minutes or until tender; drain well.

2 In a large bowl, using a food mill, electric mixer, or masher, purée the potatoes. (Do not use a food processor or they will be gummy.) Blend in the milk, egg white, salt, and black pepper, then fold in the corn, green onions, and jalapeño pepper if using. Refrigerate for at least 1 hour or until stiff enough to be shaped.

3 Preheat the oven to 300° F. Shape a generous ½ cup of the potato mixture into a disc 3 inches in diameter and ½ inch thick. Repeat until you have 8 patties. Dredge each patty in the flour and shake off the excess. In a 10-inch nonstick skillet, melt 1 ½ teaspoons of the butter over moderate heat. Cook 4 of the patties for 3 minutes on each side or until golden brown. Transfer to a baking sheet and keep warm in the oven. Repeat with the remaining 4 patties and 1 ½ teaspoons of butter. Serve with Chicken in Salsa Marinade (page 104) or Swordfish with Pineapple Salsa (page 95). Makes 8 patties.

PREPARATION TIME: 20 MIN. COOKING TIME: 25 MIN.

CHILLING TIME: 1 HR.

Per patty: Calories 107; Saturated Fat 1 g; Total Fat 2 g; Protein 3 g; Carbohydrate 21 g; Fiber 1 g; Sodium 114 mg; Cholesterol 4 mg

POTATO LOAF

Serve this simple, hearty potato loaf with a roast, or enjoy a slice for lunch accompanied by a green salad.

- ¾ cup low-fat (1% milkfat) cottage cheese
- 8 ounces mushrooms, coarsely chopped (2½ cups)
- ½ cup grated Parmesan cheese
- 6 green onions, including tops, thinly sliced (¾ cup)
- 3 large egg whites
- ⅓ cup plain dry bread crumbs
- ½ teaspoon dried marjoram, crumbled
- ¼ teaspoon each salt and black pepper, or to taste
- 6 medium-size all-purpose potatoes (1½ pounds), peeled and shredded

1 Preheat the oven to 400° F. Grease a 9″ x 5″ x 3″ loaf pan; set aside. In a food processor or blender, purée the cottage cheese for 1 minute or until smooth.

2 In a large bowl, combine the puréed cottage cheese, mushrooms, Parmesan cheese, green onions, egg whites, bread crumbs, marjoram, salt, and pepper. Fold in the potatoes. Transfer the mixture to the prepared loaf pan. Bake for 1 hour 10 minutes or until firm and a cake tester inserted in the center comes out clean. Loosen the sides with a metal spatula and invert onto a serving platter. Serves 6 to 8.

PREPARATION TIME: 15 MIN. COOKING TIME: 1 HR. 10 MIN.

Per serving (for 6): Calories 197; Saturated Fat 2 g; Total Fat 3 g; Protein 12 g; Carbohydrate 30 g; Fiber 2 g; Sodium 435 mg; Cholesterol 8 mg

Two of America's favorite vegetables acquire an appealing and healthy elegance in Potato-Corn Patties, served here with an herb-baked chicken.

POTATOES WITH THYME AND RED WINE

This modern version of a classic recipe is simple to prepare and can be baked right along with a roast or a chicken. If you wish, substitute 1 teaspoon of red wine vinegar and ½ cup chicken stock for the wine.

- 1 tablespoon olive oil
- 4 green onions, including tops, thinly sliced (½ cup)
- 5 medium-size all-purpose potatoes, thinly sliced (2 cups)
- ½ cup Chicken Stock or Vegetable Stock (page 62) or low-sodium chicken broth
- ½ cup dry red wine
- ¾ teaspoon dried thyme, crumbled
- ½ teaspoon salt
- ¼ teaspoon black pepper
- 1 tablespoon grated Parmesan cheese

1 Preheat the oven to 350° F. In a 10-inch nonstick skillet, heat the oil over moderately high heat. Stir in the green onions and potatoes and sauté, stirring constantly, for 2 minutes. Add the stock, wine, thyme, salt, and pepper and cook for 2 to 3 minutes or until the liquid boils.

2 Spoon the potatoes and liquid into a lightly greased 9-inch square baking dish and cover with aluminum foil. Bake for 1 hour. Uncover, sprinkle the top with the cheese, and bake, uncovered, 15 minutes more or until the potatoes are tender. Serve with a roast or Lemon Sole Blanketed in Mushrooms (page 94). Serves 4.

PREPARATION TIME: 12 MIN. COOKING TIME: 1 HR. 20 MIN.

Per serving: Calories 207; Saturated Fat 1 g; Total Fat 4 g; Protein 4 g; Carbohydrate 35 g; Fiber 2 g; Sodium 323 mg; Cholesterol 1 mg

The entertaining is easy when you serve Potatoes with Thyme and Red Wine alongside a bowl of Sautéed Summer Squash and a platter of London broil coated with cracked peppercorns.

SPINACH WITH SESAME-TOFU SAUCE

The sauce for this dish tastes just as creamy as sour cream but has no cholesterol. It can be made in advance and refrigerated for up to 1 week; bring to room temperature before using.

- 4 ounces soft tofu (soybean curd)
- 1 tablespoon plus 1 teaspoon sesame seeds
- 2 tablespoons water
- 1½ tablespoons cider vinegar or white wine vinegar
- 1 teaspoon sugar
- ¼ teaspoon salt
- 2 pounds fresh spinach, stems removed, leaves rinsed well

1 In a food processor or blender, whirl the tofu and 1 tablespoon of the sesame seeds for 1 minute or until the seeds are crushed. Add the water, vinegar, sugar, and salt and whirl 30 seconds longer or until well combined.

2 In a steamer or metal colander set over a large saucepan of boiling water, steam the spinach for about 3 minutes or until wilted. Drain and transfer to a serving dish. Spoon the sesame-tofu sauce over the spinach and sprinkle with the remaining teaspoon of sesame seeds. Serve with broiled fish or chicken and rice. Serves 4.

PREPARATION TIME: 7 MIN. COOKING TIME: 3 MIN.

Per serving: Calories 91; Saturated Fat 0 g; Total Fat 3 g; Protein 9 g; Carbohydrate 11 g; Fiber 7 g; Sodium 315 mg; Cholesterol 0 mg

SAUTÉED SUMMER SQUASH

The squash of summer and radishes combine here to create a colorful, crunchy vegetable dish that beautifully complements almost any type of entrée. You can also prepare this recipe with the squash sliced or cut in sticks instead of shredded; omit Step 1 and sauté the squash for 4 minutes instead of 2.

- 2 small yellow squash (8 ounces), shredded
- 2 small zucchini (8 ounces), shredded
- ¼ teaspoon salt
- 1 tablespoon unsalted butter or margarine
- 2 cloves garlic, minced
- 1 bunch (about 12 medium-size) radishes, thinly sliced
- 1 tablespoon lemon juice
- ¼ teaspoon black pepper
- ¼ cup minced parsley
- 2 tablespoons minced fresh mint or basil or 2 teaspoons mint flakes or dried basil, crumbled

1 Place the yellow squash and zucchini in a colander and sprinkle with the salt. Let drain for 15 minutes, then press out the excess water.

2 In a 10-inch nonstick skillet, melt the butter over moderately high heat. Stir in the garlic and radishes and sauté, stirring constantly, for 1 minute. Add the yellow squash, zucchini, lemon juice, and pepper and sauté another 2 minutes, stirring constantly, until the vegetables are hot but still crunchy. Stir in the parsley and mint and cook 30 seconds more. Serve with London broil. Serves 4.

PREPARATION TIME: 20 MIN. COOKING TIME: 4 MIN.

Per serving: Calories 57; Saturated Fat 2 g; Total Fat 4 g; Protein 2 g; Carbohydrate 7 g; Fiber 3 g; Sodium 146 mg; Cholesterol 8 mg

Braising vegetables brings out their natural sweetness and coats them with a rich glaze. Some ideal candidates for braising are carrots, turnips, fennel, and celery.

To prepare vegetables for braising, trim, peel, and cut them to a uniform size. Next, sauté them (cook quickly over moderate to high heat) with 1 to 3 teaspoons of oil in a nonstick saucepan or skillet for 2 to 5 minutes. For each pound of vegetables, add 1 cup of stock or water plus garlic, herbs, spices, and other flavorings such as orange or ginger if desired. Lower the heat and simmer, covered, for 15 to 25 minutes or until tender. Transfer the vegetables to a warm serving dish and boil the liquid remaining in the pan until slightly thickened; pour it over the vegetables.

For a casual evening by the fireside, cozy up with Sweet Potato Pancakes, Sweet-and-Sour Swiss Chard, and Pot Roast, New Orleans Style (page 128).

PURÉED SQUASH WITH ORANGE AND CINNAMON

1 medium-size butternut squash, peeled, seeded, and cut into 1-inch cubes (5 to 6 cups)
1 cinnamon stick, cracked
3 strips orange rind
¼ teaspoon salt
1 teaspoon grated orange rind
⅛ teaspoon each ground cinnamon and white pepper

1 In a large saucepan, combine the squash, cinnamon stick, orange peel strips, and ⅛ teaspoon of the salt. Add enough boiling water to just cover the squash, and simmer, covered, for 12 to 15 minutes or until the squash is tender. Drain in a colander, discarding the cinnamon stick and orange rind.

2 In a food processor or blender, whirl the squash for 1 minute or until smooth. Add the remaining ⅛ teaspoon of salt, grated orange rind, ground cinnamon, and pepper and purée an additional minute or until the ingredients are well combined. Transfer to a warm serving dish. Serve with roast pork, turkey, or chicken and steamed broccoli. Serves 4.

PREPARATION TIME: 10 MIN. COOKING TIME: 12 MIN.

Per serving: Calories 114; Saturated Fat 0 g; Total Fat 0 g; Protein 3 g; Carbohydrate 30 g; Fiber 5 g; Sodium 145 mg; Cholesterol 0 mg

SWEET POTATOES ROASTED WITH GARLIC

In this versatile recipe, any kind of potato can be used, and the garlic, which becomes mellow with roasting, can be squeezed from its skin and eaten right alongside. If you prefer, peel and slice the garlic cloves and add them to the pan during the last 15 minutes of roasting.

2 tablespoons olive oil
6 cloves garlic, unpeeled
4 medium-size sweet potatoes, yams, or all-purpose potatoes (1 ½ pounds), peeled and cut into 1-inch cubes
2 teaspoons dried rosemary, crumbled
¼ teaspoon salt, or to taste

1 Preheat the oven to 450° F. In a small roasting pan, combine the oil and garlic and heat in the oven for 5 minutes. Add the potatoes and rosemary and turn to coat well with the oil. Roast the potatoes, turning them frequently, for 35 minutes or until tender and brown on all sides. Sprinkle with the salt. Serve with grilled chicken or turkey and steamed spinach. Serves 4.

PREPARATION TIME: 7 MIN. COOKING TIME: 40 MIN.

Per serving: Calories 186; Saturated Fat 1 g; Total Fat 7 g; Protein 2 g; Carbohydrate 30 g; Fiber 3 g; Sodium 147 mg; Cholesterol 0 mg

SWEET POTATO PANCAKES

Sweet potatoes and carrots are perfect partners. When shredded and fried, they create a terrific-tasting, healthful alternative to home fries.

- 2 **large eggs**
- ½ **teaspoon salt, or to taste**
- 3 **green onions, slivered or sliced (⅓ cup)**
- 2 **tablespoons minced parsley**
- 2 **tablespoons minced fresh basil, or 2 teaspoons dried basil, crumbled**
- 2 **small sweet potatoes, peeled and shredded (3 cups)**
- 2 **medium-size carrots, peeled and shredded (1 cup)**
- 3 **tablespoons all-purpose flour**
- 3 **teaspoons olive or canola oil**

1 Preheat the oven to 200° F. In a large bowl, beat together the eggs and salt. Add the green onions, parsley, basil, sweet potatoes, carrots, and flour and toss until well combined.

2 In a 12-inch nonstick skillet, heat 1 teaspoon of the oil over low heat for 2 minutes. For each pancake, drop 2 tablespoons of the sweet potato—carrot mixture into the skillet, then use a spatula to flatten it slightly to about 3 inches in diameter and ¼ inch thick. Make 4 pancakes at a time and cook for 3 to 4 minutes on each side or until golden brown. Transfer to a baking sheet and keep warm in the oven. Repeat with the remaining oil and sweet potato—carrot mixture until you have 12 pancakes. Serve with roast pork or poultry. Serves 4.

PREPARATION TIME: 15 MIN. COOKING TIME: 25 MIN.

Per pancake: Calories 69; Saturated Fat 0 g; Total Fat 2 g; Protein 2 g; Carbohydrate 11 g; Fiber 1 g; Sodium 107 mg; Cholesterol 36 mg

SWEET-AND-SOUR SWISS CHARD

Nothing need be discarded when cooking with Swiss chard because both its stems and leaves are edible. Rich in beta carotene, this dish can be prepared ahead and the leaves added just before serving. If you add them sooner, they will discolor from the acid in the vinegar.

- 1 **pound Swiss chard, rinsed and patted dry**
- 2 **teaspoons olive oil**
- 1 **medium-size yellow onion, quartered and sliced**
- ¼ **cup raisins**
- 2 **cloves garlic, minced**
- 3 **tablespoons cider vinegar or white vinegar**
- 1½ **teaspoons sugar**
- ½ **teaspoon salt**
- ¼ **teaspoon black pepper**

1 Slice the Swiss chard leaves into 1-inch strips and set aside. Slice the stems diagonally ¾ inch long. In a medium-size skillet, heat the oil over moderate heat. Add the onion and cook, covered, for 5 minutes or until softened. Add the Swiss chard stems, raisins, garlic, vinegar, sugar, salt, and pepper and cook, covered, for 8 minutes. Place the leaves on top of the mixture (do not stir in), cover, and cook for 2 minutes. Remove from the heat and stir. Serve with grilled chicken and roasted potatoes or steamed rice. Serves 4.

PREPARATION TIME: 10 MIN. COOKING TIME: 15 MIN.

Per serving: Calories 89; Saturated Fat 0 g; Total Fat 3 g; Protein 3 g; Carbohydrate 18 g; Fiber 3 g; Sodium 509 mg; Cholesterol 0 mg

SOUTHWESTERN STEWED TOMATOES

These zesty, Santa Fe—style stewed tomatoes bear no resemblance to the canned variety. Make a double batch at the end of the season with the ripest tomatoes you can find; they'll keep frozen at 0° F for up to 3 months, providing a fresh, summery side dish to liven up winter entrées. If you like spicy food, add more jalapeño pepper.

- 1 tablespoon olive oil
- 3 cloves garlic, minced
- 1 small sweet green pepper, cored, seeded, and chopped (½ cup)
- 1 teaspoon chopped jalapeño pepper
- ¼ cup water
- 4 medium-size tomatoes (2 pounds), peeled, seeded, and cut into eighths
- ¼ teaspoon salt, or to taste
- 3 tablespoons minced fresh basil or 1 teaspoon dried basil, crumbled

1 In a 12-inch nonstick skillet, heat the oil over low heat. Add the garlic and cook, stirring, for 2 minutes. Add the green and jalapeño peppers and cook, stirring frequently, for 5 minutes. Add the water and cook, stirring occasionally, for 4 minutes or until the peppers soften. Stir in the tomatoes, salt, and basil, raise the heat to moderately high, and cook for 5 minutes or until the mixture is thick but the tomatoes still have some shape. If the tomatoes seem too dry, add more water. Serve with Beef, Bulgur, and Spinach Loaf (page 136). Makes 2 cups.

PREPARATION TIME: 20 MIN. COOKING TIME: 16 MIN.

Per ½ cup: Calories 86; Saturated Fat 1 g; Total Fat 4 g; Protein 2 g; Carbohydrate 12 g; Fiber 3 g; Sodium 166 mg; Cholesterol 0 mg

BROILED TOMATOES

This super-quick recipe turns the ordinary tomato into an elegant side dish for poultry, meat, or fish.

- ⅓ cup fresh basil leaves, minced, or 1½ teaspoons dried basil, crumbled
- ¼ cup parsley leaves, minced
- ¼ cup plain dry bread crumbs
- 2 cloves garlic, minced
- ¼ teaspoon salt, or to taste
- 1 tablespoon olive oil
- 4 medium-size tomatoes, halved horizontally

1 Preheat the broiler, setting the rack 6 inches from the heat. Line the broiler pan with a sheet of aluminum foil. In a small bowl, stir together the basil, parsley, bread crumbs, garlic, salt, and oil.

2 Place the tomato halves, cut sides up, on the prepared broiler pan and broil for 2 minutes. Top with the basil-crumb mixture and broil 3 minutes longer or until the topping is crisp and the tomatoes are hot. Serves 4.

PREPARATION TIME: 10 MIN. COOKING TIME: 5 MIN.

Per serving: Calories 85; Saturated Fat 1 g; Total Fat 4 g; Protein 2 g; Carbohydrate 11 g; Fiber 2 g; Sodium 194 mg; Cholesterol 0 mg

VEGETABLE KEBABS

Lightly seasoned new potatoes, zucchini, and summer squash are wonderful when broiled; in the summer consider grilling them alongside fish or poultry. If pressed for time, you can substitute 2 tablespoons of your favorite low-fat Italian dressing for the vinaigrette.

12 small or 6 medium-size new potatoes (12 ounces), scrubbed

1 medium-size zucchini (about 6 ounces), sliced ¾ inch thick (8 slices)

1 medium-size yellow squash (about 6 ounces), sliced ¾ inch thick (8 slices)

1 tablespoon plus 1 teaspoon olive oil

2 teaspoons red wine vinegar

½ teaspoon dried thyme, crumbled

¼ teaspoon each salt and black pepper, or to taste

1 Bring a stockpot of unsalted water to a boil. (If using medium-size potatoes, cut them in half.) Add the potatoes and cook for 12 to 15 minutes or until almost tender when pricked with a fork. Drain, rinse under cold water to stop the cooking, and drain again.

2 Meanwhile, place the zucchini and yellow squash slices in a bowl of cold water and let them stand for 10 minutes. Drain and pat dry with paper toweling. Arrange the potatoes, zucchini, and yellow squash alternately on four 8-inch-long skewers. The skewers may be covered and refrigerated for up to 5 hours.

3 Preheat the broiler, setting the rack 6 inches from the heat, or preheat a gas grill to high, or prepare charcoal to the white ash stage. In a small bowl, whisk together the oil, vinegar, thyme, salt, and pepper. Using a pastry brush, brush the mixture on the vegetables. Broil or grill the kebabs, turning occasionally, for 12 minutes or until browned on the edges and the squash are crisp-tender. Serves 4.

PREPARATION TIME: 10 MIN.   COOKING TIME: 25 MIN.
STANDING TIME: 10 MIN.

Per serving: Calories 128; Saturated Fat 1 g; Total Fat 5 g; Protein 2 g; Carbohydrate 20 g; Fiber 2 g; Sodium 139 mg; Cholesterol 0 mg

•

Pepper Variation: Substitute for the zucchini and yellow squash *1 small sweet green pepper, 1 small sweet yellow pepper, and 1 small sweet red pepper, cored, seeded, and cut into 1½-inch squares.* Omit the cold-water soak in Step 2. *Per serving: Calories 124; Saturated Fat 1 g; Total Fat 5 g; Protein 2 g; Carbohydrate 21 g; Fiber 2 g; Sodium 139 mg; Cholesterol 0 mg.*

No matter how you slice them, tomatoes come up a winner. Sweet and hot peppers spice up Southwestern Stewed Tomatoes, served here with Crispy Baked Fish (page 84) and potatoes roasted with garlic (for recipe, see sweet potato version, page 240).

BROILED VEGETABLE MÉLANGE

Here is an easy way to turn the best of summer into a nutritious and colorful feast. Serve these as an appetizer or side dish or make a delectable sandwich with them, adding thin slices of mozzarella or some goat cheese if you wish. The vegetables can also be cooked on a grill if you put the cherry tomatoes on skewers.

1 small eggplant (8 ounces), halved lengthwise, then cut crosswise ¾ inch thick
1 medium-size zucchini (6 ounces), halved lengthwise, then cut crosswise into 8 pieces
1 large sweet red or green pepper, cored, seeded, and cut into strips 1 ½ inches wide
8 cherry tomatoes
1 tablespoon lemon juice
2 teaspoons olive oil
1 clove garlic, crushed
½ teaspoon each dried thyme and oregano, crumbled
¼ teaspoon each salt and black pepper, or to taste

1 Preheat the broiler, setting the rack about 8 inches from the heat. Grease a shallow baking pan. Arrange the eggplant, zucchini, red pepper, and tomatoes in the pan. In a small bowl, whisk together the lemon juice, oil, garlic, thyme, oregano, salt, and black pepper and brush the mixture over the vegetables.

2 Broil the vegetables for 4 to 5 minutes on each side or until they are tender and golden brown. Remove the tomatoes after 5 minutes. Serve with Red Snapper with Black Beans (page 94). Serves 4.

PREPARATION TIME: 15 MIN. COOKING TIME: 8 MIN.

Per serving: Calories 75; Saturated Fat 0 g; Total Fat 3 g; Protein 2 g; Carbohydrate 13 g; Fiber 3 g; Sodium 143 mg; Cholesterol 0 mg

VEGETABLE MEDLEY STIR-FRY

½ cup orange juice, Chicken Stock (page 62), or low-sodium chicken broth
1 teaspoon cornstarch
2 teaspoons honey
2 teaspoons reduced-sodium soy sauce
2 teaspoons rice vinegar or white wine vinegar
¼ teaspoon hot red pepper sauce
1 teaspoon each olive and dark sesame oil
4 small carrots, peeled and thinly sliced diagonally (2 cups)
1 large sweet red pepper (8 ounces), cut into strips ¼ inch wide
1 medium-size yellow onion, halved and thinly sliced (2 cups)
8 ounces Chinese cabbage (about 5 large leaves), halved lengthwise and sliced ½ inch thick
4 ounces snow peas or sugar snap peas, trimmed
1 teaspoon toasted sesame seeds (optional)

1 In a small bowl, stir together the orange juice and cornstarch until well blended. Add the honey, soy sauce, vinegar, and red pepper sauce, stirring to combine.

2 In a large wok or 12-inch nonstick skillet, heat the olive oil and sesame oil over moderately high heat until hot but not smoking. Add the carrots, sweet red pepper, and onion and stir-fry for 8 minutes. Add the cabbage and snow peas and stir-fry for 2 minutes. Stir in the orange juice mixture and cook for 1 minute or until the sauce boils and thickens. Stir in the sesame seeds if desired. Serve with grilled poultry or fish and brown rice. Serves 4.

PREPARATION TIME: 20 MIN. COOKING TIME: 12 MIN.

Per serving: Calories 123; Saturated Fat 0 g; Total Fat 3 g; Protein 3 g; Carbohydrate 23 g; Fiber 5 g; Sodium 110 mg; Cholesterol 0 mg

SALADS

Salads are a boon to a busy person who wants to eat healthfully. Most can
be prepared in minutes and with ingredients that today are plentiful and varied the year
around. The only drawback is the classic dressing, which typically contains 3
parts of oil to 1 part vinegar. The dressings in this chapter solve this dilemma for you.
Stocks and juices have been substituted for part of the oil. Some recipes
incorporate buttermilk or low-fat yogurt or mayonnaise. So you can enjoy salads with
maximum flavor and minimal fat. Bear in mind that the more flavorful
your vinegar, the less dressing you need (see recipes for flavored vinegars on page 288).
And remember that dressings are not just for salads; you can brush our
low-calorie versions on broiled fish or chicken, or drizzle a little on a baked potato or
steamed vegetables to add pizzazz to these simply prepared foods.

A **salad is anything** you make it. Spinach, lettuce, watercress, arugula, chicory, and other greens are some obvious ingredients, but whole or cut-up vegetables or fruits, sprouts, olives, nuts and seeds, pasta or other grains, herbs, and even flower blossoms are excellent in salads too. Grilled chicken or fish, small marinated shrimp or scallops, thin strips of steak or smoked ham, cooked beans, chunks of tofu, or wedges of cheese or hard-cooked eggs turn a simple salad into a meal.

When selecting ingredients, strive for contrasting flavors, textures, and colors and match them with the right dressing. Use mild vinaigrettes for delicate greens and fruits and more intense dressings for robust ingredients such as winter vegetables, grains, and meats.

SPICED ORANGE CHICKEN SALAD

Serve this wonderful one-dish meal slightly warm, or prepare ahead and chill—either way, it's terrific.

- 4 small red-skin potatoes, scrubbed (1 pound)
- 1½ cups orange juice
- 1 tablespoon grated fresh ginger or 1 teaspoon ground ginger
- ½ teaspoon ground cumin
- 1 clove garlic, crushed
- 2 whole skinned and boned chicken breasts, halved (8 ounces each)
- 4 small carrots, peeled and cut into matchstick strips 2 inches long
- 2 tablespoons raspberry vinegar or cider vinegar
- ¼ teaspoon salt
- 2 tablespoons minced parsley or fresh cilantro (coriander)
- 1 small head red-leaf lettuce or escarole, rinsed and patted dry
- Orange slices (optional garnish)

1 Bring a medium-size saucepan of water to a boil. Add the potatoes, cover, and cook for 13 to 14 minutes or until tender. Drain and rinse under cold water; drain again. Halve, then slice ¼ inch thick.

2 Meanwhile, in a 10-inch skillet, bring the orange juice, ginger, cumin, and garlic to a boil. Add the chicken, lower the heat, cover, and simmer for 3 to 4 minutes. Turn the chicken over, cover, and simmer 3 to 4 minutes more or until the juices run clear when the flesh is pricked with a fork. With a slotted spoon, transfer the chicken to a cutting board. Add the carrots to the simmering juice, cover, and cook for 3 minutes. With a slotted spoon, transfer the carrots to a plate to cool. Remove the skillet from the heat and stir in the vinegar, salt, and parsley.

3 Cut the chicken into ½-inch strips. Arrange the lettuce on 4 individual plates, then arrange the potatoes, chicken, and carrots on top and spoon some of the dressing over each salad. Garnish with the orange slices if desired. Serve with warm crusty bread. Serves 4.

PREPARATION TIME: 20 MIN. COOKING TIME: 15 MIN.

Per serving: Calories 265; Saturated Fat 0 g; Total Fat 2 g; Protein 30 g; Carbohydrate 33 g; Fiber 4 g; Sodium 239 mg; Cholesterol 66 mg

CHICKEN AND WATERCRESS SALAD

A fresh tomato vinaigrette complements mellow chicken and the peppery flavor of watercress. You can also use pork or swordfish instead of chicken, adjusting the cooking time as needed.

For the salad:
- 1 teaspoon dried oregano, crumbled
- ½ teaspoon each ground coriander and cumin
- ¼ teaspoon salt
- 2 whole skinned and boned chicken breasts, halved (8 ounces each)
- 1 large bunch watercress, rinsed and large stems removed

For the dressing:
- 1 clove garlic, peeled
- 2 teaspoons red wine vinegar
- 2 teaspoons olive oil
- ¼ teaspoon each ground coriander and cumin and dried oregano, crumbled
- ¼ teaspoon salt
- 1 medium-size tomato, peeled, seeded, and finely chopped (¾ cup)

1 To prepare the salad: Preheat the broiler, setting the rack 6 inches from the heat. In a small bowl, combine the oregano, coriander, cumin, and salt. Rub the chicken breasts with the spice mixture and arrange them on a broiler pan. Broil on each side for 4 to 5 minutes or until lightly browned and the juices run clear when the flesh is pricked with a fork. When the chicken breasts are cool enough to handle, slice them diagonally into ½-inch strips, transfer them to a large bowl, and add the watercress.

2 To prepare the dressing: Drop the garlic into a small saucepan of boiling water and blanch for 2 minutes; drain and rinse under cold water, then mince. In a small bowl, whisk together the vinegar, oil, coriander, cumin, oregano, and salt. Whisk in the tomato and garlic. Pour the dressing over the chicken and watercress and toss until coated. Serves 4.

PREPARATION TIME: 15 MIN. COOKING TIME: 10 MIN.

Per serving: Calories 156; Saturated Fat 1 g; Total Fat 4 g; Protein 27 g; Carbohydrate 2 g; Fiber 1 g; Sodium 224 mg; Cholesterol 66 mg

TURKEY AND SWEET POTATO SALAD

For a no-fuss lunch or supper the day after Thanksgiving (or anytime), serve this savory main-dish salad.

3 tablespoons red currant jelly

½ cup Chicken Stock (page 62) or low-sodium chicken broth

1 tablespoon lemon juice

1 tablespoon olive oil

½ teaspoon dried rosemary or savory, crumbled, or poultry seasoning

¼ teaspoon salt, or to taste

12 ounces cooked turkey, cut into ¾-inch cubes (3 cups)

1 large cooked sweet potato, peeled and cut into ¾-inch cubes (2 cups)

1 cup frozen corn kernels, rinsed under hot water and drained

2 green onions, including tops, thinly sliced (¼ cup)

8 romaine or red leaf lettuce leaves (optional)

1 In a small saucepan, warm the jelly and stock over moderate heat for 2 minutes or until the jelly has melted. Whisk in the lemon juice, oil, rosemary, and salt.

2 In a large bowl, combine the turkey, sweet potato, corn, and green onions. Add the dressing and toss until well coated. Place 2 lettuce leaves on each individual plate if desired, and spoon the salad on top. Serves 4.

PREPARATION TIME: 16 MIN.   COOKING TIME: 2 MIN.

Per serving: Calories 410; Saturated Fat 1 g; Total Fat 7 g; Protein 30 g; Carbohydrate 59 g; Fiber 6 g; Sodium 229 mg; Cholesterol 59 mg

SEASIDE SUPPER

Fresh Tuna Salad

Herbed Spiral Bread
(page 300)

Honey-Peach Cup
(page 317)

Macaroon Cupcakes
(page 323)

SEAFOOD SALAD PRIMAVERA

Tender scallops and young vegetables make a refreshing salad to serve anytime. In spring, use the first slender asparagus and baby squash instead of broccoli and green beans. The pasta, vegetables, and seafood can be prepared and refrigerated up to 8 hours ahead. Toss them with the Sweet Red Pepper Sauce just before serving.

12 ounces pasta twists, penne, or medium-size pasta shells

4 ounces green beans, trimmed and cut into 1½-inch lengths (1 cup)

1½ cups broccoli florets

1 small yellow summer squash, sliced ¼ inch thick (1¼ cups)

1 pound sea scallops or shelled and deveined shrimp or a combination

1 cup Sweet Red Pepper Sauce (page 272)

Grated Parmesan cheese (optional)

1 In a large saucepan of boiling unsalted water, cook the pasta over moderately high heat for 5 minutes. Add the green beans and broccoli and cook another 2 minutes. Add the squash and seafood and cook 2 to 3 minutes more or until the seafood is opaque and the vegetables are crisp-tender. Drain, rinse with cold water to stop the cooking, and drain again. Transfer to a large bowl. Pour the sauce over the salad and toss well. If desired, sprinkle the cheese on each serving. Serves 4 to 6.

PREPARATION TIME: 15 MIN. COOKING TIME: 10 MIN.

Per serving (for 4): Calories 487; Saturated Fat 0 g; Total Fat 4 g; Protein 33 g; Carbohydrate 79 g; Fiber 4 g; Sodium 249 mg; Cholesterol 37 mg

SWEET-AND-SOUR THAI SHRIMP SALAD

Coconut and lime juice balance the spicy bite of crushed red pepper in this summer cooler. Match it with Confetti Rice Salad (page 253) and Green Bean Salad, Oriental Style (page 258) for a dazzling buffet or picnic supper.

1½ tablespoons olive oil

¼ teaspoon crushed red pepper flakes, or to taste

¼ cup bottled clam juice

2 tablespoons lime juice

12 ounces peeled and deveined medium-size shrimp

1 small head savoy cabbage or iceberg lettuce, shredded (4 cups)

1 large carrot, peeled and grated (1 cup)

4 ounces bean sprouts (1 cup)

3 tablespoons unsalted dry-roasted peanuts

3 tablespoons flaked sweetened coconut

1 green onion, including top, thinly sliced

1 Bring a large saucepan of unsalted water to a boil. Meanwhile, in a small saucepan, heat the oil over low heat. Add the red pepper flakes and cook, swirling occasionally, for 3 minutes. Strain the oil into a small bowl and whisk in the clam and lime juices; set the dressing aside.

2 Drop the shrimp into the boiling water, lower the heat, and simmer for 2 minutes or until the shrimp turn opaque. Drain the shrimp and rinse under cold water to stop the cooking, then drain well. Transfer the shrimp to a large bowl and add the cabbage, carrot, bean sprouts, peanuts, coconut, and green onion. Pour the dressing over the salad and toss to coat. Serves 4.

PREPARATION TIME: 20 MIN. COOKING TIME: 5 MIN.

Per serving: Calories 210; Saturated Fat 3 g; Total Fat 9 g; Protein 21 g; Carbohydrate 12 g; Fiber 3 g; Sodium 190 mg; Cholesterol 130 mg

FRESH TUNA SALAD

Tuna and capers are natural partners in this hearty salad. You can find capers, the unopened buds of a Mediterranean shrub, in the specialty food section of most supermarkets. Use them to lend a piquant, slightly salty flavor to seafood and chicken.

For the salad:
- 4 small red-skin potatoes, peeled and cut into eighths (about 2 cups)
- 6 ounces green beans, trimmed and cut into 1½-inch lengths (2 cups)
- 2 tuna steaks (8 ounces each), about 1 inch thick
- 1 small yellow onion, finely chopped (½ cup)
- 12 yellow or red cherry tomatoes or 1 medium-size tomato, seeded and cubed (about 1 cup)
- 2 tablespoons snipped fresh dill
- 2 teaspoons capers, rinsed, drained, and chopped

For the dressing:
- 2 tablespoons white wine vinegar
- 1 teaspoon Dijon mustard
- 1 clove garlic, minced
- ¼ teaspoon each salt and black pepper
- 1 tablespoon olive oil

1 In a large saucepan of boiling unsalted water, cook the potatoes for 1 minute over moderately high heat. Add the green beans and cook 6 minutes more or until tender. Set aside 3 tablespoons of the cooking liquid and drain the vegetables. Rinse the vegetables under cold water to stop the cooking and drain again.

2 To prepare the dressing: In a small bowl, combine the vinegar, mustard, garlic, salt, and pepper. Whisk in the reserved cooking liquid and then the oil. Or put all the dressing ingredients in a small jar, cover tightly, and shake until well blended.

3 Meanwhile, preheat the broiler, setting the rack 6 inches from the heat. Arrange the tuna steaks on a broiler pan, brush both sides of each steak with some of the dressing, and broil for 4 to 5 minutes on each side or until the fish flakes easily when tested with a fork. Transfer the tuna to a cutting board and allow to cool slightly.

4 In a large bowl, combine the potatoes, green beans, onion, tomatoes, dill, and capers. Cut the tuna into 1-inch cubes and add it to the bowl. Add the remaining dressing and gently toss to combine. Serves 4.

PREPARATION TIME: 22 MIN. COOKING TIME: 15 MIN.

Per serving: Calories 287; Saturated Fat 2 g; Total Fat 9 g; Protein 29 g; Carbohydrate 22 g; Fiber 3 g; Sodium 276 mg; Cholesterol 43 mg

Sweet-and-Sour Thai Shrimp Salad comes from the South Seas—but you can make it at home in just 25 minutes.

A **simple dressing,** such as a vinaigrette, can be greatly enhanced by whisking a crushed garlic clove or a minced shallot into the vinegar and oil; and the need for salt is lessened because of their intense flavors.

If the raw flavor of these bulbs is not to your taste, you can soften the effect by blanching. Simply drop a peeled whole garlic clove or shallot into boiling water for 2 to 3 minutes. Drain, rinse under cold water, and drain again.

ORZO SALAD WITH ARTICHOKE HEARTS

Combine sunny lemon juice, creamy feta cheese, and black olives for pasta salad "à la Grecque," or Greek style. Other small pasta shapes and green vegetables can be substituted for the orzo and artichokes.

For the salad:
- 1 cup orzo
- 1 package (9 ounces) frozen artichoke hearts
- 2 medium-size tomatoes, seeded and coarsely chopped (2 cups)
- 1 small red onion, finely chopped (½ cup)
- 2 ounces feta cheese, crumbled (½ cup)
- 8 pitted black olives, sliced (¼ cup)
- Fresh dill sprigs (optional garnish)

For the dressing:
- 2 tablespoons lemon juice
- 1 tablespoon olive oil
- 1 teaspoon Dijon mustard
- 2 tablespoons snipped fresh dill
- ¼ teaspoon each salt and black pepper, or to taste

1 In a large saucepan of boiling unsalted water, cook the orzo for 6 minutes over moderately high heat. Add the artichoke hearts and cook, stirring occasionally, 3 to 4 minutes more or until the pasta and artichoke hearts are tender. Drain, rinse with cold water, and drain again. Transfer to a large salad bowl and add the tomatoes, onion, cheese, and olives.

2 Meanwhile, prepare the dressing. In a small bowl, whisk together the lemon juice, oil, mustard, dill, salt, and pepper. Or put all the ingredients in a small jar with a tight-fitting lid and shake vigorously.

3 Pour the dressing over the salad and toss gently until well coated. If desired, garnish each serving with sprigs of fresh dill. Serves 4 to 6.

PREPARATION TIME: 18 MIN. COOKING TIME: 10 MIN.

Per serving (for 4): Calories 303; Saturated Fat 3 g; Total Fat 8 g; Protein 9 g; Carbohydrate 51 g; Fiber 2 g; Sodium 468 mg; Cholesterol 12 mg

It takes just a few black olives and sun-dried tomatoes to enhance this simple Pasta Salad with Italian Green Beans and Mushrooms.

PASTA SALAD WITH ITALIAN GREEN BEANS AND MUSHROOMS

2 tablespoons olive oil
6 ounces mushrooms, trimmed and quartered (2¼ cups)
12 medium-size pitted black olives (¼ cup), halved
¼ cup sun-dried tomatoes in oil, rinsed, patted dry, and coarsely chopped
8 ounces bow-tie or medium-size shell pasta

1 package (9 ounces) frozen Italian green beans or cut green or wax beans, thawed
2 tablespoons red wine vinegar
1 teaspoon Dijon mustard
½ teaspoon each dried oregano and marjoram, crumbled

1 In a 10-inch nonstick skillet, heat 1 tablespoon of the oil over high heat. Add the mushrooms and sauté, stirring frequently, for 5 minutes or until the mushrooms have softened and are lightly colored. Transfer to a large salad bowl and add the olives and sun-dried tomatoes.

2 In a large saucepan of boiling unsalted water, cook the pasta for 10 minutes or until tender but still firm to the bite. During the last 5 minutes of cooking, add the green beans. Drain, rinse under cold water, and drain again. Transfer to the salad bowl.

3 Meanwhile, in a small bowl, whisk together the vinegar, mustard, oregano, marjoram, and remaining 1 tablespoon of oil. Or put all the ingredients in a small jar with a tight-fitting lid and shake vigorously. Pour the dressing over the salad and toss until well coated. Serve at room temperature. Serves 4.

PREPARATION TIME: 10 MIN. COOKING TIME: 15 MIN.

Per serving: Calories 347; Saturated Fat 1 g; Total Fat 9 g; Protein 11 g; Carbohydrate 59 g; Fiber 2 g; Sodium 136 mg; Cholesterol 0 mg

COUSCOUS-VEGETABLE SALAD WITH CREAMY DILL DRESSING

If you prefer, you can make this salad with 1½ cups of cooked bulgur, rice, or orzo instead of couscous. The optional blue cheese garnish will add 3 grams of protein, 5 grams of fat, and 198 milligrams of sodium.

For the dressing:
1 clove garlic, sliced
1 tablespoon olive oil
1 tablespoon white wine vinegar or cider vinegar
1 tablespoon snipped fresh dill or 1 teaspoon dill weed
¼ cup plain low-fat yogurt
¾ teaspoon salt
6 drops hot red pepper sauce

For the salad:
½ cup couscous
1 large sweet green pepper, cored, seeded, and diced (1 cup)
1 medium-size stalk celery, diced (½ cup)
1 medium-size tomato, diced (1 cup)
6 radishes, sliced (¾ cup)
2 cups torn romaine lettuce
2 ounces blue cheese, crumbled (optional)

1 To prepare the dressing: In a food processor or blender, whirl the garlic, oil, vinegar, dill, yogurt, salt, and red pepper sauce until blended. Or mince the garlic and place it in a jar with the remaining dressing ingredients, cover tightly, and shake until well combined.

2 To prepare the salad: Cook the couscous according to package directions — about 5 minutes — then fluff with a fork. Transfer to a large bowl, add the pepper, celery, tomato, radishes, and dressing, and toss together.

3 Arrange the lettuce on individual serving plates, place the couscous mixture on top, and sprinkle with the blue cheese if desired. Serve with grilled lamb. Serves 4.

PREPARATION TIME: 20 MIN. COOKING TIME: 5 MIN.

Per serving: Calories 144; Saturated Fat 1 g; Total Fat 4 g; Protein 5 g; Carbohydrate 23 g; Fiber 5 g; Sodium 431 mg; Cholesterol 0 mg

VIVA ITALIA BUFFET

Bruschetta
(page 311)

Orzo Salad with Artichoke Hearts

Ricotta, Basil, and Pine Nut Loaf
(page 182)

Bread Sticks

Green and Red Grapes

Sparkling Spring Water

Take Panzanella on your next picnic. The toasted bread and diced vegetables, dressed with a light vinaigrette, are an immensely practical, portable, and pleasing salad.

BARLEY, CORN, AND LIMA BEAN SALAD

Here is a festive fall salad that will go equally well with beef, pork, or poultry.

2 teaspoons olive or canola oil

1 large yellow onion, coarsely chopped (1 ½ cups)

1 cup frozen lima beans

1 clove garlic, minced

½ teaspoon dried thyme, crumbled

2 tablespoons water

1 cup fresh or frozen corn kernels

1 ½ cups cooked pearl barley

½ teaspoon salt, or to taste

Pinch ground red pepper (cayenne)

2 tablespoons rice vinegar or cider vinegar

½ cup cherry tomatoes, quartered (optional)

1 In a 10-inch nonstick skillet, heat the oil over moderate heat. Add the onion and sauté for 5 minutes or until softened. Stir in the lima beans, garlic, thyme, and water. Lower the heat and simmer, covered, for 6 minutes. Stir in the corn and simmer, covered, for 2 minutes.

2 Stir in the barley, salt, and red pepper and cook, stirring, for 2 to 3 minutes or until heated through. Remove from the heat and stir in the vinegar. Add the tomatoes if desired. Marinate in the refrigerator for at least 4 hours before serving. Serves 4.

PREPARATION TIME: 15 MIN. COOKING TIME: 15 MIN.

MARINATING TIME: 4 HR.

Per serving: Calories 192; Saturated Fat 0 g; Total Fat 3 g; Protein 6 g; Carbohydrate 39 g; Fiber 7 g; Sodium 295 mg; Cholesterol 0 mg

CONFETTI RICE SALAD

Perfect for a picnic, this colorful salad also makes a great accompaniment to ribs or chicken at a backyard barbecue. To turn it into a main-dish salad, add 1 ½ cups diced Cheddar or Jarlsberg cheese or cooked chicken or pork.

For the dressing:
- 2 tablespoons white wine vinegar
- 1 teaspoon Dijon mustard
- 1 teaspoon grated lemon rind
- ¼ teaspoon each salt and black pepper
- ¼ cup Chicken Stock (page 62) or low-sodium chicken broth
- 1 tablespoon olive oil

For the salad:
- 3 cups hot cooked rice
- 1 large carrot, peeled and grated (1 cup)
- 1 medium-size cucumber, peeled, seeded, and diced (1 cup)
- 1 medium-size sweet green pepper, cored, seeded, and diced (¾ cup)
- 1 small red onion, finely chopped (½ cup)
- 2 tablespoons each snipped fresh dill and minced parsley

1 To prepare the dressing: In a small bowl, whisk together the vinegar, mustard, lemon rind, salt, and pepper. Whisk in the stock and olive oil. Or put all the ingredients in a small jar with a tight-fitting lid and shake until well blended.

2 To prepare the salad: In a large bowl, combine the rice, carrot, cucumber, pepper, onion, dill, and parsley. Add the dressing and toss to combine. Cover the bowl with plastic food wrap and chill for at least 2 hours before serving. Will keep, refrigerated, for up to 2 days. Serves 6.

PREPARATION TIME: 25 MIN. CHILLING TIME: 2 HR.

Per serving: Calories 176; Saturated Fat 0 g; Total Fat 3 g; Protein 4 g; Carbohydrate 34 g; Fiber 3 g; Sodium 125 mg; Cholesterol 0 mg

PANZANELLA

This scrumptious Italian recipe gives you starch and vegetables in one dish. And it's a great way to use day-old bread.

For the salad:
- 6 slices (1 inch thick) stale white or whole-grain French or Italian bread, toasted and cut into 1-inch cubes (2 ½ cups)
- 1 small sweet green pepper, cored, seeded, and diced (½ cup)
- 3 plum tomatoes, diced (1 ½ cups)
- 2 green onions, including tops, finely chopped (¼ cup)
- 1 medium-size stalk celery, diced (½ cup)
- 1 small cucumber, peeled, seeded, and diced (1 cup)
- 2 teaspoons drained capers, finely chopped (optional)
- ¼ cup minced fresh basil or parsley

For the dressing:
- ¼ cup Chicken Stock or Vegetable Stock (page 62) or low-sodium chicken broth
- 2 tablespoons balsamic or red wine vinegar
- 1 clove garlic, minced
- ¼ teaspoon each salt and black pepper, or to taste
- 1 tablespoon olive oil

1 To prepare the salad: In a large salad bowl, combine the bread, green pepper, tomatoes, green onions, celery, cucumber, capers if desired, and basil.

2 To prepare the dressing: In a small bowl, whisk together the stock, vinegar, garlic, salt, and pepper. Whisk in the oil. Or place all of the ingredients in a small jar with a tight-fitting lid and shake until well blended. Pour the dressing over the salad; toss lightly. Cover and chill for at least 1 hour or up to 6 hours. Serve with grilled meat, fish, or poultry. Serves 4 to 6.

PREPARATION TIME: 25 MIN. CHILLING TIME: 1 HR.

Per serving (for 4): Calories 206; Saturated Fat 1 g; Total Fat 6 g; Protein 6 g; Carbohydrate 34 g; Fiber 3 g; Sodium 494 mg; Cholesterol 0 mg

TAILGATE PICNIC

Herbed Cheese Ball
(page 310)

Whole-Grain Crackers

Crudités

Panzanella

Deviled Oven-Fried Chicken
(page 107)

Basket of Summer Fruits

Iced Tea

CARROT-TURNIP SALAD WITH CUMIN-LIME DRESSING

This refreshing mélange of vegetables in a cumin-lime dressing goes especially well with Mexican dishes, such as Turkey Quesadillas (page 121).

For the dressing:
- 3 tablespoons fresh lime juice
- 2 tablespoons olive oil
- ⅓ cup tightly packed parsley leaves
- ¾ teaspoon ground cumin or dried basil or tarragon, crumbled
- ¾ teaspoon salt
- ⅛ teaspoon black pepper

For the salad:
- 4 medium-size carrots, peeled and shredded (12 ounces)
- 2 small white turnips or 3 medium-size parsnips or carrots, peeled and shredded (8 ounces)
- 1 small red onion, slivered

1 To prepare the dressing: In a food processor or blender, whirl the lime juice, oil, parsley, cumin, salt, and pepper for 30 seconds or until the parsley is minced.

2 To prepare the salad: Bring a large saucepan of water to a boil over moderately high heat. Add the carrots, turnips, and red onion and cook for 2 minutes (the water will not return to a boil). Drain the vegetables and transfer to a large salad bowl. Add the dressing and toss until well combined. Serve warm or chilled. Serves 4 to 6.

PREPARATION TIME: 15 MIN. COOKING TIME: 2 MIN.

Per serving (for 4): Calories 124; Saturated Fat 1 g; Total Fat 7 g; Protein 2 g; Carbohydrate 16 g; Fiber 5 g; Sodium 462 mg; Cholesterol 0 mg

CAULIFLOWER, CARROT, AND PEPPER VINAIGRETTE

For the salad:
- ½ medium-size head cauliflower, cored and cut into florets (2¼ cups)
- 2 small carrots, peeled and thinly sliced (1 cup)
- 1 small sweet red or green pepper, cored, seeded, and thinly sliced (¾ cup)
- 1 green onion, including top, sliced

For the dressing:
- 3 tablespoons Chicken Stock (page 62) or low-sodium chicken broth
- 1 tablespoon plus 1 teaspoon Dijon mustard
- 1 tablespoon olive oil
- 2 teaspoons red wine vinegar

1 Arrange the cauliflower in a steamer basket, set over boiling water, cover, and steam for 3 minutes. Add the carrots and red pepper, cover, and steam 2 to 3 minutes more or until the vegetables are slightly tender. Drain and run under cold water to stop the cooking; transfer to a salad bowl and stir in the green onion.

2 To prepare the dressing: In a small bowl, whisk together the stock, mustard, oil, and vinegar. Or put all the ingredients in a small jar with a tight-fitting lid and shake vigorously. Pour the dressing over the vegetables and toss gently to coat. Serve with grilled chicken or fish. Serves 4.

PREPARATION TIME: 15 MIN. COOKING TIME: 5 MIN.

Per serving: Calories 74; Saturated Fat 0 g; Total Fat 4 g; Protein 3 g; Carbohydrate 9 g; Fiber 3 g; Sodium 155 mg; Cholesterol 0 mg

Cauliflower, Carrot, and Pepper Vinaigrette—one of the niftiest combos on the scene. It's sky high in vitamins A and C and notably low in calories.

CELERY VICTOR

Here is a smart way to serve fiber-packed celery. To develop the full flavor, this dish should be marinated for at least 3 hours or as long as overnight. If fennel is available, it makes an interesting substitute for the celery.

2 **bunches celery hearts (1 pound), trimmed and cut diagonally into 1 ½-inch lengths**	1 **teaspoon Dijon mustard**
2 **cups Chicken Stock or Vegetable Stock (page 62) or low-sodium chicken broth**	⅛ **teaspoon black pepper, or to taste**
	2 **teaspoons olive oil**
	Optional garnishes:
¼ **teaspoon salt**	2 **to 3 anchovy fillets**
1 **tablespoon lemon juice**	2 **tablespoons minced parsley or celery leaves**

1 In a medium-size saucepan, bring the celery, stock, and ⅛ teaspoon of the salt to a boil over moderate heat. Lower the heat, cover the saucepan with wax paper, and fit the lid snugly on top. Simmer for 15 to 20 minutes or until the celery is tender. Using a slotted spoon, transfer the celery to a bowl. Raise the heat to high and boil, uncovered, for 10 minutes or until the liquid is reduced to ½ cup.

2 In a small bowl, whisk together the reduced cooking liquid, the remaining ⅛ teaspoon salt, and the lemon juice, mustard, and pepper. Whisk in the oil and pour the dressing over the celery. Cover the bowl with plastic food wrap and chill for at least 3 hours or overnight. Before serving, garnish with the anchovy fillets and parsley if desired. Serve with grilled lamb, poultry, beef, or cold poached salmon. Serves 4.

PREPARATION TIME: 8 MIN. COOKING TIME: 25 MIN.

CHILLING TIME: 3 HR.

Per serving: Calories 48; Saturated Fat 0 g; Total Fat 2 g; Protein 2 g; Carbohydrate 5 g; Fiber 2 g; Sodium 330 mg; Cholesterol 0 mg

Winter is a fine season for salads; ingredients that you may have overlooked when summer greens were abundant can be enlisted for salads in January and February. Make use of plentiful onions, broccoli, cauliflower, celery, sweet potatoes, and squash. Try tossing shredded parsnips, cabbage, or carrots with Buttermilk Dressing (page 268); or matchsticks of lightly steamed turnips, rutabagas, or fennel with Zesty Italian Dressing (page 267).

Currants, raisins, and other dried fruits go well with winter's robust vegetables and add extra fiber and nutrients too. Also don't overlook canned vegetables: Artichoke hearts, corn, hearts of palm, roasted sweet red peppers, and beets can be drained, rinsed, and combined with pasta, rice, or potatoes. If you still favor greens, try them with a warm dressing to chase away winter's chill.

TRICOLOR COLESLAW

This sweet-and-sour dressing is lower in fat than the traditional mayonnaise-based type. If you prefer, substitute poppy seeds for the caraway in the dressing and 1 large sweet red pepper for the carrots in the salad.

For the dressing:
- 1 large egg white
- ⅓ cup cider vinegar or white vinegar
- 2 tablespoons brown sugar
- 2 tablespoons flour
- 1 teaspoon dry mustard
- ½ teaspoon caraway seeds
- ¼ teaspoon salt
- ½ cup water
- 2 tablespoons plain low-fat yogurt or reduced-fat sour cream (optional)

For the salad:
- 5 cups thinly sliced red and green cabbage (1½ pounds)
- 2 small carrots, peeled and shredded (1 cup)
- 2 green onions, including tops, thinly sliced (¼ cup)
- ¼ teaspoon salt (optional)

1 To prepare the dressing: In a small bowl, beat the egg white and vinegar with a fork until well blended. In a small saucepan, stir together the sugar, flour, mustard, caraway seeds, and salt, pressing the sugar to break up any lumps. Add the water and whisk until smooth.

2 Set the saucepan over moderate heat, bring to a boil, and cook, whisking constantly, for 1 minute. Remove from the heat and gradually whisk in the vinegar mixture. Return to the heat and bring to a boil, whisking constantly. Remove from the heat and let cool to room temperature. Stir in the yogurt if desired.

3 To prepare the salad: In a large bowl, toss together the red and green cabbage, carrots, green onions, salt if desired, and dressing. Marinate in the refrigerator for at least 2 hours before serving. Serves 4 to 6.

PREPARATION TIME: 15 MIN. COOKING TIME: 3 MIN.
MARINATING TIME: 2 HR.

Per serving (for 4): Calories 103; Saturated Fat 0 g; Total Fat 1 g; Protein 4 g; Carbohydrate 24 g; Fiber 5 g; Sodium 187 mg; Cholesterol 0 mg

CUCUMBERS WITH LIME-CHILI DRESSING

Small Kirby cucumbers, normally used for pickling, are called for here because they are crunchier and less watery; you can use other cucumbers and peel them if you prefer.

- 1 pound Kirby cucumbers, sliced ¼ inch thick (about 3¾ cups)
- 2 green onions, including tops, thinly sliced (¼ cup)
- 2 tablespoons Tomato Chili Sauce (page 271) or bottled chili sauce
- 1 tablespoon plus 1 teaspoon lime juice
- 2 teaspoons reduced-sodium soy sauce
- ½ teaspoon sugar
- ¼ teaspoon ground ginger
- ¼ teaspoon hot red pepper sauce

1 In a medium-size bowl, combine the cucumbers and green onions. In a small bowl, whisk together the chili sauce, lime juice, soy sauce, sugar, ginger, and red pepper sauce. Pour the dressing over the cucumbers and toss to coat. Serve with broiled fish or chicken. Serves 4.

PREPARATION TIME: 8 MIN.

Per serving: Calories 24; Saturated Fat 0 g; Total Fat 0 g; Protein 1 g; Carbohydrate 5 g; Fiber 1 g; Sodium 75 mg; Cholesterol 0 mg

DILLED CUCUMBER-CARROT SALAD

This cool, refreshing salad goes particularly well with spicy dishes such as curry and chili. If you use the long European cucumbers, you don't have to peel or seed them.

¼ teaspoon salt
4 small carrots, peeled and sliced ¼ inch thick (2 cups)
2 large cucumbers (8 ounces each), peeled, halved lengthwise, seeded, and sliced ¼ inch thick (2½ cups)

2 tablespoons snipped fresh dill or minced fresh mint or 2 teaspoons dill weed
½ cup plain low-fat yogurt
1 teaspoon olive oil
¼ teaspoon each ground cumin and coriander

1 Bring a medium-size saucepan of water to a boil, add the salt and carrots, and cook for 2 minutes. Drain the carrots, rinse under cold water to stop the cooking, and drain again. Transfer to a medium-size bowl and stir in the cucumbers and dill.

2 In a small bowl, whisk together the yogurt, oil, cumin, and coriander. Pour the dressing over the vegetables and stir until well combined. Serve chilled or at room temperature. Serves 4.

PREPARATION TIME: 12 MIN. COOKING TIME: 2 MIN.

Per serving: Calories 67; Saturated Fat 0 g; Total Fat 2 g; Protein 3 g; Carbohydrate 11 g; Fiber 3 g; Sodium 175 mg; Cholesterol 2 mg

Sweet shredded carrots and caraway seeds make Tricolor Coleslaw special. It travels readily from countertop to desk top.

257

Green Bean Salad, Oriental Style gets its Asian accent from water chestnuts and fresh ginger. Serve this distinctive salad with chicken kebabs and steamed rice.

GREEN BEAN SALAD, ORIENTAL STYLE

The tangy dressing for this crunchy combination is also good drizzled over asparagus.

For the salad:
- 1 can (8 ounces) water chestnuts, drained
- 12 ounces green beans, trimmed
- 1 sweet red pepper, cored, seeded, and slivered

For the dressing:
- 2 tablespoons orange juice
- 2 tablespoons rice vinegar or cider vinegar
- 2 teaspoons grated fresh ginger
- 1 teaspoon dark sesame oil
- ¼ teaspoon salt, or to taste
- 4 dashes hot red pepper sauce

1 Bring a large saucepan of water to a boil over moderately high heat. Place the water chestnuts in a strainer or colander and immerse them in the boiling water for 30 seconds; lift out, rinse under cold water, and slice. Transfer to a salad bowl.

2 Add the green beans to the boiling water and cook for 5 minutes. Add the sweet red pepper and cook 4 minutes longer or until the vegetables are crisp-tender. Drain and rinse under cold water to stop the cooking. Drain again and add to the salad bowl.

3 To prepare the dressing: In a small bowl, whisk together the orange juice, vinegar, ginger, oil, salt, and red pepper sauce. Or put all the ingredients in a small jar with a tight-fitting lid and shake vigorously. Pour the dressing over the vegetables and toss gently to coat. Serve at room temperature or chilled. Serves 4 to 6.

PREPARATION TIME: 15 MIN. COOKING TIME: 10 MIN.

Per serving (for 4): Calories 77; Saturated Fat 0 g; Total Fat 1 g; Protein 2 g; Carbohydrate 16 g; Fiber 2 g; Sodium 142 mg; Cholesterol 0 mg

ORIENTAL GREEN SALAD

The protein in this vegetable salad comes from the tofu in the luscious creamy dressing. To make ginger juice, put a 1/2-inch piece of fresh ginger through a garlic press or grate the ginger and press out the juice with a spoon; discard the pulp.

For the dressing:
- 4 ounces soft tofu (soybean curd)
- 1/4 cup water
- 1 tablespoon reduced-sodium soy sauce
- 1 clove garlic, crushed
- 2 teaspoons rice vinegar
- 1/2 teaspoon ginger juice
- 1/4 teaspoon sugar

For the salad:
- 1 small head romaine lettuce or 6 ounces spinach leaves, cut into 1-inch-wide ribbons (6 cups)
- 2 medium-size carrots, peeled and shredded (1 1/2 cups)
- 4 radishes, thinly sliced (1/3 cup)

1 To prepare the dressing: In a food processor or blender, whirl the tofu, water, soy sauce, garlic, vinegar, ginger juice, and sugar for 1 minute or until smooth.

2 To prepare the salad: In a large salad bowl, place the lettuce, carrots, and radishes. Pour the dressing over the vegetables and toss until coated. Serves 4.

PREPARATION TIME: 10 MIN.

Per serving: Calories 55; Saturated Fat 0 g; Total Fat 1 g; Protein 4 g; Carbohydrate 8 g; Fiber 3 g; Sodium 143 mg; Cholesterol 0 mg

•

Sesame Variation: For the dressing, omit the tofu, water, garlic, and ginger juice and add *1 1/2 teaspoons dark sesame oil, 1 1/2 teaspoons vegetable or peanut oil,* and *1 teaspoon sesame seeds.* Increase the vinegar to 1 tablespoon plus 2 teaspoons and the sugar to 1 teaspoon. In a small bowl, whisk together the soy sauce, vinegar, sugar, and sesame and peanut oils. Or put all the ingredients in a small jar with a tight-fitting lid and shake vigorously. Pour the dressing over the vegetables and toss until coated. Serves 4. *Per serving: Calories 70; Saturated Fat 1 g; Total Fat 4 g; Protein 2 g; Carbohydrate 8 g; Fiber 3 g; Sodium 141 mg; Cholesterol 0 mg.*

SPINACH SALAD WITH PEARS AND WALNUTS

A zippy yogurt dressing makes a pleasing foil for fruit and nuts. You can substitute any combination of mixed greens for the spinach and use an apple in place of the pear.

- 3/4 cup plain low-fat yogurt
- 1 clove garlic, crushed
- 1 tablespoon olive oil
- 1/4 teaspoon Dijon mustard
- 1 pound spinach, rinsed, trimmed, and torn in bite-size pieces
- 1 ripe pear, cored and thinly sliced (1 1/3 cups)
- 1/4 cup coarsely chopped walnuts (1 ounce)

1 In a food processor or blender, whirl the yogurt, garlic, oil, and mustard for 30 seconds to 1 minute or until smooth. In a large bowl, combine the spinach, pear, and walnuts. Pour the dressing over the salad and toss until coated. Serve with Herbed Cornish Hens (page 125) or Skirt Steak in a Crispy Potato Crust (page 131). Serves 4.

PREPARATION TIME: 10 MIN.

Per serving: Calories 153; Saturated Fat 1 g; Total Fat 9 g; Protein 7 g; Carbohydrate 15 g; Fiber 4 g; Sodium 131 mg; Cholesterol 1 mg

Most salad greens, but especially curly or deep-veined types such as escarole or spinach, need careful rinsing to remove concealed grit. After you have separated the leaves, plunge them into a sink filled with cold water and gently swish them around to loosen the dirt, then rinse them thoroughly under cold running water. The next step is to dry them as completely as possible because dressings slide off wet leaves and end up on the bottom of the salad bowl. A salad spinner, available in the housewares section of most department and hardware stores, quickly and thoroughly spins greens dry with little mess and without bruising them. Rolling the leaves in a clean dish towel or in paper toweling is also effective. After drying, place the greens in a salad bowl lined with paper toweling and refrigerate for at least 1 hour to allow them to crisp.

Though all salad greens should be served as fresh as possible, at the peak of flavor and nutritional content, you can refrigerate them for up to 5 days. Wash and dry the greens as soon as you bring them home. Place the leaves, layered with some paper toweling, in a large plastic bag and refrigerate until ready to use. Also, if you expect to have leftover salad, serve the dressing on the side; dressed greens don't keep well.

F **resh herbs enhance** all types of salads. Try minced rosemary, thyme, or basil in your next potato salad. Season cold meat or poultry salads with fresh oregano or rosemary. Or garnish sliced tomatoes and mozzarella or a pasta salad with basil leaves.

Fresh snipped dill and minced tarragon are fine accents for seafood and fish salads as well as greens. Mint adds just the right touch to fresh fruits and bulgur salad. Cilantro (coriander) goes well with avocado, Oriental, or Mexican salads.

If fresh herbs are not available at your grocery, visit a nursery and start your own herb garden in a sunny garden spot or window box. It takes surprisingly little space and effort to produce a bountiful crop all year round.

CURLY ENDIVE SALAD WITH WARM BACON DRESSING

Here is a French bistro standard: curly endive, or chicory, topped with toasted croutons, a classic vinaigrette, and diced bacon.

4 slices firm-textured white bread (4 ounces), crusts removed	¼ teaspoon black pepper
1 tablespoon olive oil	⅛ teaspoon salt, or to taste
2 cloves garlic, 1 halved, 1 minced	8 ounces curly endive, rinsed, patted dry, and torn into bite-size pieces
1 slice thick-cut bacon	
2 tablespoons finely chopped shallot	2 tablespoons minced fresh tarragon or chives
2 tablespoons each tarragon vinegar and water	

1 To make the croutons: Preheat the broiler, setting the rack 6 inches from the heat. Brush both sides of the bread with the oil and place on a baking sheet. Toast the slices under the broiler for 2 minutes on each side or until golden. Rub both sides of each slice with the garlic halves, then cut the bread into ½-inch squares. Set aside.

2 In a 10-inch nonstick skillet, cook the bacon over moderate heat, turning occasionally, for 5 minutes or until crisp. With tongs or a slotted spoon, transfer the bacon to paper toweling to drain. Pour off all but 1 tablespoon of the bacon drippings in the skillet. Add the shallot and minced garlic to the skillet and cook, stirring, over moderately low heat for 2 minutes or until soft. Add the vinegar, water, pepper, and salt and simmer, scraping the bottom of the skillet, for 30 seconds.

3 In a large bowl, combine the endive, tarragon, and croutons. Crumble the bacon on top. Pour the dressing over the salad and toss to combine. Serves 4.

PREPARATION TIME: 20 MIN.   COOKING TIME: 12 MIN.

Per serving: Calories 120; Saturated Fat 1 g; Total Fat 6 g; Protein 4 g; Carbohydrate 15 g; Fiber 1 g; Sodium 237 mg; Cholesterol 2 mg

Curly Endive Salad with Warm Bacon Dressing. Add French bread, sliced cold meat, olives, mustard — you have a French feast.

POTATO AND CHICK PEA SALAD

*This sensational combination can
be served warm or cold.*

For the salad:
- 1 pound red-skinned potatoes, cut into ½-inch cubes (3 cups)
- 3 green onions, including tops, white and green sliced separately
- 1 cup cooked chick peas

For the dressing:
- 2 tablespoons olive oil
- 1 tablespoon Dijon mustard
- 2 tablespoons red wine vinegar
- 2 tablespoons apple juice
- ½ teaspoon dried basil, crumbled
- ½ clove garlic, minced (optional)

1 To prepare the salad: Bring a large saucepan of water to a boil over moderately high heat, then add the potatoes. When the water returns to a boil, cook the potatoes for 6 to 7 minutes or until they are fork-tender. Add the white part of the green onions during the last minute of cooking.

2 Meanwhile, prepare the dressing. In a small bowl, whisk together the oil, mustard, vinegar, apple juice, basil, and garlic if using. Or put all the ingredients in a small jar and shake until well blended.

3 Place the green part of the onions and the chick peas in a colander and set in the sink. Drain the potatoes into the colander, then transfer the vegetables to a salad bowl and toss with the dressing. Serve warm or refrigerate for up to 3 days and serve chilled. Serves 4.

PREPARATION TIME: 15 MIN. COOKING TIME: 10 MIN.

*Per serving: Calories 234; Saturated Fat 1 g;
Total Fat 8 g; Protein 6 g; Carbohydrate 36 g;
Fiber 1 g; Sodium 103 mg; Cholesterol 0 mg*

SLIM AND TRIM POTATO SALAD

*For the zesty vinaigrette dressing in this
recipe, soup stock is substituted for some of the
oil to cut down on fat and calories.*

For the salad:
- 1 pound small red-skinned potatoes, sliced ¼ inch thick
- 1 small sweet red or green pepper, cored, seeded, and diced (½ cup)
- 1 medium-size stalk celery, diced (½ cup)
- 3 shallots, finely chopped (¼ cup)

For the dressing:
- 1 tablespoon lemon juice
- 1 tablespoon tarragon vinegar or white wine vinegar
- 1 teaspoon Dijon mustard
- 1 clove garlic, minced
- ¼ teaspoon each salt and black pepper
- ¼ cup Chicken Stock or Vegetable Stock (page 62) or low-sodium chicken broth
- 1 tablespoon olive oil
- 3 tablespoons minced fresh herbs, such as chervil, tarragon, chives, or parsley

1 To prepare the salad: Arrange the potatoes in a steamer basket, set over boiling water in a large saucepan, and steam for 8 to 10 minutes or until tender. Transfer to a large bowl. Add the sweet pepper, celery, and shallots.

2 Meanwhile, prepare the dressing. In a small bowl, whisk together the lemon juice, vinegar, mustard, garlic, salt, and black pepper. Whisk in the stock, oil, and herbs. Or put all the ingredients in a small jar and shake until well blended. Pour the dressing over the potatoes and toss gently to combine. Serve warm or chilled. Serves 4.

PREPARATION TIME: 20 MIN. COOKING TIME: 10 MIN.

*Per serving: Calories 146; Saturated Fat 1 g;
Total Fat 4 g; Protein 3 g; Carbohydrate 27 g;
Fiber 2 g; Sodium 191 mg; Cholesterol 0 mg*

A simple pleasure: Grilled Vegetable Salad with Mozzarella makes a terrific antipasto or a light meal by itself.

GRILLED VEGETABLE SALAD WITH MOZZARELLA

If you prefer to broil the vegetables, set the rack 6 inches from the heat and cook them 1 or 2 minutes longer than directed or until crisp-tender.

2 **tablespoons olive oil**	1 **small zucchini (4 ounces), sliced lengthwise ¼ inch thick**
2 **tablespoons lemon juice**	1 **medium-size sweet red pepper, cored, seeded, and quartered lengthwise**
1 **clove garlic, minced**	
½ **teaspoon each dried thyme and marjoram, crumbled**	4 **ounces fresh or smoked part-skim mozzarella cheese, thinly sliced**
½ **teaspoon salt**	
¼ **teaspoon black pepper**	8 **pitted black olives**
2 **small Japanese eggplants (3 ounces each), trimmed and halved lengthwise**	2 **tablespoons minced fresh basil or parsley**
1 **small yellow squash (4 ounces), sliced lengthwise ¼ inch thick**	1 **tablespoon balsamic vinegar**

1 In a small bowl, combine the oil, lemon juice, garlic, thyme, marjoram, salt, and black pepper. Using a pastry brush, coat the eggplants, yellow squash, zucchini, and red pepper with some of the mixture.

2 On a grill set 4 inches from glowing coals, cook the egg-plants for 3 to 4 minutes on each side or until tender. Cook the squash, zucchini, and red pepper for 2 minutes on each side or until tender.

3 Cut the red pepper into strips and arrange on a serving platter with the eggplants, yellow squash, zucchini, cheese, and olives. Whisk the basil and vinegar into the remaining oil mixture and drizzle over all. Serve with a crusty Italian bread. Serves 4.

PREPARATION TIME: 25 MIN. COOKING TIME: 10 MIN.

Per serving: Calories 175; Saturated Fat 4 g; Total Fat 13 g; Protein 8 g; Carbohydrate 9 g; Fiber 1 g; Sodium 441 mg; Cholesterol 16 mg

LENTIL SALAD WITH SUMMER SQUASH

For the salad:
- 3 cups water
- 4 small yellow summer squash or zucchini (1 pound), quartered lengthwise and thinly sliced
- 1 small stalk celery, cut into 1-inch lengths
- 2 whole cloves
- 1 cup dried brown lentils
- 2 green onions, including tops, sliced (¼ cup)
- 8 cherry tomatoes, quartered (optional)

For the dressing:
- 2 tablespoons lemon juice
- 2 tablespoons apple juice or water
- 2 tablespoons olive oil
- ½ teaspoon grated lemon rind
- ½ teaspoon salt
- ¼ teaspoon fennel seeds (optional)
- Pinch ground red pepper (cayenne)

1 To prepare the salad: In a medium-size saucepan, bring the water to a boil over moderately high heat. Add the squash and cook for 4 minutes or until crisp-tender. Using a slotted spoon, transfer the squash to a colander, rinse under cold water, and drain well; place in a large bowl.

2 Stud 2 celery pieces with the cloves and add all the celery to the boiling water. Stir in the lentils, lower the heat, cover, and simmer for 25 minutes or until the lentils are just tender. Drain well and add to the bowl with the squash; discard the celery and cloves.

3 Meanwhile, prepare the dressing: In a small bowl, whisk together the lemon juice, apple juice, oil, lemon rind, salt, fennel seeds if desired, and red pepper until smooth. Or place the dressing ingredients in a small jar, cover tightly, and shake until blended.

4 Add the dressing to the salad and toss to coat. Marinate for at least 1 hour (will keep, refrigerated, for up to 3 days). Stir in the green onions and cherry tomatoes if desired; serve chilled or at room temperature. Serves 4.

PREPARATION TIME: 20 MIN.   COOKING TIME: 30 MIN.

MARINATING TIME: 1 HR.

Per serving: Calories 252; Saturated Fat 1 g;
Total Fat 8 g; Protein 13 g; Carbohydrate 35 g;
Fiber 2 g; Sodium 291 mg; Cholesterol 0 mg

MEXICAN CORN SALAD

Serve this healthful salad with Chicken Tortilla Sandwiches (page 48) or Easy Black Bean Soup (page 72) for a super south-of-the-border lunch.

For the dressing:
- ¼ cup white wine vinegar or 2 tablespoons white wine vinegar plus 2 tablespoons balsamic vinegar
- 1 tablespoon water
- 1 teaspoon chili powder
- ⅛ teaspoon ground red pepper (cayenne), or to taste (optional)
- 1 tablespoon vegetable or canola oil

For the salad:
- 3 medium-size tomatoes, diced (3 cups)
- 3 green onions, including tops, sliced (⅓ cup)
- 1 small sweet green pepper, cored, seeded, and diced (½ cup)
- 1 medium-size cucumber, peeled and diced (1 cup)
- 1 package (10 ounces) frozen corn kernels, thawed
- 1½ cups cooked chick peas
- ⅓ cup minced fresh cilantro (coriander) or ⅓ cup minced parsley plus 2 teaspoons dried cilantro
- 1 fresh or pickled jalapeño pepper, seeded and chopped (about 2 tablepoons)

1 To prepare the dressing: In a small bowl, whisk together the vinegar, water, chili powder, and red pepper if desired. Whisk in the oil until well blended. Or put all the ingredients in a small jar, cover tightly, and shake until well blended.

2 To prepare the salad: In a large bowl, combine the tomatoes, green onions, green pepper, cucumber, corn, chick peas, cilantro, and jalapeño peppers. Pour the dressing over the salad and toss to coat. Serve chilled or at room temperature. Serves 6.

PREPARATION TIME: 22 MIN.

Per serving: Calories 120; Saturated Fat 1 g;
Total Fat 4 g; Protein 6 g; Carbohydrate 27 g;
Fiber 3 g; Sodium 101 mg; Cholesterol 0 mg

For lively salads, combine two or more of the greens shown below and on the opposite page.

Arugula: Its peppery bite combines well with that of milder greens.

Boston lettuce: The soft, buttery-flavored leaves make an attractive base in a composed salad.

Chicory (or curly endive): Its firm leaves and slightly bitter taste stand up well to heartier dressings.

Endive, Belgian: The crisp, firm, slightly bitter leaves add zest to milder greens.

TROPICAL FRUIT SALAD

Mango, pineapple, and banana splashed with a blushing grenadine dressing lighten a hearty meal. Try this salad also with raspberries or seedless grapes.

- 2 cups pineapple juice
- 2 tablespoons firmly packed light brown sugar
- 1 tablespoon plus 1 teaspoon grenadine or 2 teaspoons each orange juice and cranberry juice
- ¼ teaspoon ground ginger
- 1 large mango (1 ¾ pounds), peeled, pitted, and sliced ½ inch thick

- 1 medium-size pineapple, peeled, quartered, cored, and sliced ¾ inch thick (3 cups)
- 4 medium-size bananas, peeled and sliced ¾ inch thick (1 ½ cups)
- 1 pint strawberries, hulled and halved
- Fresh mint leaves (optional garnish)

1 In a large bowl, combine the pineapple juice, sugar, grenadine, and ginger. Add the mango, pineapple, bananas, and strawberries and toss gently to coat. Cover and refrigerate for at least 2 or up to 24 hours. If desired, garnish each serving with the mint. Serves 8.

PREPARATION TIME: 17 MIN. CHILLING TIME: 2 HR.

Per serving: Calories 206; Saturated Fat 0 g; Total Fat 1 g; Protein 2 g; Carbohydrate 52 g; Fiber 5 g; Sodium 5 mg; Cholesterol 0 mg

ARUGULA, PEAR, AND GOAT CHEESE SALAD

Pungent arugula, or rocket, marries well with a cheese and fruit combo. A member of the crucifer family, this peppery Italian green has 3 times the calcium and vitamin C of spinach. If it's unavailable, substitute chicory or watercress. Neufchâtel cream cheese can be substituted for the goat cheese, but the result will be blander.

For the dressing:
- ⅓ cup orange juice
- 2 tablespoons lemon juice
- ½ teaspoon grated orange rind
- ⅛ teaspoon each salt and pepper, or to taste
- 1 tablespoon vegetable oil or walnut oil

For the salad:
- 2 large pears (12 ounces each), halved lengthwise and cored

- 2 teaspoons lemon juice
- 4 ounces arugula, watercress, or chicory, rinsed and patted dry
- 4 ounces goat cheese, cut into 8 slices
- ⅓ cup pecan or walnut halves, toasted and chopped
- Orange zest (colored part of the rind), blanched and slivered (optional garnish)

1 To prepare the dressing: In a small bowl, whisk together the orange juice, lemon juice, orange rind, salt, and pepper; whisk in the oil. Or put all the dressing ingredients in a small jar, cover tightly, and shake until well blended.

2 To prepare the salad: Cut the pear halves lengthwise into ½-inch slices and sprinkle with the lemon juice to prevent darkening. Arrange the arugula on 4 plates, top with the pears and goat cheese, and sprinkle with the nuts. Drizzle the dressing over the salad and, if desired, garnish with the orange zest. Serves 4.

PREPARATION TIME: 15 MIN.

Per serving: Calories 301; Saturated Fat 6 g; Total Fat 18 g; Protein 8 g; Carbohydrate 31 g; Fiber 6 g; Sodium 247 mg; Cholesterol 28 mg

Wedges of sweet, juicy fruit and buttery cheese tame the peppery greens in Arugula, Pear, and Goat Cheese Salad.

SUMMER FRUIT SALAD WITH SPINACH

This delightful combination of sweet fruit, greens, and a slightly tart dressing makes a wonderful summer luncheon. Serve it with sourdough bread or corn or bran muffins.

For the dressing:
- 1 tablespoon chutney or honey
- 1 tablespoon Dijon mustard
- 2 tablespoons lime juice or rice vinegar
- 1 teaspoon grated fresh ginger or ½ teaspoon ground ginger
- ⅛ teaspoon black pepper

For the salad:
- 8 ounces spinach or curly endive, rinsed, trimmed, and torn (4 cups)
- 1 pint strawberries, hulled and quartered, or blueberries
- 8 ounces cubed honeydew or cantaloupe (2 cups)
- 1 ounce blue cheese, crumbled (optional)

1 To prepare the dressing: In a food processor or blender, whirl the chutney, mustard, lime juice, ginger, and pepper for 30 seconds or until smooth. Or mince the chutney and place it in a jar along with the other dressing ingredients, cover tightly, and shake until blended.

2 To prepare the salad: Arrange the spinach leaves on a serving platter and scatter the strawberries, honeydew, and blue cheese if desired on top. Drizzle the dressing over all. Serves 4.

PREPARATION TIME: 17 MIN.

Per serving: Calories 82; Saturated Fat 0 g; Total Fat 1 g; Protein 3 g; Carbohydrate 19 g; Fiber 4 g; Sodium 149 mg; Cholesterol 0 mg

Escarole: Similar in flavor to chicory, it can be used alone or blended with other greens.

Radicchio: Its leaves add a slightly bitter flavor and intense color to any salad.

Romaine (or cos): Hearty, succulent, and very crisp, its sweet-flavored leaves blend well with more astringent greens.

Watercress: The peppery sprigs (discard tough stems) can be used alone or with a mild lettuce such as romaine.

APPLE, CABBAGE, AND WALNUT SALAD

This cool and slightly sweet salad is a wonderful side dish with spicy Mexican or Indian food. You can prepare it too with red cabbage and green Granny Smith apples.

¾ cup plain low-fat yogurt
3 tablespoons reduced-calorie mayonnaise
1½ tablespoons honey
½ teaspoon ground ginger
1 small head green cabbage, cored and shredded (6 cups)
1 medium-size McIntosh or other red apple, cored, seeded, and cut into ¾-inch cubes (1½ cups)

1 small stalk celery, thinly sliced (about ½ cup)
⅓ cup raisins
¼ cup walnuts, coarsely chopped
Thin slices of apple, sprinkled with lemon juice (optional garnish)

1 In a large mixing bowl, whisk together the yogurt, mayonnaise, honey, and ginger. Add the cabbage, apple, celery, raisins, and walnuts and toss to coat. Chill for 30 minutes. Will keep, covered and refrigerated, for up to 2 days. If desired, arrange the apple slices on top of the salad just before serving. Serves 4 to 6.

PREPARATION TIME: 15 MIN. CHILLING TIME: 30 MIN.

Per serving (for 4): Calories 221; Saturated Fat 1 g; Total Fat 9 g; Protein 5 g; Carbohydrate 34 g; Fiber 5 g; Sodium 66 mg; Cholesterol 6 mg

ROASTED TOMATO VINAIGRETTE

Tomatoes roasted over an open fire lend an exciting new dimension to a simple vinaigrette. Add a splash to a green or vegetable salad or drizzle some over steamed seafood or grilled vegetables.

2 large ripe tomatoes
1 large shallot, finely chopped (2 tablespoons)
1 small clove garlic, minced
2 teaspoons olive oil
2 teaspoons balsamic vinegar

¼ teaspoon each salt and black pepper, or to taste
2 tablespoons minced fresh basil, parsley, or chives or a combination or 1 teaspoon dried herbs, crumbled

1 Using a long-handled fork, roast each tomato over an open flame, turning frequently, for 2 minutes or until charred all over. Or preheat the broiler, setting the rack 6 inches from the heat. Place the tomatoes on a broiler pan and broil for 2 to 3 minutes, turning once, or until charred. Peel, core, and chop the tomatoes.

2 In a food processor or blender, whirl the tomatoes, shallot, garlic, oil, vinegar, salt, pepper, and basil for 30 seconds or until well combined. Will keep, covered and refrigerated, for up to 3 days. Makes about 1 cup.

PREPARATION TIME: 10 MIN. COOKING TIME: 2 MIN.

Per tablespoon: Calories 11; Saturated Fat 0 g; Total Fat 1 g; Protein 0 g; Carbohydrate 1 g; Fiber 0 g; Sodium 36 mg; Cholesterol 0 mg

FERMENTED BLACK BEAN DRESSING

Look for fermented black beans in the imported foods section of your supermarket or in an Asian specialties store. This decidedly Oriental dressing enlivens summer greens, crisp cucumber slices, or chunks of ripe avocado.

1 tablespoon fermented black beans

2 tablespoons sherry vinegar or cider vinegar

2 tablespoons water

1 piece (about 2 inches) fresh ginger, peeled, or ¼ teaspoon ground ginger

1 tablespoon finely chopped green onion

¾ teaspoon honey

1 tablespoon plus 1 teaspoon peanut or corn oil

1 In a small bowl, combine the beans, vinegar, and water. Let stand at room temperature for 30 minutes. Meanwhile, grate the fresh ginger, then press the gratings through a fine sieve to extract the juice. (You should have about 1 teaspoon.) Discard the pulp. Stir the ginger juice, green onion, and honey into the bean mixture. Gradually whisk in the oil. Will keep, refrigerated, for up to 3 days. Whisk again just before serving. Makes about ½ cup.

PREPARATION TIME: 10 MIN. STANDING TIME: 30 MIN.

Per tablespoon: Calories 7; Saturated Fat 0 g; Total Fat 1 g; Protein 0 g; Carbohydrate 0 g; Fiber 0 g; Sodium 126 mg; Cholesterol 0 mg

ZESTY ITALIAN DRESSING

¼ vegetable bouillon cube

½ cup boiling water

1 tablespoon chopped pimiento or tomato paste

1 tablespoon minced fresh basil or ½ teaspoon dried basil, crumbled

1 clove garlic, sliced

2 tablespoons red wine vinegar or cider vinegar

1 tablespoon olive oil

1 In a food processor or blender, whirl the bouillon cube with the water until dissolved. Add the pimiento, basil, and garlic and whirl for 30 seconds or until smooth. Add the vinegar and oil and whirl 1 or 2 minutes more or until well combined. Will keep, covered and refrigerated, for up to 1 week. Whisk well before using. Makes about ¾ cup.

PREPARATION TIME: 9 MIN.

Per tablespoon: Calories 11; Saturated Fat 0 g; Total Fat 1 g; Protein 0 g; Carbohydrate 0 g; Fiber 0 g; Sodium 18 mg; Cholesterol 0 mg

Adorn your favorite salads with these three jewels from the kitchen (clockwise, from top): Zesty Italian Dressing, Fermented Black Bean Dressing, and Roasted Tomato Vinaigrette.

Olive, canola, and vegetable oils are excellent choices for salad dressings because their mild flavors blend well with most vinegars, herbs, and greens but don't overpower them.

Seed and nut oils, such as sesame and walnut, can add a special touch to a salad but should be used sparingly because their flavors are bolder and may overwhelm other ingredients. (Often they are combined with a milder oil to tone them down.) Some oils are infused with chili peppers, spices, or herbs; use these according to the subtlety or intensity of their flavors.

All oils eventually turn rancid; it's best to buy them in quantities you can use up within a few weeks. You can prolong their shelf life by storing in a cool, dark place; keep seed and nut oils in the refrigerator.

BUTTERMILK DRESSING

Use this to dress spinach, watercress, escarole, or arugula.

- ⅔ cup buttermilk
- 1 tablespoon cider vinegar
- 1 tablespoon finely chopped shallot
- ¼ teaspoon each salt and sugar
- ⅛ teaspoon ground red pepper (cayenne)
- 2 tablespoons snipped fresh chives, parsley, or dill or a combination

1 In a small jar, shake the buttermilk, vinegar, shallot, salt, sugar, red pepper, and chives until well combined. Will keep, covered and refrigerated, for up to 1 week. Makes about 1 cup.

PREPARATION TIME: 5 MIN.

Per tablespoon: Calories 5; Saturated Fat 0 g; Total Fat 0 g; Protein 0 g; Carbohydrate 1 g; Fiber 0 g; Sodium 44 mg; Cholesterol 0 mg

CREAMY TOMATO VINAIGRETTE

Satisfy your craving for traditional Russian dressing with this rich-tasting low-calorie, low-fat version.

- 1 medium-size tomato, peeled, quartered, and seeded (1 cup)
- ½ cup low-sodium tomato-vegetable juice
- ¼ cup plain low-fat yogurt
- 2 tablespoons reduced-calorie mayonnaise
- 6 drops hot red pepper sauce

1 In a food processor or blender, whirl the tomato and tomato-vegetable juice for 30 seconds or until smooth. Add the yogurt, mayonnaise, and red pepper sauce and whirl for 30 seconds more or until well combined. Will keep, refrigerated, for up to 3 days. Makes 1½ cups.

PREPARATION TIME: 7 MIN.

Per tablespoon: Calories 7; Saturated Fat 0 g; Total Fat 0 g; Protein 0 g; Carbohydrate 1 g; Fiber 0 g; Sodium 4 mg; Cholesterol 1 mg

MINTED PINK GRAPEFRUIT DRESSING

Toss your favorite fruits with this sweet-tart dressing for a refreshing first course or a quick dessert.

- 1 cup pink grapefruit juice (from 1 large grapefruit or frozen concentrate)
- ¼ cup fresh mint leaves
- 2 teaspoons honey
- 1 teaspoon minced fresh ginger
- ⅛ teaspoon salt

1 In a blender, whirl the grapefruit juice, mint, honey, ginger, and salt for 15 seconds or until well combined. Pour into a jar, cover, and chill. Will keep, covered and refrigerated, for up to 1 week. Makes about 1 cup.

PREPARATION TIME: 5 MIN.

Per tablespoon: Calories 8; Saturated Fat 0 g; Total Fat 0 g; Protein 0 g; Carbohydrate 2 g; Fiber 0 g; Sodium 17 mg; Cholesterol 0 mg

AVOCADO DRESSING

- 1 large ripe avocado, peeled, pitted, and cut into chunks (1½ cups)
- ¼ cup chopped tomato
- 2 tablespoons chopped red onion
- 2 tablespoons water
- 1 tablespoon reduced-calorie mayonnaise
- 2 teaspoons lemon juice
- ¼ teaspoon salt
- ¼ teaspoon paprika

1 In a food processor or blender, whirl the avocado, tomato, onion, and water for about 30 seconds. Add the mayonnaise, lemon juice, salt, and paprika and whirl for 1 minute or until smooth. Will keep, covered and refrigerated, for up to 4 days. Makes about 2 cups.

PREPARATION TIME: 10 MIN.

Per tablespoon: Calories 14; Saturated Fat 0 g; Total Fat 1 g; Protein 0 g; Carbohydrate 1 g; Fiber 0 g; Sodium 18 mg; Cholesterol 0 mg

SAUCES AND ACCOMPANIMENTS

"The secret is in the sauce." This old adage takes on new meaning here with recipes that taste rich and flavorful yet are healthfully low in fat. The 20 sauces in this chapter enhance any foods that are simply prepared — without breaking the calorie bank. All are low in salt too. And for those who have to be particularly careful of their sodium intake, there are two special recipes: Homemade Ketchup (page 281) and Saltless Dill Pickles (page 286). There is also a surprise mayonnaise made with tofu (page 287) and a Creamy Yogurt Spread (page 287) that can be substituted in many recipes calling for sour cream.

Feisty Tomato Chili Sauce heats up dishes to your family's taste. Make it as spicy as you like with jalapeño peppers.

HERBED TOMATO SAUCE

Fresh herbs lend flavor and color to this robust tomato sauce, which goes with just about anything, from pasta to vegetables. You'll want to have plenty of this versatile sauce on hand. It will keep, covered, in the refrigerator for up to 3 days or in the freezer for up to 2 months.

2 teaspoons olive oil	½ teaspoon each dried basil and oregano, crumbled
1 medium-size yellow onion, finely chopped (1 cup)	¼ teaspoon each salt and black pepper, or to taste
1 can (28 ounces) low-sodium crushed tomatoes with their juice	3 tablespoons minced fresh basil, chervil, or parsley or snipped chives or a combination

1 In a medium-size heavy saucepan, heat the oil over moderate heat. Add the onion and sauté, stirring occasionally, for 5 minutes or until soft. Lower the heat and add the tomatoes, dried basil and oregano, salt, and pepper and bring to a simmer. Cook, covered, stirring occasionally, for 15 minutes. Stir in the fresh basil. Serve over Cheese Polenta (page 184). Makes 3½ cups.

PREPARATION TIME: 7 MIN.   COOKING TIME: 20 MIN.

Per ½ cup: Calories 43; Saturated Fat 0 g; Total Fat 2 g; Protein 1 g; Carbohydrate 7 g; Fiber 1 g; Sodium 149 mg; Cholesterol 0 mg

•

Onions and Orange Variation: Increase the olive oil to *1 tablespoon* and the onions to *2 cups*. In a large saucepan, heat the oil over moderately low heat. Add the onions and *2 cloves minced garlic* and cook, covered, stirring occasionally, for 5 minutes. Add the tomatoes, *2 strips orange zest (2 inches long), 2 tablespoons tomato paste, ½ teaspoon sugar,* the dried basil and oregano, salt, and pepper. Bring to a boil; simmer, covered, stirring occasionally, for 30 minutes. Omit the fresh basil. Transfer the sauce to a food processor or blender and, working in batches, purée until smooth. Serve immediately or cover and refrigerate. Makes 3½ cups. *Per ½ cup: Calories 63; Saturated Fat 0 g; Total Fat 2 g; Protein 2 g; Carbohydrate 10 g; Fiber 2 g; Sodium 130 mg; Cholesterol 0 mg.*

TOMATO MEAT SAUCE

1 **clove garlic, minced**	¼ **cup minced parsley**
2 **large yellow onions, finely chopped (3 cups)**	1 **tablespoon dried basil, crumbled**
8 **ounces lean ground beef**	1 **teaspoon dried oregano, crumbled**
2 **cans (28 ounces each) low-sodium crushed tomatoes**	¾ **teaspoon salt, or to taste**
2 **tablespoons tomato paste**	¼ **teaspoon black pepper**
1¼ **cups chopped mushrooms (4 ounces)**	2 **packages (4 grams each) reduced-sodium beef broth granules**

1 In a large saucepan over moderately low heat, combine the garlic, onions, and beef, breaking up the beef with a spoon. Cook, stirring occasionally, for 8 minutes or until the meat is no longer pink. Stir in the tomatoes, tomato paste, mushrooms, parsley, basil, oregano, salt, pepper, and beef broth granules. Bring to a simmer and cook, partially covered, for 30 minutes or until thickened. Makes 8 cups or enough to serve with 2 pounds of pasta.

PREPARATION TIME: 18 MIN. COOKING TIME: 40 MIN.

Per 1 cup: Calories 101; Saturated Fat 1 g; Total Fat 2 g; Protein 9 g; Carbohydrate 14 g; Fiber 2 g; Sodium 342 mg; Cholesterol 16 mg

BARBECUE SAUCE

1 **teaspoon dry mustard**	½ **teaspoon dried oregano, crumbled**
1½ **tablespoons cider vinegar**	¼ **teaspoon salt**
1 **teaspoon olive oil**	1 **can (8 ounces) low-sodium tomato sauce**
1 **medium-size yellow onion, finely chopped (1 cup)**	1 **tablespoon Worcestershire or low-sodium soy sauce**
2 **cloves garlic, minced**	1½ **tablespoons each honey and molasses**
2 **teaspoons chili powder**	

1 In a cup, stir the mustard with the vinegar until dissolved. Let stand for at least 10 minutes. In a small saucepan, heat the oil over moderately low heat. Add the onion, garlic, chili powder, oregano, and salt. Cook, stirring occasionally, for 8 minutes or until the onion is soft.

Stir in the tomato sauce, Worcestershire sauce, honey, and molasses. Bring to a simmer; cook, partially covered, stirring occasionally, for 10 minutes or until thickened. Will keep, refrigerated, for up to 2 weeks. Makes 1¼ cups.

PREPARATION TIME: 10 MIN. COOKING TIME: 20 MIN.
STANDING TIME: 10 MIN.

Per tablespoon: Calories 20; Saturated Fat 0 g; Total Fat 0 g; Protein 0 g; Carbohydrate 5 g; Fiber 0 g; Sodium 41 mg; Cholesterol 4 mg

TOMATO CHILI SAUCE

Spoon this sauce over burgers or grilled meats, toss some with your favorite pasta, or dip a chip in it. If any is left over, store it, covered, in the refrigerator for up to 5 days.

2 **teaspoons olive oil**	1 **tablespoon ground cumin**
1 **medium-size yellow onion, finely chopped (1 cup)**	2 **large tomatoes, peeled, seeded, and chopped (3 cups) (see Tip, page 280)**
1 **large sweet green pepper, cored, seeded, and finely chopped (1 cup)**	1½ **cups low-sodium tomato sauce**
2 **tablespoons chili powder, or to taste**	½ **teaspoon salt**
1 **tablespoon minced fresh oregano or 1 teaspoon dried oregano, crumbled**	2 **medium-size jalapeño peppers, seeded and finely chopped (optional)**
	3 **tablespoons minced fresh cilantro (coriander)**

1 In a medium-size saucepan, heat the oil over moderate heat. Add the onion and green pepper and sauté, stirring occasionally, for 3 minutes. Add the chili powder, oregano, and cumin and cook, stirring, for 1 minute. Add the tomatoes, tomato sauce, salt, and jalapeño peppers if desired, and bring to a boil. Lower the heat and simmer, covered, for 20 minutes. Stir in the cilantro. Makes 4 cups.

PREPARATION TIME: 20 MIN. COOKING TIME: 25 MIN.

Per ½ cup: Calories 68; Saturated Fat 0 g; Total Fat 2 g; Protein 2 g; Carbohydrate 12 g; Fiber 3 g; Sodium 177 mg; Cholesterol 0 mg

Tomato sauces have dozens of uses. And when they're as good as these homemade versions, leftovers are never a problem. Drizzle some over broiled fish or roasted meat or poultry. Spice up meat loaf or eggs, any style. Brush a little on lightly broiled vegetables. Or top such meatless entrées as Black Bean Pancakes (page 163), Bulgur-Stuffed Cabbage (page 165), Bean Burritos (page 161), or Eggplant-Ricotta Loaf (page 175).

You can use tomato sauce on baked potatoes as a low-calorie, low-fat alternative to sour cream or butter. Pour it over polenta or rice. Add it to dips, sauces, soups, stews, marinades, and casseroles. And whisk 1 or 2 tablespoons with oil and vinegar for a zesty vinaigrette.

QUICK TOMATO-PEPPER SAUCE

This super simple sauce will brighten up any meal. Try it over Cheese Squares (page 187).

½ small sweet red pepper, cored, seeded, and cut into chunks	1 can (8 ounces) low-sodium tomato sauce
1 green onion top, cut into 1-inch lengths	4 drops hot red pepper sauce

1 In a blender or food processor, whirl the sweet red pepper, onion, tomato sauce, and red pepper sauce for 2 minutes or until smooth. Makes about 1 cup.

PREPARATION TIME: 5 MIN.

Per ¼ cup: Calories 25; Saturated Fat 0 g; Total Fat 0 g; Protein 1 g; Carbohydrate 5 g; Fiber 1 g; Sodium 17 mg; Cholesterol 0 mg

SWEET RED PEPPER SAUCE

This delectable sauce turns chicken, fish, and pasta into something special. Why not make a double batch and freeze the extra? It will keep at 0° F for up to 3 months. When unexpected guests arrive, thaw and reheat the sauce gently.

3 teaspoons olive oil	3 large sweet red peppers, cored, seeded, and thinly sliced (4½ cups)
2 medium-size yellow onions, thinly sliced (4 cups)	¼ teaspoon salt
3 cloves garlic, minced	⅛ teaspoon each ground cinnamon, ginger, and cardamom

1 In a 12-inch nonstick skillet, heat 2 teaspoons of the oil over low heat. Add the onion and cook, stirring frequently, for 5 minutes or until softened. Add the garlic and cook 5 minutes longer. Add the remaining teaspoon of oil and the peppers, salt, cinnamon, ginger, and cardamom and cook, covered, over low heat for 15 minutes or until the peppers are soft.

2 Transfer the mixture to a food processor or blender and whirl for 1 minute or until smooth. Serve with 1 pound of pasta or spoon over 4 servings of broiled fish or poached chicken. Makes 2⅔ cups.

PREPARATION TIME: 15 MIN. COOKING TIME: 25 MIN.

Per ⅔ cup: Calories 112; Saturated Fat 1 g; Total Fat 4 g; Protein 3 g; Carbohydrate 19 g; Fiber 4 g; Sodium 140 mg; Cholesterol 0 mg

For a Caribbean cookout this summer, set aside the usual barbecue sauce in favor of Jamaican Jerk Paste, a sweet-tart mixture redolent with pungent spices and garlic.

272

JAMAICAN JERK PASTE

In Jamaica jerk is a spicy, savory paste originally used to preserve pork before it was spit-roasted. Brush this paste on broiled chicken or beef as well as pork. If you have time, let the meat marinate with it for several hours or overnight.

6 green onions, including tops, sliced (¾ cup)	1 ½ teaspoons each ground allspice and cinnamon
8 cloves garlic	1 ¼ teaspoons ground ginger
¼ cup corn oil	1 teaspoon salt
2 tablespoons red wine vinegar	½ teaspoon black pepper
2 tablespoons lime juice	¼ teaspoon ground red pepper (cayenne)
2 tablespoons firmly packed dark brown sugar	

1 In a food processor or blender, whirl the green onions, garlic, oil, vinegar, and lime juice for 30 seconds or until smooth. Add the sugar, allspice, cinnamon, ginger, salt, black pepper, and red pepper and blend for 1 minute or until well combined. The paste will keep, covered and refrigerated, for up to 2 weeks. It may also be frozen at 0° F for up to 3 months (see Tip, page 286); thaw before using. Makes about 1 cup.

2 To use on chicken or turkey cutlets: Spread 1 ½ tablespoons of the paste over each cutlet before baking, broiling, or grilling. To use for roasting a chicken: Spread ½ cup of the mixture under the skin before roasting.

PREPARATION TIME: 15 MIN.

Per tablespoon: Calories 40; Saturated Fat 0 g; Total Fat 3 g; Protein 0 g; Carbohydrate 3 g; Fiber 0 g; Sodium 134 mg; Cholesterol 0 mg

BASIL-GARLIC PESTO

To cut down on fat, cottage cheese and chicken stock are used here to supplement a small quantity of oil If you are making this sauce ahead of time, do not blend the oil with the other ingredients; instead, scoop them into a container, pour the olive oil on top, cover, and refrigerate. The sauce will keep for up to 5 days. Bring to room temperature and stir well before serving.

½ cup Chicken Stock or Vegetable Stock (page 62) or low-sodium chicken broth	⅓ cup no-salt-added low-fat (1% milkfat) cottage cheese
6 large cloves garlic, thinly sliced	2 tablespoons grated Parmesan cheese
2 cups lightly packed basil leaves	¼ teaspoon salt
2 tablespoons toasted walnuts	⅛ teaspoon black pepper
	1 tablespoon olive oil

1 In a small skillet, bring the stock and garlic to a boil, reduce the heat to low, and simmer, uncovered, for 4 minutes or until the garlic is tender. Transfer the stock and garlic to a food processor or blender, add the basil, walnuts, cottage cheese, Parmesan cheese, salt, and pepper, and whirl for 30 seconds or until smooth. Add the oil and blend for 10 seconds. Serve immediately with 1 pound of pasta. Makes about 1 cup.

PREPARATION TIME: 15 MIN.   COOKING TIME: 5 MIN.

Per ¼ cup: Calories 98; Saturated Fat 1 g; Total Fat 7 g; Protein 5 g; Carbohydrate 5 g; Fiber 2 g; Sodium 224 mg; Cholesterol 3 mg

The word *pesto* comes from the Italian *pestare,* meaning "to make a paste." The rich, garlicky version made with basil is traditionally served with linguine or spaghetti. But pesto is not just for pasta. It can be a dip for raw vegetables or a sauce for cooked fish or seafood. Brush some on toasted slices of French bread for an instant appetizer. Spread it over chicken before roasting or on top of broiled pork chops. Toss steamed green beans or thinly sliced summer squash with pesto. Stir 1 or 2 tablespoons into your next omelet, soufflé, or scrambled eggs. Add it to salad dressings, soups, sauces, rice, or potatoes.

Pesto can be frozen for up to 3 months, so you can keep some on hand for quick meals. For best results when freezing, omit the cheese from the recipe and stir it in just before serving. If the pesto seems too thick, add 1 or 2 teaspoons of hot water.

CREAM SAUCE FOR PASTA

Neufchâtel cheese (a low-fat cream cheese) and a boiled potato make this sauce thick and rich without too much fat. If you prepare this recipe ahead of time, it will keep in the refrigerator for up to 3 days. Reheat it slowly over low heat.

- 2 cups water
- 1 medium-size all-purpose potato, peeled, halved, and thinly sliced (¾ cup)
- 2 cloves garlic
- ½ teaspoon salt
- 3 ounces Neufchâtel cream cheese
- 2 teaspoons snipped fresh chives
- ½ teaspoon dried oregano, crumbled

1 In a 10-inch nonstick skillet, bring the water, potato, and garlic to a boil over moderate heat. Lower the heat and simmer, covered, for about 12 minutes or until the potato is tender. Transfer the potato, garlic, and half of the cooking liquid to a food processor or blender and whirl for 1 minute or until smooth. Add the cream cheese and whirl 30 seconds longer.

2 Return the mixture to the skillet, stir in the chives and oregano, and cook over moderate heat for 1 minute or until bubbling and of a coating consistency. Serve immediately with 1 pound of pasta. Makes 2⅓ cups.

PREPARATION TIME: 7 MIN. COOKING TIME: 13 MIN.

Per ½ cup: Calories 81; Saturated Fat 3 g; Total Fat 4 g; Protein 3 g; Carbohydrate 8 g; Fiber 0 g; Sodium 303 mg; Cholesterol 14 mg

Broccoli Variation: Before cooking the pasta, bring a stockpot of water to boil. Stir in *3½ cups small broccoli florets (8 ounces)* and cook for 5 minutes or until crisp-tender. Remove the broccoli florets with a slotted spoon and add them to the skillet in Step 2 along with the chives and oregano. Bring the water to a boil again and cook the pasta. Toss the cooked pasta with the sauce; serve immediately. *Per 1 cup: Calories 76; Saturated Fat 2 g; Total Fat 4 g; Protein 4 g; Carbohydrate 10 g; Fiber 2 g; Sodium 250 mg; Cholesterol 10 mg.*

CREAMY CHICKEN GRAVY

This low-fat version of chicken gravy is sure to please. Try it over roast chicken, turkey, or veal.

- 1 tablespoon drippings from roast chicken or unsalted butter
- ¼ cup finely chopped onion
- ¼ cup finely chopped celery
- 2 tablespoons all-purpose flour
- 2 cups Chicken Stock (page 62) or low-sodium chicken broth
- 1 bay leaf
- ¼ cup skim milk
- ¼ teaspoon salt
- ⅛ teaspoon black pepper

1 In a medium-size saucepan, heat the drippings over moderate heat. Add the onion and celery and sauté, stirring occasionally, for 5 minutes or until soft. Lower the heat, stir in the flour, and cook, stirring, 3 minutes more or until golden and bubbling. Stir in the stock and bay leaf, bring to a boil, then lower the heat and simmer, stirring occasionally, for 10 minutes. Add the milk, salt, and pepper and simmer for about 2 minutes or until heated through. Remove and discard the bay leaf. If not serving right away, lay a piece of wax paper or plastic food wrap on the surface of the sauce to keep a skin from forming. Remove the paper before reheating. Makes 2⅔ cups.

PREPARATION TIME: 10 MIN. COOKING TIME: 20 MIN.

Per ⅓ cup: Calories 34; Saturated Fat 1 g; Total Fat 2 g; Protein 2 g; Carbohydrate 2 g; Fiber 0 g; Sodium 107 mg; Cholesterol 2 mg

Mushroom Variation: To the heated drippings, add *4 ounces sliced mushrooms (1½ cups)* along with the onion and celery and cook over moderately low heat, stirring occasionally, for 5 to 7 minutes or until tender. Proceed as directed. Makes 3½ cups. *Per ½ cup: Calories 43; Saturated Fat 1 g; Total Fat 3 g; Protein 1 g; Carbohydrate 4 g; Fiber 0 g; Sodium 123 mg; Cholesterol 3 mg.*

BETTER BROWN GRAVY

Your roasts and meat loaves will shimmer with this tempting gravy. The seasonings come together so beautifully, you won't believe that it is low in fat and calories. For extra-special occasions, try the variations below.

- 1 tablespoon unsalted butter
- 2 tablespoons each finely chopped carrot, celery, and yellow onion
- 2 tablespoons all-purpose flour
- 1 ½ cups beef stock or low-sodium beef broth
- 2 teaspoons tomato paste
- ¼ teaspoon dried thyme, crumbled
- 1 small bay leaf
- ¼ teaspoon salt
- ⅛ teaspoon black pepper

1 In a medium-size saucepan, melt the butter over moderate heat. Add the carrot, celery, and onion and sauté, stirring occasionally, for 5 minutes or until golden. Lower the heat, add the flour, and cook, stirring, for 3 minutes or until golden and bubbling. Stir in the stock, tomato paste, thyme, and bay leaf; bring to a boil, stirring until smooth and thickened. Lower the heat and simmer, covered, for 10 minutes. Stir in the salt and pepper. Remove and discard the bay leaf. Makes 1 ½ cups.

PREPARATION TIME: 10 MIN. COOKING TIME: 20 MIN.

Per ¼ cup: Calories 35; Saturated Fat 1 g; Total Fat 2 g; Protein 1 g; Carbohydrate 3 g; Fiber 0 g; Sodium 170 mg; Cholesterol 6 mg

•

Herb Variation: Stir in *2 tablespoons minced fresh tarragon, chives, or chervil* before serving. Makes 1 ½ cups. *Per ¼ cup: Calories 35; Saturated Fat 1 g; Total Fat 2 g; Protein 1 g; Carbohydrate 3 g; Fiber 0 g; Sodium 171 mg; Cholesterol 6 mg.*

•

Red Wine and Shallot Variation: In a small saucepan, combine *¼ cup minced shallot* with *½ cup dry red wine* and cook, uncovered, over moderately high heat until reduced to ¼ cup. Add to the above mixture at the same time as the beef stock and proceed as directed. Makes about 2 cups. *Per ¼ cup: Calories 40; Saturated Fat 1 g; Total Fat 2 g; Protein 1 g; Carbohydrate 3 g; Fiber 0 g; Sodium 129 mg; Cholesterol 4 mg.*

Incredibly light and infused with garlic, the Broccoli Variation of Cream Sauce for Pasta is the perfect foil for *pappardelle* (broad noodles).

275

An egg-based sauce should always be cooked over low heat and removed from the heat as soon as it thickens. Allowing it to boil will cause it to curdle. If curdling does occur, you can salvage the sauce by whirling it in a food processor or blender for about 1 minute.

EASY WHITE SAUCE

Here is a reduced-fat white sauce that can be used in any recipe that calls for a savory cream sauce. Try it over vegetables, chicken, or fish.

1 tablespoon unsalted butter	1 ½ cups warm skim milk
1 small shallot, finely chopped (2 tablespoons)	¼ teaspoon salt
	⅛ teaspoon white pepper
2 tablespoons all-purpose flour	⅛ teaspoon ground nutmeg, or to taste

1 In a medium-size saucepan, melt the butter over moderate heat. Add the shallot and sauté, stirring, for 3 minutes. Lower the heat, add the flour, and cook, stirring, 3 minutes more or until golden and bubbling. Pour in the milk and bring to a simmer, stirring constantly, for 5 minutes or until thickened and smooth. Add the salt, pepper, and nutmeg. Makes about 1 ½ cups.

PREPARATION TIME: 5 MIN.   COOKING TIME: 11 MIN.

Per ¼ cup: Calories 51; Saturated Fat 1 g; Total Fat 2 g; Protein 2 g; Carbohydrate 5 g; Fiber 0 g; Sodium 121 mg; Cholesterol 7 mg

•

Mustard Variation: Add *1 tablespoon plus 1 teaspoon Dijon mustard* to the finished sauce. *Per ¼ cup: Calories 55; Saturated Fat 1 g; Total Fat 2 g; Protein 3 g; Carbohydrate 6 g; Fiber 0 g; Sodium 205 mg; Cholesterol 7 mg*

•

Onion Variation: Substitute for the shallot *1 ½ cups finely chopped yellow onion (1 large onion)* and sauté it in the butter over moderate heat, stirring occasionally, for 5 minutes. Add the flour and simmer, stirring, for 3 minutes or until golden and bubbling. Stir in the heated skim milk and cook 5 minutes longer or until thickened. Transfer the sauce to a food processor or blender and whirl for 30 seconds or until smooth; return to the saucepan. Stir in *¼ cup reduced-fat sour cream or half-and-half* and bring to a simmer, stirring, over moderately low heat for 1 minute or until heated through. Makes about 2 ½ cups. *Per ¼ cup: Calories 50; Saturated Fat 2 g; Total Fat 2 g; Protein 2 g; Carbohydrate 5 g; Fiber 0 g; Sodium 80 mg; Cholesterol 4 mg;*

GREEK LEMON SAUCE

Lemon and dill combine to make a refreshing sauce that goes beautifully over steamed vegetables, roast chicken, or baked fish.

1 ½ cups Chicken Stock (page 62) or low-sodium chicken broth	1 egg yolk
	3 tablespoons lemon juice
1 tablespoon cornstarch mixed with 2 tablespoons water	2 tablespoons snipped fresh dill

1 In a medium-size saucepan, bring the stock to a boil over moderately high heat. Lower the heat, stir in the cornstarch mixture, and simmer, stirring occasionally, for 5 minutes.

2 In a small bowl, whisk together the egg yolk and lemon juice. Whisk in ½ cup of the hot stock, then pour the mixture back into the saucepan, whisking constantly. Simmer, whisking, for 1 minute (do not allow the sauce to boil or it may curdle). Stir in the dill. Makes 1 ½ cups.

PREPARATION TIME: 5 MIN.   COOKING TIME: 7 MIN.

Per ¼ cup: Calories 23; Saturated Fat 0 g; Total Fat 1 g; Protein 1 g; Carbohydrate 2 g; Fiber 0 g; Sodium 35 mg; Cholesterol 36 mg

Greek Lemon Sauce, touched with dill, heightens the simple, fresh taste of spring vegetables to perfection.

SPICY CUMBERLAND SAUCE

Cumberland sauce, made from currant jelly and red wine, is an English favorite that is served at room temperature with roasted meats. If you prefer, substitute nonalcoholic red wine or grape juice for the red wine.

¼ cup Chicken Stock (page 62) or low-sodium chicken broth	⅛ teaspoon each ground cinnamon, cloves, and ginger
¼ cup dry red wine	Pinch salt
3 tablespoons cider vinegar	¼ cup currant or grape jelly
3 green onions, including tops, chopped (⅓ cup)	1 ½ tablespoons cornstarch mixed with 1 tablespoon water
½ clove garlic, minced	

1 In a small enameled or stainless steel saucepan, combine the stock, wine, vinegar, green onions, garlic, cinnamon, cloves, ginger, and salt. Bring to a boil over moderate heat and cook, uncovered, for 6 minutes or until the sauce is reduced to about ½ cup. Strain through a fine sieve and return to the saucepan.

2 Reduce the heat to moderately low and stir in the jelly. Bring to a simmer, stir in the cornstarch mixture, and cook, stirring, for 1 minute or until thickened. Will keep, covered and refrigerated, for up to 2 weeks. Use about 1 tablespoon per serving for grilled or broiled poultry or meat. Makes about ⅔ cup.

PREPARATION TIME: 10 MIN.   COOKING TIME: 7 MIN.

Per tablespoon: Calories 27; Saturated Fat 0 g; Total Fat 0 g; Protein 0 g; Carbohydrate 6 g; Fiber 0 g; Sodium 24 mg; Cholesterol 0 mg

ELEGANT SUNDAY SUPPER

Creamy Parsnip Soup
(Page 80)

Four-Grain Rolls
(Page 304)

Broiled Ham Steak
with
Spicy Cumberland Sauce

Steamed Green Beans
and
Baby Carrots

Blueberry Clafouti
(Page 336)

Sparkling Mineral
Water

When only the richest, creamiest accompaniment will do, try yogurt-based Almond-Chive Sauce.

CUCUMBER-YOGURT SAUCE

This Middle Eastern sauce is refreshing with spicy foods. Try it with Three-Bean Terrine (page 162) or Tandoori Fish Kebabs (page 84). For a chunkier sauce, do not blend the ingredients (see Step 2), but stir them together in a bowl.

- 1 medium-size cucumber (8 ounces), peeled, seeded, and shredded
- ¼ teaspoon salt
- ⅔ cup plain low-fat yogurt
- ⅓ cup reduced-fat sour cream
- 1 clove garlic, minced
- 2 teaspoons lemon juice
- ⅛ teaspoon black pepper or ground red pepper (cayenne), or to taste
- 2 tablespoons snipped fresh dill

1 In a colander, sprinkle the cucumber with ⅛ teaspoon of the salt and let it drain for 15 minutes. Using your hands, gently squeeze the cucumber dry.

2 In a food processor or blender, whirl the cucumber, yogurt, sour cream, garlic, lemon juice, pepper, and remaining ⅛ teaspoon of salt for 30 seconds or until smooth. Transfer the sauce to a bowl and stir in the dill. Cover and refrigerate for at least 1 hour; will keep for up to 4 days. Makes about 2 cups.

PREPARATION TIME: 10 MIN. STANDING TIME: 15 MIN.

CHILLING TIME: 1 HR.

Per ¼ cup: Calories 40; Saturated Fat 2 g; Total Fat 2 g; Protein 2 g; Carbohydrate 3 g; Fiber 0 g; Sodium 92 mg; Cholesterol 1 mg

ALMOND-CHIVE SAUCE

To blanch almonds for this sauce, place them in a small bowl with enough boiling water to cover; let them stand for 1 minute, drain, then rinse under cold water. The skins should slip right off.

1 cup plain low-fat yogurt	1/4 teaspoon salt
10 whole almonds, blanched	1/8 teaspoon ground red pepper (cayenne)
1 clove garlic	2 tablespoons snipped fresh chives or minced tarragon
2 teaspoons olive oil	
1 tablespoon white wine vinegar or cider vinegar	

1 In a food processor or blender, whirl 1/4 cup of the yogurt with the almonds, garlic, oil, vinegar, salt, and red pepper for 15 seconds. Using a rubber spatula, scrape down the sides of the work bowl; whirl 15 seconds longer.

2 Transfer the mixture to a small bowl and stir in the remaining yogurt and the chives. Cover and refrigerate for at least 1 hour; will keep for up to 5 days. Serve chilled over fish, veal, or chicken. Makes about 1 1/4 cups.

PREPARATION TIME: 10 MIN. CHILLING TIME: 1 HR.

Per 1/4 cup: Calories 84; Saturated Fat 1 g; Total Fat 6 g; Protein 4 g; Carbohydrate 5 g; Fiber 1 g; Sodium 140 mg; Cholesterol 3 mg

WATERCRESS- BUTTERMILK SAUCE

When served chilled, this creamy sauce is an ideal complement to poached chicken or fish. To turn it into a salad dressing, add 1 teaspoon each of vinegar and mayonnaise.

1/2 clove garlic	1/2 teaspoon Dijon mustard
1/2 cup watercress leaves, rinsed	1 teaspoon lemon juice
1/2 cup buttermilk	3 drops hot red pepper sauce
1/3 cup low-fat (1% milkfat) cottage cheese	1/8 teaspoon salt, or to taste
2 tablespoons plain dry bread crumbs	

1 In a food processor or blender, whirl the garlic, watercress, buttermilk, cottage cheese, bread crumbs, mustard, lemon juice, red pepper sauce, and salt for 30 seconds or until smooth. Chill for at least 1 hour; will keep, covered and refrigerated, for up to 3 days. Makes 1 cup.

PREPARATION TIME: 8 MIN. CHILLING TIME: 1 HR.

Per 1/4 cup: Calories 40; Saturated Fat 0 g; Total Fat 1 g; Protein 4 g; Carbohydrate 5 g; Fiber 0 g; Sodium 216 mg; Cholesterol 2 mg

ORIENTAL BARBECUE SAUCE

For a taste of the Orient, brush 1 to 2 tablespoons of this sauce on a serving of poultry or fish during the last 5 minutes of grilling. Or toss some of the sauce (1 tablespoon per serving) with steamed vegetables.

1 tablespoon cornstarch	1/4 cup orange marmalade or currant jelly
2 tablespoons water	1 teaspoon grated fresh ginger or 1/4 teaspoon ground ginger
2 tablespoons reduced-sodium soy sauce	
2 tablespoons reduced-sodium ketchup	1/2 teaspoon minced garlic
1/4 cup cider vinegar	Pinch ground cloves

1 In a small saucepan, stir together the cornstarch and water until dissolved. Stir in the soy sauce, ketchup, vinegar, marmalade, ginger, garlic, and cloves. Bring to a boil over moderately high heat, stirring constantly, and simmer for 1 minute or until thickened. Will keep, covered and refrigerated, for up to 1 week. Makes about 3/4 cup.

PREPARATION TIME: 7 MIN. COOKING TIME: 1 MIN.

Per tablespoon: Calories 24; Saturated Fat 0 g; Total Fat 0 g; Protein 0 g; Carbohydrate 6 g; Fiber 0 g; Sodium 96 mg; Cholesterol 0 mg

Peeling and seeding tomatoes takes just a few minutes. The first step in peeling is to bring a large saucepan of water to a boil. Immerse the tomatoes in the boiling water for 10 to 15 seconds. (Firm tomatoes may take up to 30 seconds.) Using a slotted spoon, transfer them to a bowl of cold water to cool them quickly, then remove the core and peel off the skin with a small knife.

To seed tomatoes, cut them in half and squeeze the juice and seeds into a sieve set over a glass measuring cup. You can use the juice in a sauce or a vegetable-juice cocktail.

TOMATO SALSA

You may never again use bottled salsa once you've tasted this fresh and easy homemade version.

2 **large ripe tomatoes, peeled, seeded, and diced (3 cups)**
½ **cup low-sodium tomato sauce**
3 **green onions, including tops, finely chopped (⅓ cup)**
3 **tablespoons minced fresh cilantro (coriander) or 3 tablespoons minced parsley plus 1 ½ teaspoons dried cilantro**

1 **medium-size jalapeño pepper, seeded and finely chopped (about 1 ½ tablespoons)**
½ **teaspoon salt, or to taste**
1 **tablespoon red wine vinegar (optional)**

1 In a medium-size bowl, combine the tomatoes, tomato sauce, green onions, cilantro, jalapeño pepper, salt, and vinegar if desired. Refrigerate, covered, until ready to serve. This salsa is best eaten within a few hours after it is made, but it can be refrigerated for up to 2 days. Makes about 3 cups.

PREPARATION TIME: 13 MIN.

Per ¼ cup: Calories 14; Saturated Fat 0 g; Total Fat 0 g; Protein 1 g; Carbohydrate 3 g; Fiber 1 g; Sodium 96 mg; Cholesterol 0 mg

COOKED SALSA

Make this salsa during the height of tomato season and serve it whenever you want to fend off the winter chill. You can adjust the spiciness by increasing or decreasing the quantity of serrano peppers, mildly hot small green chilies.

1 **tablespoon olive oil**
1 **large yellow onion, finely chopped (1 ½ cups)**
1 **large sweet green pepper, cored, seeded, and diced (1 cup)**
1 **serrano pepper, seeded and finely chopped (¾ teaspoon) or ½ teaspoon finely chopped fresh or canned jalapeño pepper**

4 **cloves garlic, minced**
7 **medium-size ripe tomatoes, peeled, seeded, and coarsely chopped (7 cups)**
2 **tablespoons red wine vinegar**
1 **teaspoon salt**
¾ **teaspoon ground cumin**
¼ **cup minced fresh cilantro (coriander) or ¼ cup minced parsley plus 2 teaspoons dried cilantro**

1 In a large enameled or stainless steel saucepan, heat the oil over low heat. Add the onion and cook, stirring occasionally, for 7 minutes or until softened. Stir in the sweet green pepper, serrano pepper, and garlic and cook 4 minutes longer or until the peppers are softened. Stir in the tomatoes, vinegar, salt, and cumin and bring to a boil. Lower the heat and simmer, uncovered, for 5 to 7 minutes or until the sauce thickens. Stir in the cilantro and cook 1 minute longer. Let cool to room temperature before serving. Will keep, covered and refrigerated, for up to 1 week.

2 For longer storage, pour the hot salsa into seven ½-pint canning jars, leaving ¼ inch of head space between the salsa and the jar rim. Cover the jars with dome lids and rings, place them in a boiling water bath, and return to a boil. Process for 10 minutes. (See Box, page 283, for processing.) Remove from the bath and let cool. The next day, check the seals, label, and store in a cool, dry place. The salsa may also be frozen for up to 2 months at 0° F (see Tip, page 286). Makes about 6 ½ cups.

PREPARATION TIME: 25 MIN. COOKING TIME: 18 MIN.

Per ¼ cup: Calories 17; Saturated Fat 0 g; Total Fat 1 g; Protein 0 g; Carbohydrate 3 g; Fiber 1 g; Sodium 87 mg; Cholesterol 0 mg

HOMEMADE KETCHUP

Apple is the surprise ingredient in this special version of America's favorite condiment. You get a rich, tomatoey taste but very little sugar and salt.

4 **large ripe tomatoes, peeled, seeded, and chopped (about 6 cups), or 4 cans (14½ ounces each) low-sodium tomatoes with their juice**

2 **medium-size sweet apples, such as Golden Delicious, peeled, cored, and coarsely chopped (about 2½ cups)**

1½ **small yellow onions, chopped (¾ cup)**

2 **cloves garlic, sliced**

½ **cup cider vinegar**

⅓ **cup firmly packed light brown sugar**

1 **tablespoon honey**

½ **teaspoon salt**

½ **teaspoon ground coriander**

¼ **teaspoon ground cloves**

1 **cinnamon stick**

1 In a large enameled or stainless steel saucepan, combine all the ingredients. Bring to a boil over moderate heat, then lower the heat and simmer, covered, stirring occasionally, for 30 minutes or until the apples are soft.

2 Discard the cinnamon stick. In a food processor or blender, whirl the ketchup for 1 minute or until smooth. Pour the ketchup into seven ½-pint canning jars, leaving ¼ inch of head space between the ketchup and the jar rim. Cover the jars with dome lids and rings, place them in a boiling water bath, and return to a boil. Process for 10 minutes. (See Box, page 283, for processing.) Remove from the bath and let cool. The next day, check the seals, label, and store in a cool, dry place for up to 6 months. Makes about 6½ cups.

PREPARATION TIME: 25 MIN. COOKING TIME: 42 MIN.

Per tablespoon: Calories 7; Saturated Fat 0 g; Total Fat 0 g; Protein 0 g; Carbohydrate 2 g; Fiber 0 g; Sodium 11 mg; Cholesterol 0 mg

For guilt-free snacking, surround a bowl of Tomato Salsa (only 14 calories per ¼ cup) with crudités and baked (low-fat) tortilla chips.

281

CORN RELISH

Make a double or even a triple batch of this colorful relish. It keeps for up to 3 months, and you'll want a good supply on hand for yourself and to give to special friends.

1½ **cups cider vinegar**
½ **cup sugar**
½ **teaspoon salt**
½ **teaspoon each celery seeds and mustard seeds**
2 **large sweet green or red peppers (or 1 of each), cored, seeded, and chopped (2 cups)**

2 **cups fresh or frozen corn kernels**
2 **medium-size stalks celery, diced (1 cup)**
1 **small yellow onion, finely chopped (½ cup)**
1 **jalapeño pepper, seeded and finely chopped (optional)**

1 In a medium-size enameled or stainless steel saucepan, combine the vinegar, sugar, salt, celery seeds, and mustard seeds. Bring to a boil over high heat, then lower the heat and simmer, stirring, for 1 minute. Add the sweet peppers, corn, celery, onion, and, if desired, the jalapeño pepper. Bring to a boil again and cook for 10 minutes or until the vegetables are softened. Let cool to room temperature, then store, covered, in the refrigerator for up to 4 days.

2 For longer storage, pour the hot cooked relish into two 1-pint canning jars, leaving ¼ inch of head space between the relish and jar rim. Cover the jars with dome lids and rings, place them in a boiling water bath, and return to a boil. Process for 15 minutes. (See Box, opposite page, for processing.) Remove from the bath and let cool. The next day, check the seals, label, and store in a cool, dry place. The relish may also be frozen for up to 2 months at 0° F. (See Tip, page 286.) Makes about 4 cups.

PREPARATION TIME: 30 MIN. COOKING TIME: 11 MIN.

Per ¼ cup: Calories 45; Saturated Fat 0 g; Total Fat 0 g; Protein 1 g; Carbohydrate 13 g; Fiber 1 g; Sodium 73 mg; Cholesterol 0 mg

Gifts from your kitchen as gorgeous as this Corn Relish never fail to please. Remember to give some to yourself too.

RED ONION RELISH

Slather this zesty relish on hamburgers or serve it with the most elegant roast or steak. It's also wonderful with grilled vegetables.

2 teaspoons unsalted butter	⅛ teaspoon each salt and black pepper, or to taste
2 medium-size red onions, thinly sliced (4 cups)	½ cup dry red wine or chicken broth
3 tablespoons sugar	¼ cup white wine vinegar or red wine vinegar

1 In a 10-inch nonstick skillet, melt the butter over moderate heat. Stir in the onions, sugar, salt, and pepper. Lower the heat and cook, covered, stirring occasionally, for 20 minutes or until thickened. Add the wine and vinegar and simmer 15 minutes more. Raise the heat to high and cook, stirring often, for 3 to 4 minutes or until thickened. Cool to room temperature before serving. Will keep, covered and refrigerated, for up to 1 week.

2 For longer storage, pour the hot cooked relish into two ½-pint canning jars, leaving ¼ inch of head space between the relish and the jar rim. Cover the jars with dome lids and rings, place them in a boiling water bath, and return to a boil. Process for 15 minutes. (See Box, below, for processing.) Remove from the bath and let cool. The next day, check the seals, label, and store in a cool, dry place. The relish may also be frozen for up to 2 months at 0° F (see Tip, page 286). Makes about 2 cups.

PREPARATION TIME: 5 MIN. COOKING TIME: 39 MIN.

Per ¼ cup: Calories 67; Saturated Fat 1 g; Total Fat 1 g; Protein 1 g; Carbohydrate 12 g; Fiber 1 g; Sodium 37 mg; Cholesterol 3 mg

APPLE, HONEY, AND SAGE RELISH

2 teaspoons olive or canola oil	⅓ cup water
1 large yellow onion, diced (1 ½ cups)	1 teaspoon dried sage, crumbled
1 clove garlic, minced	⅛ teaspoon each salt and black pepper, or to taste
4 tart cooking apples, peeled, cored, and diced (6 cups)	2 tablespoons honey
	1 tablespoon lemon juice

1 In a large saucepan, heat the oil over moderately low heat. Add the onion and garlic and cook, covered, stirring occasionally, for 7 minutes or until golden. Add the apples, water, sage, salt, and pepper and cook, covered, stirring occasionally, for 15 to 20 minutes or until the apples are tender. Stir in the honey and lemon juice. Serve warm or cold with pork or poultry. Will keep, covered and refrigerated, for up to 2 weeks. Makes about 3 cups.

PREPARATION TIME: 15 MIN. COOKING TIME: 23 MIN.

Per ¼ cup: Calories 53; Saturated Fat 0 g; Total Fat 1 g; Protein 0 g; Carbohydrate 12 g; Fiber 1 g; Sodium 23 mg; Cholesterol 0 mg

Processing in a water bath destroys harmful organisms and allows foods to be stored for many months without refrigeration. For this procedure, it's best to use glass canning jars with metal dome lids and screw bands. You will also need a pot that holds enough water to circulate freely around the jars and cover them by 1 to 2 inches.

Wash the jars and rinse thoroughly before filling. When adding the contents, leave ¼ to 1 inch of space between the food and the rim of the jar. This head space allows for any expansion that may occur. Wipe the rims clean, seal with the lids and screw bands, and place upright in the boiling water bath. Return the water to a boil and begin counting the processing time, adding 1 minute for each 1,000 feet above sea level. After processing, use jar grippers to lift the jars straight out; tipping the contents can ruin the seal.

After 24 hours, lightly tap the jar lids; if properly sealed, they will give a clear metallic ping (unsealed jars will thud) and the lids will be rigid and slightly depressed in the center. If in doubt about any, remove the screw band and roll the contents around the neck of the jar to check for leakage. Reprocess any jars with imperfect seals. Label and store in a cool, dry place. Refrigerate after opening.

MUSHROOM-WALNUT CHUTNEY

Serve this chutney at a New Year's Day buffet and send a jar home with each guest as a treat for the year to come.

2 ounces coarsely chopped walnuts (about ¾ cup)	12 green onions, including tops, chopped (1½ cups)
2 cups cider vinegar	8 whole cloves
⅔ cup water	2 bay leaves
½ cup dry sherry or water	½ teaspoon ground allspice
½ cup sugar	½ teaspoon black pepper
2½ teaspoons coarse (kosher) salt	2½ pounds small mushrooms, halved (8½ cups)

1 Preheat oven to 400° F. Spread walnuts on a baking sheet and toast in the oven, stirring occasionally, for 5 to 7 minutes or until lightly colored; set aside.

2 In a large enameled or stainless steel saucepan, stir together the vinegar, water, sherry, sugar, salt, green onions, cloves, bay leaves, allspice, and pepper. Bring to a boil over moderate heat. Add mushrooms, return to a boil, then lower the heat and simmer, uncovered, for 40 minutes or until mushrooms are tender and liquid is reduced to a thick syrup. Stir in the walnuts. Remove and discard bay leaves. Serve hot, at room temperature, or chilled. Will keep, covered and refrigerated, for up to 5 days.

3 For longer storage, pour the hot chutney into six ½-pint canning jars, leaving ½ inch of head space between the chutney and jar rim. Cover the jars with dome lids and rings, place them in a boiling water bath, and return to a boil. Process for 10 minutes. (See Box, page 283, for processing.) Remove from the bath and let cool. The next day, check the seals, label, and store in a cool, dry place. The chutney may also be frozen for up to 2 months at 0° F (see Tip, page 286). Makes about 6 cups.

PREPARATION TIME: 15 MIN. COOKING TIME: 48 MIN.

Per tablespoon: Calories 15; Saturated Fat 0 g; Total Fat 1 g; Protein 0 g; Carbohydrate 2 g; Fiber 0 g; Sodium 23 mg; Cholesterol 0 mg

DRIED FRUIT CHUTNEY

Serve this with roast lamb or pork or as an alternative to the traditional cranberry sauce at Thanksgiving dinner. If you prefer a smoother chutney, coarsely chop the dried fruit before cooking.

12 ounces pitted prunes (2 cups)	1 cup water
7 ounces dried apricots (1 cup)	⅔ cup sherry vinegar, cider vinegar, or balsamic vinegar
4 ounces dried pears (1 cup)	1½ teaspoons ground ginger
4 ounces dried peaches (1 cup)	1½ teaspoons salt
4 ounces raisins (1 cup)	1¼ teaspoons mustard seeds
2 medium-size yellow onions, cut into 1-inch cubes (2 cups)	1 teaspoon ground turmeric
1½ cups firmly packed light brown sugar	

1 In a large enameled or stainless steel saucepan, combine the prunes, apricots, pears, peaches, raisins, onions, sugar, water, vinegar, ginger, salt, mustard seeds, and turmeric. Bring to a boil over moderate heat, then lower the heat and simmer, covered, for 40 minutes or until the fruit is tender. Let cool to room temperature. Will keep, covered and refrigerated, for up to 3 weeks.

2 For longer storage, pour the hot cooked chutney into six ½-pint canning jars, leaving ½ inch of head space between the chutney and jar rim. Cover the jars with dome lids and rings, place them in a boiling water bath, and return to a boil. Process for 10 minutes. (See Box, page 283, for processing.) Remove from the bath and let cool. The next day, check the seals, label, and store in a cool, dry place. The chutney may also be frozen for up to 2 months at 0° F (see Tip, page 286). Makes about 5½ cups.

PREPARATION TIME: 12 MIN. COOKING TIME: 45 MIN.

Per tablespoon: Calories 40; Saturated Fat 0 g; Total Fat 0 g; Protein 0 g; Carbohydrate 11 g; Fiber 1 g; Sodium 38 mg; Cholesterol 0 mg

TOMATO CHUTNEY

In India chutneys, or relishes, range from fiery to cooling, from lip-puckering sour to sweet and fruity like this one. Raisins, orange juice, and brown sugar balance the spicier ingredients to produce the perfect accompaniment for hot or cold roast meats.

1 tablespoon olive oil	1 cup raisins
2 medium-size yellow onions, coarsely chopped (about 2 cups)	¾ cup cider vinegar
	½ cup orange juice
1 large sweet red pepper, cored, seeded, and cut into 1-inch squares (1¼ cups)	4 strips orange zest (colored part of the rind), ½ by 3 inches each
1½ tablespoons minced fresh ginger	2 cinnamon sticks
	½ teaspoon salt, or to taste
8 medium-size ripe tomatoes, peeled, seeded, and coarsely chopped (8 cups) (see Tip, page 280)	½ teaspoon ground allspice
	¼ teaspoon each ground red pepper (cayenne) and ground cardamom
2 cups firmly packed dark brown sugar	

1 In a large enameled or stainless steel saucepan, heat the oil over low heat. Add the onions and sweet red pepper and cook, stirring occasionally, for 5 minutes. Add the ginger and cook 2 minutes longer. Stir in the tomatoes, sugar, raisins, vinegar, orange juice, orange zest, cinnamon sticks, salt, allspice, ground red pepper, and cardamom; bring to a boil over moderate heat. Lower the heat and simmer, uncovered, for 1 hour. Let cool to room temperature, then cover and refrigerate for 2 days to allow flavors to mellow. Serve at room temperature or chilled. Will keep, covered and refrigerated, for up to 3 weeks.

2 For longer storage, pour the hot chutney into eight ½-pint canning jars, leaving ½ inch of head space between the chutney and jar rim. Cover the jars with dome lids and rings, place them in a boiling water bath, and return to a boil. Process for 10 minutes. (See Box, page 283, for processing.) Remove from the bath and let cool.

The next day, check the seals, label, and store in a cool, dry place. The chutney may also be frozen for up to 2 months at 0° F (see Tip, page 286). Makes about 7½ cups.

PREPARATION TIME: 25 MIN.   COOKING TIME: 1 HR. 8 MIN.
CHILLING TIME: 48 HR.

Per tablespoon: Calories 22; Saturated Fat 0 g; Total Fat 0 g; Protein 0 g; Carbohydrate 5 g; Fiber 0 g; Sodium 11 mg; Cholesterol 0 mg

Clockwise, from top left: Tomato, Dried Fruit, and Mushroom-Walnut chutneys. These easy condiments turn the simplest meal or snack into something special with few added calories.

Many relishes, chutneys, and sauces can be frozen for up to 3 months at 0° F without being processed in a boiling water bath. Before freezing, let cooked mixtures cool to room temperature. To keep flavors and colors fresh, use airtight glass or plastic containers. Leave an inch of space at the top to allow for expansion of the contents during freezing.

Food freezes faster if you leave space between containers for air to circulate. Later they can be stacked closely. To thaw, leave overnight in the refrigerator.

CRANBERRY-APPLE RELISH

Before the holiday rush, make a batch of this fruity relish. The rich fragrance of orange, apple, cinnamon, and cloves simmering on the stove will put you in the spirit of the season. Serve this special cranberry sauce on both the day of and the days after a holiday feast. It dresses up cold meats, sweet potatoes, or other vegetables.

1 cup water	½ teaspoon ground ginger
⅔ cup firmly packed light brown sugar	¼ teaspoon ground cloves
½ cup cider vinegar	2 small tart, crisp apples, such as McIntosh, peeled, cored, and cut into 1-inch cubes (1⅔ cups)
⅓ cup honey	
1 tablespoon grated orange rind	
1 medium-size orange, peeled, white pith removed, and chopped (about ½ cup)	1 package (12 ounces) cranberries
	½ cup raisins
1 teaspoon ground cinnamon	½ cup chopped pecans or walnuts

1 In a large enameled or stainless steel saucepan, bring the water, sugar, vinegar, honey, orange rind, orange, cinnamon, ginger, and cloves to a boil, stirring, over moderately high heat. Lower the heat and simmer, stirring occasionally, for 2 to 3 minutes or until the sugar has dissolved. Add the apples, return the liquid to a simmer, and cook, stirring occasionally, 10 minutes more. Add the cranberries and cook at a low boil over moderate heat, stirring occasionally, another 10 to 15 minutes or until thick. Stir in the raisins and nuts; transfer to a medium-size bowl to cool. Cover and chill. Will keep, covered and refrigerated, for up to 2 weeks.

2 For longer storage, pour the hot cooked relish into four ½-pint canning jars, leaving ¼ inch of head space between the relish and jar rim. Cover the jars with dome lids and rings, place them in a boiling water bath, and return to a boil. Process for 10 minutes. (See Box, page 283, for processing.) Remove from the bath and let cool. The

next day, check the seals, label, and store in a cool, dry place. The relish may also be frozen for up to 2 months at 0° F (see Tip, this page). Makes about 3½ cups.

PREPARATION TIME: 15 MIN.   COOKING TIME: 25 MIN.

Per tablespoon: Calories 33; Saturated Fat 0 g; Total Fat 1 g; Protein 0 g; Carbohydrate 7 g; Fiber 0 g; Sodium 1 mg; Cholesterol 0 mg

SALTLESS DILL PICKLES

For those who love a crunchy dill pickle, this super simple recipe has all of the great vinegary flavor but none of the salt. Enjoy one with your favorite sandwich.

1 teaspoon coriander seeds	12 large sprigs fresh dill
1 teaspoon ground turmeric	8 small Kirby cucumbers (about 2 pounds), ends trimmed
¼ small yellow onion, sliced	3 cups water
1 small carrot, peeled and thinly sliced (24 slices)	2 cups cider vinegar

1 Divide the coriander seeds, turmeric, onion, carrot, and dill equally between 2 clean 1-quart canning jars, then add 4 cucumbers to each.

2 Meanwhile, in a medium-size enameled or stainless steel saucepan, bring the water and vinegar to a boil over high heat. Pour half of the hot liquid into each jar, leaving ½ inch of head space between the liquid and jar rim. Cover the jars with dome lids and rings, place them in a boiling water bath, and return to a boil. Process for 10 minutes. (See Box, page 283, for processing.) Remove from the bath and let cool. The next day, check the seals, label, and store in a cool, dry place for 1 month before eating. Will keep for up to 4 months. Makes 8 pickles.

PREPARATION TIME: 10 MIN.   COOKING TIME: 10 MIN.

Per pickle: Calories 22; Saturated Fat 0 g; Total Fat 0 g; Protein 1 g; Carbohydrate 9 g; Fiber 2 g; Sodium 8 mg; Cholesterol 0 mg

CREAMY YOGURT SPREAD

Draining yogurt of excess whey gives it a texture very similar to that of sour cream. Spoon a dollop of it on baked potatoes, waffles, or chili, or use it to make low-calorie dips and sandwich fillings.

32 ounces plain low-fat or nonfat yogurt

1 Line a large sieve with 4 layers of dampened cheesecloth and place it over a large bowl. Spoon the yogurt into the sieve, cover, and chill for at least 3 or up to 12 hours. (The longer it drains, the thicker it becomes.) The yogurt will keep, covered and refrigerated, for up to 1 week. Low-fat yogurt yields 2 to 3 cups; nonfat yogurt yields 1 ½ to 2 cups.

PREPARATION TIME: 5 MIN. CHILLING TIME: 3 HR.

Per tablespoon: Calories 18; Saturated Fat 0 g; Total Fat 0 g; Protein 1 g; Carbohydrate 2 g; Fiber 0 g; Sodium 20 mg; Cholesterol 2 mg

TOFU MAYONNAISE

Make this terrific low-calorie, low-fat, no-cholesterol mayonnaise without cracking even 1 egg. Use it just as you would the real thing.

8 ounces firm tofu, cubed (about 1 cup)
½ cup plain low-fat yogurt
1 tablespoon tarragon vinegar
2 teaspoons vegetable or olive oil
1 teaspoon prepared mustard
¼ teaspoon salt, or to taste
⅛ teaspoon ground red pepper (cayenne) or black pepper, or to taste
2 tablespoons minced fresh tarragon, chives, or parsley

1 In a food processor or blender, whirl the tofu, yogurt, vinegar, oil, mustard, salt, and red pepper, scraping down the sides once, for 30 seconds or until smooth. Transfer the mayonnaise to a container and stir in the tarragon. Cover and chill for 30 minutes or until thickened. Will keep, covered and refrigerated, for up to 1 week. Makes about 1 ½ cups.

PREPARATION TIME: 6 MIN. CHILLING TIME: 30 MIN.

Per tablespoon: Calories 22; Saturated Fat 0 g; Total Fat 1 g; Protein 2 g; Carbohydrate 1 g; Fiber 0 g; Sodium 30 mg; Cholesterol 0 mg

Take a leaner, low-sodium approach with two lunchtime regulars—Saltless Dill Pickles and a tuna salad sandwich made with Tofu Mayonnaise.

Vinegars were originally wines that had fermented or soured. (The word comes from the Latin *vinum,* for "wine," and *aigre,* for "sour.") Today most vinegars are made from fermented wines, ciders, or distilled spirits, which are diluted with water to a strength of about 5 percent acidity.

Vinegar flavors can be varied enormously with the addition of herbs and fruits. The recipes on this page are but a sampling of possibilities. Using flavored vinegars is one of the best ways to enhance the taste of almost any savory dish — from soup and stew to fish, poultry, and pasta — without the addition of salt or fat.

GARLIC VINEGAR

3 cups distilled white vinegar	2 teaspoons black peppercorns
20 cloves garlic, crushed, or 8 shallots, coarsely chopped	1 cup dry red wine
	Garlic chives (optional garnish)

1 Wash and sterilize a 1 ½-quart wide-mouth jar and its lid by boiling for 10 minutes. In a medium-size enameled or stainless steel saucepan, bring the vinegar to a simmer. Meanwhile, place the garlic, peppercorns, and wine in the sterilized jar. Add the hot vinegar and mix thoroughly. Let cool to room temperature, cover tightly, and store in a cool, dry place for 2 weeks. At the end of 2 weeks, strain the vinegar through a fine sieve into a sterilized 1-quart jar, add a few garlic chives for decoration if desired, and seal with a sterilized lid. Makes about 1 quart.

PREPARATION TIME: 20 MIN. COOKING TIME: 3 MIN.
STANDING TIME: 2 WK.

*Per tablespoon: Calories 5; Saturated Fat 0 g;
Total Fat 0 g; Protein 0 g; Carbohydrate 1 g;
Fiber 0 g; Sodium 1 mg; Cholesterol 0 mg*

•

Basil or Oregano Variation: Substitute *1 cup dry white wine* for the red wine and *3 cups loosely packed fresh purple basil, green basil, or oregano* for the garlic and peppercorns. If desired, add *basil or oregano sprigs* for decoration.

•

Mint Variation: Substitute *1 quart cider vinegar* for the distilled white vinegar and red wine and *3 cups loosely packed mint leaves* for the garlic and peppercorns. If desired, add *mint sprigs* for decoration.

ROSEMARY VINEGAR

If you wish, substitute thyme or tarragon for the rosemary.

1 quart rice vinegar	1 teaspoon black peppercorns
1 bunch fresh rosemary sprigs (1 cup)	Rosemary sprig (optional garnish)
2 small shallots, thinly sliced (¼ cup)	

1 Follow the instructions in Garlic Vinegar (left) for sterilizing a jar and preparing and storing the vinegar. At the end of 2 weeks, before sealing the jar, add a rosemary sprig for decoration if desired. Makes about 1 quart.

PREPARATION TIME: 13 MIN. COOKING TIME: 3 MIN.
STANDING TIME: 2 WK.

*Per tablespoon: Calories 4; Saturated Fat 0 g;
Total Fat 0 g; Protein 0 g; Carbohydrate 1 g;
Fiber 0 g; Sodium 1 mg; Cholesterol 0 mg*

FRUIT VINEGAR

*This vinegar smells as wonderful as it tastes.
Use it in a vinaigrette to dress tender baby greens
or the first fruits of early summer.*

2 cups distilled white vinegar	2 cups raspberries, strawberries, or blueberries
½ cup dry white wine	Raspberries for garnish (optional)
¼ cup sugar	

1 Sterilize a 1-quart wide-mouth jar and its lid by boiling them for 10 minutes. In a medium-size enameled or stainless steel saucepan, bring the vinegar, wine, and sugar to a boil and simmer, stirring, for 1 minute or until the sugar has dissolved.

2 In a medium-size bowl, mash the raspberries with the back of a spoon and transfer them to the sterilized jar; stir in the vinegar. Let cool to room temperature, cover tightly, and store for 2 weeks in a cool, dry place.

3 At the end of 2 weeks, strain the vinegar through a fine sieve into a sterilized 1-quart bottle. Add a few raspberries for decoration if desired, and seal with a sterilized lid. Use within 6 to 12 months. Makes about 3 cups.

PREPARATION TIME: 15 MIN. COOKING TIME: 4 MIN.
STANDING TIME: 2 WK.

*Per tablespoon: Calories 9; Saturated Fat 0 g;
Total Fat 0 g; Protein 0 g; Carbohydrate 2 g;
Fiber 0 g; Sodium 0 mg; Cholesterol 0 mg*

BREADS

Of all life's cooking pleasures, bread baking is one of the best. The aroma
and sense of satisfaction it creates are hard to beat. And in today's health-conscious
world, we know that breads, especially those that incorporate whole
grains, seeds, vegetables, and/or fruit, provide incomparable nourishment. The better
the bread, of course, the less necessary it is to slather it with fat-laden
spreads. The following pages contain a tempting choice of "better bread" recipes;
Basil-Parmesan Biscuits, Lemon-Sesame Muffins, Herbed Spiral Bread, and
Four-Grain Rolls are just a few of the choices. If the time it takes to make them seems
an extravagance in a busy life, consider that perhaps you and your family are
worth the pleasure and good health such an endeavor can bring.

Patting out biscuit dough with your hands instead of rolling it out is an easy shortcut, although it gives the biscuits a slightly rougher texture on top. To save even more time, you can make square biscuits. Simply pat the dough into a rectangle of the recommended thickness, then cut it into 2- to 3-inch squares.

BASIL-PARMESAN BISCUITS

These extraordinary biscuits call for dried basil that has been warmed in oil to bring out the flavor. If available, 1 tablespoon of minced fresh basil could be substituted.

1 ½ cups all-purpose flour	2 tablespoons canola or corn oil
½ cup whole-wheat or all-purpose flour	1 teaspoon dried basil, crumbled
1 ½ teaspoons each baking powder and baking soda	2 cups plain low-fat yogurt
½ teaspoon salt	1 tablespoon low-fat (1% milkfat) milk or water
2 tablespoons plus 2 teaspoons grated Parmesan cheese	

1 Preheat the oven to 450° F. In a large bowl, stir together the all-purpose and whole-wheat flours, baking powder, baking soda, salt, and 2 tablespoons of the cheese.

2 In small skillet, heat 1 tablespoon of the oil over moderate heat. Add the basil and cook for 1 minute; transfer to a small bowl and let cool slightly. Stir in the yogurt, milk, and remaining 1 tablespoon of oil. Add the basil mixture to the dry ingredients and stir until just combined.

3 Place the dough on a well-floured surface. Using a lightly floured rolling pin, roll out the dough until ½ inch thick. Using a 2 ¼-inch biscuit cutter or glass, cut out rounds, gently rerolling the scraps, to form 12 biscuits. Place the biscuits on an ungreased baking sheet, spacing them 1 inch apart. Sprinkle with the remaining 2 teaspoons of cheese and bake for 12 to 15 minutes or until golden. Serve warm. Makes 12 biscuits.

PREPARATION TIME: 15 MIN. COOKING TIME: 12 MIN.

Per biscuit: Calories 121; Saturated Fat 1 g; Total Fat 4 g; Protein 5 g; Carbohydrate 17 g; Fiber 1 g; Sodium 286 mg; Cholesterol 3 mg

CARROT-GINGER BISCUITS

Here is an unusual biscuit with which to surprise family and friends. It goes especially well with roast turkey or chicken.

1 ½ cups all-purpose flour	1 small carrot, peeled and shredded (½ cup)
½ cup whole-wheat or all-purpose flour	2 cups plain low-fat yogurt
1 ½ teaspoons each baking powder and baking soda	2 tablespoons canola or corn oil
1 ½ teaspoons ground ginger	2 teaspoons honey or sugar
½ teaspoon salt	

1 Preheat the oven to 450° F. In a large bowl, stir together the all-purpose and whole-wheat flours, baking powder, baking soda, ginger, and salt. In a small bowl, stir together the carrot, yogurt, oil, and honey. Add carrot mixture to dry ingredients and stir until just combined.

2 Place the dough on a well-floured surface. Using a lightly floured rolling pin, roll out the dough until ½ inch thick. Using a 2 ¼-inch biscuit cutter or glass, cut out rounds, gently rerolling the scraps, to form 12 biscuits. Place the biscuits on an ungreased baking sheet, spacing them 1 inch apart. Bake for 12 to 15 minutes or until golden. Serve warm. Makes 12 biscuits.

PREPARATION TIME: 15 MIN. COOKING TIME: 12 MIN.

Per biscuit: Calories 120; Saturated Fat 1 g; Total Fat 3 g; Protein 4 g; Carbohydrate 19 g; Fiber 1 g; Sodium 261 mg; Cholesterol 2 mg

HERBED BUTTERMILK BISCUITS

Fresh herbs transform simple biscuits. If fresh dill is unavailable, however, 1 teaspoon of dill weed will serve nearly as well.

1 ⅓ cups all-purpose flour
⅓ cup toasted wheat germ
2 teaspoons sugar
1 ½ teaspoons baking powder
½ teaspoon baking soda
¼ teaspoon salt

1 tablespoon each snipped fresh dill, parsley, and chives or green onion tops
2 tablespoons unsalted butter, cut into pieces
⅔ cup buttermilk
2 tablespoons olive oil

1 Preheat the oven to 450° F. Lightly grease a baking sheet and set aside. In a large bowl, stir together the flour, wheat germ, sugar, baking powder, baking soda, and salt. Stir in the dill, parsley, and chives.

2 Using a pastry blender or 2 knives, cut in the butter until the mixture resembles coarse crumbs. With a mixing spoon, make a well in the center of the dry ingredients and pour in the buttermilk and oil. Stir until just combined.

3 Place the dough on a lightly floured surface. Using a lightly floured rolling pin, roll out the dough until ½ inch thick. Using a 3-inch biscuit cutter, cut out rounds, gently rerolling the scraps, to make 9 biscuits. Transfer the biscuits to the prepared baking sheet and bake for 10 to 12 minutes or until golden. Makes 9 biscuits.

PREPARATION TIME: 10 MIN. COOKING TIME: 10 MIN.

Per biscuit: Calories 140; Saturated Fat 2 g; Total Fat 6 g; Protein 4 g; Carbohydrate 17 g; Fiber 1 g; Sodium 180 mg; Cholesterol 8 mg

•

Sun-Dried Tomatoes and Olives Variation: In Step 1, decrease the sugar to *1 teaspoon;* substitute *¼ teaspoon black pepper, 1 tablespoon grated Parmesan cheese, 1 teaspoon dried basil, ¼ cup coarsely chopped black olives,* and *2 tablespoons chopped sun-dried tomatoes* for the dill, parsley, and chives. Makes 9 biscuits. *Per biscuit: Calories 156; Saturated Fat 3 g; Total Fat 7 g; Protein 5 g; Carbohydrate 19 g; Fiber 1 g; Sodium 220 mg; Cholesterol 9 mg.*

Get just-baked freshness in minutes: roll out a batch of Herbed Buttermilk Biscuits for dinner tonight.

FOUR-GRAIN MUFFINS

*In this recipe, all-purpose and rye
flours, oat bran, and cornmeal combine to
create nutty-tasting muffins that have
a slight crunch. If you like, substitute
whole-wheat flour for the rye flour.*

Nonstick cooking spray
¾ cup all-purpose flour
½ cup each rye flour and
   oat bran
¼ cup cornmeal
3 tablespoons firmly
   packed brown sugar
2½ teaspoons baking
   powder
½ teaspoon salt
1 cup low-fat (1%
   milkfat) milk
¼ cup vegetable oil
1 large egg, lightly
   beaten

1 Preheat the oven to 400° F. Lightly coat twelve 2½-inch muffin cups with cooking spray or insert cupcake liners. In a large bowl, stir together the all-purpose flour, rye flour, oat bran, cornmeal, sugar, baking powder, and salt until well combined. With a mixing spoon, make a well in the center.

2 In a small bowl, stir together the milk, oil, and egg, then pour the mixture into the well of the dry ingredients. Stir until just combined.

3 Spoon the batter into the prepared muffin cups, filling them ⅔ full. Bake for 20 minutes or until a toothpick inserted in the center comes out clean. Let the muffins cool in the pan for 5 minutes, then turn them out onto a wire rack to cool. Makes 12 muffins.

PREPARATION TIME: 12 MIN. COOKING TIME: 20 MIN.

*Per muffin: Calories 132; Saturated Fat 1 g;
Total Fat 6 g; Protein 3 g; Carbohydrate 18 g;
Fiber 1 g; Sodium 174 mg; Cholesterol 19 mg*

LEMON-SESAME MUFFINS

*You can mix the dry ingredients for
these or any muffins ahead of time and store
them in an airtight container in a cool, dry place
for up to 3 months. Add the oil, eggs, liquids,
and lemon rind just before baking.*

Nonstick cooking spray
2½ cups all-purpose flour
1 teaspoon each baking
   powder and baking
   soda
½ teaspoon salt
2 tablespoons sesame
   seeds, toasted (see
   Tip, page 312)
⅓ cup brown sugar
1 tablespoon each
   vegetable and dark
   sesame oil
1 cup low-fat (1%
   milkfat) milk
2 large egg whites
2 teaspoons grated
   lemon rind
2 tablespoons lemon
   juice

1 Preheat the oven to 400° F. Lightly coat twelve 2½-inch muffin cups with cooking spray or insert cupcake liners. In a large bowl, stir together the flour, baking powder, baking soda, salt, and 1½ tablespoons of the sesame seeds.

2 In a medium-size bowl, stir together the sugar, vegetable oil, and sesame oil until smooth. Add the milk, egg whites, lemon rind, and lemon juice and stir until well blended. Add this mixture to the dry ingredients and stir until just combined.

3 Spoon the batter into the prepared muffin cups and sprinkle with the remaining sesame seeds. Bake for 18 to 20 minutes or until a toothpick inserted in the center comes out clean. Let the muffins cool in the pan for 5 minutes, then turn them out onto a rack to cool. Serve warm. Makes 12 muffins.

PREPARATION TIME: 15 MIN. COOKING TIME: 18 MIN.

*Per muffin: Calories 153; Saturated Fat 1 g;
Total Fat 4 g; Protein 4 g; Carbohydrate 26 g;
Fiber 1 g; Sodium 207 mg; Cholesterol 1 mg*

Wake your family's appetite in the morning with fiber-rich Fig-Bran Muffins (left) and Lemon-Sesame Muffins. They're good just plain or with your favorite no-sugar-added fruit preserve.

FIG-BRAN MUFFINS

Figs and bran are fine companions, especially at the breakfast table. For variety, you can make crusty English muffins with this same recipe. On a lightly greased baking sheet, spoon the batter into 10 English muffin rings or tuna cans cut off at both ends and bake as directed. For easy removal, lightly grease the metal rings.

Nonstick cooking spray	¾ cup buttermilk
12 small dried figs (½ cup, packed)	2 tablespoons canola or corn oil
1½ cups all-purpose flour	3 tablespoons honey
½ cup wheat bran or whole-wheat flour	2 tablespoons molasses
½ cup oat bran	1 large egg white
2 teaspoons baking soda	½ teaspoon vanilla extract
¾ teaspoon salt	

1 Preheat the oven to 400° F. Lightly coat twelve 2½-inch muffin cups with cooking spray or insert cupcake liners. Place the figs in a small heatproof bowl, cover with boiling water, and let soak for 15 minutes. Drain, trim the ends, and coarsely chop.

2 In a large bowl, stir together the flour, wheat bran, oat bran, baking soda, and salt. In a small bowl, whisk together the buttermilk, oil, honey, molasses, egg white, and vanilla until well blended. Stir in the figs. Add the buttermilk mixture to the dry ingredients and stir until just combined.

3 Spoon the batter into the prepared muffin cups, filling them ⅔ full. Bake for 15 to 18 minutes or until a toothpick inserted in the center comes out clean. Serve warm. Makes 12 muffins.

PREPARATION TIME: 15 MIN. COOKING TIME: 15 MIN.
SOAKING TIME: 15 MIN.

Per muffin: Calories 143; Saturated Fat 1 g; Total Fat 3 g; Protein 4 g; Carbohydrate 28 g; Fiber 2 g; Sodium 293 mg; Cholesterol 1 mg

Pair Buttermilk-Pepper Corn Bread with Quick Turkey Chili (page 123) for a fast feast.

MARMALADE-BRAN MUFFINS

A dollop of orange marmalade cooked into the center of these healthful muffins adds a lovely fruity flavor. You can also blend the marmalade into the batter in Step 2 if you prefer.

Nonstick cooking spray	1 cup buttermilk
2 cups all-purpose flour	1 large egg
2 teaspoons baking powder	¼ cup melted unsalted butter or margarine
1 teaspoon baking soda	3 tablespoons firmly packed light brown sugar
½ teaspoon salt	
1 cup bran cereal flakes	¼ cup orange marmalade

1 Preheat the oven to 375° F. Lightly coat twelve 2½-inch muffin cups with the cooking spray or insert cupcake liners. In a large bowl, stir together the flour, baking powder, baking soda, salt, and bran cereal flakes.

2 In a medium-size bowl, whisk together the buttermilk, egg, butter, and sugar. Add the liquids to the dry ingredients and stir until just combined.

3 Spoon half the batter into the prepared muffin cups, filling each cup about ⅓ full. Spoon 1 teaspoon of the marmalade into the center of each muffin. Top with the remaining half of the batter. Bake for 18 to 20 minutes or until the tops of the muffins are golden and a toothpick inserted in the center comes out clean. Let the muffins cool in the pan for 5 minutes, then turn them out onto racks to cool. Makes 12 muffins.

PREPARATION TIME: 10 MIN. COOKING TIME: 20 MIN.

Per muffin: Calories 164; Saturated Fat 3 g; Total Fat 5 g; Protein 4 g; Carbohydrate 26 g; Fiber 1 g; Sodium 267 mg; Cholesterol 30 mg

BUTTERMILK-PEPPER CORN BREAD

Spicy jalapeños and sweet peppers add a little kick and a lot of color to this delightful corn bread. Serve it with chili, or top it with cheese and beans for a simple meatless entrée.

2 teaspoons olive oil	1¾ cups all-purpose flour
1 small yellow onion, finely chopped (½ cup)	1¼ cups cornmeal
	2 tablespoons sugar
1 small sweet green pepper, cored, seeded, and diced (½ cup)	2 teaspoons baking powder
	¾ teaspoon baking soda
1 small sweet red pepper, cored, seeded, and diced (½ cup)	½ teaspoon salt
	2 cups buttermilk
1 teaspoon finely chopped jalapeño pepper	¼ cup vegetable oil
	1 large egg
½ cup frozen corn kernels, thawed	2 large egg whites

1 Preheat the oven to 375° F. Lightly grease a 13" x 9" x 3" baking pan and set aside. In a 12-inch skillet, heat the oil over moderate heat. Add the onion and sauté, stirring frequently, for 5 minutes or until softened. Add the green, red, and jalapeño peppers and sauté, stirring frequently, 3 minutes longer. Stir in the corn and cook 1 minute more. Remove from the heat and set aside.

2 In a large bowl, stir together the flour, cornmeal, sugar, baking powder, baking soda, and salt until well combined. Stir in the pepper mixture. With a mixing spoon, make a well in the center. In a small bowl, stir together the buttermilk, oil, egg, and egg whites until well combined. Pour this mixture into the well and stir until just combined.

3 Scrape the batter into the prepared pan. Bake for 25 minutes or until a toothpick inserted in the center comes out clean. Serve hot or warm. Makes 12 servings.

PREPARATION TIME: 18 MIN. COOKING TIME: 33 MIN.

Per serving: Calories 204; Saturated Fat 1 g; Total Fat 7 g; Protein 6 g; Carbohydrate 31 g; Fiber 2 g; Sodium 257 mg; Cholesterol 19 mg

CARROT, RAISIN, AND PECAN BREAD

2 cups all-purpose flour	⅓ cup vegetable oil
1 tablespoon baking powder	1 large egg
	1 large egg white
1 teaspoon ground cinnamon	⅔ cup sugar
	¼ cup evaporated skim milk
½ teaspoon ground allspice	1 teaspoon vanilla extract
½ teaspoon salt	½ cup each raisins and chopped pecans
2 medium-size carrots, peeled and shredded (2 cups)	

1 Preheat the oven to 350° F. Lightly grease a 9" x 5" x 3" loaf pan and set aside. In a large bowl, stir together the flour, baking powder, cinnamon, allspice, and salt.

2 In a medium-size bowl, stir together the carrots, oil, egg, egg white, sugar, milk, and vanilla. Add the carrot mixture to the dry ingredients and stir until just combined. Fold in the raisins and pecans.

3 Pour the batter into the prepared loaf pan and bake for 1 hour or until a toothpick inserted in the center comes out clean. Let the loaf cool in the pan for 5 minutes, then turn it out onto a rack to cool completely. Makes twelve ¾-inch slices.

PREPARATION TIME: 15 MIN. COOKING TIME: 1 HR.

Per slice: Calories 234; Saturated Fat 2 g; Total Fat 10 g; Protein 4 g; Carbohydrate 34 g; Fiber 2 g; Sodium 195 mg; Cholesterol 18 mg

S lightly stale bread, bagels, and muffins can be made fresh-tasting again in less than a minute in the microwave. Just wrap a piece in a slightly damp paper towel and heat on high (100% power) for 15 seconds.

Breads can also be refreshed in a conventional oven preheated to 325° F. Place the bread in a brown paper bag, sprinkle the bag with water, and warm for 10 to 15 minutes.

Three quick breads—Pumpkin-Oat, Lemon-Zucchini, and Prune-Applesauce—score high marks in nutrition, fiber, and, above all, taste.

PUMPKIN-OAT BREAD

Puréed pumpkin adds a good measure of cancer-fighting beta carotene to this moist, flavorful loaf.

1¼ cups all-purpose flour	1 cup canned pumpkin purée
2 teaspoons baking powder	1 large egg
½ teaspoon baking soda	1 large egg white
½ teaspoon salt	¼ cup vegetable oil
½ teaspoon ground cinnamon	¾ cup firmly packed brown sugar
¼ teaspoon ground mace	¼ cup orange juice
⅛ teaspoon ground cloves	2 teaspoons grated orange rind
¾ cup oat bran	½ cup chopped walnuts (2 ounces)

1 Preheat the oven to 350° F. Lightly grease a 9″ x 5″ x 3″ loaf pan. In a large bowl, stir together the flour, baking powder, baking soda, salt, cinnamon, mace, and cloves. Stir in the oat bran.

2 In a medium-size bowl, combine the pumpkin, egg, egg white, oil, sugar, orange juice, and orange rind. Add the pumpkin mixture to the dry ingredients and stir until just combined. Fold in the walnuts.

3 Pour the batter into the prepared loaf pan and bake for 1 hour or until a toothpick inserted in the center comes out clean. Let the bread cool in the pan for 5 minutes, then turn it out onto a rack to cool. Makes twelve ¾-inch slices.

PREPARATION TIME: 15 MIN. COOKING TIME: 1 HR.

Per slice: Calories 197; Saturated Fat 1 g; Total Fat 8 g; Protein 4 g; Carbohydrate 30 g; Fiber 2 g; Sodium 194 mg; Cholesterol 18 mg

LEMON-ZUCCHINI BREAD

Serve this luscious tea bread just plain or spread with lemon curd or raspberry preserves. Bake and freeze a couple of loaves for future picnics or unexpected guests. Wrapped in heavy-duty aluminum foil, they will keep for up 2 months in the freezer.

- 2 cups all-purpose flour
- 2 teaspoons baking powder
- 1 teaspoon baking soda
- 1 teaspoon ground cinnamon
- ½ teaspoon salt
- ¼ teaspoon ground nutmeg
- ⅛ teaspoon ground cloves
- ⅓ cup each brown and granulated sugar
- 1 large egg
- 1 large egg white
- ⅓ cup vegetable oil
- 1 tablespoon grated lemon rind
- 1 large zucchini, shredded (2 cups)

1 Preheat the oven to 350° F. Lightly grease a 9" x 5" x 3" loaf pan. In a large bowl, stir together the flour, baking powder, baking soda, cinnamon, salt, nutmeg, and cloves.

2 In a medium-size bowl, stir together the brown and granulated sugars, egg, egg white, oil, and lemon rind. Fold in the zucchini. Add the zucchini mixture to the dry ingredients and stir until just combined.

3 Pour the batter into the prepared loaf pan and bake for 1 to 1 ¼ hours or until a toothpick inserted in the center comes out clean. Let the bread cool in the pan for 5 minutes, then turn it out onto a rack to cool completely. Makes twelve ¾-inch slices.

PREPARATION TIME: 15 MIN. COOKING TIME: 1 HR.

Per slice: Calories 179; Saturated Fat 1 g; Total Fat 7 g; Protein 3 g; Carbohydrate 27 g; Fiber 1 g; Sodium 225 mg; Cholesterol 18 mg

PRUNE-APPLESAUCE LOAF

- 1 cup all-purpose flour
- 1 cup rye or whole-wheat flour
- 1 teaspoon each baking powder and baking soda
- ½ teaspoon each ground cinnamon and nutmeg
- ½ teaspoon salt
- ⅓ cup chopped walnuts or pecans
- ⅓ cup chopped prunes or currants
- 1 ¼ cups unsweetened applesauce
- ⅔ cup light brown sugar
- 3 egg whites
- 3 tablespoons canola, vegetable, or olive oil

1 Preheat the oven to 325° F. Lightly grease a 9" x 5" x 3" loaf pan and cut a piece of wax paper to fit the bottom. In a large bowl, stir together the all-purpose flour, rye flour, baking powder, baking soda, cinnamon, nutmeg, salt, walnuts, and prunes.

2 In a medium-size bowl, stir together the applesauce, sugar, egg whites, and oil until blended. Add the applesauce mixture to the dry ingredients and stir until just combined.

3 Spoon into the prepared pan. Bake for 60 to 65 minutes or until a toothpick inserted in the center comes out clean. Let the loaf cool in the pan for 5 minutes, then turn it out onto a rack to cool. Serve warm or at room temperature. Makes twelve ¾-inch slices.

PREPARATION TIME: 20 MIN. COOKING TIME: 1 HR.

Per slice: Calories 188; Saturated Fat 1 g; Total Fat 6 g; Protein 3 g; Carbohydrate 32 g; Fiber 1 g; Sodium 204 mg; Cholesterol 0 mg

Leaveners, which under the right circumstances cause bubbles of carbon dioxide gas to form, are what make doughs and batters rise. Yeast is a powerful leavener because it is a living fungus. To become active, yeast must be dissolved in water; warm water works faster than cool, but hot water (above 115° F) will kill it. As it grows, yeast feeds on sugar and/or the starch in flour. If bread dough does not rise, it is because the yeast is inactive. The dough can be salvaged by dissolving fresh yeast in water and kneading it into the dough, then adding a little extra flour to absorb the excess liquid. (Yeast's rising action is stopped by oven heat during baking.)

Quick breads rely on baking soda and baking powder as leaveners. Carbon dioxide bubbles form as soon as baking soda is combined with an acid such as buttermilk. Baking powder begins to work the moment dry ingredients are mixed with a liquid. (Over time, baking powder loses its leavening power. It should be purchased in small quantities and replaced often.)

Most bread doughs require 2 risings, or proofs — one after kneading and one after the dough has been shaped into loaves or rolls. For the first rising, transfer the dough to a lightly greased large bowl, turn to coat with the grease, and cover loosely with plastic food wrap. Set the bowl in a warm (80°–85° F), dry, draft-free place for 1 to 1½ hours or until doubled in bulk. The usual test is to press 2 fingers about ½ inch into the dough; if an indentation remains, it has risen enough. Punch down the dough to its original size, form into the desired shape, and let rise an additional 45 minutes to 1 hour before baking.

PEAR AND PECAN LOAF

This fragrant bread can also be made with equal amounts of applesauce and walnuts instead of pear purée and pecans.

6 dried pear halves (about ½ cup)	**½ teaspoon each ground cinnamon and cloves**
1 large ripe pear, peeled, cored, and cubed, or 2 canned pear halves in juice, drained	**½ teaspoon salt**
	⅔ cup pecans, toasted and coarsely chopped
1 cup each all-purpose and whole-wheat flour	**⅔ cup firmly packed dark brown sugar**
1 teaspoon each baking powder and baking soda	**3 tablespoons canola, hazelnut, or corn oil**
	3 large egg whites

1 Preheat the oven to 325° F. Lightly grease a 9" x 5" x 3" loaf pan and cut a piece of wax paper to fit the bottom. In a small heatproof bowl, soak the dried pears in enough boiling water to cover for 15 minutes; drain and chop.

2 Meanwhile, in a food processor or blender, whirl the fresh pear for 30 seconds or until puréed. In a large bowl, combine the dried pears, all-purpose flour, whole-wheat flour, baking powder, baking soda, cinnamon, cloves, salt, and pecans. In a medium-size bowl, beat together the pear purée, sugar, oil, and egg whites until blended. Add this mixture to the dry ingredients and stir together until just combined.

3 Spoon the batter into the prepared pan. Bake for 60 to 65 minutes or until a toothpick inserted in the center comes out clean. Let the loaf cool in the pan for 5 minutes, then turn it out onto a rack to cool. Serve warm or at room temperature. Makes twelve ¾-inch slices.

PREPARATION TIME: 20 MIN.   COOKING TIME: 1 HR.

SOAKING TIME: 15 MIN.

Per slice: Calories 217; Saturated Fat 1 g; Total Fat 8 g; Protein 4 g; Carbohydrate 35 g; Fiber 3 g; Sodium 203 mg; Cholesterol 0 mg

INDIAN CRANBERRY BREAD

2 packages (¼ ounce each) active dry yeast	**1 teaspoon salt**
¾ cup lukewarm water (105°–115° F)	**½ cup each whole-wheat flour and cornmeal**
¼ cup molasses	**⅓ cup chopped dried cranberries, dried cherries, or golden raisins**
2 cups all-purpose flour	
3 tablespoons low-fat dry milk powder	**3 tablespoons chopped toasted walnuts**

1 In a large bowl, stir together the yeast, water, and molasses. Let stand for 5 minutes or until foamy. Beat in the all-purpose flour, milk powder, and salt until smooth. Stir in the whole-wheat flour and cornmeal until a soft dough forms. Knead until smooth and elastic — about 4 minutes by hand or 2 minutes with an electric mixer. (See Box, page 301, for kneading.) Transfer to a lightly greased large bowl, turn to coat with the grease, and cover loosely with plastic food wrap. Let rise in a warm, draft-free place for 45 minutes to 1 hour or until doubled in bulk.

2 Lightly grease a baking sheet. Punch down the dough, place it on a lightly floured surface, and knead lightly. Roll out to a 9- by 13-inch rectangle with the long side facing you. Sprinkle the cranberries and walnuts over the dough and roll up, jelly-roll style. Place the loaf on the baking sheet, seam side down, and tuck under the ends. Cover loosely and let rise for 45 minutes to 1 hour or until doubled in bulk.

3 Preheat the oven to 375° F. Bake for 30 minutes or until the loaf is brown and sounds hollow when tapped on the bottom. Let cool on a wire rack. Makes one 12- to 13-inch loaf or sixteen ¾-inch slices.

PREPARATION TIME: 25 MIN.   COOKING TIME: 30 MIN.

STANDING AND RISING TIME: 1 HR. 35 MIN.

Per slice: Calories 156; Saturated Fat 0 g; Total Fat 2 g; Protein 4 g; Carbohydrate 32 g; Fiber 2 g; Sodium 187 mg; Cholesterol 0 mg

ORANGE-FENNEL BREAD

1 **cup cold water**	1 **package (¼ ounce) active dry yeast**
1 **tablespoon fennel seeds**	3 **tablespoons firmly packed light brown sugar**
1 **tablespoon unsalted butter**	¼ **cup lukewarm water (105°–115° F)**
1 **teaspoon salt**	2 **cups all-purpose flour**
½ **cup orange juice**	2 **cups rye flour**
2 **teaspoons grated orange rind**	

1 In a small saucepan, combine the cold water, fennel seeds, butter, and salt. Bring to a boil over moderate heat, lower the heat, and simmer for 5 minutes. Transfer to a large bowl and mix in the orange juice and orange rind.

2 In a small bowl, stir together the yeast, sugar, and luke-warm water. Let stand for 5 minutes or until foamy. Stir the yeast mixture into the orange-fennel liquid until thoroughly blended. Gradually work in the all-purpose flour, then the rye flour, until a soft dough forms. Knead the dough until smooth and elastic—about 10 minutes by hand, 6 minutes with an electric mixer, or 45 seconds in a food processor. (See Box, page 301, for kneading.) Transfer the dough to a lightly greased large bowl, turn to coat with the grease, and cover loosely with plastic food wrap. Let rise in a warm, draft-free place for 1 hour or until almost doubled in bulk.

3 Lightly grease a baking sheet. Punch down the dough, shape into a ball, and place on the baking sheet. Cover loosely and let rise until doubled in bulk. Preheat the oven to 350° F. Make 4 parallel diagonal slashes in the top of the loaf, then make 4 more slashes to form diamonds.

Bake for 50 minutes or until the loaf is crusty and makes a hollow sound when tapped on the bottom. Let cool on a rack. Makes one 9-inch loaf or twelve ¾-inch slices.

PREPARATION TIME: 25 MIN.   COOKING TIME: 57 MIN.

RISING TIME: 1½ HR.

Per slice: Calories 160; Saturated Fat 1 g; Total Fat 2 g; Protein 4 g; Carbohydrate 33 g; Fiber 1 g; Sodium 181 mg; Cholesterol 3 mg

Redolent with sweet citrus and licorice, Orange-Fennel Bread makes a tasteful impression at breakfast or teatime.

HERBED SPIRAL BREAD

*A cheesy, savory whorl runs through
every slice of this beautiful loaf. Try other herb
combinations — rosemary and thyme, oregano
and basil — or substitute rye flour and caraway seeds
for the whole-wheat flour and fennel seeds.*

1 package (¼ ounce)
  active dry yeast
¼ cup lukewarm water
  (105°–115° F)
1 teaspoon honey
1 cup buttermilk
2½ cups all-purpose flour
¾ cup whole-wheat flour
2 tablespoons plus 1
  teaspoon olive or
  canola oil

1¼ teaspoons salt
½ cup minced parsley
1½ teaspoons dried
  oregano, crumbled
½ teaspoon crushed
  fennel seeds
¼ teaspoon black pepper
3 tablespoons grated
  Parmesan cheese

Make an extra-
ordinary sandwich
with Herbed Spiral
Bread and Neufchâtel
cream cheese; try it also
with one of the spreads
on pages 54 and 55.

1 In a large bowl, combine the yeast, water, and honey. Let stand for 5 minutes or until foamy. Add the buttermilk, 1¼ cups of the all-purpose flour, all of the whole-wheat flour, 2 tablespoons of the oil, and the salt and mix thoroughly. Gradually work in enough of the remaining all-purpose flour to make the dough firm enough to handle.

2 Knead the dough until smooth and elastic—about 4 minutes by hand or 2 minutes with an electric mixer. (See Box, opposite page, for kneading.) Transfer the dough to a lightly greased large bowl, turn to coat with the grease, and cover loosely with plastic food wrap. Let rise for 45 minutes to 1 hour or until doubled in bulk.

3 Lightly grease a 9" x 5" x 3" loaf pan. In a small bowl, combine the parsley, oregano, fennel seeds, and pepper. Punch down the dough, place it on a lightly floured surface, and knead lightly. Roll it out to a 9- by 12-inch rectangle with the short side facing you. Sprinkle all but 1 teaspoon of the cheese over the dough, leaving a ½-inch border on all sides uncovered. Sprinkle the herb mixture on top and roll up the dough, jelly-roll style. Place the roll, seam side down, in the pan. Cover and let rise for 45 minutes to 1 hour or until doubled in bulk.

4 Preheat the oven to 375° F. Brush the loaf with the remaining 1 teaspoon of oil and sprinkle the remaining cheese over the top. Bake for 35 minutes or until the loaf is brown and sounds hollow when tapped on the bottom. Remove from the pan, place on a foil-covered baking sheet, and bake 5 minutes more for a crisp crust. Let cool on a rack. Makes one 9-inch loaf or twelve ¾-inch slices.

PREPARATION TIME: 20 MIN. COOKING TIME: 40 MIN.
STANDING AND RISING TIME: 1 HR. 35 MIN.

*Per slice: Calories 156; Saturated Fat 1 g;
Total Fat 4 g; Protein 5 g; Carbohydrate 26 g;
Fiber 2 g; Sodium 275 mg; Cholesterol 2 mg*

SPINACH-TOMATO BREAD

*Unveil this spectacular spiral loaf on
Christmas Eve or at a New Year's brunch.
It is definitely worth the extra time it takes
to knead 2 doughs. The mashed potatoes in
Step 1 can be prepared the day before.*

2 medium-size all-purpose potatoes, peeled and sliced (about 2 cups)
4 cloves garlic, crushed
1¾ cups cold water
2¼ teaspoons salt
2 packages (¼ ounce each) active dry yeast
2 tablespoons sugar
1 cup lukewarm water (105°–115° F)

¾ cup low-fat (1% milkfat) milk
3 tablespoons olive oil
6 cups all-purpose flour
1 package (10 ounces) frozen chopped spinach, thawed and squeezed dry (¾ cup)
3 tablespoons tomato paste
1 egg, beaten with 1 tablespoon water

1 In a small saucepan, combine the potatoes, garlic, cold water, and ¼ teaspoon of the salt and bring to a boil over moderate heat. Cook, uncovered, for 10 minutes or until the potatoes are tender. Drain, reserving ¼ cup of the cooking liquid. Mash the potatoes with the garlic; you should have about 1⅓ cups.

2 In a large bowl, combine the yeast, sugar, and luke-warm water and let stand for 5 minutes or until foamy. Stir in the mashed potatoes, reserved cooking liquid, remaining 2 teaspoons of salt, the milk, and oil. With a wooden spoon or an electric mixer set on low speed, beat in 3 cups of the flour, then gradually add enough of the remaining flour to make a soft dough. Divide the dough in half and transfer to a lightly floured surface.

3 Knead the spinach into half of the dough until smooth, elastic, and well combined—about 10 minutes by hand or 6 minutes with an electric mixer. (See Box, this page, for kneading.) Transfer to a lightly greased large bowl, turn to coat with the grease, and cover loosely with plastic food wrap. Let rise in a warm, draft-free place for 45 minutes or until doubled in bulk. Repeat with the tomato paste and remaining half of the dough.

4 Lightly grease a baking sheet. Punch down the spinach dough, place on a lightly floured surface, and pat the dough out to a 12- by 14-inch rectangle. Place the tomato dough on top and pat it out to a 12- by 13-inch rectangle. Roll up the 2 layers, jelly-roll style, to form a loaf 6 by 13 inches. Place on the baking sheet, seam side down, tuck under the ends, cover loosely, and let rise for 30 minutes or until light and puffy.

5 Preheat the oven to 400° F. Brush the top of the loaf with the beaten egg. Bake for 50 minutes or until the loaf is golden brown and crusty and sounds hollow when tapped on the bottom. Let cool on a wire rack. Makes one 12- to 13-inch loaf or sixteen ¾-inch slices.

PREPARATION TIME: 40 MIN. COOKING TIME: 1 HR.

STANDING AND RISING TIME: 1 HR. 20 MIN.

*Per slice: Calories 221; Saturated Fat 1 g;
Total Fat 4 g; Protein 7 g; Carbohydrate 40 g;
Fiber 2 g; Sodium 352 mg; Cholesterol 14 mg*

K **neading dough** evenly distributes ingredients and binds together the strands of gluten, or protein, in the flour, giving bread its elasticity and texture. Before kneading, dust your hands and work surface with just enough flour to prevent the dough from sticking. Form the dough into a ball and place it on the floured surface. Push the dough down and away from you with the heels of your hands. Then fold it in half, bringing the top half toward you. Give the dough a quarter turn and continue to push, fold, and turn it for 1 minute, then let it rest for about 10 minutes to absorb the flour. Continue kneading for 4 to 8 minutes or until the dough is smooth and elastic and bounces back when you press down.

Speedier and easier kneading is possible with either an electric mixer or food processor. To knead with a mixer requires a dough hook; beaters will not do the job except for a very light batter bread. After the last addition of flour, let the dough rest for 1 minute. At medium speed, knead the dough for 6 to 8 minutes, adding flour if it seems too sticky.

With a food processor, the blunt plastic blade attachment is most effective for bread-making because the dough sticks to the sharp edges of a metal blade. A large processor can handle up to 6 cups of flour. Place dry ingredients and shortening in the bowl and whirl for about 30 seconds or until the mixture resembles oatmeal. Pour the yeast mixture, then the other liquids down the feed tube and whirl for 45 seconds or until the dough forms a ball. Kneading longer can overheat the dough and kill the yeast.

OLIVE-CHEDDAR BREAD

Swiss, Monterey Jack, and other semihard cheeses are good alternatives to use in this hearty bread.

1 **package (¼ ounce) active dry yeast**	1 **tablespoon olive oil**
¼ **cup lukewarm water (105°–115° F)**	¾ **teaspoon black pepper**
1 **teaspoon honey**	½ **teaspoon salt**
2¼ **cups all-purpose flour**	½ **cup shredded Cheddar cheese (2 ounces)**
1 **cup whole-wheat flour**	3 **tablespoons chopped black olives**
1 **cup skim milk**	

1 In a large bowl, stir together the yeast, water, and honey. Let stand for 5 minutes or until foamy. Stir in 1¼ cups of the all-purpose flour, all of the whole-wheat flour, the milk, oil, pepper, and salt. With a wooden spoon or an electric mixer set on medium speed, beat until smooth. Mix in the cheese, olives, and as much of the remaining all-purpose flour as needed to make the dough firm enough to handle. Knead the dough until smooth and elastic—about 4 minutes by hand or 2 minutes with an electric mixer. (See Box, page 301, for kneading.) Transfer the dough to a lightly greased large bowl, turn to coat with the grease, and cover loosely with plastic food wrap. Let rise for 1 hour or until doubled in bulk.

2 Lightly grease a baking sheet. Punch down the dough, place on a lightly floured surface, and knead lightly. Roll out to a 9- by 13-inch rectangle. With the long side facing you, roll up, jelly-roll style. Place the loaf on the baking sheet, seam side down, and tuck under the ends. Cover loosely; let rise for 1 hour or until doubled in bulk.

3 Preheat the oven to 375° F. Cut diagonal slashes across the top of the dough about ¼ inch deep and 1 inch apart. Bake for 40 minutes or until the loaf is golden and sounds hollow when tapped on the bottom. Let cool on a rack. Makes one 12-inch loaf or sixteen 1-inch slices.

PREPARATION TIME: 20 MIN. COOKING TIME: 40 MIN.

STANDING AND RISING TIME: 2 HR. 5 MIN.

Per slice: Calories 116; Saturated Fat 1 g; Total Fat 2 g; Protein 5 g; Carbohydrate 20 g; Fiber 2 g; Sodium 101 mg; Cholesterol 4 mg

WHOLE-WHEAT, OAT, AND MOLASSES BREAD

Batter breads such as this one give you homemade goodness without kneading and with only a single rising. In just over 2 hours, you can have a warm, crusty loaf.

1 **package (¼ ounce) active dry yeast**	3 **tablespoons corn or vegetable oil**
⅓ **cup lukewarm water (105°–115° F)**	1¼ **teaspoons salt**
½ **teaspoon sugar**	1 **egg**
½ **cup low-fat (1% milkfat) milk**	2 **cups whole-wheat flour**
⅓ **cup molasses**	¾ **cup all-purpose flour**
	½ **cup rolled oats**

1 In a small bowl, combine the yeast, water, and sugar. Let stand for 5 minutes or until foamy. Meanwhile, lightly grease a 9" x 5" x 3" loaf pan and set aside. In a small saucepan, heat the milk, molasses, oil, and salt over low heat for about 45 seconds or just until lukewarm.

2 In a large bowl, with an electric mixer set on low speed, beat together the yeast and milk mixtures. Beat in the egg. Gradually work in the whole-wheat flour, all-purpose flour, and oats. Beat the dough at moderate speed for 4 minutes or until smooth and elastic. Scrape the dough into the prepared pan, cover with lightly greased plastic food wrap, and let rise in a warm, draft-free place for 1 hour or until the dough almost reaches the top of the pan.

3 Preheat the oven to 350° F. Bake for 50 minutes or until the loaf is crusty and sounds hollow when tapped on the bottom. If the loaf appears to be browning too quickly, cover with aluminum foil during the last 15 minutes of baking. Let cool on a wire rack. Makes one 9-inch loaf or twelve ¾-inch slices.

PREPARATION TIME: 15 MIN. COOKING TIME: 50 MIN.

STANDING AND RISING TIME: 1 HR. 5 MIN.

Per slice: Calories 184; Saturated Fat 1 g; Total Fat 5 g; Protein 6 g; Carbohydrate 31 g; Fiber 4 g; Sodium 235 mg; Cholesterol 18 mg

POTATO-OAT ROLLS

1 ¼ cups boiling water
2 teaspoons dry mustard
½ cup warm mashed potato
1 package (¼ ounce) active dry yeast
2 tablespoons honey
2 ½ to 2 ¾ cups all-purpose flour
¾ cup oat bran
1 teaspoon salt
1 to 2 tablespoons skim milk

1 In a 1-pint glass measuring cup, combine the water and mustard and let stand for 10 minutes. In a large bowl, with a wooden spoon or an electric mixer set on low speed, gradually beat the hot liquid into the potatoes. Let the mixture cool to lukewarm (105°–115° F). Blend in the yeast and honey and let stand for 5 minutes or until foamy.

2 Add 1 cup of the flour, the oat bran, and salt to the potato mixture and beat until smooth. Gradually work in as much of the remaining flour as needed to make the dough firm enough to handle. Knead the dough until smooth and elastic — about 4 minutes by hand or 2 minutes with an electric mixer. (See Box, page 301, for kneading.) Transfer to a lightly greased large bowl, turn to coat with the grease, and cover loosely with plastic food wrap. Let rise in a warm, draft-free place for 1 hour or until doubled in bulk.

3 Lightly grease a baking sheet. Punch down the dough, place on a lightly floured surface, and knead lightly. Roll into a 10-inch log and cut the log into 10 pieces; shape each piece into a ball or one of the shapes illustrated at right and arrange them 1 ½ inches apart on the baking sheet. Cover and let rise for 35 minutes.

4 Preheat the oven to 350° F. Brush the tops of the rolls with the milk. Bake for 30 to 35 minutes or until golden. Place on a wire rack to cool. Makes 10 rolls.

PREPARATION TIME: 20 MIN. COOKING TIME: 30 MIN.

STANDING AND RISING TIME: 1 HR. 45 MIN.

Per roll: Calories 175; Saturated Fat 0 g; Total Fat 1 g; Protein 6 g; Carbohydrate 38 g; Fiber 2 g; Sodium 298 mg; Cholesterol 0 mg

Shaping rolls into twists and pretzels is easy. After the first rising, divide the dough into the number of rolls the recipe will make and follow the directions below.

To make twists, use your hands to roll each piece of dough into a strip 12 inches by ¾ inch. Fold the strip in half and twist as shown. Pinch ends together.

To make pretzel-shaped rolls, use your hands to roll each piece of dough into a strip 10 inches by 1 inch. Form a circle and overlap the ends as shown.

Give these Potato-Oat Rolls a twist or tie them in knots for special occasions (see Tip, right).

Bread dough can be refrigerated or frozen, well greased and tightly covered, for later baking. You can refrigerate the dough immediately after mixing and kneading or after one rising. When you're ready to bake, follow the procedures for rising and shaping, allowing an extra 20 minutes for the cold dough to rise.

To freeze dough, punch it down after the first rising, place it in a plastic freezer bag or airtight container, and freeze at 0° F for up to 3 months. Transfer the dough to the refrigerator to thaw 24 to 48 hours before you wish to bake it. Shape the dough, follow the procedure for the second rising, and bake as usual.

FOUR-GRAIN ROLLS

If rye or buckwheat flour is unavailable, you can increase the other flours proportionately.

- 2 packages (¼ ounce each) active dry yeast
- 1½ cups lukewarm water (105°–115° F)
- 1 tablespoon light brown sugar
- ⅓ cup nonfat dry milk powder
- 2 teaspoons caraway seeds
- 1½ teaspoons salt
- 1½ cups all-purpose flour
- 1 cup each whole-wheat, buckwheat, and rye flour
- 1 egg white, beaten with 1 teaspoon water
- 1 tablespoon all-purpose flour

1 In a large bowl, combine the yeast, ½ cup of the water, and the sugar and let stand for about 5 minutes or until foamy. Stir in the remaining water, the milk powder, caraway seeds, and salt. Mix in 1 cup of the all-purpose flour and all of the whole-wheat, buckwheat, and rye flours, working in as much of the remaining all-purpose flour as needed to make a soft dough.

2 Knead the dough until smooth and elastic — about 7 minutes by hand or 3 to 4 minutes in an electric mixer. (See Box, page 301, for kneading.) Transfer to a lightly greased large bowl, turn to coat with the grease, and cover loosely with plastic food wrap. Let rise in a warm, draft-free place for 1 to 1½ hours or until doubled in bulk.

3 Lightly grease and flour a baking sheet. Punch down the dough, transfer to a lightly floured surface, and roll it into a 12-inch log. Cut the log crosswise into 12 pieces. Shape each piece into a ball, twist, or knot (see page 303) and arrange 2 inches apart on the baking sheet. Cover and let rise for about 1 hour.

4 Preheat the oven to 400° F. Brush the rolls with the egg white and sift the tablespoon of flour over them. Bake for about 15 minutes or until golden. Makes 12 rolls.

PREPARATION TIME: 25 MIN. COOKING TIME: 15 MIN.

STANDING AND RISING TIME: 2 HR. 5 MIN.

Per roll: Calories 169; Saturated Fat 0 g; Total Fat 1 g; Protein 7 g; Carbohydrate 35 g; Fiber 3 g; Sodium 285 mg; Cholesterol 0 mg

ROSEMARY DINNER ROLLS

- 1¼ cups skim milk
- ¼ cup unsalted butter or margarine, at room temperature
- 1 package (¼ ounce) active dry yeast
- 2 tablespoons light brown sugar
- 1 teaspoon salt
- 2 teaspoons dried rosemary, crumbled
- 2 cups all-purpose or bread flour
- 2 to 2½ cups whole-wheat flour

1 In a small saucepan, warm the milk and 3 tablespoons of the butter over low heat until the butter melts. Transfer to a large bowl and let cool to lukewarm (105°–115° F). Add the yeast, sugar, salt, and rosemary to the milk-butter mixture and let stand for 5 minutes or until foamy. Stir in the all-purpose flour and 2 cups of the whole-wheat flour, adding more whole-wheat flour as needed to make a soft but manageable dough. Knead the dough until smooth and elastic — about 7 minutes by hand or 3 to 4 minutes with an electric mixer. (See Box, page 301, for kneading.) Transfer to a lightly greased large bowl, turn to coat with the grease, and cover loosely with plastic food wrap. Let rise in a warm, draft-free place for 1½ hours or until doubled in bulk.

2 Lightly grease four 8-inch round pans. Punch down the dough, place it on a lightly floured surface, divide it in half, and roll each half into a 12-inch log. Cut each log crosswise into 10 pieces. Shape the pieces into balls and arrange 5 in each pan, leaving about 1 inch between them. Cover and let rise for 1 hour or until doubled in bulk.

3 Preheat the oven to 425° F. Melt the remaining 1 tablespoon of butter and brush the roll tops with it. Bake for 15 minutes or until golden brown. Remove from the pans and let cool on wire racks. Makes 20 rolls.

PREPARATION TIME: 27 MIN. COOKING TIME: 15 MIN.

STANDING AND RISING TIME: 2 HR. 40 MIN.

Per roll: Calories 116; Saturated Fat 2 g; Total Fat 3 g; Protein 4 g; Carbohydrate 20 g; Fiber 2 g; Sodium 116 mg; Cholesterol 7 mg

APPETIZERS, SNACKS, AND BEVERAGES

The best appetizers and snacks satisfy the urge to nibble, yet provide wholesome nutrients and few calories. They can also help you maintain your ideal weight or stay with a weight-loss program by preventing you from becoming overly hungry and eating too much at mealtime. Fulfilling this purpose are crisp vegetables or fat-free crackers served with dips and spreads such as Mushroom Mousse (page 308) or Mexicali Bean Spread (page 309). But if noshing to you means potato chips and popcorn, try the fabulous low-calorie versions on page 313. To accompany your nibbles, whirl up one of the beverages on pages 317–320; they take a bit more time than opening a soft drink, but the benefits to your health are worth it.

Decorative scoring adds a festive touch to vegetables used for appetizers and salads. A 5-hole zester makes delicate, closely spaced grooves and creates curls that can be used as garnishes. For more pronounced scoring, use a 1-hole zester, which makes deep grooves. Both are illustrated below.

1. To score with a 5-hole zester, hold the cucumber and zester as illustrated and scrape toward you, applying even pressure. Repeat, starting each new set next to the previous one.

2. To score with a 1-hole zester, hold the cucumber and zester as illustrated and scrape toward you; repeat every ¼ inch. (If you are left-handed, hold the cucumber in your right hand; start at the top and scrape away from you.)

CUCUMBER-CHEESE FLOWERS

Crunchy cucumber slices make appealing low-calorie servers for a spicy cheese mixture. If you prefer, you can peel the cucumbers before hollowing and filling them.

3 medium-size cucumbers (about 1 ¼ pounds), scrubbed
1 package (7 ½ ounces) farmers cheese
2 tablespoons reduced-fat sour cream
2 tablespoons plain dry bread crumbs
½ clove garlic, minced
1 teaspoon dried marjoram, crumbled

1 teaspoon reduced-sodium Worcestershire or soy sauce
⅛ teaspoon hot red pepper sauce
3 tablespoons each finely chopped radishes, parsley, and celery

Optional garnishes:
¼ cup finely chopped sweet red pepper
¼ cup minced parsley

1 Score the cucumbers lengthwise with a 1-hole or 5-hole zester (see Tip, left) or the tines of a fork. Trim ½ inch off each end and cut the cucumber in half crosswise. Using a melon baller or small spoon, scrape out the seeds in the center of each cucumber, leaving a hollow about ½ inch across. Pat the cucumbers dry with paper toweling and set aside.

2 In a food processor or blender, whirl the farmers cheese, sour cream, bread crumbs, garlic, marjoram, Worcestershire sauce, and red pepper sauce for 1 minute or until smooth. Transfer the mixture to a medium-size bowl and stir in the radishes, parsley, and celery.

3 Using a small spatula or spoon, pack the cheese mixture into the 6 cucumber halves. Wrap well in plastic food wrap and refrigerate for at least 4 hours or up to 12 hours. To serve, slice crosswise ½ inch thick and arrange on a platter. Sprinkle with the chopped red pepper or parsley if you wish. Makes 36 appetizers.

PREPARATION TIME: 25 MIN. CHILLING TIME: 4 HR.

Per appetizer: Calories 22; Saturated Fat 1 g;
Total Fat 2 g; Protein 1 g; Carbohydrate 1 g;
Fiber 0 g; Sodium 34 mg; Cholesterol 5 mg

ENDIVE BOATS

This recipe calls for feta, a pungent Greek goat cheese. A milder goat cheese or even Neufchâtel cream cheese is also suitable. The filling can be mixed and refrigerated up to 4 hours ahead, and the boats assembled and refrigerated up to 1 hour before serving.

1 small sweet green or red pepper, cored, seeded, and finely chopped (½ cup)
3 large radishes, finely chopped (½ cup)
1 small carrot, peeled and grated (½ cup)
1 large shallot, finely chopped (2 tablespoons)
2 ounces feta cheese, finely crumbled (½ cup)

¼ teaspoon black pepper
⅛ teaspoon salt
2 tablespoons snipped fresh dill
1 tablespoon lemon juice
1 tablespoon olive oil
2 medium-size heads endive, trimmed, rinsed, and separated into 20 leaves
Sprigs fresh dill (garnish)

1 In a medium-size bowl, combine the sweet pepper, radishes, carrot, shallot, cheese, black pepper, salt, and snipped dill. In a small bowl, whisk together the lemon juice and oil and pour it over the mixture; stir to combine.

2 Spoon 1 tablespoon of the filling into the bottom ⅔ of each endive leaf. Garnish each leaf with a small sprig of dill. Makes 20 appetizers.

PREPARATION TIME: 15 MIN.

Per appetizer: Calories 19; Saturated Fat 1 g;
Total Fat 1 g; Protein 1 g; Carbohydrate 1 g;
Fiber 0 g; Sodium 49 mg; Cholesterol 2 mg

•

Seafood Variation: Add ½ cup diced shrimp, lobster, or crabmeat to the filling in Step 1. *Per serving: Calories 22; Saturated Fat 1 g; Total Fat 1 g; Protein 1 g; Carbohydrate 1 g; Fiber 1 g; Sodium 57 mg; Cholesterol 9 mg.*

CHICKEN-CASHEW STUFFED POTATOES

Scooped-out new potatoes make handy containers for a variety of fillings. All the recipes below can be prepared a day ahead and the potatoes stuffed and refrigerated up to 8 hours before serving.

2 pounds small new potatoes, unpeeled
1 cup diced cooked chicken breast
¼ cup shredded carrot
¼ cup finely chopped celery
2 green onions, including tops, chopped (¼ cup)
2 tablespoons finely chopped unsalted cashews or almonds

1½ teaspoons rice vinegar or cider vinegar
1 teaspoon grated orange rind
2 tablespoons reduced-fat sour cream or Creamy Yogurt Spread (page 287)
¼ teaspoon salt

1 In a large saucepan of boiling water, cook the potatoes for 20 to 25 minutes or until tender. Drain and let stand until cool enough to handle, then cut each potato in half. Trim the bottoms so that the potatoes will sit flat, cut side up. Using a melon baller or small spoon, hollow out the center of each half, leaving a ⅜-inch shell. Save the potato centers for another use.

2 In a medium-size bowl, stir together the chicken, carrot, celery, green onions, cashews, vinegar, orange rind, sour cream, and salt until well blended. Spoon 1 tablespoon of the mixture into each hollowed-out potato half. Makes 32 appetizers.

PREPARATION TIME: 10 MIN. COOKING TIME: 20 MIN.

Per appetizer: Calories 39; Saturated Fat 0 g; Total Fat 1 g; Protein 2 g; Carbohydrate 6 g; Fiber 1 g; Sodium 23 mg; Cholesterol 4 mg

•

Shrimp Variation: Follow Step 1 as directed. In Step 2, stir together *4 ounces cooked shrimp, finely chopped, ¼ cup finely chopped water chestnuts or celery, ¼ cup finely chopped sweet red pepper, 2 green onions, including tops, finely chopped (¼ cup), 2 tablespoons reduced-fat sour cream, 1½ teaspoons drained*

prepared horseradish, and *¼ teaspoon salt*. Fill the potatoes as directed. Makes 32 appetizers. *Per appetizer: Calories 31; Saturated Fat 0 g; Total Fat 0 g; Protein 1 g; Carbohydrate 6 g; Fiber 0 g; Sodium 29 mg; Cholesterol 7 mg.*

•

Guacamole Variation: Follow Step 1 as directed. In Step 2, whirl *1 cup low-fat (1% milkfat) cottage cheese* and *half of a small avocado (6 ounces)* in a food processor or blender until smooth. Add *2 tablespoons medium-hot salsa, 1 tablespoon lime or lemon juice, 2 tablespoons minced fresh cilantro or parsley,* and *2 sliced green onions, including tops,* and process until blended. Add the remaining *avocado half* and whirl until chunky. Fill the potatoes as directed. Makes 32 appetizers. *Per appetizer: Calories 40; Saturated Fat 0 g; Total Fat 1 g; Protein 2 g; Carbohydrate 6 g; Fiber 1 g; Sodium 34 mg; Cholesterol 0 mg.*

Spotlight your culinary talents with this show-stopping (but easy) array of appetizers: Cucumber-Cheese Flowers, Endive Boats, and Chicken-Cashew Stuffed Potatoes.

Low-fat Neufchâtel cream cheese makes the rich taste of Smoked Salmon Spread go a long way. Serve with toast points or raw vegetables.

MUSHROOM MOUSSE

To further enhance the flavor of this inviting mousse, add 2 tablespoons of dry sherry before cooking off the liquid.

- 1 tablespoon unsalted butter
- ⅓ cup finely chopped shallots (3 medium-size)
- 8 ounces mushrooms, chopped (2 ⅓ cups)
- 1 clove garlic, minced
- ¼ teaspoon each salt and black pepper
- 4 ounces Neufchâtel cream cheese, softened

Optional garnishes:
- 2 tablespoons minced parsley
- 1 hard-cooked egg, finely chopped

1 In a 10-inch nonstick skillet, melt the butter over moderate heat. Add the shallots and cook, stirring, for 1 minute. Add the mushrooms, garlic, salt, and pepper and cook, stirring occasionally, for 5 minutes or until the mushrooms have released their juices. Raise the heat to high and cook for 3 to 5 minutes or until the mixture is almost dry. Remove from the heat and let cool.

2 In a food processor or blender, whirl the mushroom mixture with the cream cheese for 30 seconds or until smooth. Transfer the mousse to a serving dish and garnish with the parsley and chopped egg if desired. Cover and chill for 2 hours or until firm. Serve as a spread with assorted crackers. Makes about 1 ¼ cups.

PREPARATION TIME: 15 MIN. COOKING TIME: 10 MIN.

CHILLING TIME: 2 HR.

Per tablespoon: Calories 25; Saturated Fat 1 g; Total Fat 2 g; Protein 1 g; Carbohydrate 1 g; Fiber 0 g; Sodium 50 mg; Cholesterol 6 mg

MINTED SPINACH DIP

A platter filled with a colorful assortment of crisp raw vegetables and served with a creamy piquant dip like this one is bound to get mouths watering and the party going.

- 1   cup low-fat (1% milkfat) cottage cheese
- ½   cup chopped fresh spinach (4 ounces), blanched and drained, or 2½ ounces frozen chopped spinach, thawed and squeezed dry
- ¼   cup plain low-fat yogurt or reduced-fat sour cream
- ¼   cup minced fresh mint or ¼ cup minced parsley mixed with 1 teaspoon dried mint
- 1   green onion, white part only, chopped (1 tablespoon)
- 1   clove garlic, minced
- ¼   teaspoon grated lemon rind
- ¼   teaspoon salt
- ⅛   teaspoon ground red pepper (cayenne)

1 In a food processor or blender, whirl all the ingredients for 30 to 45 seconds or until smooth. Transfer the dip to a small bowl, cover, and chill until ready to serve. Makes about 1¼ cups.

PREPARATION TIME: 15 MIN.

Per tablespoon: Calories 12; Saturated Fat 0 g; Total Fat 0 g; Protein 2 g; Carbohydrate 1 g; Fiber 0 g; Sodium 79 mg; Cholesterol 1 mg

SMOKED SALMON SPREAD

Serve this tempting spread with assorted crackers or toast points. To make toast points, trim the crusts off slices of sandwich bread, toast, and cut into triangles.

- 6   ounces Neufchâtel cream cheese, softened
- 4   ounces smoked salmon, diced
- 2   tablespoons reduced-fat sour cream
- 2   to 3 teaspoons fresh lemon juice, or to taste
- ⅛   teaspoon each salt and white pepper, or to taste
- Optional garnishes:
    Reduced-fat sour cream
    Sprigs fresh dill

1 In a food processor or blender, whirl the cream cheese, salmon, sour cream, 2 teaspoons of the lemon juice, the salt, and pepper for 30 to 45 seconds or until smooth. Taste and add more lemon juice, salt, or pepper if you like.

2 Transfer the spread to a small serving bowl, cover, and chill for 2 hours or overnight. Before serving, garnish with the sour cream and dill if desired. Makes 1⅓ cups.

PREPARATION TIME: 7 MIN. CHILLING TIME: 2 HR.

Per tablespoon: Calories 33; Saturated Fat 2 g; Total Fat 3 g; Protein 2 g; Carbohydrate 0 g; Fiber 0 g; Sodium 90 mg; Cholesterol 8 mg

MEXICALI BEAN SPREAD

This snappy spread is a welcome change from cheese and contains no fat. You can keep it for up to 5 days in the refrigerator.

- 1½ cups cooked red kidney beans
- 3   tablespoons water
- 1   tablespoon tomato paste
- 1   tablespoon lemon juice
- 1   teaspoon ground cumin
- ¾   teaspoon dried oregano, crumbled
- ¼   teaspoon hot red pepper sauce
- Pinch ground cinnamon

1 In a food processor or blender, whirl the kidney beans, water, tomato paste, lemon juice, cumin, oregano, red pepper sauce, and cinnamon for 1 minute or until smooth. Serve as an appetizer, accompanied by tortilla chips or pita bread, or make sandwiches with it, garnishing them with sliced cucumber and lettuce. Makes 1½ cups.

PREPARATION TIME: 5 MIN.

Per tablespoon: Calories 15; Saturated Fat 0 g; Total Fat 0 g; Protein 1 g; Carbohydrate 3 g; Fiber 0 g; Sodium 6 mg; Cholesterol 0 mg

Low-fat tortilla chips, wonderful with dips and spreads, are easy to make at home. All you need are corn tortillas (available in the frozen or refrigerated food section of most supermarkets) and nonstick cooking spray. The secret to these tasty chips is that they are broiled, not fried.

Preheat the broiler, setting the rack 6 inches from the heat. Lightly coat the tortillas on both sides with nonstick cooking spray. Salt them lightly if you wish. Cut the rounds into 6 wedges and arrange them on a baking sheet. Broil for 3 minutes or until crisp; there is no need to turn them over. When cool, they can be stored in an airtight container for up to 2 weeks.

HERBED CHEESE BALL

If possible, start this beautiful appetizer the day before you wish to serve it so that it has sufficient time to chill. For easier preparation, have the cheeses at room temperature.

1 package (7 ½ ounces) farmers cheese	1 tablespoon minced fresh rosemary or 1 teaspoon dried rosemary, crumbled
4 ounces plain goat cheese or ½ cup small-curd low-fat (1% milkfat) cottage cheese	½ teaspoon dry mustard
½ cup shredded Cheddar cheese (2 ounces)	⅛ teaspoon black pepper
	⅓ cup minced parsley
	8 strips roasted red pepper, 3 inches by ½ inch (optional)

1 In a food processor, whirl the 3 cheeses, rosemary, mustard, and black pepper for 30 seconds or until smooth. Line a small bowl with a 12-inch square of plastic food wrap and scrape the mixture into the bowl. Gather up the plastic food wrap around the cheese mixture and shape the mixture into a ball. Chill for 8 hours or overnight.

2 Adjust the shape of the cheese ball if needed. Remove the plastic food wrap. Sprinkle the parsley on wax paper and roll the cheese ball in it to coat. Place on a small plate and press the strips of red pepper into the ball for decoration if desired. Serve with whole-wheat or rye crackers and slices of tart apple. Serves 12.

PREPARATION TIME: 15 MIN.   CHILLING TIME: 8 HR.

Per serving: Calories 74; Saturated Fat 4 g; Total Fat 6 g; Protein 4 g; Carbohydrate 1 g; Fiber 0 g; Sodium 139 mg; Cholesterol 19 mg

•

Miniature Cheese Ball Variation: Prepare the cheese mixture as directed. Shape it into a log 12 inches long, wrap with plastic food wrap, and chill for 8 hours or overnight. Remove the plastic food wrap, cut the log into 12 slices, and shape each slice into a ball. Roll the balls in the parsley and serve with toothpicks.
Per ball: Calories 74; Saturated Fat 4 g; Total Fat 6 g; Protein 4 g; Carbohydrate 1 g; Fiber 0 g; Sodium 139 mg; Cholesterol 19 mg.

MINI PIZZAS

Topped with mozzarella and Parmesan cheese, these little pizzas are elegant enough for a party, yet simple enough for snacks just about anytime. To use the leftover bread for bread crumbs, let it dry overnight, then whirl the pieces in a food processor for 30 seconds. Store in an airtight container.

6 slices whole-wheat or white bread	¼ teaspoon each salt and black pepper, or to taste
1 tablespoon olive oil	1 cup shredded part-skim mozzarella cheese (4 ounces)
1 clove garlic, crushed	1 tablespoon grated Parmesan cheese
2 medium-size plum tomatoes, cut crosswise into 12 slices	Sprigs fresh thyme, oregano, or parsley (optional garnish)
2 tablespoons minced fresh basil or 2 teaspoons dried basil, crumbled	
½ teaspoon dried oregano, crumbled	

1 Preheat the oven to 425° F. Using a 2-inch biscuit cutter or small glass, cut 2 rounds from each slice of bread. With a rolling pin, gently flatten the rounds. In a small bowl, combine the oil and garlic. Using a pastry brush, coat each bread round with a little of the mixture. Arrange the rounds on a baking sheet and bake for 5 minutes or until slightly crisp.

2 On each round of bread, layer a slice of tomato, a sprinkling of basil, oregano, salt and pepper, a heaping tablespoon of mozzarella cheese, and ¼ teaspoon Parmesan cheese. Bake the mini pizzas for 7 to 10 minutes or until the mozzarella cheese is melted. Transfer the pizzas to a serving dish and garnish with sprigs of fresh herbs if desired. Makes 12 pizzas.

PREPARATION TIME: 20 MIN.   COOKING TIME: 12 MIN.

Per pizza: Calories 72; Saturated Fat 1 g; Total Fat 3 g; Protein 4 g; Carbohydrate 7 g; Fiber 1 g; Sodium 159 mg; Cholesterol 6 mg

BRUSCHETTA

- 3 tablespoons olive oil
- 2 tablespoons water
- 2 tablespoons minced fresh basil
- 2 cloves garlic, minced
- 1 loaf Italian bread (10 ounces), cut into 20 slices
- 2 medium-size tomatoes, peeled (see Tip, page 280), seeded, and coarsely chopped (1¾ cups)
- ½ teaspoon salt Basil leaves (optional garnish)

1 Preheat the oven to 400° F. In a small saucepan, heat the oil and water over low heat. Add the basil and garlic and cook, uncovered, for 4 minutes. Remove from the heat and let stand for 10 minutes. In a sieve set over a bowl, strain the mixture, pressing on the solids to extract all the liquid. Set aside both the solids and liquid.

2 Using a pastry brush, coat 1 side of each bread slice with the reserved liquid and arrange on a large baking sheet. Bake for 10 minutes or until crisp.

3 In a small bowl, combine the tomatoes and salt. Add the reserved solids to the tomatoes and let stand for 30 minutes. Spoon a heaping tablespoon of the mixture onto each piece of toast and garnish with whole basil leaves if you like. Makes 20 appetizers.

PREPARATION TIME: 15 MIN.   COOKING TIME: 14 MIN.

STANDING TIME: 40 MIN.

> Per appetizer: Calories 61; Saturated Fat 0 g;
> Total Fat 2 g; Protein 2 g; Carbohydrate 9 g;
> Fiber 1 g; Sodium 127 mg; Cholesterol 0 mg

EGGPLANT CAVIAR

This mildly spicy and smoky dish is a great make-ahead for company. It will keep for a week in the refrigerator.

- 4 cloves garlic, unpeeled
- 1 eggplant (1 pound)
- 3 tablespoons finely chopped walnuts
- 2 teaspoons lemon juice
- 1 teaspoon olive oil
- ½ teaspoon each ground coriander and cumin
- ¼ teaspoon paprika
- ⅛ teaspoon each ground cinnamon and salt

1 Preheat the oven to 400° F. Wrap the garlic cloves in aluminum foil. Prick the skin of the eggplant a few times with a fork and place it on a baking sheet along with the garlic. Bake for 30 minutes or until the garlic packet feels soft. Bake the eggplant an additional 20 minutes or until soft. Let cool.

2 Unwrap the garlic, squeeze the cloves into a medium-size bowl, and mash them. Halve the eggplant and scrape the flesh into the bowl, discarding most of the seeds. With a fork, mix in the walnuts, lemon juice, oil, coriander, cumin, paprika, cinnamon, and salt. Spoon into a small serving bowl and serve at room temperature or chilled with whole-wheat crackers. Makes about 1 cup.

PREPARATION TIME: 8 MIN.   COOKING TIME: 50 MIN.

> Per tablespoon: Calories 20; Saturated Fat 0 g;
> Total Fat 1 g; Protein 1 g; Carbohydrate 2 g;
> Fiber 0 g; Sodium 18 mg; Cholesterol 0 mg

Today's entertaining can be both easy and healthful. Two appetizers that prove the point are Herbed Cheese Ball, served with whole-wheat crackers and apple slices, and Bruschetta, Tuscan-style toasts topped with tomatoes, basil, and garlic.

Sesame seeds are fine flavor enhancers of crackers and breads and are even better when toasted. To toast them, place a single layer of seeds in a heavy skillet and cook over moderate heat for 1 to 2 minutes, shaking or stirring, until lightly browned. Or place the seeds in a microwave-safe glass measuring cup and heat on high (100% power) for 3 to 4 minutes, stirring occasionally, until golden. (These same techniques can be used for other seeds and wheat germ.)

SESAME-HONEY CRACKERS

These crunchy little bites of sesame and honey can be stored in an airtight container for up to a week.

1 2/3 cups all-purpose flour
1/3 cup sesame seeds, toasted (see Tip, left)
2 tablespoons wheat germ
3/4 teaspoon salt
1/4 teaspoon baking powder

1/4 teaspoon dry mustard
2 tablespoons unsalted butter
1/4 cup low-fat (1% milkfat) milk
3 tablespoons honey
2 tablespoons canola or corn oil

1 In a large bowl, stir together the flour, sesame seeds, wheat germ, salt, baking powder, and mustard. With a pastry blender or 2 forks, cut in the butter until the mixture resembles coarse crumbs.

2 In a glass measuring cup, combine the milk, honey, and oil. Make a well in the center of the dry ingredients and pour in the liquid; stir just until combined. Spoon half the dough onto a sheet of plastic food wrap and shape into a log 2 inches in diameter and 6 inches long. Roll up the log in the plastic wrap. Repeat with the remaining half of the dough. Freeze the logs for 1 hour.

3 Preheat the oven to 400° F. Lightly grease 2 baking sheets. Remove the plastic wrap from the logs, slice them 1/4 inch thick, and arrange the slices on the prepared baking sheets. Bake for 5 to 6 minutes, then turn them over and bake 5 to 6 minutes more or until brown on both sides. Transfer to wire racks to cool. Makes 48 crackers.

PREPARATION TIME: 10 MIN. COOKING TIME: 10 MIN.
FREEZING TIME: 1 HR.

Per cracker: Calories 36; Saturated Fat 0 g; Total Fat 2 g; Protein 1 g; Carbohydrate 5 g; Fiber 0 g; Sodium 36 mg; Cholesterol 1 mg

Alone or with a slice of low-fat cheese, Sesame-Honey Crackers give you satisfying crunch in a bedtime or anytime snack.

SPICY WONTON CRACKERS

When baked, a wonton wrapper (used to make the dumpling known as wonton) becomes as crisp as a cracker. Wonton wrappers are available in the produce or frozen food section of many supermarkets. If you cannot find 3-inch-square wrappers, buy 6-inch squares and quarter them.

¼ teaspoon hot chili powder	1 tablespoon olive, corn, or peanut oil
¼ teaspoon salt	1 tablespoon water
⅛ teaspoon each ground allspice and cloves	16 wonton wrappers (3-inch squares)

1 Preheat the oven to 400° F. Line a baking sheet with aluminum foil. In a small cup, combine the chili powder, salt, allspice, cloves, oil, and water. Using a pastry brush, coat the wonton wrappers on each side with the mixture. Place the wontons on the prepared baking sheet and bake for 5 minutes or until crisp. Makes 16 wonton crackers.

PREPARATION TIME: 6 MIN. COOKING TIME: 5 MIN.

Per cracker: Calories 31; Saturated Fat 0 g; Total Fat 1 g; Protein 1 g; Carbohydrate 4 g; Fiber 0 g; Sodium 34 mg; Cholesterol 0 mg

CHILI POPCORN

This low-calorie snack is made with corn popped in a hot-air popper. If prepared ahead, it can be recrisped on a baking sheet in a 300° F oven for 6 to 8 minutes just before serving.

1 teaspoon paprika	1 tablespoon grated Parmesan cheese
½ teaspoon chili powder	10 cups popped corn, without salt or oil (½ cup unpopped)
¼ teaspoon salt	
⅛ teaspoon garlic powder	
Pinch ground red pepper (cayenne), or to taste	Butter-flavored nonstick cooking spray or water

1 Preheat the oven to 350° F. In a small bowl, combine the paprika, chili powder, salt, garlic powder, red pepper, and Parmesan cheese. Spread the popcorn in an even layer on 2 large baking sheets and coat lightly with the nonstick cooking spray or water from a spray bottle. With a fork, sprinkle the herbs over the popcorn and toss to coat. Bake for 5 to 10 minutes or until crisp. Serve immediately or store in an airtight container. Makes ten 1-cup servings.

PREPARATION TIME: 10 MIN. COOKING TIME: 5 MIN.

Per serving: Calories 29; Saturated Fat 0 g; Total Fat 0 g; Protein 1 g; Carbohydrate 5 g; Fiber 0 g; Sodium 66 mg; Cholesterol 0 mg

HOMEMADE POTATO CHIPS

Feel free to indulge yourself with these fabulous, guilt-free munchies.

2 medium-size russet potatoes (about 1 pound), sliced ¹⁄₁₆ inch thick	1 tablespoon grated Parmesan cheese
	1 teaspoon paprika

1 Preheat the oven to 350° F. Lightly grease a nonstick baking sheet. Arrange the potato slices in 1 layer on the baking sheet and bake, turning occasionally, for 45 minutes or until golden brown.

2 In a small bowl, combine the cheese and paprika and sprinkle the mixture over the potatoes. Bake 5 minutes more, let cool, and transfer to a serving dish. Makes about 2 cups or 120 chips. Serves 4 to 6.

PREPARATION TIME: 7 MIN. COOKING TIME: 50 MIN.

Per serving (for 4): Calories 81; Saturated Fat 0 g; Total Fat 1 g; Protein 2 g; Carbohydrate 17 g; Fiber 2 g; Sodium 33 mg; Cholesterol 1 mg

•

Spiced Variation: Substitute *1 teaspoon each chili powder* and *cumin* for the Parmesan cheese and paprika. Add *⅛ teaspoon ground red pepper (cayenne)*, or to taste. *Per serving: Calories 77; Saturated Fat 0 g; Total Fat 0 g; Protein 2 g; Carbohydrate 17 g; Fiber 2 g; Sodium 11 mg; Cholesterol 0 mg.*

Popcorn — low in calories — is an ideal snack food when cooked in an air popper without oil or butter. And a little goes a long way: just ½ cup of kernels yields up to 10 cups of popped corn.

Kernels for popping are larger than other corn kernels because they have a bit of moisture trapped inside. When heat is applied, the moisture expands, causing the kernels to burst. If you have kernels that do not pop, they may have dried out and need to be refreshed. Put them in an airtight container and add 1 teaspoon of water for every cup. Seal and leave for a few days, shaking occasionally. When all the water has been absorbed, the corn is ready for popping.

DEVILED SHRIMP

Cooking the shrimp in their shells gives a richer flavor to this spicy appetizer. If you wish to prepare it a day ahead, just complete Step 1, then cover and refrigerate the shrimp. Shell and devein them just before serving.

3 cups water
1 medium-size yellow onion, chopped (1 cup)
1 medium-size stalk celery, chopped (½ cup)
6 allspice berries
6 black peppercorns
1 bay leaf
2 tablespoons lemon juice
1 tablespoon white wine vinegar
½ teaspoon red pepper flakes
¼ teaspoon salt
1 pound large shrimp in their shells, rinsed (about 36)
½ recipe Tomato Salsa (page 280) or 1 ½ cups bottled salsa (optional)

1 In a large saucepan, bring the water, onion, celery, allspice, peppercorns, bay leaf, lemon juice, vinegar, red pepper, and salt to a boil over moderate heat. Lower the heat and simmer for 15 minutes. Add the shrimp, bring the liquid to a boil, then simmer, stirring, for 1 to 2 minutes or until the shrimp are opaque and just firm to the touch. Remove from the heat and let the shrimp cool in the liquid.

2 Shell and devein the shrimp (see Tip, page 100). Arrange on a platter, and serve with the salsa on the side if desired. Makes about 36 shrimp.

PREPARATION TIME: 10 MIN. COOKING TIME: 20 MIN.

Per shrimp: Calories 16; Saturated Fat 0 g; Total Fat 0 g; Protein 3 g; Carbohydrate 1 g; Fiber 0 g; Sodium 35 mg; Cholesterol 19 mg

TOMATO-BASIL MOLD

This lovely aspic looks even more attractive when garnished with fresh sprigs of herbs and a dollop of Creamy Yogurt Spread (page 287) or reduced-calorie mayonnaise. It makes a refreshing, low-calorie starter for a summer supper.

3½ cups low-sodium tomato juice
1 small yellow onion, finely chopped (½ cup)
1 small stalk celery, finely chopped (⅓ cup)
½ teaspoon each dried basil and thyme, crumbled
6 black peppercorns
2 whole cloves
¼ teaspoon salt
⅛ teaspoon ground red pepper (cayenne), or to taste
4 teaspoons plain gelatin (1 ½ envelopes)
3 tablespoons dry white wine or water
3 tablespoons minced fresh basil, dill, or parsley
Sprigs fresh dill, basil, or parsley (garnish)

1 In a medium-size saucepan, bring the tomato juice, onion, celery, dried basil and thyme, peppercorns, cloves, salt, and red pepper to a boil over moderately high heat. Lower the heat and simmer for 15 minutes.

2 Meanwhile, in a small bowl, combine the gelatin and wine and let stand for 5 minutes. Add the gelatin mixture to the tomato mixture and simmer for 5 minutes. Strain through a fine sieve into a heatproof bowl, stir in the fresh basil, and let cool to room temperature.

3 Rinse a 3-cup decorative mold with cold water and pour in the tomato-herb mixture. Refrigerate, covered, for 3 hours or until set. To unmold, dip the mold in a large pan filled with hot water for 5 to 10 seconds, place a serving plate over the mold, then invert the mold onto the plate. Garnish with sprigs of fresh dill, basil, or parsley. Makes 6 to 8 appetizer servings.

PREPARATION TIME: 10 MIN. COOKING TIME: 20 MIN.
COOLING AND CHILLING TIME: 3½ HR.

Per serving (for 6): Calories 43; Saturated Fat 0 g; Total Fat 0 g; Protein 3 g; Carbohydrate 8 g; Fiber 2 g; Sodium 112 mg; Cholesterol 0 mg

CHICKEN KEBABS WITH MANDARIN ORANGES

This tempting appetizer is served on 24 wooden or bamboo skewers. To make the kebabs even more flavorful, place a leaf of fresh mint or coriander between each chicken and orange segment.

¼ cup orange juice
2 teaspoons grated orange rind
1 tablespoon soy sauce
1 clove garlic, minced
1 teaspoon minced fresh ginger
1 teaspoon honey
1 ½ teaspoons Dijon mustard

1 pound skinned and boned chicken breast, cut into 1-inch cubes
2 ½ teaspoons dark sesame oil
½ cup reduced-calorie mayonnaise
1 can (11 ounces) mandarin oranges, drained

1 In a medium-size bowl, combine the orange juice, orange rind, soy sauce, garlic, ginger, honey, and 1 teaspoon of the mustard. Add the chicken and toss to coat. Refrigerate, covered, for 2 hours or overnight.

2 Preheat the broiler, setting the rack 6 inches from the heat. Drain the chicken and pat it dry with paper toweling. In a small bowl, toss the chicken with 2 teaspoons of the sesame oil. Arrange the chicken on the broiler pan and broil, turning once or twice, for 7 minutes or until firm.

3 Meanwhile, in a small bowl, whisk the mayonnaise with the remaining ½ teaspoon of sesame oil and ½ teaspoon of mustard and transfer to a serving dish.

4 Arrange 2 pieces of chicken alternately with 2 orange segments on each of 24 wooden or bamboo skewers. Arrange the skewers on a platter and serve with the mayonnaise for dipping. Makes 24 appetizers.

PREPARATION TIME: 15 MIN. COOKING TIME: 7 MIN.
MARINATING TIME: 2 HR.

Per appetizer: Calories 49; Saturated Fat 0 g; Total Fat 2 g; Protein 5 g; Carbohydrate 3 g; Fiber 0 g; Sodium 64 mg; Cholesterol 13 mg

Chicken Kebabs with Mandarin Oranges tantalize the eye and the appetite. Dip one into a light and zippy sauce of mustard and reduced-calorie mayonnaise.

Apples, with their high fiber content, are a very good snack food. They are filling yet low in calories, help maintain a good blood-sugar balance, and are available year round. Apples are at their best, of course, during the harvest season of late summer through autumn. This is the period when you can find a wider selection, especially local types. Though thousands of apple varieties exist, only a few are produced in sufficient quantity for supermarket distribution.

Apples in the United States used to be sprayed with the chemical protective agent alar, but the practice was stopped in 1989. For this reason, some apple varieties may appear more blemished than in the past.

At room temperature, apples ripen quickly. To keep them fresh longer, store them in a plastic bag in the refrigerator.

RASPBERRY APPLESAUCE

This simple dish can be enjoyed anytime. Try it for breakfast, accompanied by vanilla yogurt; have it for a pick-me-up in mid-morning or afternoon; serve it as a condiment with roast pork or poultry; or present it for dessert, warmed and topped with a scoop of vanilla ice milk or frozen yogurt.

- 6 medium-size tart apples, such as Granny Smith or greening, peeled, cored, and thickly sliced (about 6 cups)
- 1/3 cup apple juice or water
- 1/4 teaspoon ground cinnamon
- 1/8 teaspoon ground cloves
- 3 tablespoons seedless raspberry jam
- 2 tablespoons honey
- 1 tablespoon lemon juice

1 In a medium-size saucepan, bring the apples, apple juice, cinnamon, and cloves to a simmer over moderately low heat. Cook, covered, stirring occasionally, for 15 minutes or until tender. Break apart any large chunks of apple with a spoon. Stir in the jam, honey, and lemon juice. Serve warm or chilled. Will keep, covered and refrigerated, for up to 2 weeks. Makes 4 cups.

PREPARATION TIME: 12 MIN. COOKING TIME: 15 MIN.

Per 1/2 cup: Calories 103; Saturated Fat 0 g; Total Fat 0 g; Protein 0 g; Carbohydrate 27 g; Fiber 2 g; Sodium 2 mg; Cholesterol 0 mg

APPLE-BUTTER CHEW

Pack a couple of these chewy fruit treats in school or work lunch boxes. Pear butter works well too.

- 1/2 cup dried currants or golden raisins
- 1 cup apple butter
- 1/4 teaspoon ground allspice
- 1 tablespoon honey
  Nonstick cooking spray

1 In a small heatproof bowl, soak the currants in boiling water to cover for 10 minutes or until softened. Drain, then let dry on paper toweling for several minutes. In a food processor, whirl the currants, apple butter, allspice, and honey for 1 minute or until smooth.

2 Preheat the oven to 175° F. Spread a sheet of plastic food wrap on a 10- by 16-inch baking sheet and lightly coat with the cooking spray. Spread the apple mixture in a thin, even layer on the baking sheet. (The thinner it is, the more quickly it will dry.) Bake in the center of the oven for 4 to 6 hours or until the leather is pliable and stretches slightly before tearing. Cool, cut into 1- by 4-inch strips; wrap in plastic food wrap. Will keep in an airtight container in a cool, dry place for up to 1 month. Makes 16 strips.

PREPARATION TIME: 6 MIN. COOKING TIME: 4 HR.
SOAKING AND DRYING TIME: 15 MIN.

Per strip: Calories 54; Saturated Fat 0 g; Total Fat 0 g; Protein 0 g; Carbohydrate 14 g; Fiber 0 g; Sodium 0 mg; Cholesterol 0 mg

Watch the big game with these two healthful snacks on your team — Honey-Peach Cup and Chili Popcorn (page 313).

KIWI-PINEAPPLE SMASH

Be sure to use soft, ripe kiwis to make this fruity beverage that's as cool and refreshing as a tropical breeze.

- 3 kiwis, peeled and chopped (1 ½ cups)
- 1 cup drained fresh or canned pineapple chunks
- 1 cup pineapple juice
- 1 tablespoon lime juice
- 1 tablespoon grenadine syrup or cranberry-apple juice
- 1 cup ice cubes
- 1 kiwi, sliced (optional garnish)

1 In a food processor or blender, whirl the chopped kiwis, pineapple, pineapple juice, lime juice, grenadine, and ice for 1 minute or until thick and frothy. Pour the mixture into tall glasses and garnish with a slice of kiwi if desired. Serves 4.

PREPARATION TIME: 5 MIN.

Per serving: Calories 92; Saturated Fat 0 g; Total Fat 0 g; Protein 1 g; Carbohydrate 23 g; Fiber 2 g; Sodium 4 mg; Cholesterol 0 mg

HONEY-PEACH CUP

- 1 small peach, peeled and cubed, or ½ cup drained and diced canned peaches
- 1 can (5 ½ ounces) peach nectar
- 1 tablespoon honey, or to taste
- ¾ teaspoon grated fresh ginger or ¼ teaspoon ground ginger
- 1 cup seltzer

1 In a food processor or blender, whirl the peach, nectar, honey, and ginger for 1 minute or until smooth. Divide the mixture between 2 tall glasses. Add ½ cup of seltzer to each glass and stir until well blended. Fill each glass with ice. Serves 2.

PREPARATION TIME: 5 MIN.

Per serving: Calories 93; Saturated Fat 0 g; Total Fat 0 g; Protein 0 g; Carbohydrate 24 g; Fiber 1 g; Sodium 8 mg; Cholesterol 0 mg

SPARKLING FRUIT PUNCH

To vary this spritely combination of fruit juices and mineral water, you can substitute reconstituted frozen lemonade or raspberry daiquiri mix for the cranberry juice.

2 cups cranberry juice cocktail	6 orange slices
1 cup orange juice	6 lime slices
1 cup sparkling mineral water or seltzer	Sprigs fresh mint (optional garnish)

1 In a 1-quart pitcher, stir together the cranberry juice, orange juice, and mineral water. Fill 6 tall glasses with ice cubes, then fill almost to the top with the punch. Add 1 orange and 1 lime slice to each glass and top with a sprig of fresh mint if desired. Serves 6.

PREPARATION TIME: 6 MIN.

Per serving: Calories 80; Saturated Fat 0 g; Total Fat 0 g; Protein 1 g; Carbohydrate 20 g; Fiber 1 g; Sodium 4 mg; Cholesterol 0 mg

ORANGE SLUSH

You can delight in this cooling refresher on any hot summer day. Try it with other fruit juices too.

1 cup orange juice	1 tablespoon each granulated and light brown sugar
4 ice cubes	
3 tablespoons nonfat dry milk powder	

1 In a food processor or blender, whirl ½ cup of the orange juice with the ice, milk powder, and sugars for 1 minute or until smooth. Add the remaining ½ cup orange juice and whirl for 30 seconds or until combined. Serves 2.

PREPARATION TIME: 4 MIN.

Per serving: Calories 126; Saturated Fat 0 g; Total Fat 0 g; Protein 3 g; Carbohydrate 29 g; Fiber 1 g; Sodium 38 mg; Cholesterol 1 mg

MOCHA SHAKE

Consider having this instead of your usual morning brew. It's almost like having dessert for breakfast.

½ cup strong brewed coffee	2 teaspoons unsweetened cocoa powder
4 ice cubes	½ cup low-fat (1% milkfat) milk
1 tablespoon malted milk powder (optional)	
1 tablespoon each sugar and honey	

1 In a food processor or blender, whirl the coffee, ice cubes, malted milk powder if desired, sugar, honey, and cocoa powder for 1 minute or until smooth. Add the milk and blend just until combined. Serves 2.

PREPARATION TIME: 5 MIN.

Per serving: Calories 86; Saturated Fat 0 g; Total Fat 1 g; Protein 2 g; Carbohydrate 19 g; Fiber 0 g; Sodium 32 mg; Cholesterol 3 mg

A buffet of appetizers presents a wealth of entertaining opportunities, from celebrations of holidays and birthdays to informal gatherings of neighbors. Here are simple ways to make a buffet festive — with imagination, not expense.

Use flowers in unexpected ways. Try arranging them in containers other than vases — a water pitcher, terrine, or pretty teakettle, for example. Lay one or two buds, backed by a spray of greens, on a serving tray. And float edible flowers, such as nasturtiums and day lilies, in a punch bowl.

An effective centerpiece can be candles of different colors and heights grouped in a variety of holders. (This is an attractive way to use up half-burned candles from other events.) Or feature a basket filled with flowering plants, their pots covered with dried moss. Or make an arrangement of seasonal fruits or vegetables.

You can also hollow out fruits or vegetables and use them as servers for dips. (If you surround the dips with bite-size vegetables and fruits instead of chips, your table will be not only more colorful but healthful too.) And if you line serving plates or platters with the leaves of sturdy greens, such as kale or cabbage, or patterned linen napkins, they will look nice and seemingly abundant, even after many of the appetizers have been eaten.

CRANBERRY FIZZ

This sparkling blend of fresh fruit, juice, and seltzer is better tasting than bottled sodas and better for you.

1 ¼ cups fresh or frozen cranberries (5 ounces)

5 strips orange zest (colored part of the rind), each 3 inches by ¼ inch

1 cup water

½ cup orange juice

⅓ cup sugar

3 slices fresh ginger, each the size of a quarter

½ vanilla bean, split lengthwise, or 1 teaspoon vanilla extract

1 ⅓ cups seltzer

1 In a medium-size saucepan, bring the cranberries, orange zest, water, orange juice, sugar, ginger, and vanilla bean to a boil over high heat (if using vanilla extract, add it in Step 2). Lower the heat, cover, and simmer for 10 minutes or until the berries are soft.

2 Strain the mixture over a medium-size heatproof bowl. Using the back of a spoon, press the solids to extract as much liquid as possible, then discard them. You should have about 1 ⅓ cups of liquid. (Stir in the vanilla extract if using.) Let the liquid cool to room temperature. For each serving, pour ⅓ cup of the cranberry mixture into a tall glass, add ⅓ cup of the seltzer, and stir to blend. Add ice if desired. Serves 4.

PREPARATION TIME: 6 MIN. COOKING TIME: 10 MIN.

Per serving: Calories 97; Saturated Fat 0 g; Total Fat 0 g; Protein 0 g; Carbohydrate 25 g; Fiber 0 g; Sodium 4 mg; Cholesterol 0 mg

Raise a toast at your next celebration with refreshing Cranberry Fizz.

GAZPACHO COOLER

Beat the heat with this lively blend of fresh vegetable juices. Make plenty—it keeps for up to 5 days in the refrigerator, but it disappears fast.

1 small sweet green pepper, cored, seeded, and diced (½ cup)	2 tablespoons lemon juice
1 small sweet red pepper, cored, seeded, and diced (½ cup)	1 clove garlic
	⅛ teaspoon ground red pepper (cayenne), or to taste (optional)
½ medium-size cucumber, peeled, seeded, and diced (½ cup)	2½ cups low-sodium tomato juice
1 green onion, including top, sliced	

1 In a food processor or blender, whirl the sweet green and red peppers, cucumber, green onion, lemon juice, garlic, and, if desired, the ground red pepper for 1 minute or until well combined. Add the tomato juice and whirl 30 seconds more or until smooth. Serve over ice. Serves 4.

PREPARATION TIME: 15 MIN.

Per serving: Calories 42; Saturated Fat 0 g; Total Fat 0 g; Protein 2 g; Carbohydrate 10 g; Fiber 3 g; Sodium 17 mg; Cholesterol 0 mg

CITRUS SPICED TEA

Serve hot in the winter, over ice in the summer. To warm your teapot, fill it with boiling water while the spices are simmering, then drain just before making the tea.

4 cups water	2 cinnamon sticks, split lengthwise
8 strips lemon zest (colored part of the rind), each 3 inches by ¼ inch	8 whole cloves
	½ teaspoon each ground ginger and allspice
8 strips orange zest, each 3 inches by ¼ inch	3 bags black tea

1 In a small saucepan over high heat, bring the water, lemon zest, orange zest, cinnamon stick, cloves, ginger, and allspice to a boil. Lower the heat, cover, and simmer for 10 minutes. Pour into a warm teapot, add the tea bags, and steep for 10 minutes. Pour the tea through a sieve into teacups or let cool and strain over ice. Serves 4.

PREPARATION TIME: 7 MIN. COOKING TIME: 10 MIN.
STANDING TIME: 10 MIN.

Per serving: Calories 6; Saturated Fat 0 g; Total Fat 0 g; Protein 0 g; Carbohydrate 2 g; Fiber 0 g; Sodium 8 mg; Cholesterol 0 mg

SPICY MULLED CIDER

This hot and sassy brew will warm you up on frosty winter days.

1 quart apple cider	8 whole cloves
6 slices fresh ginger, each about the size of a quarter (optional)	2 cinnamon sticks, cracked
	2 tablespoons honey
3 strips orange zest (colored part of the rind)	2 tablespoons lemon juice

1 In a large saucepan over moderate heat, stir together the cider, ginger if desired, orange zest, cloves, cinnamon sticks, and honey. Bring the mixture just to a simmer, reduce the heat to low, and cook, partially covered, for 25 minutes. Stir in the lemon juice and strain through a sieve into another heatproof container or individual mugs. Serve hot. Makes 1 quart.

PREPARATION TIME: 5 MIN. COOKING TIME: 25 MIN.

Per cup: Calories 150; Saturated Fat 0 g; Total Fat 0 g; Protein 0 g; Carbohydrate 39 g; Fiber 1 g; Sodium 8 mg; Cholesterol 0 mg

DESSERTS

Help yourself to Neufchâtel Cheesecake (page 325) or Chocolate
Angel Food Cake (page 323), just 2 of some 30 recipes in this chapter that prove
you can have your cake and eat it too — you *can* eat healthfully
and still enjoy dessert. Several, such as the frozen desserts on pages 333–334,
Fruited Bread Pudding (page 329), or Blueberry Clafouti and Poached
Fruit in Ginger Syrup (page 336), can be enjoyed every day. Others, such as Chocolate
Glazed Cocoa Cake (page 322) and Lemon Mousse Pie (page 327), are
for special occasions. The secret, of course, is that all of these recipes are lower
in fat and sugar and higher in protein than the average bakery product,
ice cream, or other confection heavy with cream, butter, and egg yolks. So go ahead
and indulge yourself now and then without guilt.

When nothing but the deepest, darkest chocolate flavor will do, satisfy your craving with moist Chocolate-Glazed Cocoa Cake.

CHOCOLATE-GLAZED COCOA CAKE

1 ¾ cups all-purpose flour
1 cup granulated sugar
⅔ cup unsweetened cocoa powder
1 teaspoon baking soda
¼ teaspoon ground nutmeg
¼ teaspoon salt
½ cup olive or canola oil
¼ cup honey
2 large egg yolks
1 cup skim milk
1 ½ teaspoons vanilla extract

6 large egg whites
½ teaspoon cream of tartar
½ cup no-sugar-added apricot or raspberry preserves

For the glaze:
1 ¾ cups confectioners sugar
¼ cup unsweetened cocoa powder
¼ cup skim milk
1 tablespoon honey
¾ teaspoon vanilla extract

1 Preheat the oven to 350° F. Lightly grease two 8-inch round cake pans and dust with flour. Into a large bowl, sift together the flour, sugar, cocoa powder, baking soda, nutmeg, and salt. Make a well in the center of the dry ingredients and add the oil, honey, egg yolks, milk, and vanilla. Stir just until combined and smooth.

2 In a perfectly clean medium-size bowl, beat the egg whites with an electric mixer set on high speed until foamy. Add the cream of tartar and continue beating until stiff peaks form — about 5 minutes. Stir ¼ of the egg whites into the batter, then gently fold in the remaining egg whites. Divide the batter between the prepared pans.

3 Bake for 35 to 38 minutes or until a toothpick inserted in the center of the cake comes out clean. Place the pans upright on wire racks for 5 minutes, then invert the cakes onto the racks and let cool completely.

4 Place 1 layer, upside down, on a serving plate. Cut 4 strips of wax paper and slide them under the edges of the cake to protect the plate from the glaze. Spread the preserves on top of the layer and top with the second layer, right side up.

5 To prepare the glaze: In a small saucepan, combine the sugar and cocoa powder. Whisk in the milk, honey, and vanilla and cook over low heat for 1 to 2 minutes or just until smooth. (Do not cook the glaze longer or it may become grainy.) Using an icing spatula or wide knife and working quickly, frost the top, then the sides of the cake with the glaze. Let stand for 30 minutes or until hardened. With a sharp knife, score a line around the bottom edge of the cake and remove the wax paper. Serves 12.

PREPARATION TIME: 25 MIN. COOKING TIME: 36 MIN.
STANDING TIME FOR GLAZE: 30 MIN.

Per serving: Calories 370; Saturated Fat 2 g; Total Fat 11 g; Protein 6 g; Carbohydrate 65 g; Fiber 1 g; Sodium 149 mg; Cholesterol 36 mg

CHOCOLATE ANGEL FOOD CAKE

You can dust this heavenly cake with confectioners sugar or top each serving with a dollop of Creamy Whipped Topping (page 335).

1 cup sifted cake flour	1 ½ teaspoons cream of tartar
1 ¼ cups granulated sugar	2 teaspoons vanilla extract
⅓ cup unsweetened cocoa powder	2 tablespoons sifted confectioners sugar (optional)
¾ teaspoon ground cinnamon	
½ teaspoon salt	
1 ½ cups egg whites (about 12 large eggs)	

1 Preheat the oven to 325° F. In a medium-size bowl, sift together the flour, ¾ cup of the granulated sugar, the cocoa, cinnamon, and salt.

2 In a perfectly clean large bowl, beat the egg whites with an electric mixer set on high speed until foamy. Add the cream of tartar and beat until soft peaks form. Gradually add ¼ cup of the remaining sugar in a steady stream and continue beating until the whites are stiff and glossy but not dry. Beat in the vanilla. Sprinkle the remaining ¼ cup of sugar over the top of the whites and fold in gently. Gently fold in the flour mixture.

3 Spoon the batter into an ungreased 10-inch tube pan and bake for 45 minutes or until a toothpick inserted in the center comes out clean. Invert the pan and let cool. Transfer the cake to a serving platter and dust with the confectioners sugar if desired. Serves 12.

PREPARATION TIME: 15 MIN. COOKING TIME: 45 MIN.

Per serving: Calories 133; Saturated Fat 0 g; Total Fat 1 g; Protein 5 g; Carbohydrate 29 g; Fiber 0 g; Sodium 147 mg; Cholesterol 0 mg

MACAROON CUPCAKES

What could be better for an afternoon treat than freshly baked coconut cupcakes? You can use either sweetened or unsweetened coconut in this recipe. Unsweetened coconut is available in specialty food stores.

Nonstick cooking spray	1 teaspoon almond extract
1 ½ cups sifted cake flour	½ teaspoon vanilla extract
1 ½ teaspoons baking powder	½ cup low-fat (1% milkfat) milk
6 tablespoons (¾ stick) unsalted butter or margarine, at room temperature	½ cup shredded sweetened coconut
⅔ cup granulated sugar, sifted	Sifted confectioners sugar (optional)
2 large eggs, separated	

1 Preheat the oven to 350° F. Lightly coat eighteen 2¼-inch muffin cups with the cooking spray or insert cupcake liners. Sift the flour and baking powder onto a sheet of wax paper and set aside. In a large bowl, cream the butter with an electric mixer set on medium speed. Gradually add about ½ cup of the granulated sugar in small amounts, beating until the mixture is light and fluffy. Add the egg yolks and almond and vanilla extracts and beat until well combined.

2 In a perfectly clean medium-size bowl and with clean beaters, beat the egg whites with the electric mixer set on high until they form soft peaks. Add the remaining granulated sugar in small amounts and beat until the egg whites are stiff and glossy but not dry.

3 Add the flour mixture and milk to the butter mixture. Fold in the coconut and egg whites and spoon the batter into the prepared muffin cups, filling them ⅔ full. Bake for 20 to 25 minutes or until a toothpick inserted in the center of a cupcake comes out clean. Let cool to room temperature; dust with the confectioners sugar if desired. Makes 18 cupcakes.

PREPARATION TIME: 15 MIN. COOKING TIME: 20 MIN.

Per cupcake: Calories 122; Saturated Fat 4 g; Total Fat 6 g; Protein 2 g; Carbohydrate 16 g; Fiber 0 g; Sodium 45 mg; Cholesterol 35 mg

Perfect cakes demand careful techniques. It is especially important to measure ingredients accurately. For dry ingredients, fill cups and spoons to the top and level them with a knife; if your recipe calls for sifted flour, sift *before* measuring, then sift again if the directions call for this step. When measuring liquid ingredients, use a glass cup and view the measuring line at eye level.

Follow the instructions for mixing precisely. If you undermix, the ingredients may not be distributed evenly; overmixing may produce a tough cake that won't rise fully.

Set cake pans in the oven at least 1 inch apart and let the minimum baking time elapse before opening the oven door. Even a brief opening may cool the oven enough to make the cake fall.

A cake is done when a toothpick inserted near the center comes out clean. It's ready to frost when thoroughly cool; wait at least 30 minutes after removing the cake from the oven.

CHIFFON CAKE WITH STRAWBERRY MOUSSE

You can serve this feather-light cake with sumptuous strawberry mousse and fresh fruit, as directed below, with a chocolate glaze (see Chocolate-Glazed Cocoa Cake, page 322), or dusted with 2 tablespoons of confectioners sugar.

For the cake:
- 1 ½ cups sifted cake flour
- 1 cup plus 2 tablespoons granulated sugar
- 2 ¼ teaspoons baking powder
- ¾ teaspoon salt
- ¼ teaspoon baking soda
- ¼ cup plus 2 tablespoons vegetable oil
- 2 large egg yolks
- ½ cup plus 1 tablespoon buttermilk
- 2 teaspoons vanilla extract
- 7 large egg whites

For the mousse:
- 1 envelope (¼ ounce) unflavored gelatin
- ¼ cup water
- 1 package (12 ounces) frozen unsweetened strawberries, thawed, or 3 cups fresh strawberries, hulled
- ⅓ cup granulated sugar
- 8 ounces plain nonfat yogurt
- 2 tablespoons confectioners sugar
- 5 large strawberries, hulled and halved
- 1 ½ cups blueberries

1 Preheat the oven to 325° F. Lightly grease a 10-cup Bundt pan or 10-inch tube pan and lightly dust with flour. In a large bowl, sift together the flour, 1 cup of the sugar, the baking powder, salt, and baking soda. Make a well in the center of the dry ingredients and add the oil, egg yolks, buttermilk, and vanilla. Stir until combined.

2 In a perfectly clean medium-size bowl, beat the egg whites with an electric mixer set on high speed until foamy. Gradually beat in the remaining 2 tablespoons of sugar until the whites are stiff and glossy but not dry. Stir ¼ of the egg whites into the batter, then gently fold in the remaining egg whites. Spoon batter into the prepared pan.

3 Bake for 1 hour or until a toothpick inserted in the center of the cake comes out clean. Set the pan upright on a wire rack for 30 minutes or until cool. Run a metal spatula gently around the sides of the pan and under the edge of the bottom; invert the cake onto a serving plate.

4 While the cake is baking, prepare the mousse. In a small bowl, sprinkle the gelatin over the water and let soften for 5 minutes. In a food processor or blender, whirl the strawberries for 30 seconds or until puréed. You should have 1 cup; if not, add water to make 1 cup. Pour ½ cup of the purée into a small saucepan, add the granulated sugar, and bring to a boil over moderate heat.

5 Add the softened gelatin to the saucepan and stir until dissolved. Transfer the mixture to a medium-size bowl and stir in the remaining ½ cup of strawberry purée. Set the bowl in a large bowl filled with ice water and stir occasionally until syrupy — about 20 minutes. Fold in the yogurt and refrigerate for 2 hours or until firm.

6 Using a serrated knife, cut away some of the center of the cake until the hole is about 4 inches in diameter. Spoon the mousse into the hole; dust the cake with the confectioners sugar. Arrange some of the strawberries and blueberries on top of the mousse and the remaining fruit at the base of the cake. Serves 12.

PREPARATION TIME: 50 MIN. COOKING TIME: 1 HR.
COOLING TIME: 3 HR.

Per serving: Calories 277; Saturated Fat 2 g; Total Fat 8 g; Protein 6 g; Carbohydrate 47 g; Fiber 2 g; Sodium 275 mg; Cholesterol 36 mg

Most cakes will keep at room temperature for up to 3 days. It's best to cover a frosted cake with a cake box or a large inverted bowl. If you must use plastic food wrap or aluminum foil, insert toothpicks into the top of the cake so that the wrapping does not stick to the frosting. A cake with a cream-based topping or filling should always be refrigerated.

Wrapped in heavy-duty aluminum foil, many cakes will keep for up to 3 months in the freezer at 0° F. The best way to freeze a cake is to wrap unfrosted layers individually. But if you prefer to frost the cake first, use a butter-cream icing (any frosting or filling that contains artificial flavorings, egg whites, fresh fruit, or brown sugar should not be frozen). First, freeze the cake unwrapped, then carefully wrap it. To defrost a cake, unwrap and let it stand at room temperature for 1 to 2 hours.

NEUFCHÂTEL CHEESECAKE

In this luscious cheesecake, both calories and cholesterol are reduced by substituting egg whites for whole eggs and low-fat milk and yogurt for heavy cream. Garnish this delightful treat with fresh strawberries or raspberries.

For the crust:
- 1 cup graham cracker crumbs (12 double wafers, crushed)
- 3 tablespoons sugar
- 3 tablespoons unsalted butter or margarine, melted
- ½ teaspoon ground cinnamon

For the filling:
- 1 tablespoon plus 1 teaspoon unflavored gelatin
- ½ cup evaporated or fresh skim milk
- 1 pound Neufchâtel cream cheese, at room temperature
- 1 cup plain low-fat yogurt
- 1 teaspoon grated lemon rind
- 1 teaspoon vanilla extract
- ½ cup sugar
- ¼ cup water
- 3 large egg whites

1 Preheat the oven to 350° F. Lightly grease a 9-inch springform pan. To prepare the crust: In a small bowl, combine the graham cracker crumbs, sugar, butter, and cinnamon. Using your fingers, press the mixture evenly onto the bottom and sides of the pan. Bake for 10 minutes or until the crust is lightly colored. Let cool.

2 Meanwhile, prepare the filling. In a small heatproof bowl, sprinkle the gelatin over the milk and let soften for 5 minutes. In an 8-inch skillet, bring ½ inch of water to a simmer. Place the bowl in the simmering water and stir until the gelatin is dissolved.

3 In a food processor or blender, whirl the cream cheese, yogurt, gelatin mixture, lemon rind, and vanilla, scraping down the sides if necessary, for 30 seconds or until smooth. Transfer the mixture to a large bowl.

4 In a small heavy saucepan, combine the sugar with the water. Bring the mixture to a boil over moderately high heat and cook, occasionally washing down the sides of the pan with a pastry brush dipped in cold water (see Tip, page 330), for 6 minutes or until a candy thermometer registers 240° F or ¼ teaspoon of the syrup dropped into a saucer of cold water forms a soft ball.

5 In a perfectly clean large bowl, beat the egg whites with an electric mixer set on high speed for 2 to 3 minutes or until they form soft peaks. With the mixer running on medium-high, add the sugar syrup in a stream and beat for 4 to 5 minutes or until the mixture is cool and looks thick and glossy. Fold the whites into the cheese mixture. Pour the filling into the crust and chill, covered with plastic food wrap, for 3 to 4 hours or until firm. Serves 10 to 12.

PREPARATION TIME: 25 MIN. COOKING TIME: 18 MIN.
CHILLING TIME: 3 HR.

Per serving (for 10): Calories 267; Saturated Fat 9 g; Total Fat 15 g; Protein 9 g; Carbohydrate 24 g; Fiber 0 g; Sodium 269 mg; Cholesterol 47 mg

Chiffon Cake with Strawberry Mousse is a sensational presentation for any special occasion, from Mother's Day to Valentine's Day.

CRANBERRY-PEAR UPSIDE-DOWN CAKE

*Moist, tender, colorful, and refreshingly fruity —
what more could you ask of a cake that is also easy to
prepare? Consider too that you're getting some
fiber and vitamins as part of the bargain. To please those
for whom just cake is never quite enough, add a dollop
of Creamy Whipped Topping (page 335).*

- ½ **cup packed light brown sugar**
- 1 **tablespoon unsalted butter or magarine, melted**
- 1 **tablespoon lemon juice**
- 1 **can (1 pound) pear halves in juice**
- 1 **cup fresh or frozen cranberries (4 ounces)**
- 1 ½ **cups all-purpose flour**
- ½ **cup rye or all-purpose flour**
- 1 **teaspoon each baking powder and baking soda**
- ½ **teaspoon salt**
- ⅓ **cup granulated sugar**
- 3 **tablespoons honey**
- 3 **tablespoons canola or vegetable oil**
- 2 **large egg whites**
- 2 **teaspoons grated lemon rind**
- 1 **tablespoon lemon juice**

1 Preheat the oven to 350° F. Lightly grease a 9-inch round cake pan. In the cake pan, stir together the brown sugar, butter, and lemon juice, then spread the mixture evenly over the bottom.

2 Drain the pears, reserving ¾ cup of the juice, and cut them in half lengthwise. Place the pears on top of the butter-sugar mixture with the rounded sides down, arranging them like the spokes in a wheel. Scatter the cranberries in a single layer around the pears.

3 In a medium-size bowl, combine the all-purpose flour, rye flour, baking powder, baking soda, and salt. In a large bowl, whisk together the granulated sugar, honey, oil, egg whites, lemon rind, lemon juice, and reserved pear juice until well blended.

4 Add half of the flour mixture to the sugar-egg mixture and stir just until blended; add the remaining flour mixture and blend, being careful not to overmix. Scrape the batter into the prepared pan, spreading it evenly over the fruit, and bake for 30 to 35 minutes or until a toothpick

Light up a meal's end with the sunny taste of Lemon Mousse Pie, made with a zesty gingersnap crust.

inserted in the center comes out clean. Place the pan upright on a wire rack and let cool for 5 minutes. Invert the cake onto a serving plate and serve warm. Serves 10.

PREPARATION TIME: 20 MIN. COOKING TIME: 30 MIN.

*Per serving: Calories 245; Saturated Fat 2 g;
Total Fat 6 g; Protein 3 g; Carbohydrate 47 g;
Fiber 1 g; Sodium 239 mg; Cholesterol 3 mg*

PINEAPPLE UPSIDE-DOWN GINGERBREAD

You can substitute for the pineapple some peeled and sliced firm pears or baking apples, such as Rome or Granny Smith.

1 tablespoon unsalted butter or margarine, melted
⅓ cup firmly packed light brown sugar
1 tablespoon lemon juice
9 rings canned pineapple in juice, drained
1¾ cups all-purpose flour
¼ cup cornstarch
1 teaspoon each ground cinnamon and ginger

½ teaspoon each baking powder and baking soda
½ teaspoon salt
⅓ cup molasses
⅓ cup granulated sugar
¼ cup canola or vegetable oil
2 large egg whites
1 cup low-fat (1% milkfat) milk
Creamy Whipped Topping (page 335) (optional)

1 Preheat the oven to 350° F. Lightly grease a 9" x 9" x 2" baking pan. In the pan, stir together the butter, brown sugar, and lemon juice, then spread the mixture evenly over the bottom. Arrange the pineapple rings on top.

2 Into a medium-size bowl, sift together the flour, cornstarch, cinnamon, ginger, baking powder, baking soda, and salt. In a large bowl, whisk together the molasses, granulated sugar, oil, and egg whites.

3 Add half of the flour mixture and half of the milk to the molasses mixture and stir just until blended. Repeat with remaining flour and milk, taking care not to overmix. Pour the batter into the prepared pan, spreading it evenly over the fruit. Bake for 35 to 40 minutes or until a toothpick inserted in the center comes out clean. Set the pan upright on a wire rack and let cool for 5 minutes, then invert onto a serving platter. Serve warm, topped with a dollop of Creamy Whipped Topping if desired. Serves 9.

PREPARATION TIME: 20 MIN. COOKING TIME: 35 MIN.

*Per serving: Calories 251; Saturated Fat 2 g;
Total Fat 8 g; Protein 4 g; Carbohydrate 41 g;
Fiber 1 g; Sodium 214 mg; Cholesterol 5 mg*

LEMON MOUSSE PIE

For the filling:
1 cup plain nonfat yogurt
1 envelope (¼ ounce) unflavored gelatin
2 tablespoons water
½ cup lemon or lime juice
⅔ cup sugar
1 large egg
4 large egg whites

1 tablespoon unsalted butter or margarine

For the crust:
24 gingersnap cookies, crushed (1½ cups)
1 tablespoon sugar
2 tablespoons unsalted butter, softened
2 tablespoons vegetable or olive oil

1 To prepare the filling: Spoon the yogurt into a fine sieve set over a bowl; refrigerate and let drain for at least 2 hours or overnight. In a small bowl, sprinkle the gelatin over the water and let soften for 5 minutes. In the top of a double boiler, whisk together the lemon juice, sugar, egg, and egg whites; set the pan over, not in, simmering water. Cook, whisking constantly, for 6 to 8 minutes or until light and thickened. Stir in the gelatin and cook 1 minute more.

2 Remove the mixture from the heat and transfer to a heatproof bowl. Stir in the butter, set the bowl in ice water, and whisk occasionally for 15 minutes or until cool and thickened. Lightly whisk the drained yogurt and fold it into the lemon mixture. Cover the bowl with plastic food wrap and refrigerate while you make the crust.

3 To prepare the crust: Preheat the oven to 400° F. In a medium-size bowl, using a fork, thoroughly combine the gingersnap crumbs, sugar, and butter. Add the oil and stir until the crumbs are evenly coated. Press onto the bottom and sides of a 9-inch pie plate. Bake for 8 minutes or until firm and set. Let cool to room temperature.

4 Spoon the lemon mixture into the pie shell, smooth the top, and refrigerate for at least 3 hours before serving. Will keep, refrigerated, for up to 3 days. Serves 8.

PREPARATION TIME: 20 MIN. COOKING TIME: 15 MIN.

STANDING AND CHILLING TIME: 5¼ HR.

*Per serving: Calories 277; Saturated Fat 3 g;
Total Fat 13 g; Protein 6 g; Carbohydrate 35 g;
Fiber 1 g; Sodium 161 mg; Cholesterol 39 mg*

Mousses and other creamy desserts usually have a custard base, one thickened with eggs. A smooth custard requires gentle cooking and close attention. Use a double boiler, setting the pan over, not in, simmering water, and watch carefully to make sure that the custard doesn't boil, which will cause it to curdle. Stir constantly, lifting the spoon now and then to check thickness. The custard is done when it thickly coats the spoon.

Everyone loves this old-fashioned favorite. Pear-Apple Crisp evokes memories of crisp fall days and perhaps aromas from Grandma's kitchen.

PEAR-APPLE CRISP

This sweet-tart fruit crisp, served warm or at room temperature, only gets better with a dollop of Creamy Whipped Topping (page 335). It will taste terrific reheated the next day too—if you have any left.

3 ripe pears, peeled, cored, and thinly sliced (about 3½ cups)

2 tart apples, such as Granny Smith, Jonathan, or greening, peeled, cored, and sliced (about 2½ cups)

2 tablespoons lemon juice

2 tablespoons bourbon, applejack, brandy, or apple cider

1 teaspoon vanilla extract

¾ cup all-purpose flour

⅓ cup sugar

½ teaspoon ground cinnamon

¼ teaspoon ground allspice

2 tablespoons unsalted butter or margarine, chilled

1 tablespoon vegetable oil

1 Preheat the oven to 350° F. In a large bowl, toss together the pears, apples, lemon juice, bourbon, and vanilla. Transfer to a 9-inch pie plate.

2 In a medium-size bowl, stir together the flour, sugar, cinnamon, and allspice. With a pastry blender or 2 knives, cut in the butter until the mixture resembles coarse crumbs, then stir in the oil. Spoon the mixture on top of the fruit. Bake for 30 minutes, then remove from the oven and spoon some of the juice that has collected over the topping. Bake 15 minutes more or until the fruit is soft and the topping is crisp. Serves 6 to 8.

PREPARATION TIME: 20 MIN. COOKING TIME: 45 MIN.

Per serving (for 6): Calories 239; Saturated Fat 3 g; Total Fat 7 g; Protein 2 g; Carbohydrate 42 g; Fiber 4 g; Sodium 1 mg; Cholesterol 11 mg

APRICOT CRISP

*With dried apricots, you can make this fruity
crisp any time of year. Drying intensifies the sweetness
of fruit, so only a small amount of sugar is
needed in this recipe. Try other dried fruits too –
apples, pears, peaches, or a mixture.*

12 ounces dried apricots (2 cups)
1 cup orange juice
¾ cup water
1 tablespoon plus 1 teaspoon finely chopped candied orange peel (optional)
¾ cup all-purpose flour
¼ cup firmly packed light brown sugar
½ teaspoon each ground cardamom and ginger
2 tablespoons unsalted butter or margarine, chilled
1 tablespoon vegetable oil

1 In a medium-size heavy saucepan, bring the apricots, ¾ cup of the orange juice, the water, and orange peel if using to a boil over moderate heat. Lower the heat and simmer, covered, for 30 minutes or until the apricots are soft and most of the liquid has been absorbed. Remove the mixture from the heat and stir in the remaining ¼ cup of orange juice.

2 In a medium-size bowl, stir together the flour, sugar, cardamom, and ginger. With a pastry blender or 2 knives, cut in the butter until the mixture resembles coarse crumbs, then stir in the oil. Spoon the mixture on top of the fruit. Bake for 20 minutes, then remove from the oven and spoon some of the juice that has collected over the topping. Bake 10 minutes more or until the topping is crisp. Serve warm or at room temperature. Serves 6.

PREPARATION TIME: 10 MIN. COOKING TIME: 1 HR.

*Per serving: Calories 296; Saturated Fat 3 g;
Total Fat 7 g; Protein 4 g; Carbohydrate 59 g;
Fiber 5 g; Sodium 10 mg; Cholesterol 11 mg*

FRUITED BREAD PUDDING

*Fiber and flavor rich, this easy old-fashioned dessert
is a comforting conclusion to a hectic day. It also makes
a great breakfast. In summer, peaches or nectarines
can be substituted for the apple and pear.*

6 slices whole-wheat bread, cut into 1-inch cubes
1 each McIntosh apple and Bosc pear, peeled, cored, and sliced (about 2 cups)
1 tablespoon lemon juice
½ cup raisins
3 cups skim or low-fat (1% milkfat) milk
2 large eggs
1 large egg white
⅓ cup granulated sugar
1 teaspoon vanilla extract
1 teaspoon grated lemon rind
½ teaspoon ground cinnamon
2 tablespoons sifted confectioners sugar (optional)

1 Lightly grease an 11" x 9" x 2" baking dish. Scatter half the bread cubes on the bottom. In a medium-size bowl, toss the fruit with the lemon juice and raisins. Spoon the fruit over the bread and top with the remaining bread.

2 In a large bowl, whisk together the milk, eggs, egg white, granulated sugar, vanilla, lemon rind, and cinnamon and pour the mixture over the bread, pressing the cubes with the back of a spoon to soak them completely. Cover with aluminum foil and let stand for 30 minutes at room temperature or overnight in the refrigerator.

3 Preheat the oven to 350° F. Set the baking dish in a large pan and add enough hot water to come halfway up the sides of the dish. Bake, covered, for 30 minutes. Uncover and bake 30 minutes more or until puffed and golden. Let cool to warm, then dust with the confectioners sugar if desired. Serves 6 to 8.

PREPARATION TIME: 15 MIN. COOKING TIME: 1 HR.
STANDING TIME: 30 MIN.

*Per serving (for 6): Calories 246; Saturated Fat 1 g;
Total Fat 3 g; Protein 10 g; Carbohydrate 47 g;
Fiber 5 g; Sodium 273 mg; Cholesterol 73 mg*

A **cooked meringue of** egg white and sugar syrup gives a wonderful texture and richness to such desserts as chocolate mousse; for the recipes in this chapter, it substitutes for the usual whipped cream, thus keeping fat calories to a minimum.

The procedure is to bring sugar and water to a boil, stirring until the sugar is dissolved and the syrup is clear. Once the syrup begins to boil, do not stir, or the sugar may crystallize. Some crystals will form on the sides of the saucepan during cooking. These can be washed down periodically with a pastry brush dipped in cold water. Cook until a candy thermometer registers 240° F or ¼ teaspoon of syrup dropped into a saucer of cold water forms a soft ball.

Beat the hot syrup gradually into egg whites that have already been whipped to the soft peak stage. The whites become slowly cooked in the process, forming a rich, creamy substance (and one free of any salmonella that the uncooked eggs may have harbored).

COUSCOUS PUDDING

Couscous replaces rice in this grown-up version of a childhood favorite. Faster-cooking than rice, couscous also has a smoother texture. The nuts and grated orange rind add just the right touch.

- 1 large egg
- 1 large egg white
- ¼ cup sugar
- 2¾ cups low-fat (1% milkfat) milk
- 1 teaspoon grated orange rind
- ¼ teaspoon salt
- 1 cup uncooked couscous
- 3 tablespoons golden raisins
- 2 tablespoons pine nuts or coarsely chopped pistachios or almonds
- 1 teaspoon vanilla extract

1 In a medium-size bowl, beat together the egg, egg white, and 2 tablespoons of the sugar. In a medium-size saucepan, combine the milk, the remaining 2 tablespoons of sugar, the orange rind, and salt and bring to a simmer over moderate heat. Slowly pour the warmed milk into the egg mixture, whisking constantly.

2 Return the mixture to the saucepan and cook over moderate heat, stirring constantly, for 4 minutes or until thickened. Add the couscous and cook, stirring constantly, 6 minutes more. Remove from the heat, cover, and let stand for 6 minutes or until the couscous is tender. Stir in the raisins, pine nuts, and vanilla. Serve warm or at room temperature. Makes eight ½-cup servings.

PREPARATION TIME: 10 MIN. COOKING TIME: 12 MIN.
STANDING TIME: 6 MIN.

Per serving: Calories 186; Saturated Fat 1 g; Total Fat 3 g; Protein 8 g; Carbohydrate 31 g; Fiber 4 g; Sodium 126 mg; Cholesterol 30 mg

CHOCOLATE MOUSSE

- 4 ounces dark sweet or semisweet chocolate, cut into bits
- 1 tablespoon unsweetened cocoa powder
- ¼ cup evaporated or fresh skim milk
- 2 teaspoons grated orange rind
- ½ cup sugar
- ⅓ cup water
- 3 large egg whites

1 In the top of a double boiler set over simmering water, melt the chocolate with the cocoa and milk, stirring, about 4 minutes or until smooth. Add the orange rind and transfer the mixture to a large bowl.

2 In a small heavy saucepan, bring the sugar and water to a boil over moderately high heat; cook, occasionally washing down the sides of the pan with a pastry brush dipped in cold water (see Tip, left), for 6 minutes or until a candy thermometer registers 240° F or ¼ teaspoon of the syrup dropped into a saucer of cold water forms a soft ball.

3 In a perfectly clean large bowl, beat the egg whites with an electric mixer set on high speed for 2 to 3 minutes or until they form soft peaks. With the mixer running on medium-high, add the sugar syrup in a stream and beat for 4 to 5 minutes or until the mixture is cool and looks thick and glossy. Fold the whites into the chocolate mixture. Spoon the mousse into 6 individual bowls. Chill, covered with plastic food wrap, for 2½ hours or until firm. Serves 6.

PREPARATION TIME: 20 MIN. COOKING TIME: 11 MIN.
CHILLING TIME: 2½ HR.

Per serving: Calories 169; Saturated Fat 0 g; Total Fat 6 g; Protein 4 g; Carbohydrate 29 g; Fiber 0 g; Sodium 41 mg; Cholesterol 0 mg

Peppermint Variation: In Step 1, substitute *¼ teaspoon peppermint extract, or to taste,* for the orange rind. In Step 3, after folding the whites into the chocolate mixture, fold in *½ cup crushed peppermint candy* and proceed as directed. *Per serving: Calories 206; Saturated Fat 0 g; Total Fat 6 g; Protein 4 g; Carbohydrate 38 g; Fiber 0 g; Sodium 44 mg; Cholesterol 0 mg.*

CHOCOLATE-CHESTNUT BAVARIAN CREAM

Chestnuts are much lower in fat and calories than other nuts, containing fewer than one-third the calories of walnuts for example. For easy preparation, use canned chestnut purée, usually available in both sweetened and unsweetened forms in the baking section of a supermarket.

1 tablespoon plus 1 teaspoon unflavored gelatin	1 ounce dark sweet chocolate, melted
¼ cup plus 2 tablespoons cold water	½ cup unsweetened chestnut purée, pressed through a sieve
2 large eggs, separated	1 teaspoon vanilla extract
½ cup sugar	Shaved chocolate (optional garnish)
1 ½ cups low-fat (1% milkfat) milk, heated to the boiling point	

1 In a small heatproof bowl or custard cup, sprinkle the gelatin over ¼ cup of the water and let soften for 5 minutes. Meanwhile, in an 8-inch skillet, bring ½ inch of water to a simmer. Place the bowl in the simmering water and stir until the gelatin is thoroughly dissolved.

2 In a medium-size bowl, whisk together the egg yolks and ¼ cup of the sugar for 2 to 3 minutes or until light. Whisk in the milk, then transfer the mixture to a medium-size saucepan. Cook, stirring, over moderately low heat for 5 minutes or until thick enough to coat a spoon. Transfer the custard to a large bowl and stir in the gelatin mixture, chocolate, chestnut purée, and vanilla. Chill, stirring occasionally, for 15 to 20 minutes or until thickened.

3 Meanwhile, in a small heavy saucepan, bring the remaining ¼ cup of sugar and the 2 tablespoons of water to a boil over moderate heat; cook, occasionally washing down the sides of the pan with a pastry brush dipped in cold water (see Tip, opposite page) for 2 minutes or until a candy thermometer registers 240° F or ¼ teaspoon of the syrup dropped into a saucer of cold water forms a soft ball.

4 In a perfectly clean medium-size bowl, beat the egg whites with an electric mixer set on high speed until they form soft peaks. With the mixer running on medium-high, add the sugar syrup in a stream; beat for 5 minutes or until cool, thick, and glossy. Stir ¼ of the whites into the custard to lighten it, then fold in the remaining whites.

5 Rinse a 1-quart decorative mold with water, add the Bavarian cream, and tap the mold to release any air bubbles. Chill, covered with plastic food wrap, for 3 hours or until set. Dip the mold in hot water for 15 seconds, cover with a serving dish, and invert onto the dish. Decorate with chocolate shavings if desired. Serves 4 to 6.

PREPARATION TIME: 25 MIN. COOKING TIME: 7 MIN.

CHILLING TIME: 3¼ HR.

Per serving (for 4): Calories 279; Saturated Fat 1 g; Total Fat 6 g; Protein 10 g; Carbohydrate 48 g; Fiber 2 g; Sodium 82 mg; Cholesterol 110 mg

Chocolate Mousse tastes sinfully smooth and rich, yet contains not a drop of cream nor a trace of egg yolk. Enjoy a dishful of guilt-free indulgence.

SWEET POTATO SOUFFLÉ

What could be nicer than having dessert and a hefty serving of vitamin A too. Your soufflé will be higher if you let the egg whites come to room temperature before beating them.

¼ cup plus 2 teaspoons sugar

4 large sweet potatoes (2¼ pounds), baked and peeled, or 2 cans (23 ounces each) sweet potatoes, drained and rinsed

⅓ cup milk

1 teaspoon ground cinnamon

½ teaspoon ground allspice

½ teaspoon salt

¼ teaspoon ground ginger

⅛ teaspoon ground nutmeg

3 tablespoons finely chopped crystallized ginger

4 large egg whites

⅛ teaspoon cream of tartar

1 Preheat the oven to 375° F. Lightly grease a 1½-quart soufflé dish or deep baking dish; dust with 2 teaspoons of the sugar. In a food processor or blender, whirl the potatoes, 2 tablespoons of the remaining sugar, the milk, cinnamon, allspice, ¼ teaspoon of the salt, the ground ginger, and nutmeg for 45 seconds or until smooth. Transfer to a large bowl and stir in the crystallized ginger.

2 In a perfectly clean medium-size bowl, beat the egg whites with an electric mixer set on high until foamy. Add the remaining ¼ teaspoon of salt and the cream of tartar and beat for 1 minute or until very soft peaks form. Gradually add the remaining 2 tablespoons of sugar, beating continuously for 3 more minutes or until the whites are stiff and glossy but not dry. Stir ¼ of the egg whites into the sweet potato mixture to lighten it, then gently fold in the remaining egg whites. Scrape the mixture into the prepared dish and bake for 45 minutes or until puffed and golden brown. Serve immediately. Serves 8.

PREPARATION TIME: 20 MIN. COOKING TIME: 45 MIN.

Per serving: Calories 180; Saturated Fat 0 g; Total Fat 1 g; Protein 4 g; Carbohydrate 40 g; Fiber 4 g; Sodium 180 mg; Cholesterol 1 mg

When summer sizzles, cool off in minutes with a picture-perfect Frozen Yogurt Parfait. It's popular with all ages.

FROZEN YOGURT PARFAIT

1 **pint fresh raspberries, strawberries, or blueberries or 1 package (12 ounces) frozen unsweetened berries, thawed**	1 **tablespoon lemon juice**
	1 **teaspoon grated lemon rind**
	1 **pint frozen vanilla yogurt, slightly softened**
3 **tablespoons sugar**	

1 In a food processor or blender, whirl half of the raspberries with the sugar, lemon juice, and lemon rind for 15 seconds or until puréed. Transfer the purée to a medium-size bowl and stir in the remaining berries.

2 Layer the purée with the frozen yogurt in four 8-ounce parfait glasses. Place in the freezer for 45 minutes or until the parfait is firm. Serves 4.

PREPARATION TIME: 10 MIN. FREEZING TIME: 45 MIN.

Per serving: Calories 179; Saturated Fat 2 g; Total Fat 4 g; Protein 3 g; Carbohydrate 34 g; Fiber 3 g; Sodium 63 mg; Cholesterol 2 mg

APRICOT SHERBET

⅓ **cup sugar**	½ **cup chopped dried apricots**
1 **teaspoon unflavored gelatin**	
	3 **tablespoons honey**
1 **can (5½ ounces) apricot nectar**	2 **teaspoons lemon juice**
	2 **cups buttermilk**

1 In a medium-size saucepan, combine the sugar and gelatin. Stir in the nectar, apricots, and honey. Bring to a simmer over moderately low heat and cook for 1 minute. Remove from the heat and let stand for 15 minutes or until the apricots are softened.

2 Transfer the mixture to a food processor or blender. Add the lemon juice and whirl for 30 seconds or until smooth. Add the buttermilk and whirl 15 seconds more or until blended. Transfer to an ice cream maker and freeze according to the manufacturer's instructions. Or transfer to an 8″ x 8″ x 2″ pan, cover with plastic food wrap, and freeze for 2 hours or until the center is almost frozen. Remove the sherbet from the freezer and beat until smooth (see Tip, right). Return to the freezer for 45 minutes more, then beat again until smooth. Freeze 2 to 3 hours longer or until firm. Makes six ½-cup servings.

PREPARATION TIME: 12 MIN. COOKING TIME: 2 MIN.
STANDING TIME: 15 MIN. FREEZING TIME: 5 HR.

Per serving: Calories 149; Saturated Fat 0 g; Total Fat 1 g; Protein 4 g; Carbohydrate 34 g; Fiber 1 g; Sodium 89 mg; Cholesterol 3 mg

MOCHA ICE

2½ **cups water**	½ **teaspoon ground ginger**
½ **cup firmly packed dark brown sugar**	
	¼ **teaspoon salt**
⅓ **cup granulated sugar**	1 **tablespoon strong brewed coffee**
⅓ **cup unsweetened cocoa powder**	1 **teaspoon vanilla extract**

1 In a medium-size saucepan, bring the water, brown sugar, granulated sugar, cocoa, ginger, and salt to a boil over moderate heat. Cook, uncovered, for 5 minutes or until syrupy. Let cool to room temperature, then stir in the coffee and vanilla.

2 Pour into an 8″ x 8″ x 2″ pan, cover with plastic food wrap, and freeze for 2 hours or until almost firm but the center is still mushy. Remove the mixture from the freezer and beat until smooth. Cover and freeze 2 to 3 hours more or until firm. Remove from the freezer and let stand at room temperature for 5 minutes before serving to allow it to soften slightly. Makes eight ½-cup servings.

PREPARATION TIME: 15 MIN. COOKING TIME: 7 MIN.
FREEZING TIME: 4 HR. STANDING TIME: 5 MIN.

Per serving: Calories 92; Saturated Fat 0 g; Total Fat 1 g; Protein 1 g; Carbohydrate 23 g; Fiber 0 g; Sodium 71 mg; Cholesterol 0 mg

An ice cream maker is ideal for making sorbets, ices, and sherbets, as well as ice cream. But if you don't have one, you can make a satisfactory product in the freezer compartment of your refrigerator by following this procedure: Have the freezer temperature at its lowest setting. Pour the prepared mixture into ice cube trays (dividers removed) or baking pans, and freeze, covered, for 1 to 2 hours or until nearly firm. Transfer the mixture to a large chilled bowl and beat with an electric mixer or whirl in a food processor for 2 to 3 minutes or until light colored and smooth. This breaks up any ice crystals that may have formed. Return to the trays and freeze 2 to 3 hours more or until firm. For an even smoother result, repeat the beating process 1 or 2 times more.

A **low-calorie dessert** topping that can be used as an alternative to Creamy Whipped Topping (opposite page) is canned evaporated skim milk. Have the milk, beaters, and bowl thoroughly chilled. Beat the milk until slightly thickened, then add 1 tablespoon of confectioners sugar and 1 teaspoon of vanilla for each cup of milk. Continue beating until thick.

PEAR SORBET

Late summer's sweet, juicy fruits make wonderful sorbets and ices. Try the "plum perfect" variation below too.

- 3 medium-size ripe pears, peeled, cored, and thinly sliced (about 4 cups)
- ¾ cup water
- ½ cup lemon juice
- ½ cup granulated sugar
- 3 tablespoons firmly packed light brown sugar
- 1 bay leaf
- 1 teaspoon vanilla extract

1 In a large saucepan, bring the pears, water, lemon juice, granulated sugar, brown sugar, and bay leaf to a boil over moderate heat. Lower the heat and simmer, uncovered, for 25 minutes or until the pears are very tender. Let cool. Remove and discard the bay leaf and stir in the vanilla.

2 Transfer the mixture to a food processor or blender and whirl for 1 minute or until puréed. Pour into an 8" x 8" x 2" pan, cover with plastic food wrap, and freeze for 2 hours or until the center is almost frozen. Remove the mixture from the freezer and beat until smooth (see Tip, page 333). Return to the freezer for 45 minutes, then beat until smooth again. Freeze 2 to 3 hours more or until firm. Makes six ½-cup servings. Serves 6.

PREPARATION TIME: 16 MIN. COOKING TIME: 27 MIN.

FREEZING TIME: 5 HR.

Per serving: Calories 142; Saturated Fat 0 g; Total Fat 0 g; Protein 0 g; Carbohydrate 37 g; Fiber 2 g; Sodium 2 mg; Cholesterol 0 mg

•

Plum Variation: Substitute *8 large sweet plums, such as Santa Rosa, peeled, pitted, and thinly sliced (about 4 cups)*, for the pears. In a large saucepan, bring the plums, *¾ cup red wine or cranberry juice, ¼ cup water, 2 tablespoons lemon juice,* the sugars, and bay leaf to boil over moderate heat. Continue as directed. *Per serving: Calories 171; Saturated Fat 0 g; Total Fat 0 g; Protein 1 g; Carbohydrate 38 g; Fiber 2 g; Sodium 4 mg; Cholesterol 0 mg.*

BERRY SORBET

Sorbets, made only from fruit and sweetener — no milk — are fat and cholesterol free. You'll always have room for a dessert as light and refreshing as this one.

- ½ cup lime juice
- ⅓ cup sugar
- 2 tablespoons grenadine syrup or 2 tablespoons water plus 1 tablespoon sugar
- ⅓ cup water
- 1 package (12 ounces) frozen unsweetened raspberries, thawed
- 1 package (12 ounces) frozen unsweetened strawberries, thawed

1 In a medium-size saucepan, bring the lime juice, sugar, grenadine, and water to a boil over moderate heat. Cook about 1 minute or until the sugar is dissolved.

2 In a food processor or blender, whirl the raspberries and strawberries for 30 seconds or until puréed. Press the fruit through a fine sieve to eliminate the seeds. You should have 2 cups of purée; if not, add enough water to make 2 cups.

3 Stir the purée into the sugar syrup until well combined. Transfer the mixture to an 8" x 8" x 2" pan, cover with plastic food wrap, and freeze for 2 hours or until the center is almost frozen. Remove the sorbet from the freezer and beat until smooth (see Tip, page 333). Return to the freezer for 45 minutes, then beat again until smooth. Freeze 2 to 3 hours more or until firm. Makes six ½-cup servings.

PREPARATION TIME: 8 MIN. COOKING TIME: 3 MIN.

FREEZING TIME: 5 HR.

Per serving: Calories 125; Saturated Fat 0 g; Total Fat 0 g; Protein 1 g; Carbohydrate 33 g; Fiber 4 g; Sodium 1 mg; Cholesterol 0 mg

CREAMY WHIPPED TOPPING

Spoon this smooth, all-natural topping over fresh berries, fruit crisps, your favorite cake, or pudding. It is low in fat and has none of the additives of non-dairy toppings. It keeps, covered, for up to 5 days in the refrigerator without becoming watery.

½ teaspoon unflavored gelatin
1 tablespoon water
1 cup low-fat (1% milkfat) cottage cheese
1 tablespoon honey
1 tablespoon firmly packed brown sugar
¼ teaspoon vanilla extract

1 In a small heatproof bowl or custard cup, sprinkle the gelatin over the water and let soften for 5 minutes. Meanwhile, in an 8-inch skillet, bring ½ inch of water to a simmer over low heat. Place the bowl in the simmering water and stir until the gelatin is dissolved.

2 In a food processor or blender, whirl the cottage cheese, honey, sugar, and vanilla, scraping down the sides once, for 1 minute or until creamy. Add the gelatin and whirl for 30 seconds or until smooth. Scrape into a small bowl, cover, and chill, stirring occasionally, for 2 hours or until thickened. Makes 1 cup.

PREPARATION TIME: 10 MIN.   CHILLING TIME: 2 HR.

Per tablespoon: Calories 18; Saturated Fat 0 g; Total Fat 0 g; Protein 2 g; Carbohydrate 2 g; Fiber 0 g; Sodium 58 mg; Cholesterol 1 mg

From the left — Berry, Plum, and Pear Sorbets — who could say no to any one of these refreshing treats?

BLUEBERRY CLAFOUTI

This light confection of French origin should be served warm. It is wonderful topped with a dollop of vanilla low-fat yogurt or Creamy Whipped Topping (page 335).

2 cups blueberries, cranberries, or pitted Bing cherries	1 teaspoon grated orange rind
½ cup granulated sugar	1 teaspoon vanilla extract
1 cup skim milk	½ teaspoon ground cinnamon
½ cup all-purpose flour	2 tablespoons sifted confectioners sugar
2 large eggs	

1 Preheat the oven to 375° F. In a medium-size bowl, combine the blueberries with 2 tablespoons of the granulated sugar and let stand while preparing the batter.

2 In a food processor or blender, whirl the remaining granulated sugar, the milk, flour, eggs, orange rind, vanilla, and cinnamon for 30 seconds or until smooth. Or put all the ingredients in a medium-size bowl and stir just until blended.

3 Lightly grease a 9-inch pie plate and arrange the blueberries on the bottom. Spread the batter evenly over the blueberries and bake for 35 to 40 minutes or until puffed and lightly golden. Sprinkle with the confectioners sugar. Serves 4 to 6.

PREPARATION TIME: 10 MIN. COOKING TIME: 35 MIN.

Per serving (for 4): Calories 258; Saturated Fat 1 g; Total Fat 3 g; Protein 7 g; Carbohydrate 52 g; Fiber 2 g; Sodium 68 mg; Cholesterol 108 mg

POACHED FRUIT IN GINGER SYRUP

When you want a light ending to a hearty meal, serve poached apples and pears drizzled with a ginger-citrus sauce.

2 cups water	2 medium-size Granny Smith or McIntosh apples, peeled, cored, and thinly sliced (2 cups)
½ cup sugar	
1 strip orange zest (colored part of the rind), 3 inches long	
1 strip lemon zest, 2 inches long	2 medium-size Bosc or Anjou pears, peeled, cored, and thinly sliced (2 cups)
¼ cup orange juice	
1 stick cinnamon, cracked	½ cup raisins or diced dried apricots
1 tablespoon plus 1 teaspoon minced fresh ginger or 1 teaspoon ground ginger	1 tablespoon lemon juice
	1 teaspoon grated lemon or orange rind
	Thin strips lemon or orange zest (optional garnish)

1 In a large stainless steel or enameled saucepan, bring the water, sugar, orange zest, lemon zest, orange juice, cinnamon stick, and ginger to a boil over moderately high heat. Lower the heat and simmer for 10 minutes.

2 Add the apples to the liquid and simmer for 3 minutes. Add the pears and simmer 2 to 3 minutes more or until just tender. Stir in the raisins and let the mixture cool.

3 Pour the syrup through a sieve into a small bowl and discard the cinnamon sticks and strips of zest. Transfer the fruit to a serving dish. Return the syrup to the saucepan and cook over moderate heat for 5 minutes or until reduced to ½ cup. Add the lemon juice and rind and pour the syrup over the fruit. Chill, covered, for 2 hours or overnight. Spoon into dishes and garnish with strips of zest if desired. Serves 4 to 6.

PREPARATION TIME: 20 MIN. COOKING TIME: 20 MIN.

CHILLING TIME: 2 HR.

Per serving (for 4): Calories 228; Saturated Fat 0 g; Total Fat 1 g; Protein 1 g; Carbohydrate 60 g; Fiber 4 g; Sodium 3 mg; Cholesterol 0 mg

The next time little ones clamor for cookies and milk, give them homemade Cranberry-Apricot Bars and Double-Ginger Cookies (page 339). You'll both be happy.

CRANBERRY-APRICOT BARS

For the base:
- 4 ounces Neufchâtel cream cheese, at room temperature
- ⅓ cup canola or vegetable oil
- ½ cup packed light brown sugar
- ¼ teaspoon ground nutmeg
- ¼ teaspoon salt
- 1 ¼ cups all-purpose flour
- ¼ cup cornstarch

For the filling:
- 2 cups fresh or frozen cranberries (6 ounces)
- ½ cup chopped dried apricots
- ¼ cup honey
- ¼ cup granulated sugar
- ½ teaspoon each ground allspice and cinnamon
- 2 teaspoons grated orange rind
- ¼ cup orange juice

For the topping:
- 3 tablespoons granulated sugar

1 Preheat the oven to 375° F. Lightly grease a 9" x 9" x 2" baking pan. To prepare the base: In a medium-size bowl, using an electric mixer set on medium speed, beat the cream cheese, oil, sugar, nutmeg, and salt for 1 minute or until smooth. Stir in the flour and cornstarch just until combined. Scrape the mixture into the prepared pan, reserving ½ cup. Place a sheet of wax paper on top and press the mixture until level. Bake for 15 minutes.

2 Meanwhile, prepare the filling. In a small saucepan, bring the cranberries, apricots, honey, sugar, allspice, cinnamon, orange rind, and orange juice to a boil over moderate heat. Cook, stirring occasionally, for 8 minutes or until thickened. Spoon the filling over the cooked base, spreading it evenly.

3 To make the topping: Using a fork, work the sugar into the reserved base mixture until crumbly. Sprinkle the mixture evenly over the filling. Bake for 20 to 25 minutes or until the topping is golden. Let cool in the pan, then cut into bars about 1 by 2 ¼ inches. Makes 32 bars.

PREPARATION TIME: 25 MIN.   COOKING TIME: 45 MIN.

Per bar: Calories 89; Saturated Fat 1 g; Total Fat 3 g; Protein 1 g; Carbohydrate 15 g; Fiber 0 g; Sodium 32 mg; Cholesterol 3 mg

To keep cookies fresh after baking, store them at room temperature in a tightly covered container. Most types will keep this way for up to 2 weeks. Keep chewy cookies soft by placing a piece of bread in the cookie jar. Refresh crisp cookies if necessary by briefly heating them in a 300° F oven.

For longer storage, use the freezer. Since most cookies will keep, tightly covered, for up to 3 months in the freezer at 0° F, you can get a head start on your holiday baking in October.

COCONUT THUMBPRINT COOKIES

Toasted coconut gives these cookies a nutty and rich flavor.

1 cup flaked sweetened coconut (3 ounces)	½ teaspoon grated lemon rind
¼ cup plain dry bread crumbs	3 egg whites
2 tablespoons sugar	2 teaspoons lemon juice
	4 teaspoons no-sugar-added raspberry jam

1 Preheat the oven to 400° F. Spread the coconut on a baking sheet and toast in the oven about 8 minutes, stirring after 4 minutes, or until golden brown. Transfer to a food processor or blender; let cool to room temperature. Reduce the oven temperature to 350° F.

2 Add the bread crumbs, sugar, and lemon rind to the coconut and whirl for 30 seconds or until the coconut is fine. Add the egg whites and lemon juice and whirl until the mixture comes together in a mass.

3 Lighty grease a baking sheet. Using a rounded measuring teaspoon for each cookie, roll the dough with dampened hands into balls and place them 1 inch apart on the baking sheet. With your thumb, make an indentation in the center of each cookie and spoon ¼ teaspoon of jam into the imprint. Bake for 20 to 23 minutes or until firm and golden. Let cool for 3 minutes on the baking sheet, then transfer to a wire rack to cool completely. These cookies can be stored in an airtight container for up to 3 days at room temperature or in the freezer for up to 3 months. Makes sixteen 1¾-inch cookies.

PREPARATION TIME: 12 MIN. COOKING TIME: 30 MIN.

COOLING TIME: 5 MIN.

Per cookie: Calories 49; Saturated Fat 2 g; Total Fat 2 g; Protein 1 g; Carbohydrate 7 g; Fiber 0 g; Sodium 37 mg; Cholesterol 0 mg

Coconut-Almond Variation: In Step 1, substitute ½ cup *unblanched almonds (3 ounces)* for half of the coconut and toast as directed. Transfer the almonds to the food processor and set the coconut aside. Add *2 tablespoons sugar* and *2 tablespoons plain dry bread crumbs* to the almonds (omit lemon rind) and whirl for 30 seconds or until coarsely ground. Add *2 egg whites* and *1 teaspoon vanilla extract* (omit lemon juice) and whirl 10 seconds more. Stir in the coconut. Continue as directed in Step 3. Makes 16 cookies. *Per cookie: Calories 54; Saturated Fat 1 g; Total Fat 3 g; Protein 1 g; Carbohydrate 5 g; Fiber 1 g; Sodium 21 mg; Cholesterol 0 mg.*

FUDGY BROWNIES

These rich and chewy treats are quickly prepared in a single bowl.

¼ cup unsweetened cocoa powder	1 teaspoon vanilla extract
⅓ cup warm water	½ teaspoon baking powder
¼ cup vegetable oil	¼ teaspoon salt
⅓ cup granulated sugar	¾ cup all-purpose flour
⅓ cup firmly packed light brown sugar	⅓ cup coarsely chopped walnuts or pecans
2 egg whites	

1 Preheat the oven to 350° F. Lightly grease an 8″ x 8″ x 2″ baking pan. In a large bowl, stir together the cocoa and water and let stand for 5 minutes. Stir in the oil, granulated sugar, brown sugar, egg whites, and vanilla. Add the baking powder, salt, and flour and stir for 2 minutes. Fold in the nuts, then pour the mixture into the prepared pan.

2 Bake for 20 minutes or until set and a toothpick inserted in the center comes out clean. Let cool in the pan, then cut into 2-inch squares. Makes 16 brownies.

PREPARATION TIME: 10 MIN. COOKING TIME: 20 MIN.

STANDING TIME: 5 MIN.

Per brownie: Calories 105; Saturated Fat 1 g; Total Fat 5 g; Protein 1 g; Carbohydrate 14 g; Fiber 0 g; Sodium 52 mg; Cholesterol 0 mg

DOUBLE-GINGER COOKIES

2 cups all-purpose flour
1½ teaspoons baking soda
1 teaspoon ground ginger
½ teaspoon each ground cinnamon and cloves
¼ teaspoon salt
6 tablespoons (¾ stick) unsalted butter or margarine, softened
¾ cup packed light brown sugar
1 tablespoon finely chopped crystallized ginger (optional)
¼ cup molasses
1 large egg white

1 Preheat the oven to 375° F. In a medium-size bowl, stir together the flour, baking soda, ground ginger, cinnamon, cloves, and salt.

2 In another medium-size bowl, using an electric mixer set on medium speed, cream the butter, sugar, and crystallized ginger if using until smooth and light. Add the molasses and egg white and beat until combined. Stir in the flour mixture just until combined.

3 Using a measuring teaspoon, drop rounded spoonfuls of batter onto large ungreased baking sheets, spacing them 1 inch apart. Bake for 7 minutes or until crispy on the edges and slightly soft in the centers. Let cool on the pans for 2 minutes; remove with a spatula and let cool completely on racks. Makes about 4 dozen 1½-inch cookies.

PREPARATION TIME: 15 MIN. COOKING TIME: 7 MIN.

Per cookie: Calories 48; Saturated Fat 1 g;
Total Fat 2 g; Protein 1 g; Carbohydrate 8 g;
Fiber 0 g; Sodium 40 mg; Cholesterol 4 mg

•

Fruit Topping Variation: Peel, core, and slice *3 ripe sweet apples or pears.* In an 8-inch nonstick skillet, melt *1 tablespoon unsalted butter or margarine* over moderately low heat. Add the fruit and *½ teaspoon ground cinnamon.* Cook, stirring occasionally, for 5 to 7 minutes or until tender. In each of 4 individual serving dishes, place two Double-Ginger Cookies. Top with some of the fruit and *¼ cup frozen vanilla yogurt.* Serves 4. *Per serving: Calories 241; Saturated Fat 5 g; Total Fat 9 g; Protein 3 g; Carbohydrate 41 g; Fiber 3 g; Sodium 112 mg; Cholesterol 18 mg.*

PINEAPPLE-STUFFED DATES

These filled treats make wonderful finger food for a party. You can make them up to 4 days in advance and refrigerate until ready to serve.

1 can (8¼ ounces) crushed pineapple in juice
2 ounces Neufchâtel cream cheese, softened
1 tablespoon honey
1 tablespoon finely chopped almonds or pistachios (optional)
¼ teaspoon ground ginger
⅛ teaspoon almond extract
4 ounces pitted dates (about 20)
1 tablespoon flaked sweetened coconut (optional garnish)

1 Drain the pineapple in a sieve over a bowl, pressing with the back of a spoon to remove as much juice as possible. (Reserve the juice for another use.) Transfer to a double layer of paper toweling to finish draining. In a small bowl, stir together the pineapple, cream cheese, honey, almonds if desired, ginger, and almond extract until blended. Refrigerate, covered, for 2 hours or until firm. Or chill in the freezer for 30 minutes.

2 Meanwhile, split the dates lengthwise, cutting not quite all the way through. Fill each date with a slightly rounded ½ teaspoon of the pineapple mixture. Sprinkle the coconut over the filling if desired, and arrange the dates on a serving plate. Makes 20 dates.

PREPARATION TIME: 15 MIN. CHILLING TIME: 2 HR.

Per date: Calories 37; Saturated Fat 0 g;
Total Fat 1 g; Protein 0 g; Carbohydrate 8 g;
Fiber 1 g; Sodium 12 mg; Cholesterol 2 mg

TOPSY-TURVY TEA PARTY

Salmon-Cucumber Sandwich
(page 51)

Herbed Cheese and Watercress Sandwich
(page 52)

Coconut Thumbprint Cookies

Pineapple-Stuffed Dates

Assorted Teas

GRANDPARENTS' DAY DINNER

Cream of Broccoli Soup
(page 78)

Roast Chicken with Orange Rice Stuffing and Citrus Sauce
(page 102)

Mixed Greens with Buttermilk Dressing
(page 268)

Fudgy Brownies

Sparkling Fruit Punch
(page 318)

CREDITS

The editors are grateful to the following for their courtesy in lending items for photography. Items not listed below are privately owned.

Page 30: Cup, saucer, and plate — *Wedgwood*. **Page 36:** Cup, saucer, and plate — *Wedgwood*; small pitcher — *Orrefors Inc.*, available at *Royal Copenhagen/Georg Jensen Silversmiths*; tablecloth — *Le Jacquard Français*. **Page 49:** Plate — *Eigen Arts Inc.* **Page 50:** Sandwich tray — *Wedgwood*. **Page 58:** Plate — *Eigen Arts Inc.* **Page 66:** Rim soup bowl and underliner — *Waterford Wedgwood USA Inc.* **Page 69:** Tureen — *Wedgwood*. **Page 70:** Square plate — *Eigen Arts Inc.* **Page 81:** Rim soup bowl and dinner plate — *Wedgwood*; spoon — *Jean Couzon Inc.* **Page 86:** Condiment bowl — *Royal Copenhagen/Georg Jensen Silversmiths*. **Page 88:** Skillet — *Nordicware Inc.* **Page 99:** Tablecloth — *Le Jacquard Français*. **Page 102:** Platter and square bowl — *Spode*; carving set — *Jean Couzon Inc.* **Page 108:** Oval bowl — *Spode*. **Page 111:** Tablecloth — *Le Jacquard Français*; fork — *Jean Couzon Inc.* **Page 115:** Pitcher — *Eigen Arts Inc.* **Page 118:** Platter, oval bowl, and plates — *Spode*; tablecloth — *Le Jacquard Français*. **Page 125:** Round and small oval platters — *Royal Worcester*. **Page 129:** Tablecloth — *Le Jacquard Français*. **Page 130:** Salad bowl — *Royal Copenhagen/Georg Jensen Silversmiths*; glass bowl — *Simon Pearce U.S., Inc.*; towel — *Le Jacquard Français*. **Page 136:** Platter and small oval dish — *Wedgwood*. **Page 138:** Skillet — *Doug Hendrickson*; towel — *Le Jacquard Français*. **Page 143:** Oval platter — *Wedgwood*. **Page 144:** Plate — *Wedgwood*. **Page 157:** Skillet — *All-Clad Metalcrafters Inc.* **Page 175:** Plate — *Wedgwood*. **Page 176:** Bowls, plates, and platter — *Royal Copenhagen/Georg Jensen Silversmiths*. **Page 192:** Plate — *Wedgwood*. **Page 206:** Runner and napkin — *The Museum of Modern Art Design Store*. **Page 209:** Platter and plates — *Spode*. **Page 217:** Serving dish — *Wedgwood*. **Page 218:** Tablecloth — *Le Jacquard Français*; bowl and tray — *Wedgwood*; stemware — *Waterford*. **Page 223:** Pepper mills and canisters — *The Museum of Modern Art Design Store*. **Page 294:** Soup bowl — *Eigen Arts Inc.* **Page 296:** Pitcher — *Eigen Arts Inc.* **Page 322:** Cup and saucer, teapot, and plate — *Wedgwood*; tablecloth — *Le Jacquard Français*.

INDEX

Page numbers in *italic* type refer to illustrations.

Page numbers in *italic* type refer to illustrations.

Page numbers in *italic* type refer to illustrations.

Page numbers in *italic* type refer to illustrations.

EQUIVALENTS AND YIELDS OF FRESH INGREDIENTS

FOOD	AMOUNT	APROXIMATE MEASURE	FOOD	AMOUNT	APROXIMATE MEASURE

Almonds
  in shell
  shelled, blanched
	1 lb
	5 1/3 oz
		1–1 1/4 cup nutmeats
		1 cup
			Cranberries	8 oz	2 cups

			Cucumbers	1 whole	6 oz, 3/4 cup seeded and sliced, 1 cup chopped
Apples	1 lb	3 medium, 3 cups peeled, sliced	**Egg, large**	1 whole 1 white	3 tbs 2 tbs
Apricots, dried	4 oz	1/2 cup chopped			
Bananas	1 lb	3 medium, 1 3/4 cups mashed	**Eggplant**	1 small 1 medium 1 large	6 oz, 1 1/2 cups diced 12 oz, 3 1/2 cups diced 1 1/2 lb sliced, 7 cups diced
Beans, green, fresh	1 lb	3 cups uncooked, 2 1/2 cups cooked			
Beans, kidney, dried	1 lb	2 1/2 cups uncooked, 6 cups cooked			
Beans, navy, dried	1 lb	2 cups uncooked, 6 cups cooked	**Flour, all-purpose**	1 lb	3 1/2 cups unsifted, 4 cups sifted
Berries	1 dry pt	2 1/3 cups	**Flour, cake**	1 lb	4 1/2 cups sifted
Bread crumbs, dry	1 slice bread	1/4 cup	**Flour, whole wheat**	1 lb	3 1/2 cups unsifted

Bread crumbs, soft	1 slice
	bread
		1/2 cup	**Green onions**
			  white part only
			  including top
				1 medium
				1 medium
					1 tbs chopped
					2 tbs chopped

Broccoli	1 lb	2 cups cooked	**Herbs, fresh**	1 tbs	1 tsp dried
Butter or margarine	4 oz	1 stick or 8 tbs	**Lemon**	1 medium	3 tbs juice, 1 tbs grated rind
Cabbage	1 lb	1 small, 4 cups shredded	**Lentils**	1 lb	2 cups uncooked, 6 cups cooked
Carrots	1 large 1 lb	1/2 cup chopped 3 cups shredded, 2 1/2 cups diced	**Lime**	1 medium	1 1/2–2 tbs juice, 1 tsp grated rind
			Mushrooms, fresh	1 lb	6 cups sliced uncooked, 2 cups cooked

Celery	1 stalk
	1 bunch
		1/2 cup chopped
		4 1/2 cups chopped
			Noodles
			  broad
			  macaroni
				8 oz
				8 oz
					3 1/2 cups cooked
					4 cups cooked

Cheese, Cheddar	4 oz	1 cup shredded			
Cheese, cottage	1 lb	2 cups	**Oatmeal**	1 cup	1 3/4 cups cooked
Cheese, Parmesan	1 oz	1/4 cup grated	**Onion**	1 small 1 medium 1 large	1/2 cup chopped 1 cup chopped 1 1/2 cups chopped
Chicken, broiler-fryer	3 1/2 lbs	2 cups diced, cooked			
Coconut, flaked	7 oz	2 2/3 cups			